D1250034

Adaptation-Level Theory

Adaptation-Level Theory

AN EXPERIMENTAL AND SYSTEMATIC APPROACH TO BEHAVIOR

HARRY HELSON
KANSAS STATE UNIVERSITY

HARPER & ROW, PUBLISHERS, New York, Evanston, and London

E-0

TO LIDA, HENRY, AND MARTHA

Contents

stimulus as member of series   Minimally effective and interpolated stimuli   Reciprocity of frequency and magnitude   Various stimulus distributions   Range and density of series stimuli   Dispersion of series stimuli   Practice and past experience   Series effects in discrimination   Effects of order on fractionation data

General considerations   Nonstimulating energies   Physiological stimuli   Subliminal stimuli   Field stimulation   Higher-order stimulation   Substitute or conditioned stimuli   Aesthetic, emotional, and sexual stimuli   Reduced stimulation   Internal states as stimuli   Paradoxical, illusory, and hallucinatory stimuli   Less well-defined stimuli

Preface

In this book I have endeavored to systematize the results of studies in which the concept of adaptation level has proved useful both in devising and in interpreting experiments in various areas of psychology. This volume thus serves to bring together material published in various sources as well as a number of studies and ideas that have not previously appeared in print. Problems of adaptation have occupied me since the beginning of my scientific career when, in the fall of 1924, Dr. Deane B. Judd and I constructed a sphere large enough to admit an observer's head and a light source for the purpose of studying total chromatic adaptation with constant light flux to all parts of the retina. Later, studies in which subjects wore colored goggles for a number of hours while going about their everyday activities and studies in which subjects viewed nonselective papers in strongly chromatic illumination showed that while there was loss of chroma in the colors associated with the dominant wave-lengths of the stimuli, there was simultaneously heightened sensitivity to wave-lengths responsible for complementary colors. Indeed, under certain conditions, the eye may supply complementary colors when there are no specific stimuli for them. Adaptation thus has a double effect in which there is reduced response to dominant stimulation and heightened response to complementary stimulation. These studies convinced me that adaptation involves much more than the decrement in response envisaged in the classical formulation of this concept. The discovery of neutral points or regions revealed in our studies of chromatic adaptation supplied the critical concept needed for extension of adaptation level to all psychophysical judgments. This, in turn, led to the postulate that all responses can be viewed as positive or negative gradients from equilibrium conditions.

By taking the level of adaptation as a fulcrum or origin with respect to which behavior is organized, an analytical approach to problems of patterning or Gestalt becomes possible. Thus, if we know the brightness, loudness, or weight that is judged medium or indifferent in a series of stimuli then we can order all other members of the series with respect to these qualities. The relation of any stimulus to prevailing level determines its perceived magnitude and quality. By defining adaptation level as a weighted mean of all stimuli affecting behavior, past as well as present, it becomes a quantitative, operational concept for handling the varied adaptations and adjustments of organisms to the conditions confronting them.

From the fields of sensory processes and psychophysical judgments it was natural to extend the concept of adaptation to other areas of behavior. Experiments by my co-workers and myself were accordingly made dealing with problems of perception, affectivity, learning, cognition, and interpersonal relations conceived as modes of adaptation to focal, contextual, and residual stimuli. Our emphasis has always been on concrete, quantitatively verifiable aspects of behavior, with the result that many problems which had previously been discussed in purely verbal or qualitative fashion were found amenable to quantitative treatment within a systematic conceptual framework. Among such problems are the order effects of classical psychophysics, the hues perceived in strongly chromatic illumination and in passing from daylight to various artificial sources of illumination, the von Bezold spread or assimilation effect, and phenomena of transposition and learning. Our manner of handling these and other problems will be shown in the pages that follow.

The concept of adaptation level seems to have been interesting and useful not only to those with whom I have come into direct contact but also to others working in various areas. Some of the most exciting results have been obtained by younger psychologists working independently at various institutions. I have tried to take into account all studies relevant to the theory without forcing them into a preconceived schema. A number of studies which have appeared since this book went to press could not be included, and some earlier ones may have escaped me; but no omissions have been intentional.

Some of the experiments which have appeared in the technical journals and others reported here for the first time should be regarded as initial explorations or models suggested by the theory. Better experiments may be performed within the framework of the theory in areas we have initially explored, and there is also the possibility of extending the theory to areas where it has not yet been applied.

This book was made possible through my appointment as Research Scholar of the Hogg Foundation for Mental Health during the academic year 1956–1957, which enabled me to devote full time to research and writing. I am grateful to Dr. Wayne H. Holtzman, Associate Director of the Hogg Foundation, for his interest and support in getting this book under way. A grant from the Texas Research Institute also aided materially in furthering work on the book during the first semester of 1959–1960.

My debt to my co-workers, Drs. Deane B. Judd, Walter C. Michels, Robert R. Blake, and Martha A. Wilson, is evident in the extent to which I have drawn from both their own and our joint publications. From my association with Dr. Judd and Dr. Michels I learned something of how physicists tackle and solve problems. Without the cooperation of Dr. Blake I would not have ventured into the field of personality and social psychology. Since coming to Kansas State University, I have had the benefit of closer association with Dr. William Bevan whose contributions to adaptation-level theory are outstanding in their originality. And I must also express my deep appreciation to Dr. J. P. Guilford who has contributed to my thinking in many ways over the years through correspondence and personal discussions. Finally, I am happy to acknowledge the contributions made by students, research assistants, and colleagues whose names appear in our joint publications.

Dr. Gardner Murphy, psychology editor for Harper & Row, read the entire manuscript and made suggestions that improved the presentation in divers ways. I would like here to express my admiration for his tolerance and kindness during the preparation of this book for publication.

Manhattan, Kansas   HARRY HELSON
January, 1964

Adaptation-Level Theory

1 *Introduction*

Psychology today is properly classed among the sciences because it uses experimental methods in establishing its facts and orders many of its findings according to theoretical schemata. Scientific knowledge constitutes a true Gestalt; that is, it is a whole in which each part influences and in turn is influenced by every other part. In other words, scientific knowledge is systematized and not a mere collection of independent facts, laws, or theories. Although bits of unrelated information may be valuable for didactic or practical purposes, they do not have scientific significance until they are shown to be necessary parts of a conceptual whole. If facts have systematic implications, they are scientifically important; otherwise they remain empirical findings. Thus Estes points out that "the experimental findings which survive will be those which are organized around laws, principles, or concepts of some generality, in short, those which lead to theory construction" (1956, p. 1). Psychologists are becoming increasingly aware of the necessity for systematic constructs to order data, which are accumulating at an ever increasing rate.

Pure empiricism is found in reports of experimental data without supporting theory or conceptualization, e.g., in correlations between variables that cannot be shown to be rationally related on any other basis and in purely statistical evaluations of data obtained under conditions that permit no analysis other than tests of significance. Examples of empiricism are not hard to find, and they multiply fast when some new tool such as a test, a method of computation, or a new set of operations appears. Jensen points out that much work has been done in the study of attitudes through an easy-to-use measuring device that impinges upon a large number of dimensions of personality with the result that

. . . in past years ethnic prejudice and authoritarianism . . . have been shown to be significantly related to rigidity, concreteness, narrowness of thinking and problem solving, premature closure of perception, intolerance of ambiguity, distortion of memory, intelligence, xenophobia, family ideology, anxiety, re-enlistment intent, cooperation in experimentation, and leadership qualities . . . resulting in the accumulation of so many findings with the F scale that are now practically impossible to interpret. Much of the research on authoritarianism has consisted in correlating one unknown with another (1958, p. 306).

The same writer asks:

How can one even begin theoretically to relate the observations (a) that Ss with high need achievement show greater preference on the strong Vocational Interest Blank for occupations involving financial risk than Ss with low n Ach and (b) that Ss with high n Ach prefer colors blue and green over red and yellow, while this not true of Ss with low n Ach? (Jensen, 1958, p. 311).

Regarding the belief that it is possible to proceed fruitfully without any theory whatsoever, Miller writes:

Pure empiricism is a delusion. A theorylike process is inevitably involved in drawing boundaries around certain parts of the flux of experience to define observable events and in the selection of the events that are to be observed. Since multitudinous events could be observed and an enormous number of relationships could be determined among all of these events, gathering all the facts with no bias from theory is utterly impossible. Scientists are forced to make a drastic selection, either unconsciously on the basis of perceptual habits and the folklore and linguistic categories of the culture, or consciously on the basis of explicitly formulated theory (Miller, 1959, p. 200).

The alternative, then, to an explicitly formulated theory is not total lack of theory, but rather the making of implicit assumptions never brought to the surface to reveal their full implications. Where no theory is explicitly stated in connection with empirical studies, one runs the risk that others will construct the theory that seems to follow from the data, methodology of the experiment, or discussion of results. More often than not most empiricists deny that they make the assumptions attributed to them. If an empiricist attributes the changes in judgment following an introduction of anchoring stimuli to the way the observer uses a rating or numerical scale or to a change in semantics without recognizing the possibility that sensory magnitude is a function of background or contextual stimuli as well as of focal stimulus, he may be accused of making the old-fashioned stimulus error or, in Köhler's terminology, holding to the constancy hypothesis. The empiricist would probably deny categorically that he harbors such assumptions. We know that a stimulus may be red against one background and bluish green against another, loud in one context and soft in another, or heavy following a light anchor and light following a heavy anchor. If one discusses such phenomena in terms of "errors of observation" or "changes in scale factors" or merely "semantic usage," he must assume that a constant stimulus has a constant effect under all conditions or he would not have recourse to these explanations. Unless the empiricist brings his assumptions out into the open, he runs the risk of having them stated by others.

The lack of general basic theories often leads to expressions of dissatisfaction with psychology by laymen, psychologists, and scientists in other fields. Although the reason most frequently given is that "there are too few facts" in psychology, actually, empirical studies abound and there is no dearth of facts concerning the behavior of humans, primates, rats, and many submammalian organisms. Technical publications in psychology are filled with facts gleaned from experiments on humans and infrahumans, and from psychometric measurements, factor analyses, tests, case histories, interviews, questionnaires, behavior of natural and artificially contrived groups, and free associations of patients undergoing psychoanalytic treatment! Psychology suffers from a plethora of facts that have yet to be systematized and related to each other. What the critics mean, therefore, is not that there are no facts in psychology but that the ones we have do not hang together. We lack simple basic schemata to give meaning and order to facts. By way of contrast, consider the atomic and relativity theories in physics and the many facts that find their place in them. Even individuals lacking technical training in physics and chemistry sense that everything hangs together in these sciences. Certainly this is not true of that amorphous subject, present-day psychology.

Progress in the physical sciences is greatly accelerated because theories already exist for dealing with new facts and, when existing theory is not adequate, it is traditional to formulate theories to bring new data into the already organized body of knowledge. Compare this way of thinking with the empiricism prevalent in much present-day psychology, where even in the oldest and best-established areas, e.g., psychophysics and perception, we find a plethora of empirical results unordered in any systematic context. On the other hand, we often account for data by attributing them to the influence of intervening variables such as "set," "attitude," or individual differences—concepts devoid of systematic power.

Although we lack theories capable of bridging different areas, we do have many special theories, such as those of vision, hearing, and learning. Psychology needs constructs to bring facts of perception, learning, and social and deviant behavior within a common frame of reference. We have nothing corresponding to the physicist's formally identical equations for electrical and mechanical phenomena. The Gestalt psychologists proposed laws of organization to serve for perception, thinking, memory, and other processes, but only in a qualitative way. Since the same organism makes psychophysical judgments, learns lists of nonsense syllables, behaves in conformity with social norms, and becomes psychotic, the chances are very good that certain basic principles will be found to hold for all behavior. In addition to having special theories, we must seek wider generalizations to bring larger and larger classes of facts together in meaningful fashion.

SYSTEMATIC VS. SPOT INVESTIGATIONS

Nowhere does pure empiricism manifest its weaknesses so clearly as in the failure to study the whole range of variables in experimental investigations. Reference to Fig. 1.1 shows how two investigators may reach different conclusions regarding the relation between two variables when each studies a restricted range of the independent variable. Experimenter A, working with values $X_1—X_3$, finds that the relation of Y to X is a negatively accelerated, monotonically increasing function and concludes that the regression of Y on X is positive and fairly high. Experimenter B, working with values $X_4 — X_6$, concludes that the increase in Y with increase in X is negligible and that there is no significant correlation between the two variables.

Lest this example be regarded as farfetched, consider the conflicting generalizations prior to 1938 regarding the colors of objects in strongly chromatic illumination. Some writers asserted that only colors corresponding to the hue of the illuminant are seen, while others maintained that those that are complementary predominate in monochromatic illumination. Not until the complete range of object and background reflectances was investigated could these opposing views be reconciled:

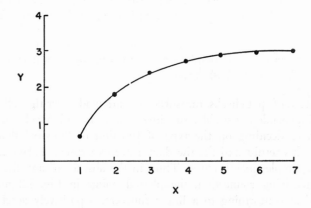

FIG. 1.1. The regression of Y on X is positive and significant if values from $X_1 - X_4$ only are considered but if values $X_4 - X_7$ are considered the correlation between Y and X is nearly zero and not significant.

With black background, illuminant hues predominate; with white background, complementary hues predominate (Helson, 1938; Helson and Jeffers, 1940). Let us take another example from the field of learning. In considering the relation between stimulus intensity and response strength, Johnsgard (1957) pointed out that although the majority of investigators found a negatively accelerated function, one reported a positive linear relationship, another reported both positive linear and positive negatively accelerated functions, still another found an S-shaped function, and a few reported no relationship! When it was realized, however, that contrast between stimulus and background might play a role in stimulus-intensity dynamism, a more thorough exploration was made of varying degrees of stimulus-background contrasts. As a result of experiments employing small as well as large contrasts and white on black as well as black on white contrast, Johnsgard concluded that the conflicting reports in the literature arose from investigations of restricted stimulus ranges.

Spot-check investigations are inadequate—not only for purposes of scientific generalization but also for practical purposes. In this connection Wood states:

> The literature in the field of human factors is full of information that is apparently very correct but which represents only one point on what should have been a curve showing how one variable is functionally related to another. . . . Human factors engineering is being held back more by this deficiency than any other, and there is more to be gained at the present by attempting to put data that are now available into the form of such meaningful functional relationships rather than in collecting new scattered points (1957, in an unpublished report).

If, instead of spot checks, measurements are made over the full range of the independent variable, the investigator is still faced with the problem of deciding on the type of function or "theory" that best describes his results and fits the data, since experimental data seldom fall on a simple smooth curve. Thus, in the absence of any theory of their underlying connection, the plotted points in Fig. 1.2 may be regarded as conforming to a linear function, a positively accelerated function, or a negatively accelerated function. If one believes that the relation is linear, he will regard the sixth value as a deviation due to experimental error; if one favors a positively accelerated function, the sixth value will represent a true determination, but the second value will be regarded as due to experimental error; if one thinks the data fit a negatively accelerated function, he will regard the second value as a true determination and the third, fourth, and sixth values as chance variations.

There is no purely mathematical basis for deciding which type of curve is the best scientific description of a set of data. Consider this with regard to the relation between intensity of stimulation and reaction time as summarized by Teichner, who, after pointing out that reaction time decreases with increase in intensity of stimulation, says: "Attempts have been made to fit the intensity data into mathematical, theoretical frameworks, with exponential, hyperbolic, and parabolic functions, *all being used more or less successfully on the same sets of data"* [italics ours] (Teichner, 1954, p. 132).[1] Need we add that only theory based on the substantive principles underlying data can serve as a basis for choosing one mathematical function over another? Tests of fit such as the smallest sum of squares of differences between observed and theoretical values and determinations of significant com-

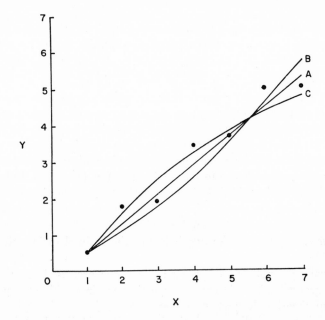

FIG. 1.2. The set of points in this graph may be fitted by any one of the three curves, A, B, or C, depending upon what theory of the relation between X and Y is held.

ponents (linear, quadratic, cubic, etc.) by trend analyses hold for the specific data entering into the computations but may not be valid for replicated data. Since there are no formal criteria for determining the mathematical function that should be taken as the proper description of scientific data, recourse must be had to theoretical considerations rooted in the *nature* of the problem under investigation.

[1] Among the illustrious workers who are referred to by Teichner as having tried their hands at the problems are Hull, Piéron, and Rashevsky!

STAGES IN GENERALIZATION AND THEORY BUILDING

Philosophers of science often assert that experiments are never undertaken unless an explicit hypothesis is being tested. This generalization confuses the ideal with the real, for a large number of experiments are constantly reported without any underlying rationale. To formulate hypotheses requires a certain amount of knowledge which may not be available until after the observations have been made. Although the formulation or testing of a law, principle, or theory should be the aim of every experiment, some experiments are performed to answer specific questions concerning fact as well as theory or to satisfy the scientist's curiosity. An example from the writer's experience may serve to show that theory building may come after as well as before experimentation. Some years ago it occurred to me that the two-point limen is smaller when the stimuli straddle the mid-line of the body than when measured, as is usual, on one side only. Results with two *S*s confirmed the hunch with reference to the forehead and chest regions, but were inconclusive with a third *S*. At present the finding stands only as an empirical result; if confirmed,[2] it will require further investigation to formulate a reasonable hypothesis of why sensitivity is greater in simultaneous stimulation of the two halves of the brain than in unilateral stimulation.

Actually generalization is not an all-or-none process. Even though broad generalizations do appear from time to time without apparent buildup, theories always have a history. A number of phases in scientific thinking generally precede the formulation of full-fledged theories; these are roughly identified in the sections that follow.

Subsumption. Perhaps the first stage beyond pure empiricism is what we may refer to as *subsumption*. When a fact or class of facts is shown to be a member of a larger class with which it has something in common, we may say it is *subsumed* under the larger class. Even though the larger class of facts may not be fully understood, subsumption of isolated facts often helps to direct thinking into the proper channels. Thus, in understanding polio and developing a vaccine, a considerable advance was made when the disease was subsumed under the larger class of virus diseases. On the other hand, subsumptive terms

[2] Since this was written the fact has been confirmed by Mr. C. K. Adams, one of my students at Kansas State University, and a major study is now under way.

explain nothing in themselves and must not be mistaken for laws or theories. Such terms as "constancy," "conditioning," "frame of reference," and "organization" are subsumptive rather than explanatory.

Correlation. This term covers a wide range of relationships, from the most tenuous to the most solid that can be found between variables. When two events are correlated, there is usually thought to be some underlying connection between them; but this need not be true. Not even perfect correlation denotes functional dependency because some events that are perfectly correlated are known to have nothing to do with one another. We must therefore distinguish between statistical and functional correlations. When events are functionally related, one event depends materially upon the other and an underlying connection exists between them. The establishment of functional correlations is a step in generalization, for when two variables are correlated, either they both belong to a larger more general group of phenomena or one serves as the ground of the other.

Analogical thinking. When similarities are perceived between different types of phenomena, they are said to be analogous, and reasoning based on similarities is said to be reasoning by analogy. Because this type of reasoning may be faulty, as indeed is true of all types of reasoning under certain circumstances, some logicians and scientists regard all analogical thinking as *ipso facto* bad. Since it has been such a fertile source of generalization in science, let us consider analogical reasoning in some detail, noting its good and bad points. Analogy originally meant identity of relations. If the relations are assumed to be the same in two different cases, what follows from a relation in one case follows from the relation in the other case. If the relations happen to be quantitative, the reasoning is mathematical in character and "such reasoning is necessary, like any other mathematical reasoning" (Joseph, 1916, p. 532). The danger in analogical thinking is that two domains similar in one respect or at one level (phenotypical) may be different in other respects or at another level (genotypical) and inferences drawn from one may not hold for the other. But analogical inferences may be fruitful in suggesting things to look for which are not clearly evident in one domain but are clear in the other. Moreover, the *direction* of analogical inference is extremely important. If one side of the analogy concerns entities and relations that are well known and firmly established, it is fairly safe (and fruitful) to approach the other, less-known side of the analogy with knowledge gained from the strong side. But it is unsafe to proceed from a weak or uncertain area to another area, even if the second is a well-established domain.

Analogical models are widely used in physics. In this connection, Michels and Patterson justify the analogy between motion under a constant acceleration and the energy of a compressed spring:

> When the analogy is complete . . . reasoning by analogy provides one of the most powerful methods of science. We judge that an analogy is complete when we can recognize that a number of variables in one problem are related to one another by *exactly the same mathematical relations* as those which connect an entirely different set of variables in another problem. If this is the case the two problems, although quite different physically, have the same mathematical treatment. The mere fact we do not need to repeat the mathematical discussion for the second of the two analogous problems leads, of course, to a great saving in time, but that perhaps is not the most important feature of an analogy. We may recognize in one physical situation an interesting feature which might be hidden in another problem. The analogy would encourage us to look for the hidden feature in the second problem and that feature when uncovered may be of great interest (1951, p. 136).

One of the most widely used analogies in physics and engineering is that between mechanical and electrical phenomena. It is often possible to visualize and understand mechanical systems by translating them into their electrical analogues or vice versa. Indeed the properties of mechanical systems are often pictured on an oscilloscope for ease and speed in studying changes in components of the mechanical systems. Through the use of analogy it is possible to show that *formally* identical laws are operative in widely different types of physical phenomena. Consider first the differential equation expressing the relations between the input considered as a time-varying force and the behavior of the elements of a mechanical system consisting of a mass attached to a spring free to oscillate:

$$Kx + F\frac{dx}{dt} + M\frac{d^2x}{dt^2} = f(t) \qquad (1)$$

and next consider the differential equation governing the behavior of an electric current in a simple oscillating circuit:

$$Cq + R\frac{dq}{dt} + L\frac{d^2q}{dt^2} = e(t) \qquad (2)$$

The symbols in Equations (1) and (2) have the meanings given them in Table 1.1. We see that these equations are formally identical and that each of the terms in Equation (1) has its analogue in Equation (2). Since the *relations* of the components in the two systems are identical, it becomes possible to describe the behavior of an electric current in a system containing inductance, resistance, and capacity in terms of the actions of a mass attached to a spring that is given an initial push or pull; and, conversely, to describe the elements of a mechanical system having mass, friction, and a spring in terms of an electrical circuit when a voltage is applied to a capacitance in series with an inductance and a resistance.[3] Differences in the nature of the physical phenomena

TABLE 1.1.   Electromechanical Analogues

	Mechanical		Electrical
f	Force	e	Electromotive force
F	Friction	R	Resistance
x	Position	q	Electric charge
dx/dt	Velocity	dq/dt	Current
d^2x/dt^2	Acceleration	d^2q/dt^2	Rate of change of current
K	Stiffness constant	C	Capacitance
M	Mass	L	Inductance

SOURCE: From Michels and Patterson, *Elements of Modern Physics*, Copyright 1951, D. Van Nostrand Company, Inc., Princeton, N. J.

are not allowed to obscure similarities in their *dynamic* or functional aspects, and the analogy does not imply that the one set of phenomena has been identified with or reduced to the other. We need therefore have no fear that the use of mathematical or physical models, when properly understood, will entail reduction of one system to another or that there will be an unwarranted extension of properties of simple systems to more complex configurations having totally different properties. Indeed, it is possible to consider systems insofar as they are alike according to a common model and at the same time to be fully aware of their differences.

The equations we have just discussed are, as Fitts points out (1951), system equations that can be used to determine how component parts

[3] Those interested in a complete working through of the analogy between mechanical and electrical systems at an elementary level should refer to Michels and Patterson (1951, pp. 523 ff.).

of systems behave under various conditions. He also indicates that the systems described by these equations provide a suggestive model for understanding the role of the human organism, in spite of its great complexity, in control tasks such as tracking by means of manually operated handwheels. Other models have also been suggested for the human as a tracking operator, and all rest on the use of analogy!

Analogy, when properly employed, can help to understand one system in terms of another that has formally similar properties. For example, Sherrington, as pointed out by Lloyd (1946b) used the analogy of facilitation and inhibition of motor spinal reflexes to speculate on how the retina functions. New insights often develop which expedite treatment of certain problems by means of analogical thinking. All theoretical constructs and models require analogical modes of thinking, since the properties of the model are held to represent or to be analogous to certain aspects of the phenomenon to be explained. In psychology there has been too little carry-over from the simpler, hard-core areas to the more complex fields of investigation. Often it is assumed that behavior in a social context must be basically different from behavior in a psychophysical experiment, although the behavior in both may actually be governed by the same principles. Not all transfers of ideas are analogical, and in this book we employ few analogies. But if some reader is tempted to dismiss all transfer of methods, principles, and ideas from one area to another area as "mere analogical thinking," we would remind him that if this point of view prevailed in physics, physics would be the empirical amorphous subject that psychology, for the most part, still is today. Proper use of analogy helps extend knowledge and may lead to generalizations having wide significance.

Hypotheses and theories. After a sufficient body of facts has been established, and the inner relations of the facts determined, the formulation of theories becomes possible. Theories without facts—like concepts, according to Kant—are empty; and facts without theories are sterile. Often one may not know the precise line of demarcation between fact and theory. The ideal of theory in science is a statement in mathematical form, for only in mathematics are the terms, operations, and relations univocal. Propositions in terms of psychological entities and processes without quantitative formulations are difficult, if not impossible, to test and validate. Quantitative predictions permit precise validations, and if they have psychological content, grounds for the predictions can be said to exist in a theory. Theories in quantitative form therefore possess a double virtue: They can be tested within precise limits, and, being mathematical, they are formal in character and applicable to wide classes of facts. Space in this work does not permit differentiation among theories according to such characteristics as the nature and number of assumptions on which they rest, the generality of their applications, and their verifiability.

GENERALITY OF EXPERIMENTAL–QUANTITATIVE THEORIES

Our discussion of the prevalence of empiricist thinking in psychology should not be taken to imply that psychology is totally lacking in general systematic approaches; this is by no means true. What is striking in the present situation is that experimental-quantitative systematizations come almost entirely from two areas of psychology: perception and learning. This is revealed by a glance at representative general theories: Pavlov's theory of conditioned reflex; Wertheimer's theory of Gestalt; the learning theories of Hull, Spence, and Tolman; and S-R theories, such as those of Miller and his colleagues (1959). The theories that have dominated thinking in the field of personality and social psychology (stemming chiefly from Freud) can hardly be regarded as general systematizations of psychology because they have so far failed to throw light on some of the most basic areas of behavior—perception, judgment, learning, thinking, and concept formation. Contrary to popular belief, and even the belief of some professional psychologists, the socalled "dynamic" systems of psychology of Freud, Jung, Adler, and their many followers are more narrowly based and have fewer implications than some of the theories based on (academic) experimental-quantitative approaches. Similarly, fields in which global approaches have predominated (such as personality and interpersonal relations) have been, as one writer puts it, "test rich and integration poor" (Mann, 1959) and consequently have not provided systematizations extending beyond their own areas.

A strong personal element enters into theory building and attitudes toward theories. Theories rest upon the assumptions that one is willing to make, and they will not be accepted by those to whom any of the assumptions are repugnant. The assumption of the constancy of the speed of light as a cardinal postulate in relativity theory has been rejected or questioned by a number of theoreticians (including A. N. Whitehead) who have formulated relativity theories without it. Immediately questions of simplicity and economy in applications of the theory arise, and although they may be extralogical, they are important in everyday scientific work. An assumption unacceptable to a mathematician may be taken in stride by a physicist, who must consider specific uses of the theory as well as its logical or mathematical elegance. What one individual is willing to accept as a postulate may be acceptable to another only as a theorem, as shown by the opposed treatments of the problem of "insight" by S-R learning theorists and Gestalt theorists.

Many psychologists mistrust transfer of concepts and methods from one field of psychology to another. There are psychophysicists who regard applications of basic principles to (what they consider) the more complicated, less "scientific" areas to be unwarranted, if not dangerous; there are social and personality psychologists who regard transfer of facts and concepts from psychophysics to interpersonal relations to be the result of loose, analogical thinking. But the systematist searching for unity in diversity is mindful that the same organism makes psychophysical judgments, learns lists of nonsense syllables, conforms to, or departs from social norms, and sometimes consults a psychiatrist. These facts seem to the systematist to establish a high probability that a single theoretical basis may be found for ordering and understanding many different aspects of behavior. A theory should not be judged on its origins but rather on its adequacy and fruitfulness in whatever area it is applied.

There is no reason why knowledge gained from laboratory experiments is precluded from aiding in understanding facts of everyday behavior. If pure research does not enable us to understand classes of phenomena other than the ones investigated, it is not because the research is "pure" but because it is too narrowly based and interpreted. The fault lies not with the area investigated or the experimental method qua method, but with the investigator and his insight. The success with which physical scientists have been able to transfer facts and theories from pure research to everyday use is so well known as to need no repetition here. But let us digress for a moment to show how physicists have been able to explain phenomena occurring in distant nebulae on the basis of, or by analogy to, phenomena observed in their own laboratories (Oort, 1957). Pictures of the Crab nebula made with different filters revealed two different types of phenomena with regard to the light emitted by this nebula. One filter, which transmits wave lengths mainly associated with hydrogen and helium atoms, yields a line spectrum; the other yields a continuous spectrum over a fairly wide band of wave lengths. The nebula is known to consist of rarefied gases that always emit light at discrete wave lengths. What is the origin of the continuous radiation from this nebula? The answer came from an experiment dealing with electrons moving at high speed in a magnetic field created in a synchrotron. Whereas light that comes from vibrations of electrons in small orbits within an atom gives off discrete spectral lines, radiation due to acceleration or bending of electrons from a straight path is continuous. As reported by Oort (1957), a Russian physicist suggested that the continuous radiation came from electrons affected by strong magnetic fields and furthermore that the same synchrotron action could account for the strong radio emissions from the Crab nebula. At first this theory was questionable because it seemed implausible that a very specialized laboratory effect also operates in the stars. But a further check known from synchrotron experiments was applied to the slightly lower (radio) emissions from the nebula. Light from electrons in the synchrotron was polarized, and when the light from Crab nebula was found to be polarized, a double check was provided on the hypothesis of the strong magnetic or synchrotron forces at work in the nebula. Later pictures showed that all the continuous radiation from the nebula was in fact polarized! Oort concluded, "We have every reason, then, to believe that the continuous light of the Nebula is actually synchrotron light" (1957, p. 56).

Psychology, too, is not without its successes in achieving understanding of distant phenomena on the basis of knowledge gained in the laboratory. Much has been learned through experimentation about the ways in which judgments, attitudes, and intra-organismic norms are formed and how they may be changed under both laboratory and everyday conditions. For example, the repulsion effects of background stimuli have been found to be formally identical in studies of sensory processes, psychophysical judgments, aesthetic responses, and responses involving symbolic and verbal materials (Helson, 1959). Laboratory findings are often not appreciated by laymen and professional psychologists because they seem to be obvious replications of phenomena encountered in daily life. The systematist, however, sees in such cases the underlying unity of responses evoked under different conditions and takes delight in discovering common theoretical bases for phenomena that differ phenotypically but are genotypically the same. The transfer of knowledge from one area of psychology to another, or from pure research to everyday life, gives evidence of both the validity and the fruitfulness of many theoretical constructs.

Quantitative generalizations are comparatively rare in psychology for a variety of reasons. Because we are aware of individual variability, we often are so concerned with making sure that two samples did or did not come from the same population ("population" being defined in terms of attributes or behaviors exhibited by individuals as a result of some treatment or selection process) that after they have been analyzed statistically no further quantification seems necessary. Although tests of significance of differences between populations may serve to establish the *fact* of difference, they do not reveal either the nature of the functional relations underlying the difference or the principle governing the phenomenon investigated. Granting the great power of, and necessity for, statistical analysis in the sciences dealing with living organisms, we must nevertheless recognize its limitations as regards theory building. If we are interested in developing a quantitative formulation, it is not enough to establish significant differences between attributes or magnitudes at one point, or to show that a trend is statistically significant; rather, the ground of the difference, or the trend, must be embodied in mathematical formulations such that the observed data follow from permissible mathematical operations. The process of inference from initial mathematical hypotheses is the most trustworthy guide in scientific theorizing because such inference "runs in the trustworthy channels of rules of calculation learned once and for all" (Joos, 1934).

Additional considerations also enter into quantitative theories, some of which were noted in an earlier publication:

Quantitative theories must contain more than purely formal, mathematical relations to be of value in an experimental science. They must have psychological content. The degree of mathematical sophistication in a theory is not necessarily highly correlated with its power of interpreting data or its power to suggest new experiments, or its ability to yield new information. A simple mathematical formulation may have more power than a complicated model if the one deals with fundamental relations while the other deals with minutiae or trivia. Examples of both types of theory are not difficult to find in contemporary theorizing. The Weber and the Weber-Fechner laws are examples of extremely simple mathematical formulations which have decisively influenced psychology and sensory physiology because of the basic nature of the problems with which they coped.

In constructing quantitative models in psychology one may begin with some fundamental, general characteristic of behavior and then subsume specific cases under it by showing how this characteristic enters into them; or, one may begin with the minutiae of some domain, such as perception or learning, and by successive postulations attempt to encompass wider and wider classes of phenomena. Each approach has been tried and there is no *a priori* basis on which to assess their relative merits. They can only be judged by the results they achieve (Helson, 1959, p. 576).

One of the advantages of quantitative formulations is their definiteness and simplicity, at least as compared with verbal statements. Often various transformations, particularly log transformations, are resorted to in order to express quantitative relations as simply as possible. Mathematical as well as verbal and conceptual simplification has its dangers in the experimental sciences. For example, polynomials of the nth degree which have $n - 1$ turns can be transformed into straight lines by taking logs of both sides of the equation. A power function with one variable:

$$Y = BX^n \tag{3}$$

gives a linear function by taking logs of both sides:

$$\log Y = \log B + n \log X \tag{4}$$

Although this transformation is perfectly sound mathematically, a good deal of concrete information may be lost if one is unable to visualize the original function. We may be interested in inflection points where curves change their direction or in absolute values rather than in their logs. In this connection Sholl (1954) pointed out that the power function "is highly adaptable and can be fitted to many arrays of very variable configurations. In some senses it is a very non-specific curve, and only the most general type of information can be derived from its parameters. . . . The striking differences between situations . . . tend to be concealed under the double logarithmic transformation" (pp. 226–227). If the same data are plotted on an ordinary Cartesian grid, the enormous differences between data yielding different values of the slope, n, in the log-log transformation become obvious.

As soon as data are transformed, the form of the resultant relationship is quite arbitrary and, indeed, can be made into anything one pleases as shown by the transformations in Figs. 1.3 and 1.4 from Taylor

and Birmingham (1959). The data represent tracking performance as
a function of the type of aid given the operator shown in the figures.
From these figures it is seen that the difference between concave, convex, and sigmoidal, as well as that between linear and concave upward,
is merely a matter of scale factor. The curves in Fig. 1.3 are semi-log

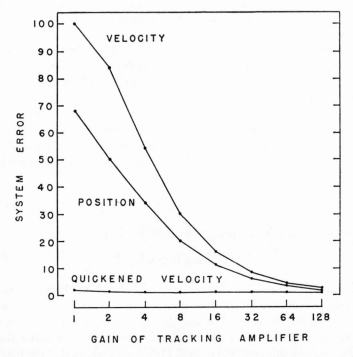

FIG. 1.3.   Performance of three systems as a function of the gain of the "man"
when a linear scale is employed for the ordinate values. Compare the two upper
curves with the same data plotted on a logarithmic ordinate in Fig. 1.4. (From
Taylor and Birmingham, 1959. With the permission of the American Psychological
Association.)

plots of the data plotted in log-logs in Fig. 1.4. Analytically, the change
in ordinate is represented by changing from $Y = \log X$ to $\log Y = \log$
X. In Fig. 1.3 the curve for velocity is slightly sigmoidal, that for
position tracking is concave upward, and that for quickened velocity
is almost flat. When the ordinate is changed from a linear to a log
scale, the curve for velocity changes from sigmoidal to concave down-

ward, the curve for position changes from concave upward to concave downward, and the quickened velocity curve becomes concave upward! Generalizations based on the shapes of curves involving log and

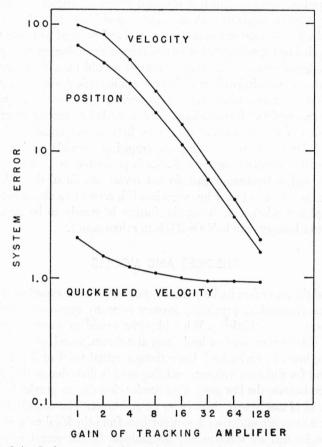

FIG. 1.4. Performance of three systems as a function of the gain of the "man." Note that the two upper curves which were concave upward when a linear ordinate was employed (Fig. 1.3) are now concave downward when a logarithmic ordinate is employed. (From Taylor and Birmingham, 1959. With the permission of the American Psychological Association.)

other transformations must therefore be viewed with the knowledge that almost any shape may be given any functional relation through choice of scale factors.

Rational vs. empirical formulas. A distinction is often made between a rational formula, which is derived from explicitly stated assumptions from which the mathematical expression necessarily follows, and an empirical formula, which is obtained by fitting curves to observed data by various methods such as averages and least squares. The numerical value of constants in both empirical and rational formulas must be supplied by experimentation or observation since there is no a priori knowledge of what values these constants should take. Consequently even purely postulational or deductive mathematical systems contain empirical constants when applied to specific areas of investigation. However, empirical formulations, often regarded as merely shorthand expressions for experimental data, may have power equal to that of rational formulations. Certainly an empirical formula showing the quantitative *relation* between variables is preferable to a mere display of data and to treatments that do not reveal functional dependencies among the variables under investigation. If it comes to a choice between an empirical relation or none, the former is greatly to be preferred (since to a hungry man half a loaf is better than none).

THEORIES AND MODELS

Good theories often make it unnecessary to perform experiments and are thus economical, providing answers to many questions purely by the operations of thinking. What physicist would measure the rate of fall of objects composed of lead, iron, aluminum, wood, or feathers to test the law of gravitation? Even though actual rates of fall may be different for different volumes and shapes of bodies, due to differences in air resistance, the law governing acceleration due to gravity is based on the ideal case where there is no air resistance. The complexities of concrete cases are understood as departures from the ideal case, and the reasons for this are subsequently determined. Of the recent successful orbital flights by the two astronauts Glenn and Carpenter one physicist said with tongue in cheek, "They proved that Newton was right." Space flight has verified under previously untried conditions many laws of physics and chemistry which were formulated on the basis of laboratory experiments. How many general laws are we likely to discover with the present empirical approaches to problems? Too many investigations in our discipline are merely replications, differing from each other only in the minutiae of concrete events, and would be unnecessary if we had good theories to draw upon. Too many experiments provide answers only to specific questions because no general theoretical issues are posed. Except in restricted areas, we have not learned to strip away nonessentials in order to establish the pure or ideal case. Impressed with the difficulties and complexities of their subject matter, many psychologists will have nothing to do with theories that embody ideal cases. In our zeal for total understanding and useful applications we miss the importance of studying the crucial and basic problems which alone can provide the knowledge for a *science* of behavior.

Although theories often provide "models" of the facts they explain, this is not, as is often assumed, a necessary attribute of theories. The term "model" suggests mechanism and mechanical gadgets and representations of *structures* that are readily visualized. There are theories based on operations or definitions which, strictly speaking, do not provide models of anything beyond themselves because they generate the entities and relations of which they are constituted. Cantor's "theory" of transfinite numbers is an example: classes are defined by operations that determine whether the classes are finite or infinite and that also determine the order of potency of infinite classes. An infinite class is defined as a class all of whose members can be put into one-to-one correspondence with a part of itself according to a stated rule. This is obviously not true of any finite class of objects. Thus the integers are an infinite class because all members can be matched by the subclass of even integers:

 1   2   3   4   5   6   7   8   9   .   .   .   .   .
 2   4   6   8 10 12 14 16   .   .   .   .   .   .

Every member in the total set can be matched by a member of the subset. The same definition or set of operations is used to demonstrate the existence of infinities of higher potency. For example, the points on a line represent an infinity of higher order than does the infinity of integers. In the unit right-angled triangle, the hypotenuse, by the Pythagorean theorem, is equal to the square root of the sum of the sides squared; but since the square root of 2 is an irrational number (not expressible as an integer or as the quotient of two integers), the line contains irrational as well as rational numbers.[4] A whole new field

[4] It is not necessary for the point being made here to show that the set of irrational numbers is infinite in itself and hence that a line contains at least a double infinity of points since points on the line can be matched with the rational and irrational numbers.

of mathematics was opened up by Cantor's definition of infinite sets, which rests on the operation of one-to-one correspondence of a set with a proper part of itself.[5] Since this definition gave rise to "a body of theorems presenting a clear, rounded, and systematic view" of transfinite numbers, it can properly be called a theory of transfinite numbers, although it can hardly be regarded as a "model."

Without pretending that this work will have the consequences for behavioral science that Cantor's work has had for mathematics, I present in this book a definition that entails determination of adaptation level and I explore its manifestations in the main areas of behavior. Because of the extent and variety of its applications, the concept may be regarded as having the status of a theory in the dictionary sense given in the above quotation. It has suggested some quantitative models but does not stand or fall with any one of them. It may suggest physiological models to theorists better equipped than I am to speculate in that area.[6]

THE PROBLEM OF DYNAMICS IN PSYCHOLOGY

Since the advent of psychoanalytic, hormic, and similar concepts in psychology, much has been written concerning the necessity for dealing with the dynamic aspects of behavior. Even behaviorists have now embodied in their systems need, drive, motivation, goal seeking, and similar concepts having dynamic connotations. Apparently such intervening variables are supposed to indicate the source of power, push, pull, or movement exhibited by organisms. To deal successfully with dynamic events we must formulate mathematical expressions incorporating the dynamic relations exhibited in the events. In other words, the trick, if so it may be called, consists in formulating a mathematico-static description of movement and change. We can illustrate what this means by the following equations for motion of a falling body under the influence of gravity (neglecting air resistance). The distance, s,

---

[5] For an exciting elementary treatment of transfinite numbers, see Gamow (1957). It should also be mentioned that rules must be given for choosing the subset and for matching to the whole set.

[6] The concepts of pooling and interaction, so central to the theory of adaptation level, would seem to require some type of physiological interaction as opposed to concepts of discretely acting physiological units.

covered in a period of time, *t,* following start of fall, is given by the equation

$$s = \frac{1}{2}gt^2 \tag{5}$$

where *g* is the gravitational constant. For every instant of fall, the traversed distance is given by this equation. Moreover, the rate of fall is given by taking the first derivative of the distance with respect to the time:

$$\frac{ds}{dt} = gt \tag{6}$$

so that the rate of fall can be determined at every instant as well as the distance. Finally, the acceleration due to gravity is given by the second derivative:

$$\frac{d^2s}{dt^2} = g \tag{7}$$

The mathematical expression of the functional relations between space and time observed for bodies falling under the influence of gravity has yielded far more information than has the concept of motion per se. The highly successful and elaborate theoretical structure of physics is based upon many such relations between variables expressed in mathematical language. Just as a roll of film can reproduce motion when properly projected—although each picture on the screen is static—so equations of motions of bodies yield information concerning the dynamics of movement. Dynamic relations usually concern variations in magnitude of variables. Unless the degree to which an observed variable manifests itself can be specified as a function of known conditions, we cannot be said to have an understanding of its "dynamics."

To deal with the dynamics of behavior one must do more than verbally employ terms that have dynamic connotations. Concepts must be formulated so as to make possible the determination of the functional relations between relevant variables in the dynamic situation— and what objects of study are not in some sense dynamic? In this book the dynamic concept of adaptation or adjustment is central, and an attempt is made to show how it may be used to yield quantitative data wherever it is applied.

Theoretical models. Theories make explicit or implicit use of models that are usually simpler than the phenomena they are designed to explain. They help to visualize essential relations between phenomena on the premise that the underlying nature of the phenomena is similar or analogous to the model. Since the beginnings of modern experimental psychology we have had mechanical, electrical, mathematical, chemical, hydrodynamical, and other types of models for special senses, learning, memory, attention, and even for gross approach and avoidance patterns of behavior. Whether or not certain descriptive systems can be regarded as models (e.g., Lewin's topological and hodological constructs and Freud's inner dynamisms), they serve many workers as principles of explanations and as cognitive maps for ordering phenomena. Some models have persisted over the years and seem to have astonishing vitality in spite of their admitted shortcomings (e.g., the tri-receptor theory of color vision) and others barely outlive their authors (e.g., McDougall's drainage theory of attention and Wertheimer's short-circuit theory of the phi phenomenon).

That models have value in spite of their short lives cannot be denied. The longevity of models depends upon a number of factors, and the more dependent a model is upon specific entities and relations, the shorter will be its period of usefulness. Models that permit modification or outright substitution of substantive elements and relations have the best chances of survival. One of the most striking examples is the membrane theory of nerve conduction, which, like the one-horse chaise, still persists although almost every element in the theory has been changed several times. Originally the membrane was conceived to be a semipermeable, linear, two-dimensional conductor, with hydrogen ions free to pass through the membrane while carbonate ions were held inside during the resting state of the nerve. The theory further assumed that there was a state of equilibrium between inner and outer electrical charges as long as the elements of the membrane were polarized and that excitation of the nerve at one point destroyed the polarization of the membrane, allowing the hydrogen and carbonate ions to pass freely through the membrane. The point-by-point continuation of this process of depolarization-disequilibrium constituted the passage of the impulse along the nerve fiber. Soon the hydrogen ions gave way to potassium ions as the elements believed able to traverse the semipermeable membrane in the polarized state, and negative ions of a potassium salt were thought to be contained inside the membrane. Later, the belief in the negative potassium ions gave way to the thought that sodium ions were inside the membrane, and still later acetylcholine was thought to be the active agent in depolarization. Moreover, the original belief in a two-dimensional system has now given way to belief in a tridimensional volume conductor in which the inside and the outside of the membrane act alternately as source and sink to allow the current to pass radially *across* the membrane as well as longitudinally along the nerve fiber (cf. Troland, 1930; Lloyd, 1946*a;* and Brink, 1951). The membrane theory of nerve conduction survives today because its formal structural features persist in spite of almost complete change in the entities and relations in the original statement of the theory.

The history of the membrane theory of nerve conduction illustrates nicely the difference between the formal and the material aspects of theories and models. Material properties postulated in theories may change while formal properties remain; and it is the formal properties that are usually of importance in a theory. Few models in psychology have permitted modification of details while preserving their formal structure. Even models that are abstract in character may be tied so closely to specific assumptions that they cannot survive if the assumptions prove to be untenable. Consider the formal model of the way a rat learns a maze in which one of the basic assumptions is the goal gradient hypothesis. According to this assumption, the rate of progression of the animal increases as the goal is approached. If rats run at a constant rate toward the goal or the rate of running maximizes somewhere along the run *before* the goal is reached, a theory based on goal gradient obviously will not hold generally. But if the theory provides a parameter for rate of progression through the maze without specifying where the maximum must occur, or even that there must be a maximum, the theory may be adapted to fit any rate functions found in maze learning.

It may be asked how theories and models that are formal in character can yield concrete predictions. Depending on the type of model, there are a number of ways in which they can do so. Thus the formal statement of the universal law of gravitation is that the force of attraction between any two bodies having masses m and M is

$$F = \frac{mM}{r^2} C \qquad (8)$$

where r is the distance between the centers of the masses (assuming them to be spherical) and C is a constant. If the value of the constant, C, is known, the formula ceases to be a purely formal construct, and specific values of F can be determined for particular masses at known distances. Similarly it is possible to construct purely formal postulational systems that do not have any content until the symbols are given concrete interpretations. In general, we can say that theories and models may be more or less formal and may be built to provide more or less latitude in interpretation. Models that are too specific or too complicated have less chance of squaring with wide classes of facts than do more abstract, simple formulations.[7]

Physical vs. psychological dimensions. Quantitative methods require units and scales of measurement, and these, in turn, involve dimensions that define what is being measured. The fundamental dimensions of physics are length, time, and mass,[8] and they can be expressed in centimeter-gram-second, meter-kilogram-second, or other systems employing fundamental quantities such as force or electrostatic units (see Michels and Patterson, 1951). Many behavioral phenomena can be measured in appropriate physical units, and there need be no conflict between behavioral and physical variables so long as they are seen to be distinct. Thus learning may be measured in units of time, and maternal drive in terms of the electric shock (in electromotive units) that stops a rat from going to her litter. But we cannot identify physical intensity with psychological intensity, e.g., sound pressure with loudness, physical distance with psychological distance, physical time with experienced time. Behaviorally, a period of two hours may be short or long and the distance between two places may be small or large, depending upon psychological factors that interact with the physical quantities involved.

The problem is further complicated because many psychological dimensions have as yet no known physical dimensions. Thus arithmetic problems may be arranged along a difficulty continuum and individuals may be rated according to intelligence, though there are no physical units for measuring either difficulty of arithmetic problems or amount of intelligence. In such cases we must resort to methods of scaling which involve the behavior of living organisms, and we must use

[7] One of my colleagues in mathematics once remarked that he did not see how a theory as complicated as Einstein's theory of relativity could possibly be true!

[8] Others have also been suggested but these three are sufficient for the argument.

psychophysical and statistical methods developed for scaling purposes. The application of experimental-quantitative methods to many areas of behavior still awaits identification of their relevant psychological dimensions and the development of scaling techniques appropriate for measuring them.

The dimensional approach to psychological problems has often been charged with being a form of reductionism, with all the onus that attaches to destroying the properties of wholes. As Chein has defined it, reductionism consists in stripping the phenomenon to be explained of its phenotypic and unique characteristics and subsuming it under a broader class of phenomena. In line with this definition, Chein (1947) described several forms of reductionism, all equally objectionable: (1) crossing from a higher to a lower level, as in the assertion, "thinking is a reflex"; (2) crossing from a lower to a higher context, as in the declaration "behavior is just an expression of culture"; and (3) crossing at the same level from one context to another, as in the statement, "fighting is just human nature." Although many psychologists have been alert to reductionism of the first type, they have often failed to see the fallacy in crossing from lower to higher levels or from one context to another on the same level. The fallacy of reductionism lies in its implication that phenomena are "nothing but" something or other, when in reality no object or event can be *completely* described or analyzed into anything other than itself. Yet the task of science is to describe and analyze phenomena so as to bring order and simplicity into them. Although water is more than two atoms of hydrogen combined with one of oxygen, the chemist's task is to account for the properties of water in as simple and general terms as possible. The atomic hypothesis was a beginning, and now solid-state physics can predict properties of various combinations of atoms.

Dimensionalism, then, is not "bad," provided we do not identify totalities with partial aspects of systems. On the contrary, dimensionalism in psychology has many things to its credit, such as bringing order and simplicity into the study of sensory processes and identifying variables for control and measurement. The remedy for a dimensionalism that is too narrow, as I have pointed out elsewhere (1951), lies in the development of a richer dimensionalism, not in a flight from dimensional to global thinking. Paradoxical as it may seem, one of the chief shortcomings of early dimensionalism was its reluctance to admit the existence of new sensory dimensions, which forced it to turn to higher memorial processes for explanations of perceptual phenomena. Many of the phenomena that the older dimensionalism accounted for in terms of memory images, memory colors, and past experience have been shown to involve new dimensions and/or to be due to interactions of known sensory processes or their underlying physiological events. As new dimensions of stimulation are discovered and field effects are taken into account, there will be less need of molar processes to account for behavioral phenomena.

The dimensional approach was employed from the very beginning in the study of sensory processes, but its use in the study of personality and social behavior has lagged chiefly for two reasons: (1) In the areas of personality and interpersonal relations there is a strong urge for the development of practical instruments, with the result that would-be scientists have been diverted from scientific analysis to applied work. (2) There is a strong tradition in favor of global approaches to human problems which is antagonistic to scientific analyses. There are many spot checks of personality and social behavior in the literature, but systematic investigations in these areas are relatively rare. These two tendencies have retarded analysis of the fundamental variables operative in personality and in interpersonal contacts. Although much has been written about intraversion and extroversion, about anxiety and defense mechanisms, about the neurotic and the psychotic personalities, and about authoritarian and permissive types of individuals, almost nothing is known to yield answers to some of the most elementary questions in these areas, e.g., what is the functional relation between variables X and Y? How much change in X is associated with a given change in Y? Is the relation between X and Y direct or inverse? To answer such questions as these, one must identify variables and dimensions and make careful measurements. The *scientist* concerned with personality and social behavior may have to isolate and measure what seem to be obvious relations, and he may have to endure the charge that he is concerned with minutiae having little relation to global problems; but this has been the lot of all pioneers and is something to be taken in stride. The followers of experimental-quantitative methods are content to learn as they go along, step by step, slowly but surely, and they eschew what William James called "cheap and wholesale" explanations. Reliance on the ultimate value of this approach rests upon faith, but a faith that has more than justified itself in the solid progress of the experimental sciences, including psychology.

Validity of experimental approaches. At various times since the beginnings of modern scientific psychology there have been critics both of laboratory psychology in general and of particular experimental approaches to behavior. First the analytical introspective psychology of Wundt and Titchener was attacked by those who saw the need for long-section concepts like goal, purpose, and *Aufgabe* to supplement cross-section analyses; by those who maintained that behavior was determined by subconscious as well as by conscious processes; by those who objected to analysis of immediate data of experience whether by the observer or by the experimenter; by those who believed that behavior, rather than mind or consciousness, was the proper subject matter for psychological study; and by those who distrusted experimental methods and wished to study human beings in the clinic, in the psychiatrist's office, or in everyday noncontrived situations. Usually the critics themselves were attacked when *their* programs proved as artificial and restrictive in *their* way as the older introspective psychology was in its way. Usually nonexperimental approaches to various areas of psychology tend to become experimental as the need for basic knowledge reasserts itself. Thus psychoanalytic concepts like repression have been subjected to experimental test and projective materials have been investigated as experimental variables. The best answer to criticism of experimental-quantitative procedures has been to extend experimentation and quantification to areas previously handled by nonexperimental methods.

It is contended by some, however, that there are areas of psychology in which experimental-quantitative methods, although desirable, are still not possible because of the complexity of the interacting factors. Such attitudes are frequently found among workers concerned with social behavior and interpersonal relations, where the problems are admittedly very complex. But the complexities in these areas may be no greater than the problems faced by the early workers in sensory processes when a few hardy pioneers started out by performing simple and obvious experiments, thereby developing analytical methods and tools. What an achievement it was in the last century to reduce the almost infinite variety of colors to three fundamental dimensions of hue, brightness, and saturation, and how inadequate this analysis must have seemed to the aestheticians, painters, interior decorators, stage designers, and industrialists of that day. Yet now individuals in all areas where color is of importance come to the colorimetrist, the psychologist, and the chemist for advice and help in solving practical color problems. Similarly, the field of memory was opened to scientific investigation by Ebbinghaus when he introduced the nonsense syllable, making possible experimental control and quantification of this important activity. How artificial and obvious Ebbinghaus' experiments must have seemed to many of his contemporaries, who surely already knew that it takes longer to learn a long list of items than a short one! Yet the exact determination of the functional relationship between such variables as number of syllables and the time or number of repetitions necessary to learn them must be counted one of the great achievements of the scientific method. No one today scoffs at the simplicity and obviousness of Ebbinghaus' experiments, for he made it possible for his successors to study the learning process in more realistic ways and by means of more sophisticated tools than he employed.

The problem of relativity in psychology.   The history of science is littered with absolute concepts that have had to be discarded or modified as knowledge of environing influences and interaction effects has increased, forcing the abandonment of self-sufficient, independent entities and relations. Relativity theory in physics outmoded the concept of absolute space, time, and mass; and modern techniques in biology have destroyed the concept of the independence of nucleus and cytoplasm in the living cell. In psychology, the concepts of sensation and reflex as independent units have largely disappeared. Fechner's law is often cited as an expression of the relativity of judgment in psychophysics because it states that intensity of sensation is proportional not to absolute magnitude of stimulus but to the logarithm of the magnitude. Although Fechner's law can be regarded as a first step in the direction of a relativistic psychophysics, it cannot be regarded as a completely relativistic theory because of its assumption of a fixed zero for all magnitudes within a given sensory modality.

In spite of the realization of the complexities and interdependencies among behavioral phenomena, the search for solid unchangeable absolutes still goes on as is evidenced by attempts to determine the inner core of personality by means of tests, by the belief that the attitudes of individuals toward various issues may be univocally determined, by the attempt to specify the *real* colors of objects, and in general, by trying to extrapolate on the basis of insufficient data. Scientific findings are relative to the conditions under which they are obtained. At one time many of us thought that the integral of the normal probability function was the only psychometric function relating stimuli to the intensitive dimension of sensory processes, but recently quite a different function has been proposed as the proper expression for *the* psychophysical law (Stevens, 1957). Yet new psychophysical methods will undoubtedly lead to still other psychophysical functions in the future.

A truly relativistic approach to behavioral phenomena must state to what frame of reference phenomena are relative. Measurements of mass, space, and time are relative to the speed of light in Einstein's theory of relativity. Behavioral phenomena are relative to the state of the organism. In postulating adaptation level as the referent with respect to which behavioral phenomena are relative, psychology possesses an even more thoroughgoing relativity than does present-day physics. In relativity theory it is assumed that the speed of light has an absolute value in all systems whereas the concept of adaptation level provides for a *moving* zero to which measurements of behavior are referable.

A truly relativistic approach to behavioral phenomena must incorporate not only quantities defining the stimulus but also quantities specifying the state of the organism in laws expressing stimulus-response (S-R) relationships. Inconvenient as it may be to give up the notion of S-R relationships that omit the organism as an integral factor, it will have to be done in the interests of (1) closer approximations to experimental data and (2) better theories for dealing with large classes of facts. The domains of experimental error, individual differences, and even ignorance may be narrowed as the role of the organism is recognized and assessed.

Behavioral relativity does not imply that the relations between stimulus and response variables are capricious or fortuitous. Rather it makes possible translation of data obtained under one complex of conditions into the frame of reference demanded by other complexes of conditions. Thus a weight may feel heavy when it is the topmost stimulus in one series and light when it is the bottom stimulus in another series, not merely because it occupies different positions in the two series but because the organism shifts its zero when confronted with different sets of stimuli. Behavioral relativity as conceived here is not to be equated with experimental error or with deviations from expected outcomes due to extraneous factors; it should be considered rather as relativity that is lawful, ordered, and predictable from situational and personal factors which influence prevailing adaptation levels.

Scaling and scale factors. The problem of relativity of judgment is intimately related to the problem of scaling and of scale factors. Since the beginning of modern experimental psychology with the work of Weber, the problem of measurement has been central, first with respect to sensory magnitudes and later with respect to intelligence, attitudes, and personality traits. Advances along various fronts have occurred either concomitantly with or because of the development of more adequate methods of measurement. To measure is essentially to scale, and to scale is to order, although not all ordering involves scaling or measurement. In psychology we measure various aspects of behavior by a variety of measuring devices ranging from physical instruments to psychophysical methods involving human responses. Human beings act as measuring devices by making estimates of magnitudes, by comparing objects and relations, and, in general, by making judgments that furnish the basis for various types of scaling (cf. Stevens, 1951, 1957; Michels and Helson, 1953). Unlike physical measuring devices (excluding for the moment changes in length, mass, and time with speed, which are taken into account by the theory of relativity), living organisms change their scales as their level of adaptation changes. Just as relativity theory makes provision for measurements of fundamental physical quantities in systems traveling at different speeds, so the concept of adaptation level takes into account changes in sensitivity, judgment, and performance with changes in level of adjustment.

Different scales are (and should be) used for different orders of magnitude. Thus a man of 5 ft. 8 in. is said to be of average height in our western culture; one 6 ft. is "tall," and one 6 ft. 6 in. is very very tall. But we speak of a man 7 ft. tall as a "giant" because the usual scale of height no longer suffices. Similarly, when we deal with physical magnitudes, different physical scales are used for different orders of magnitude. We express small lengths in centimeters or inches, larger magnitudes in meters or feet, and still larger ones in miles. When we come to astronomical distances, we are obliged to incorporate time in our measure of spatial magnitude in order to obtain the convenient working unit *the light year,* which is the distance traveled by a beam of light in one year or six trillion miles. In each scale there are values we regard as small, intermediate, or large, depending partly on the units of the scale, partly on the objects measured, and partly on the experience of the individual using the scale. The farad, the unit of capacity in electrical circuits, is so large that ordinary condensers are rated in microfarads (millionths of a farad) or micromicrofarads. On the other hand, classes of objects possess characteristic magnitudes of their own, so that the same unit is large with respect to one class and small with respect to another: a millimeter is large when applied to wave lengths of light and small when applied to wave lengths of audible sounds. Individual experiences influence not only judgment but actual perceptions of magnitude. Americans perceive European automobiles as small, accustomed as they are to larger domestic cars.

When human beings scale objects, it must be remembered that the zero of the scales is not necessarily the functional zero with respect to which the judgments are actually made. Thus, if we ask Ss to find a stimulus equal to a standard tone, weight, or light, the chances are small that they will choose a stimulus equal to the standard. This may be regarded either as an error in judgment or as an indication that the judgment is a function of the level at which the organism is functioning under the prevailing conditions of stimulation.

Measurement and the use of scales involving different orders of magnitude offer no problem to the physicist since the zero of physical scales does not vary as a result of personal factors. When the properties of the organism enter into the use of scales, as in psychophysical judgments, psychometric ratings, and experimental, clinical, and everyday evaluative procedures of all kinds, the organism shifts its zero in accordance with the class of objects or events to which it is responding. A giant is not merely a larger man, he is a deviant, a monstrosity, perhaps something to be feared; all judgments regarding giants may be modified by the fact that giants and the usual run of men belong to different classes of objects. Experience provides organisms with ranges of objects that constitute definite classes. Within each class there is a range of magnitudes from very small to very large. An object that falls outside of the range usually experienced belongs *ipso facto* to another class or is regarded as novel or outré, with resultant changes in scale factor. Since, according to the theory elaborated in this book, there is a different adaptation or adjustment level for every distinguishable class of objects, it follows that the functional zero of the organism enters into psychological scaling as well as into all other types of behavior.

Change of scale often involves qualitative as well as quantitative considerations, and this often gives rise to conflicting views regarding the possibility of measuring qualities. For example, our usual standards of the virtues enable us to classify most of the people we know on a scale ranging from very bad, through average, to very good. But a large majority of the world's population rate their religious leaders so far above ordinary humans that they elevate them to saintly, Brahman, or divine status. Such individuals are obviously not judged by the same scales as the rest of us and are accordingly placed in different classes from most other mortals.

Our argument at this point may seem to concern matters of no scientific or even practical importance, but consider the attempts made in the early part of this century to assign measures of intelligence to the greats of history who were long since dead. Goethe was given an IQ of 185, Galileo only rated 145, and Newton barely managed to make 130; Mozart and Longfellow were given IQs of 150, but Laplace was given 145 and Faraday, only 105 (Terman and Cox, 1925). These early examples of overenthusiastic use of a tool should not detract from the great contribution made by Terman and his collaborators in the measurement of intellectual capacity. But is not a similar mistake being made today by those who assume that individuals can employ the number system over great ranges in scaling sensory magnitudes? Is the distance from 90 to 100 the same as the distance from 990 to 1000 psychologically? If not, what is the function that changes the scale factor when one judges sensory or other magnitudes using large numbers?

We cannot agree with laymen or psychologists who maintain that measurement is impossible where there are qualitative differences. Even intensive continua involve qualities (if only a single quality on each continuum) like brightness, pitch, or saturation. There are various ways of handling qualitatively different continua as attested by the large number of psychological scaling methods now in common use (see Guilford, 1954a). Perhaps the simplest and most universal type of scale that reflects the organism's change of zero or scale factor with different classes of objects is the category rating scale in which absolute or relative terms may be employed. In both the absolute and relative category rating scales the zero is fixed by the class of objects being judged and there is no problem regarding use of numbers over a wide range of values. Thus in using rating scales, a *small* elephant means something very different from a *small* cat and a medium-sized man suggests a different order of magnitude from a medium-sized giant. Scale factors and qualitative characteristics of different classes of objects are immediately conveyed in rating scale types of judgments;

hence this type of scale appears to be the most primary and universal of psychological scales. Such judgments also have the merit of transmitting more definite behavioral information than do scales involving the number system. A psychophysical experiment is not necessary to determine which of the following two commands would be executed more satisfactorily: "Make that radio *half* as loud as it is now" or "Make that radio much, much softer; it's altogether too loud." Scales based on number estimates are valuable within certain limits, but it must not be assumed that the organism responds in accordance with the properties of the system of natural numbers. Evidence is presented in Chapter 4 that ratio estimates made by the constant sum method vary with the absolute size of the numbers entering into the ratios.

SUMMARY

Present-day psychology has a plethora of facts and a paucity of theories by which the former may be ordered, related, and understood. This state of affairs is partly due to the difficulty and complexity of the subject matter with which psychology deals, partly to the lack of systematic investigations yielding sufficient data for valid generalizations, and partly to stereotyped modes of handling and thinking about data. Interest in presence or absence of significant differences between populations, in discovery of mere correlations without an attempt at understanding the bases of the relationships, and in purely empirical approaches to problems have hindered development of experimental-quantitative theories. We have fruitful theories in special areas, e.g., vision, hearing, and learning, but we lack the more general formal types of theory found in the other sciences which give unity and coherence to many different kinds of facts. Empirical formulas are valuable as well as rational formulas in thinking about problems and in suggesting new experiments, and they should be more widely used and taught, especially in dealing with *dynamic* phenomena. More can be learned about dynamic processes if functional relations between basic variables are put into quantitative form than if terms having only qualitative connotations are used.

Problems having systematic importance, viz., dimensionalism, the generality and validity of experimental approaches, relativity of behavioral phenomena, and scaling and scale factors, are discussed in this chapter as background for later developments.

2 *The Concept of Adaptation*

Some years ago a widely read magazine carried an article entitled "Men Who Need Your Friendship," based on hospital records of mentally ill war veterans (Hogan and Moulton, 1949). Among the cases discussed was a litter patient who clenched his teeth against food the army nurses offered him but ate the same dishes when tendered by civilian volunteers. Another patient was sullen and dispirited, caring nothing for his personal appearance until an attractive girl, an office worker not connected with the hospital, started visiting and reading with him one evening a week.

A student once came to me in deep distress after frequenting the bars and night "dives" of a large city and walking the streets until early morning, not caring what she did or what might happen to her, ready to end her life because nothing mattered and the future seemed to hold only the prospect of endless monotony and vacuity. After a number of sessions in which the satisfactions and rewards of "normal" activities were stressed, followed by a summer in a completely different environment, she returned to college with a normal outlook and zest for life.

On the day following the 1956 election in which a *Republican* President and a *Democratic* Congress were elected, two colleagues remarked to me that the voters were becoming more discriminating in splitting their ballots. But the two individuals did not mean the same thing by the remark, for one was a stanch Republican and the other a strong Democrat. The first referred with satisfaction to the election of a

Republican President; the second approved the election of a Democratic Congress.

These four cases have certain formal features in common, although they differ in material content. They illustrate the operation of intra-organismic norms and personal standards and the extent to which differences in frames of reference are responsible for individual modes of response. The last example, particularly, shows that identical responses by two individuals may mean different things, depending upon the individual's scale of values, where he draws the line between good or bad, acceptable or unacceptable. Even under conditions of laboratory investigations, individual reference systems are decisive in determining responses to specific stimuli. The experimental literature concerned with the operation of internal norms in all types of responses is now large enough to constitute a challenge to present-day psychology. We cannot understand how individual reference systems develop and function without a direct study of such systems and a theory of their origin and *modus operandi.*

The basic premise of this book is that an individual's attitudes, values, ways of structuring his experiences, judgments of physical, aesthetic, and symbolic objects, intellectual and emotional behavior, learning, and interpersonal relations all represent modes of adaptation to environmental and organismic forces. These forces do not act willy-nilly upon the organism from without, nor do they erupt spontaneously from within. Stimuli impinge upon organisms already adapted to what has gone before, and internal states depend upon previously existing internal conditions as well as external inciters to action. Furthermore, stimuli do not act singly even if they are in different sense modalities. Even the simplest sensory experiences are more or less complex, containing focal, contextual, and organic components. The pooled effect of these three classes of stimuli determines the adjustment or adaptation level underlying all forms of behavior. Before attempting a precise, quantitative definition of our central concept, let us consider some of its main connotations in biology, physiology, and sensory psychology.

CONNOTATIONS OF ADAPTATION

Adaptation, a time-honored term, came into psychology from biology, where it is used in a broad, general sense as adjustment to the conditions under which species must live in order to survive, and from sensory physiology, where it is used in the much more restricted sense of decrement in intensity of sensation or muscular response as a result of steady-state stimulation or continued responses. Let us first consider its broad, general meaning and then turn to its more restricted usage.

Adapt comes from Latin *adaptare,* meaning to *adjust.* The original meaning of adaptation is therefore adjustment. Among synonyms given for the verb adapt are: accommodate, adjust, arrange, attune, conform, fashion, fit, harmonize, prepare, proportion, set, and suit (Funk and Wagnalls *Standard Universal Dictionary,* 1941). In biology, adaptation refers to favorable organic modifications suiting a plant or animal to its environment (*Gould's Practitioner's Medical Dictionary,* 1918). Adaptation as adjustment to environing conditions finds concrete expression in Dobzhansky:

> The more one studies living beings, the more one is impressed by the wonderfully effective adjustment of their multifarious body structures and functions to their varying ways of life. From the simplest to the most complex, all organisms are constructed to function efficiently in the environment in which they live. The body of a green plant can build itself from food consisting merely of water, certain gases in the air and some mineral salts taken from the soil. A fish is a highly efficient machine for exploiting organic food resources of water, and a bird is able to get the most from its air environment. The human body is a complex, finely coordinated machine of marvellously precise engineering, and through the inventive abilities of his brain man is able to control his environment. Every species, even the most humble, occupies a certain place in the economy of nature, a certain adaptive niche which it exploits to stay alive (1950, p. 32).

Psychologists, no less than biologists, have recognized the ubiquity of adaptive mechanisms when they equate practically all forms of behavior, from the simplest reflexes to the highest accomplishments of the cortex, with adaptation. In this vein Piéron writes:

> Reflexes, partial and stereotyped responses, operate in general as adaptive directive mechanisms, either in an appetitive sense (like the sucking or grasping of the newborn), or in a protective sense (like the different reflexes of defense), or finally in a regulative sense (like the straightening of posture or the alteration of walking which one observes from the first hours after birth). The role of the cortex is essentially that of conditioning which permits adaptive anticipation . . . (1950, p. 76).

In lower organisms it is difficult to distinguish between sensory adaptation and learning. Schneirla asks: "Has an amoeba learned in any important sense when in the course of repeated head-on exposures to a beam of light it extends progressively fewer pseudopodia? . . . The phenomenon appears to resemble light adaptation more closely than it does learning in a higher animal" (1949, p. 247 f.). But should we distinguish between learning and adaptation even in the higher animals? Many psychologists would answer in the negative. Piéron and many other psychologists regard all learning as adaptive in nature. Yerkes, in his definitive monograph on multiple-choice learning in chimpanzees (1934), used the term "adaptation" where other psychologists usually use "conditioning" and "learning." Similarly, Minami and Dallenbach speak of putting their animal subjects "into the practice box for 10 minutes to 'adapt' to the experimental situation" (1946); they could just as well have said "to become familiar with, or to learn about, the experimental situation." Harlow relates learning sets and adaptation even more explicitly:

The construct of learning sets is of importance in the understanding of adaptive behavior. . . . Training on several hundred specific problems has not turned the monkey into an automaton exhibiting forced, stereotyped, reflex responses to specific stimuli. These several hundred habits have, instead, made the monkey an adjustable creature with an increased capacity to adapt to the everchanging demands of a psychology laboratory environment. . . . Learning sets acquired by man in and appropriate to his environment have accounted for his ability to adapt and survive (1949, pp. 59, 65).

In a broad sense psychologists and biologists recognize that all organic activities, from the lowest to the highest, aid in adapting individuals and species to the environments in which they live. Human and animal subjects adjust to situations confronting them under the restricted and artificial conditions of laboratory experimentation as well as under the free natural conditions of living.

The many ways in which animals adapt to their environments must be studied in detail to be understood. Prosser and Sherman (1958) point out that physiologists study adaptation to environmental changes largely in terms of responses of the total organism and in terms of specific function systems; plant physiologists emphasize selection of genetic varieties as the principal mode of adaptation in plants; bacterial physiologists have noted genetic adaptation to physical factors while concentrating on adaptations to changed nutrients. Widely different species, however, may employ similar mechanisms in adapting to their environments, e.g., the enzymatic mechanisms of temperature adaptation found in fish and in yeast. Because adaptation occurs in many different ways, there are difficulties in using one definition of adaptation for all cases (plants and animals); yet the concept of adaptation persists and is widely used in all branches of biology.

Anticipating, in a broad sense, the general adaptation syndrome of Selye (1950), Jelliffe stressed the adaptive nature of mental disease when he asserted that abnormal as well as healthy individuals adapt to the conditions in which they live. He insisted that adaptation is not limited to physicochemical and sensori-motor systems, but occurs also in response to sociogenic and symbolic factors in the environment and in the person. Ecology, according to Jelliffe, not only considers the adjustments of individuals and species to their environments, but also studies communities or the "adaptation of whole to wholes" (1937). It is evident that many authorities have used the concept of adaptation to cover the whole range of animal adjustments, from the simplest responses of sensori-motor systems to the most complex interactions within and among individuals and societies.

Homeostasis.   The great class of adaptations to which Cannon gave the name "homeostasis" are the steady physiological states in mammals which enable them to counteract changes both in external environing conditions and in internal bodily processes. Homeostatic processes are essentially compensatory in nature. If the outside temperature falls, blood is withdrawn from the surface of the body by vasoconstriction to prevent cooling so that the internal temperature remains constant; if the outside temperature rises, vasodilation allows blood to flow to the surface capillaries, and the sweat glands also function to cool the body. Similarly, the pH content of the blood is kept constant by buffer mechanisms, and its sugar level is maintained constant by regulatory storage and excretion mechanisms. Homeostasis is also found at higher, behavioral levels of activity. Perceptual and cognitive processes make us aware of danger and bring into play autonomic and endocrine systems that enable us to meet or avoid emergencies. Activities leading to satisfaction of basic needs (e.g., food, water, shelter, sex) and involving the somatic as well as the autonomic systems are now regarded as bona fide instances of homeostasis. Indeed, Dempsey asserts "voluntary activity, instinctive reactions, and even intellectual behavior of a high order cannot be excluded from consideration" as homeostatic mechanisms, and he suggests that "the adjustments of societies to their physical environments and to each other show the operation of homeostatic principles" (1951, p. 231).

Cannon's concept of homeostasis has wider importance than is implied by an enumeration of physiological steady states and the specific mechanisms effecting them. The concept of homeostasis introduced order and unity into what was a welter of conflicting data. Dempsey says:

Viewed empirically, the physiological reactions of mammalian organisms present an array of contradictory and paradoxical phenomena. The heart rate and cardiac output may increase while the blood flow in a given region increases, decreases, or remains static. An accelerated respiratory rate may accompany muscular activity (exercise) or inactivity (panting). The glucose concentration of the blood may rise during depletion of the glycogen stores of the body, or, conversely, while the carbohydrate reserves are being augmented. Taken without reference to the total needs of the individual, these reactions can but bewilder the systematist. It is understandable, therefore, that a generalization rationalizing these and many other observations would be received gratefully by physiological investigators (1951, p. 209).

This unifying concept proved to be the "general law of constancy of the internal environment." Phenomena that appeared paradoxical and contradictory by themselves were ordered and understood when seen as manifestations of homeostasis.

The second great contribution implicit in the concept of homeostasis is its demonstration of physiological interactions at various levels of complexity. Blood-sugar level is regulated by more or less discrete organs and functions and is the result of relatively simple, low-order integrations, but mobilization of the organism for emergencies involves complex interactions of chemical, endocrine, and neural systems. Physiological pooling of many systems is, therefore, a prime condition for maintaining the steady internal states necessary for survival of mammalian organisms (see Dempsey, 1951). Pooling must be considered a fundamental principle governing physiological processes at the simplest as well as the most complex levels of functioning and is responsible for the adaptive nature of homeostatic processes.

SENSORY ADAPTATION

Contrasted with homeostasis is sensory adaptation, which represents a more restricted type of adaptation because specific receptor systems are involved rather than the whole organism. Yet certain features of sensory adaptation are also present in the most complex types of behavior.

   Adaptation and fatigue. The concept of adaptation commonly used by psychologists stems from nerve physiology, where the decline in rate of discharge of receptors under constant stimulation is defined as adaptation. Usually the plateau rate of discharge after various periods of stimulation, depending upon the end organs in question, is taken as the adapted state of the end organ, although the initial rapid decline in receptor discharge is also considered as part of the process of adaptation. The question immediately arises: where is the line to be drawn between adaptation and its closely related process, fatigue? Both terms refer to performance decrement following repetition of stimulus or response. Phenomena of fatigue and adaptation are difficult to distinguish except on the basis of explicit criteria applicable to specific areas of investigation. Ruch (1946) states that it is common to designate any decrement in response resulting from *activity* as "fatigue." When stretch stimuli are slowly applied to muscle, the rate of discharge from the muscle receptors is initially high and then grows progressively slower—an *adaptation* effect, according to Ruch, because no activity has occurred in the muscle. Fatigue is also distinguished from adaptation on the basis of temporal onset and recovery, fatigue being a slower process than adaptation. Other differences between fatigue and adaptation concern chemical changes in the end organs and physiological changes that may not be distinguishable psychologically (see Bronk, 1935). Granting that sense organs show two types of activity decrement, fatigue and adaptation, we need not at present attempt to distinguish them. After an extensive review of the literature dealing with fatigue at the behavioral level, Bartley and Chute (1947) come to the conclusion that fatigue is almost always a psychological phenomenon tantamount to frustration. Supporting this view are the findings of Carmichael and his co-workers (1949) who were unable to demonstrate fatigue in prolonged reading and other long-continued sensori-motor tasks. Fatigue may be regarded as a special kind of adjustment or in its strict physiological sense when the latter is more appropriate.

   Transient and steady phases of adaptation. Although adaptation is often considered to be the end result of long-continued stimulation, nerve and sensory physiologists recognize the initial rapid changes in nerve and receptor activity as part of the adaptive process. Both the transient and the steady phases of adaptation appear clearly in the classical curves depicting light and dark adaptation. The cone and rod portions of the dark adaptation curve(*s*) show an initial rapid decline in the amount of light needed for threshold vision, followed by a slower, almost imperceptible drop. The initial gain in sensitivity upon entering a dark room from lighted surroundings is so rapid that subjects (*Ss*) cannot rotate the control of the Nagel adaptometer fast enough to keep the stimulus light invisible. Hecht emphasized the importance of adaptation in acquainting the organism with fast transient changes in the environment when he stated that the sensory system "acts so as to transmit any rapid changes in the environment, but which hides any long-maintained conditions" (1934, p. 739). This rapid initial phase of adaptation has been practically overlooked by the majority of psychologists, who mention only the steady homogeneous phase of adaptation. We must recognize that adaptation is a mechanism for acquainting us with *changes* in the environment. If the same stimulation continues, adaptation gradually counteracts its effects to the point where it may no longer be sensed or its quality becomes neutral.

The complete course of adaptation from the initial rapid change in sensitivity to the steady state is best exemplified in the dark adaptation curves of rods and cones, as we have already pointed out. Action potentials of touch and other receptors also show the initial rapid change in activity of receptors when first subjected to new stimulation. Measurements at the behavioral level are usually confined to the steady state because of the difficulty of measuring the initial rapid changes in sensitivity and because the steady state is easier to identify introspectively. Studies of steady (or equilibrium) states often yield beautifully ordered data, even when they are affected by a multiplicity of conditions. Consider the data from Zigler (1932) which appear in Table 2.1, giving the times of complete disappearance of tactile sensation as a function of weight and size of stimuli. With size of stimuli constant, the length of time necessary for complete adaptation increases with the weight of the stimulus, but with weight constant, the time decreases with increasing size of stimulus. As in vision, greater intensities of stimulation require longer periods to reach the steady end-state than do weaker intensities of stimulation. Although end-states with different weights and sizes of stimuli appear identical, different adaptation levels are established in each instance, as shown by the differences in sensitivities and recovery times following adaptation to the various conditions of stimulation.

TABLE 2.1.　Times of Disappearance of Sensation as a Function of Weight and Size of Tactile Stimuli

	Time in Seconds, Size Constant[a]			
Weight (mg.)	Back of Hand	Forearm	Forehead	Cheek
50	2.42	2.31	5.07	5.71
100	3.82	3.28	6.22	6.37
500	6.01	4.86	9.96	11.63
1000	6.71	5.60	10.43	13.51
2000	9.52	7.76	16.03	19.36

	Time in Seconds, Intensity Constant[a]	
Diameter (mm.)	Forehead	Cheek
5	18.9	21.2
10	16.1	16.5
15	14.6	14.4
20	12.3	12.2
25	9.9	10.3

[a] Values are averages for eight Ss.
SOURCE: From Zigler, 1932. With the permission of the *American Journal of Psychology*.

Several other important facts emerge from Zigler's study of the steady state in tactile sensitivity. What looks like a simple, unidimensional stimulus may often be a sum, product, or ratio of several dimensions. The data for weight and size indicate that the *effective* tactile stimulus is *density,* or mass per unit volume, not weight or size per se. Density has also been found to be the effective stimulus in lifted weights (Furth, 1960). Furthermore, adaptation time depends upon the part of the body stimulated, e.g., the back of the hand and forearm require about half as much time as the forehead and cheek for complete adaptation. Individual differences do not appear in Table 2.1, where the values are averages for eight subjects. Zigler reports that individual differences in adaptation times vary widely; one S may take from 8 to 15 times longer to adapt than another; some Ss adapt quickly in all regions, others take longer in all regions, and still others adapt quickly in some regions and slowly in others.[1] Evidently individuals cannot be typed even so far as this simple sensory function is concerned.

Consideration of the transient and the steady phases of adaptation has shown that whereas the initial phase of adaptation serves to acquaint the organism with changes and differences in the environment, the final phase results in wiping the slate clean. The classical view of adaptation as an index of receptor activity that is lowered by increments of stimulation and raised by decrements of stimulation emphasizes the steady end-state established under constant stimulation. We may reformulate the classic statement to make the temporal nature of the process with its changing rates more explicit: For every condition or complex of conditions in which a receptor system is stimulated, there is an initial rapid change in activity and sensitivity, which is followed by a constant level of activity and sensitivity if the stimulation is continued at a constant intensity. Conversely, all receptor activities and sensitivities are referable to steady states that are reached if stimulation remains constant. This statement relates the transient part of the adaptive process to the steady state, and thereby makes it possible to understand how departures from level are related to the equilibrium state.

Adaptation is not always complete in the sense that steady stimulation is neutralized. Intense visual stimuli may lose chromaticness and lightness, but they do not fade out to neutral gray, as is often asserted (cf. Troland, 1921; Helson and Judd, 1932). In such instances, the steady state represents an equilibrium between stimulus and receptor activity wherein stimulus quality is reduced but not entirely obliterated. Complete adaptation probably occurs only with stimuli of weak to moderate intensities.

For many years psychologists doubted that adaptation occurred in all sense modalities, particularly with auditory and pain stimulation. It is now definitely established, however, that the loudness of a steady auditory stimulus decreases with time (Harris and Rawnsley, 1953; Carterette, 1956) and that afterimages, so characteristic of adaptation in vision, also occur in hearing (Rosenblith, Miller, Egan, Hirsh, and

[1] Such differences among Ss as Zigler reports may be important practically in tasks requiring tactile discrimination because, as Ruch points out, "rapid adaptation may be an advantage to an exploratory sense such as touch where, after contacts are perceived the slate is wiped clean by adaptation and made ready to receive a new impression" (1946, p. 313).

Thomas, 1947). Similarly, adaptation to pain, at least to cutaneous pain, has been definitely established by Burns and Dallenbach (1933).

On the other hand, important differences exist among the various sense modalities in rates of adaptation, recovery times, and the presence or absence of positive and negative afterimages. Rosenblith and his co-workers (1947) were able to demonstrate auditory afterimages only by the change in timbre of such familiar sounds as a handclap, a typewriter noise, and voices following high-intensity buzzing lasting one or two minutes, but not by direct observation. No afterimage has yet been demonstrated in olfaction, unless increased sensitivity to one odor following adaptation to another is to be regarded as an afterimage phenomenon. We need not present an exhaustive survey of likenesses and differences among the sense modalities with respect to all phenomena of adaptation as this information can readily be obtained from many sources (Boring, 1942; Stevens, 1951; Woodworth and Schlosberg, 1954).

In addition to the different phenomena of adaptation among sensory systems there are the "adaptive" phenomena in the central nervous system. Steady-state stimulation of the central nervous system leads to phenomena different from those found when peripheral nerves and receptors are studied and makes the problem of adaptation even more difficult and complicated than it was thought to be before the recording of brain potentials. Bagchi points out, "In the brain there is no decrease in frequency of rhythm following the disturbance occasioned by continued stimuli but rather a regaining of potential value" (1936, p. 467). Perhaps the term "readjustment" is preferable to "adaptation" to cover observations of central neural changes following continued stimulation. In any case, adjustment or adaptation at the behavioral level must be the end result of a complicated process in which adaptive phenomena may differ from stage to stage.

Two aspects of adaptation.   Even at the sensory level, the concept of adaptation as decrement in sensitivity and/or response fails to do justice to the fact that adaptation is as much a sensitizing process as a desensitizing one. Coincident with decrement in response of some receptors following durative or repeated stimulation there is found heightened response on the part of other receptors: Adaptation (decreased sensitivity) to red makes us more sensitive to blue-green; adaptation to light makes us more sensitive to dark; adaptation to warm makes us more sensitive to cold; and so on through the whole gamut of simultaneous and successive contrasts. Only recently have the practical implications of the double aspect of adaptation been realized; e.g., to increase sensitivity to small differences in colors, each color should be presented on a background of a *complementary* color (White, 1949). Though it is a truism that adaptation to a given quality results in enhancement of the complementary quality, there are still psychologists who define adaptation solely as a desensitizing process. This one-sided view is based on effects of localized stimulation with no thought given to spatial or temporal parameters. Desensitization of any given spot is accompanied by heightened sensitivity to complementary qualities of neighboring spots, and there is heightened sensitivity of the spot itself following the adapting stimulus. The Hering theory of color was expressly designed to account for both the sensitizing and the desensitizing effects of adaptation. A law of compensation seems to be generally at work whereby loss in one direction is counterbalanced by gain in another.

On the response side, the tendency of stimuli to lose their effectiveness with repetition or duration is known as habituation or negative adaptation. An interesting example of this type of adaptation was given by Humphrey: If the cage containing a number of frogs is tapped at intervals of about two seconds, the frogs react by jumping; if the test is repeated, reaction soon ceases (1930*b*). But repetition does not always result in diminution of response for if this were the case, there would be only one-trial learning. As documented in E. Gibson's review (1953), many studies have demonstrated improvement of both sensory and motor functions with repetition or practice, e.g., in visual acuity, two-point tactile threshold, judgments of two-dimensional length and visual extent, reduction of visual illusions, absolute judgments of magnitude, stereoscopic depth perception, visual range estimations, and veridicality of perception under impoverished conditions of viewing. Although some of the improvement may be attributed to learning, cognitive, and judgmental factors, the fact remains that improvement does occur with repetition or controlled training.

We must therefore recognize that adaptation is a two-way process involving heightened as well as lowered performance of receptors or sensori-motor systems. Traditionally, adaptation has been assigned the role of a leveling process, and contrast the role of an accentuating process. But since these two processes are never found apart it is, operationally, meaningless to separate them. Attesting to the sensitizing effects of adaptation are the simultaneous appearance of surround and complementary colors in colored shadows; the presence of illuminant, achromatic, and complementary colors in strongly chromatic sources of illumination with nonselective stimuli on backgrounds of intermediate reflectance; and many other cases of what Gibson (1937*a, b*) called "adaptation with negative aftereffect" (also found in space perception and color perception).

Appreciation of absolute levels of stimulation. Although stimuli that coincide with level are neutral and sometimes not sensed as such, there is an appreciation of absolute levels of stimulation and response. While a sheet of paper looks white in both bright and dim illuminations and all other objects in the field of view are perceived to be the same, we are nevertheless aware of whether the level of illumination is high or low. We perceive reflectances, which are constant properties of objects, while we perceive levels of illuminance as they change from time to time. Similar distinctions are made in motor activities where quite different rates of activity may seem "normal": the natural rate of walking is slower than the natural rate of running, yet both feel equally "right." In performing at different levels, each level seems normal for the type of activity involved. Because the organism adjusts to levels of stimulation and to rates of response, the deleterious effects of extreme or long-continued stimuli and responses may not be manifested before considerable damage to the organism has occurred. Adjustment to extreme levels may hide the long-term cost of working at maximum output or in abnormal environments. Awareness of differences in level, therefore, has biological utility just as perception of constant properties of objects and responses has its biological utility.

HOMEOSTASIS, EQUILIBRIUM, AND ADAPTATION–LEVEL THEORY

Theories of behavior which assume that all responses are directed toward the attainment of fixed levels of equilibrium must not be confused with the theory forming the central core of this book. Although they have something in common, they differ in important respects. At the physiological level, in many biological and in some sociological phenomena, departures from fixed values of certain constants, or from equilibrium, are signs of abnormality. We are ill if our internal temperature rises or falls a few degrees from its normal value of 98.6° F or if the pH content of the blood varies much from its normal value of 7.40. Similarly, strife between groups in any society is fraught with danger, whereas peaceful coexistence denotes a condition of equilibrium within a society devoutly to be wished. Mechanisms exist for maintaining and restoring fixed values of certain physical and chemical constants associated with vital bodily processes and for peaceful relations between groups, classes, and nations. The equilibriums associated with these fixed levels are dynamic; in fact, these levels cannot represent static equilibriums because of the ongoing changing nature of processes in the individual and in the give-and-take of interpersonal relations.

Although recognizing such concepts as homeostasis, striving toward equilibrium, desire for rest, and other more or less steady states, we must not forget that individuals and groups strive for variety, change, and novelty as well as for rest, quiet, and the familiar. To infer from our theory that all behavior is directed toward the attainment of equilibrium or fixed end-states is wrong. The desire for pleasure, action, objects, possessions, change of situation, fame, recognition, and all the other things for which men strive is not satisfied by reaching a state of equilibrium (which would be paralleled psychologically by feelings of neutrality or indifference) but rather by attaining greater variety and intensity of satisfactions which come from activities and objects associated with higher levels of adjustment. A person strives for $1,000 when he has nothing, $10,000 when he has $1,000, and $1,000,000 when he has $500,000, not because the larger amount of money will bring equilibrium and quiescence, but because, in his opinion, it holds possibilities for new sources of enjoyment. As Peak (1955) and others have pointed out, impulsion to action (and enjoyment) comes not from situations giving rise to neutral states of the organism but rather from the disparity between stimulation and prevailing adaptation level. Magnitude of response depends upon this difference from level, not only in perceptual phenomena but in emotional and motivational states as well.

How then does adaptation level differ from homeostasis and from concepts that envisage behavior as always changing in the direction of greater stability? The point of view enunciated here asserts that equilibrium states represent the reference points or zeros from which behavior is measured, predicted, and understood, without implying that the *goal* of behavior is a state of equilibrium. The adaptation level represents the zero or origin to which gradients of stimulation are referable. The steeper the gradient is, the greater the impact of the stimulus on the organism and the greater the response to it. Repeated or long-continued stimulation is reduced in effectiveness and sometimes completely neutralized because the organism brings its level as close as possible to the level (a weighted mean) of stimulation. With very intense (and sometimes very weak) stimuli complete adaptation does not occur. The adjustment level does not rise high enough or sink low enough to negate stimuli completely, except near the lower absolute threshold. There is survival value in remaining aware of such extremes in the environment as the deafening roar of an explosion or the quiet hiss of a rattlesnake. Since level tends to approximate a weighted mean of all stimuli, it never corresponds to zero or complete absence of stimulation. This is true even in cases where there is no stimulation, e.g., in complete darkness, because of fine and gross bodily activities and residual factors within receptors. Adaptation thus occurs with respect to a given segment or region of stimulation, reducing its effectiveness but at the same time accentuating stimuli above and below the critical region. Thus, far from being only a neutralizing process, as in the classical concept, adaptation is also a sensitizing process that enhances some stimuli at the same time that it negates others.

Sensory adaptation thus differs from homeostasis, as do other forms of adjustment, in being labile and in having reference to continua rather than to fixed values. Adaptation level furnishes reference points, as does homeostasis, for understanding complex interactions of many simultaneously operating factors in the organism.

MOTOR ADAPTATIONS

Organisms adopt various postures and make movements indicative of the type of adaptation made to the conditions facing them at the moment. Each bodily posture represents a type of adjustment to stimulation, just as sensory and judgmental responses do. Too often the concept of equilibrium is equated with static symmetrical balance, which is usually not the most stable equilibrium for tasks the organism must perform. A person standing bolt upright with hands at sides and head erect may be in perfect equilibrium, but he can be knocked over much more easily than if he crouches with head low, foot forward, and arms bent, in the stance of the prize fighter. Organisms as a rule maintain bodily balance in off-center positions, a point generalized by Gesell (1946) in his principle of functional asymmetry:

> The principle of functional asymmetry is a special inflection of the principle of reciprocal interweaving and is inseparable therefrom. Bilateral and ipsilateral members must be brought into parallel and diagonal coordination. This takes an enormous amount of dovetailing, which is accounted for by the principle and process of neuromotor interweaving.
>
> But man, in spite of his bilateral construction, does not face the world on a frontal plane of symmetry. He confronts it at an angle and he makes his escapes also, obliquely. He develops monolateral aptitudes and preferences in handedness, eyedness, footedness, and other forms of unidexterity. Perfect ambidexterity, if it exists, would seem to be almost an abnormality, because effective attentional adjustments require an asymmetric focalization of motor set. The behavioral center of gravity always tends to shift to an eccentric position. Unidexterity of hand, foot, or eye does not so much represent an absolute difference in skill as a predilection for stabilized psychomotor orientations.
>
> These orientations are fundamentally postural sets; and they are asymmetric. Ideally reciprocal interweaving operates to preserve harmony and balance; but in actuality there is superadded ontogenetic deflection to insure the greater efficiency of functional asymmetry (p. 307).

Is it mere coincidence that most motor adjustments involve asymmetric bodily coordinations and that the point of subjective equality (PSE) of psychophysical judgments is usually *below* the midpoint of symmetrical distributions of the stimuli being judged? May not both of these phenomena be manifestations of the same basic principle of organic functioning?

Most motor coordinations, particularly those constituting the best ways to accomplish tasks, must be learned. The infant learns to orient head and mouth for suckling; the child learns to walk; the youth learns to play ball; the adult learns the best way to run a lathe or to play the piano. All stages of the learning process are adaptations in which the individual does as well as he can with what he has and what he knows. The two-year-old grasps the pencil or crayon in his fist and makes sweeping arm movements in his attempts to write or draw; only after considerable practice does he hold the instrument with his fingers and restrict the writing movements to the minimum necessary for the task. No one can watch young children learning to walk, write, draw, climb, or manipulate objects without becoming aware of the successive adaptations that enter into learning processes. The adaptive nature of learning would have been recognized and would have received theoretical consideration long ago had psychologists been as interested in *motor* behavior as in verbal and discriminatory behavior. *Learning* has become almost synonymous with *behavior,* for according to most learning theorists almost everything we do is a product of learning. But consideration of the ways in which motor coordinations are refined through learning reveals their adaptive nature and shows the necessity for subordinating learning to adaptation as the more general concept.

ADAPTATION AS AN ACTIVE PROCESS

Up to this point we have treated adaptation as the adjustment of the organism to the environment, as if, to quote Hecht, "the stimulus adapts the organism to itself" (1923, p. 577). Cohen has argued against this point of view:

> Whatever the value of the principle of equilibrium in physiology where it arose, whether it is called constancy, stability, homeostasis or negative feedback, its explanatory value in the domain of mind is limited. . . . It serves to express the important elements of stability and resistance to change, but it does nothing to convey the part played by instability and the impulse to change in human life. These are just as fundamental, and without them social change would be inconceivable (1958, pp. 19–20).

But adaptation is not the static one-way process implied by Cohen, and the theory propounded in this book differs from the principle of homeostasis because it stresses *changing levels.* Furthermore, the theory provides for internal as well as for external initiators of action. Internal stimuli drive organisms to seek food, water, shelter, comfortable temperatures, and release from the tensions built up by accumulation of waste products within the body. Organisms are in continual movement so that even in a constant environment actual stimulation varies from moment to moment. We move our limbs, head, trunk, eyes, hands, and feet in order to see, hear, taste, smell, feel, and manipulate objects, and also to modify our position or orientation in space. We turn away or otherwise protect ourselves from excessive stimulation, and we take appropriate action to intensify stimulation that is not seen, heard, or otherwise sensed clearly. Although the flow of energy is from the environment to the organism, our powers of selection, our ability to "gate" stimuli as Bruner has put it, and our ability to change the environment by moving about in it allow us to determine to a large extent the nature and degree of stimulation that we receive.

The sympathetic and parasympathetic systems, in maintaining the various vegetative and equilibratory processes necessary for life, act as energizers both for normal internal activities and for sudden emergency responses involving visceral and somatic systems. Closely allied with autonomic functions are the humoral agents that act on specific organs and (more generally) by way of the circulation. Neural and circulatory mechanisms are thus the source of internally initiated changes, often triggered and guided by sensory and cognitive processes. Adaptation must therefore be regarded as the product of both internally and externally initiated energies and as a dynamic, not static, process. Far from regarding the organism as a piece of putty molded by environmental forces, many writers who stress the importance of adaptation also recognize as a source of the organism's activities "internal disequilibria" that act as "sensitizing components in behavior determination" (Nissen, 1951, p. 355). Dynamic equilibrium in living organisms, as opposed to static equilibrium, is described as follows by Lillie:

The living substance is continually changing; its stability is dynamic rather than static: "all living structure is actively maintained structure" quoting Haldane. An old comparison is that with candle flames, vortexes, fountains, and other systems which preserve constant structural and active characters in spite of continual change of material. Such systems have been classed . . . as "stationary systems"; each represents not a static but a kinetic (or dynamic) equilibrium—what we now often call a "steady state"; there is a balance of constitutive and dissipative processes (1945, p. 28).

Constitutive and dissipative processes, however, are not in perfect balance at all times, especially when stimulation is changing and the organism is active. The permissible range of steady states is much greater at the behavioral level, even in sensory adaptation, than at the vital physiological level with which homeostasis is mainly concerned. Whereas life can function only with relatively small variations from normal values of blood sugar, internal temperature, and oxygen tension of the blood, the eye may function over a range of 10,000 to 1 and surface temperature may vary over a range of 25 degrees or more without harm. Moreover, the organism does not come into equilibrium with extreme or changing stimulation, since complete adaptation occurs only with medium intensities and constant stimulation. To maintain constant stimulation, sense organs as well as stimuli must be immobilized. Even with constant stimulation, adaptation level lags behind stimulation level, with the result that it is always below intense stimuli and often above weak stimuli.

In recognizing the power of organisms to initiate action from within, we must not overlook sources of outside stimulation. Some stimuli serve as sensitizing agents. They do not initiate action or elicit specific responses, but they do prepare the organism to react to stimuli that may come at another time. Nissen (1951) gives the following illustration of a sensitizing stimulus: When carbon dioxide is added to the water of their aquarium, Daphnia ordinarily rise to the surface, but if the aquarium is lighted from below, they move to the bottom of the tank. Movement is, therefore, initiated, and its direction determined, by light; but the carbon dioxide is the stimulus that makes the organism receptive to the light stimulus. Nissen further points out that "extreme intensities of any sensory modality may disturb homeostasis and thus may both initiate and direct behavior" (1951, p. 356).

Adaptation is, therefore, a two-way affair. Effects of stimulation initiate changes within the organism. These changes adapt the organism to prevailing conditions, but may also actuate the organism from within. It is doubtful that stimulation is ever received completely passively by the organism. Anyone who has been seriously ill knows how differently stimuli affect us during sickness. Music, which is a delight to a healthy individual, cannot be borne when vital energies are low. Responses reflect the state of the organism as well as the properties of stimuli and hence must be regarded as the results of active adjustive processes. Thus by its own neural, humoral, visceral, muscular, and somatic activities the organism varies internal and external stimuli; therefore, it can hardly be regarded as a passive recipient of energies or as a mechanism that merely reflects, transduces, or modifies energy in the manner of a mirror, filter, or prism. On the contrary, the organism utilizes the energies and the information it receives in accordance with its own purposes, goals, and wishes. We not only see with our eyes, we look; we not only feel, we explore and fashion with our hands; we not only perceive, we utilize what is given to reach our immediate or long-term ends.

It may seem to the reader that only the passive role of the organism is stressed in our approach to behavior since we deal mainly with the *results* of actions and processes rather than with the dynamisms themselves. This is in line with a descriptive quantitative treatment which is common in scientific work. As pointed out earlier, the trick is to capture dynamisms in *descriptive* terms the way phenomena of physics, such as motion and magnetic attraction and repulsion, are described in mathematical formulas. By narrowing our sights we may hope to achieve a penetration into crucial basic aspects of behavior that can lead to a better understanding than has hitherto been achieved by global thinking.

THE CONCEPT OF LEVEL

Adaptation and level are co-ordinate terms, for every state of adaptation corresponds to a given level of activity. Conversely, level of activity is a reflection of the state of adaptation. The activity may be neural, humoral, receptor, effector, or sensori-motor; it may be manifested in sensory processes, phenomena of judgment, affectivity and expression of attitudes, learning, habit formation, intelligence, and thinking. As we shall see later, there is adaptation to level of difficulty of intelligence tests (Heim, 1955) and to degrees of social pressure exerted on individuals under various conditions (Rosenbaum and Blake, 1955; Helson, Blake, Mouton, and Olmstead, 1956; Helson, Blake, and Mouton, 1958*a, b*), just as there is adaptation to level of luminance or to the sound "level" that prevails in the determination of the half-loudness of a series of auditory stimuli. To clarify the concept of level as it is employed in this book, let us consider it in a number of other contexts.

Quantitatively, whenever two sets of measures differ significantly from each other, they are said to represent different levels of the variables being measured. Often the term level indicates rate as well as amount, higher rates being taken to indicate higher (integrated) amounts, as in forecasts of employment or industrial productivity. In psychology, the concept of level has been most explicit in studies of sensory processes, but it has not been absent from the fields of personality and clinical psychology. Indeed, the classical division of temperaments into sanguine, choleric, phlegmatic, and melancholic suggests different levels of activity among the four types of personality. For example, the phlegmatic individual is slower and more even in his responses than the choleric. Whether or not this classification of personality types is valid, measurements of simple types of responses reveal

individual differences in reactive levels. The data of Table 2.2 indicate
that individual *B* responds more slowly than individual *A* to auditory,
tactile, and olfactory stimulation. Wherever measures differ significantly, whether in the field of threshold measurements or in the field
of social and interpersonal relations, we are justified in speaking of
differences in level.

TABLE 2.2.   Reaction Times (in Milliseconds) of Two Individuals
to Auditory, Tactile, and Olfactory Stimulation

	A	B
Noise	165	185
Touch	187	214
Odor	210	390

SOURCE: From Woodworth and Schlosbreg, 1954. With the
permission of Henry Holt and Co.

Measures of level depend upon the conditions of measurement and
upon the variables being measured. Negatively correlated variables
yield opposite (but not necessarily contradictory) conclusions regarding
level. For example, in beginning practice with mirror-tracing, speed
and accuracy are inversely related, with the result that high accuracy
is accompanied by slow speed. In this case we would say that level of
accuracy is high while level of speed is low. When qualities form oppositional series (pleasant-unpleasant, loud-soft, light-dark) or when
reciprocal values are in question, high level of one quality or value
implies low level of the other, and vice versa. Although these considerations are elementary, they must be kept in mind when speaking about
"high" or "low" adaptation levels.

Occasionally levels interchange, one variable yielding lower values
than another at one end of a continuum and higher values than the
other at the opposite end of the continuum. Thus the relation between
visual acuity and retinal illumination reveals higher acuity with a
grating than with a C-type test object up to about 1.25 log trolands; but
beyond this value the C curve rises above the grating curve (Bartley,
1951). Even in this paradoxical instance, the definition of levels in
terms of sets of values which differ significantly holds. That is, even
though the curves for the two types of test objects cross, visual acuity
is definitely higher with the grating from about 0.001 to 30 trolands and

definitely lower than the C-type test object above 30 trolands. Such instances as these are relatively rare, but they do indicate the necessity for specification of limits, breaking points, overlapping regions, and crossing points of performance curves in using the concept of levels, since a given stimulus or condition may not be superior to another throughout the whole range of variables tested.

The concept of level is subject to a variety of interpretations, and its meaning should be stated when it is not clear from its context. Measures of level of a given variable are not necessarily identical, particularly if different formulas or operations are used in their determination. Threshold values, point of subjective equality (PSE), and interval of uncertainty depend upon the particular formulas used in their calculation (see Woodworth and Schlosberg, 1954). Measures of level may be in physical units, as in measurement of sensory processes and psychophysical judgments; in terms of frequencies of response or numbers of individuals responding in certain ways; in terms of scale values derived from frequencies or physical measures; and so on through the whole gamut of measures found in present-day psychology. We may specify level in terms of central tendency or variability or by comparing slopes of curves. We may use absolute numbers, ratios, or any other meaningful quantities to denote levels. We shall use a number of different measures of level in this book, but their being different does not vitiate their value. Nor is the usefulness of the concept of adaptation level impaired because it is stated sometimes in physical units, sometimes in terms of absolute or relative frequencies, and at other times in terms of conditions that elicit neutral or indifferent responses.

BEHAVIORAL ADAPTATION: DEFINITION AND ASSUMPTIONS

Adaptation defined in the general biological sense as the "adjustment of internal to external relations" is too broad to serve the purposes of an experimental-quantitative approach to problems of behavior. To be most fruitful, the concept of adaptation must be given an operational, quantitative definition. Moreover, it must cover all significant cases of behavioral adjustment. We are thus faced with the problem of formulating a quantitative definition of adaptation which will be significant and meaningful for the science of behavior. What aspect of behavior shall we choose that is characteristic of all adjustments and lends itself to quantitative treatment? Although all choices of fundamental postulates are more or less arbitrary, the systematist is usually guided by salient facts in the organized body of knowledge constituting his science. It has been found in studies of sensory adaptation, in numerous studies of perception and judgment, in studies of psychophysical methods, and in studies of expressions of attitudes and of conforming behavior, that there are neutral or indifference levels in all those modes of response. When these neutral levels are known, many important phenomena that have stood as disparate facts can be ordered within a single frame of reference.

Just as the general biological definition of adaptation is too broad, so is the concept of adaptation in its narrowest sense of sensory adaptation too narrow for our purposes. We need a definition of adaptation which will encompass not only sensory adaptation but also many other phenomena of behavioral adaptation.

Recognition of the complexity and variety of the phenomena of sensory adaptation is necessary, but it is not sufficient for solving the problem of organization and adjustment with which we began this chapter. Most of the studies of sensory adaptation have been concerned with measurement of thresholds as functions of specific conditions of stimulation, such as luminance and area of visual stimuli and duration and temperature of thermal stimuli. In general such studies have concentrated on effects of local stimulation and on judgments of single stimuli in relation to a standard without regard to the broader context, i.e., other stimuli that are present or were previously experienced or the state of the organism when an individual enters into a psychological experiment or when he is modified by the experiment. We need a definition of adaptation that includes the state of the organism along with quantitative aspects of stimulation since the *net effect* of stimulation depends upon the state of the organism.

We stated earlier (p. 37) that the level of adaptation is the pooled effect of three classes of stimuli: (1) focal stimuli; (2) background or contextual stimuli; and (3) residual stimuli. The behavioral adaptation level is then defined as a weighted product of these three classes of stimuli:

$$A = \overline{X}^p B^q R^r \tag{1}$$

or, in log form:

$$\log A = p \log \overline{X} + q \log B + r \log R \tag{2}$$

where A is the adaptation level; $\overline{X}$ is the geometric mean of the focal stimuli; B is the background stimulus, or the geometric mean of contextual stimuli in cases where there is no uniform background; R is the residual stimulus; and p, q, and r are weighting coefficients denoting the relative contributions of the three classes of stimuli to level. We may normalize the values of the weighting coefficients by letting $p + q + r = 1$. From Equations (1) and (2) it is evident that adaptation level is defined as a weighted geometric mean of all stimuli impinging upon the organism from without and all stimuli affecting behavior from within. This definition, as is shown later, has provided good approximations to experimentally determined values of adaptation level in judgments of time intervals, lifted weights, sound intensities, tactile density, achromatic levels with various backgrounds in strongly chromatic illumination, and of level operative in construction of veg, bril, and sone scales, and in evaluations of PSE and other cognate values of adaptation level obtained by various psychophysical methods. Since any variations whatsoever in conditions of stimulation may affect adaptation level, it may be necessary to incorporate additional terms or weighting coefficients in Equations (1) and (2) in defining level. Thus stimuli may be weighted to take account of frequency and order of presentation, area, recency, duration, position in series, and other dimensions of stimulation that affect level.

The division of stimuli into three classes (focal, background, and residual) is largely a matter of convenience and depends upon the "sense" of the experimental situation. In identifying sources of variance in behavior, presumably focal and background stimuli are experimentally controlled, leaving all other sources of variance to be classed as residuals. What is focal at one moment may become background or residual at the next moment, and what is background at one time may become focal at another time. The particular class to which stimuli are referred is far less important than is the determination of the contribution made by stimuli to level, regardless of what they are called. It is obvious from Equations (1) and (2) that the weighting constants may be greater for background or residual stimuli than for focal stimuli, and in such cases the former are more important, as far as formation of level is concerned. Stimuli may be assigned to one of the three classes in accordance with their average or predominant role, thus obviating the necessity for taking minor fluctuations in function into account. Pursuing the same line of reasoning, residual stimuli may be assigned to one of the other two classes of stimuli as soon as they are identified and controlled. For example, in most experiments on visual sensitivity choroidal pigmentation has not been noted and correlated with threshold measurements and hence has presumably acted as a random variable to be classed among the residual determiners of visual sensitivity. When pigmentation is noted and found to correlate with sensitivity (see Helson and Guilford, 1933) it can be treated as a focal or background variable. Only considerations of simplicity and economy of thinking limit the number of explicitly specified variables entering into the formation of adaptation level in any given situation. In some cases it may be wise to omit variables having only second-order effects on level.

The weighted logarithmic mean has been most frequently used as the definition of adaptation level for a number of reasons. First, it approximates a wider variety of experimentally observed values of adaptation level than any other a priori value. Second, the logarithmic mean is affected by both range and density of a set of values, something that is not true of either the arithmetic mean or the median when the distribution is symmetrical. Third, the log mean increases less rapidly than does the arithmetic mean as larger and larger values are added to a set of numbers, thus mirroring the lag in adaptation level when extreme stimuli are introduced. The log mean automatically incorporates the law of diminishing returns which, while not universally true, is a good first approximation to the relation between stimulus intensity and magnitude of sensation or response (Fechner's law). Other reasons may be advanced for the use of the log mean as the fundamental definition of adaptation level, but enough has been said to show that it embodies a number of properties which are found in a large variety of responses. On the other hand, it must be remembered that usually neither the simple unweighted log nor the arithmetic mean furnishes a good approximation to observed adaptation levels and each must be modified or supplemented in various ways. For example, the log mean is affected by size of step-interval between stimuli (density of series), but it is not sufficiently affected by density of series stimuli to yield good values of adaptation level, so a constant must be introduced to take account of this factor (Helson, 1947). All in all, however, the log mean has been found to be an easy and convenient base with which to start. Other definitions, such as the power mean (Behar and Bevan, 1961) and the median (Parducci, Calfee, Marshall, and Davidson, 1960) are also compatible with adaptation-level theory and may be useful in certain cases.

The ease and simplicity with which differential weighting factors may be incorporated into various types of means to take account of variations in stimulus conditions that affect level are immediately apparent from the following general definition of mean functions: if ϕ is an increasing function, convex or concave, for $x > 0$, $[\phi(0) = 0]$ we may say for data $x_1, x_2, \ldots x_n$

$$\phi^{-1}\left[\frac{1}{n}\sum_1^n \phi(x_j)\right] = M_\phi(x_1, \ldots x_n) \tag{3}$$

If $\phi(x) = x$, this is the arithmetic mean; if $\phi(x) = \log x$, this is the geometric mean; and if $\phi(x) = x^n$, this is the "power" mean. Other means, such as the harmonic mean, may be similarly defined, and weighting coefficients may be introduced to yield weighted means as desired.

It is evident that adaptation level is a single value or rather a single value within a finite interval. If only the value of adaptation level is known, all we can say is that the stimuli coinciding with level are neutral or ineffective; stimuli above level elicit one kind of response, and stimuli below level elicit an opposite kind of response. To specify responses to stimuli *exactly*, the function relating stimulus and response variables must be known. The manner in which judgments distribute over the stimulus continuum, whether responses show "assimilation" or "contrast," and the fineness of discriminations are given by the shapes of stimulus-response curves, a topic which will be discussed below.

The definition of adaptation level as a weighted mean immediately implies that every stimulus displaces level more or less in its own direction, providing that counteracting residuals are not operative. If a stimulus is above level, the level is displaced upward; if below level, downward; and if it coincides, it does not change level. Since effectiveness of stimulation depends upon gradients from level, it follows that stimulation, especially repeated stimulation, negates itself to some degree by reducing its distance from level. The fact that adaptation level is a weighted mean of external and internal stimuli implies that the influence of one class of stimuli may be counteracted by sufficient emphasis on other classes of stimuli.

There now are formulas embodying adaptation level as a parameter (Helson, 1948; Helson and Michels, 1948; Michels and Helson, 1949; Helson, Judd, and Warren, 1952; Attneave, 1953) so that values of adaptation level can be determined from experimental data (Philip, 1949; Furth, 1960); however, the weighted mean definition is still of use in determining the values of the constants p, q, and r, which denote the relative contributions of focal, background, and residual stimuli to level, and this has been done in a number of studies (Michels and Helson, 1954a; Bevan and Darby, 1955; Philip, 1949; Furth, 1960; Helson, 1947; and others).

SUMMARY

The concept of adaptation as adjustment to environing conditions has been used by biologists as well as psychologists for many years and antedates the concept of physiological decrement. The restriction of the concept of adaptation to effects of long-continued stimulation neglects the important rapid, transient stages of adaptation, which must be taken into account when considering sensory phenomena. Similarly, the important double aspect of behavioral adaptations has often been neglected, viz., increased sensitization to complementary qualities along with decreased response to predominant stimulation as an adaptive phenomenon. Finally, we must recognize that adaptation is affected by reaction of the organism to stimulation, as well as by action of stimulation upon the organism. The concept of adaptation, to be maximally fruitful for the behavioral scientist, must be broader than the concept of sensory decrement, and must be given a more concrete meaning than is contained in the general biological concept of adaptation as adjustment to the environment. In addition a quantitative definition of adaptation is necessary if the concept is to be operational. If responses denoting equilibrium or neutral states are used to indicate the state of the organism, it becomes possible to define adaptation level as a weighted mean of all stimuli, present and past, affecting behavior.

We may summarize the consequences of this definition of behavioral adaptation as follows:

1. In every situation confronting the organism there is established an adaptation level that is a weighted mean of focal, background, and residual stimuli.

2. Adaptation level represents the zero of function, and, since it is

always associated with positive values of stimulation, stimuli *below* as well as *above* level exert positive effects on behavior.

3. Responses to stimulation are manifestations of positive or negative gradients from level.

4. Intensity of response is a function of distance from, or ratio of stimulation to, prevailing level; the greater the magnitude of the ratio or distance, the steeper is the excitation gradient and the greater is the response.

5. With positive gradients of excitation responses are of one kind, e.g., blue-green, pleasant, approach; with negative gradients they are of the opposite kind, e.g., red, unpleasant, avoid; and with zero gradients responses are neutral, indifferent, or absent, e.g., gray, affectively neutral, no response. Behavior is therefore basically bipolar in nature.

6. Level of output tends to match the level of input stimulation; i.e., the adaptation level is a weighted mean of input stimulation unless inner (residual) factors are very strong.

7. Organisms are space-time averaging mechanisms in which all dimensions of objects and events contribute differentially to the formation of levels. Among the more obvious and important weighting factors are area, intensity, frequency, nearness, recency, order of stimulation, and affective quality. Less obvious but often important in fixing levels are task, instructions, self-instructions, organic states, cognitive systems, and genetic factors.

8. Group behavior can be conceived as the resultant of pooled individual behaviors and hence as functions of individual modes of adjustment. Just as individual levels are established with respect to prevailing conditions, so group levels, conceived as weighted means of individual levels, are established with respect to situations involving interpersonal interactions.

9. Cognitive acts, sensori-motor responses, skills, and learning are differentially affected by focal, background, and residual stimuli and hence are functions of prevailing level no less than perception and judgment. Similar considerations apply to affective and emotional behavior.

These and other implications of the definition of adaptation level are elaborated in succeeding chapters where supporting experimental evidence for them is presented.

3 *Seven Basic Characteristics of Behavior*

Whereas perception, memory, judgment and interpersonal behavior have been accorded chapters in textbooks and even whole volumes, certain other basic modes of behavior have received hardly any attention, have been treated as subsidiary topics under the better-known subjects, and often are regarded as accidental or deviant forms of response. The characteristics of behavior to which I have reference cut across sense modalities and specialized effector systems; they are manifested in all types of content and in all sorts of motor patterns. These modes of response depend upon the properties of sensori-motor systems and represent ways in which human organisms have adapted to their conditions of life. Some of them also appear in the behavior of the lowest and simplest organisms. Briefly, these modes of behavior can be characterized as (1) bipolarity of responses; (2) pooling, interaction, or integration of elements; (3) differential weighting of stimuli and responses; (4) nonlinearity of responses vis-à-vis stimulation; (5) variability and oscillation in levels; (6) optimal levels of function; and (7) output-input matching. Let us turn to a consideration of these characteristics of behavior and evidence supporting our contention that they are basic manifestations of adaptive mechanisms.

THE BIPOLARITY OF BEHAVIOR

In considering behavior as adjustment we are struck by the fact that all animals "avoid some types of stimulation, generally injurious, and approach other types which are generally adaptive or beneficial" (Schneirla, 1949, p. 258). Approach and avoidance need not be all-or-none responses but may manifest varying degrees of acceptance or rejection.[1] Primitively, animals approach weak energies and withdraw from intense sources of stimulation. What is effectively weak or strong depends upon the adaptive state of the organism, a fact which Schneirla has referred to as the "principle of differential organic thresholds underlying adaptive orientation of behavior" (p. 262). This principle applies to vertebrate as well as lower organisms: "systems of approach and withdrawal behavior are widely adaptive on all animal levels." We can summarize these characteristics of behavior by saying that behavior is bipolar with neutral, indifferent, or zero responses as indicators of stimuli and situations to which the organism is adapted.

The concept of approach-avoidance implies more than mere change in distance between the organism and the object. Approach involves carrying on activities of all sorts, and withdrawal means that the object is dismissed, cast out, done with. Similarly approach is usually associated with pleasantness and avoidance with unpleasantness but there are exceptions, such as wrestling with a hated adversary or facing a tough intellectual problem, where physical approach is unpleasant but necessary to achieve later satisfaction.

Lest it seem that we are overemphasizing the ubiquity and importance of these types of behavior, consider the fundamental roles of approach and avoidance in such widely different systems of psychology as those represented by Lewin, who speaks of positive and negative valences, Hull, who formulated the goal gradient hypothesis and posited positive and negative reinforcers as incitors or inhibitors of activity, and Miller, who has based a theory of conflict on theorems concerned with rates of approach and withdrawal. Boring, in seeking

---

[1] Schneirla refers to the point made by Hess that there is a gradual decrease from a maximum of approach reactions in the light responses of earthworms toward a maximum frequency of withdrawal when the source of light is changed from low to high intensity (W. Hess, Reactions to light in the earthworm, *Lumbricus Terrestris L. J. Morphol. Physiol.*, 1924, **39**, 515–542).

for an objective definition of "demand" character defined it as "that property of an object by virtue of which it attracts or repels an individual" (1936) thus making approach-avoidance the basic behavioral criterion for the "demand" properties of objects described by Gestalt psychologists in phenomenological terms.

Categorizing and scaling. Approach-avoidance responses, whether overt or covert, are primitive forms of categorizing since they serve to dichotomize objects into positive and negative classes. In accepting or rejecting objects organisms engage in a primitive form of scaling. Rudiments of order appear as soon as any discrimination whatsoever is made with respect to the world about us. We may diagram the most primitive type of scaling as a division of objects into two classes, approach-pleasant and avoid-unpleasant, as follows:

Approach	*Neutral*	*Avoid*
Pleasant		*Unpleasant*

Some objects evoke indifferent responses or none at all. In the case of newborn human and lower organisms the number of objects in the approach class is small compared to the number in the avoid class.

While this account of categorizing and discrimination may seem to be purely theoretical, it accords with conclusions reached by workers concerned with simple conditioned responses:

The doctrine of qualitative, categorizing, "rating scale" type of CR gradient . . . is based upon a statistical and logical analysis of total evidence, which . . . demonstrates that there is a true CR gradient, but this gradient is very qualitative and very crude, consisting of only a few steps, perhaps more steps in human beings than in dogs, but few just the same. Apparently, when human beings or dogs that have been conditioned to some stimulus or object are confronted with some new non-conditioned but in some way related stimulus or object, they categorize or rate the new stimulus on some sort of crude similarity-dissimilarity scale. With human subjects, introspections actually reveal such categorizing as "similar," "dissimilar," "very dissimilar," and the like attitudes that apparently control or even initiate the generalization responses. And . . . some such categorizing behavior is operative also in animals (Razran, 1949, p. 362).

Hofstätter (1956) also stresses human categorizing (arriving at decisions) as predominantly binary in character as shown by the classical lists of opposites (love-hate, warm-cold, dry-wet); two-valued classical logic (a proposition is true or false; there is no third alternative); polar definitions of phenomena; the division of numerous primitive groups into halves (the moieties); the dual motive in mythology and ancient cosmology; and the preference for dichotomous personality types (extravert-introvert; normal-abnormal) in human typology.

As organisms advance both ontogenetically and phylogenetically, their discriminations become finer and more numerous, with the result that more and more properties of objects are differentiated. With greater differentiation all-or-none behavior gives way to graded responses. Thus we pass from the crude plus-minus dichotomizing to the highest types of discrimination involving as many categories as there are just noticeable differences in perception. The two-division scale becomes an n-division scale as shown schematically in the following diagram:

$$\cdots\cdots-6 \quad -5 \quad -4 \quad -3 \quad -2 \quad -1 \quad 0 \quad +1 \quad +2 \quad +3 \quad +4 \quad +5 \quad +6\cdots\cdots$$

Just as the number and size of the scale divisions on a meter indicate the fineness of measurement of which it is capable, so the number of categories in rating scales determine the fineness with which discriminations can be made. If Ss judge a set of stimuli by means of few categories, the resultant discriminations are coarse. As the number of categories is increased, discrimination of stimuli becomes finer until the limit of discriminability is reached. Conversely, to ascertain the limits of discriminability under given conditions of observation, Ss must have the proper language in which to respond. Psychophysical scaling is a function of the language and the constraints imposed upon Ss as much as it is a function of stimulus variables. The varieties of judgments in psychophysics as well as in everyday life attest to the many ways in which primitive approach-avoidance behavior has proliferated.

Approach-avoidance responses vary in many ways and become differentiated into, or associated with, a variety of properties of objects and events. Animals move toward or retreat from objects at various rates (see goal gradient hypothesis); they occupy themselves with objects or avoid them for various periods of time; they exhibit various intensities of response or effort; they show effects of maturation and learning in both approaching and avoiding objects. Out of primitive approach-avoidance tendencies are developed all other differentiations such as similarity-dissimilarity, beautiful-ugly, far-near, up-down, past-future, justice-injustice, and so on through all the nuances of language and judgment.

The bipolar nature of language finds expression in many forms, such as antonyms, prefixes, and negatives, and special phrases and constructions that convey contrary meanings. In the Egyptian language, as pointed out by Freud (1953), there are words that unite antithetical meanings, such as *strong* and *weak,* in a single word that has the meaning of only one of the terms. This language possesses other compound terms in which two words having opposite meanings are united without change into one word, with only one meaning. For example, "oldyoung" means *young;* "farnear" means *near;* and "bindloose" means *bind.* The contradictory concepts are not combined to create a third concept, Freud says, but only to express the meaning of one of the contradictory members. The explanation of this paradoxical usage of words was given by Abel in terms of the fundamental bipolarity of cognition:

Were it always light we should not distinguish between light and dark, and accordingly could not have either the conception of, nor the word for, light. . . . It is clear that everything on this planet is relative and has independent existence only insofar as it is distinguished in its relations to and from other things. . . . Since every conception is thus the twin of its opposite, how could it be thought of first, how could it be communicated to others who tried to think of it, except by being measured against its opposite? . . . Man has not been able to acquire even his oldest and simplest conceptions otherwise than in contrast with their opposites; he only gradually learned to separate the two sides of the antithesis and think of the one without conscious comparison with the other (quoted by Freud, 1953, pp. 184 ff.).

While nature presents us with such contrasts as night and day, warm and cold, and summer and winter, an explanation of the origin of the bipolarity of behavior must be sought within the organism itself. If a mechanism did not exist within the organism for transmitting and responding to contrasts and periodicities, their existence in nature would not be sufficient to account for them in behavior. It follows from our definition of adaptation level as the neutral region of response continua that behavior is bipolar because stimuli above level are responded to in one way and stimuli below level in an opposite way. When the zero of function shifts to either the high or low extreme of the continuum, responses are all of one kind and behavior is unipolar. Thus a professional weight lifter, whose functional zero for weights is very high, judges ordinary objects as light whereas an office worker classes ordinary objects as heavy, medium, or light. Bipolarity of responses follows from the fact that organisms usually establish their zero points within the range of stimuli presented them.

Bipolarity is also clearly evident in the expression of feelings and emotions. Michotte (1950) divided all emotions into two groups: integrative and segregative. Sympathy, love, and friendship belong to the integrative class, for they result in identification, union, possession (approach). Antipathy, disgust, hate, and fear belong in the segregative class, for they result in apartness, segregation, repulsion (avoidance). He pointed out that the motor reactions of the first group involve approach, contact, embrace, clasp of the hand, keeping near the beloved object, while the characteristic reactions of segregative emotions are the opposite, i.e., movements away from or breaking and destroying the disliked objects. Inanimate objects moving along a simple path were reported by his *S*s as having approach and avoidance characteristics. The movements of people and of objects in approach and avoidance, Michotte believes, are perceived as properties distinct from direction and distance in that one may *approach* with *hostile* intent making the act really a form of negation.

Similarly, Buytendijk (1950), in discussing forms of feeling as modes of "replying" to situations, pointed out that in our encounters with that which "limits our existence" we are aware of either resistance or lack of resistance. From these two modes of experience there arise four modes of feeling pleasant and four modes of feeling unpleasant. According to Buytendijk feeling pleased encompasses (1) being-with-something or being one with something or someone, (2) flowing-on, flowing-out existence, (3) expansion of the self, and (4) taking to oneself, assimilating, including as one's own. Feeling displeased involves: (1) being thrown back, (2) being subdued, (3) being injured, and (4) losing or abandoning a part of oneself. The various forms of pleasantness and unpleasantness are illustrated in Buytendijk's article by many concrete examples that show the range and variety of emotional situations covered by this classification. The phenomenological and behavioristic approaches to feelings and emotions come together in the analyses of Michotte and Buytendijk because both men start from the bipolar nature of responses in affective behavior.

Bipolarity of sensory phenomena. Paralleling approach-avoidance behavior are the many manifestations of bipolarity in sensory responses to stimulation. Negative afterimages of lightness, chromaticness, and movement in vision; warmth and coldness in the temperature senses; relaxation and strain in kinesthesis—in short, all simultaneous and successive contrasts point to the bipolar nature of sensory systems. Whether or not aftereffects of stimulation are like the original stimulus or complementary to it depends upon the relation of succeeding stimulus conditions to the previous level of stimulation. Adaptation to a high temperature results in perception of cold when we are exposed to a lower temperature; the Plateau spiral appears to contract when rotation is stopped if it was previously perceived to expand; and the noise of airplane engines is at first deafening if the previously prevailing sound level was low.

Judgmental responses usually have their roots in, and reflect the nature of, sensory processes. Because of changes in adaptation level, the same stimulus may evoke different, sometimes contradictory, judgments of its attributes. Thus a 300-grm. weight lifted after a 900-grm. weight feels light, but lifted after a 90-grm. weight it feels heavy and is judged accordingly. What of responses that are largely verbal-cognitive in character and do not seem to be determined primarily by the nature of their sensory content but shift with changes in background or contextual stimulation? Thus a man is large with respect to a mouse and small with respect to an elephant. The judgment of an object is said to be relative to that with which it is being compared. But the principle of relativity of judgment is itself a special case of the principle that the attributes of stimulation depend upon their relation to prevailing organismic levels. Mice, men, and elephants represent classes of objects having different ranges of sizes, each with its own magnitudes of what will be judged large, medium, or small. If, for purposes of comparison, mice, men, and elephants are brought into a single class, then within this class there is established a level with respect to which large and small are differentiated. If these objects are compared with the earth or the sun, all are judged vanishingly small because of the change of level following inclusion of the new object within the class of stimuli being judged. Verbal-cognitive responses also have their roots in perceptual processes; for example, within any given class of objects some *look* large, some *look* medium, and some *look* small, in accordance with the principle previously stated that adaptation level tends to assume some intermediate value between extremes of stimulation.

Rating scales and bipolarity of behavior. The bipolarity of behavior is probably best expressed in rating-scale types of judgment which have a neutral or zero incorporated in the scale. Such scales may be numerical or qualitative, absolute or comparative. A set of stimuli or a class of objects may be judged in terms of numbers or in terms of qualitative categories. Various restrictions may be imposed on rating scales or they may be employed with a minimum of constraints; e.g., the largest stimulus in a series may be given the number 10, and the smallest the number 1; or the largest may be categorized as extremely large, and the smallest as extremely small; or one end of the scale may be tied down, the other left open. Occasionally the neutral, zero, or midpoint of the scale is assigned to a certain value of stimulus as well as the end points. It should be remembered that every constraint placed on the use of a scale may influence the shape of the stimulus-judgment function; e.g., a negatively accelerated curve obtained with an open-ended scale may change to a positively accelerated curve if the scale is narrow and the top value of the scale is assigned to the top member of the series.

When individuals judge a series of objects, all objects of a more or less similar nature that are present determine, for the most part, the way in which the categories or numbers of the scale are employed, i.e., what will be judged medium or neutral and which members of the series will be assigned the other scale units. If, however, the objects of judgment are not immediately present to sense, as is the case with many judgments in everyday life, the individual himself defines the universe of discourse. The extreme range of variation in judgments as well as individual differences in the use of scales, which occur in such cases, was brought out in a study by Sheppard (1954). As seen from Table 3.1, individual estimates of distances vary much more when the universe of discourse is unrestricted than when it is restricted, e.g., by telling *S*s to judge distance as "if you were going for a walk."

Variations in individual interpretation of the language of the scale were also studied by Sheppard. *S*s were asked to indicate the positions of the following categories on a straight line: extremely good, very good, rather good, good, average, rather bad, bad, very bad, extremely bad. Two teachers, *A* and *C,* interpreted the modifier "rather" in quite different fashion, with the result that the "average" category was much wider for C than for A, as shown in Fig. 3.1. C made "rather" synonymous with "very" while A regarded it as a weak modifier. The width of the "average" category for a third subject, S, also a teacher, fell between the widths assigned it by A and C.

TABLE 3.1.　Effects of Restricted Universe of Discourse on Estimates of Distances

	Very Near	Near	Rather Near	Neither Far nor Near	Rather Far	Far	Very Far
				Unrestricted Universe			
Smallest	4×10^{-9}	1 yd.	¼ mi.	150 yd.	6 mi.	2 mi.	100 mil. 1000 light
Largest	200 yd.	2 mi.	20 mi.	63 mi.	to moon	to sun	years
				Restricted Universe			
Smallest	2 yd.	15 yd.	20 yd.	300 yd.	440 yd.	¾ mi.	3 mi.
Largest	3 mi.	5 mi.	7 mi.	10 mi.	20 mi.	50 mi.	100 mi.

SOURCE:　From Sheppard, 1954. With the permission of the *British Journal of Psychology*.

Group differences may also be revealed in the way members of different economic classes, countries, or cultures employ rating scales, as was also shown by Sheppard. One of his rating scales concerned the amount

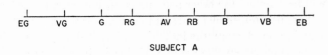

SUBJECT A

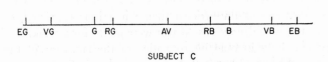

SUBJECT C

FIG. 3.1.　How two Ss assigned different widths to the categories of a rating scale. The symbols from left to right stand for the following terms: extremely good, very good, good, rather good, average, rather bad, bad, very bad, extremely bad. (From Sheppard, 1954. With the permission of the *Quarterly Journal of Experimental Psychology*.)

"a single man would have to earn in a week" to be described as very poor to very rich. Comparison of the replies given to this question by different economic groups within the same country or by similar groups in different countries should reveal the economic standards or levels of the groups in question. Individuals in one income group might be surprised at the discrepancy between their concepts of an adequate "average" income and those of members of other groups.

Much has been written concerning the construction, use, and ways of handling data gained from the various types of rating scales. For further information the reader is referred to Guilford (1954a) who has given a detailed account of various forms of rating scales and the rules for constructing each type as well as the constant tendencies of judgment which appear in their use, the peculiarities shown by raters, and a general evaluation of rating methods. The bipolar nature of psychophysical judgments is clear in the absolute and comparative rating methods, in the method of constant stimulus differences, in the method of paired comparisons, and in the rank order method of scaling. It is my belief that *all psychophysical scaling methods are fundamentally bipolar rating scales with the neutral or zero category supplied by the organism whether or not it is incorporated in the scale.*

POOLING, INTERACTION, AND INTEGRATION

It is a fact of common experience that complex objects are judged as if they were simple, unitary wholes. Paintings, musical compositions, literary works, persons, jobs, foods, and so on, may be given absolute ratings or placed in an order-of-merit scale although many different attributes affect the decision. Usually, only individuals with specialized training are able to analyze complex objects in order to assess the relative contributions of the individual components affecting the over-all judgment. Over-all judgments can be made and are dependable due to the fact that the attributes of the object pool or fuse into a single impression. Phenomena of pooling and interaction have long been studied in sensory psychology where they have been treated under the headings of fusion, assimilation, complication, and synesthesia (Ryan, 1940; Gilbert, 1941). The Gestalt psychologists recognized the fundamental nature of interaction and made it a basic postulate of their system of psychology. Pooling may range from complete fusion of components, with loss of their individual identities, to interactions involving the facilitative or inhibitive effects of one stimulus on another, with preservation of the components. Without attempting to draw sharp lines between the various degrees of pooling let us turn to some illustrative examples.

Sensory fusions and interactions. The coalescence of sensory qualities to produce new qualities has been known as fusion in classical introspective psychology. In general, fusions arise when stimuli are very closely juxtaposed in space or time, as in mosaic mixture of colors and in color mixture by means of Maxwell discs. Thus red and yellow yield orange, and proper combinations of yellow and blue, red and blue-green, black and white all produce gray. Less known to the younger generation of students of psychology are the fusions from stimulation of receptors in the skin: warmth and pressure give rise to oiliness; coldness and pressure to wetness; warmth and coldness to heat sensation. Similarly, fusion of component frequencies is responsible for emergence of timbre and formant qualities of single musical tones, and fusion of whole tones in chords is at least partly responsible for the consonance of the musical intervals, according to Stumpf (1883; 1890).

There are other interaction effects that are usually not classed with the fusions. We do not speak of fusion where area and brightness interact in determining visual thresholds nor in the case of the Bezold-Brücke effect where brightness influences hue. It has long been axiomatic that one sensory dimension is affected by all the others in greater or lesser degree. Indeed, so pervasive are interaction effects in sensory processes it is almost impossible to study a single sensory dimension in isolation from the rest. Phenomena of sensory facilitation, such as binocular and binaural summation, phenomena of inhibition, such as the Fry-Bartley effect (where borders at right angles inhibit each other), and visual and auditory masking all give clear evidence of peripheral or central interactions among the component processes aroused by more or less discrete stimuli.

In visual space perception objects at first seem to have spatial characteristics (size, position, distance, etc.) that are independent of those of other objects in the field of view. Both everyday observation and results of numerous experiments prove the contrary, i.e., spatial attributes of objects interact no less than do their color attributes. The distortions found in the figures of Poggendorff, Müller-Lyer, Zöllner,

Wundt, and Hering arise from interactions among spatial attributes of figures. "Illusions" of length, size, direction, and perspective all attest to the potency of spatial pooling. Künnapas has shown (1957) that the elliptical shape of the visual field may be at least partially responsible for the so-called vertical-horizontal illusion in which vertical lines appear longer than equal horizontal lines. He reasoned that this is because the visual "frame" is smaller in the vertical than in the horizontal direction—after having previously shown that perceived length of lines depended upon the size of the frame in which they were perceived (1955). If this assumption is correct, the illusion should disappear in dark viewing owing to the disappearance of the visual frame. Using an L-shaped stimulus, he found that the vertical equal to a horizontal of 50 mm. was 46.46 mm. in light and 47.61 mm. in the dark. A significant decrease in the illusion was thus found with a dark field, showing that the frame of the visual field influences perceived length. It is not necessary to present the many other examples of spatial interactions in vision and other sense modalities; the fact is that pooling occurs in space perception no less than in the fusions and interactions of other sensory qualities.

Cross-modality interactions. The mutual influences of sight and sound, vision and kinesthesis, and other cross-modality effects too numerous to mention are well known, yet their role in determination of adaptation levels has been recognized by only a few psychologists. The systematic implications of cross-modality pooling were stated by Gilbert in his review of intersensory interactions when he said:

. . . modern psychophysics has produced overwhelming evidence of the inadequacy of the traditional static relationship between stimulus and response, wherein each attribute of a sensory response was conceived of as determined simply by the value of the corresponding physical dimension of the "adequate" stimulus. . . . Actual experimental evidence . . . has shown that the dimensions of stimulation are interdependent in affecting a sensory response, and that sensation may be dependent on the interaction of excitations, on mental set, physiological state of the organism, practice, and numerous other factors, all interrelated and in a constant state of flux (1941, p. 404).

Let us consider, as a first example of cross-modality interactions, evidence demonstrating that tactile and kinesthetic impulses from both the intrinsic and extrinsic muscles of the eyes play an important role in perceptions of visual size, position, direction, and distance. A simple experiment, described by F. B. Hofmann (1920) and repeated by the writer (1935), shows the effect of accommodation on visual size and distance: If a finger is held from 3 to 6 in. before one eye as the other eye is occluded and the gaze is shifted from, say, a window on the far side of the room to the finger, the window appears to shrink and recede as the accommodation changes from far to near. The change in width of the window may be as much as 33 percent if the finger is held sufficiently close to the eye. Although the pupil of the eye contracts with increasing accommodation and thereby lessens the amount of light in the retinal image, the reduction in size cannot be attributed wholly to the reduced light flux; this is proved by what happens with constant light flux in the following experiment: If a bright object is fixated *through* a pinhole held close to the eye, the perceived size of the object is larger than when the *pinhole* is fixated. The kinesthetic impulses accompanying accommodation in fixating the pinhole are stronger than in fixating the object through the pinhole, and presumably they exert an effect on the perceived size.

That position and convergence of the eyes influence apparent size of the moon was demonstrated by Holway and Boring (1940*a*, *b*) in their investigation of the classical "moon illusion" wherein the moon appears to be larger at the horizon than when it is overhead. While Boring (1943) has been willing to say only that convergence and change of regard above or below the horizon may be partly responsible for the apparent decrease in size of the moon, Hermans (1954) believed that torsional movements associated with changes in elevation together with those in convergence account for the moon illusion. Although some observers reported an increase in apparent size with increase in elevation of the eyes, Hermans concluded that kinesthetic input cannot be disregarded as an important factor determining visual size.

The induction of movement of the visual field through stimulation of the semicircular canals by rotation or by syringing the ears with warm or cold water is well known. I have often observed an analogous effect in elevators, though here the kinesthetic impulses must originate through stimulation of the end organs of the utriculus and sacculus since the motion is one of translation. Fixating a spot on the wall of the elevator to reduce eye movement to a minimum, one can *see* the inside of the moving room *as a whole* rising or falling even though all points of the visual environment remain stationary relative to the retina! Small overt or incipient eye movements would not explain perception of movement of the whole room in this observation. There must be a direct influence of kinesthesis on vision, from the vestibular and semicircular organs to the visual mechanism.

Visual localization and direction can be strongly influenced by sound stimuli and localization of sound may be influenced by visual stimuli. Ryan (1940) referred to a study in which sound and light presented close together in a dark room induced a constant displacement in the localization of the sound toward the light of about 0.9 cm. when the two were separated by 4.0 cm., an effect amounting to almost 25 percent. An experiment by Witkin, Wapner, and Leventhal (1952) employing conflicting visual and auditory cues to localization also showed that a visual stimulus may displace an auditory signal. Sounds were conducted by means of tubes to the ears of *S*s who saw *E*'s face in a mirror directly behind them. When the sounds were in phase for the two ears, *S*s localized the sound in the direction of *E*'s face. Threshold of shift of the sound out of the median plane with *E*'s face visible in the median plane compared with threshold with eyes closed furnished a measure of the influence of the visual anchor on the position of the sound. With eyes closed the angle of displacement from the median plane was 17° in the case of men *S*s and 18° in the case of women *S*s. But with eyes open the angle of displacement was 28° for the men and 38° for the women (thus showing greater dependence of the women on the visual impression). The admittedly high displacement thresholds were attributed to the fact that the auditory stimulus was shifted constantly. While part of the effect reported in this experiment may be attributed to the fact that *S*s were presented with a divided task, i.e., to watch the face and to report on the first noticeable displacement of the sound from the median position, it must be granted that interaction between vision and hearing was clearly demonstrated.

Although movement and touch often serve to correct distortions of visual position and direction, Ivo Kohler (1956) found that distortions of the visual field following prolonged wearing of half-prismatic lenses were communicated to tactile impressions so that the objects were distorted to touch as well as to vision.

Sensory conditioning also offers evidence of central pooling across sense modalities. Various degrees of intermodal effects were found in studies by Brogden (1947; 1950) and Brogden and Gregg (1951). In the first study Brogden paired a light stimulus with a sound stimulus and then paired the sound stimulus with electric shock. Subsequently the light stimulus aroused the conditioned response to shock although it was never directly paired with shock, an example of second-order conditioning. In a second study Brogden paired a tone stimulus with a light stimulus which increased in intensity while the tone was on. A control group was given only the tone stimulus. Both groups were then given 30 presentations of tone alone, 10 of light alone, and 10 of tone alone. Subsequently, auditory thresholds were determined with tone and light and also with only the tone stimulus present. Ss in the experimental group had lower auditory thresholds when the light accompanied the tone than when the tone was presented alone, whereas the control group showed no significant difference in thresholds in the two tone conditions. Since the gain in auditory threshold by the experimental group was a function of the initial trials in which tone and light were presented together, the inference is that some relation between tone and light was established. These results were later confirmed in a study by Brogden and Gregg (1951). Interaction or pooling of effects seems very likely in these studies since stimulation intervened between the original paired stimuli and the critical trials.

Heteromodal figural aftereffects have also been reported. Figural aftereffects have been extensively investigated, first in vision, and then in the kinesthetic-tactile modality. As is well known, steady fixation of a visual figure results in displacement of other figures away from the adapted area. Similarly, if the fingers are first run along two raised diverging strips of aluminum and then along parallel strips, the latter will appear to converge. Jaffe (1956) has shown that if Ss view a strip of white paper on black background of the same width as the standard, parallel strips, there is no effect of vision on the tactile figural aftereffect; but if the visual stimulus is wider or narrower than the tactile stimulus, the latter shows a contrast effect. Jaffe concluded that concurrent visual stimulation can induce significant kinesthetic figural aftereffects.

The electrotonic model proposed by Köhler and Wallach (1944) for figural aftereffects was criticized by Jaffe because it is couched in terms of specific projection areas of the brain. On the basis of this model heteromodal interactions would require too great an electrotonic spread over the brain. The concept of pooling to form level seems to Jaffe to furnish a more labile model:

. . . the contrast between the visual objects resulted in a change in the general frame of reference, and this in turn influenced the kinesthetic judgment. In terms of . . . "adaptation-level" one might assume that the action of the visual stimuli is not limited to visual [areas] alone. These stimuli contribute to a common pool of past and current effects of stimulation and thereby may produce alterations in all modalities. . . . adaptation-level does provide a potential basis for the explanation of intermodal influences in perception. This broader application is possible since a specific physiological mechanism has not been invoked that is limited to a single sensory process (1956, p. 75).

Qualitative fusions across sense modalities reach their apex in synesthetic perceptions. Among those reported in the literature the most common is "colored hearing" in response to musical tones, in which specific hues are assigned to specific pitches. Colored pains have also been reported: a needle prick was described as "pinkish" by a young child (Helson, 1933), and massive large pains as "blue" by an acquaintance of the writer. Just as fusions of taste and smell are not cases of mere temporal juxtaposition or association, so the synesthetic experiences of numerous observers do not appear to be purely associative in character. The neurological basis for synesthesia is, of course, unknown; but it must consist of a more intimate interaction between different central sensory areas than is commonly supposed. Since physiological short-circuiting has been invoked for so many learning and perceptual phenomena, it may not be amiss to advance it again for the phenomenon of synesthesia.

We have so far discussed the pooling of qualities that produce fusions and new emergent qualities. Whether or not we may speak of pooling of the different sensory dimensions (quality, time, spatiality, intensity) is problematical since they all have more or less direct representation in their underlying neurological processes. Be this as it may, there are phenomena involving the basic dimensions of perceptual processes which argue for substitutability of one dimension for another if not for actual fusion of dimensions.

Probably the best known examples of dimensional interactions (we shall refer to them as such even though we have questioned the propriety of doing so) are expressed in the law of photographic reciprocity, $It = k$, and Ricco's law, $AI = k$. From the first law it is evident that at the lower threshold a decrease in intensity, I, can be compensated by an increase in time of exposure, t, up to about $\frac{1}{5}$ sec. From Ricco's law, and similar expressions concerning absolute threshold luminance and area of the stimulus, the larger the area, the less intense need the stimulus be for liminal vision. In these, and many other cases, increase in one dimension permits decrease in another.

Somewhat different relations among dimensions are operative in Korte's laws governing the perception of movement from successively exposed stationary slits of light:

$$s \sim i$$
$$i \sim \frac{1}{t}$$
$$t \sim s$$

where s refers to the spatial interval between the illuminated slits, i to the luminance of the slits, and t to the time interval between the extinction of the first slit and the appearance of the second. Here increases in the distance between the slits must be accompanied by an increase in their luminance or by an increase in the time interval if the perception of movement is to be preserved; otherwise there is only partial movement of each of the slits. An increase in the luminance of the slits requires a decrease in the time interval between exposures for optimal movement to be preserved. But it is in so-called delta movement where interaction of dimensions is great enough to allow substitution of one dimension for another. In ordinary phi movement the direction of movement is from the first light exposed to the second; but in delta movement the direction of perceived motion is opposite to the objective order of exposure due to the fact that the second stimulus is either larger or more intense than the first. Here area or intensity predominates over temporal order to determine the direction of movement. This result may not seem paradoxical until it is realized that in order for motion to be perceived from stationary stimuli, *both* stimuli must be physiologically effective, if not actually perceived. Although the first stimulus is necessary for the perception of motion, it is not adequate in delta movement to determine the direction of the perceived motion. Difficult as it has been to account for simple phi phenomenon (each of the several theories was shown to be inadequate by its successor), it is even more difficult to construct a model to account for perceived motion in which the objective order of stimulation is reversed without assuming dimensional pooling as a primary postulate.

The classical example of perceptual reversal of objective temporal order is found in Wundt's complication experiment, so called because two different sense modalities are involved, where the subject reports the position of a pointer moving around the face of a clock at the time a stimulus is sounded. If the subject attends to the pointer, the sound is reported later than it occurred objectively, and if he attends to the sound, he reports it earlier. In other words, the stimulus not attended to lags in perception. We have evidence here of the influence of inner factors ("attention") upon the perceived position of the pointer relative to the sound under two sets. This phenomenon, known as "prior entry," carries over into reaction times, that is, if one has to respond to a stimulus by pressing a key, the reaction time is shorter if attention is on the movement to be made (motor set) than if it is on the stimulus (sensory set).

In an unpublished experiment performed thirty-five years ago, I found that reaction times to a stimulus were lengthened when a second stimulus was interpolated between the primary stimulus and the response. A light stimulus was introduced about 75 msec. following a sound stimulus (or vice versa) to which the subject was to respond by pressing a key. The reaction times to the first stimulus were invariably lengthened even though Ss were not instructed to pay attention to, or to respond to, the second stimulus. The interesting aspect of this finding is that presumably the reaction to the primary stimulus has started before the second stimulus appears since the total reaction time to light is about 180 msec. and to sound, against silent background, about 120 msec. Evidently the second stimulus overtakes the first stimulus and lengthens its reaction time. A more systematic study of this phenomenon has now been made (Helson and Steger, 1962) in which it was found that the second stimulus may be given as long as 170 msec. after the first and still lengthen reaction time to the first as seen in Fig. 3.2.

Experiments by Needham (1934a, b; 1936) dealing with prior entry within a single sense department gave results which may involve interactive inhibition of the same type that was operative in our reaction-time experiments. Needham sounded a tone of 1100 cps for 250 msec. five times in succession with silent intervals of 250 msec. between the stimuli. A second sound, from a buzzer, was given in different positions relative to the sounds and the silent intervals. The five positions of the buzzer were as follows: (A) coincident with the third tone; (B) halfway through the third tone and into the silent interval between the third and fourth tones; (C) coincident with the silent interval between the third and fourth tones; (D) during the latter half of the

silent interval before the fourth tone and into the fourth tone; and
(*E*) coincident with the fourth tone. Judgments of position of the
sound of the *buzzer* were distributed as follows: 58 percent showed
negative error, i.e., were reported too early or before the correct position; 23 percent were correct; and the remaining 19 percent showed
positive error or were reported too late. Omitting condition *C*, Needham pointed out that 63 percent of the reports were negative, 27 percent

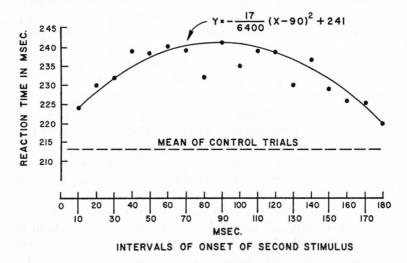

$$Y = -\frac{17}{6400}(X-90)^2 + 241$$

MEAN OF CONTROL TRIALS

MSEC.

INTERVALS OF ONSET OF SECOND STIMULUS

FIG. 3.2. The inhibitory effect on reaction time (RT) of a second stimulus that
follows the primary stimulus to react. The lengthening of RT to the first stimulus
is statistically significant when the second stimulus is given as much as 170 msec.
after the first. (From Helson and Steger, 1962. With the permission of the American Psychological Association.)

were correct, and 10 percent were positive. Hence, the stimulus tends
to be anticipated. Another interpretation of the results is that responses
to the series tones are inhibited or delayed by the buzzer. The results of
this experiment parallel our findings regarding the effects of an interpolated stimulus on the reaction time to a signal.

Spatiotemporal pooling. The dependence of space on time and of
time on space (a deduction in relativity theory from the constancy of
the speed of light) can be demonstrated in direct experience. Perceived
distance between successive tactile stimuli was first shown by Gelb
(1914) to be dependent upon the temporal interval between stimuli in

this way: When three collinear spots on the skin are tapped in succession, the perceived distances between the spots vary with the temporal intervals between stimulations. Helson and King (1931) measured the phenomenon and called it the "Tau" effect. They found that depending on whether the time interval between the second and third stimulus was greater or less than that between the first and second stimuli, the distance was perceived to be greater or less. Space was perceived to expand or contract in accordance with the temporal intervals between the stimuli. If the stimulated spots were at the apexes of an equilateral triangle, the perceived sides of the figure were distorted as the temporal intervals between stimulations were varied. The reverse of the Tau effect, i.e., dependence of perceived time on spatial interval, was first studied by Abe (1935) in Japan, and by Cohen, Hansel, and Sylvester (1953) in England, the latter naming it the "Kappa" effect. Scholtz (1924) had shown earlier that visually perceived space was influenced by the temporal intervals between flashing light stimuli; and Price-Williams (1954) demonstrated that temporal intervals between flashing visual stimuli were underestimated as the distance between them decreased (Table 3.2).

TABLE 3.2.   Estimated Time Interval as a Function of the Distance between Visual Stimuli

Distance between Stimuli in Inches	Time Interval between Stimuli in Seconds				
	Objective				
	7.0	8.0	9.0	10.0	11.0
	Estimated				
8	5.93	6.50	7.06	7.67	8.39
16	6.39	7.15	7.22	8.51	9.11
32	7.07	8.05	8.28	8.99	9.49

SOURCE: From Price-Williams, 1954. With the permission of *Nature*.

If the Tau effect is operative in two-point discrimination, thresholds should be larger with shorter times between stimulations. Jones (1956) found that the *longer* the time interval between tactile stimuli, the *smaller* the two-point threshold. Thus with about 1 sec. between stimuli the two-point threshold averaged 3.75 cm. for two Ss, and with 2.1 msec. between stimuli it rose to 11.4 cm. (Table 3.3).

TABLE 3.3.   Influence of the Tau Effect on Judgments of Positions on the Skin

Interval between Stimuli (msec.)	Minimum Separation Judged Different on Skin (Mean Distance, cm.)	
	Subject F	Subject M
2.1	11.0	11.8
3.0	10.6	10.3
12.0	10.2	10.9
102.0	7.1	7.7
1001.0	4.5	3.0

SOURCE: From Jones, 1956. With the permission of *Science*.

Perception of velocity which is primarily temporal in character was shown by Brown (1931) and by Johansson (1950) to be influenced by spatial factors. Brown found that perceived velocity depended upon the spatial dimensions of the moving objects—larger objects appearing to move faster than smaller—even when the comparisons were made successively. Johansson reported that the perceived velocity of an object was influenced by the movement of another object in the same field. When spatial and temporal factors were in conflict, the latter were more important in perceived velocity than the former, something we would expect since velocity is primarily temporal in character.

The systematic importance of spatiotemporal pooling can hardly be overestimated because spatial and temporal dimensions are involved in all behavioral processes. Evidence that spatial dimensions depend upon time and that the temporal dimension depends upon space argues for a more thorough relativity theory of behavioral processes than is envisaged in the Weber-Fechner law and in theories that make behavioral relativity an epiphenomenon by regarding it as an attitudinal, semantic, or judgmental effect. The place and function of an element in a pattern are affected by spatiotemporal interactions. Thus the "local sign" of a spot on the skin or of a visual stimulus on the retina is not sufficient to specify its position even though its spatial quality is considered to be derived from a pattern because the very pattern in which it appears depends upon the temporal as well as the spatial relations among the elements of the pattern. Spatiotemporal pooling, constituting the very warp and woof of physical phenomena, provides a basis for the fundamental nature of pooling processes underlying all behavioral phenomena.

Cognitive pooling. We have already noted that pooling occurs in time as well as in space in discussing apparent movement, perception of velocity, and the Tau and Kappa effects. Temporal pooling is not limited to perceptual phenomena and the simpler motor responses such as are found in determinations of reaction time. The highest forms of affective, cognitive, and adjustive behavior also depend upon temporal pooling. The handling of spoken and written language, the solution of problems of all levels of complexity, the acquisition of skills, and the appreciation of music (to mention only a few) all require temporal pooling if patterns are to be formed from discrete units. As Hearnshaw pointed out (1956), little is known concerning the actual process of pooling by which this is achieved. The Gestalt people, he asserts, did not quite succeed in dealing with the problem because of the extraordinary dominance of spatial concepts in their thinking; and learning theory people have not recognized it because of their preoccupation with material that can be handled repeatedly. But World War II forced psychologists to deal with situations that moved with dramatic speed and that required fast manipulation of mechanical devices for control and prediction, and the importance of temporal pooling was recognized thereafter.

One of the most important functions of adaptive behavior is to anticipate future events. As Hearnshaw says, "We are constantly having to summate our experiences, evaluate them, and make predictions as to the future on the strength of them, and in doing this we necessarily have to integrate temporally separated events" (1956, p. 9). Experimental studies of the use of manipulanda necessary for carrying out skilled acts (some requiring accurate fast judgments, as in piloting planes) have thrown considerable light on temporal integrations involving utilization of sensory data. Studies dealing with decision making, probability learning, and information theory can contribute to an understanding of pooling at the cognitive level.

Disturbances in temporal integration range all the way from inability to see objects in motion to the language difficulties of the aphasic. Many of the patients studied by Gelb and Goldstein (1920) and Poppelreuter (1923) after World War I suffered from defects in pooling functions. One patient saw moving automobiles only as a succession of static images; another was unable to perceive words as wholes by means of vision and had to trace letters by means of eye and head movements as if he were writing the words; a third patient was unable to continue a series of digits unless he started with number one. The reading difficulties found in so many of our school and college students point to defects in ability to form temporal patterns. The lame halting manner, devoid of rhythm, inflection, and proper pauses, in which such individuals read aloud reflects the absence of extended unit-formations necessary for rapid smooth handling of verbal materials.

So far in our discussion of pooling we have employed this concept to indicate interaction, integration, connectedness, and fusions of various kinds. In some cases, pooling occurs to such an extent that the components are completely lost, as in the fusion of blue and yellow to yield gray; at other times it is partial, for example, the modifications of space by time and time by space as in the *Tau* and *Kappa* effects. It is apparent that various degrees of pooling occur, and in the world in which we live and because of the way we are built, these are necessary for various purposes. Coalescence by an individual of all objects into undifferentiated wholes impairs discriminatory responses. When objects are not separated in space and time in accordance with their objective structure, resultant behavior may be inadequate and in extreme cases psychotic. Normal adjustment requires the ability to discriminate degrees or amounts of properties belonging to specific objects. In an unpublished study by Kaplan and Helson it was found that psychotic *S*s selected for frontal lobotomy were unable to judge lifted weights on an absolute scale because of their inability to distinguish between the anchor stimulus, which was presented first, and the variable stimulus, which came second. In such cases series weights from 200 to 400 grm. were all judged heavy with a 900 grm. anchor, while with an anchor weight of 90 grm. they were all judged light, due to obvious confusion of anchor and series stimuli. Here the difficulty seemed to be opposite to the difficulties of the aphasic patients studied by Head (1926). His brain-injured patients lacked the power to combine both verbal and concrete materials. The psychotic subjects in our study were unable to differentiate stimuli that were very different from each other and were separated in time as well.

We thus find two extreme types of disturbance with respect to temporal integration. At one extreme are the individuals who are unable to pool units to form temporal patterns necessary for normal activities;

at the other extreme are the individuals who fail to discriminate objects because of excessive pooling. The latter cannot distinguish, separate, and localize objects in the environment. Between these two extremes are the normal integrations that result in pattern formation while preserving the individuality of the components.

Many phenomena which appear to be unitary wholes and seem to be grasped "immediately" are actually products of rapid temporal pooling. Hebb (1949) has stressed this point in his theory of form perception, contrary to the common view that form is an immediately intuited datum. Thus reading, which appears to be a simple, forward-moving process, is shown by eye-movement records to require many oculomotor adjustments. Ryan and Schwartz (1956) found that recognition thresholds were lowest when common objects were represented by cartoons and highest when represented by photographs, with schematic drawings falling between. (Cartoons may fail in their purpose if they contain too many details. Since everything in a cartoon is emphasized by the very nature and purpose of the caricature the reader should not be called upon to synthesize more than is absolutely necessary for the intended message of the artist. Whatever results in easy, rapid, temporal integration contributes, not only to ease of perception, but also to comprehension of cognitive materials and appreciation of aesthetic objects.)

Since pooling is necessary for the establishment of level, the following question arises: Over what temporal period, and over how many items does the pooling process extend in the formation of adaptation levels? There is, of course, no single general answer to this question since it depends upon conditions of stimulation and the extent to which past effects of stimulation persist. Some writers have supposed that only present or immediately preceding stimuli pool with incoming stimuli, thus making level synonymous with the integrated effect of events in the specious present. But this restriction on level formation neither fits the facts nor follows from adaptation-level theory. Beebe-Center (1932) concluded that the affective value of a stimulus could not be predicted on the basis of simple contrast with the immediately preceding stimulus but could be predicted by reference to the "general" level established by all the preceding stimuli in the experimental session. Pratt (1933b) pointed out that stimuli judged by Ss two or three weeks earlier affected subsequent judgments of sound intensities. Garner (1953) found that the response to a stimulus might be raised when the preceding stimulus was higher, and lowered when the preceding stimulus was lower, than the one judged, and had to conclude that the response to a stimulus is actually a response to the weighted mean of the present stimulus and the one preceding it. In the light of considerable evidence it is not unreasonable to proceed on the assumption that all stimuli pool more or less to form level—even remote stimuli. Considering the extent of temporal pooling this is not an unreasonable assumption.

Interaction and pooling as varieties of adaptation. Interaction effects are so closely related to effects of adaptation that they cannot be separated; what happens in any local region affects and is affected by what happens in neighboring areas. The visibility of a spot of light depends upon surround luminances as well as upon its own luminance; the audibility of a sound depends upon the presence or absence of other sounds; the number of warm and cold spots in any area of the skin depends upon size of the thermal stimulus and upon the temperature of other areas. Areal interactions have been called "lateral adaptation" by Evans (1948), and I have suggested the term "pooling" (1947) to cover both temporal and spatial interactions. Temporally, every stimulus leaves an aftereffect that modifies incoming stimulation by pooling with it. Thus every movement of the eyes leaves a positive or negative afterimage from previous stimulation upon the newly fixated object, and every taste, odor, sound, or touch is modified by what has preceded it. Although sensory processes are basically quantal in nature, temporal carry-over and pooling may explain why experience is introspectively continuous and does not appear to be made up of discrete units.

Pooling may result in facilitation or inhibition of interacting processes, as shown by many well-known examples of summation and inhibition in both sensory and motor responses. Some of the most striking examples of spatial and temporal interactions are found in conditioned reflexes. Even in simple Pavlovian conditioning, independent discrete stimuli interact to yield conditioned responses. The conditioned stimulus (CS) by interacting with the unconditioned stimulus (US) calls forth the response originally made only to the US. The affinity of excitations that occur simultaneously or in close succession (sometimes after considerable intervals, providing they are paired) is evidence of the strength and pervasiveness of the pooling tendency. So strong is this tendency that often extraneous stimuli are conditioned and call forth conditioned response (CR) in their own right. Conditioning, viewed as the result of arbitrary pairings of stimuli, appears to be a purely mechanical effect impressing itself on a passive organism. But if behavior is fundamentally a process of adaptation in which stimuli pool to form level, it is understandable why the same response is eventually made to CS as well as to US and why even extraneous stimuli may be unwittingly conditioned in some unguarded experimental situations.

WEIGHTING AND DISTINCTIVENESS

That stimuli are not equally weighted in perception, memory, and thinking is well known from everyday experience. The classical concept of attention which has almost completely disappeared as a chapter heading in textbooks of psychology emphasized the fact that some stimuli make greater claims, stand out more, and elicit more intense or more frequent responses than do other stimuli. Introspective psychology noted many determinants of attention, such as size, position, intensity, novelty, movement, and vividness, but provided no theory by which the diverse determinants could be included within a single frame of reference. Nor did the behavioristic concept of attention as focalized response explain why some stimuli are neutral and others are predominant or why the same stimulus differs from time to time in its ability to arouse responses. Neurologically, Boring pointed out, "what is wanted and wanting here is some reasonable conception of a facilitation that will show why a loud noise, a pretty face, and an interesting idea have more command than their neutral competitors upon the neural activity that leads to discriminatory response" (1933, p. 198). In our terms, many of the facts embraced under the concept of attention, figure-ground, demand character, effects of organization and grouping, and many factors determining learning, recall, and "distinctiveness" are cases of *differential weighting* of stimuli with respect to levels of functioning. Although this statement is qualitative as it stands, it has the virtue of being capable of quantitative formulation.

It follows from the concept of adaptation level that the effectiveness of stimuli is greater the more they differ or the farther they are from prevailing level; conversely, the less stimuli differ from level the more neutral or indifferent they are. Distance from adaptation level has been taken by Nachmias as a measure of degree of distinctiveness (1958, p.

578) and Murdock's definition of distinctiveness as the "sum of all differences of a given stimulus from other members of its group" emphasizes, along with adaptation-level theory, "the effect that all stimuli in a group have upon one particular stimulus" (1960, p. 17). These writers, in agreement with our position, take account of degree of deviation in the negative direction (below level) as well as deviation in the positive direction (above level) in measuring distinctiveness. Thus Nachmias showed that words of intermediate frequency according to the Thorndike-Lorge word count were recalled less frequently than words of *lower or higher* frequencies and Murdock's quantitative formulation of distinctiveness yields low values for items near the center of a group and higher values for end items. Since we shall discuss these studies later, this brief mention of them must suffice at this point.

A   **B**

FIG. 3.3. The black filling in *B* is redundant from the point of view of information theory but is not redundant in perception in that *B* is perceived differently from *A* in tachistoscopic exposures, under reduced illumination, and even under ordinary conditions of viewing.

The necessity for taking the properties of the organism and its subsystems into account to arrive at a proper estimate of weighting is brought out in the following illustration touching upon some basic differences between a purely informational approach to the problem of redundancy and a behavioral approach. Consider the two forms in Fig. 3.3. From the point of view of information theory the black filling in the right-hand figure is redundant since it adds no new information once the border is crossed in any direction. But the two figures are weighted very differently in perception: they are perceived differently under ordinary conditions of viewing and even more so under tachistoscopic exposure; their recognition thresholds are different; they suffer different distortions in brief exposures and under conditions of reduced illumination; and they give rise to different contrast and afterimage effects! Hence the filling that is "redundant" from the informational point of view is highly efficacious from the behavioral point of view.

Every perceived difference arises from differential weighting with respect to level and in turn exerts differential effects on level. This proposition is supported by one of the simplest changes which can be made in a stimulus: rotation about its own axis. It was noted by Mach (1886) that a square resting on one of its sides was a different figure in perception from one standing on one of its corners. Rotation of the square through an angle of 45° changes it from square to diamond. Furthermore gamma movement of the diamond is very different from that of the square: in the latter, the sides are perceived to move; in the former, the corners. Modern information theory which is presumably

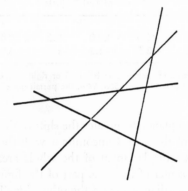

FIG. 3.4. It is difficult not to perceive order patterns in lines drawn at random.

able to account for figural differences has not yet accounted for "Mach properties" that arise from changes in spatial orientation involving no inner changes in figures. Koffka (1935) stressed the importance of the gravitational vertical and horizontal, calling them preferred positions in space. But it is difficult, if not impossible, to eradicate directionality even in randomly arranged, nonvertical, nonhorizontal lines. Thus, although in Fig. 3.4 the lines have been drawn without regard to any specific direction and there is no true vertical or horizontal line among them, subpatterns can be seen in the areas enclosed by the various lines. Form, shape, pattern, order, and direction emerge whenever there is differential weighting of elements within a field. *Differential weighting* with establishment of level precedes organization and Gestalt.

Two studies by Bruell and Albee (1955a and 1956) demonstrate the effectiveness of weighting on the position of the median plane in vision.

These writers followed up an observation made by Roelofs (1935) that if a plane surface is placed with one edge tangent to the median plane, the perceived median shifts toward the center of the surface. Using a vertical line, 1.5 × 20 cm., as a control, and three test rectangles (20 × 20 cm., 40 × 20 cm., and 60 × 20 cm.) they placed one edge of the rectangles in the objective median plane and determined the position of the apparent median for each of the figures. The stimuli were luminous and were viewed in a dark room at a distance of 200 cm. The results, given in Table 3.4, show that the larger the area on one side of

TABLE 3.4. Shift of Apparent Median Plane as a Function of Area of Test Objects

Area of test object	−60.0	−40.0	−20.0	0.0	+20.0	+40.0	+60.0
Deviation	−6.5	−3.5	−1.2	+1.3	+6.0	+7.4	+10.9

Note: Signs indicate area of rectangle to left (−) or right (+) of median plane.
SOURCE: From Bruell and Albee, 1955a. With the permission of *Perceptual and Motor Skills.*

the objective median plane, the greater the shift of the apparent median toward the center of the area. Concomitant with the shift of the perceived median was a displacement of the whole area. As the median shifted toward the center of the area, part of the figure appeared to be located *beyond* the median plane on the other side. Thus an area having its left edge in the objective median appeared to extend into the left half of the visual field owing to the perceived shift of the median toward the center of the figure on the right. In their second study, Bruell and Albee varied the area of the rectangle continuously by removing a masking panel exposing more and more of the figure. All but one of their twenty-three subjects saw movement of the edge of the panel away from the median plane as more of the figure was exposed to view.

Social weighting. Weighting is of importance in studies of the person and in interpersonal relations no less than in perception, judgment, and learning. Just as physical stimuli differ in their dimensional attributes, so social stimulation varies in time, in intensity, and in extent. Individuals affect others in varying degrees and in various situations, as shown by studies of propaganda, conformity behavior, and in the "action" studies discussed later in this book. Certain individuals exert predominant influence on their fellow men in the social, economic, religious, aesthetic, and intellectual spheres and function as focal or anchor stimuli. Thus a statement by the President of the United States or the Secretary of the Treasury regarding business outlook can send the stock market up or down; Emily Post for years determined the position of the left hand and arm for millions of diners; and Comstock's judgments as to which books were fit for public consumption and which should be banned as obscene had almost as much force as legal statutes during the heyday of his power. The ability of individuals to influence others changes with changes in their status; e.g., the pronouncements of politicians carry far less weight after they leave office than before. High-status individuals are more potent sources of stimulation than are ordinary individuals, although the latter may have high status in circumscribed areas, e.g., as parents or employers. The old expression that so-and-so "likes to throw his weight around" supports our thesis that the concept of weighting is as applicable in the field of interpersonal behavior as in the study of the classical laboratory topics in psychology.

We have discussed weighting largely in terms of the relative contributions of various components of the stimulus situation; but internal sources of stimulation are often more important than external sources in determining adaptation levels. The stimulating value of food is much greater for a hungry than for a satiated organism. Stimuli associated with the so-called primary drives or with tissue needs vary greatly in their appeal and effectiveness, depending largely on the state of the organism. Also to be reckoned with organic determiners are pre-existing affective levels and cognitive systems which have greater weight than do stimulus dimensions in the determination of many responses. We have classed such determinants of behavior among the residual factors, not because they are less important than focal and background stimuli, but because usually they are neither manipulated as independent variables nor evaluated as dependent variables in experimental procedures. In properly controlled experiments all external stimuli are presumably accounted for, so it is not unreasonable to assign residual sources of variance to factors within the organism. In any case the quantitative treatment of residuals is the same whether their origin is inside or outside the organism. The task facing the student of behavior is evaluation of the relative weights of focal, background, and residual stimuli, through which he may understand and predict responses of individuals in specific situations.

Weighting also makes possible better manipulation and control of conditions affecting behavior. Since behavior depends upon the pooled effect of all stimuli, once the relative contributions of the three classes of stimuli are known, the amounts by which one class must be weighted to compensate or overbalance the other classes are known. I have stated in a previous work that in the field of personality and interpersonal relations, "the critical problem . . . is to understand how residuals develop, how they interact with present stimulation to modify behavior, and how they can be modified or counteracted by appropriate control or manipulation of environmental factors to make possible adjustment of the organism to changing . . . conditions" (1955a, p. 99). The concept of weighting provides for the emphases made by the individual in his encounters with situations and also for the impacts made by situations on the individual. Determination of weighting of situational and personal factors in responses is therefore fundamental to a quantitative approach to behavior.

NONLINEAR RESPONSE TENDENCIES

Nothing is more certain in psychology than that the behavior of living organisms is not always in accord with "facts." Fortunately for the science of psychology, however, many deviations of responses from so-called objective criteria exhibit definite patterns and are found to be lawfully determined. If one-to-one correspondence existed between stimuli and perception, judgment, cognition, or memory, responses would be linear with stimulation; but this occurs only in special cases. The Weber and Weber-Fechner laws—as well as earlier findings going back to Aristotle in tactile, visual, kinesthetic, and auditory illusions— attest the nonlinearity of the simplest sensory processes with their antecedent stimuli. Moreover, the less intimate the connection between stimulus and response, as in cognitive and memorial processes, the less correspondence we expect between them. On the other hand, uniformities have been discovered in such nonlinear stimulus-response relations as positive and negative time-order error, time error, space error, central tendency of judgment, and hysteresis effect. Most of these departures from linearity of response concern overestimation or underestimation of magnitudes, intensities, qualities, and spatial properties of stimuli. In this section we shall be concerned chiefly with overestimation (O tendency) and underestimation (U tendency) of magnitudes of various sorts, tendencies that appear in many types of materials and activities.

One of the most striking departures from linearity of responses to stimulation is found in overestimation of small magnitudes and underestimation of large magnitudes, with an intermediate range where "error" is minimal or absent. This double deviation from linearity of response usually takes the form of a negatively accelerated curve in which the lower part of the curve lies above the straight line of unit slope and the upper part of the curve lies below (see Fig. 3.5). Holling-

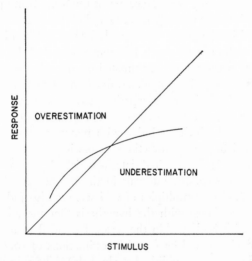

FIG. 3.5. Departures from linearity of stimulus-response functions tend to result in overestimation of small quantities and underestimation of large quantities as shown in this negatively accelerated curve.

worth (1910) made this discovery in a study of motor behavior and referred to it as the "central tendency" effect. In this study, Ss reproduced three series of linear extents by means of arm-hand movements ranging from 10 to 70 mm., 30 to 150 mm., and 70 to 250 mm. Smaller distances in each series were overshot, and the larger distances were undershot. *Within each series was a neutral region with minimal errors.* This early finding of Hollingworth's was replicated nearly 50 years later in motor responses by Weiss (1954) in a study of tracking behavior. Using a joy stick, Ss centered a spot of light which appeared at one place and then reappeared at another place. Ss could correct their guess upon the reappearance of the spot. "A 3° distance underestimated in one condition where it was one of the longer distances (e.g., in a 0°–3° series) tended to be overestimated in another condition where it was one of the shorter distances (e.g., in a 0°–12° series)" (1954, p. 223). Such effects have been called "series" effects; but the clue as to which members of a series will be over- or underestimated is given by the position of the region of minimal errors, which is our adaptation level. As we shall see later, O judgments for small values and U judgments for large values of stimuli are found only when the adaptation level lies within, and usually near the center of the series being judged. Central tendency is thus a special case of O and U departures from linearity as exemplified in negatively accelerated plots of S-R relationships.

For many years a vain search has gone on to find the time interval that is neither over- nor underestimated on the supposition that there is a "specious present" innately determined. William James pointed out that "in every list of intervals experimented with there will be found what Vierordt calls an 'INDIFFERENCE POINT' [caps in original!]; that is to say, an interval which we judge with maximum accuracy . . . and away from which, in both directions, errors increase their size" (1890, Vol. I, pp. 616–617). James cited data in which IP ranged from 0.35 to 0.75 sec. with most of the intervals in the neighborhood of 0.75 sec., and he suggested that multiples of 0.75 sec. are also judged more accurately. In accordance with the hypothesis that the adaptation level tends to establish itself within the series, I decided to test whether O and U tendencies would be found in estimations of time intervals as long as 26 to 90 sec. (unpublished study, 1946). The stimuli and activities engaged in by the 10 Ss are given in Table 3.5, along with the actual times, the times estimated by Ss, and the percentage of error. Although the estimates are contaminated by different kinds of "filling," it is nevertheless striking that the shortest interval (26 sec.) was overestimated 17.8 percent on the average, and the longer intervals (60, 80, and 90 sec.) were underestimated 20.3, 25, and 26.9 percent respectively. The IP seems, therefore, to be between 26 and 60 sec. under the conditions of this experiment. Admittedly these data are only suggestive; but they show the need for investigating longer temporal intervals than have been employed in the past, and they cast doubt on the concept of an absolute temporal indifference interval. The specious present may be a minute, an hour, or almost any value, depending upon the circumstances under which time is estimated.

TABLE 3.5. Average Estimates of Temporal Intervals Made by Ten Ss
under Nine Conditions

	Time in Seconds		
Stimuli or Activity	Actual	Estimated	Error (Percent)
1. Empty interval	26.0	36.5	+40.0
2. Fast classical music	26.0	27.5	+ 5.8
3. Answering questions on passage read	60.0	47.0	−21.7
4. Fast classical music	90.0	72.5	−19.4
5. Tapping	80.0	60.0	−25.0
6. Jazz music	60.0	55.5	− 7.5
7. Writing	90.0	59.0	−34.4
8. Slow classical music	60.0	41.0	−31.7
9. Listening to tapping	26.0	28.0	+ 7.7

Deliberate, systematic forcing of *O* and *U* tendencies was shown to be possible in a study by Noble and Broussard (1955). *S*s turned a ¾-in. micrometer by an amount necessary to receive a total numerical score of 200 after 30 turns. Scores were contingent upon feedback from *E* concerning *S*s' performance on preceding trials. The instructions explained that 200 constituted the goal score, that size of score increased with number of turns, that each trial would start from zero, and that a uniform type of response was required. Three groups of *S*s received information regarding their supposed performance according to values derived from the constants of the power equation $Y = aX^b$, with *b* assuming a value of 1, giving a linear function, a value of 0.25, giving a negatively accelerated function, or a value of 4.0, giving a positively accelerated function. (The actual equations contained additional constants to yield convenient values.) Thus, one group was given correct information (according to the linear function), another group was given inflated values that gradually decreased until they were short of actual performance (negatively accelerated curve), and the third group was given low values that increased rapidly beyond their actual performance (positively accelerated curve). As was expected, the positively accelerated group first overshot the target and then improved in accuracy by discrete corrections, while the negatively accelerated group undershot the target at the beginning and then gradually corrected their undershooting. The performance of the zero group (no distortion) was superior to that of the other two groups throughout, though at first they undershot and then quickly came in on zero deviation from goal. The "plus" group showed more oscillation than the other two groups, and on the whole their performance was unsymmetrical due to predominance of undershooting. We have here a beautiful example of effects of feedback in modes of responding to fixed goals.

Judgments of rates of work in industry have revealed overestimation of slower and underestimation of faster rates in a study by Lifson (1953). He pointed out that in judging how much time should be required to accomplish specified amounts of work it is necessary to determine the "normal time," *i.e.,* the time taken to do the work at a "normal pace." This is done as follows: The time-study man records the amount of time taken by the operator and also makes a judgment of the work pace of the operator. Then the time is adjusted in accordance with the judgment of work pace so that the adjusted time is representative of normal performance. Thus, if the pace is judged 30 percent faster than normal, the performance is rated 130, and the observed work time is multiplied by 1.30, bringing the shorter time up to "normal." Lifson pointed out several sources of error in this procedure: (1) Different observers have different "concepts" of "normal" work pace and tend to rate consistently high or low. (2) Different jobs may appear easier to some observers than to others, and this variation may be superimposed on a high or low rating bias on the part of the observer. (3) Different workers maintaining the same objective tempo on a job may be rated differently. (4) Different paces are not linearly rated, lower paces are rated too high and higher paces are rated too low. Furthermore, a normal pace for one worker may be too high or difficult for another. Finally, although time-study people and workers would be presumed to have opposite biases regarding work rates, both groups overrated low paces and underrated high paces!

That *O* and *U* modes of behavior are not solely due to distorting effects of cognitive and judgmental processes is proved by their presence in tasks requiring direct report of perceptual data. Thus, Minturn and Reese (1951), in common with others working in this area, found that groups of 1 to 6 dots exposed tachistoscopically were reported correctly, groups of 7 to 11 dots were overestimated, groups of 11 to 20 dots were again correctly estimated, and groups of more than 20 dots were underestimated. The curve for an experimental group which was reinforced by being told the correct number of dots after each judgment had the same shape as the curve for the nonreinforced control group, but the experimental group did not over- or underestimate as much as the control group.

In a task involving the use of a scale with numbers 1 to 11 to specify the over-all impression of number of dots of a given color ("color mass"), Philip (1941) found that the numerical responses did not utilize the full scale but ranged from 3.32 to 9.02 on the average. Ss avoided numbers toward the ends of the scale although the maximum number of dots of one color was 23, far above the maximum of the scale, 11. Had the responses been linearly related to the scale values, the number 1 could have been assigned to the minimum number of dots of one color, 13; 2 assigned to 14; and so on up to 11 for 23, the maximum number of one color. In addition, the middle of the numerical scale, 6, would have been assigned to 18 dots. Actually, the number 6 was assigned, on the basis of calculations made by me (1948), to 17.4 dots, indicating a clear displacement of the response scale below the middle of the numerical scale given Ss. In terms of the older psychophysical concepts, a negative time-order error was present, if it is permissible to employ this concept for this type of judgment. We have here another example of the fact that the organism tends to center its responses at stimulus values below the arithmetic or simple geometric mean of a series of stimuli.

With O and U tendencies so firmly anchored in sensory responses it is not surprising that they are also found at more complicated levels where cognitive and memorial processes are known to intervene in forming judgments. Engen (1956) required Ss to translate differences in length between pairs of lines into ratios formed by using 100 as the base number. Relatively small differences between lines were overestimated, e.g., 45:55 was assigned to a pair that actually had the ratio 40:60, and large differences were underestimated. The same tendencies have been found in responses involving memory and creative processes. Attneave's Ss overestimated the less frequently occurring letters of the alphabet in common English writing and underestimated the more frequently occurring letters (1953). When Thorndike (1949) asked college students to make words beginning with various initial letters such as *ba, bi,* and *ind,* he found that rare words according to the Thorndike-Lorge word count were mentioned more frequently and common words less frequently than expected, in accordance with the principle that one overreacts to small values and underreacts to large values.

These double departures from linearity of responses are found with sophisticated as well as naïve individuals and in statistics derived from mass as well as individual reactions. In a betting game wherein Ss were informed of the amounts to be won by the throw of dice and the probability of winning, Preston and Baratta (1948) found that mathematically sophisticated Ss overbet on the smaller "objective" prizes and underbet on the larger ones to the same extent that naïve Ss did. Thus for all values of prizes from \$5 to \$1,000 and with probabilities of winning from .01 to .99, hence with objective expectations ranging from .05 to 990.00, the mean winning bid for the prizes exceeded the mathematical expectation for small values of probability (less than .25) and was less than the mathematical expectation for large values of probability (above .25). Essentially similar modes of behavior have been found to characterize mass reactions. Betting behavior at race tracks was analyzed by Griffith (1949) and here the objectively poorer risks, on the basis of past performance, were overbet and the better ones were underbet by most of the people who "played" the horses. It has been asserted by market analysts that in the stock markets, another great sphere of "betting," lower-priced stocks are bid much higher than their intrinsic worth warrants and higher-priced stocks are underbid in relation to their future possibilities. It would appear that the O and U tendencies of judgment uncovered long ago in psychophysical studies are not artifacts of laboratory procedures or mere errors of estimation. Rather, they represent fundamental modes of adjustment that are ubiquitous.

So far we have considered what are probably the most frequent types of judgment, overestimation of small magnitudes and underestimation of large magnitudes relative to the range of stimuli under observation. Cases where small magnitudes are understimated and large magnitudes are overestimated are less frequent. Stevens (1956) reported that faint tones were underestimated and extremely loud tones were overestimated when Ss judged loudness in terms of a numerical scale. Whether this result was due to the fact that subjects were told that a 90 db. sound was to be rated 10, the range being 30 to 120 db., or to some other factor in the experiment is hard to say on the basis of the information given.

Occasionally all stimuli in a group are overestimated or underestimated, deviations from linearity occurring in one direction only. As in the case of double deviations, either O or U tendency may be found not only in simple perceptual judgments but also in more complicated types of responses. Thus Clausen (1950) reported that all time intervals were overestimated, but no intervals shorter than 5 sec. were employed in his study. On the other hand, in the study by MacLeod and Roff (1935) Ss devoid of all external stimulation underestimated, on the whole, elapsed time in a soundproof room. Apparently sources were available for estimation of time from their own activities, e.g., eating, writing, thinking, defecating, sleeping, and probably also from the intra-organic cues furnished by breathing, heart rate, and movement of limbs. These writers concluded that "the individual lives not merely in a present time, but in a present time which is imbedded in a larger temporal structure. Thus, each present event, insofar as it is apprehended as present, is apprehended in a certain position within this structure" (p. 414).

Overestimation by all members of a group has been reported by Anastasi (1936) and by Paterson and Tinker (1938). Anastasi found a pronounced tendency to match figures with a standard of larger area— irrespective of the shape of the figure used as standard or of the variable —in the case of nine different shapes. In the study by Paterson and Tinker, students estimated the amount of page devoted to print in 400 textbooks evenly divided between literature and history. The overwhelming majority of students believed that 60 percent or more of the page was devoted to print, the modal judgment being 75 percent, when the actual amount was 52.8 percent. They then tested this finding experimentally by using cards of different sizes with black center on white, and white center on black. Both black and white centers were overestimated relative to the margins to the extent of 18 percent for all conditions. Since the centers occupied from 43 to 72 percent of the total area, it would be interesting to replicate this experiment by presenting a series containing greater areas in the margins as well as in the centers to determine if U and O tendencies appear with this type of material as they do with many other kinds of stimuli.

Certain features in situations or certain information possessed by Ss may force whole classes of stimuli to be either over- or underestimated. We have already seen how information fed back to Ss regarding their performance resulted in O or U responses in the study by Noble and Broussard (1955). Gaier and Bass (1956) found that when cities were matched for size, estimates of familiar cities were significantly higher than estimates of unfamiliar places. Familiarity thus served as a weighting factor or anchor; what was otherwise a negatively accelerated function was transformed into a positively accelerated one when the cities were known to *S*s.

Can the varieties of over- and underestimation be subsumed to a single principle, or must we be content with calling them "errors"? Let us consider some simple sensory phenomena that have the same formal structure as *O* and *U* patterns of response. A set of gray stimuli on black background appears lighter than the same set on white background, hence the former may be said to be overestimated relative to the latter. On a background of medium reflectance, the grays below background reflectance appear darker (underestimation) than their counterparts on black background, while the grays above background reflectance appear lighter (overestimation) than their counterparts on white background. Whether or not the lightness of a gray stimulus will be overestimated or underestimated relative to another depends upon the relations of the two stimuli to the adaptation levels (among other things) prevailing at the time of judging them. Similar considerations apply to sensory modalities in which anchor stimuli at the high end of a continuum lower the judgments of series stimuli by raising adaptation level and those at the low end raise judgments by lowering adaptation level. Depending upon the position of adaptation level and the composition of series stimuli, *U* or *O* tendencies or both may be found in psychophysical judgments and also in more complex responses, as we have seen in this section.

VARIABILITY AND OSCILLATION

A fundamental characteristic of living things is their variation in structure and function. Not only are no two members of the same species exactly alike in all ways, but the same individual does not respond identically to repeated identical stimuli. At least two types of variability should be distinguished. The first type arises from random determiners and is random in nature; the second type exhibits uniformities that cannot be ascribed to chance. The first may be called random variability, the second, ordered variability. Ordered variation may be as short as milliseconds or as long as the seasons and may occur only once or may be cyclical in nature. When ordered variability is observed under constant conditions of stimulation, the sources of the variability must be sought within the organism. While specific mechanisms are the source of much variability, some variations arise from systemic conditions, such as accumulation of acids within the body (see Williams, 1956), or from environmental sources. In short, there are many types of ordered variability.

The distinction between random and ordered variability has been recognized by other writers. Holway, Smith, and Zigler (1937*a*) say that "one way of treating variation-indices has been to associate them with such words as 'indeterminacy,' 'experimental error,' 'uncontrollable variation,' and even 'freedom'; in effect to relegate them almost completely to the limbo of ignorance" (p. 377). They suggest that variation may be expressed as a function of some well-controlled and experimentally defined variable, and if a uniform relation is found to exist, it must be a biological invariant. Fiske and Rice (1955) came to the conclusion, after an exhaustive survey of types and sources of variability, that variability is related to *the degree of adaptation to the stimulus,* a view that we share.

Paradoxical as it may seem, much of the variability displayed by organisms serves to maintain constancy of over-all function. Changes in pupillary size serve to counteract increases or decreases in luminance thereby maintaining a more constant light flux on the retina; the amount of blood reaching the surface capillaries varies inversely with ambient temperature, thus conserving internal heat with low external temperatures and facilitating heat loss in high temperatures. These and many other examples of the "wisdom of the body" were expressed by Cannon (1939) in the principle of "homeostasis." To maintain constant internal conditions, organisms possess tremendous powers of compensatory adaptations that counteract variations in external conditions. Not only must the body be able to withstand excessively intense stimuli, it must also be responsive to weak energies to maintain a state of vigilance at the behavioral level. These two ends are served by adaptation, which has a double aspect: Repeated or intense stimuli elicit less and less response from receptors, nerves, and muscles and are thereby diminished in their *effective* stimulating power; but stimuli that are weak relative to the general level of stimulation are amplified in order to be perceived often with qualities complementary to those associated with similar intense stimuli. Thus variations within the organism at reflex and higher levels serve to balance extremes of stimulation.

Rhythmicity of responses. Many sensory and sensori-motor processes have very rapid rhythms and are oscillatory in nature, although they may appear to be continuous to introspection. Thus most people are never aware of the oscillatory nature of their visual processes. Ordinary observation reveals at most only the well-known positive and negative afterimages following change of visual stimulation; but with very brief exposures and proper field conditions several additional phases of the afterimage can be observed which reveal the oscillatory nature of the visual mechanism. Much easier to observe is the succession of colors known as "flight of colors" which appears in the dark after intense visual stimulation. Fluctuations of liminal stimuli, illusions of reversible perspective, and reversals in figure-ground relationships all attest to the underlying rhythmical character of receptor and nerve activities.

Rhythmical changes are not confined to sensory phenomena but are also found in motor responses. Action potential records show different frequencies and rates with various degrees of muscular contraction, and even when muscles are completely relaxed, there is a steady stream of nerve impulses to maintain their tonicity. When motor nerves are severed and tonic innervations cease, true paralysis ensues and the muscles become flaccid and atrophy. The pupil of the eye changes in size by a series of expansions and contractions until a steady size is reached, and even constant pupillary diameter is maintained by rhythmical oscillations. The eyeball itself, as shown by Ratliff and Riggs (1950), makes oscillatory movements even when fixating a steady stimulus. Under conditions of steady fixation these workers recorded eye tremors ranging from 17.5 sec. of arc with frequencies of 30–70 cps to 10 min. of arc with periods of 3–4 sec.

What of higher-order voluntary activities, especially those continued over fairly extended periods of time? From much of the literature on fatigue and work decrement it might be inferred there is always steady decline after peak performance is reached; but there is no hint of the cyclical nature of many types of activity which may, on an average, show no deterioration after hours of continuous work. In the Foxboro studies of handwheel tracking we found that on the average accuracy was maintained during three or more hours of continual handwheel turning! Examination of the tracking records revealed why there seemed to be no evidence of fatigue. Poorer runs were compensated by better runs with the result that accuracy averaged over 15-min. periods was maintained at a level characteristic of the operator in shorter periods of work interspersed with rest periods. And little evidence for fatigue has been found in various other activities (cf. the reading studies of Carmichael and Dearborn, 1947; and the review of fatigue by Bartley and Chute, 1947). However, the cyclical nature of performance did not receive the attention it deserved except by a few workers. Snoddy (1926) was one of the first to report that accuracy in the stylus maze during continuous tracing varied in cycles spanning several runs.

The notion of a natural or optimal interval between repetitions of an act was introduced by Scripture (1936) on the basis of Miyake's results with tapping:

> When a person is asked to repeat an act continuously with no specification of the interval between acts he unconsciously selects an average interval. . . . The successive individual intervals are never exactly alike; they vary around the average. If we ask the person to repeat the action with smaller or larger intervals, we find the average variation from the newly chosen interval increases with the amount of difference from the natural interval (p. 235).

Scripture formulated the relation governing the variation in performance when intervals other than the natural interval are employed as follows:

$$r = R \frac{1 + c (u - T)^2}{-u}$$

where r is the average percentage variation of u, T is the natural interval, u is any other interval, R is the percentage variation of the natural interval, and c is a constant depending upon the person, the type of activity, and other factors. The equation shows that the natural interval is easiest, yielding the smallest variability, and it also enables us to determine what intervals are two, three, or more times as variable as the natural interval.

Studies of skilled acts in servomechanisms, initiated during World War II and continued to the present, have shown that lag and oscillation, two important properties of control systems, are also found in the performances of human operators. Lag concerns the time delay between input and output sides of a transmission or control system and oscillation concerns an output that overshoots the correct position before it settles down (Fitts, 1951). Fitts pointed out that equations which express the relations between input and output of systems have been used to describe the behavior of isolated muscle preparations and of intact human limbs, and he also suggested (in keeping with the position taken here) that homeostatic processes and general neural activities of the body are also subject to analysis as rhythmic dynamic processes. Human systems are governed largely by feedback loops which involve interoceptive and especially proprioceptive feedback supplementing primary visual data. In Fig. 3.6 the oscillatory nature of the simple

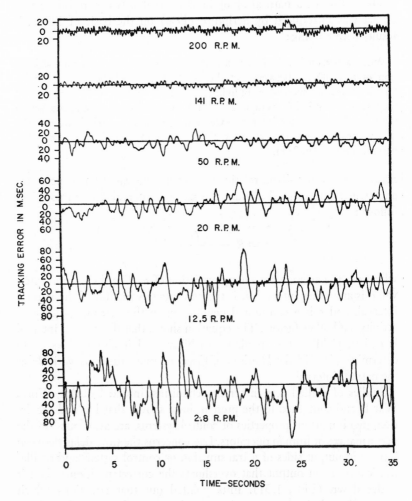

FIG. 3.6. Effect of handwheel speed on pattern of tracking error. (From Helson, 1949. With the permission of the *American Journal of Psychology*.)

sensori-motor task of turning a handwheel at constant speed to keep a moving target aligned with a stationary index is brought out. Both the frequency and amplitude of tracking error are affected by the gear ratios, which fix the speed of turning necessary to maintain the target in alignment with the stationary index (Helson, 1949). Inertia in the control system, by providing kinesthetic feedback either from the hand-wheel itself or from the flywheel, also affects frequency and amplitude of the tracking motion as shown in Fig. 3.7. We may regard feedback

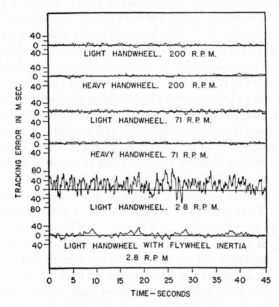

FIG. 3.7. Tracking pattern as affected by inertia. (From Helson, 1949. With the permission of the *American Journal of Psychology*.)

as a factor which is superimposed on the natural variations in rhythm of tracking performance, often profoundly altering it as can be clearly seen from the tracking curves in Figs. 3.6 (from Helson, 1949, p. 480) and 3.7 (from Helson, 1949, p. 485).

Optimal patterns of response in sports and many of the skilled motions required in industry are rhythmical in character. Time and motion studies of optimal arm and hand movements in various tasks reveal patterns which are not only symmetrical but which must be carried out in rhythmical fashion for maximum efficiency. In studies of tracking, two types of skilled movements have, in general, been distinguished: (1) a slow "continuous-control" movement which is subject to correction during its course; and (2) a fast ballistic movement which is triggered at the beginning but thereafter goes to its completion without further correction (Fitts, 1951; Gibbs, 1954). Feeding a steel rod to a cutter in a lathe is an example of the first type of movement and swinging a bat to hit the ball is an example of the second. The first type of movement can be monitored by visual and kinesthetic feedback; the second cannot be. However, as Gibbs has argued, rapid movements may occur in phases each of which is monitored by integrating the feedback signals giving the rate of movement for each phase. Gibbs pointed out that "The problems of learning, in relation to high-grade skill, may therefore hinge upon relatively small time differences in the feedback from vision and kinesthesis, and upon the anticipatory characteristics of kinesthetic discharge" (1954, p. 38).

Whether motor responses are of the continuous-control or ballistic type, they involve an appreciation of, and reaction to, position, rate, and acceleration of both the objects being responded to and the members of the body which are moved. Thus to throw a ball, one aims (position) and then throws it with a certain velocity. Purposeful movements involve positioning as well as displacement of both objects and limbs. There are many activities which require appreciation of accelerations as well as of rates of movement. The sprinter must know how much to accelerate in order to pass an opponent, and the driver of a car must know his car's accelerative power in order to be able to pass another. In the Foxboro studies of tracking (Helson, 1949) target motions were employed requiring high accelerations and reversals of the handwheel controls. Analyses of the performance of skilled operators in these studies left no doubt of their ability to perceive and respond to acceleration as well as to rate of visual targets.

Most striking and perhaps least understood are the longer physiological and behavioral periodicities ranging from days to months and years, although their adaptive function is clear in many cases. Brown (1959), among others, regards the innumerable diurnal rhythmic changes in plants and animals as manifestations of adaptive mechanisms which bring the organism into optimal relations with rhythmic fluctuations in the environment, e.g., changes in light intensity, temperature, tides, and probably levels of radiation. Movements of plant leaves and petals, "spontaneous" activity in numerous animals, emergence of flies from their pupal cases, color changes in the skin of crabs, and wakefulness in man are examples of bodily rhythms in phase with the 24-hr. solar day. Examples given by Brown are the adaptations to the 24-hr. 50-min. lunar rotation found in intertidal organisms whose lives are governed by the ebb and flow of the ocean tides and the lunar-month periodicity of 29.5 days exemplified in the menstrual cycle of the human and the breeding rhythms of numerous marine organisms. Still other periodicities in animals exist and all "adapt them so nicely to their geophysical environment with its rhythmic fluctuations in light, temperature, and ocean tides" (1959, p. 1535). Even stronger evidence for the adaptive nature of these periodicities according to Brown, appears in the phenomenon of *autophasing* by which organisms readjust their periodicities to suit altered environmental conditions. Thus animals that are kept under constant conditions of light and temperature may shift their precise 24-hr. period by as much as plus or minus 4–6 hours. For example, animals may have a 24-hr. period under some constant temperature but as the temperature is adjusted to higher or lower levels, the animals shift their periods away from their 24-hr. cycle as a function of the temperature change. These minor variations in periodicity, which are examples of autophasing, are also adaptive in nature; that is, they are trial adjustments to achieve a new periodicity better adapted to the changed conditions. Autophasing is the mechanism by which the organism introduces periodicity by changing its sensitivity to constant stimulation, or in Brown's words:

Under the hypothesis of autophasing, it is postulated that the organism uses its daily rhythmic fluctuations in sensitivity to light (for example) to effect a daily shift in its phase relation relative to its environmentally imposed 24-hour periodicity. The manner of action, in general terms would be as follows: The organism reaching a "light-sensitive" phase in its daily cycle, and encountering the illumination of a constantly illuminated environment, would be given a shifting stimulus whose strength, within limits, would be a function of the level of the illumination. Though physically the light is held constant, in stimulative effectiveness for the organism it is rhythmic as a consequence of rhythms in the organism's own responsiveness (p. 1542).

Periodicities as long as months are found in changes in the thickness of fur of animals in northern latitudes and high elevations, and periodicities as long as years are found in the life cycles of such animals as the seventeen-year locust. Rhythmic variations in human output appear at all behavioral levels, from the diurnal variations in performance of the factory worker to the productivity of creative thinkers whose cycles of activity may encompass years. In this connection Kretschmer noted the following:

> No form of mental and spiritual activity, especially if it be the creative force of genius, flows evenly and constantly through the whole course of life. Rather, in the intellectual life of great men, is there usually a peculiar wave-like course, a coming and going, a welling-up of passionate excitement and an exhausted sinking down again. . . . This periodic undulation is a definite characteristic peculiarity of much of the work of genius (including scientific genius)—of really productive mental work in contrast to the re-productive, daily, bread-and-butter activities of the average man . . . (1931, p. 107).

Kretschmer ascribes periods of productivity in men of genius to periodicities both in nature and in their own bodies, especially to fluctuations associated with the sexual life, i.e., puberty, maturity, and change of life. A detailed study of Goethe's periods of productivity convinced Kretschmer that they were associated with the poet's love affairs, not that the poetry was written because of these affairs but rather that when Goethe became fired over his work he became amorous! Short of direct testimony by the individuals concerned, and this may not always be reliable, I believe there is no way of settling this issue. Ideas, like mines, can be exhausted and the individual must come up with new ideas to make new contributions. The problem is not restricted to men of genius; average individuals have their good days, months, or years.

The physiological basis of oscillation and variability in behavior is just beginning to be fully appreciated. Certain general states such as excited emotion, alert attentiveness, and relaxed wakefulness have been correlated with alpha rhythms; and very specific types of response involving very short durations, e.g., brightness enhancement of flashing stimuli, have also been correlated with alpha activity (Lindsley, 1952); but as yet no basis has been found for the ordered variabilities of repetitive performances over long periods (hours), e.g., mirror tracing or the diurnal variations in work output. Eventually cyclical activities having periods of hours, days, months, or years may be correlated with physiological activities that are physical, chemical, or neurological in character. It is conceivable that at least some behavioral cycles that are not extremely slow may actually be the envelopes or beat frequencies of faster oscillatory neural events much as audio frequencies arise from modulation of high-frequency carrier waves. While oscillation and variability are basic in behavior, they are as yet imperfectly understood.

OPTIMAL LEVELS AND RANGES OF FUNCTIONS: THE U–HYPOTHESIS

The diversity of forms, structures, and functions in the plant and animal kingdoms is evidence of the great variety of ways in which organisms have adapted to the conditions of life in which they have evolved. Both durative and transient changes in the environment require constant readjustments on the part of living things to maintain and advance life in the individual and in the species. Almost all types of animals can function within fairly wide limits provided certain vital supports, such as oxygen, food, and water are not withdrawn. Fishes that have evolved in the depths of the sea under tremendous pressures literally blow up when brought to the surface, showing that adaptations are more or less specialized. Within the fairly wide limits under which animals are able to survive there are optimal zones, regions, or levels of functioning, where demands of the environment are met with ease, accuracy, comfort, and with the least cost as gauged by long-term effects on the organism.

Optimal ranges of sensitivity to stimulation appear in the photopic and scotopic luminosity functions for vision and in the minimal and maximal sound-pressure curves for hearing. Differential sensitivity as measured by the just noticeable increment or decrement in wave length (hue discrimination) and in frequency (pitch discrimination) is a complex function, representing specialized adaptations which are as yet imperfectly understood. Sensory adaptations involve interaction of a number of variables in the receptor processes as well as further complications in the central nervous system. As Harris (1950) pointed out, sense organs have no true zero; the state of balance of receptor systems shifts with changes in level of stimulation. There is a time parameter in all phenomena of adaptation, for the sensory system does not come into equilibrium with the stimulus immediately. Thus it takes from 20 to 30 min. for dark adaptation and about 5 min. for light adaptation. It may take hours for the skin to come to equilibrium with ambient temperature when passing from cold to warm. It is extremely doubtful if sensory systems ever come into complete equilibrium with extremely high intensities of stimulation since they do not "adapt out" completely under these conditions.

Complete adaptation to a stimulus is signalized by neutralization of the impinging energy. With steady sound or pressure stimulation nerve impulses decline in rate and perhaps in amplitude, and there is a concomitant change in perceived intensity, quality, and area (figural aftereffect) of the stimulus. Following intense or prolonged stimulation decline in sensitivity may be noticeable for days if the original intensity is very great; e.g., exposure to 110–130 db. for 8 min. may result in a hearing loss of 60 db. which is not fully regained for a week.

We are justified in saying that there is an optimal band of stimulus frequencies, wave lengths, or energies for every level of adaptation. Thus the maximum brightness sensitivity of the eye is 555 mμ at levels above .01 ml., decreasing on either side of this value; at levels below .01 ml. maximum sensitivity shifts to 511 mμ. Usually the differential threshold is smallest in the immediate vicinity of the adaptation level (AL), although large displacements of AL toward extremes of sensory continua may result in loss of sensitivity to that portion of the continuum to which the neutral zone has shifted (cf. Woodworth and Schlosberg, pp. 286 ff., and other discussions of adaptive effects in this book).

On the motor side we find that there are optimal ranges of variables just as there are in the various sense modalities. Within these ranges performance tends to be more accurate, more efficient, and usually more comfortable than with values of variables outside these ranges. In a previous publication (1949) I referred to the generalization regarding optimal ranges in performance as the U-hypothesis because when the measure of performance is in terms of errors or time, the plots of performance as a function of the independent variable are roughly U-shaped; if accuracy or sensitivity is plotted, inverted U-shaped curves are found. For small values of the independent variable the curve is high, and as it increases, the curve descends rapidly, then remains flat over a considerable range of values, and then rises steeply with further increase in the independent variable. Fig. 3.8 shows a plot of tracking error as a function of the speed of handwheel necessary to offset the movement of a cursor which was displaced from zero position at a constant rate, thus requiring constant rate of turning for perfect per-

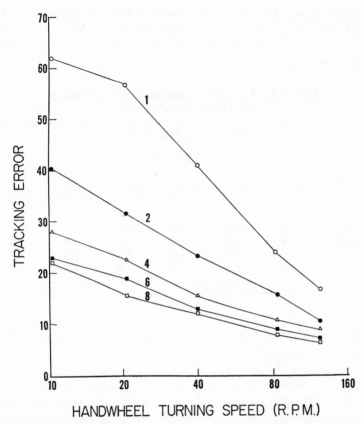

FIG. 3.8. Tracking error as a function of handwheel turning speed with hour of practice as the parameter in the curves. After the first hour of practice it is seen that there is a broad band of turning speeds within which performance is optimal. The sharp increase in error above 150 rpm is not shown because of individual differences in breaking points at the higher turning speeds.

formance.[2] The right branch of the U-curve is not given because of marked individual differences in breaking point where the curve rises abruptly. The flat portion of this curve extends from about 36 rpm to

[2] Each curve in Fig. 3.8 represents hour of practice, the curves for the third and seventh hours having been omitted because of overlapping in whole or in part with those for the fourth and sixth hours. Fig. 3.8 should be compared with Fig. 7.3 where the same data are plotted as a function of hours of practice with turning speed as the parameter.

about 200 rpm and is fairly wide, though it does not appear so in the plot because the abscissa is in log units. The superiority of the 36–200 range appears in Table 3.6 which gives the results for 15 min. of continuous turning.

TABLE 3.6. Average Time Errors for Continuous Tracking with Five Speeds of Turning

Speed (rpm)	Time Error in Milliseconds					
	Tracking Periods					
	3 min.	6 min.	9 min.	12 min.	15 min.	Mean
2.8	25.5	23.0	27.0	28.2	27.6	26.3
12.0	12.9	12.2	13.8	13.3	14.4	13.3
35.5	5.4	6.2	5.9	6.1	5.9	5.9
71.4	4.8	4.9	4.6	4.8	5.3	4.9
200.0	5.3	5.2	4.8	4.7	4.5	4.9

SOURCE: From Helson, 1949. With the permission of the *American Journal of Psychology.*

In quite a different type of task, Holway, Smith and Zigler (1937*b*) obtained an inverted U-curve when DL for lifted weights was plotted against rates of lifting stimuli. The rates ranged from 30 to 240 lifts per min. Sensitivity increased to a maximum between 90 and 120 lifts per min., decreasing on either side of the region of greatest sensitivity.

Results also supported the U-hypothesis for aiding time constants, i.e., the time required by a servomechanism to double the operator's input (cf. Fig. 7.1). The optimal band of aiding-time constants extended from about 0.10 to 1.0 sec. (neglecting the inversion of the error scores at 0.18 sec.). The U-hypothesis was found to hold by Swartz, Norris, and Spragg (1954) for radii of turning cranks, with the maximum optimal size of their cranks (2–3 in.) falling somewhat below the maximum found in the Foxboro studies (4.5 in.). Battig, Nagel, and Brogden (1955) reported that error was minimal between .16 and .24 in. per degree of stick displacement and became greater above and below this range. Fitts (1954) reported that performance, evaluated by the information output of the human motor system, was relatively constant over a central range of amplitudes in a tapping test in which *S*s tapped alternately against two strips separated by various distances and also in a task involving transfer of a disc from one spindle to another. He concluded that this relation holds for most perceptual and motor activities. In his experiments the level of optimum performance varied only between 10 and 12 bits per sec. He suggested that "the fixed information handling capacity of the motor system probably reflects a fixed capacity of central mechanisms for monitoring the results of ongoing motor activity while at the same time maintaining the necessary degree of organization with respect to the magnitude and timing of successive movements" (1954, p. 391).

The concept of a central monitoring mechanism is supported by the fact that conditions that differ in content but are formally or functionally similar have similar effects. Magnification, whether visual or kinesthetic, reduced tracking error. It makes little difference whether visual magnification consists of actual increase in target motion or is obtained by optical means. Similarly, increase of arm motion is beneficial whether obtained through use of large handwheels or by use of gear ratios requiring faster turning speeds or higher angular motions of arm and hand as in the Foxboro studies and the study by Hartman and Fitts (1955), where the elbow rested on the pivot of a horizontal lever. In the Foxboro studies the motion of the arm was either parallel or at right angles to the line of sight, while in the Hartman and Fitts study the motion was sidewise and at right angles to the line of sight; yet in all conditions, larger movements resulted in reduced tracking error.

When a U-curve is obtained under given conditions, the lowest, flat portion of the curve does not always represent an absolute level of performance, for with change in conditions the U-curve for a given variable may shift downward. A family of U-curves is obtained at various stages of learning or practice or if a variable which was previously held constant is altered. Thus the two U-curves in Fig. 7.1, for 1:1 and 4:1 magnifications of target motion, show different levels of optimal performance. The optimal regions of U-curves may shift to right or left to yield different optimal ranges of the independent variable. From Fig. 7.1 it appears that a wider band of aiding time constants is optimal with 4:1 than with 1:1 magnification. There is thus both lowering and widening of the curve with greater magnification. Optimal ranges of individual variables depend, therefore, on all conditions underlying performance.

Optimal values of a variable such as size of handwheel depend upon their interactions with other variables. Low levels of illuminance do not appear to be deleterious if the task does not require detailed vision or if the material presents high contrasts. When this is not the case, higher illuminances are necessary for comfort and efficiency. In this connection a study by Mackworth on the effects of temperature on accuracy of reception of Morse code messages at high transmission rate (one letter or number per second) is of interest. The *S*s were acclimatized to temperature approximating *tropical* levels every day for two or three months. The optimal temperature, as seen from Table 3.7, was found at a dry/wet bulb ratio of 90/80, a rather high value when compared with what might be expected if the *S*s had been acclimatized to temperate-zone conditions. Since the purpose of this study was to determine the extent to which air conditioning should

TABLE 3.7.   Accuracy of Morse Code Reception as a Function
of Room Temperature

Dry/wet bulb temperature, °F	85/75	90/80	95/85	100/90	105/95
Average mistakes per hour per man	12.0	11.5	15.3	17.3	94.7

SOURCE: From Mackworth, 1952. With the permission of the author.

be provided for effective performance of men working in abnormally hot rooms of ships, the range of temperatures studied was properly chosen. Here the optimal value required adaptation to a fairly high temperature and should therefore not be regarded as representative of the optimal for all types of work. Thus in a test situation in which *S*s raised and lowered a 15-lb. weight, the optimal temperature was the lowest studied, 65/60, even though the men had been acclimatized to hotter temperatures. Effects of acclimatization to cold were also studied by Mackworth. Men acclimatized to cold weather by working out of doors perceived twoness at a smaller separation than indoor men not acclimatized but tested under the same cold conditions. The former required an increase of only 1 mm. over indoor threshold, while the latter required a 7-mm. increase. Acclimatization to cold as measured by the numbness index (two-point threshold) required about five weeks.

It is not to be expected that the U-hypothesis will hold for all variables. Thus friction is bad in any amount, and as friction in a control system is increased from zero onwards, performance becomes poorer.[3]

Par and standards of performance. Tracking studies have demonstrated that individuals act in accordance with intra-organismic norms that determine their standards of excellence or what they consider to be "par" for the task. When performance falls, or appears to fall, below the standard that the individual sets for himself, he exerts greater effort to bring the error within his tolerance limits. Thus an operator of a tracking device who is satisfied with his performance as long as the discrepancy between cursor and target does not exceed ¼ in. will not be satisfied when his error is magnified so that he perceives a ¾-in. discrepancy. Figure 7.1 shows that 4:1 magnification of target motion resulted in reduction of error to less than half throughout the whole range of aiding-time constants. Tolerance levels for error depend not only upon sensory input and the properties of the receptor mechanism but also upon the nature of manipulanda, the properties of effector systems, and internal states. There are individual differences in ability to handle load, inertia, high rates of turning, cranking, and other movements involved in sensori-motor tasks and in the extent to which individuals put up with, adjust to, or compensate for defects in equipment and personal irritations (Helson, 1949). All must be taken into account in considering efficiency and comfort of workers.

Numerous studies have shown that intra-organismic norms are raised or lowered by the feedback that Ss receive from their own responses. Two kinds of feedback concerning performance were studied by Payne and Hauty (1955a): (1) *directive feedback* defined as S's perception of the quality of his own performance, and (2) *incitive feedback* or motivation defined in terms of appraising S of his progress relative to his own previous performance, in relation to the performance of others, or in relation to a standard set by E. Payne and Hauty found both types of feedback were highly significant in a multidimensional pursuit task in which Ss had to scan four cam-driven simulated aircraft instruments and to counteract the drifts in the instruments by the coordinated adjustment of simulated aircraft controls. Three levels of both types of feedback were studied. In directive feedback (1) Ss were given no outside information and had to detect drift in the instruments by their own scanning; (2) a single peripheral visual signal was provided whenever a deviation occurred, but it provided no indication of the deviant instrument among the four; (3) the signal provided

[3] Further discussion of the U-hypothesis will be found in Chapter 7.

information of drift and of the actual instrument on which it occurred. In incitive feedback (1) general, hazy, self-informed notions of progress were gleaned by the Ss themselves; (2) information was given regarding S's standing relative to a group norm; (3) in addition to the group norm, the Ss' standings in previous runs were kept in view. The results of this study demonstrated that standards of performance can be controlled to a significant extent through manipulation of the feedback to Ss. The same authors reported in another study (1955b) that groups performed better when there was an expectation of a 4-hr. period of work than did groups who expected a 17-hr. work period.

The concept of par or tolerance for error has certain points in common with the concept of level of aspiration. Insofar as explicitly formulated standards are concerned, the two concepts seem to be identical. But in addition we stress implicit standards that are established more or less automatically. Consciously formulated aspirations constitute only one class of determinants of intra-organismic norms. Conversely, aspiration levels may, in part, be determined by the mode of adjustment of the individual to the task confronting him.

What an individual will tolerate . . . depends not only upon motivational factors but also upon his perceptual and motor capacities and the data and tools furnished him. Together all of these factors interact to produce patterns of behavior which we label inadequate or adequate, good or bad, acceptable or unacceptable. The aim in controlling behavior should be to make objective as well as "subjective" conditions so favorable that the worker's par will be near his physiological limit without excessive cost to him (Helson, 1949, pp. 496–497).

Level of aspiration according to this view goes into the pool of factors affecting behavior and, in turn, is affected by prevailing adaptations.

Evidence for additivity of external and internal determiners of behavior which sustain performance level is found in the studies by Payne and Hauty referred to above. They reported,

. . . in general . . . multiple influences . . . have cumulative, if not additive effects. . . . The performance of control Ss contrasted with that of Ss operating under a combination of conditions involving specific cue feedback (directive), motivational (incitive) feedback, and cerebral stimulation (by means of the drug dextroamphetamine sulfate) (1955b, pp. 388–389).

The control group steadily declined in performance over the 4-hr. period while the experimental group improved during the first 90 min., stayed high for more than another hour, and then declined to a level about equal to their beginning level, which was superior to that of the control group. Hence, it appears that factors as diverse as types of feedback and chemical agents may pool in predictable ways to influence optimal levels of performance.

OUTPUT–INPUT MATCHING

One of the most basic characteristics of organic adjustment is that the level of stimulation tends to be matched by the level of response. This principle is demonstrated most strikingly in sensory and judgmental processes: within wide limits physiological zero, or the stimulus that elicits neither warm nor cold responses, coincides with the ambient temperature; the level of visual adaptation is a weighted mean of all luminances and chromaticities in the field of view; what feels light or heavy corresponds with a weighted mean of the weights being judged; probabilities of stimulation are matched more or less by probabilities of response. The range over which most of the senses are efficient is enormous due to the ability of sense organs to keep pace with changing stimulation. The eye responds to energies as low as 1/10,000 and as high as 1,000,000,000 candles per sq. cm., and the ear responds to intensities of sound ranging from 1/10,000 to 10,000,000 dynes per sq. cm. (Harris, 1950). William Stern said in this connection:

> The human psychophysiological constitution, capable of elaborating only a finite number of stimuli and stimulus degrees within the infinity of the world as a whole, is not related accidentally and haphazardly to these particular stimulus ranges, but has achieved the relationship through continual commerce with the world and by constant self-adaptation (1938, p. 180).

As Stern implied, at each level of adaptation there is a limited number of just noticeable differences, but their range is extended by changes in level. Michels and I have pointed out there is a reciprocal relation between range of adaptation levels and number of JND's within any given level:

> ... organs with high static sensitivity show great adaptive shifts, and those with low static sensitivity show low shifts. Thus a hundred-fold variation in the intensity of light uses up the full scale of responses in a rating scale with the eye in a given state of adaptation. Actually we find it necessary to respond to intensity over a million-fold range. Changes in the adaptation level

allow us to make judgments over any part of this (extended) range. On the other hand, in hearing we need a range of ten thousand-fold to evoke the full range of responses and adaptive effects are much less marked than they are in vision. (Michels and Helson, 1953, p. 6).

Variations in AL thus serve both to extend the range of responses and to refine them within given ranges of stimulation.

Change in any condition of stimulation results in some change in level, though it may be small. Hunt and Flannery (1938) found that variability of affective judgments increased as the number of stimuli increased from three to twelve and also as the number of categories used by *S*s increased. On the other hand, variability decreased during successive presentations of color stimuli. Paralleling variability of judgment, Hunt and Flannery reported variability in the reaction time necessary to make the judgments. Response time became stable as the judgments became less variable. When a new series of colors was introduced, reaction times increased at first, then decreased with repetition. Similar results in a totally different type of judging behavior appeared in a study of decision making by Irwin and Smith (1956). Their *S*s had the task of judging the mean value of numbers on cards with packs so constructed that the mean values were -1.5, -0.5, 0.0, $+0.5$, and $+1.5$. Each mean value was associated with two distributions of numbers, one having a standard error of 2.0 and the other of 7.5. Irwin and Smith regarded the process of deciding the means of the packs as the formation of an adaptation level, and this assumption seemed borne out by the results. Trials to learn were higher with packs having larger, than with packs having smaller standard deviations (SD's), showing that formation of stable levels was more difficult with greater range of stimulation. This result follows from the definition of AL as a weighted log mean of the stimuli. They found that packs with plus and minus numbers having means of zero required the largest number of trials to learn, indicating again that greater variability of stimulation delayed formation of stable levels.

Something akin to the principle of output-input matching was expressed by Brunswik as follows: "One of the . . . tasks of a molar environmental psychology is to find out the extent to which environmental hierarchies of probabilities of object-cue as well as of means-end relationships find a counterpart in similar hierarchies of evaluation by the organism" (1943, p. 259). The principle of output-input matching may be regarded as a principle of *functional isomorphism* between levels of stimulation and response. It covers matches of rates of change, amounts of stimulation and patterns of stimulation, as well as responses to individual stimuli.

The importance of homologous relations between stimulus patterns and movement patterns was shown in two brilliant papers by Fitts and his co-workers (Fitts and Seeger, 1953; Fitts and Deininger, 1954), who found that optimal levels of performance were attained when "sets of stimuli and responses form a congruent match." The first paper tested the hypothesis that "effective performance depends to a large extent upon the unique characteristics of S-R ensembles rather than on specific aspects of particular stimulus or response sets" (Fitts and Seeger, 1953, p. 201). They employed three stimulus patterns which could be responded to by means of one of three response arrangements. Each stimulus pattern was matched by a response pattern isomorphic with it, $S_A — R_A$, $S_B — R_B$, $S_C — R_C$, but also had to be responded to by the other two movement patterns. The patterns of responses were prescribed by means of three response panels which permitted movements from the center of the panels to the position of a light or lights that came on in the stimulus pattern. The several stimulus and response patterns are shown in Fig. 3.9 (from Fitts and Seeger, 1953, p. 203). The performance of Ss was scored in terms of mean reaction time, percentage of errors, and the information lost, which was computed as the theoretical information in the stimulus minus the calculated value for information transmitted. The results showed that reaction time and errors are minimal when the response pattern is isomorphic with the stimulus pattern or is most highly compatible with it.

The experiment was then continued to determine whether the differences between various S-R combinations were transitory or permanent, in other words, the goodness of the learning of the various S-R combinations. A new experiment was performed with new Ss and extended over a period of 2.5 months and involved performance under distraction as well as under normal conditions. Here it was found that throughout all the trials of the 32 training sessions reaction-time was lowest and errors less with $S_A — R_A$ as against $S_B — R_A$ and $S_C — R_A$. The permanence of the learned effects seems best explained, say Fitts and Seeger, by reference to the capacity to learn to deal with sets of probabilities.

The response that a person makes to a particular stimulus event can be considered to be a function of two sets of probabilities: (*a*) the probabilities (uncertainties) appropriate to the situational constraints established by *E's* instructions, by the reinforcements experienced in the experimental situation, and by other aspects of the immediate situation; and (*b*) the more general and more stable expectancies or habits based on *S's* experiences in many other situations. . . . A person's behavior is never entirely relevant to the particular constraints of specific situations; instead *S* acts as if additional possibilities were present (1953, p. 208).

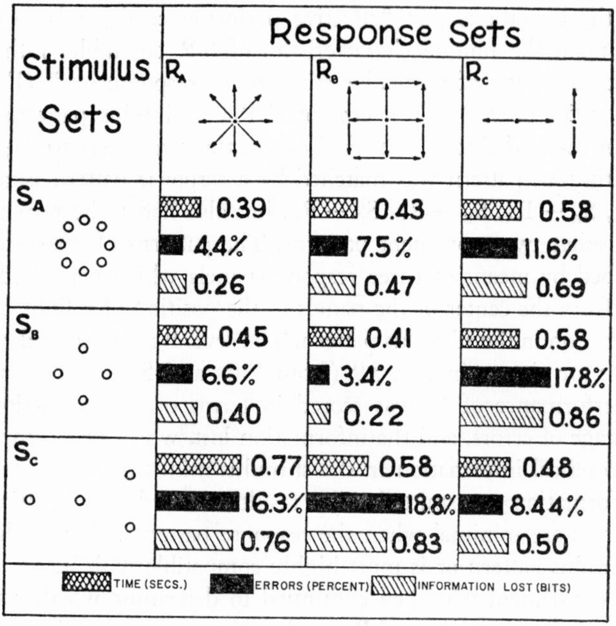

Stimulus Sets	Response Sets		
	R_A	R_B	R_C
S_A	0.39 4.4% 0.26	0.43 7.5% 0.47	0.58 11.6% 0.69
S_B	0.45 6.6% 0.40	0.41 3.4% 0.22	0.58 17.8% 0.86
S_C	0.77 16.3% 0.76	0.58 18.8% 0.83	0.48 8.44% 0.50
	TIME (SECS.)	ERRORS (PERCENT)	INFORMATION LOST (BITS)

FIG. 3.9. Performance is better when stimulus and response sets are isomorphic according to three different criteria than when they do not match. (From Fitts and Seeger, 1953. With the permission of the American Psychological Association.)

They concluded that stimulus and response sets are optimally matched when the resulting ensemble agrees closely with the basic habits or expectancies of individuals.

In the second study, Fitts and Deininger (1954) varied the types of stimulus and response sets by employing several symbolic stimulus sets which consisted of numbers and three-letter first names requiring movement responses in predetermined directions. Again it was found that compatibility of S-R sets made for best processing of information and fastest and most accurate responses. One of the implications of this work, they say, is that S-R compatibility might well replace older concepts of meaningfulness and belongingness in specifying conditions of motor learning. Thus in studies of transfer of training it may be important to specify that the task to be learned is one for which there is (or is not) a strong population stereotype, or that transfer is from a relatively compatible to a relatively incompatible task.

A study by Hake and Hyman (1953) illustrates the operation of output-input matching at the cognitive level. Subjects were required to predict whether the symbol H or V would appear next on each of 240 trials. The proportion of trials in which each letter appeared was varied from series to series. The Ss in all groups began by predicting about equal occurrence of the two symbols, but gradually they adjusted their predictions to conform to the actual probabilities of the appearance of the symbols in each series.

One of the most important practical considerations involving output-input matching concerns anticipations of future events. Manufacturers and retailers must anticipate future buyer demands because industrial products have to be planned and fabricated long in advance of actual sale to consumers. Almost all human decisions, made by and concerning individuals, groups, or governments, depend upon presumed behavior for situations that may arise. The basis for making decisions may be immediately available, may be extrapolated from past experience (which is often not a reliable guide), or may be logically deduced from facts or hypotheses. Knowledge of basic human reaction tendencies can be utilized in predicting how others will act in various situations.

The modes of behavior discussed in this chapter are manifested in daily life as well as under laboratory conditions. In a sense, the mode of behavior which we have called output-input matching is basic to all the other modes. If stimuli elicited univocal responses in all cases, there would be no variability in behavior, no over- or underestimation in judgment, and linear functions would be adequate for all types of S-R relationships. Fortunately, the deviations from one-to-one correspondence between stimuli and responses are for the most part orderly, as we have seen from the seven modes of behavior discussed in this chapter. Other behavioral characteristics could have been covered, but

I have restricted the discussion to modes for which a considerable body of experimental knowledge exists. Succeeding chapters show that changes in sensory adaptation levels, internal norms, and modes of adjustment to complex situations are responsible for much of the variability in behavior frequently attributed to chance, experimental error, or *ad hoc* attitudinal, judgmental, and cognitive processes.

SUMMARY

Supporting evidence has been given for seven basic behavioral phenomena associated with establishment of and changes in adaptation levels. These are important in various types of behavior: Categorizing and scaling are found to have their origins in the bipolarity of both sensory and motor responses; pooling of sensory, cognitive, and sensori-motor data results in the formation of adaptation levels; in the pooling process stimuli keep their individuality, and their distinctiveness depends upon their difference from or their relation to level; because the organism's equilibrium points seldom coincide with the arithmetic means of the stimuli impinging upon it, responses are in general nonlinear, with overestimation of small quantities and underestimation of large quantities most common; variations in adaptation level are in part responsible for oscillation and variability in performance; most performances are optimal with more or less broad bands of conditions, but above and below these, performance is poor and is carried out at greater cost to the individual; and finally, level of output tends to match the level of input as shown by the fact that the value of adaptation level is a weighted mean of the stimuli impinging upon the organism.

4 *Psychophysical Judgment*

Essentially, classical psychophysics as well as most current approaches to measurement of sensory processes are oriented toward specific stimuli. Thus absolute and relative thresholds represent specific values of stimuli and are not necessarily related to stimuli other than the standard. In a similar vein, scaling procedures have been concerned with determinations of given fractions or multiples of specific stimuli in an endeavor to construct sensory scales having general applicability. This approach to stimuli regards psychophysical functions as uniquely determined by stimulus magnitudes formulated on the assumption that no explicit parameter is required to take into account the level of function of the organism. Departures from fixed relations are treated as errors in judgment or as semantic artifacts. Each sense modality is presumed to have its own fixed sensitivity or scale modulus, which holds throughout the range of magnitudes to which it responds. The organism, according to this view, functions only as a meter or transducer of energy in the S-R relationships expressed in psychophysical functions. One of the implications, seldom if ever realized, is that equally spaced stimuli should elicit equal frequencies of judgments, with the result that asymmetries in responses are treated as artifacts. This position has also been responsible for the failure of most workers in the classical tradition to appreciate the systematic importance of time-order and space-order effects (TOE and SOE), the decentered position of indifference points (IPs) and points of subjective equality (PSEs), and other phenomena for which classical psychophysics had no adequate explanation.

Contrasted with the above orientation is the frame-of-reference approach, which regards stimuli as members of classes. Interest centers on the way each stimulus is ordered both as a function of membership in its class and as a result of the adjustment made by the organism to the class as a whole. The basic assumption is that stimuli are judged with respect to internal norms representing the pooled effects of present and past stimulation in specified universes of discourse. Thus within classes (houses, dogs, men, automobiles) some members are large, some are medium, and some are small; and what is large in one class may be small compared with the members of other classes. Only when there is doubt concerning the class to which a stimulus belongs is there question as to how it should be judged. In cases where classes do not overlap, it does not make sense to use the same scale to describe or measure them (a loud whisper is in no sense a very soft thunderclap).

It follows immediately from the frame-of-reference view that all judgments (not only judgments of magnitude) are relative, i.e., based on the relation of stimulation to prevailing adaptation levels. Thus, a 4-oz. fountain pen is heavy, but a baseball bat must weight about 40 oz. to be heavy because in judging the pen only finger and hand muscles are involved while in judging the bat these muscles plus those of the arms, shoulders, back, and legs are involved. There is a unique adjustment level for each class of stimuli which is largely determined by the kind of response it evokes. A scale of heaviness based on data obtained under the usual laboratory conditions cannot be expected to hold for most of the objects lifted and otherwise manipulated in everyday life. Similarly, a single scale does not suffice for judging sizes of rectangles and sizes of houses especially when functional considerations enter into the judgments. A house that is large for a family of two is small for a family of eight and will be so perceived. The more functional considerations enter into judgments, the more necessary it is to know the actual frame of reference of the individual respondent.

Judgments of size, weight, intensity, duration, and other magnitudes change not only between classes but also as a result of conditions affecting the members of a single class. It does not require radical changes in adjustment or posture (as in hefting pens and bats) to invalidate psychophysical findings when they are generalized beyond the conditions under which they were obtained. Psychophysical judgments are affected by mere change in frequency, order of presentation, or spacing of stimuli; by variations in instructions, constraints placed on the use of scaling categories, the type of judgment demanded; and by many other more or less subtle nuances in procedure, as well as by the very act of responding, especially if time is involved (cf. Guilford, 1954*a*). A concept is needed that makes possible a reduction in the number of variables that must be considered if they are to be handled at other than the verbal level and made amenable to quantitative treatment. The concept of adaptation level meets these requirements in that it represents the pooled effect of all members of a class. It provides a single value that is sensitive to all conditions affecting responses, and it makes possible a quantitative treatment of psychophysical phenomena previously regarded as artifacts of judgmental and attitudinal processes. The rest of this chapter concerns quantitative formulations in the frame-of-reference approach to psychophysics.

QUANTITATIVE FORMULATION

Two tasks face us in formulating the concept of adaptation level to serve as frame of reference for a theory of judgment and for prediction of psychophysical data. First, we must define adaptation level operationally and in quantitative terms; second, we must derive functions embodying AL as a parameter which show the relations between stimuli and responses for various conditions and types of judgments. We may define AL a priori by a mathematical expression; we may determine it experimentally as a single value on a continuum (e.g., in terms of the stimulus judged indifferent, neutral, equal, or PSE); or we may derive it as one of the constants in an equation fitting experimental data. It has been handled in each of these ways in various studies.

Since AL has been assumed to be a pooled effect of all stimuli impinging upon the organism both from without and within and includes residuals from past experience, it is reasonable to make the further assumption that it is a weighted mean of all these stimuli. A weighted mean, whether it is arithmetic, geometric, power, or harmonic, has many advantages, chief of which is that it provides for differential weighting of various factors in judging situations and the weighting coefficients can be used as measures of contributions to level.

In addition, the concept of the mean immediately implies a pooling or averaging mechanism which is central to AL theory.

We shall first explore the possibilities of a weighted log mean of focal, background, and residual stimuli as an approximation to experimentally determined ALs or cognate measures such as PSE, after which we shall consider several stimulus-response functions based on the assumption that judgments of stimuli depend upon their relation to prevailing AL.

Before proceeding with the weighted log mean definition of AL let us review some of the ideas that were basic in its development. Fundamental to the theory is the assumption that effects of stimulation form a spatiotemporal configuration in which order prevails. For every excitation-response configuration we assume that there is a stimulus which represents the pooled effect of all the stimuli and to which the organism may be said to be attuned or adapted. Stimuli near this value either fail to elicit any response from the organism or bring forth responses that are indifferent, neutral, doubtful, equal, or the like, depending upon the context of stimulation. Such stimuli are said to be at adaptation level. Conversely, adaptation level may be quantitatively specified by giving a value of stimulus eliciting the neutral response. Stimuli above AL give rise to positive gradients of excitation and responses of one kind, while stimuli below AL give rise to negative gradients of excitation and responses of an opposite kind. Depending upon the momentary value of AL, a stimulus may at one time be above it, at another time below. The effect of stimulation thus depends upon its relation to prevailing level. It follows that the distinctiveness of stimuli is a function of either the distance or the ratio of any given excitation to AL. Since every stimulus tends to displace AL in its own direction, repeated and durative stimuli adapt or satiate, within limits, and lose their distinctiveness. Stimuli far above or below the average may displace level to such an extent that the character of other stimuli may be profoundly altered as seen in the modifications in color which objects undergo when viewed against chromatic backgrounds and in the dependence of vowel quality of words on the formant frequencies in words preceding them.

The concept of AL, as pointed out in an earlier chapter, is not restricted to effects of prolonged stimulation resulting in reduced capacity for response as an end-state. *AL is a function of all aspects of present and past stimulation and is modified by feedback from the responses made to stimuli.* There is thus a changing AL at every moment of time, just as the threshold varies from moment to moment; and values assigned to AL, as well as to thresholds, must be regarded as mean values about which the actual values fluctuate. Like the threshold, AL denotes a region rather than a point on a continuum, although we shall speak of it as having a single fixed value under specified conditions for the sake of brevity.

WEIGHTED LOG MEAN DEFINITION OF AL

A good approximation to the achromatic point in vision is obtained by taking a weighted log mean of the reflectances of all stimuli and the background in the field of view. Choice of a log mean is in keeping with the well-established law of diminishing returns both in the field of sensation and in other areas where rate of output is a decreasing function of input. The formula predicting the reflectance perceived to be achromatic in strongly chromatic illumination was found to be as follows:

$$\text{AL} = K(A_0{}^3 \bar{A})^{\frac{1}{4}} \tag{1}$$

where K is a fractional constant, A_0 is the reflectance of the background, and $\bar{A}$ is the logarithmic mean of the reflectances of the stimuli (Helson, 1938). From this formula it is seen that AL is a weighted geometric mean in which background is weighted three times as heavily as the log mean of all other stimuli in the field. Rewriting Equation (1) in logarithmic form and changing the symbols so as to facilitate discussion in terms of lifted weights we have

$$\log \text{AL} = \log K + \left[\frac{\left(k_1 \sum_{1}^{n} \log X_1 / n \right) + k_2 \log C}{k_1 + k_2} \right] \tag{1A}$$

where K is a constant, X_i refers to the series stimuli, C is an anchor or comparison stimulus, and k_1 and k_2 are constants. There is a lower limit to values of X_i and C which may be used in Equation (1A) and the following equations owing to the fact that stimuli somewhere in this region do not reduce AL further.[1] When a standard or anchor is not effective, or when none is present, as in the so-called

---

[1] We shall take this point up again later in the discussion.

absolute method, the C term becomes zero and is dropped in Equation (3) below.

It is possible to eliminate one of the constants in Equation (1A) by dividing both numerator and denominator by k_2 and defining a new constant $k = k_1/k_2$. The weighting coefficient for the series stimuli becomes k and the coefficient for the comparison stimulus becomes 1.0 with the denominator now equal to $k + 1.0$.

When Equation (1A) was applied to lifted-weight data, it was necessary to weight the log mean of the series more than the comparison stimulus in order to obtain a good fit. If we consider the anchor stimulus the analogue of the background in vision, then at first sight this change in weighting seems paradoxical. Consideration of the visual situation, however, reveals why the background is weighted more than the stimuli being judged. Background in vision bounds each stimulus on all sides and is effective as long as the stimulus is perceived. In situations involving successive presentations as in lifted weights the anchor stimulus either precedes or follows the series variables in time and is therefore less effective than the visual background. Moreover, the series stimuli, being the object of judgment, tend to form a group leaving the anchor stimulus more or less outside. Hence we give greater weight to the series than to the anchor stimulus in successive judgments. The best value of the coefficient for series weights was found to be the same as was formerly used for visual background (three), and this proved to hold for a variety of lifted-weight data as will be shown below.

Another change in Equation (1A) found necessary to fit psychophysical data concerns the constant K which was a fractional constant in the visual data serving to lower the weighted log mean. For lifted-weight data it was found necessary to replace this constant by an additive constant, cd, which proved to be related both to size of step interval between stimuli and to the order of presentation. The symbol d denotes the step interval between stimuli and c is a fractional constant. Consideration of the gradients established when judging in the two time orders shows that if there is a preponderance of positive gradients with standard first, variable second (S_1V_2), there must be a reversal in the other time order, variable first, standard second (V_1S_2). The gradient effect, d, may be positive in one time order and negative or zero in the other time order. In judgments of lifted weights and sound intensities the d factor is zero in the second time order (V_1S_2). The best value of cd fitting a wide variety of data was found to be

0.75 d for S_1V_2 and, as stated above, zero for V_1S_2. Due to the logarithmic formulation we put the d factor on the left-hand side of Equation (1) giving

$$\log (\text{AL} + 0.75d) = \frac{\left(3.0 \sum_{1}^{n} \log X_i/n\right) + \log C}{4} \tag{2}$$

The importance of the size of step interval between stimuli has been recognized by Wever and Zener: "It seems probable that the absolute impression (in method of absolute judgment) is no constant affair, but is responsive to a change in the magnitude or the range of the stimuli used in a given situation" (1928, p. 471). The d factor, as well as the log formulation, accounts for differences in level with changes in density (spacing) of series stimuli and for reversals in excitation gradients as a result of changes in time order. A paradoxical result encountered by Newhall (1940) in determining the lightness-reflectance function seems to be accounted for by the d factor. In using *whole* Munsell value (lightness) steps at the lower end of the scale (Munsell 1–6) he obtained one function, and in using *half* Munsell steps at the higher end (6.5–9.0) he obtained another function. From our analysis we would expect different levels to be operative in judgments of lightness when size of the step interval between stimuli changes. Although the d factor was introduced into the first formulation of the weighted log mean definition of AL (Helson, 1947) it has been omitted by some workers who have employed the definition in dealing with experimental data.

Some important consequences follow from differential weighting of series and anchor, or background stimuli. First, AL is neither the arithmetic nor geometric mean; nor is it the midpoint of the stimuli, except in special cases, e.g., in judgments of numbers and types of stimuli where feedback in the act of responding is minimal (cf. Parducci, 1959; 1960). Second, Equation (2) provides for shift of AL in the direction of the anchor stimulus; but even when the anchor is the standard it does not completely determine AL, e.g., in methods involving direct comparisons. The fact that the series as a whole is weighted more heavily than C also means that AL is not simply a function of the anchor *even to a first approximation* as has often been assumed. With constant series and variable C the AL varies as the fourth root of C, as a transformation of Equation (2) into arithmetical form will show.

Third, Equation (2) shows that any single series stimulus affects AL less than the anchor stimulus does because series stimuli receive a weight of $3/n$ as against 1.0 for the anchor. We therefore expect less shift from a stimulus when it is a member of the series than we do when it is the anchor stimulus.

One final deduction from Equation (2) should be mentioned at this point. If no anchor stimulus is employed as in the method of single stimuli (the *absolute* method) the anchor term, C, drops out and AL becomes simply the logarithmic mean minus the d factor:

$$\log (\text{AL} + 0.75d) = \frac{\sum_1^n \log X_1}{n} \tag{3}$$

If we choose C such that the resultant value of AL is identical with (or near) AL given by Equation (3), then we expect the two methods to yield identical results. This consequence of the theory was verified experimentally, thus bridging the gap between the comparative method and the method of single stimuli.

Equation (2) enables us to calculate any one of the three variables from the other two thus making it possible to determine effects of "mental" anchors. An observer presented with a series of stimuli and an anchor normally judges with AL determined in accordance with Equation (2). Sometimes, however, he brings into the experiment some idea of what is heavy, very heavy, or light; or he may have judged another series of stimuli which combine with present stimuli in establishing AL. In such cases if the remote anchor has magnitude Z, a properly weighted geometric mean of C and Z can be used in Equation (2) giving

$$\log (\text{AL} + 0.75d)$$
$$= \frac{\left(3.0 \sum_1^n \log X_1/n\right) + (w_1 \log C + w_2 \log Z)/(w_1 + w_2)}{4} \tag{4}$$

where w_1 and w_2 are weighting factors. Data to be discussed give some indication that unless the observer makes a deliberate attempt to neglect an anchor (as when an interpolated stimulus is inserted between standard and variable), $w_1 = w_2$. If w_1 is not equal to w_2 it is possible to reduce w_2 to unity and the denominator of this fraction to $w + 1$ by dividing w_1 by w_2 and defining $w_1/w_2 = w$ as was done with k_1 and k_2 above. Equation (4) must then be extended accordingly.

Equations (2), (3), and (4) may be used to calculate AL as described above from given values of series and comparison stimuli. An even more important use of these equations concerns the evaluation of factors which have hitherto not been given quantitative expression. Assumptions concerning remote anchors, general frames of reference, and past experience can be tested and quantitatively evaluated. Thus we may treat experimentally found values of AL as knowns, and *C, Z,* or both as unknowns, to determine the extent to which factors outside the concretely given stimuli affect AL. If the values of *C* or *Z* are found to differ from actual anchors employed or require new weighting coefficients to fit observed data, then we know to what extent additional factors are affecting judgment. Data from Pratt (1933*a*) and Guilford and Park (1931) will be utilized below to illustrate such uses of these formulas.

Absolute and relative methods.   One of the first deductions from AL theory to be tested experimentally was that AL should be the same in the method of absolute judgment and the relative method when the standard is chosen equal to or near the log mean of the series, a consequence that follows from Equations (2) and (3).[2] Since the AL in these cases is below the midpoint of the series it also follows that the same asymmetry in judgments should be found with both methods. These consequences of the theory are confirmed in Fig. 4.1, where results with the single-stimuli method and results with a 300 background stimulus are seen to be almost the same throughout. For strict test of the theory a background stimulus of 254 grm. should have been used instead of the 300-grm. stimulus actually employed, as shown by the slightly lower judgments when the background stimulus was introduced.

Wever and Zener (1928), using a series consisting of 88, 92, 96, 100, and 104 grm., found that the PSE was below the midpoint of the series in the absolute method and nearer the midpoint when a standard of 100 grm. was employed. Similarly, Fernberger (1931) obtained lower values for the point of symmetry (PS) in the absolute method than in the relative method when a standard above the midpoint of the series was employed. Wever and Zener, in agreement with the theory pre-

[2] Provided the *d* factor on the left-hand side of these equations is taken into account.

sented here, stated they would have expected PSE to be below the midpoint in the relative series if they had used a standard at the midpoint. From Fernberger's data we obtain a calculated AL of 92.6 as

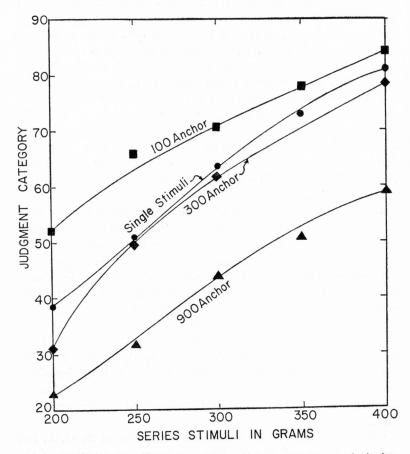

FIG. 4.1. Shifts in scale values of stimuli in the comparative and absolute methods and with different standards. (From Helson, 1947. With the permission of the *American Journal of Psychology*.)

against an observed 92.0 grm. with absolute method, and 93.7 as against 95.1 grm. with the comparative method from Equations (1) and (2).

The asymmetry in judgments with and without a centered background stimulus appears clearly in Fig. 4.1: the greater portion of the

two middle curves lies above adaptation level. The shift in scale values
due to use of anchors outside the series range is also shown in this
figure in the plots of data obtained with 100-grm. and 900-grm.
anchors. With the 100-grm. anchor judgments are shifted upward,
with 900 grm. downward—clearly demonstrating the repellant effect
of anchors. These are analogous to the background effects found by
the writer with strongly chromatic illuminants.

TABLE 4.1. Shifts in AL with Change in Comparison Stimulus and Identity of
PSE in Absolute and Comparative Methods when the Standard is Near AL
According to the Formula
$\log (AL + 0.75d) = [(3.0 \, \Sigma \, \log X_i/n) + \log C]/4$

Condition	Theoretical AL	Observed Medium	Urban Limen	Geometric Mean
Single stimuli (200, 250, 300, 350, 400 grm.)	253.9	249.0	251.0	291.0
Anchor:				
300 grm.	256.0	250.0	261.0	296.0
100 grm.	185.5	197.0	184.0	171.0
900 grm.	348.8	349.0	345.0	512.0
Single stimuli (88, 92, 96, 100, 104 grm.)	92.8	96.2	96.2	95.8
Anchor:				
96 grm.	92.7	95.4	95.0	95.8
40 grm.	74.0	77.0	63.9	61.9
260 grm.[a]	120.0	——	138.9	157.8
5 grm.[a]	42.7	——	37.3	21.9

[a] The observed values are so far below 5.0 that extrapolation does not yield a reliable
figure for medium in these cases.
SOURCE: From Helson, 1947. With the permission of the *American Journal of Psychology*.

To show the agreement between theory and observation, data are
given in Table 4.1 for the 200–400 grm. series and for a lighter series,
88–104 grm., with anchors of 5, 40, 96, and 260 grm. Table 4.1 contains
the calculated AL; the observed "medium" stimulus determined by
linear interpolation between the values immediately below and above
AL, which is given the numerical value of 5 in the judgment scale;
the Urban threshold; and the geometric mean. From these data it is
seen that the agreement between theory, observation, and the Urban
values is excellent in the 200–400 grm. series and fair in the 88–104

grm. series. Theoretical values of AL in the 88–104 grm. series are too low by the *d* factor, as comparison with observed medium judgment shows. This discrepancy may be the result of individual variation since groups judging identical stimuli may differ, on the average, by as much as a whole category step or one unit on the judgment scale.

Inspection of the geometric means given in Table 4.1 shows they do not agree with either the observed or the calculated values. It therefore appears that the geometric mean (GM) cannot be taken as the center of psychological scales even in the case of the single-stimuli method, where the indifference point usually comes nearest to GM. We find from Table 4.1 that the Urban values depart more and more from calculated values of AL the more asymmetrical the observed data become. In the case of the 88–104 grm. series, the shifts in scale value were so pronounced with the different anchors that judgments tended to be very high or very low; that is, well above or below 5. As a result the Urban threshold in these cases represents extrapolations well beyond observed values. Since the Urban fit is based on the phi-gamma function which is symmetrical about the 50 percent point, it is easy to understand why we cannot expect a good extrapolation to such data. Hence we regard the discrepancies between our calculated AL and the Urban values in the 88–104 grm. series as of no consequence for the theory presented here.

The profound change in sensory character of the series stimuli indicated by the observed changes in AL is borne out by the comments of *S*s in the experiments. These comments showed they were unaware of the purpose of the experiments and believed the series weights were different when different anchors were employed. For example, one *S* reported that the observations were much less fatiguing with the 900-grm. anchor than with the single-stimuli method "because the weights are so much lighter now." Actually the total weight lifted with the 900-grm. standard was 6000 grm. per series as against 1500 grm. with the single-stimuli method! Theories which imply that we are dealing here merely with shifts in judgment or verbal categories do not account for the sensory changes that accompany shifts of AL. With change in *sensory character* of the stimuli there must be a difference in physiological process. For this reason we have chosen the term "adaptation level" to stress the basic nature of the phenomena.

Equal weighting for primary and interpolated anchors. In some cases an interpolated stimulus acts as a second anchor with an importance equal to the first and the two anchors may be given equal weighting coefficients. To make a test of the importance of the interpolated anchor when *S*s were left uninstructed concerning the two anchors, the following procedure was employed: A series of five weights ranging from 200 to 400 grm. with a 50-grm.-step interval between stimuli was given to two groups of four *S*s. Both groups first judged the stimuli without anchors and then as follows: the first group judged the stimuli with anchors of 900 grm., 900 and 800 grm., 800 and 900 grm., 900 and 600 grm., and 600 and 900 grm., the second group judged the stimuli with anchors of 90 grm., 90 and 100 grm., 100 and 90 grm., 90 and 133 grm., and 133 and 90 grm. (The anchors were randomized as far as possible among the four *S*s in each group.) The choice of these anchors was to determine whether it was necessary to take account of the order in which they were presented; that is, whether 900 and 800 grm. followed by the variable would give different results from 800 and 900 grm. followed by the variable. Furthermore, it was also an open question whether simple logarithmic averaging of double standards, as provided by the *C* terms in Equation (4), was adequate for relatively large as well as relatively small differences between anchors, e.g., 900 and 600 grm. vs. 900 and 800 grm. As the results in Table 4.1 show, neither the differences between the anchors nor their order of presentation required new parameters in the formulation since the simple log average of the anchors was used in deriving the predicted ALs. It is evident that *S*s, without special instructions to this effect, treated the double anchors about equally, regardless of time order or differences in weight. It must be remembered that the anchors always preceded the series stimuli in this experiment and that there is no implication here that order of presentation and stimulus gradients may not be important in even slightly different experimental situations. On the contrary, order and gradients of stimulation often are of prime importance and require special treatment as will be shown later in this chapter.

Stimulus as standard vs. stimulus as member of series. From Equation (2) it is seen that series stimuli receive a weight of $3/n$ while the anchor stimulus is weighted with unity. Since n is greater than 3, as a rule this means that a stimulus is weighted less when it is a series stimulus than when it is an anchor, and this is reasonable since the anchor is presented more frequently than is any series stimulus. Hence series stimuli should affect AL less than anchors. This consequence of the theory is borne out by the data in Table 4.2. Thus the stimulus judged medium in the 200–400 grm. series is 250 grm. but it rises to 313 grm. when a 900-grm. stimulus is made a member of the series. The stimulus judged medium rises still higher to 338 grm. when the 900-grm. stimulus is employed as anchor. Comparable downward shifts occur when a 90-grm. stimulus is employed as a member of the 200–400 grm. series (AL = 211 grm.) and as an anchor (AL = 185 grm.) as seen in Table 4.2. Similar results are found with a lighter set of stimuli, 88–104 grm., when 40- and 260-grm. stimuli are added to the series stimuli or are made anchors. The greater effect of anchors is reflected in scale values of all members of the series as shown by the curves in Fig. 4.1. The complete displacement of the curves upward or downward as a result of stimuli outside the range of series stimuli whether as members of the series or as anchors is evidence for the operation of a common norm in all the judgments.

TABLE 4.2.   Theoretical and Experimental Values of AL to Show Effect of a Stimulus as Member of a Series and as a Comparison Stimulus

Condition	Theoretical AL	Observed Medium
Single stimuli (200, 250, 300, 350, 400 grm.)	253.9	250.0
Single stimuli with 900 grm. included	314.0	313.0
900-grm. anchor	349.0	338.0
Single stimuli with 90 grm. included in series	202.0	211.0
90-grm. anchor	180.0	185.0
Single stimuli (88, 92, 96, 100, 104 grm.)	92.8	96.2
Single stimuli with 40 grm. included in series	79.9	92.7
40-grm. anchor	74.0	77.0
260 grm. included in series[a]	110.2	
260-grm. anchor[a]	120.0	

[a] The observed values are so far below 5.0 that extrapolation does not yield a reliable figure for medium in these cases.

SOURCE: From Helson, 1947. With the permission of the *American Journal of Psychology*.

The adequacy of the theory in accounting for greater shifts with a stimulus as anchor than as series member appears from comparison of observed and predicted values of AL in Table 4.2. The predictions for 200–400 grm. series are within one category step in all cases and almost as close for the 88–104 grm. series.

Minimally effective and interpolated stimuli. The question explicitly raised by Pratt (1933*a*) was how small a stimulus anchor could cause upward displacements of the indifference point of a psychophysical scale. Actually the problem dates almost to the beginnings of psychophysics, as Black and Bevan (1960) point out: "From the inception of psychophysics, it has been held that the absolute threshold provides the limiting criterion in the identification of the stimulus-correlates of the several magnitudes of sensory experience" (p. 262). The original Fechner law made the unit of sensory magnitude the absolute threshold, which was taken as the first step above sensory zero. Interest was manifested in the effects of subliminal stimuli on a number of different responses, e.g., on verbal behavior (Baker, 1937), on muscular responses (Davis, 1950), on autonomic changes (Lazarus and McCleary, 1951), and in the *New Look* studies dealing with the influence of inner factors, such as needs, values, and hunger, on perception and recognition thresholds (reviewed by Helson, 1953). On the basis of the concept of pooling, subliminal stimuli should have an effect on level, albeit less effect than supraliminal stimuli.

The problem of effects of subliminal stimuli on judgment is closely linked with effects of interpolated stimuli which may range from zero to subliminal to clearly supraliminal intensities. Pratt (1933*a*) found that a stimulus of 15 grm., interpolated between a standard of 100 grm. and series weights of 92, 100, and 108 grm., yielded a larger number of heavy judgments than when no interpolated stimulus was employed; hence the 15-grm. stimulus pooled with the series and standard stimuli and reduced AL. The question was further investigated (Helson, 1947) using a 5-grm. anchor with a series of weights ranging from 200 to 400 grm. in 50-grm. steps. The large preponderance of "heavy" judgments with the 5-grm. anchor showed that this very light anchor was effectively pooled with the series weights and lowered AL. However, when an anchor weighing 0.5 grm. was employed with the 200–400 grm. series the results were almost identical with those obtained when no anchor was employed, hence AL was not lowered in this case and the 0.5-grm. stimulus had no effect. Hence, with lifted weights a stimulus between 5.0 and 0.5 grm. ceases to affect AL, although it must not be assumed from these results that subliminal stimuli do not affect AL.

The power of subliminal stimuli to lower AL was definitely shown in a study by Black and Bevan (1960), who employed two groups of Ss. The first, a control group, judged the intensity of five electric shocks of 1500, 1800, 2100, 2400, and 2700 μamp. presented 20 times in random order at 20-sec. intervals. The second, an experimental group, received the intensities given the control group plus interpolated stimuli at the midpoint of the 20-sec. interval between the supraliminal shocks. The intensities of the subliminal stimuli were 50 percent of each S's individual threshold. Checks were also made by recording GSR (galvanic skin response) deflections for all stimuli and during the intervals between stimulations. Fitting the Black and Bevan data

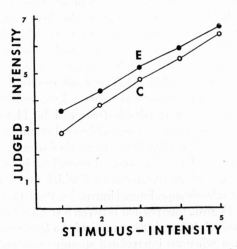

FIG. 4.2. Average judgments of intensity of five supraliminal stimuli with and without the interpolation of a subliminal anchor. The physical intensities varied from 1500 to 1700 μamp. in 300-μamp. steps. (From Black and Bevan, 1960. With the permission of the *American Journal of Psychology*).

by Equation (39) yields ALs of 2.36 (1909 μamp.) for the control group and 1.79 (1740 μamp.) for the experimental group; the plots in Fig. 4.2 show that the experimental group judged the supraliminal shocks to be greater in every case than did the control group. Both the reports of Ss and GSR data indicated that the experimental Ss were not aware of the subthreshold stimuli that decisively influenced perceived intensity.

Three conclusions drawn by Black and Bevan from this study should be noted: (1) The results are inconsistent with traditional psychophysical assumptions that the absolute threshold is a limiting value in the generation of psychophysical functions. (2) The organism may incorporate subliminal stimuli along with supraliminal stimuli in the formation of norms underlying judgment. (3) The criterion of perceptibility cannot be applied in defining the properties relevant for pooling.

They also pointed out that once again a behavioral measure was a more sensitive indicator of a physical variable than a physiological measure (which in this case was GSR).

The effects of subliminal anchors in modifying perceived attributes of stimulation should not be confused with better-than-chance reports of subliminal stimuli that are not sensed as such. The subliminal anchor effects discussed in this section and elsewhere in this book are referable to their influence on adaptation level and are thus assumed to have much the same effects on level as suprathreshold stimuli do. Since the subliminal stimuli are not perceived and Ss are not asked to report them, they belong with the class of physiological stimuli discussed later which exert physiological effects without coming to awareness. With the finding that subliminal stimuli pool with supraliminal stimuli to form level we have added evidence of the basic physiological nature of adaptation levels underlying perceptual and judgmental processes. That shifts in judgment resulting from the introduction of background or anchor stimuli represent only semantic reformulations seems less and less credible as information on effects of subliminal anchors accumulates.

Up to this point we have evidence (1) that weak or subliminal stimuli sometimes pool to lower level, thus raising judged intensities, and (2) that such stimuli sometimes may not affect level. The contradiction is only an apparent one and disappears on closer examination of the intensity relations in the various cases. Thus in the cases where very weak or zero stimulation did not lower level (the 0.5-grm. anchor with the heavy series of weights and the interpolated silent interval between the supraliminal sounds) the stimuli were far below 50 percent of absolute threshold! A stimulus of 0.5 grm. is practically the same as zero by comparison with the 200 grm. stimulus, the lightest in the series, and with the weight of the hand itself, which must not be left out of consideration. The same argument applies with even greater cogency to the silent interpolated interval between Pratt's supraliminal sounds. But the shocks in Black and Bevan's study were effective in that they were a considerable fraction (50 percent) of the threshold values even though they did not give rise to perceptions or GSRs. With this type of stimulation as well as with the lifted-weight and sound stimuli one needs only to reduce the intensity of shock to smaller and smaller fractions of threshold values to arrive at some value that fails to lower AL.

Reverting to the lifted-weight data, it appears that somewhere between 5.0 and 0.5 grm. there is a critical value or region where stimuli become too weak to change level. This situation introduces a discontinuity in the weighted log mean definition of AL in that the anchor term drops out and AL becomes the geometric mean of the series stimuli minus the d factor. The discontinuity was also found experimentally as indicated. For this reason the C term in Equation (2) must be restricted to some lower limit below which it is equal to zero, making Equation (2) identical with Equation (3). We have already pointed out that this result leads to the prediction that series stimuli will be judged the same whether without anchor or with an anchor stimulus introduced at or near the log mean of the series stimuli—a prediction that was verified experimentally.

It is evident that any condition that reduces the net effectiveness of stimulation also lessens its contribution to level. The weighted log mean definition of level enables us to determine the contributions to level of stimuli under various conditions of presentation, particularly conditions that are not directly measurable in physical units such as effects of instructions and residuals from past experience. Use of the weighted log mean to determine the contribution made by an interpolated stimulus that was neglected by Ss as a result of instructions given them is seen in the following example from Guilford and Park (1931). In their experiments Ss were presented with three weights and *instructions to judge whether the third was heavier or lighter than the first.* "This instruction was carried out," Guilford and Park say, "to the extent that frequently the Ss reported: 'The second weight tends to drop out, to be ignored.'" Three series of stimuli were presented as follows: series N: 185, 190, 195, 200, 205, 210, and 215 with 200 grm. as the standard; series A: 185, 195, 205, and 210 grm. with 200 grm. as the standard and 400 grm. as the interpolated weight; and series B: 185, 190, 200, 205, and 215 grm. with 200 grm. as the standard and 400 grm. as the interpolated weight. In view of the instructions given Ss and the reports of the Ss, the standard and interpolated weights are not expected to contribute equally to AL (PSE). Solving Equation (4) to obtain the values of the weighting coefficients we find that in series A the standard and interpolated stimulus must be weighted 7.5

to 1 and in series B the coefficients are 5.5:1 in order to obtain the experimentally observed values of PSE (199.2 and 188.2 grm.). We are thus able to evaluate the effects of instructions and attitudes quantitatively by means of the weighted log mean definition.

We have just seen how instructions given Ss can reduce the effective value of stimulation. Still other elements in experimental situations may act to reduce some stimuli and enhance others. What has been called "ego involvement" is often a matter of the extent to which Ss are called upon to do something in the experimental or test situation. We would not expect stimuli to be as effective when Ss are merely allowed to see or observe them as when they are called upon to discriminate, judge or remember them. But in accordance with the assumption that all stimuli pool to form level it is erroneous to infer from AL theory, as Parducci did (1959), that stimuli merely laid before Ss in a given order would have no effect when they were subsequently asked to judge them. Exposure to stimuli leaves residual effects that may be effective after a lapse of days or weeks and their contributions to level may be evaluated (*vide infra*). In the study by Parducci Ss were shown a series of 43 sticks, 10 mm. wide, 5 mm. thick, and from 32 to 298 mm. in length. They were placed horizontally before Ss on a 22 by 28 in. poster board ruled with horizontal lines 10 mm. apart in either short-to-long (S-L) sequence or long-to-short (L-S) sequence. When called upon to judge the lengths of the sticks in terms of a five-category scale consisting of very long, long, medium, short, and very short, the Ss judged either in S-L or L-S order. In accordance with expectations based on AL theory both order of presentation and order of judgment affected AL, the stimulus judged "medium" being shifted in the direction of the stimuli first presented and first judged. We can make a rough estimate of the relative importance of presentation order vs. judgment order by comparing the average differences between ALs in S-L and L-S *orders of judgment* (confounding orders of presentation) with average differences between ALs in S-L and L-S *orders of presentation* (confounding orders of judgment). These turn out to be (from Table 4.3) 24.5 for order of judgment as against 10.0 for order of presentation. Hence while order of judgment is 2.5 times as effective in determining level as order of presentation, the latter by no means makes a negligible contribution. Although we treat stimulus distributions in another section, it should be noted in passing that ALs are lower in positively skewed distributions (an excess of smaller lengths) than in negatively skewed distributions (Table 4.3) a finding also in accord with theory.

TABLE 4.3. Effects of Order of Presentation, Order of Judgment, and Skewedness on Adaptation Level

Judgment Order	Presentation Order			
	Short to Long		Long to Short	
	Mean AL	SD	Mean AL	SD
	Positively Skewed (GM = 115)			
Short to Long	113.7	9.5	123.0	14.5
Long to Short	136.1	10.5	151.4	16.5
	Negatively Skewed (GM = 178)			
Short to Long	174.9	17.7	188.6	15.1
Long to Short	205.2	16.0	207.5	14.3

SOURCE: From Parducci, 1959. With the permission of the American Psychological Association.

We come now to the case where the interpolated stimulus has zero value. Both Lauenstein (1933) and Pratt (1933a) regarded this case as crucial for any theory of judgment. Lauenstein, on the basis of the assimilation theory, predicted that PSE should be lower with a silent interval interpolated between standard and variable tones than with a soft interpolated sound. Pratt found the contrary to be true in accordance with the theory presented here. In Pratt's experiments a pendulum falling from 37°, 41°, 45°, 49°, and 53° was used as the source of sound. The standard was 45°, the loud interpolated sound was 70°, and the soft sound was 20°. In applying the weighted mean definition to Pratt's data we use Equation (2) providing for only a single anchor since the interpolated interval has the value of zero. The soft interpolated sound requires Equation (4) which provides for two comparison stimuli. No information is available for weighting the two standards differently, hence we give each a unit weighting. The d factor in both formulas is zero, as in the case of V_1S_2 for lifted weights, in accordance with previous findings that in sound intensities time-order effect is either zero or positive. Turning to Table 4.4 which gives Pratt's observed PSE and the calculated ALs for the three conditions, we find that not only is the *order* of PSE correctly predicted for these three conditions but the theoretical values approximate the observed so closely as to leave no doubt that the present formulation gives the correct prediction for this crucial case.

TABLE 4.4.   PSE (AL) Predicted Higher with Silent Interpolated Interval than with Soft Interpolated Sound

Interpolated Stimulus	Observed PSE[a]	Calculated AL
Soft	42.2°	40.4°
Silent	44.1°	44.7°
Loud	48.2°	46.5°

[a] Average for three observers.
SOURCE: From Pratt, 1933a. With the permission of the *American Journal of Psychology.*

Reciprocity of frequency and magnitude.   According to Equation (1*A*) the value of AL is largely a function of the frequency and magnitude of the series and background stimuli. It should therefore be possible to determine for any given set of series stimuli and any arbitrarily chosen value of background stimulus the number of times the background stimulus must be presented with the series stimuli to preserve any given AL. This information can be derived from the weighted log mean equation by inserting explicit parameters for frequency and solving for the unknown, which is frequency of background presentation, as follows:

$$\log (A + 0.75d) = \frac{\Sigma f_i X_i + f_b \log \beta}{\Sigma f_i + f_b} \tag{5}$$

where f_i and f_b are the frequencies of presentation of series and background stimuli respectively, and the other symbols have the same meanings as in Equation (2). Transposing we get

$$(\Sigma f_i + f_b) \log (A + 0.75d) = \Sigma f_i X_i + f_b \log \beta \tag{6}$$

and

$$\log \beta = (\Sigma f_i + f_b) \log (A + .75d) - \frac{\Sigma f_i X_i}{f_b} \tag{7}$$

It is obvious that the value of β is given by Equation (7) for any choice of *frequency* of series stimuli and for any arbitrarily chosen frequency of presentation of the background stimulus. On the other hand, if we assign values to and predetermine the number of presentations of the series and background stimuli, we can determine from

Equation (7) the value of background stimulus that will leave A unchanged. Reasoning in this way, Bevan and Darby (1954) determined the frequency with which various background stimuli would have to be presented with a given "core" of stimuli to preserve the same value of AL. They called this deduction from the weighted log mean definition the "reciprocity law."

Using a set of series stimuli weighing 220, 260, 300, and 340 grm., Bevan and Darby explored the limits of the reciprocity law and found it held as follows:

. . . between 312.1 grm presented 200 times for each core and 314.4 grm presented 100 times for each core at one extreme, and 1010 grm. presented 1.16 times, and 1231 grm. presented once for each core at the other extreme . . . It . . . can be confidently stated that all magnitude presentation values between 314.4/100 and 1010/1.16 constitute a family of equivalent stimulus conditions so far as preserving the same value of AL is concerned (Bevan and Darby, 1954, p. 580).

Agreement between theory and observations was remarkably good in the case of three of the six experimental groups and off by only 15 percent in the case of the remaining three groups of Ss. The agreement is all the more remarkable when we consider that the largest values of background stimuli were nearly four times the mean of the series stimuli while the number of presentations of the background stimuli ranged from 1 to 200! Since the core stimuli were presented only three times while the background frequencies varied over a much greater range this study showed that decided asymmetries in the experimental conditions can be compensated so as to preserve constant AL.

A somewhat similar use of the reciprocity principle in determination of AL was made previously by Levin (1952). He found that if his Ss each lifted a light and heavy weight simultaneously (one in each hand) and then lifted equal weights, the equal weights were underestimated by the hand that had first held the heavy weight and overestimated by the other hand. Levin employed a design in which different weights were presented to the two hands with (1) the sum of the weights in a cycle constant, (2) the frequency of presentation the same for both hands while the sum was equal, or (3) frequency of presentation the same while the sum was different. He was able to study effects of weight differential as well as frequency differential between the hands on estimations of the second set of weights. By equalizing weight differential he was able to study effects of frequency differential and vice versa. He found that frequency-weight and weight conditions were very similar as against the frequency condition alone. He concluded that the weight-differential summation, rather than relative frequency, was the effective factor in influencing subsequent judgments of stimuli. Considering the differences in conditions, we cannot regard the Bevan and Darby experiments and the Levin experiments as conflicting. Rather they both demonstrate the extent to which dimensions of stimulation pool to form predictable levels.

Various stimulus distributions. Stimulus distributions of different types offer particularly good tests of the theory presented here. We have already considered asymmetries in judgment due to the use of variables and anchors far removed from series range and have found they can be satisfactorily predicted by the theory. However, observations made by Johnson (1944) with truly normal, J-shaped, I-shaped, rectangular, and skew distributions make a direct test of the theory possible in a wider variety of stimulus constellations than we have yet considered. Although Johnson's data represent only one *S* in each case, his observed limens and our calculated ALs are in very good agreement as shown in Table 4.5. Calculated values of AL might have been

TABLE 4.5. Theoretical and Experimental Values of Adaptation Level
for Rectangular, Skew, I-Shaped, J-Shaped, and
Approximately Normal Distributions

Series (grm.)	Theoretical AL	Experimental Limen	Error (Percent)
20, 25, 30, . . . 55	31.9	29.7	+ 7
60, 65, 70, . . . 100	74.7	76.3	− 2
20, 25, 30, . . . 100	50.5	48.1	+ 5
20, 30, 40, 50(3), 60(5)	39.2	41.2	− 5
60, 70, 80, 90(3), 100(5)	80.5	75.4	+ 7
75(5), 80(3), 85(3), 90(2), 95, 100	78.8	77.4	+ 2
20(4), 25, 30, 35, 40(4)	25.0	26.8	− 7
40(3), 45, 50, 55, 60, 65, 70(6)	53.0	58.3	− 9
20, 30(3), 40(5), 50(3), 60	30.9	37.2	−17
40, 50(2), 60(4), 70(4), 80(2), 90	56.1	61.7	− 9
		Average	7.0

Note: Numbers in parentheses following stimulus values indicate repetitions within series to give the desired distribution.

SOURCE: From Johnson, 1944. With the permission of the American Psychological Association.

closer to the observed values if the d factor had been determined with precision in the distributions where stimuli were presented an unequal number of times. The d factor was assumed to be $0.75\times$ step interval in all cases without regard to number of repetitions. The average error in the predicted values is 7 percent, which is slightly higher than Johnson's 6.2 percent, from values derived from an equation which is admittedly restricted to these data. Consideration of the discrepancies between theory and observation reveals the predicted values are on the whole low, indicating that $0.75d$ is larger than the d factor that would best fit these data. The errors in prediction do not appear to be associated with any particular type of distribution; e.g., one of the two normal types has the largest and one has average errors. Again it is found that the unweighted log mean is not a good approximation to the center of psychological scales, for with Johnson's data this value is too high in every case but one.

Range and density of series stimuli. Changes in adaptation level are expected with changes in range and density of a series of stimuli on the log mean definition since the log mean is lowered when the density is increased by making the step interval between stimuli smaller. Thus AL for the stimuli 300, 350, 400, 450, and 500 grm. is the log mean minus the d factor (37.5) or 356.5. If we extend the range, keeping the interval between stimuli constant, so that the series becomes 200, 250, 300, 350, 400, 450, 500, 550, and 600 grm., AL is 340.5. With the extended range we therefore expect a larger number of heavy judgments than with the original range of stimuli since AL has dropped from 356.5 to 340.5.

Now let us see what the effect is of decreasing the step interval between stimuli. Instead of a step interval of 50 grm. between stimuli, let the interval be 25 grm., giving the following series: 300, 325, 350, 375, 400, 425, 450, 475, and 500 grm. The value of AL (376.25) is now greater than in the original series (356.5) because the d-factor is 18.75 (0.75×25) instead of 37.5. Since AL is nearer the center of the denser stimulus series we expect a more symmetrical distribution of judgments in this case than with the original series.

In order to make a valid test of these predictions these or similar stimulus distributions should be judged by Ss using an absolute rating scale. Such data are not available at the time of writing but data based on somewhat different conditions of judging furnish a partial validation. Engen (1956) studied the effects of range and absolute magnitude on ratio scaling by using the constant-sum method in which *S*s divide 100 into the same proportions that the stimuli seem to bear to one another. Four groups of *S*s judged lengths of lines shown in Table 4.6.

TABLE 4.6. Design of Experiment to Show Effect of Absolute Magnitude and Ranges of Stimuli on Ratio Judgments by Constant-sum Method

Group	0.5	0.67	1.0	1.5	2.0	3.0	4.5	6.0	9.0	13.5	18.0
I	X	X	X	X	X	X	X	X	X	X	X
II	X	X	X	X	X						
III				X	X	X	X	X			
IV							X	X	X	X	X

Note: Crosses indicate stimuli presented to each of the groups.
SOURCE: From Engen, 1956. With the permission of the *American Journal of Psychology*.

Group I was given the whole range of stimuli and the other groups were given restricted ranges covering the low, middle, and high values of the total series. The situation is therefore complicated in that the series stimuli for the various groups differ both in range and in mean values. An important fact emerges from the data given in Table 4.7: scale values are smaller with the long (complete) range than with the short ranges. Identical stimulus ratios do not necessarily yield

TABLE 4.7. Ratio Estimates by Four Groups of *S*s of Stimuli Given in Table 4.6

Stimulus Ratios	Estimated Ratios	
	Group I	Groups II–IV
1.000	1.000	1.000
1.333	1.402	1.437
2.000	2.053	2.222
3.000	2.932	3.385
4.00	3.772	4.399
6.00	5.542	6.752
9.00	8.075	10.227
12.00	10.588	13.667
18.00	15.751	20.797
27.00	22.612	31.125
36.00	29.559	41.755

SOURCE: From Engen, 1956. With the permission of the *American Journal of Psychology*.

identical psychological ratios. The ratios assigned identical stimulus pairs depend upon the level and range of stimuli in which they appear and not solely upon the individual pairs being judged. Since the complete range of stimuli has the lowest AL, the higher ratios should be smaller in this series than the ratios in the shorter series, a deduction verified by Engen's data.

Dispersion of series stimuli. Closely related to density and range of series stimuli is the magnitude of the spread, or standard deviation, of the stimuli around the mean value. It is obvious that with constant density, the standard deviation increases with the range of stimuli, but with constant range, the standard deviation decreases as step interval between stimuli decreases. Since the geometric mean is affected by both range and density of a series it follows immediately that variations in these parameters will affect AL. We expect, on this basis, to find different values of AL with changes in *SD* of a series even though the mean of the series remains constant. A study by Irwin and Smith (1956) bears on this point. In this experiment cards were drawn from a pack containing positive and negative numbers distributed normally around mean values of either 1.5, 0.5, 0.0, −0.5, or −1.5. In each case there were two experimental packs having the same mean value, but one had an SD of 2.0 and the other of 7.5. The task of the Ss was to tell, after seeing numbers on individual cards, whether the mean value of the numbers on the cards was greater or less than zero.

The number of cards necessary to reach a correct decision on whether the mean was greater or less than zero was found to be inversely related to the absolute value of the mean of the sets, being greatest for a mean of zero and least for a mean of plus or minus 1.5. Further, more presentations were required to arrive at a correct decision regarding the mean for the sets having an SD of 7.5 than for the sets having an SD of 2.0. While Irwin and Smith regard the process by which the mean is determined as the formation of an AL, they believe that the larger number of exposures necessary with higher SDs requires an additional concept, namely, that of *strength*. But it is not necessary to invoke additional concepts to account for their findings because they have erroneously assumed that sets having the same arithmetic means will have the same ALs; in addition, it is highly desirable to keep the number of primitive concepts in any theory as low as possible. From what we know a priori of the relation between range and SD of stimulus distributions to AL, we would expect the ALs to differ more from the arithmetic means in sets with large SDs. To bring AL toward the arithmetic means of the sets (a requirement laid down by the demands of the experiment) would therefore necessitate more trials in the case of the sets with large SDs. This is what was found by Irwin and Smith! Their study demonstrates both the necessity of distinguishing between the properties of arithmetic and geometric means and also the importance of the d factor in the weighted log mean function.

Practice and past experience. It is generally recognized that judgments are affected by past experience and practice, even in simple psychophysical experiments. Ss bring into the experimental situation ideas of loud, soft, heavy, light, pleasant, and unpleasant from their former experiences due to residuals of stimuli from previous experimental sessions. In addition, judgments of stimuli change with practice although they usually stabilize rather quickly (Johnson, 1949; Rambo and Johnson, 1963). Unless such terms as "practice effect," "past experience," and "general frames of reference" can be evaluated quantitatively, their scientific usefulness is questionable. The theory of adaptation level takes into account remote standards and effects of previous stimulation and provides a means for specifying their effects quantitatively. Data from studies by Pratt, by Long, and by Nash will be considered in this connection.

In the first study, Pratt (1933a) asked Ss to judge the intensity of the sound made by a falling pendulum by the method of single stimuli in two series and by the comparative method in a third series. In series I the angles of fall were 78°, 72°, 66°, and 53°, with psychological (loudness) values of 8, 7, 6, 5, and 4; in series II the angles were 41°, 37°, 32°, 26°, and 18° with values of 2.5, 2.0, 1.5, 1.00, and 0.5; in series III they were 37°, 34.5°, 32°, 29°, and 26°, with values of 2.0, 1.75, 1.50, 1.25, and 1.00. The Ss judged in terms of categories from 1 to 9, with 5 for the middle, 9 for the loudest, and 1 for the softest sound. In series I, PSE was found to be 5.37 (62.2°), a value below the average loudness, 6 (66.0°). Series II was much softer than the first—PSE was 1.61 (32.6°), which was above the midpoint of the series, 1.6 (32.0°). In series I the time-order effect was obviously negative and in series II it was positive. After pointing out that sinking traces would not explain these results, Pratt (1933b, p. 809) asserted (in line with our theory) that "the factor which would produce a negative time-error in the first case and a positive time-error in the second would be a general level of standard reference lying *between* the two series" (5.37 and

1.61). Pratt assumed that the value of this general level was 3.0. We
have a double way of checking both his assumption of a level intermediate between series I and II and the value he assigned to it. We
may use Equation (4) to calculate the remote standard affecting series
II by using PSE found experimentally and solving for C, which yields
the value 3.1 (46.0°). Or we may assume that series I coalesced with
series II to form a single AL and extend the summation in Equation
(4) to cover both series to obtain the value 2.9 (43.9°). Both applications of Equation (4) yield the same value of level and this proves to
be precisely the value assumed by Pratt. We are thus able to put into
quantitative form what Pratt could only refer to "as a general level
of reference built up in the past which serves as a basis for alignment
for all impressions constituting a more or less homogeneous mass."
Hence the influence of traces and remote frames of reference can be
quantitatively evaluated by means of the weighted log mean formulation.

Pratt found that previous practice effects were apparently overcome
in the third series when a standard at the midpoint of the series (1.5)
was employed: PSE dropped to 1.39 thus showing a normal negative
time-order effect. These findings strongly suggest that the reversal in
time-order effect found by Woodrow was a practice effect operating
within the complicated series-standards patterns used in his experiments.

The second study by Long (1937) contains results similar in principle to Pratt's but perhaps more striking due to the fact that scale
values of stimuli were a function of their position in the series. Long
also used sounds as stimuli and studied the effect of series on series.
In one series, the intensities ranged from 20 to 40 db. in 2-db. steps
with 30 db. as the standard; another series ranged from 30 to 50 db. in
2-db. steps with 40 db. as the standard. Hence the 30–40 db. stimuli
were common to both series. The calculated AL for the 30-db. series
is 29.5 and for the 40-db. series 39.6. We should therefore expect 30, 32,
and 34 db. to be judged somewhat louder than medium in the 30-db.
series, since they were slightly above AL, and to be judged much
softer in the 40-db. series, where they were definitely below AL. Long
reported that in the 30-db. series these values were "slightly underestimated," and that in the 40-db. series they were "more underestimated," a trend in keeping with our prediction. Even more striking
were the judgments of 38 and 40 db. in the two series: in the 30-db.

series they were greatly overestimated (well above the AL) and in the 40-db. series they were underestimated (somewhat below the AL). We find, therefore, that we have accounted both quantitatively and qualitatively for effects of previous experience as reported in the experiments by Pratt and by Long.

Residuals from previous experience play a more or less important role in all responses. It is possible to control and study effects of previous experience by subjecting individuals to stimulation at a given time which will function as "past experience" at a later time. Clear evidence for the influence of past experience on present behavior appears when Ss judge ordered ascending and descending magnitudes, as in the study by Nash (1950b). Two groups of Ss judged successive sets of weights either in ascending or descending order. The first group judged a set of five weights ranging from 400 to 600 grm. with 50-grm. step intervals, and after five random presentations of each stimulus they judged a set of weights ranging from 350 to 550 grm. After five presentations of this series the top stimulus was again discarded and a lighter one added and this was repeated until a set from 100 to 300 grm. was reached. The second group of Ss began with a set of weights ranging from 100 to 300 grm.; after five random presentations of each member of the set they were given a set ranging from 150 to 350 grm., and so on until the last set, which consisted of weights ranging from 400 to 600 grm. Each group of Ss thus began with stimuli that served as the end set for the other group; conversely each group ended with the set that was first for the other group as shown in Table 4.8. The weights were judged on a nine-category rating scale ranging from very very

TABLE 4.8. Effects of Preceding Stimulation upon
Judgments of Weights

Sets (grm.)	Ascending AL	Descending AL
400–600	361	418
350–550	332	384
300–500	301	356
250–450	257	315
200–400	227	269
150–350	202	232
100–300	165	186

SOURCE: From Nash, 1950b. With the permission of the author.

heavy, through medium, to very very light. Numbers from 1 to 9 were assigned to the categories for purposes of computation and values of AL were determined by least-squares fit to Equation (39) below (Helson, 1948; Helson and Himelstein, 1955).

The results show that the level against which any set of weights was judged was a function of preceding stimulation levels, the ascending sets having lower ALs in every case than the descending sets. Remembering that judgments of "heavier" are inversely related to magnitude of AL it is seen that weights in ascending sets were judged heavier than sets judged in descending order.

The effects of preceding series upon succeeding series can be classed with practice effects even though they involve sets of stimuli differing in magnitude from series to series. Repetition of the same series of stimuli has also been found to involve adaptation as Woodrow has pointed out. Summarizing his extensive research on estimation of temporal intervals, he wrote:

> The total range of times used is extremely important because of the tendency to become adapted to an interval repeatedly presented. As a consequence of adaptation to times of one length, judgments of other lengths may be altered. Practice alone may cause a pronounced change in the magnitude of the time-order errors or a reversal in their direction. In the course of a long experiment the indifference interval tends to move towards the average length of the intervals constituting the total series. . . . In one study . . . 110 subjects were given 120 comparisons of empty intervals with a standard of 1.0 sec. and variables of 0.8, 0.9, 1.0, 1.1, and 1.2 sec. The pooled data show that if the indifference interval were calculated from the first 60 trials it would fall below 0.8 sec. (as estimated by extrapolation). During the last 60 trials, however, the responses were what might be expected if the variables were being compared with a standard of about 0.94 sec. With practice the indifference interval moved towards the average length of all the intervals presented during the entire sitting, namely, 1.0 sec. (Woodrow, 1951, p. 1227).

Woodrow's explanation of the change of the indifference time interval is entirely in accord with our fundamental position. We differ from Woodrow on one point: instead of assuming that the arithmetic mean of the stimuli represents the general time level, we assume that it is represented by a weighted log mean function which, with the d factor, yields 0.915 as the indifference level of the whole series—a value nearer to Woodrow's observed value of 0.94 than to the arithmetic mean, 1.0 sec. Lest this difference be overemphasized, it should be pointed out that Woodrow's concept of a "weighted general level" as the effective standard underlying judgments of time is similar to the position taken here.

Whether we are dealing with an ordered succession of stimuli, as in Nash's study, or with haphazard presentations, as in Woodrow's and other studies, we find that the judgment of any stimulus or series of stimuli is influenced by both immediate and remote contexts of stimulation. It has been erroneously assumed that psychophysical judgments are subject only to contrast effects of stimuli immediately preceding or contiguous to the judged stimulus, but this assumption runs counter to our assumption that AL is the pooled effect of remote as well as of adjacent stimuli. Thus Garner (1953) found that judgment of loudness of a stimulus may be raised following a loud stimulus and lowered following a soft stimulus, a finding that appears to contradict the position taken here unless the level established by all preceding stimuli is taken as the basis of judgment. Harris (1929) pointed out that judgments of pleasantness of individual colors could not be predicted as simple contrasts with immediately preceding stimuli but could be predicted if the affective level of all the colors preceding the judged color was taken as the frame of reference. Whether affective or sensory dimensions of stimuli are being judged, the influence of remote as well as immediate contexts of stimulation must be taken into consideration.

Series effects in discrimination. It was suggested by Pratt (1930) that tones of low pitch were localized nearer to the ground than were tones of high pitch. As pointed out by Pedley and Harper (1959), this fact was utilized by fliers using an instrument in which rising pitch meant that the plane was climbing, falling pitch that it was descending. To test if position in a pitch series would affect the height localization of pitches, Pedley and Harper constructed three series of seven pitches, each containing two critical frequencies, 900~ and 1400~. In the 100 to 1400~ series the critical pitches were the top members; in the 240 to 3400~ series they were the "middle" members; in the 900 to 12,500~ series they were the lowest members. The localizations were made on a 7-ft. vertical scale in 1-ft. intervals from the floor. The results indicated clear-cut series effects on localization: When the critical pitches were at the top of the series they were localized a little above five on the scale; when they were at intermediate positions in the series their average localization was a little more than four; and when they were the lowest members in the series their average localization was a little over three. By analogy with anchor stimuli in lifted weights and background stimuli in vision, another experiment is immediately suggested. Using a single series of pitches throughout, the shifts in height localization could be determined as a function of low, intermediate, and high anchoring pitches. Under these conditions we would expect the *whole series* to be displaced upward with the low anchor and downward with the high anchor. There should be an anchor somewhat below the mean of the pitches which would exert no effect or would yield the same localizations that are found with the single-stimuli method, when no anchor is presented.

Discriminability of stimuli, as expressed in mel, veg, bril, and other "ratio-type" scales, has been assumed to be determined largely if not solely, by the type of the receptor mechanism mediating the sensory process. But direct tests of discrimination of pitches picked by Hartman (1954) according to the mel scale revealed that contextual stimuli are as important in discriminating pitch as background luminance is in discriminating brightness (Evans, 1948).

Wedell (quoted by Hartman, 1954) reported that his average S could not learn to identify 13 tones which were 111 DLs apart in pitch; but Hartman found Ss could identify 9 tones about 106 DLs apart and under some conditions with separations of only 70 DLs between stimuli. Hartman concluded that the difficulty experienced by Wedell's Ss was caused not by pitch separation but by the absolute number of stimuli comprising the series. He tested this conclusion as follows: Frequencies of 1330, 1700, and 2104~ separated by 200 mels were presented in different positions in 50-, 100- and 200-mel series. As seen from Table 4.9 these frequencies occupy positions 1, 5, and 9 in the 50-mel group, positions 3, 5, and 7 in the 100-mel group, and positions 4, 5, and 6 in the 200-mel group. Hartman reasoned as follows: If the tones were confused equally often in the different series, then the conclusion would have been that confusion (discrimination) is due to a given pitch separation irrespective of the position of the tones in the series; but if degree of confusion varied systematically with the position of the tones in the series, the conclusion should have been that pitch separation is only one of the factors causing confusion in a serial situation and not the most important one. The data in Table 4.9 show that stimuli separated by equal pitch separations are not confused equally in the three mel series: 1, 5, and 9 are never confused in the 50-mel series but they are confused as much as 28 percent of the time in the 200-mel series.

TABLE 4.9. Confusions of Equal Pitch Distances (200 Mels) in Three Mel Groups

Mel Group	Stimuli	Confusions	
		Number	Percent
50	1330–1700(1–5)	0	0.0
	1700–2104(5–9)	0	0.0
	1330–2104(1–9)	0	0.0
100	1330–1700(3–5)	7	7.0
	1700–2104(5–7)	4	4.0
	1330–2104(3–7)	1	1.0
200	1330–1700(4–5)	20	21.0
	1700–2104(5–6)	27	28.0
	1330–2104(4–6)	3	3.0

SOURCE: From Hartman, 1954. With the permission of the *American Journal of Psychology*.

Discrimination is therefore not an absolute capacity dependent only upon sense modality and type of psychophysical judgment required of *S*s, important as these may be. Discrimination depends upon the adjustment level and the relations of specific stimuli to prevailing level at the moment of judging.

Effects of order on fractionation data. It has long been known that absolute and differential thresholds have quite different values depending upon whether one approaches the threshold from above or below in the method of limits and whether the variables are presented first and the standard second or vice versa in the constant method. Thus Clausen, Gjesvik, and Urdal (1954) found that pain thresholds measured seriatim on different parts of the body on three different days were affected by the order in which they were determined. The thresholds in Table 4.10 show significant order effects, seven of the twelve differences being significant at the 1 percent level and one at the 5 percent level. *Thresholds determined later were significantly lower than those determined earlier on all areas measured.* If we rearrange the data in *A* of Table 4.10 by body area, as shown in *B* of the same table, we see that order effects can wipe out differences due to

TABLE 4.10.

A. Pain Thresholds for Three Body Areas[a]

Session I			Session II			Session III		
Arm	Forehead	Leg	Forehead	Arm	Leg	Leg	Arm	Forehead
226	221	196	234	213	198	220	213	217

B. Pain Thresholds from A Rearranged by Body Area to Show Order Effects

Order	Arm	Forehead	Leg
I	226	234	220
II	213; 213	221	
III		217	196; 198

[a] In millicalories per second per square centimeter.
SOURCE: From Clausen, Gjesvik, and Urdal, 1954. With the permission of the *Journal of General Psychology*.

body area. While the physiological mechanisms suggested by the authors may be partially responsible for the lower successive thresholds, they bear a striking resemblance to other well-known adaptation effects. Woodrow (1935) found that along with pronounced shift in TOE in the positive direction as a result of practice there was an increase in upper and lower DLs for estimation of temporal intervals. Woodrow's explanation of such results in terms of change in the effective standard seems a more plausible explanation of the findings reported by Clausen, Gjesvik, and Urdal than an explanation in terms of peripheral receptor or afferent mechanisms.

Starting point and direction of stimulation affect all types of thresholds. Measuring the size-weight illusion, Nyssen and Bourdon (1956) found that the magnitude of the illusion varied greatly with order of presentation of the stimuli. Using a standard of 500 grm., measuring 21 × 5 × 2 cm., and 13 variables, measuring 21 × 5 × 7 cm. and ranging from 500 to 1100 grm. in 50-grm. steps, Ss compared the large, less dense variables with the standard. In the ascending order, beginning with large 500-grm. stimulus, it required large 750-grm. stimulus to equal the small 500-grm. standard. But in the descending series, beginning with large 1100-grm. stimulus, the large stimulus judged equal to the small standard was about 825 grm. Hence the illusion was greater when measured in the descending order than in the ascending order. Averaging the results of ascending and descending series, as is usually done in such cases, is quite unjustified because the average value does not necessarily coincide with threshold found in haphazard presentation of the variables. Estimations of a time interval of 1 sec. by normal and schizophrenic *S*s were also found to depend on the order in which the temporal magnitudes were presented (Weinstein, Goldstone, and Boardman, 1958). As seen from Table 4.11 the time interval judged

TABLE 4.11.   Geometric Means of Estimated Seconds by Normal and Schizophrenic Groups Following 0.1- and 2.0-Second Starting Times

Group	Origin (Sec.)	Geometric Mean of Estimated Seconds Normals	Patients
I	0.1	0.442	0.238
	2.0	0.671	0.450
II	2.0	0.584	0.516
	0.1	0.577	0.211

SOURCE: From Weinstein, Goldstone, and Boardman, 1958. With the permission of the American Psychological Association.

to be 1 sec. was always longer when, using the method of limits, the starting time was 2 sec. than it was when the starting time was 0.1 sec. In general, schizophrenic *S*s were more affected by order of stimulation than were normal *S*s and their estimations were always shorter than those of the normals.

Order effects have now been proved to be as important in the fractionation methods as in the limiting, constant, and rating-scale methods. In classical psychophysics and for many modern workers effects of order of stimulation are merely "errors" of judgment which should be eradicated; but for us TOE and SOE have deeper significance. So-called time-order and space-order errors arise from the decentered position of adaptation level and are therefore manifestations of lawful underlying mechanisms. The importance of order of stimulation for the determination of equilibrium conditions of judgment was not realized so long as order effects were regarded as sources of error. The systematic nature of such effects rules out the "error" view of their origin. Not only threshold values but psychophysical functions and scales are in large part determined by order of stimulation. In accordance with our assumption that every stimulus that impinges on the organism pulls AL more or less in its own direction, we expect lower ALs in series of ascending order of magnitude than in descending series. Interacting with order of stimulation are effects of frequency, recency, and intensity and effects of stimulus distributions, i.e., whether normally distributed or positively, or negatively skewed. We shall be concerned in this section chiefly with effects of order of stimulation unconfounded by factors that are discussed in other sections of this chapter.

The predominant influence on judgment of the first stimulus of a pair with relatively short interval and the decreasing influence on judgments of half pitches with longer interval were strikingly brought out in a study by Cohen, Hansel, and Sylvester (1954). Ss were required to determine the half-pitch of a variable stimulus presented between two tones. The end tones varied in order of presentation as follows: 1000 and 3000~; 3000 and 1000~; 2000 and 4000~; and 4000 and 2000~. In addition to the influence of order and pitch of the end stimuli on the half pitch, the time intervals between the first tone and the variable and between the variable and the third tone were found to influence the judged half pitch. The experimental values in Table 4.12 show that "when the observer is adjusting the second tone so that it seems to him intermediate in pitch between the first and third

TABLE 4.12.   Calculated and Observed Values of Tones Bisecting Two Tonal Intervals in Ascending and Descending Orders

t_2/t_1	First and Third Tones	Mean Half-pitch		Discrepancy (Percent)
		Observed	Calculated	
0.5	1000–3000	1676	1742	+3.4
0.5	3000–1000	1921	1930	0.0[a]
0.5	2000–4000	2628	2660	+1.2
0.5	4000–2000	2837	2850	0.0[a]
1.0	1000–3000	1874	1828	−2.5
1.0	3000–1000	1838	1834	0.0[a]
1.0	2000–4000	2693	2746	+2.0
1.0	4000–2000	2808	2764	−1.5
2.0	1000–3000	2068	1999	−3.3
2.0	3000–1000	1725	1673	−3.0
2.0	2000–4000	2786	2917	+4.7
2.0	4000–2000	2674	2593	−3.0

Note: Calculated values are derived from the equation
$$I = 0.918t_1 - 0.369d - 0.0858rd$$
[a] Less than ½ of 1 percent.
SOURCE: From Cohen, Hansel, and Sylvester, 1954. With the permission of *Nature*.

tones, he makes the tones which are presented closer together in time farther apart in frequency, regardless of the ascending or descending order of the tones" (1954, p. 643). The effect of a shorter time interval between tones is to displace the pitch of the second tone in the direction of the first with the result that the observer compensates by choosing a half pitch displaced in the opposite direction. Thus when the second time interval between 1000 and 3000~ was half the first, the half pitch was judged to be 1676~; but when the second interval was double the first, the half pitch was judged 2068~. Hence the longer the time interval between the first tone and the top tone the less the first tone is weighted. The half pitch is therefore influenced by the order of presentation of the end tones as well as by their frequencies and also by the time relations between the intermediate and end tones.

We can determine the relative contributions of the various factors entering into the estimated half pitch between two given tones by assuming that the intermediate tone is equal to some function of the first tone, another function of the tonal interval that is to be bisected, and a third function of the product of the ratio of the time intervals between the tones to the difference between the first and third tones as follows:

$$I = a_1t_1 + a_2d + a_3rd \qquad (8)$$

where I is the frequency of the half pitch; a_1, a_2, and a_3 are the weighting constants we are seeking; t_1 is the frequency of the tone first sounded; d is the difference between the first and third tones *taken with regard to sign;* and r is the ratio of the time interval between the second and third tones to the time interval between the first and second tones. To obtain the best values of the constants according to the least-squares criterion, we solve the following normal equations for a_1, a_2, and a_3:

$$\Sigma(t_1I) = a_1\Sigma t_1^2 + a_2\Sigma(dt_1) + a_3\Sigma(rdt_1) \qquad (9)$$

$$\Sigma(dI) = a_1\Sigma(dt_1) + a_2\Sigma d^2 + a_3\Sigma(rd^2) \qquad (10)$$

$$\Sigma(rdI) = a_1\Sigma(rdt_1) + a_2\Sigma(rd^2) + a_3\Sigma(r^2d^2) \qquad (11)$$

Solution of Equations (9) to (11) gives

$$I = 0.918t_1 - 0.369d - 0.0858rd^3 \qquad (12)$$

[3] I am indebted to the late Dr. Ralph Lane for the hypotheses and their solution as given here.

The calculated values in Table 4.12 are derived from Equation (12) and are, on the average, within 1.5 percent of the intermediate tones found experimentally by Cohen, Hansel, and Sylvester. From the values of the constants, a_1, a_2, and a_3, it is seen that the first tone is about 10 times as important as the ratio of the time intervals between the tones and about 2.5 times as important as the interval to be bisected. Stated otherwise, the first stimulus is most important, next comes the width of the tonal interval between the end tones, and last in importance is the time interval between the tones.

Since the weighting constant fixing the contribution of the stimulus first presented to the subjects is much greater than the weighting constants for the other two factors entering into the bisection data of Cohen, Hansel, and Sylvester, it is evident that there can be an inherent asymmetry in fractionation procedures due to the predominant effect of the first stimulus. Thus in the ascending order, 1000–3000, the half pitch is 1676∼, but in the descending order, 3000–1000, the half pitch is 1921∼, a difference of 245∼ or nearly 15 percent. The half pitch is thus closer to the first tone perceived than to the second end tone. It might be thought that this asymmetry can be overcome by averaging the intermediate tones yielded by the two orders of presentation but with such a large difference the average of these frequencies will not appear to be halfway between the end tones when either the high or the low member of the pair is presented first. Even when the time intervals are equal, consider the predominant effects of the first stimulus: In the order 1000–3000 the intermediate tone is 1874∼, but in the order 3000–1000 it is 1838∼, a discrepancy of only 36∼; but with 2000–4000 the intermediate tone is 2693∼, and with 4000–2000 it is 2808∼, a discrepancy of 215∼! Similarly, Engen and Tulünay (1957) obtained very different half weights in ascending and descending orders of presentation as shown in Table 4.13. We thus find that pitch, a "metathetic" continuum, is as subject to order and hence to adaptation effects as are loudness and kinesthesis, which are presumably "prothetic" senses.

The form of the pain scale obtained by successive fractionation changes as a result of adaptation and with different orders of stimulation as was decisively shown by Swartz (1953). After establishing the absolute threshold for pain in tooth pulp (by means of electrical stimulation) and the upper limit of tolerance for pain, Ss adjusted the current eliciting the pain halfway between these limits. Then the half pain

TABLE 4.13. Half Weights of Various Standards in Ascending and Descending Orders of Presentation of the Variables

Standard (grm.)	Mean of Ascending Order	Mean of Descending Order
150	82.7	104.3
300	140.0	178.8
550	306.5	344.2
900	501.7	581.6

SOURCE: From Engen and Tulünay, 1957. With the permission of the American Psychological Association.

between the first half pain and the absolute threshold was determined to obtain the quarter pain. Says Swartz: "On the day following the determination of the pain-range threshold, adaptation was frequently noted. It was therefore necessary to determine a new threshold before scaling could begin. This meant that for most Ss the range bisected was smaller than the original pain range" (1953, p. 290). More important still was his finding that the results of the first day's bisections were fitted by *negatively* accelerated curves whereas on the second day the bisections were fitted by *positively* accelerated curves due to the fact that the order of determination was different in the two sessions. In the first session the order was: absolute threshold, upper limit, half pain; in the second session it was: upper limit or previously established half pain, then threshold value, followed by determination of the half pain between the latter and the former. *The curve of bisection was concave downward or concave upward depending upon the order of determination within the same sense modality.*

The influence of order of stimuli is not limited to psychophysical judgments in the strict sense as shown in a study of the influence of preceding formant frequencies of vowels on recognition of succeeding vowels (Broadbent, Ladefoged, and Lawrence, 1956). Vowels are distinguished from one another mainly by the frequencies of the formants or regions of the auditory spectrum in which there is a comparatively large amount of energy. According to these writers it has been hypothesized recently that when a listener identifies a vowel in a particular word he does so, not by considering the absolute values of the two lowest formant frequencies of other vowels, but by "assessing the frequencies of these formants in relation to the formant frequencies of other vowels which he has heard pronounced by that speaker. On this hypothesis, the identification of a particular sound depends upon the acoustic structure of the neighboring sounds" (1956, p. 815). In their experiments two versions of the phrase "please say what this word is" were synthesized followed by the same test sound consisting of words formed by the letter *b* followed by a vowel and ending with the letter *t*. The ranges of the first formants in the two versions of the introductory phrase were 300–675 cps and 150–400 cps. The results for a group of 15 *S*s who heard the two versions separated by an interval of 5 *min.* are given in Table 4.14. Fourteen of the fifteen

TABLE 4.14.   Vowel Sounds Reported by 30 Ss

First Formant of Preceding Word (cps)	Test Word Heard		
	Bit	Bet	Bat
300–675	20	10	0
150–400	0	19	11

SOURCE: From Broadbent, Ladefoged, and Lawrence, 1956. With the permission of *Nature*.

*S*s reported hearing different words in the two versions despite the fact that the stimulus was reproduced from a recording and was therefore identical. In the first version "bit" was reported most often, "bet" next, and "bat" not at all; in the second version "bit" was not reported at all, "bet" was reported most often, and "bat" next in frequency. When the two versions were separated by only a 10-sec. interval the number of test *S*s in a second group of 15 who reported different words dropped to 7. Context thus can be as important in discrimination of auditory quality as background is for visual quality.

LOCUS OF NEUTRAL POINTS

In accordance with the assumption that the neutral point changes with every change in focal, background, or residual stimuli, we expect the neutral point to move along predictable loci as a function of systematic variations in dimensions of stimulation. Thus as weights become heavier the stimulus judged medium moves up; as the skin becomes warmer or cooler physiological zero changes accordingly. There are limits to the movement of the neutral point which are set by the extent to which adaptation can counteract extreme stimulation. With a set of very heavy weights all may be judged heavy and none medium or light, or with sufficiently high temperatures all may be judged hot because the limits of adaptation have been exceeded. Usually the limits of adaptation are not reached and values of AL tend to approximate a weighted mean of impinging stimuli. The locus of neutral or indifferent points conveys considerable information in that it demarcates opposite qualities such as bright-dim, pleasant-unpleasant, warm-cold, heavy-light, tall-short, or, in general, positive-negative attributes on bipolar continua. The locus of ALs also serves to denote the conditions giving rise to judgments of equality which are important in the determination of many psychophysical data. Determinations of loci of neutral points over a wide range of stimuli and for different stimulus-background conditions have been made in studies by Helson and Michels (1948), Guilford (1954*b*), Guilford and Smith (1959), Furth (1960), and Rambo and Johnson (1963). Let us consider the varieties of information obtained from these studies.

Turning first to the determination of the locus of indifferent states dividing pleasant from unpleasant tones by Guilford, we see from Fig. 4.3 that the isohedonic line with a value of zero (neither pleasant nor unpleasant) divides the intensity-frequency plane into two regions, the upper comprising the region of combinations of intensity and frequency yielding varying degrees of unpleasantness, the lower containing the pleasant combinations of intensity and frequency. Regarding the neutral locus Guilford says: "For all tones with combinations of frequency and intensity above and to the right of this curve we would predict a judgment of 'unpleasant.' For all tones with frequency and intensity below and to the left of this curve, we would predict a judgment of 'pleasant'" (1954*b*, p. 694). The locus of neutral points thus divides the plane into two regions such that any point in the plane immediately denotes the conditions of frequency and loudness that are judged pleasant or unpleasant.

Isohedonic curves for colors, similar to those for tones, have been constructed by Guilford and Smith (1959) for a large number of colors based on their extensive investigations of color preferences. The loci of the indifference points as functions of brightness and saturation are found to vary with the hues of the stimuli and the sex of *S*s (see p. 361 where graphs for red, yellow-red, and yellow have been reproduced from Guilford and Smith). The practical utility of such plots is apparent in a field where definite information regarding the relations between hue, lightness, and saturation and the affects has not been available.

Neutral visual stimuli take on various hues when viewed against strongly saturated surrounds, so the following question arises: What are the conditions for perceiving an achromatic color against a strongly

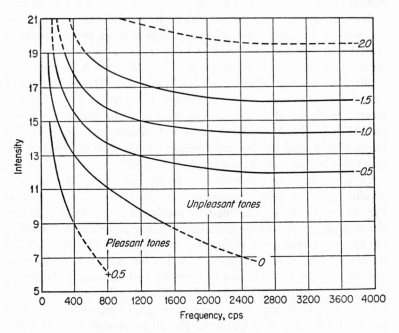

FIG. 4.3. An isohedon chart, showing the loci of constant affective value levels at one-half sigma intervals for various combinations of frequency and intensity of pure tone stimuli separated by the locus of neutral points. (From Guilford, 1954b, based on data from Singer and Young, 1941. With the permission of the *American Journal of Psychology*.)

chromatic background? The locus of achromatic points in the C.I.E. trichromatic mixture diagram as a function of the brightness of a spot 1° 35′ perceived to be achromatic (black, gray, or white) in large, strongly chromatic surrounding fields was determined in a study by Helson and Michels (1948). Ss sat facing the inside of a semicylindrical booth 4 ft. in diameter and 6 ft. high, lined with fairly matt, nonselective, highly reflective cardboard (daylight white) in the center of which was an aperture, the exit pupil, of a colorimeter set flush with the surround. The task of the Ss was to adjust the amounts of red, green, and blue primaries of the colorimeter so that the color of the aperture was achromatic when set initially at high, medium, and low luminance levels. The luminance of the surround was varied by means of a lamp-filter combination from 0.10 to 8.63 apparent footcandles. Its hue was either red, yellow, green, or blue though not all luminances

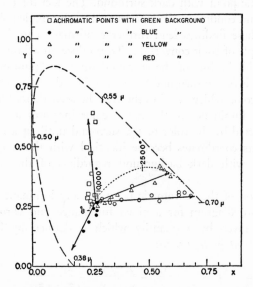

FIG. 4.4. Achromatic loci: The dashed curve shows the spectral locus, with wave lengths in microns; the dotted curve is the locus of blackbody radiators, with temperatures in degrees Kelvin; the solid lines join the "white point" with the background points. (From Helson and Michels, 1948.)

were possible with all the hues due to the differences in transmissions of the filters. The aperture spot was also adjusted to achromaticity against a completely dark surround and against a near-white surround illuminated by light from 2854° K illumination. Four different chromaticities and two to five luminances were employed with three Ss making the total number of conditions investigated 47, including the observations with dark surround.

The results show certain regularities as seen from Fig. 4.4. The trilinear coordinates of the spot seen as achromatic when its luminance is *low* compared to that of the surround, about 1/10 or less, approximate the trilinear coordinates of the surround. With high luminances of the spot relative to that of the surround, about 10:1, its coordinates approximate the trilinear values of the achromatic spot with dark surround, showing that there is no color contrast when the foveal stimulus is sufficiently bright. In Fig. 4.4 these facts are manifested in the locus of achromatic points which run from the surround points to the achromatic point with dark surround. The loci for the four chromatic surround conditions all intersect at the achromatic point for dark surround. These findings lend further confirmation to the generality of the principle of color conversion: To produce an achromatic spot in a colored field the hue of the surround must be "pumped" into the spot when it is *below* surround luminance in order to negate the complementary color which would otherwise be seen there. On the other hand, as the luminance of the foveal color increases it becomes less and less affected by the color of the surround until, at a ratio of 10:1 and above, its coordinates become identical with those of the white point found with dark background regardless of the color of the surround.

The position of the achromatic point for any luminance in the trilinear mixture diagram for a given luminance and chromaticity of surround is given by a quantity which is defined by Helson and Michels as the *adaptation* ratio:

$$r = \frac{x_s - x_o}{x_b - x_o} = \frac{y_s - y_o}{y_b - y_o} = \frac{z_s - z_o}{z_b - z_o} \tag{13}$$

where x, y, and z are trilinear coordinates in the C.I.E. diagram, and the subscripts s, b, and o refer to the achromatic spot, the background, and the achromatic spot as found with a dark surround ($x_o = 0.269$; $y_o = 0.269$; $z_o = 0.462$). In turn, r depends upon the ratio (R) of the luminance of the spot to that of the ground, which is given by

$$R = \frac{X_s + Y_s + Z_s}{X_b + Y_b + Z_b} \tag{14}$$

where the capital letters represent tristimulus values of spot and surround as in the preceding equation. The dependence of r upon R is given by the expression

$$r = \frac{1}{1 + 0.21 R^2} \tag{15}$$

This function is plotted in Fig. 4.5 (Helson and Michels, 1948) and resembles, but is not, a sigmoid curve.

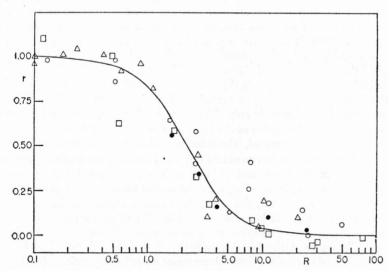

FIG. 4.5. Adaptation ratio as a function of stimulus sum ratio: the points are keyed to the various backgrounds as in Fig. 4.4. The solid curve is that of $r = 1/(1 + 0.21R^2)$. (From Helson and Michels, 1948.)

Using short flashes of the light of the variable and a null method in which the spot seen in the chromatic field by one eye was matched to an achromatic spot seen by the other eye in a neutral field, MacAdam (1949) verified the findings of Helson and Michels but suggested as a better fit for the dependence of r on R the equation

$$r = \frac{1}{1 + 0.54R^3} \tag{16}$$

Considering the differences in observation conditions it is not surprising that a somewhat different function provides a better fit to the MacAdam data than does Equation (15) based on the earlier data.

We now find that the principle of color conversion, which was originally stated only qualitatively, can be deduced directly from Equation (15).

The principle, based on work with reflecting samples on nonselective surfaces states: In every viewing situation there is established an adaptation level or neutral region such that stimuli with reflectances above this level are tinged with the hue of the source of illumination, stimuli with lower reflectances take the afterimage complementary to the hue of the illuminant, and stimuli with reflectances near AL are either achromatic or weakly saturated and of uncertain hue. In order that a highly reflecting surface appear achromatic it is necessary that its spectral reflectance be such that, when multiplied by the spectral energy distribution of the illuminant, it yield the specifications of the corresponding achromatic point. But highly reflecting surfaces necessarily depart from this condition toward the hue of the illuminant. According to Equation 15 a stimulus of very low reflectance would be achromatic only if its spectral reflectance, multiplied by the spectral energy distribution of the illuminant, were to yield the chromaticity coordinates of the surround. The reflectance of selective surfaces can depart from this requirement in one of two ways: (1) favoring the dominant wavelength of the illuminant and yielding high reflectance, and (2) favoring other wavelengths, thus causing the color to shift toward the complement of the illuminant. However, this effect alone cannot explain the behavior of nonselective surfaces of low reflectance. The color of such surfaces must be due to the afterimage complementary effect noted with spots of low brightness. The results obtained in this study therefore agree with the principle of color conversion obtained from observations on reflecting surfaces (slightly modified from Helson and Michels, 1948, pp. 1031–1032).

Another class of phenomena can also be deduced from Equation (15). As seen from Fig. 4.5, the plot of this equation is fairly flat at and above spot-surround luminance ratios of 10:1 and 1:0.1, and it is steepest at intermediate values of r. Where the curve is flat large changes in spot-surround luminance ratios have little effect—hence the perceived color is "constant" beyond intermediate ratios of luminances, i.e., ratios above 10:1 and below 0.1:1 of foveal to surround luminances. At the high end the spot holds its dark surround color and at the low end it holds the color complementary to the hue of the surround. In between these ratios there is a range of luminances of about 100:1 wherein the color of the spot changes in accordance with the principle of color conversion.

From Equations (13), (14), and (15), which define the loci of neutral colors, it is possible to calculate the trilinear coordinates of the foveal color that will be perceived to be achromatic with any ratio of luminances of the foveal and surround colors and for any background chromaticity. Determination of the loci of achromatic colors viewed against backgrounds of different chromaticities not only has resulted in a quantitative statement of the conditions determining achromaticity but has also furnished a quantitative basis for the principle of color conversion.

A third study concerned with loci of ALs is that of Furth (1960), to which we have referred previously. In this study the locus of ALs as a function of the *density* of anchor stimuli was determined with a fixed set of series weights. As shown by the curves in Fig. 4.6, both PSE and

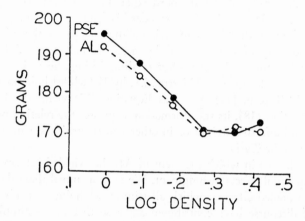

FIG. 4.6. Adaptation level and point of subjective equality in lifted weights as a function of log of density of standards. (From Furth, 1960. With the permission of the American Psychological Association.)

its cognate value, AL, approach an asymptote with decreasing density of anchor stimuli, thus demonstrating that the size-weight illusion has limits beyond which *increase* in size is no longer accompanied by decrease in perceived weight. Remembering that the series weights were 152, 176, 200, 224 and 248 grm. throughout and the six standard weights were always 200 grm. but differed in volume so that their densities were 1.017, 0.804, 0.651, 0.540, 0.452, and 0.385, it is possible to express the "effect of variation in density of standards in terms of an equivalent change of weight with density held constant." If the ALs are known, we can convert the log mean equation for AL:

$$\log (AL + .25d) = \frac{\left(3.0 \sum_{1}^{n} \log C_o/N\right) + \log St}{4} \tag{17}$$

in which d is the average step interval between stimuli, C_o refers to the series stimuli, and St is the standard, to the following form by substituting the known values of series stimuli:

$$\log St = 4 \log (AL + 6.0) - 6.8843 \qquad (18)$$

Given the value of AL for any value of density of standard and solving for St, the *effective* weight of the standard can be determined. Thus with density of the standard equal to 0.540 and AL equal to 170.4, the effective weight of the standard is found to be 126.3 grm. As elucidated by Furth, "This conversion allows one to say that diminishing the density of the standard by nearly a half ($St = .540$ vs $St = 1.017$) has the equivalent effect of diminishing the weight of the standard from 200 grm. to 125 grm., i.e., by ⅜ [while] holding density constant" (1960, p. 153). Whereas Equation (17) yields the locus of ALs, Equation (18), its transformation, expresses the relation between density and effective weight or in other words furnishes a measure of the size-weight *illusion*.

A fourth area in which the locus of ALs has yielded information is with sequential effects in judgment. We have assumed that adaptation level is a pooled effect to which all stimuli belonging to a given universe of discourse have contributed and also that every stimulus impinging upon the organism pulls established ALs in its own direction. If a given stimulus is repeated a sufficient number of times or exposed for a sufficient length of time, AL moves in the direction of the stimulus and nullifies its action to a considerable extent. Since only with weak to moderate stimuli is complete adaptation found, the value of AL approaches an asymptote short of the highest intensity of stimulation. There is also evidence that AL stabilizes when a series of stimuli is repeated again and again even though none of the members of the series are very intense as was first shown by Johnson (1949). Both Johnson and others have found that when Ss are asked to judge a set of pitches, weights, etc. the "reference scale" is relatively quickly established; in other words AL changes very rapidly as the first few stimuli are beng judged and then assumes a relatively stable value. A study by Rambo and Johnson (1963) again shows that AL reaches a stable value fairly soon after Ss become familiar with the stimuli. In this study Ss judged a series of 9 cards bearing from 5 to 65 dots. Judgments were made in terms of a rating scale from "very small" through "average" to "very large." In the first trial AL was in the neighborhood of 8.5–10.5 dots. (There were two independent experiments with minor variations which will be treated as one.) By the fourteenth trial AL rose to about 20 dots and then rose more slowly to stabilize at about 21.5 dots from about trial 25 through trial 45.

Plotting the locus of ALs from the first through the forty-fifth trials gave a hyperbolic function of the following type:

$$AL = \frac{T}{a + bT} \qquad (19)$$

The actual fitted equations were

$$AL = \frac{T}{0.483 + .0472T} \qquad (20)$$

$$AL = \frac{T}{.0451 + .0755T} \qquad (21)$$

where T refers to trials and the numerical constants were determined by least-squares fit. The two fitted equations are reproduced here to show how closely two independent experiments utilizing slightly different sets of stimuli yielded very similar values of the constants of the fitted hyperbolas. Rambo and Johnson suggest that a crude estimate of the extent to which a scale has achieved stability may be gauged by comparing AL on any trial with the terminal AL (TAL) as given by the asymptote ($1/b$ in Equation 19) of the fitted hyperbola.

Since judgments of individual stimuli depend upon the magnitude of AL it follows that sequential effects in judgment can be studied through the changes in AL over time, repetitions, or other dimensions of stimulation. The number of repetitions necessary to reach TAL should correlate highly with difficulty of judging various types of materials, with individual differences in acquiring stable frames of reference, and with other variables in the judging process.

FACTORS AFFECTING PSYCHOPHYSICAL FUNCTIONS

Stevens and Galanter (1957) proposed to divide judgmental continua into two fundamental classes based on the distinction between perception of intensity vs. perception of quality, or "size vs. sort." In the first class, which they call *prothetic,* they include magnitudes like heaviness, loudness, and brightness, on the assumption that the underlying physiological mechanism is additive; presumably here the same receptors are involved: as perceived magnitudes increase, excitation is added to excitation. In the second class, which they call *meta-thetic,* they include such "qualities" as pitch, visual position, inclination, and proportion, on the assumption that a substitutive mechanism is at work at the physiological level. This distinction rests on assumed differences in the form of the stimulus-judgment functions sometimes found. Continua in the first class are supposed to yield nonlinear magnitude scales while continua in the second class may be linear, but not necessarily so.

Opposed to the division of sensory continua into prothetic and metathetic types is the fact that the curves fitting magnitude and quality judgments are often the same. There is much evidence showing that curves are affected more by conditions of judgment than by the difference between so-called metathetic and prothetic dimensions. Judgments of loudness, which involve magnitude, are affected by composition of the variables judged (Garner, 1954) and by standards or anchors; judgments of pitch, which involve quality, are affected in the same way by these factors. Christman (1954) reported shifts in pitch following prolonged stimulation with pure tones as shown in Table 4.15. In his experiment, a standard or satiating tone was presented for two seconds followed by a two second interval after which the variable was presented for two seconds. In other cases longer satiating periods of one and two minutes were employed. From Table 4.15 it is seen

TABLE 4.15.   Average PSE for Five Observers for Three Satiating Pitches

	Standard-ization	Satiating Tones			Restandard-ization
	600	400	500	800	600
Mean	595.8	603.8	603.8	584.0	595.3

SOURCE: From Christman, 1954. With the permission of the *American Journal of Psychology*.

that if the adapting tone (400 or 500 ∼) is *below* the standard of 600 ∼, the latter is judged higher (603.8 ∼) and if it is *above* (800 ∼) the standard, the latter is judged lower (584.0 ∼) than under standardizing conditions. Christman concluded that the pitch of the standard tone is lowered by satiating tones of higher frequency than the standard and raised by satiating tones of lower frequency. The magnitude of the effect varied directly with the duration of the satiating tones and inversely with the time between satiation and testing. Hence pitch, a metathetic dimension, behaves exactly like loudness, a prothetic dimension. The distinction between prothetic and metathetic continua therefore does not stand up in the light of such results as these.

Further evidence against dividing sensory continua into prothetic and metathetic dimensions comes from an experiment concerned with evaluations of pitch, loudness, and time differences of auditory stimuli by Guilford and Cotzin (1941). They found that the difficulty of evaluating pitch, loudness, and time differences between auditory stimuli (Seashore tests) obeyed the same law. Ss chose weights to denote the difficulty of making the judgments so that the harder the judgment, the heavier the weight chosen. The results of scaling the stimuli denoting the difficulty of the judgments led to a most interesting finding: "No matter whether S is judging difficulty of discriminations of pitch, intensity, or time intervals, for an item of the same objective difficulty he will select the same average weight to match" (Guilford and Cotzin, 1941, p. 44). In the light of the analysis made by Guilford and Cotzin, there is no basis for distinguishing between magnitude and quality judgments of either small or large differences between stimuli.

Far from the "pure" scales envisaged by some present-day workers, it appears from several lines of evidence that Ss adjust to the series and background stimuli presented, to the type of judgment or operation which constitutes the method, and to many other factors in psychophysical experiments. The scale with which one emerges is a function of all factors determining the adaptation level prevailing during its determination. Canter and Hirsch (1955) showed that if a separate AL is assumed for each of the Harper and Stevens veg determinations, their values are closely approximated by the author's weighted log mean formula for the adaptation level for lifted weights. These writers suggest the following:

. . . the experimental question which should be asked is not whether *the* psychological scale for weight is a positively or negatively accelerated function, but rather what it is about the conditions under which ratio judgments are made that produces the one function and what it is about the conditions that produces the other function when methods of successive intervals or constant stimuli are used (pp. 648–649).

Enough has now been learned from experiments such as those of Helson (1947), Doughty (1949), and Garner (1954) to show that the context of stimulation importantly affects psychological scale values of stimuli. Doughty showed that the percentage of judgments of higher and louder for tones increases as the asymmetry in frequency of presentation of the stimuli becomes more positive and decreases as asymmetry becomes more negative (negative asymmetry being a preponderance of lower tones than the standard and positive of higher.) Furthermore, context effects were similar for loudness and pitch, arguing against the Stevens distinction between magnitude and quality continua. Garner's determinations of the half loudness of a standard tone of 1000 cycles at 90 db. sound pressure level, or SPL (db. re 0.0002 microbar) showed that Ss chose as the half loudness an intensity close to the mean of the series of tones presented. As seen from Table 4.16 "Each of the three groups . . . shows a complete dependence of

TABLE 4.16.   Mean, Median, and SD of Tones Judged Half as Loud as the Standard[a] by Three Groups of Ss

Group	Series Range (db.)	Mean	Median	SD
I	55–65	60.4	59.8	1.8
II	65–75	69.9	69.8	1.6
III	75–85	80.2	79.9	2.7

[a] 90-db. sound-pressure level.
SOURCE: From Garner, 1954. With the permission of the American Psychological Association.

the half-loudness value on the context of variable stimuli presented . . ." (p. 220). Garner pointed out that individual differences are large and statistically significant, a finding we would expect in view of the room for disagreement of what they were to regard as the "half loudness" and what various individuals regard as "loud," "soft," etc. That residual factors were important is shown by protocols from individuals who changed their judgments of what was "too loud" or "not loud enough" as the experiment progressed.

The Canter and Hirsch results and the Garner results agree that the values chosen to bisect intervals are largely determined by the series of stimuli presented to Ss and that Ss choose values near the arithmetic or log mean of the series.

Similar conclusions were reached by Baker and Dudek (1955) who required Ss to judge ratios both directly and by the constant sum method. They concluded that "the effect of changing the way in which ratio judgments are expressed is to make the curve relating psychological scale values to physical measurement more positively accelerated and to change from predominantly underestimation of physical values to predominantly overestimation" (p. 301). They also found that the order in which weights were presented affected the judgments in accordance with classical findings. After comparing a number of weight scales, two of their own and five others, they concluded that "different methodologies permit different sets of judgment determinants to operate; thus none of the scales agrees completely with any other scale" (p. 308). Similarly, Guilford and Dingman (1955) concluded that "the form of psychophysical law is a function of the psychophysical method used. This means that scaling by different methods does not necessarily yield psychological values that are linearly related" (p. 454). In our terms any conditions that significantly affect the adjustment level of the S will tend to change the judgment-stimulus function.

The influence of context on fractionation has also been shown in studies of other sense modalities. Engen and Tulünay (1957) set out to try to settle the differences between Garner (1954) and Stevens and Poulton (1956). Engen and Tulünay repeated Garner's work with lifted weights (Garner had used tone stimuli) and also employed sophisticated as well as naïve Ss. In their first experiment the half weight for a standard of 300 grm. was to be picked either from a series of light variables, 78, 100, 110, 120, 139, and 150 grm. or from a series of heavy variables, 150, 165, 175, 185, 200, and 210 grm. The results appear in Table 4.17 and fully support Garner's contention that the

TABLE 4.17. Weight Judged Half of 300 grm.

	Naïve Ss	Sophisticated Ss
Light Series	130.4	144.5
Heavy Series	191.8	192.5

SOURCE: From Engen and Tulünay, 1957. With the permission of the American Psychological Association.

stimulus judged half of a standard depends upon not only the standard weight but also on the series of stimuli from which Ss must pick the half weight. Sophisticated Ss are no less free from context effect than are naïve subjects. In this experiment contextual stimuli outweighed residual effects of practice stimuli as shown by the lack of

significant difference in the half weight chosen. *S*s given a light practice series (78, 100, and 110 grm.) and *S*s given a heavy practice series
(185, 200, and 210 grm.) chose the half weight of 300 grm. from a
common series, 102, 139, 150, 165, 175, and 185 grm. These authors
summarized the results of these two experiments as follows: "Regardless of the absolute value of the comparison weight, *S* had a tendency
to judge it to be more than half as heavy if it was one of the heaviest
in the series and to be less than half as heavy if it was one of the lightest in the series."

Anchors or backgrounds usually exert even greater effects on judgments of individual stimuli than do contextual stimuli since the latter
differ less from the stimuli being judged. Little has been done to determine the effects of backgrounds on fractionation of visual intervals.
In bisecting the lightness interval between a white and a black stimulus
Graham and Helson (unpublished study) found that the reflectance
of the background against which the end stimuli were viewed exerted
a decisive effect on the stimulus judged to be halfway between them.
*S*s adjusted the proportions of black and white on a color mixer to
yield a gray halfway between a white of 71.2-percent reflectance and
a black of 4.5-percent reflectance when viewed against backgrounds
having reflectances of 83.0, 13.7, and 3.8 percent. The gray bisecting the
interval had a reflectance of 40.6 percent with white background, 36.8
percent with gray background, and 34.8 percent with black background. The differences between the bisecting stimuli with white and
gray backgrounds were significant between the 5 and 1 percent levels;
but that between the gray and black backgrounds was not statistically
significant because the gray background with reflectance of 13.7 percent
was too close to the black background with reflectance of 4.5 percent.
It thus appears that a ratio scale of "brightness" depends upon the
background against which bisected stimuli are viewed just as does the
lightness function (Newhall, Nickerson, and Judd, 1943). Michels
(1954) has also shown that the lightness scale is affected by the mul-
tiple defining the scale, e.g., $\frac{1}{3}$, $\frac{1}{2}$, $\frac{2}{3}$. Plots of lightness against black,
gray, and white backgrounds yield parallel straight lines (Michels and
Helson, 1949) and ratio scales embodying identical multiples should
yield parallel curves, no matter what their shape, one for each background reflectance in the light of the work by Graham and myself.

Results from the determination of veg scales based on ratio judgments given by Guilford (1954) show that this scale is by no means

fixed; therefore one cannot refer to *the* veg scale. The best-fitting equations for the veg, determined by three methods given by Guilford (1954, p. 219), are as follows:

Fractionation (halving): $\log V = 1.234 \log S - 2.495$ (22)

Constant sum (two stimuli)[4]: $\log V = 1.0637 \log S - 2.0982$ (23)

Constant sum (five stimuli): $\log V = 1.1760 \log S - 2.2692$ (24)

From the different slope constants in these equations it is seen that vegs vary in size, depending upon the method employed in their determination, the number of stimuli on which the ratio judgments are based, and other factors. From the equations above, vegs are largest by the fractionation method and smallest by the constant-sum method when only two stimuli are being judged. Whenever differences are found which spring from sources such as these, we may be quite sure that different adjustment levels are operative during the process of judging.

Two studies by Guilford and Dingman of ratio-judgment methods (1954) also showed that psychophysical functions established by one method of judging stimuli do not necessarily hold for other methods of judging. They found that Fechner's law was not validated by the method of fractionation but was validated when a modification of the method ef equal-appearing intervals was employed. Woodworth and Schlosberg also pointed out (1954) that equal sense scales, integrated JND's, and halving yield different scales. No one scale, however carefully it is established, can be considered better than other scales obtained under different conditions of judging. The best that can be done is to define the conditions under which a given scale is established. Acceptance of this basic principle would go far toward clearing much of the confusion in present-day psychophysics evidenced by the plethora of concepts, assumptions, and *ad hoc* explanations advanced to account for departures from scales or laws assumed to be universally valid.

Form of psychophysical functions and order of presentation. In a series of experiments, Bevan, Barker, and Pritchard (1963) have shown that the form of ratio scales depends upon temporal and spatial orders of presentation of stimuli. *S*s judged weights in ascending (light to

[4] In the constant-sum method subjects divide 100 in the same ratio that the stimuli bear to one another.

heavy) and descending (heavy to light) orders arranged to be hefted from left to right. Under these conditions Bevan, Barker, and Pritchard obtained an upward bowing curve with ascending order of weights and a downward bowing curve with descending order of weights as

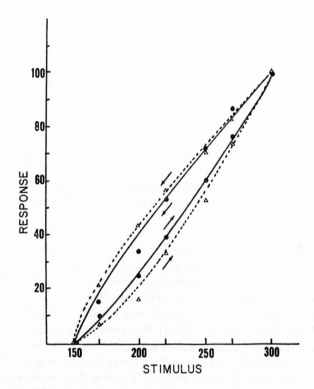

FIG. 4.7. Data of the ascending and descending orders of experiment I are compared with corresponding functions generated from the assumption that the judged difference between stimuli of successive pairs reflects a difference between a shifting adaptation level and the process representing the variable stimulus (second member of each pair). The solid lines indicate the empirical values, the dotted the predicted values. (From Bevan, Barker, and Pritchard, 1963. With the permission of the *Journal of General Psychology*.)

shown in Fig. 4.7. They pointed out that the veg scale corresponds most closely to the upward bowing curve, while JND scales correspond to the downward bowing curve. The Newhall ratio method of responding was employed, in which the end points of the scale are fixed and S adjusts a marker to indicate where the series stimuli fall, and it appears, by this method at least, that ratio scaling can yield positively or negatively accelerated curves depending upon the spatio-temporal order of presentation of stimuli. The opposite curvatures found in the ascending and descending orders of judging also resemble the hysteresis loops of Stevens (1957), which must therefore be regarded as order effects.

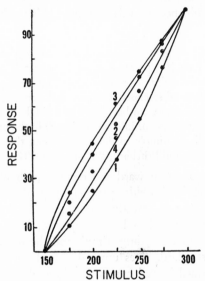

FIG. 4.8. Functions for the four conditions of time and space orders of lifting: (1) L-H, L-R; (2) H-L, R-L; (3) H-L, L-R; (4) L-H, R-L. (From Bevan, Barker and Pritchard, 1963. With the permission of the *Journal of General Psychology*.)

In a second experiment Bevan, Barker, and Pritchard studied additional effects of time and space orders on the hysteresis loops by adding a fourth condition as follows:

1. Light to heavy weights and left to right spatial order
2. Heavy to light weights and right to left spatial order
3. Heavy to light weights and left to right spatial order
4. Light to heavy weights and right to left spatial order

In this experiment only the first stimulus was assigned a scale value, the lightest in ascending order being zero and the heaviest in descending order being 100.

The results shown in Fig. 4.8 confirmed the first experiment and yielded additional information: in light-to-heavy orders upward bowed curves (1 and 4) were found, and in heavy-to-light orders downward bowed curves (2 and 3) were found. The greatest curvatures (1 and 3) were obtained with the left-to-right spatial orders, but the curvatures were opposite due to the effect of heaviness order. Stevens' assumption (1957) that bowing is due to poorer discrimination at the higher end of the scale resulting in greater use of the upper categories cannot apply to these results because this argument holds only for downward bowing curves.

The bowing that Stevens associates with category scales of prothetic dimensions and which is a prerequisite of hysteresis is nowhere apparent [in left to right spatial order of presentation]. The mean settings from left-to-right orders correspond so closely to those of the complementary arrangement that both sets of data seem best fitted by a single straight line. . . . It is clear that it is the direction of intensitive change in the presentation orders of successive stimuli, not simple spatial arrangement, that gives rise to hysteresis (Bevan, Barker, and Pritchard, 1963, pp. 103–104).

An explanation of the upward and downward bowing in terms of shifting adaptation level yields quantitative predictions close to the observed data. Taking the effective stimulus as the difference between the variables being judged and the adaptation level, calculated as a weighted mean of the preceding stimuli and the immediately preceding stimulus as standard, gives upward bowed curves for ascending series and downward bowed curves for descending series of stimuli according to Bevan, Barker, and Pritchard. The divergence between theory and observation (shown in the curves and points in Fig. 4.7) averages 4.3 percent which they consider a highly creditable account of the phenomenon of hysteresis. Bowing cannot, therefore, be written off as due to differences in discriminability for different parts of the stimulus continuum. Rather, bowing depends upon whether the greater stimulus follows or precedes the lesser. The difference between two weights is judged to be greater when the lighter one is presented first than when the heavier is presented first. And this effect, in turn, is related to the decentered position of AL (PSE).

The results reported by Bevan, Barker, and Pritchard, who used a ratio method of judging, confirmed the findings of Guilford (1954), who used the method of paired comparisons, as shown in Table 4.18 and Fig. 4.9. Seven stimulus weights were compared with each stimulus serving as standard. The plots of the data in Fig. 4.9 show that bowing

TABLE 4.18. Proportion Matrix for Seven Lifted Weights Judged by Pairs[a]

Standard Stimuli	185	190	195	200	205	210	215
185	.48	.65	.78	.92	.93	.95	.99
190	.35	.50	.69	.80	.85	.97	.94
195	.22	.31	.48	.63	.72	.89	.91
200	.08	.20	.37	.52	.67	.78	.86
205	.07	.15	.28	.33	.54	.64	.74
210	.05	.03	.11	.22	.36	.46	.62
215	.01	.06	.09	.14	.26	.38	.54

Note: Values in the table represent the number of times that top stimuli were judged heavier than side stimuli.

[a] One subject judged each pair in both time orders a total of 200 times.

SOURCE: From Guilford, Psychometric Methods, 1954a. With the permission of McGraw-Hill Book Company, Inc.

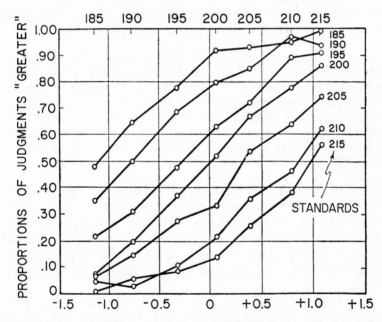

FIG. 4.9. Bowing of curves as a function of AL: With anchors at the low end of the series the curves tend to be negatively accelerated, and with anchors at the high end of the series the curves become positively accelerated. (From Guilford, Psychometric Methods, 1954. With the permission of McGraw-Hill Book Company, Inc.)

depends on position of the standard and hence on PSE or AL. With the three lightest standards, 185, 190 and 195 grm., the plots are negatively accelerated, concave downward curves; with the two intermediate standards, 200 and 205 grm., the curves are fairly linear; and with the two heaviest standards, 210 and 215 grm., the curves are positively accelerated, concave upwards. Thus we find concave, convex, and linear curves in a single sense modality by using the same method of judging when the standards and their resultant ALs change from low, to intermediate, to high values.

While the forms of the curves both in the Bevan, Barker, and Pritchard studies and in the Guilford study are in part determined by certain constraints either in the scales given to *S*s or in the use of percents, similar results have been obtained in determinations of JND's as a function of surround brightness. The usual sigmoid curve showing the number of discriminable brightness steps as a function of the logarithm of intensity of stimulation has, as Evans pointed out (1948),

> . . . little practical significance . . . [because it was obtained] with a relatively small area of light surrounded by a large field in which no light was present. As soon as light is permitted to be present around the split field and the experiment is repeated, radically different results are obtained . . . the presence of a surrounding intensity . . . increases very much the intensity necessary . . . to be perceived as present at all in the central patch, as well as the difference that must be present to be seen as a difference (pp. 104–105).

Instead of the single, S-shaped curve of brightness difference as a function of log intensity, each surround brightness yields its own sensitivity curve. With a completely black surround the curve is negatively accelerated, and as intensity of the surround increases, it changes to a sigmoid curve. At the highest intensity where it is impossible to perceive anything brighter than the surround, the curve becomes positively accelerated.

In the visual situation there is no doubt that the shape of the JND curve is a function of the surround brightness level and with what is known regarding effects of adaptation in all sense modalities it is hard to believe that the *shape* of psychophysical functions is not influenced by factors affecting adaptation levels. The reader interested in some of the practical consequences of these matters should read the entire section in Evans' book devoted to adaptation (1948, pp. 121–129).

Frequencies of judgments. When *S*s judge a series of equally spaced stimuli the judgments are usually not evenly distributed either around the mean judgment or with respect to the stimuli. If the value of PSE is less than the standard, the judgments of series stimuli show a preponderance of greater, heavier, or louder judgments; and if PSE is greater than the standard, there will be a preponderance of smaller, lighter, or softer judgments. Symmetrically spaced stimuli, therefore, do not elicit equal frequencies of judgment categories. It is to be expected that the greater the asymmetry of the series stimuli, whether due to biased magnitudes or to the fact that the stimuli are not presented equally often, the greater will be the asymmetry in the distribution of judgments (cf. Doughty, 1949). In accordance with what we expect, Parducci (1959) obtained more judgments of "larger" when the stimuli were positively skewed (preponderance of smaller stimuli) than with a negatively skewed distribution.

Opinions of various workers are in conflict regarding the possibility of compensating for, or eradicating, so-called "biased" judgment distributions. Doughty asserted that "the experimenter cannot compensate for this psychological asymmetry . . . because he does not know the direction and magnitude of the change . . . occurring as a function of the independent variable" (1949, p. 729). However, Stevens (1956) seemed to believe that "biases" can be overcome because he gave minute directions for achieving a pure category scale. According to the view presented here all distributions of judgments, whether from asymmetrical or symmetrical series of stimuli, may be accounted for by evaluating the contributions of stimulus and residual factors. It is illogical to expect equal frequencies of judgmental categories under all conditions. When AL does not coincide with the mean or median of a set of stimuli we cannot expect a symmetrical or equal-frequency distribution of judgments and the more decentered AL is the more aymmetrical should be the frequencies with which various judgmental categories are employed. Even with symmetrical sets of stimuli we cannot expect equally frequent use of judgmental categories because AL does not usually coincide with the mean or median stimulus of the set. Thus what are regarded by some workers as "biased" judgmental distributions are seen to be natural consequences of decentered ALs.

Resolution of a paradox. Morinaga and Noguchi (1960) found that judgments of lightness of stimuli on white, gray, and black backgrounds increased as the illuminances on the stimuli increased from 4 to 160 lux. In view of this finding they believed that the level of illuminance should be incorporated in the weighted log mean definition of adaptation level because the reflectances of the stimuli did not (of course) change. That such a complication of the definition is unnecessary is immediately apparent from a priori considerations as well as from experimental results obtained earlier by Helson and Kelly (unpublished study, 1955). The difference between *adaptation reflectance* and *adaptation luminance* must be kept in mind when dealing with visual problems, as is evident from the data in Table 4.19. The judgments of 20 grays on black, gray, and white backgrounds in daylight with an illuminance of 2650 ft.L. were higher on all backgrounds than they were when viewed with an illuminance of 0.21 ft.L. in accordance with the findings of Morinaga and Noguchi. Paradoxically, as seen in Table 4.19, the *adaptation reflectances* are lower in daylight than in dim illumination, but this must occur to yield higher lightness values in daylight when lightness is calculated by Judd's formula embodying AL (Helson, 1938). Hence no additional terms are needed in either the weighted log mean definition or the lightness formula to account for such findings as those of Morinaga and Noguchi and ourselves.

The lower *adaptation reflectances* in high illuminance as compared with the adaptation reflectances in dim viewing conditions may appear paradoxical but the data in Table 4.19 show that the *adaptation lumi-*

TABLE 4.19.   Adaptation Reflectance vs. Adaptation Luminance
under Conditions of High and Low Illuminance

Condition of Observation	Adaptation Reflectance			Adaptation Luminance (mL)		
	Background			Background		
	White	Gray	Black	White	Gray	Black
Daylight	27.0	24.8	21.5	716.6	658.0	570.8
Dim fluorescent	31.5	28.1	25.8	0.07	0.06	0.05

SOURCE: From Helson and Kelly, 1955.

nances were very much higher in the brighter illuminance. Although the ratio of black to white backgrounds employed in this study was 33:1, the ratio of adaptation reflectances was only 7:5. This result points to a high degree of lightness constancy, partly due to the use of a fixed numerical scale for judging under all conditions. The lightness judgments varied far less than did either the reflectances of the backgrounds or the illuminances. The great differences in level between bright and dim viewing conditions are shown in the *adaptation luminances* which were as follows: 716.6 and 0.07 ft.L. with white backgrounds; 658.0 and 0.06 ft.L. with gray backgrounds; 570.8 and 0.05 ft.L. with black backgrounds. The average ratio of ALs in bright to dim illuminance was over 10,000:1 and hence was not far from the ratio of illuminances (12,620:1). This finding provides additional evidence in support of the principle that ALs tend to approximate levels of stimulation.

Determination of the weighting constants by fitting to data. Since the value of AL depends upon stimulus conditions and personal factors, the constants of the weighted log mean equation must be determined by experimentation. The demand, often made that a theory should "predict" values of constants in equations, while naïve, is not entirely unreasonable. Do the constants that fit a given set of conditions hold for other conditions? If series stimuli are weighted more heavily than background stimuli in one sense modality, will they also be weighted more heavily in another sense modality? Do the weighting coefficients change when another psychophysical method is employed? Such questions are legitimate and can be answered within the framework of AL theory. There is no way of specifying the values of constants in advance of experimentation unless they follow from constants previously established. Thus weighting the log mean of series stimuli by three and the background stimuli by unity and using 0.75×step-interval between weights gave good approximations to the stimulus judged medium in a wide variety of conditions as shown in Tables 4.1, 4.2, and 4.5. If more complicated tasks, different psychophysical methods, or other types of stimuli are employed, different weighting coefficients for series and background stimuli may be necessary to fit obtained data. Furthermore, residual effects that could be ignored here may be very important in other situations.

The fact that the weighted log mean equation predicted the neutral stimulus for a wide variety of series-background conditions and various distributions of series stimuli (including skewed, square, linear and normal distributions) with a single set of weighting constants served to establish the validity of the fundamental hypothesis of AL theory: the organism performs as an integrating (averaging) mechanism in the manner postulated by the theory. If exact determination of AL is desired, the constants in the weighted log mean equation should not be assumed a priori but should be determined a posteriori from experimental data just as thresholds, PSE, and other psychophysical parameters are derived. This was done by Philip (1949) who used the weighted log mean definition of AL to determine the relative contributions of three variables entering into judgments of time from data previously published by Turchioe (1948). In this experiment Ss were required to duplicate time intervals of 780, 1,010, and 1,390 msec. The average intervals reproduced by the subjects for each comparison stimulus, C, were taken by Philip to be the observed ALs. The time interval between cessation of the standard and the reproduction was first 1 sec. and later 2 sec., S_1 and S_2. The comparison or standard stimuli were presented in random order; Philip therefore assumed that they pooled as series stimuli and their log mean was taken as a series effect. Since the observations were made in two sessions, the data of each session were evaluated separately by the following equations:

$$\log A_1 = \frac{k_1 \Sigma \log X_1}{3} + k_2 C + k_3 S_1 \tag{25}$$

$$\log A_2 = \frac{k_1 \Sigma \log X_i}{3} + k_2 C + k_3 S_2 \tag{26}$$

Setting $k_1 + k_2 + k_3 = 1$ and substituting experimental values for A_1, A_2, X_i, C, S_1, and S_2, Philip found the following weighting coefficients for each of the experimental variables by solving the resultant simultaneous equations:

$$\log A_1 = \frac{0.3068 \Sigma \log X_i}{3} + 0.6549 \log C + 0.0383 \log S_1 \tag{27}$$

$$\log A_2 = \frac{0.3604 \Sigma \log X_i}{3} + 0.6015 \log C + 0.0381 \log S_2 \tag{28}$$

From the values of the constants, it is apparent that the comparison stimulus being judged was about twice as important in influencing the time interval reproduced by the Ss as was the pooled effect of all the standards. It is also apparent that the interval from the end of the comparison stimulus to the beginning of the response had a constant but very small effect. Furthermore, the change in value of the weights for the series and comparison stimuli showed that residuals of comparison stimuli exerted somewhat more effect on the judgments in the second session than in the first session. This was at the expense of the comparison stimulus in the immediate focus of attention. These conclusions could not have been reached if the usual methods had been applied to Turchioe's data. Philip agreed with the view of the author:

> An important use . . . of these equations concerns the evaluation of factors which hitherto have not been given quantitative expression and so have not been capable of experimental verification. Assumptions concerning remote anchors, general frames of reference, and past experience can now be tested and quantitatively evaluated (Helson, 1947, p. 7).

FUNCTIONS EMBODYING ADAPTATION LEVEL

Since the value of adaptation level merely fixes a point or narrow region on the stimulus continuum, exact prediction of all responses must be determined by means of stimulus-response functions covering the whole continuum. While certain broad generalizations can be made concerning types of responses once the value of the adaptation level is known, other more detailed predictions can be made only if the exact shape of the stimulus-response function is known. The shape of the stimulus-judgment curve depends on many factors, e.g., on the stimuli being judged, the task given Ss, the psychophysical method, the method of treating experimental data, the position of the adaptation level or PSE. Important characteristics of judging and responding are revealed in the shapes of the curves fitting experimental data. Since AL may be incorporated into any function as a parameter, let us consider some of the chief types of stimulus-response relations.

1. When equally spaced stimuli give rise to equally spaced judgments throughout the stimulus range a straight line fits the data. This is something that seldom happens and usually only over restricted ranges of the stimulus continuum.

2. If changes in magnitude of "small" stimuli give rise to greater changes in judgment than do equal changes in larger stimuli, negatively accelerated curves fit the data. Such curves may be made linear by taking the logs of the stimuli. These curves show spreading of judgments at the low end of the stimulus range and assimilation at the high end.

3. If differences in stimuli at the low end of the continuum are less

well discriminated than are similar differences at the high end, positively accelerated functions fit this case. Judgments at the low end of the stimulus range are bunched while those in the medium and high ranges are spread out. Power functions or their related log-log inverses fit these first three cases, the exponent of the power function, or the slope of the log-log inverse, being less than unity for negatively accelerated curves, greater than unity for positively accelerated curves, and unity for linear functions.

4. When judgments are bunched at both the low and the high ends of the stimulus continuum but spread out in the intermediate range, S-shaped or ogive curves may furnish good fits to such data. This type of curve also is found when frequencies of responses are plotted as percentages because of the limiting values 0 and 100 percent. The method of constant stimuli with the data plotted as percentages yields ogive curves.

Still other types of functions may yield good fits to experimental data. Measures equivalent to AL, such as PSE in the constant method, may be derived from rating-scale procedures. We shall consider a number of functions that yield measures of AL or cognate values.

In rating-scale procedures Ss judge a series of stimuli by means of verbal categories, such as very very light, through medium, to very very heavy, or by means of numbers. The categories may be employed freely by Ss who may assign any category to any stimulus; or various constraints may be introduced such as requiring Ss to assign certain categories to certain stimuli, e.g., the highest category or numerical value to the heaviest stimulus and the lowest to the lightest stimulus. Since the distribution of judgments depends greatly upon the manner in which Ss are instructed to use rating scales, the shape of the curve embodying the relation between stimuli and responses will be affected by the constraints imposed on the use of the categories. Thus free use of a numerical scale for judging loudness may yield a negatively accelerated curve but the requirement that the number 1 be assigned to the softest sound and the number 20 to the loudest sound may yield an S-shaped curve though the stimuli are the same in the two cases.[5] Or if the number assigned to the loudest stimulus is successively lowered, a family of parallel curves is obtained showing that judgments

[5] This statement is based partly upon results reported by W. R. Garner (personal communication).

of all the stimuli have shifted downward (Long, 1937). The shape of the psychophysical function may be varied by still other constraints.

Psychophysical functions, therefore, are not quantitative statements of pure sensitivity or scales embodying only fixed psychological intervals, sense distances, or ratios. They involve more than relations of psychological magnitudes to physical magnitudes and they also reveal the manner in which Ss respond under the conditions of judgment imposed by E. All conditions combine to determine the response level of the organism and if AL is introduced as a parameter in psychophysical functions, many factors affecting responses can be subsumed under a single concept.

Two functions (Helson, 1948; Michels and Helson, 1949) embodying AL which yield negatively accelerated curves will first be discussed. In deriving these functions a continuum of some measurable attribute of a set of stimuli was assumed such that X_i is any given value of stimulus, and A is the value of adaptation level under the given conditions of stimulation. The value of A need not have the value of any stimulus in the set. We also assume that a finite number of stimuli elicits judgments representative of the continuum. The step intervals between stimuli need not be equal and the standard or anchor stimulus may be one of the series stimuli or may lie entirely outside the series. The judgment scale may be either qualitative or quantitative; but if qualitative categories are employed, they should be equally spaced and symmetrical about the middle category. However, Jones, Peryam, and Thurstone (1955) have shown these conditions are not necessary in judging some types of stimuli. Ss may interpolate or add categories especially at the extremes. In our experiments Ss were never asked to *scale* stimuli; they were asked only to judge how heavy weights felt, how light or dark neutral or colored papers appeared, or how loud sounds were. Scaling was only a by-product of the judgments. In this respect our procedure has differed from the usual scaling procedures.

The two functions embodying AL as a parameter discussed in this section have been employed in fitting data obtained by a variety of methods (Helson, 1948; Michels and Helson, 1949; Helson, Michels, and Sturgeon, 1954; Helson and Himelstein, 1955). They have been found especially applicable to data obtained from the so-called absolute method of judgment and the method of comparative ratings in which variables are judged with respect to standards. For example, the following verbal rating scales have been widely used with the numerical values assigned them for purposes of computation:

Absolute Judgments of Single Stimuli		Comparative Ratings with a Standard	
Very very light	1	Very much lighter	1
Very light	2	Much lighter	2
Light	3	Lighter	3
Medium-light	4	Little lighter	4
Medium	5	Equal	5
Medium-heavy	6	Little heavier	6
Heavy	7	Heavier	7
Very heavy	8	Much heavier	8
Very very heavy	9	Very much heavier	9

Both types of scales have considerable flexibility in that they may be modified in various ways. The absolute scale may be left open so that Ss may introduce more extreme categories at both ends with numbers assigned them accordingly. The comparative rating scale allows introduction of smaller steps between categories if desired, e.g., "barely equal," with numbers assigned in accordance with the fraction of the whole interval implied by the interpolated category.

The first function was derived on the following assumptions (Helson, 1948): (1) Response to, or judgment of, a stimulus depends upon its "distance" from AL which, in physical units, is equal to $X_i - A$. (2) Psychological distance of a stimulus from AL is related to the number of JND's in the interval $X_i - A$. (3) The JND is a function of both the stimulus being judged and AL, or $\Delta A = f(X_i, A)$. Dividing $(X_i - A)$ by $f(X_i, A)$ yields the desired psychophysical interval reflected in the response to a stimulus, so we write

$$J = \frac{X_i - A}{f(X_i, A)} \qquad (29)$$

where J is the judgment in terms of a linear numerical scale. We now have to determine $f(X_i, A)$ to obtain an expression yielding J as a function of the stimuli and AL. In the original derivation it was assumed that $f(X_i, A)$ was the Weber constant, k, operating on the *average* of the stimulus and AL giving

$$f(X_i, A) = \frac{k(X_i + A)}{2} \qquad (30)$$

This assumption involves equal weighting of the stimulus and AL, an assumption that may or may not be true and later will be shown to be unnecessary. Since k is a constant, we may transfer $k/2$ from the denominator to the numerator, calling it K, so that Equation (30) becomes

$$J = \frac{K(X_i - A)}{X_i + A} \qquad (31)$$

According to Equation (31) when $X_i = A$, $J = 0$. This means that a stimulus coinciding with AL evokes a zero or neutral response and this value of X_i fixes the equilibrium point of the organism for the

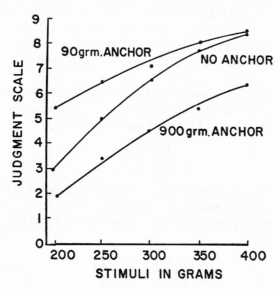

FIG. 4.10. Lifted-weight data fitted by negatively accelerated curves [Equation (39)] showing typical anchor effects: a very heavy anchor with resultant high AL depresses judgments; a very light anchor with resultant low AL raises judgments. The curve for judgments of series stimuli without anchor falls between the other two curves.

conditions under which the judgments are made. The J vs. X_i curve yielded by Equation (31) is a negatively accelerated curve differing from both the linear function of Weber and the ogive function of Müller and Urban. As seen from Fig. 4.10 this curve is not symmetric with respect to A and thus squares with the usual finding that PSE, which is equivalent to A, does not coincide with the arithmetic mean of the series stimuli.

So far it would appear that the J values yielded by Equation (31) simply express the number of JND's between A and the stimulus, X_i. This would be true if Ss actually based their judgments on the number of JND's between stimuli and AL when using rating scales. Since Ss are not able to make such estimates, the usefulness of Equation (31) is extremely limited. It possesses properties that make it unnecessary to use actual values of the Weber fraction although it did enter into the derivation of this equation. K simply becomes a scale factor if (1) the numerical scale into which qualitative categories are transformed is a linear one, (2) qualitative categories are linear with the numerical scale chosen for purposes of computation, and (3) K is the topmost value of the numerical scale with the center of the rating scale represented by a value equal to $0.5K$, the judgment elicited by the stimulus at AL.

To prove that all numerical scales satisfying the above conditions are equivalent and yield identical values of A by the least-squares criterion we transform Equation (31) into linear form giving

$$\frac{K+J}{K-J} = \frac{X_i}{A} \tag{32}$$

Let Q be the topmost value of any numerical scale other than the K scale such that $Q = cK$. Then all J values in the Q scale are multiplied by c so that the J values in the Q scale become $J' = cJ$. We have to show that

$$\frac{K+J}{K-J} = \frac{Q+J'}{Q-J'} \tag{33}$$

Substituting cK and cJ for Q and J' we obtain

$$\frac{K+J}{K-J} = \frac{cK+cJ}{cK-cJ} \tag{34}$$

or

$$\frac{K+J}{K-J} = \frac{c(K+J)}{c(K-J)} \tag{35}$$

which is seen to an identity. Furthermore, since the left-hand side of Equation (35) is dimensionless, we no longer need to know the value of the Weber constant, k, in order to use Equation (32). We can, there-fore, choose our numerical scale arbitrarily so far as the computations are concerned; but if Ss judge in numerical terms the scale should be linear and symmetrical and should satisfy various other requirements necessitated by the task.

Returning to Equation (32) we note that it is a linear function of the form $Y = mX + b$ where $Y = (K + J)/(K - J)$, $m = 1/A$ and $b = 0$. Since we shall use Equation (32) to determine the best value of A from experimental data by the method of least squares, the con-stant b should be retained in order to utilize the added degree of free-dom it affords in getting the best-fitting curve. When b is added explicitly to Equation (32), it is necessary to substitute A' for A giving

$$\frac{K + J}{K - J} = \frac{X_i}{A'} + b \qquad (36)$$

With the explicit introduction of b, the y intercept, into Equation (36) and rewriting Equation (36) to leave only J on the left-hand side, we have

$$J = \frac{K(X_i - A' + bA')}{X_i + A' + bA'} \qquad (37)$$

If this equation is solved for $X_i = A(J = 0)$ we find that

$$A = A' - bA' \qquad (38)$$

Rewriting Equation (37) in terms of A instead of A' we have

$$J = \frac{K(X_i - A)}{X_i + (1 + b/1 - b)A} \qquad (39)$$

We now see that the assumption that X_i and A are equally weighted in determining J is no longer necessary since b is derived from observed data. We have thus been able to replace the original assumptions in-volving the Weber constant and JND's by the single simple assumption expressed in Equation (39): Rating scale judgments are given by the difference between any stimulus and prevailing AL divided by a suit-ably weighted sum of the values of the stimulus and AL. Only when $b = 0$ are the weighting coefficients for X_i and A equal in determin-ing J.

Best-fitting values of A and b in Equation (39) can be obtained by the method of least squares, as shown in the worked example of Table

A in the Appendix, through the use of Equation (41) below. If a numerical scale of 1–10 is employed, the work of fitting is considerably shortened through the use of the tabled values of the left-hand side of Equation (41) given in Table B of the Appendix.

So far the development has been in terms of numerical scales such that a stimulus equal to A, $X_i = A$, will yield a J value of zero and this means that the numerical scale is centered at zero and J values are plus or minus deviates from the center of the scale. If it is desired to eliminate negative J's and yet let the center of the scale represent the judgment of the stimulus coinciding with A, we must add $0.5K$ to Equation (37) giving

$$J = \frac{K(X_i - A' + bA')}{X_i + A' + bA'} + 0.5K \tag{40}$$

which, when transformed into linear form is

$$\frac{0.5K + J}{1.5K - J} = \frac{X_i}{A'} + b \tag{41}$$

In determining the best fitting values of A' and b by the least-squares method the Y-values are now the left-hand side of Equation (41) and the slope, m, is equal to $1/A'$. A table of values of the function $(0.5K + J)/(1.5K - J)$ has been published (Helson and Himelstein, 1955) and is reproduced in Table B of the Appendix for a numerical scale in which the topmost value, K, is equal to 10. Since Equation (41) is in linear form we can use the normal equations for the slope and Y intercept of linear functions to determine the best-fitting values of A' and b as follows:

$$\frac{1}{A'} = \frac{\Sigma XY - nM_x M_y}{\Sigma X^2 - nM_x^2} \tag{42}$$

and

$$b = M_y - \frac{1}{A'} M_x \tag{43}$$

These equations have been used to determine values of AL from experimental data (Helson, 1948; Helson and Rohles, 1959; and Helson and Himelstein, 1955). For theoretical purposes, however, a much more powerful tool will be found in the reformulated Fechner law (Michels and Helson, 1949) to which we now turn.

The reformulated Fechner law. The second function embodying AL as a parameter proved to be formally identical with the Fechner law but materially the two are very different. The Fechner law,

$$S = K \log \frac{R}{R_o} \qquad (44)$$

where S is the magnitude of sensation evoked by the stimulus, R, and R_o is the stimulus at absolute threshold, assumes that the absolute threshold functions as a constant in the determination of all sensory magnitudes. In the reformulated law, which will be derived presently, the absolute threshold is replaced by AL as the origin with respect to which judgments are made and sensory magnitudes are determined. AL can be anywhere on the stimulus continuum and is affected by all the stimuli being judged as well as by personal, residual factors. Furthermore, with AL as the origin in place of the absolute threshold, the difficulty of negative sensory magnitudes, one of the chief objections to the Fechner law, is no longer present. Stimuli below AL arouse positive responses no less than do stimuli above AL. Sense modalities exhibiting bipolar continua with neutral regions separating positive and negative qualities such as vision and the temperature senses are accounted for without special assumptions in the reformulated law. Similarly, the present theory differs also from the Müller-Urban psychometric function which can handle only one type of judgment category at a time, such as "heavier" or "lighter." Other properties of the present function will be discussed following its derivation.

In deriving the reformulated Fechner law five assumptions were made by Michels and Helson (1949):[6]

1. The Weber law is valid within sufficiently broad limits to be applicable.

2. The judgment "neutral" or "medium" belongs to the stimulus $X = A$, where A is the adaptation level.

3. The judgment scale and the stimuli encountered are *equivalent* in the sense that the scale is broad enough to include judgments of all the stimuli encountered and yet is so narrow that its extreme values do not fall outside the range of judgments elicited by any of the stimuli.

4. When an observer adjusts his responses to a series of $2N + 1$ categories ($2N$ steps), symmetrically placed about "neutral," he does

[6] The following account is reprinted with the permission of the *American Journal of Psychology.*

so by choosing as the first step below "neutral" the response corresponding to a stimulus of intensity $(1 - 1/N)A$. In other words, he responds as if he had divided the stimulus A into N equal parts and had used all but one of these for his first step below "neutral."

5. In forming his judgments, the observer can make comparisons only in terms of the judgment scale. This means that all subsequent steps will have the same size on the judgment scale as the first step and that the adaptation level will be determined by a *mean of judgments* rather than by a mean of stimuli.

The assumptions are sufficient to determine a relation between judgment and stimulus under constant conditions of adaptation. In accordance with the first and fifth assumptions, the steps corresponding to equal changes ΔJ in the judgment J are connected with changes ΔX in the stimulus X by the relation

$$\Delta J = \frac{k\Delta X}{X} \tag{45}$$

where k is a constant. The fourth assumption supplies a value for the constant of Equation (45) since we have

$$-1 = \frac{k(-A/N)}{A} = \frac{-k}{N} \tag{46}$$

where $k = N$ and

$$\Delta J = \frac{N\Delta X}{X} \tag{47}$$

Applying this relation to find the stimuli which correspond to unit steps on the judgment scale, we find near the adaptation level the following sequence:

Judgment (J) . . . ,
$C - 2$, $C - 1$, C, $C + 1$, $C + 2$, . . .
Stimulus (X) . . . ,

$$A\left(\frac{1-1}{N}\right)^2, \quad A\frac{1-1}{N}, \quad A, \quad \frac{A}{1 - 1/N}, \quad \frac{A}{(1 - 1/N)^2} \cdots$$

where C is the "neutral" judgment. It is clear that the judgment X_n which invokes a response $J_n = C + n$ is

$$X_n = A(1 - 1/N)^{-n} \tag{48}$$

This relation holds for both positive and negative n and it may be easily shown by induction that it holds for all permissible values of n (that is, $-N \lessgtr n \lessgtr N$). Passing to logarithms and solving for n, we find that

$$J_n = C + n = C + K \log \frac{X_n}{A} \qquad (49)^{[7]}$$

where

$$K = \frac{-1}{\log (1 - 1/N)} \qquad (50)$$

It follows immediately that if the adaptation level is determined by a group of s stimuli X_i, *of equal statistical weight*, the adaptation level will be the geometric mean of the stimuli. According to assumption 5, the "neutral" judgment C is the mean of the individual judgments J_i. Hence,

$$C = \sum_1^s i\frac{J_i}{s} = C + \frac{K}{s} \sum_1^s i \log X_i - K \log A \qquad (51)$$

Since the summation occurring in the second term on the right is the logarithm of the product of the X_i which, in turn, is s times the logarithm of the geometric mean X_m of the X_i, we have

$$C = C + K \log \frac{X_m}{A} \qquad (52)$$

an identity which is satisfied only if

$$X_m = A \qquad (53)$$

If the stimuli which determine the adaptation level are not of equal statistical weight, a weighted geometric mean must be taken. Such cases occur, for example, when the adaptation is to a group of stimuli which differ in spatial or temporal remoteness from the stimulus being judged.

In using Equation (51) to find the adaptation level, one precaution must be used if the stimuli vary over a wide range. The lowest judgment on the scale is

$$J_{-N} = C + K \log \frac{X_{-N}}{A} \qquad (54)$$

[7] In this and all subsequent equations in the derivation of the reformulated Fechner law, the logarithms are to the natural base e.

Hence all stimuli of intensity less than that given for X_{-N} by the equation

$$\log X_{-N} = \frac{J_{-N} - C + K \log A}{K} \qquad (55)$$

will be judged as equivalent to X_{-N} and must be so counted in computing A. In particular, when the judgment scale is represented by the integers 0, 1, 2, . . . , 2N, we have $C = N$ and $J_{-N} = 0$, so that

$$\log X_{-N} = \log A - \frac{N}{K} = \log A + N \log \frac{1 - 1/N}{N} \qquad (56)$$

If N is large, this reduces to the approximate expression

$$\log X_{-N} = \log A - 1 \qquad (57)$$

so that all stimuli lower than the adaptation level by a factor of more than $1/e$ (e = Naperian base) will evoke zero judgment.

Similarly, it may be shown that the highest rating on the judgment scale, J_N, belongs to all stimuli of intensity greater than that given by Equation (55) with J_{-N} replaced by J_N. In the case of the zero to 2N scale with N large, all stimuli which are greater than e times the adaptation level evoke this maximal response. Combining our results for the upper and lower limits of distinguishable stimuli, we see that the ratio of these extremes is e^2 for the case of N large, or is somewhat greater than this for N small. This result is in accord with the commonly observed fact that satisfactory judgments of the relative intensities of rapidly changing stimuli cannot be made if the range of stimuli is appreciably greater than one decade.

It is clear that the slope of the J vs. $\log X$ curve will depend upon the judgment scale used. As the number of categories is increased, the slope K is also increased, in accordance with Equation (50). There is, however, an upper limit to the slope for a particular type of stimulus, since a single step cannot be smaller than the just noticeable difference. In other words, $1/N$ in Equation (50) cannot be smaller than the Weber constant. If attempts are made to use a continuous scale of judgment or one of a very large number of steps, we can expect that the scale will be equivalent to one of $(1 + 2/w)$ steps, where w is the Weber constant. The slope of the J vs. $\log X$ curve will therefore be $-1/\log(1 - w)$. If w in such cases is much less than unity or if N in any case is much greater than unity, Equation (50) can be approximated closely by putting $\log(1 - 1/N)$ equal to $-1/N$, so that the slope becomes $K = N$ or $K = 1/w$.

The above equations were derived under the assumption of constant adaptation. In practice, however, we cannot expect the adaptation level to remain constant since it will be affected by the stimulus being judged. Thus, in visual observations, the eye begins to adapt itself to the brightness of a reflecting sample very quickly, so that the sample grows lighter or darker during the early part of the observation, depending on whether the adaptation level at the beginning of the observation was below or above the reflectance of the sample. Similar effects occur with other types of stimuli. Suppose that the adaptation level before it is affected by adaptation to the stimulus (X) is A'. We may group the effects of all residual and background stimuli into this A'. Let the relative weight of the stimulus in determining the adaptation level be p, which we shall call the *self-adaptation coefficient*. Then, according to Equation (51) the adaptation level is determined by the relation

$$\log A = (1 - p) \log A' + p \log X \qquad (58)$$

Substitution of this value into Equation (49) gives

$$\begin{aligned} J &= C + K \log X - K(1 - p) \log A' - Kp \log X \\ &= C + K(1 - p) \log X - K(1 - p) \log A \end{aligned} \qquad (59)$$

We may rewrite this equation as

$$J = C + K' \log \frac{X}{A'} \qquad (60)$$

by making

$$K' = K(1 - p) \qquad (61)$$

We therefore see that the effect of self-adaptation is to change the slope of the J vs. $\log X$ curve from the value K, determined by the judgment scale used, to the observable slope K'. The linearity of the curve is maintained, and the observed adaptation level (i.e., the stimulus which elicits the "neutral" judgment) is identical with that which would have been observed had there been no self-adaptation. These results are of interest in connection with the conclusions of Judd (1940) and Spencer (1943) that there is in visual judgments a separate adaptation level for each stimulus intensity. According to the present treatment, the variation of A with X does not prevent the direct determination of the constant A'.

It follows from Equation (51) that the adaptation level may be expressed in terms of the three classes of stimuli as

$$A = X^p X_b{}^q X_r{}^r \tag{62}$$

Hence

$$\log A = p \log X + q \log X_b + r \log X_r \tag{63}$$

By comparison of Equations (58) and (63) we see that

$$\log A' = \frac{q \log X_b + r \log X_r}{1 - p} \tag{64}$$

Finally, since we have included in our three classes all stimuli affecting the adaptation level we see that the sum of the three weighting factors must be unity, or that

$$p + q + r = 1 \tag{65}$$

Let us consider one of the applications of the reformulated Fechner law which enables us to solve a difficulty in the classical Fechner law. In Equation (49) adaptation level replaces the absolute threshold as the origin or unit of measurement. Guilford (1954) fitted a log function to numerousness data obtained by the method of equal-appearing intervals in which cards containing groups of dots ranging from 15 to 74 had to be sorted into *nine* piles. The equation of best fit was:

$$R = 9.41 \log S - 9.36 \tag{66}$$

where R is the response to the stimulus S. Treating the constant, 9.36, as is usually done in applications of the Fechner law, Guilford found the absolute threshold (S_o) as follows:

$$9.36 = 9.41 \log S_o$$

or

$$\log S_o = \frac{9.36}{9.41} = 0.995 \tag{67}$$

from which S_o turns out to be 9.9 or 10 dots at absolute threshold. But the absolute threshold for perception of a group of dots, especially under the conditions of observation in Guilford's experiment, was certainly not 10 dots. Guilford suggested that perhaps S_o is not the absolute threshold but rather the threshold of change in perception of dots, found by Taves (1941) at about 7 dots. But this raises the question, as Guilford pointed out, of whether the discrepancy between 7 and 10 is significant.

We may apply the reformulated Fechner law as given in Equation (49) above by assuming with Guilford that the piles represent category scale values and, further, that the average or median number of dots on the cards in the fifth pile represents the response coinciding with AL. We can then solve Equation (49) for the stimulus coinciding with AL (S_A) by letting $C = 5$, giving

$$5 = 9.41 \log S_A - 9.36$$

or

$$\log S_A = \frac{14.36}{9.41} = 1.5260 \qquad (68)$$

By taking the anti-log of 1.5260 we find that the theoretical number of dots acting as the frame of reference was 33.6 which is close to the observed median value of 5.0 given to 32 dots. The value of 33.6 is also close to the value of 34.2 found by fitting Equation (39) to the same data. We can now interpret the value of S_o found by Guilford as the number of dots one step below the first category used in his experiment rather than as the absolute threshold.

The reformulated Fechner law has provided theoretical interpretations of the bril scale (Michels, 1954), the veg scale (Michels and Helson, 1954b), and comparative loudness measurements (Michels and Doser, 1955). It has also been extended to data obtained by the comparative rating scale (CRS) wherein ratings are made with respect to standard stimuli. Space permits detailed discussion of applications of the present theory only to TOE and CRS to which we shall turn following consideration of salient experimental findings regarding time-order effects and comparative rating judgments.

TIME–ORDER EFFECTS (TOE) AS MANIFESTATIONS OF LEVEL

From a logical and physical point of view identical stimuli are equal yet they do not always appear to be so in perception, for if Ss are asked to judge identical sounds, weights, brightnesses, temporal intervals, and so on, they are usually perceived to be different when presented successively. Mere differences in position also suffice to make identical objects appear different. Effects due to order and position of stimuli have long been known as time-order and space-order "errors" (TOE and SOE). A typical time-order effect appears when one judges two weights by lifting first one, then the other. The second may feel heavier 70 percent of the time and either lighter or equal in the remaining 30 percent. The weight judged equal to a standard of 100 grm. is about 98.0 grm. By employing a set of comparison stimuli it is possible to determine the value of stimulus perceived to be equal to the standard (S). This value of stimulus is usually called the point of subjective equality (PSE). When PSE is less than S, there is said to be a negative TOE, and when greater a positive TOE. With variables symmetrically grouped around the standard it is evident that negative TOE entails a preponderance of overestimations and positive TOE entails a preponderance of underestimations of the standard since TOE = PSE — S. Since PSE represents the value of stimulus evoking an equality or null response, PSE and AL are identical. The value of PSE or AL thus indicates whether there is an excess of over- or underestimations in psychophysical judgments.

Traditionally it was believed that TOE arose, as its name implies, from the effect of the time between presentations of standard and variables; but when TOE was found with the method of single stimuli where stimuli are judged without reference to an external standard, this view had to be abandoned. For example, if stimuli are judged singly in terms of a numerical or qualitative rating scale, the average or central stimulus is not usually assigned the central value of the scale. That is, when the organism is stimulated symmetrically, it does not respond symmetrically; responses usually center on a lower value than the mean or median of the stimulus distribution.

In discussing so-called time-errors it is necessary to distinguish between effects on judgments due to order of presentation of standard and variables and effects due to time as such. It is now agreed that effects of time require an interval greater than 3 sec. between standard and variable whereas TOE appears in much shorter intervals. TOE is more common because most psychophysical judgments involve less than three sec. intervals between standard and variables. Our discussion will be limited to TOE which is usually negative in lifted weights and often not found at all in experiments with sounds, although both positive and negative TOE have been reported in this sense modality. Needham, in his review of time errors in comparison judgments felt that "a single explanatory concept should suffice for both positive and negative time errors" (1934, p. 239). The theory proposed here is an attempt to arrive at such a single explanatory concept.

We have seen that Equations (2), (3), and (4) give values of AL *below* the center of the series in time-order S_1V_2 with lifted weights when judgments are made with or without anchors or comparison stimuli; hence negative TOE is immediately derived from the weighted log mean definition of AL without further assumptions. Data from Woodrow (1933) showing negative TOE are presented in Table 4.20

TABLE 4.20. Prediction of Negative Time-Order Effect

Series with 110-grm. Standard			Series with 200-grm. Standard		
	Percent Heavier			Percent Heavier	
Stimuli	V First	V Second	Stimuli	V First	V Second
106.7	28	45	194.0	28	45
110.0	40	60	200.0	37	63
113.3	56	73	206.0	56	77
116.6	65	86	212.0	74	89
119.9	78	91	218.0	81	97
50% observed	112.1	108.7		204.1	195.7
AL calculated	112.4	109.9		204.3	199.8

SOURCE: From Woodrow, 1933. With the permission of the *American Journal of Psychology.*

as an example of the normal case accounted for by Equation (2). Percentages of heavier judgments are given for lifted weights in two time orders, S_1V_2 and V_1S_2. Observed 50 percent points calculated by linear interpolation and ALs calculated by Equation (2) are also given. In calculating AL for S_1V_2, $0.75d$ is used to take account of the step interval between series stimuli, and for V_1S_2, since the step intervals are reversed, d is assumed to be zero. Agreement between observation and theory in Table 4.20 is remarkably close. Since the standards were below the centers of the series in both cases we have accounted for the asymmetry in judgments due both to TOE and to decentered standards. Normal negative TOE is thus correctly predicted by AL theory for both S_1V_2 and V_1S_2 orders of presenting series and standard stimuli.

In the study from which these data were taken, Woodrow presented results showing reversal of TOE from negative to positive as the weights of standards and series were reduced. Woodrow's experimental design consisted in mixing variables and standards over a very wide range indiscriminately (though each stimulus in a series was always compared with its own standard). The experimental situation is therefore too complicated to apply Equation (4) since many assumptions are possible regarding the interactions of the stimuli and standards. Furthermore, the results are presented as averages of two series and standards, which may conceal differences important for theory. No attempt will be made therefore to predict these other data of Woodrow although his discussion of them is in line with the theory proposed here. Woodrow uses the concept of level in accounting for his results, and he postulates an underlying set towards a certain intensity as comparisons are made which "tends to approximate the average intensity of all the preceding stimuli of the entire series from the beginning of the experimental sitting" (1933, p. 409). He also points out that this average must be thought of as a *weighted average* in which the most recent stimuli have greater weight than earlier stimuli and the last stimulus carries greatest weight of all (Woodrow, 1935; 1937; Woodrow and Stott, 1936).

Although TOE appears in results obtained by the method of absolute judgment where no time interval between standard and variables is involved, there can be no question that the time factor, when present, can influence judgments to a marked degree through its influence on the effective standard. A study by Needham (1935) on the effect of temporal interval between standard and variables on judgments of loudness of four sets of stimuli, each with its own standard, provides clear demonstration of shift away from the comparison stimulus toward the AL of all the stimuli acting as the effective standard. In Needham's study the stimuli in each of four sets were grouped symmetrically about the comparison stimulus in steps of plus or minus 2, 1, and 0 db. The standard or comparison stimuli were 30, 40, 50, and 60 db. above threshold. The 20 pairs of stimuli were presented *in haphazard order* with respect to both intensive level and position within each series thus favoring establishment of an AL determined by all the sets. Intervals of 1, 3, and 6 sec. between standard and variable stimuli were introduced, observations with one time interval being completed before another was employed. The results show that with increasing time between comparison and variable stimuli the number of *weaker* judgments increased in the 30- and 40-db. series while the number of *louder* judgments increased in the 40- and 50-db. series with increase in time interval between standard and variables, thus showing a shift toward the AL determined by all four sets of stimuli and away from the standards serving as the specific objects of comparison!

In quantitative terms, the AL of each series of stimuli with its own standard is 29.25 for the 30-db. series, 39.25 for the 40-db. series, 49.25 for the 50-db. series, and 59.25 for the 60-db. series by weighting the standards three times as heavily as the average of the series stimuli and subtracting the *d* factor which equals .75 db. But the AL of the four sets of stimuli and standards combined is 44.25. Hence if AL of all the sets exerts greater influence on judgment with increasing time intervals between variable and standard stimuli, or conversely, if the influence of the standards declines, then there should be, according to our formulation, more judgments of weaker in the two lower sets and more judgments of louder in the two higher sets of stimuli as the general AL becomes increasingly effective since it is higher than the ALs of the lower sets and lower than the ALs of the higher sets of stimuli. Needham's own explanation of his results fits our interpretation: ". . . as the time interval becomes longer between standard and comparison stimuli, the various comparison stimuli are judged less upon the basis of their respective standards, and more by reference to the total range of preceding stimulation" (1935, p. 540).

It is thus not possible to generalize concerning TOE on the basis of restricted conditions of observation. TOE is often said to be negative in judgments of loudness and absent or positive in judgments of pitch and brightness. But Needham's results show that TOE depends upon both the specific series of stimuli being judged and the level established by more remote sets of stimuli as well as upon the time interval between standard and comparison stimuli. Woodrow had earlier shown that TOE was negative with sets of weight stimuli above 130–140 grm., zero at this level, and positive with stimuli of 110–120 grm. (1933). And Postman (1947) has shown that sign and magnitude of TOE depend upon the particular psychophysical method employed in determining PSE. A standard tone of 1000 cycles at 75 db. and 11 variable tones symmetrically distributed in 1-db. steps around the standard were employed with the method of constant stimulus differences. The same standard was employed for the method of average error but here

*S*s were required to adjust the intensity of a variable tone to the standard. The results in Table 4.21 show that there is a definite trend in TOE with the constant method: It is slightly positive with 0- and 1-sec. intervals, and becomes increasingly negative with increasing time. On the other hand, with the method of average error, the TOEs are all positive and have no definite trend.

TABLE 4.21.   TOE as a Function of Method and Time Interval between Standard and Variables

Time Interval	Average TOE (db.)	
(Sec.)	Average Error	Constant Method
0	0.10	0.95
1	0.10	0.68
2	—0.12	1.15
4	—0.55	1.00
6	—0.98	1.00

SOURCE: From Postman, 1947. With the permission of the *American Journal of Psychology.*

Individual differences also complicate the picture. Koester and Schoenfeld (1946) found positive TOE with lower pitches and negative TOE with higher pitches in the case of naïve subjects, but the reverse was true for some practiced *S*s (cf. Peak, 1939).

In the light of work by several investigators—showing that TOE varies with time interval between standard and variables, with the psychophysical method employed, and with the relations of series to series when more than a single set of stimuli is employed—TOE does not appear to be an inherent property of either specific sense modalities or different attributes (e.g., loudness vs. pitch) within a single modality. The attempt to divide sensory continua into different classes on the assumption that TOE is always positive, zero, or negative for specific dimensions cannot be regarded as justified in the light of all the evidence. Rather, TOE must be regarded as a manifestation of decentered position of adaptation level. We have seen that as conditions of stimulus presentation vary, adjustment levels change with resultant effects on judgment. Looked at from a systematic point of view, departures from equal or symmetrical distributions of judgments are seen to be lawful concomitants of decentered levels of which TOE is one of the oldest and best-known phenomena. Perhaps the "E" in TOE will eventually be recognized as an "effect" and not as an error in the light of what is now known.

Having considered some typical experimental findings regarding TOE let us turn to the quantitative theory of this phenomenon proposed by Michels and Helson (1954*a*).

QUANTITATIVE THEORY OF TOE[8]

It has been demonstrated (Helson, Michels, and Sturgeon, 1954) that the judgment, *J*, expressed as the ordinal number in a progressive rating scale which is symmetrical about "equal," can be expressed as a logarithmic function of the stimulus *X* as follows:

$$J_1 = C + K' \log \frac{X}{A_1} \qquad (69)$$

Here *C* has the numerical value assigned to the equality judgment, K' is a constant, and A_1 is the *comparative adaptation level* (CAL), which is the AL when the members of a series are compared with a standard. The value of A_1 depends both on the series adaptation level A' and on the standard *S* with which the stimulus *X* is being compared.

It will be noticed that Equation (69) predicts that the equality judgment will be aroused by a stimulus equal to the CAL, rather than by a stimulus equal to the standard. Hence the point of subjective equality is higher than the standard if CAL is more than *S,* and is lower if CAL is less than *S.* It has also been shown that

$$\text{CAL} = A_1 = S^s A'^t \qquad (70)$$

where A' is the series adaptation level (SAL) which would be found by the so-called method of absolute judgment, and *s* and *t* are the relative weights of *S* and SAL in determining A_1 and are subject to the condition

$$t = 1 - s \qquad (71)$$

Hence A_1 lies between SAL and *S.* We therefore expect either a positive or negative TOE may be found depending on whether SAL lies above or below *S.* The relative positions of SAL and *S* will depend on a

---

[8] The following discussion is reproduced from Michels and Helson by permission of the *American Journal of Psychology.*

number of factors, such as the adaptation coefficients and the relative magnitudes of the residual and standard stimuli. The negative TOE found in this experiment and in most comparisons of weights by classical methods is accounted for by the fact that the residual stimulus for lifted weights is lower than the mean of the stimuli usually employed in the comparisons (Nash, 1950). Hence the SAL for the series of weights is likely to be less than a standard which falls at or near the center of this range.

The comparative rating scale technique can be used to considerable advantage in the study of TOE. Suppose that a series of n stimuli $X_i (i = 1, 2, 3, \ldots n)$ are presented for judgment in comparison with a standard S, the standard being presented immediately before each $X_i (S_1 V_2)$. It has been shown that the CAL is then specified by

$$\log A_1 = s \log \frac{S}{A'} + \log A' \tag{72}$$

and that the predicted judgments are

$$J_1 = C + K' \log \frac{X}{A'} - K's \log \frac{S}{A'} \tag{73}$$

The point of subjective equality is clearly A_1, as we may verify by setting $J_1 = C$ and $A_1 = X$ in Equation (73) to obtain Equation (72).

Now suppose that a new set of judgments is made, S being presented immediately after each X_i ($V_1 S_2$) and that the judgment is of S relative to X_i. The stimulus being judged now has a constant magnitude S, but the comparison adaptation level will be different for each X_i. The roles of S and X_i have been interchanged, and we can predict the new judgments by interchanging the two symbols representing them in Equation (73) to obtain the predicted judgments:

$$J_2 = C + K' \log \frac{S}{A'} - K's \log \frac{X}{A'} \tag{74}$$

To find the new CAL for the series, we set $J_2 = C$ and set $X = A_2$ to obtain

$$\log A_2 = \frac{1}{s} \log \frac{S}{A'} + \log A' \tag{75}$$

The value of A' in Equations (73) and (74) cannot be determined directly from comparisons, nor can absolute judgments of the series be expected to yield the correct value of A', since the AL of the series will be changed both by the introduction of the standard and by the emphasis placed on the standard by the instructions. Fortunately, however, a symmetry condition exists and may be used to eliminate A'. Regardless of the existence of a time-order error, a stimulus which is physically equal to the standard cannot be distinguished from the standard. It is possible that the stimulus will be judged heavier (or lighter) than the standard if presented as S_1V_2, but then the standard must be judged heavier (or lighter) than the stimulus if presented as V_1S_2. This statement would be true if the classical technique were used; with the present method it can be extended to state that the two judgments will be quantitatively equal to each other, though neither may be the equality judgment.

In view of these considerations, we can state unambiguously that $J_1 = J_2$ when $X = S$. In other words, the two curves of J vs. log X should intersect at a point which has an abscissa log S. The consistency of the equations with this statement is shown if we replace X by S and equate J_1 and J_2, in which case we obtain an identity.

We now find it advantageous to rewrite Equation (74) in a form analogous to Equation (69), with the help of Equation (75). This procedure yields

$$J_2 = C - K's \log \frac{X}{A_2} \tag{76}$$

A comparison of Equations (69) and (76) brings out two interesting points. In the first place, the plots of the judgments obtained with the S_1V_2 and V_1S_2 procedures should exhibit slopes of K' and $-K's$, respectively. Hence the ratios of the observed slopes may be used to determine the weight s of the standard in determining CAL. Secondly, by setting $J_1 = J_2$ and replacing X by S, we find that

$$\log \frac{S}{A_1} = -s \log \frac{S}{A_2} \tag{77}$$

or

$$s = \frac{\log S - \log A_1}{\log A_2 - \log S} \tag{78}$$

This relation gives us a second method of determining s for any particular combination of stimuli and standard.

Verification. Figs. 4.11 and 4.12 show plots of the data obtained with 350- and 400-grm. standards respectively. The lines shown have been fitted to the experimental points by the method of least squares. The last two columns of Table 4.22 contain the parameters K' and AL as they have been fitted. It will be noticed that the curves in Fig. 4.11 for the two time orders intersect almost exactly at log S. The deter-

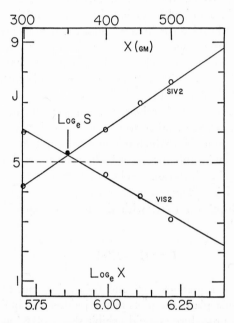

FIG. 4.11. Comparative judgments of five stimuli (350-grm. standard). The solid lines are least-square fits to the experimental points. The average judgment shown by the black circle was identical for the two orders. The J values for S_1V_2 represent judgments of X relative to S; the J values for V_1S_2 represent judgments of S relative to X. (From Michels and Helson, 1954. With the permission of the *American Journal of Psychology*.)

mination of s from the ratio of the slopes gives a value of 0.8; a second determination, based on Equation (78), gives 0.9, a very satisfactory agreement for the 350-grm. standard. In Fig. 4.12 the point of intersection for the two time orders departs from log S only by an amount within the experimental error. In Equation (78) the value of s obtained is 1.0. The ratio of the slopes gives $s = 0.7$, so that the agreement is not

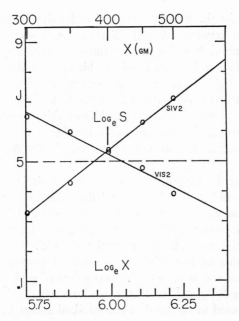

FIG. 4.12. Comparative judgments of five stimuli (400-grm. standard). The solid lines are least-square fits to the experimental points. The *J* values for S_1V_2 represent judgments of *X* relative to *S*; the *J* values for V_1S_2 represent judgments of *S* relative to *X*. (From Helson, Michels and Sturgeon, 1954. With the permission of the *American Journal of Psychology*.)

TABLE 4.22. Average Comparative Scale Ratings of Stimulus Weights by 12 Ss with Two Standards and Two Time Orders

Standard (grm.)	Order [a]		Stimulus Weight (grm.)					AL (PSE)	Slope
			300	350	400	450	500		
350	S_1V_2	*J*	4.2	5.3	6.1	7.0	7.7	338	6.6
		σ_m	0.11	0.06	0.14	0.16	0.16		
	V_1S_2	*J*	6.0	5.3	4.6	3.8	3.1	365	−5.5
		σ_m	0.13	0.07	0.10	0.20	0.09		
400	S_1V_2	*J*	3.3	4.3	5.3	6.3	7.1	381	7.5
		σ_m	0.38	0.14	0.10	0.16	0.16		
	V_1S_2	*J*	6.5	5.9	5.4	4.8	3.9	417	−5.0
		σ_m	0.14	0.15	0.14	0.06	0.10		

[a] The values of σ_m in this table were obtained by using the averages of each of the 12 Ss. The inter-S variability is obtained if these values are multiplied by 3.46.
SOURCE: From Michels and Helson, 1954a. With the permission of the *American Journal of Psychology*.

as satisfactory for the 400-grm. standard as for the 350-grm. standard. The difference between 1.0 and 0.7 does not, however, exceed the experimental error. It is hoped that future experiments, in which a wider range of stimuli are used and in which the standards are further from SAL, will give more precise determinations of *s*, and will indicate whether or not it depends on the separation of *S* and SAL.

The average value of *s* as obtained from this experiment is 0.85 ± 0.07. The appreciable departure of this value from unity indicates that SAL, as well as *S*, is an important factor in the establishment of PSE.

The fact that the experimental points fall so nicely along straight lines on the semi-logarithmic plot and that reasonable consistency is obtained in the various determinations of the weighting coefficient indicates the successful application of rating-scale techniques and of adaptation-level theory to the determination of TOE.

Average value of the TOE. An important consequence of this treatment is that the average of the two points of subjective equality, obtained by the S_1V_2 and the V_1S_2 procedures with a given standard, cannot be expected to be equal to the standard except in very special cases. Since the two curves of J vs. $\log X$ intersect at $\log X = \log S$, and since they have different slopes, the separation of $\log A_2$ and $\log S$ is different from that of $\log S$ and $\log A_1$. This fact is apparent in Fig. 4.11, in which the point at which the V_1S_2 curve crosses the ordinate $J = 5$ is clearly further removed from $\log S$ than is the crossing point of the S_1V_2 curve. If TOE is negative, as it is in this case, the intersection of the two curves must fall *above* the equality judgment, and we have the inequality relation

$$\log A_2 - \log S > \log S - \log A_1 \quad \text{or} \quad \frac{A_2}{S} > \frac{S}{A_1} \quad (79)$$

Hence *S* is *less* than the geometric mean of A_1 and A_2. Since the geometric mean is *always* less than the arithmetic mean, it follows, *if TOE is negative,* that

$$S < \frac{A_1 + A_2}{2}$$

If TOE is positive, no such general conclusion can be drawn. In this case, the two curves must intersect *below* the equality judgment, so that

$\log A_2 < \log S < A_1$. Because of the lower slope of the curve obtained with the $V_1 S_2$ procedure, we find the inequality

$$\log S - \log A_2 > \log A_1 - \log S$$

It follows that S is *higher* than the geometric mean of A_1 and A_2 *if TOE is positive,* but we cannot say whether it falls above or below the arithmetic mean unless we have the numerical magnitudes of A_1, A_2, and s.

Whenever TOE is small, say less than 5 percent of S, both the effect of the different slopes and the difference between the geometric and arithmetic means will also be small. Under these circumstances, the mean PSE will be very close to the standard and the usual averaging procedure is justified. In all other cases, the advantage of the comparative-rating-scale method is that it demonstrates by how far the mean departs from the standard; it makes possible determination of S from A_1 and A_2 by the use of Equation (78) whenever the standard cannot be measured directly.

THE COMPARATIVE RATING SCALE (CRS) AND THE METHOD OF CONSTANT STIMULUS DIFFERENCES

Although the method of absolute judgment was introduced by Wever and Zener in 1928, it was not until 1948 that a theory of this type of judgment was formulated (Helson, 1948) and later incorporated in the reformulation of the Fechner law (Michels and Helson, 1949). In the method of absolute judgment, qualitative categories or numbers are employed to designate stimuli without explicit reference to external standards. The qualitative categories are of the following type: very very heavy, very heavy, heavy, medium heavy, medium, medium light, light, very light, and very very light. For purposes of computation numbers are assigned to the categories on the assumption that the step intervals between the categories are equal. Insofar as the assumption of linearity is not met, the fit to observed data will be poorer, so this assumption is essentially a conservative one. The quantitative theory underlying the method of absolute judgments was extended (Helson, Michels, and Sturgeon, 1954) to the case where series stimuli are compared with an external standard. In this method such comparative ratings are employed as very very much heavier, very much heavier, much heavier, heavier, a little heavier, equal, a little lighter, lighter, much lighter, very much lighter, and very very much lighter. If the theory of absolute judgment is adequate to comparative types of judgment, then the way is open for quantitative treatment of such psychophysical problems as time-order effects which have hitherto stood as isolated phenomena (cf. the preceding section on TOE).

The data in Table 4.23 were obtained by using comparative judgments of weights with reference to explicitly given standards. They are averages of comparative judgments translated into a numerical scale as described above and they show a monotonically increasing heaviness judgment as the stimuli increase from 300 to 500 grm. In this respect (as pointed out by Helson, Michels, and Sturgeon) the

TABLE 4.23.   Average Comparative Scale Ratings of Weight Stimuli by 12 Ss with Two Standards

| Standard | Stimulus (grm.) | | | | | AL |
(grm.)	300	350	400	450	500	(PSE)
400	3.3	4.3	5.3	6.3	7.1	381
SD_m[a]	0.38	0.14	0.10	0.16	0.16	
350	4.2	5.3	6.1	7.0	7.7	338
SD_m[a]	0.11	0.06	0.14	0.16	0.16	

[a] The values of SD_m in this table were obtained by using the averages of each of the 12 Ss. The interobserver variability is obtained if these values are multiplied by 3.46.

SOURCE: From Helson, Michels, and Sturgeon, 1954. With the permission of the *American Journal of Psychology.*

results obtained by the comparative-rating-scale technique are formally similar to the classical method of constant stimulus differences. The two methods differ, however, in that the classical method is designed for and usually employs only three comparative judgments (such as heavier, equal, and lighter) and the quantitative data are percentages expressing the relative frequencies of the categories. In the comparative-rating procedure the quantitative data translate directly back to the originally given categories of judgment. The values of stimulus eliciting any one of the categories in the rating scale may then be determined from the data. Hence the comparative rating scale yields a much wider range and variety of judgments than does the classical method and it should therefore be correspondingly more useful. Since the fitted values are so close to the experimental data, only the fitted values are given in the table along with the standard errors of the means. From the data it can be seen that the method of comparative ratings is sufficiently sensitive to reveal the usual time-order effects. The adaptation level with a standard of 400 grm. is 381 grm. and with a standard of 350 grm. it is 338 grm. Since the TOE is generally regarded as a small (though not negligible) effect in measuring thresholds, its clear presence in the values of PSE obtained with the comparative-rating method shows that this method is capable of yielding differences as fine in sensitivity as are the longer more tedious constant methods.

Data for comparison of the CRS and the method of constant stimulus differences were obtained by Smith and Helson (1953) under the following conditions: The series stimuli consisted of a set of weights, 200, 210, 220, 230, and 240 grm. with 220 grm. as the standard; they were judged by Ss by the comparative-rating-scale (CRS) procedure (Helson, Michels, and Sturgeon, 1954) and by the Urban method. A nine-category scale was employed in the CRS method: very much heavier, much heavier, heavier, a little heavier, equal, a little lighter, lighter, much lighter, and very much lighter. Two time orders were used: S_1V_2 (standard first, variable second) and V_1S_2 (variable first, standard second). In the CRS method the categories were assigned numbers from 9 to 1 for purposes of computation and the values of stimulus eliciting the various response categories were computed by fitting to Equation (39). The adaptation level was given by the stimulus eliciting the "equal" judgment which was assigned the value 5 on the numerical scale.

In the Urban method only three categories of judgment, heavier, equal, or lighter, were permitted and the percentages of each of these types of response were utilized to determine limens for lighter and heavier by the usual method of fitting to the ogive function using Urban's weights (Guilford, 1954a) and the value of PSE was determined.

Table 4.24 shows the results by the two methods of judging, the observed and calculated percentages of heavier and lighter judgments by the method of constant stimulus differences, and the category ratings by the CRS method, as well as the percentage of heavier, equal, and lighter for each of the stimuli and their corresponding numerical category ratings. The threshold for "lighter" by the constant method (not given in Table 4.24) is 210.7 grm., which is close to the value of stimulus (207.5 grm.) eliciting the category rating "a little lighter"; the threshold for "heavier" is 228.8 grm., which is a little below the stimulus (231.6 grm.) eliciting the category rating "a little heavier." The comparative rating scale thus reflects discriminations as well as the method of constant stimulus differences does, but with far greater economy in number of observations and time spent in calculations than with the Urban method.

TABLE 4.24.   Comparison of Values Obtained by Two Psychophysical Methods

I.   Judgments as Functions of Stimuli

| Stimuli (grm.) | Comparative Rating Scale | | Constant Method (Urban) Percentages | | | |
| | | | Heavier | | Lighter | |
	Observed	Calculated	Observed	Calculated	Observed	Calculated
200	3.2	3.2	7.7	6.0	69.0	69.0
210	4.3	4.0	17.6	18.0	51.2	52.0
220	5.2	5.3	33.1	35.0	33.7	32.0
230	5.9	6.1	52.3	55.0	18.6	18.0
240	6.6	6.4	71.0	68.0	9.2	11.0

II.   Stimuli and Percentages Corresponding to Categories

| Comparative Rating-scale Category | | Stimuli | Percentages | | |
			Heavier	Lighter	Equal
Lighter	3.0	198.5	6.7	70.9	22.4
A little lighter	4.0	207.5	14.4	55.7	29.9
Equal	5.0	218.3	31.0	36.4	32.6
A little heavier	6.0	231.6	56.0	17.4	26.6
Heavier	7.0	247.8	82.7	4.7	12.6

SOURCE: From Smith and Helson, 1953.

Identity of PSE and AL.   The identity of PSE and AL, which was deduced on theoretical considerations, is supported in this study employing two methods of judging. PSE, calculated from the percentages (cf. Boring, 1917) is 219.8 grm. while AL, calculated from the CRS data fitted to Equation (39) is 218.3 grm. The difference between PSE and AL is so far below the Urban thresholds as to be insignificant.

Additional experimental evidence supporting the identity of PSE and AL comes from a study by Furth (1960) in which a series of weights, 152, 176, 200, 224, and 248 grm. were compared with six standards weighing 200 grm., differing in size and hence in density.

Variable density standards were used to determine effect of *apparent* differences in weight on AL. CRS judgments were employed and the data fitted to the Michels and Helson reformulated Fechner equation (1949). The frequencies of the four "heavier" categories were pooled into one category "heavier" and similarly the lighter judgments were pooled to obtain values of PSE by the Spearman method as given by Woodworth and Schlosberg (1954). The identity of PSE and AL is shown in the close correspondence of the two curves in Fig. 4.6 (Furth, 1960).

It is evident from the comparison of results of CRS and method of constant stimulus differences that the former yields as much information as the latter and with far less work. In addition CRS employs a scale that is widely used in everyday life and has immediate meaning for everyone. CRS is not limited to judgments of sensory dimensions but may also be employed with affective, aesthetic, attitudinal, and verbal responses. It may be necessary to scale nonphysical stimuli by one of the other psychophysical methods to calibrate them as independent variables but once they are measured, CRS can be employed to assess the responses of Ss for scientific or practical ends.

QUANTITATIVE THEORY OF CRS[9]

An implicit assumption in the derivation of the reformulated Fechner law (Michels and Helson, 1949) was that the judgments of single stimuli are made in terms of the adaptation level as a standard. At first glance, it might appear that, when comparative judgments are made involving a standard and a set of variables, the standard would merely replace the adaptation level as the basis of comparison. Such an expectation would require, however, the further assumption that the person forming the judgment has been completely successful in suppressing all adaptation effects except those resulting from the standard stimulus. Since adaptation is known to play a highly significant role in all perception, it would be very surprising if this complete success were achieved. It seems more reasonable to suppose that in comparative judgment neither the adaptation level (AL) found in single stimulus judgments (SAL) nor the standard (S) will be the effective AL and evoke the equality judgment, but rather that a new compara-

[9] The following discussion is taken from Helson, Michels and Sturgeon (1954) and is reprinted by permission of the *American Journal of Psychology*.

tive adaptation level (CAL) will be established. We may expect the CAL to lie between SAL and S, its exact location depending on the relative weights of SAL and S in establishing the new AL.

Judgments of a series of stimuli, assuming a properly constructed rating scale, can be represented by the relation:

$$J = C + K' \log \frac{X}{A'} \qquad (80)$$

where J is the judgment value on a rating scale running from 1 to 1 $+ 2N$, $C = 1 + N$; X is the magnitude of the stimulus; A' is the series adaptation level (SAL); and K' is a determinable function of N and of the conditions under which the judgments are made. Equation (80) has been tested under a variety of conditions and has been found to be valid to a fairly high degree of accuracy.

In accordance with the discussion of the theory of TOE, we must replace A' by the comparison adaptation level (CAL) if a comparative scale is used. The relation of CAL, S, and SAL is indicated by the fact that the adaptation level is found to be a weighted geometric mean of all the stimuli, past or present, which affect the judgment. Hence we can probably take CAL as a weighted geometric mean of A' and S, that is,

$$\text{CAL} = A_1 = S^s A'^t \qquad (70)^{10}$$

where

$$s + t = 1 \qquad (71)$$

The exponent s is then a measure of the influence of the standard stimulus, t is a measure of the influence of the SAL. If the judgments are completely in terms of the standard, we shall have $s = 1$, $t = 0$; if the standard has no effect, we shall have $s = 0$, $t = 1$. In any practical case, we may expect values between these limits.

We may now rewrite Equation (80) in a form applicable to comparative judgments. We first express the quality of Equation (70) in logarithmic form:

$$\log A_1 = s \log S + t \log A' = s \log S + (1 - s) \log A'$$
$$= s \log \frac{S}{A'} + \log A' \qquad (72)$$

---

[10] Equations identical with those discussed above in the theory of TOE are given the same numbers as before.

Substitution of A_1 into Equation (72), in place of A' gives

$$J = C + K' \log \frac{X}{A_1} \tag{69}$$

$$= C + K' \log \frac{X}{A'} - K's \log \frac{S}{A'} \tag{73}$$

as the prediction of the comparative judgment J as a function of the stimulus, the standard, and the series adaptation level. Equations (69)

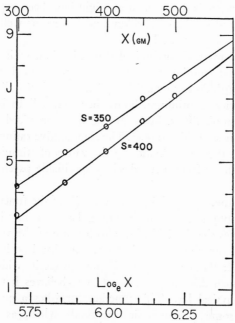

FIG. 4.13. The solid lines are least-square fits to the data, and follow the relations: $J = 6.6 \log_e X - 33.4$ for the 350-grm. standard; $J = 7.5 \log_e X - 39.6$ for the 400-grm. standard. (From Helson, Michels, and Sturgeon, 1954. With the permission of the *American Journal of Psychology*.)

and (73) do not give a complete determination, however, since A' is not the same as the adaptation level of the series *without a standard*. Hence the only prediction that we can make without further information is that the curve of comparative judgments against log X should be parallel to the corresponding curve obtained for the series by the method of single stimuli and therefore parallel to each other when different standards are used.

Fig. 4.13 shows a plot of the data obtained with the two standards.

The lines shown have been fitted to the experimental points by the method of least squares. Their slopes are 7.5 for the 400-grm. standard and 6.6 for the 350-grm. standard. While these values are not in perfect agreement, they do not depart from each other to a significant extent, and the curves are close to parallelism as expected from theory.

The comparative rating scale has an advantage over the method of absolute judgment because it provides a stimulus standard which helps to stabilize the adaptation level and therefore the judgments of stimuli. This advantage is not as great as might have been expected because series stimuli and residual or background factors, as well as the standard, affect the comparative adaptation level.

The classical methods of liminal determination, while they provide methods for determining thresholds or number of JND's above or below a standard, do not establish equivalence of stimuli and response in a psychological continuum. Thus they may tell us by how many JND's two stimuli differ, but only the most practiced subject could even make a guess at this number. The comparative-rating-scale method makes possible the determination of the values of stimulus which will be judged to differ from a standard by specifiable psychological intervals.

The power law.   One of the most versatile of the functions proposed as "the psychophysical law" is the power law, not only because of the variety of curves that it yields, but also because of the variety of interpretations that can be given to the terms entering into its formulation. Guilford (1932; 1936) was one of the first to see its wide applicability to psychophysical data, and Stevens (1962) believes it to be the only valid psychophysical law. This function furnishes a good fit to data obtained by some psychophysical methods when, as Stevens now admits, it makes provision for effects of adaptation and contrast when it embodies a proper origin or zero.

Guilford formulated the power law as follows:

$$\Delta R = KR^n \qquad\qquad (81)$$

where ΔR is the JND or some cognate measure of discriminal sensitivity, R is the standard, K is the Weber constant, and n is a constant depending upon the type of sensation involved. Guilford pointed out that K can be used as a constant index of sensitivity once the exponent n is known because $K = \Delta R/R^n$. If $n = 1$, the generalized power law reduces to the Weber law, and if it equals 0.5 it becomes, as Guilford showed, the square root law of Fullerton and Cattell.

In 1950 Attneave showed that AL can be introduced into the power law by assuming that the JND is proportional to some average of the stimuli being judged or to their pooled effect regarded as the adaptation level, A, and the standard:

$$\frac{\Delta R}{f(R,A,)} = K \tag{82}$$

where ΔR is the JND, R is the standard, and K is the Weber constant. If the function f is a weighted log mean we may write Equation (82) as

$$\frac{\Delta R}{R^n A^{1-n}} = K \tag{83}$$

Since A^{1-n} is a constant, it may be combined with K giving

$$\frac{\Delta R}{R^n} = K' \tag{84}$$

or

$$\Delta R = K'R^n \tag{84A}$$

which is Guilford's generalized nth power law.

If instead of ΔR we write S,

$$S = kR^n \tag{85}$$

we have Stevens' power law wherein S is psychological magnitude, k depends on the choice of units in which the stimulus R is measured, and n has fixed values for various sense modalities. The versatility of the power function appears at once; it yields negatively accelerated curves when n is less than unity, a linear function when it is unity, and positively accelerated curves when n is greater than unity. If logs are taken of both sides, the power function yields families of straight lines:

$$\log S = \log k + n \log R \tag{85A}$$

wherein n is the slope and $\log k$ is the y intercept. According to Stevens (1957) if S is the sensation ratio (determined by the method of ratio production) and r is the corresponding stimulus ratio, then

$$n = \frac{\log S}{\log r} \tag{85B}$$

According to Stevens "this law is simply that equal stimulus ratios produce equal subjective ratios" (1956, p. 1). In his most recent discussion of the power law (1962) he recognizes that adaptation and contrast affect the value of the exponent n and may be included in this value; but adaptation level does not appear explicitly in this formulation, which is as follows:

$$S = k(\phi - \phi_o)^n \tag{86}$$

where S is psychological magnitude, ϕ is physical magnitude, k is a constant determined by choice of units, *n varies with the modality and also with such parameters as adaptation and contrast,* and the value of ϕ_o is determined by "the effective 'threshold' that obtains under the conditions of the experiment" (Stevens, 1962, p. 32). As shown by Canter and Hirsch (1955) for the veg scale, Michels (1954) for the bril scale, Michels and Doser (1955) for the sone scale, Helson (1947) and Helson and Michels (1949) for rating-scale data, and Helson, Michels and Sturgeon (1954) for comparative rating scale data, and other types of judgments discussed in this chapter, since AL is the "effective threshold" in terms of stimulus units, ϕ_o and k may be eliminated as such if we introduce AL explicitly into the power law which then becomes

$$S = AR^n \tag{87}$$

or, in log form

$$\log S = n \log R + \log A \tag{87A}$$

where A is the adaptation level.

Woodworth in 1938 formulated a law which is formally identical with the power law and he included in his equation a term for the functional zero which he likened to the zero of the thermometer! The A term in the power law is exactly analogous to Woodworth's zero (which was neither the absolute threshold nor zero intensity). Consider Woodworth's formula

$$s = s_o r^n \tag{88}$$

where s is magnitude of sensation, r is equal to the Weber constant plus 1 ($r = k + 1$), n is the number of DL steps or JND's above any arbitrarily chosen level or standard s_o; r may be any value, not necessarily involving the Weber constant, e.g., 2, when judging octaves (1938, p. 436).

Inspection of the relevant curves published by Stevens (1962) shows that shifts in adaptation level displace plots of sensory magnitudes in accordance with Equation (87A) which contains one less constant than Stevens' latest formulation. In addition explicit introduction of A in the power law makes it possible to make one parameter do for the influence of many variables affecting psychophysical judgments.

ASSIMILATION VS. CONTRAST IN PSYCHOPHYSICAL JUDGMENTS

On the basis of data obtained with lifted weights, it has been claimed by Sherif, Taub, and Hovland (1958) that the *two* processes at work in psychophysical judgments are *contrast and assimilation,* which are manifested in opposed effects. Displacement of judgments of a series of stimuli *away* from the judgment of an anchor is a manifestation of contrast, while displacement of judgments *toward* judgment of the anchor is a manifestation of assimilation. Using weights of 55, 75, 93, 109, 125, and 141 grm. and a number scale from 1 to 6, these writers found that when they required Ss to call 6 the top member of the series (141 grm.), higher judgment categories predominated as compared with the "no anchor" series, thus showing assimilation. In a second experiment the lightest stimulus of the series (55 grm.) was dropped and similar but not so striking results were obtained. Here the bottom member of the series (75 grm.) was employed as anchor and assigned the number 1. There was an increase in lower judgment categories as compared with the no-anchor condition. As the anchor stimulus was moved farther and farther above or below the end stimuli of the series the judgments were displaced more and more away from the judgment assigned to the anchors. Sherif et al. generalized their results as follows:

When an anchor is introduced at the end or slightly removed from the end of the series, there will be a displacement of the scale of judgment toward the anchor and assimilation of the new reference point in the series. When, however, the reference point is too remote there will be displacement in the opposite direction (i.e., away from the anchor), with a constriction of the scale to a narrower range (p. 150).

Whereas Sherif, Taub, and Hovland stated that assimilation was not easily explained in terms of "indifference points" or "neutrality regions," Parducci and Marshall (1962) in replicating their experiment exactly and with additional checks found that "assimilation is consistent with the contrast principles described by the theory of adaptation level" (p. 435).

It is evident from both the original study (Sherif et al.) and from the study by Parducci and Marshall that assimilation effect can be traced to the constraints put upon Ss to assign the topmost category, 6, to the heaviest weight and the lowest category, 1, to the lightest weight. Parducci and Marshall hypothesized as follows:

Since the experimental instructions used by Sherif et al. (1958) state that the anchoring stimulus is to be judged with the heaviest category, PSE is by definition the physical value of the stimulus actually judged with the heaviest category. According to the theory of adaptation level, PSE is equal to a weighted logarithmic mean of the standard and comparison stimuli. . . . When the standard is identical to the heaviest comparison weight, PSE will be below the value of the standard since any weighted mean of the stimulus values would have to be lower than the standard. But if PSE is below the actual physical value of this anchoring stimulus, the heaviest comparison weight is perceived to be heavier than the anchor, [hence] perceptual contrast. The anchoring conditions employed by Sherif et al. thus lower the value of the stimulus to which the "heaviest" category of judgment is applied, and the entire scale of judgment is shifted downward [with a larger number of heavy judgments] (Parducci and Marshall, 1962, pp. 426–427).

The same argument applies, *mutatis mutandis,* to the case where the lightest member of the series and stimuli below the series must be assigned the lowest category of the judgment scale.

Experimental confirmation of the adaptation-level interpretation of the assimilation effect was forthcoming in the replication by Parducci and Marshall of the conditions of Sherif et al. AL in the no-anchor condition was found to be 103 grm.; but when the topmost stimulus in the series had to be called "6," AL shifted downward to 87 grm., with consequent increase in the number of higher category judgments as expected. Similarly, when the lightest stimulus in the series had to be assigned the lowest category, "1," AL was 105 grm., with a slight increase in the light judgments. When Parducci and Marshall employed the comparative rating scale (CRS) suggested by Michels and Helson (1954) for use with the method of constant stimulus differences, the curve for light standard (55 grm.) plotted completely *above* the curve for heavy standard (141 grm.), showing that only the usual "contrast" effect is found with light and heavy anchors under these conditions of judging. We therefore conclude with Parducci and Marshall that assimilation no less than contrast is a phenomenon of level rather than a separate unique effect that must be postulated in addition to contrast to explain psychophysical judgments. We shall return to the question of contrast and assimilation in propaganda effects of social communications in Chapter 10.

The important contribution made in the study by Sherif, Taub, and Hovland, which was worked out in greater detail in the study by Parducci and Marshall, concerns the effects of the psychophysical method, scale of judgment, and the constraints placed on the S's mode of judging, on the distribution of judgments and on the categories used by Ss. Thus if specific categories are assigned to certain stimuli, whether members of the series or stimuli outside the series, different use will be made of the judgment scale than if S is free to employ the categories as he wishes. The assimilation effect found by Sherif et al. thus appears to be an artifact of the instructions given Ss. On the other hand, when CRS is employed, results are very similar to those obtained by the "absolute" method if the anchors are comparable in the two methods of judging.

Some implications of the pooling process. A number of consequences follow from the assumption that level is the result of pooled stimulation and that stimuli coinciding with level are indifferent, neutral, or may go unnoticed. The extent to which any stimulus determines level depends upon its intensity, area, frequency, duration and all other conditions of its appearance as well as its relation to other stimuli affecting the organism. Every stimulus pulls prevailing level in its own direction, thus nullifying itself to some extent. The word "bread" repeated rapidly 15 or 20 times loses its meaning, and a long fixated color loses hue, saturation, and lightness and takes on a filmy appearance with indefinite localization. Conversely, the more any stimulus departs from level, the greater is its attention-getting power; the more distinctive it is, the greater is its power of arousing response (hence the well-known effects of sudden, intense, or short stimuli). If stimuli are repeated again and again and again or are durative, they lose their distinctiveness, interest in them fades, and they may induce drowsiness or sleep. Vigilance depends upon conditions of stimulation and the resultant state of the organism. What will be heard as a sudden intense stimulus depends upon the level of stimulation to which the organism has been and is being exposed. If one has been subjected to a series of sudden, intense, sounds, another stimulus of the same kind will have less effect than if it appears against a quiet sound environment. We shall return to the quantitative treatment of distinctiveness as a function of level in Chapter 7.

In memory and recall an understanding of the formation of levels and the relation of stimulation to level is of importance. It used to be said that memory depended on "good impression, retention and recall of what has been experienced." In general, distinctive stimuli are impressed and retained better than neutral or indifferent stimuli. But the distinctiveness of stimuli depends upon their relation to prevailing levels. Retention depends upon impression and upon the state of the organism following impression. Recall depends upon the conditions of impression, retention, and the state of the organism at the time of attempted recall. Reproduction depends upon all the conditions, internal and external, affecting impression, retention, and recall; in addition, it depends upon special abilities and skills because material may be recalled without being reproduced, e.g., a musical composition or a painting. We thus see that memory is no less than judgment a function of levels prevailing during and following original stimulation and at the time of recall and reproduction.

Still another area in which pooling has been shown to be important is that of reinforcement as shown in the Bevan-Adamson theory (1961) which will be discussed in Chapter 7. According to these writers reinforcement depends not merely upon the number and intensities of rewards (or punishments) but also upon their relation to prevailing levels of stimulation. We shall be concerned with many other applications of the pooling model in the rest of this book.

Classical psychophysics and current work in this area that is based on the same tradition have been regarded as a specialized, if not an esoteric, branch of psychology having little to do with behavior outside the laboratory. As a result there has been an almost unbridgeable chasm between psychophysicists and personality, social, and clinical psychologists. With recognition of the importance of internal norms in psychophysics, a common theoretical framework is available for all forms of behavior. Frame-of-reference psychophysics, far from being restricted to measures of sensitivity and estimations of sensory magnitudes, has found application in personality testing (George and Bonney, 1956*a*; 1956*b*; Murstein, 1959; Dollin and Sakoda, 1962), in studies of interpersonal interactions (see Chapter 10), and in abnormal states (Goldstone, Boardman, and Lhamon, 1959). The differences in emphasis and approach between classical psychophysics and frame-of-reference psychophysics are well summarized by one clinical psychologist in the following quotation:

It is clear that any attempt to understand sensory experience that is dominated by attention to the physical stimulus will add little to our understanding of human experience. A sensory psychology that emphasizes the inviolate stimulus and looks upon the organism as a threshold value views people as sources of error and the goal of psychological measurement the scaling of human fallibility. Traditional psychophysics focused upon sensitivity measures with the subject seen as a passive organic meter. Although psychophysics has long sought out functional relationships between the experiences or responses of people and the stimulus energies that inform them of their surroundings, devotion to method has resulted in the conclusion that the cold psychology of the acoustic laboratory is no place for the more humanistic student of human behavior. Thus, while the psychophysical and scaling renaissance has reached several applied areas of behavior measurement it has bypassed, or been bypassed by, people interested in psychopathology. It is possible and potentially fruitful to reconcile psychophysical methods and theories with the methods and observations of psychopathologists. The classical methods that used the organism as a "null instrument" offer little to the clinician who is searching for tools with which to measure and understand experience. It is suggested that the more recently emphasized absolute method represents a more appropriate experimental analogue to the judgments involved in day-to-day complex, conceptual transactions. Whereas the comparison method offers a ready-made frame-of-reference to a metering receiver, the absolute method may be used to obtain information about concepts, subjective scales, or intra-organismic norms. The absolute judgment requires a subject to compare an external stimulus with an internal norm or concept, and the judgment reflects the status of the internal standard. Recent focus upon this single-stimulus, conceptual approach to psychophysics has led to more relativistic interpretations of stimulus-response relationships . . . the absolute judgment is a function of a pooling process involving the contemporary stimulus configuration including foreground and background, and past experience with relevant stimuli. Whereas traditional psychophysics attempted to "train out" or ignore residual effects of past experience or immediate background influences, [adaptation-level theory] brought these factors into the forefront of a quantitative psychology of sensation and perception. If anything, the psychopathologist is more interested in peoples' ability to make use of remote experience, and the impact of anchoring distractions, noises or irrelevant cues, than he is in ascertaining specific sensitivity defects in responding to foreground environmental energies. The ability to control and vary these factors in a quantitative frame-of-reference approach focuses upon the perception-conception relationship, and has permitted the development of an operational approach to the clinically useful concept of reality in terms of the scaling of absolute judgments.

When the clinician speaks of *reality* he is describing the scaling of a patient's absolute judgments of his environment in accordance with cultural norms. It is presumed that people learned these norms and have them available within accepted limits. Stimuli are compared with these internal standards and the perceptual response is scaled with respect to appropriateness and accepted range. The delusion and hallucination of the psychotic, the confusion of the toxic state, the exaggerations or denials of the neurotic, and the ineffectiveness accompanying personality disorder and mental defect all reflect absolute judgments that do violence to either the nature of an accepted norm or the accepted range of that norm and are classified in terms of reality. With the *adaptation level* formulation . . . it is possible to locate alterations in absolute judgment either in the subject's response to his contemporary foreground or background, or residual effects of past experiences, the latter reflecting the norm or concept. This focus upon the concept [of] residuals and background anchor effects permits the investigator to derive theoretically useful attributes of concepts (Goldstone, 1962, pp. 263–264).[11]

SUMMARY

In this chapter the basis is laid for a psychophysics of classes, or frame of reference, as opposed to the classical psychophysics of stimuli. Many phenomena which were regarded as artifacts of judgment, errors, or mere semantic products in classical psychophysics can be brought together, so that their significance is apparent in the psychophysics of classes. By taking into account effects of stimulation on adaptation level, quantitative predictions can be made regarding effects of standards, anchors, interpolated stimuli, predominant stimuli, interactions of frequency and magnitude, various types of stimulus distributions, range and density of series stimuli, series effects, order, practice, and past experience. The weighted log mean definition of adaptation level makes possible evaluation of the contributions of focal, contextual, and re-

[11] In L. J. West (Ed.), *Hallucinations*. New York: Grune & Stratton, 1962.

sidual stimuli to level. The locus of neutral points has yielded information regarding the conditions under which colors and their complementaries are perceived, the range over which "constancy" of color is found, the relations between density and effective (perceived) weight, and the domains of pleasantness and unpleasantness of tones as a function of their pitch and loudness.

It is also shown that adaptation level may be determined by least squares from all the data in an experiment by fitting to functions embodying adaptation level as a parameter. In the reformulated Fechner law, adaptation level serves as the point of origin in place of the absolute threshold, thereby resolving the paradox of "negative" sensations and other difficulties in the classical derivation. The reformulated law has yielded quantitative formulations for time-order effects, judgments obtained by the comparative rating scale, and ratio-scaling methods. In addition frame-of-reference psychophysics has relevance for other areas of psychology.

5 *Perception*

Perception has traditionally been regarded as consisting of sensory components, aroused directly by energies that stimulate receptors, and nonsensory components supplied by past experience or imagination, i.e., from arousal of central nervous processes. It has been claimed that perception is also affected by needs, values, and attitudes; by activities such as attending or not attending and taking account or not taking account of cues; and by special analytical and synthetic processes. In accordance with this tradition, perception was bifurcated into (1) peripheral processes that could be controlled and measured on dimensional continua such as intensity, duration, and extensity, and (2) inner central processes that could not be operationally defined and manipulated since they were regarded as purely personal in nature. Under the influence of early sensory physiology interest has centered on localized focal stimuli, to the neglect of contributions of contextual and background stimuli, with the result that molar explanations have been advanced for perceptual phenomena that could not be accounted for in terms of receptor processes directly excited by stimulus energies.

From the foregoing it appears that the main task facing the systematist is to give a unified account of perception that will provide for personal as well as situational factors within a single frame of reference. A monistic theory of perception also requires that inner molar constructs be evaluated dimensionally or in terms of equivalent dimensional measures. In most cases there is a dimensional *equivalent* for effects ascribed to molar processes. The concept of adaptation level as the pooled effect of focal, contextual, and residual sources of stimulation has provided a unitary account of perception by making possible the evaluation of all sources of variance in behavior within a single universe of discourse. Consider, for example, how the weighted log mean definition of AL was used to evaluate residual as well as background factors in judgments of lightness of reflectances on white, gray, and black backgrounds (Michels and Helson, 1949). Evaluation of the weighting coefficients in Equation (5) below yielded .28 for the stimuli being judged, .16 for the backgrounds, and .56 for the residual contribution to the adaptation levels operative in this situation. Here the residual was found to be twice as important as the log mean of the reflectances being judged and three and one-half times as important as the backgrounds. The equivalent reflectance of the residual stimulus was found by calculation to be 28 percent, a value higher than the geometric mean (20.5 percent) of the three background reflectances. This value, with its large weighting coefficient, points to the predominant role of personal factors in judgments of lightness by untrained *S*s using an open-ended category scale. We thus see that residual or personal contributions to perception may be quantitatively evaluated. Before proceeding with further discussion of the pooling model in the field of perception we must analyze the concept of stimulus and consider the types of phenomenology which have at one time or another inspired various approaches to perception.

THE CONCEPT OF STIMULUS

General considerations. Since the beginnings of modern experimental psychology, stimulus has been defined as energy or change in energy capable of arousing responses. The concept of stimulus has now outgrown this precise but narrow definition. The difficulties in arriving at a suitable working definition for all types of stimuli are apparent when one considers the great variety of conditions that incite or inhibit action. Shall we include among stimuli, oxygen deprivation, poisons, narcotics, and endocrines that act by way of the circulation? Conditions of temperature and humidity? Organic and functional diseases that produce transient or chronic changes in behavior? The problem is further complicated because stimuli are modified by other stimuli, and their effectiveness depends upon the state of the organism as well as upon their own properties. These are but a few of the complexities we encounter in attempting to clarify the concept of stimulus.

Traditionally, stimuli have been defined according to the types of energies that excite receptors: light waves for vision; sound waves for audition; mechanical and chemical energies for the "contact" senses, such as the skin, its underlying tissues, and the mucous membranes lining the orifices of the body; motion and gravity for kinesthesis; and so on through the various senses. Since adaptation more or less negates steady stimulation, it is usually said that *change* in energy is necessary and often sufficient for stimulation. Sometimes stimuli are identified only with perceived energy or, with energy that elicits overt reactions, because biological systems respond only to restricted portions of the energy spectrum. As a first approximation, the definition of stimulus as energy (or change in energy) applies to effects of stimulation of receptors before the central nervous system is affected. To predict responses following stimulation, we must take into account more than localized stimulus energies, for we know that other conditions attending stimulation are important, e.g., order or pattern of stimulation, information transmitted by the stimulus, and interactions between receptors and elements of the central nervous system.

Stimuli are often regarded as fixed or constant; in reality they are variable either because of the quantal nature of energy or because receptors and nervous system are in a constant state of change. For example, we know that the eyes are in constant movement even with so-called constant fixation (Ratliff and Riggs, 1950) and that the organism by its own activities may cause steady stimulation to have variable effects. In this connection, Hahn and Bartley (1954) found that in total darkness Ss distinguished a luminous tilted circle from an ellipse having the same major-minor axes as the image of the tilted circle on the retina. Since stimuli for discriminating the two objects were lacking, the basis for differentiating them must have come from the slight differences in the images occasioned by eye tremors or grosser eye movements, or perhaps from converging eye movements. We can speak of "constant" visual stimulation only with the briefest tachistoscopic exposures, and even here we must be certain that the eyes are not in movement at the moment of exposure. The difficulties in achieving constant stimulation in the other sense modalities are as great as in vision, and it is probable that the *effective* stimulus can never be uniquely specified. Hence the measured value of stimulus must be regarded as an *approximation* to the *effective* stimulus. Realization of the difference between *measured* stimulus and *effective* stimulus may provide new sources of explanation for perceptual phenomena in stimulus and receptor activities.

There is little doubt that much of the variability found at all levels of behavior and now attributed to personal or intervening variables or experimental error will be correlated with stimulus or situational variables as more is learned about these latter variables. One of the first steps in getting more information about stimuli as sources of variance in behavior is to formulate a concept that is more adequate than the classical view of stimulus as a source of energy. We may define stimulus by intensional definitions, which have the virtues of formal logical constructs but may be outgrown operationally long before they are modified in accordance with actual usage, or by extensional definitions, which merely cite instances and lack rigor. We shall not attempt an intensional redefinition of the classical energy concept of stimulus; instead we shall discuss the chief classes of stimuli in order to arrive at an extensional point of view, which is more adequate for the facts in the light of present-day usage.

The problem of identifying and measuring stimuli that determine adjustment levels is complicated because we do not always have simple suprathreshold stimuli with which to deal. The stimulus-response (S-R) approach to psychology has been concerned almost entirely with effects of specific supraliminal stimuli capable of eliciting either verbal reports or easily identifiable responses such as salivation or eating. The typical condition usually investigated is at the top of the S-R hierarchy of clearness, simplicity, and univocality. But sensory data (or in S-R terms, responses) which cannot be correlated with effects of local stimulation and positive behavioral effects from withdrawal of stimulation and many other varieties of *environmental-organismic* relations must be considered in a systematic treatment of behavior. Let us, therefore, consider the chief classes of stimuli which must eventually be handled experimentally and quantitatively in a systematic approach to behavior theory.

The following classes of stimuli are neither mutually exclusive nor exhaustive, but they show the need for a broader concept than the definition of stimulus in terms of energies impinging on the various receptors.

Nonstimulating energies. We begin, paradoxically, with energies that do not stimulate in the sense of exciting receptors to immediate action. Our bodies are constantly bombarded by energies that normally do not affect behavior. Overexposure to very high energies that do not excite sense organs, such as X-rays, gamma, and other types of ionizing radiation, may have harmful effects on sense organs and other bodily tissues; but they cannot be said to be stimuli, or even to exist in the behavioral environment, except as they influence behavior through their untoward effects. Some energies, normally ineffective, may have sensory effects if they are made sufficiently intense. For example, the limits of normal visual energies lie between 380 and 760 mμ, but lately it has been shown that energies up to 1000 mμ may be perceived if made sufficiently intense (see Bartley, 1951). There are, however, energies that pass through living organisms without directly exciting sensory or motor systems no matter how intense they may be. Some of these types of energy are "sensed" by means of physical aids (such as Geiger counters, fluorescent screens, and photographic emulsions) which translate energy from one form into a form capable of exciting sensory systems. These sources of energy are important in research, in medicine and in other practical uses, even though we cannot sense them directly.

With the advent of the atomic age there is now much interest in the effects of ionizing radiation on the human organism. Tolerance levels for large single doses and for smaller chronic doses of such radiation are now being determined and their effects on health, learning, and various types of performance are being studied. Because of exposure to high-level energies that cannot be sensed directly—an inevitable consequence of increased use of atomic sources of energy—mankind will have to learn how to cope with probably the most dangerous hazard it has ever faced.

Physiological stimuli. It has been established beyond question that there are "stimuli" that are not perceived although they evoke bodily changes by exciting sense organs and act through the central nervous system in the manner of ordinary sensory stimuli. Two studies by Davis demonstrated recordable bodily changes following stimulation of which *S*s were totally unaware. In the first study (1948) Davis found that moderate and strong auditory stimuli produced muscular tensions that appeared in electromyographic tracings. In the second study (1950) he found that stimuli far below threshold levels evoked action potentials from four different muscle groups. In these experiments the sounds were not anticipated or temporarily conditioned, and there were residual or carry-over effects from previous stimulation as shown by the fact that the tension threshold depended upon the logarithm of the previous state of tension. A corollary from this study is that the physiological threshold of stimulation, i.e., the weakest stimulus that excites receptor and muscular elements, may be below the stimulus for sensation or verbal report. Let us call these *physiological* stimuli to distinguish them from *subliminal* stimuli which are discussed below.

Subliminal stimuli. Stimuli may be below the conscious threshold and yet be reported correctly more often than are guesses. Our justification for calling these *subliminal* stimuli is that in threshold determinations they may be perceived occasionally even though Ss do not sense them each time they are presented. There are also cases where Ss who are not aware of being stimulated are able to report correctly beyond chance expectation when called upon to "guess." This phenomenon has been demonstrated under a variety of conditions that leave no doubt of its authenticity. Subjects looking at a one-way screen thought they were only guessing at what they were reporting, but they actually named cards exposed behind the screen at subthreshold values (Miller, 1939). Moreover, as the luminance of the cards increased, the percentage of correct reports increased, although Ss were not aware of seeing the stimuli. After the Ss were told that cards were being flashed behind the screen, the awareness thresholds dropped perceptibly. In Miller's experiments no previous conditioning was responsible for the subthreshold detections.

By conditioning procedures subliminal stimuli may be "discriminated," in the sense that they evoke different bodily responses. McGinnies, using tachistoscopic exposures, found larger galvanic skin responses (GSR) for emotionally toned words than for neutral words below the threshold of awareness (1949). This study was criticized by Howes and Solomon (1950) on the ground that the Ss may have withheld verbal responses to the socially taboo words. Howes and Solomon also maintained that since such words are used less frequently by Ss, they should elicit fewer responses and should have longer reaction times than normal words. Lazarus and McCleary (1951) devised an experiment using nonsense syllables as conditioning stimuli to avoid use of socially taboo words. The tachistoscopic exposures allowed 100 percent recognition of the syllables at the slowest speed and only chance recognition at the fastest speed. Subjects had to make a choice of one syllable from among the ten syllables previously learned. Five of the syllables were conditioned by electric shock to yield GSR. When the conditioned and neutral syllables were exposed in random order at each of the five speeds, galvanic skin responses occurred with the conditioned syllables even when the *S*s were unable to report the syllables. Hence, Lazarus and McCleary substantiated the main result of McGinnies' experiment, viz., that responses can be made to stimuli that are below the threshold of *awareness*.

There is thus ample evidence that stimuli not sensed elicit a hierarchy of responses ranging from changes in muscular tension, to autonomic responses, to verbal reports that stimuli are not perceived, to awareness of supraliminal stimuli by *S*s. We must assume that subthreshold stimulation pools with effects of supraliminal stimulation to explain many phenomena. We shall discuss some of these phenomena, and we shall find later that complex social stimulation below the level of conscious awareness may also influence individual behavior.

Field stimulation. In many quarters the term "stimulus" has come to be synonymous with localized spot stimulation, and the responses to such stimuli have been regarded as more basic than responses to extended areas of stimulation. Following the tradition of Helmholtz and the sensory physiologists, analytical introspective psychologists analyzed experience into a few elements and correlated these elements with specific dimensions of stimuli. In general, sensory qualities that correlated with activities in end organs were given the status of "real" palpable psychological elements. Since receptors consist of very small anatomical units, simple pointlike stimuli were used to establish the responses of the various sensory systems. Much has been and still can be learned from this approach, which simplified and brought order into the welter of everyday experiences and opened the way for experimental control of more complicated patterns of experience. But many sensory phenomena, although definitely localized, cannot be accounted for in terms of local stimulation. An aperture in a large white ground illuminated by red light is seen as blue-green although the light coming from the aperture may be weak red or white when seen against a dark field. Here we cannot account for the color of the local stimulus without taking into account the chromaticity and luminance of the surrounding field. Illusions of extent, direction, and perspective, as well as various types of apparent movement, require field considerations for their explanation. Interactions are, however, not limited to color and space perceptions. Temporally extended and successive stimuli pool to give rise to perception of properties over and above those possessed by the individual stimuli. The form qualities of spatial and temporal patterns were recognized by von Ehrenfels and the Gestalt psychologists. Koffka (1922) saw the importance of the "general level" for patterned perception as the following quotation shows:

> The general level holds together the whole group of phenomena corresponding to the scale of stimuli. Although they may rise or fall from this level, the phenomena never lose their existential connection with it . . . further . . . this level adapts itself automatically to the scale and this process of adaptation must therefore be explicable in terms of our general physiological theory (p. 580).

But Koffka provided no way of specifying this "level," and for him it was a qualitative intuitive concept. Nor did he envisage level as the key to analyzing the problem of organization and patterning. We now know that the properties of elements vaguely attributed to their position in the whole or to organization can be accounted for in terms of the relations of the elements to prevailing ALs.

Higher-order stimulation. In one sense there are no absolutely simple single stimuli, for all stimuli represent some degree of complication. There are, however, as Meinong and other members of the Graz school pointed out half a century ago (cf. Helson, 1925; 1926), objects (Superiora) which depend for their existence upon other objects (Inferiora), the latter being discriminable units in their own right. Melodies depend upon individual tones and their harmonic relations and can be regarded as objects of higher order than their tonal components. On the other hand, musical tones depend upon the relative strengths of their partials (fundamental and overtones) and may be regarded as objects of higher order with respect to their components. Many times there is no univocal relation between objects of lower and higher order, a fact that the Graz school referred to as Gestalt ambiguity (Gestaltmehrdeutigkeit). Thus the four dots in Fig. 5.1*A* may be perceived as a square, two horizontal or vertical lines, a triangle with an element outside, two oblique lines, etc. The very simplicity of the dots facilitates the perception of many objects of higher order and thus contributes to Gestalt ambiguity.

If the dots in Fig. 5.1*A* are replaced by units having pronounced directional properties, as in Fig. 5.1*B,* the number of easily perceived patterns shrinks. The four wings or angles in Fig. 5.1*B* are easily perceived to form objects of higher order in the horizontal direction, less easily in the vertical direction, and practically not at all in the oblique direction. The "directedness" of the wings, which is lacking in the dots, imposes constraints on the number of perceptual patterns that may be formed from them. Generality and abstractedness go hand in hand with simplicity of units and relations: *the more simple an element or relation, the larger the number of objects of higher order into which it may fit*. This principle holds for verbal and cognitive materials as well as for sensory data, as shown by the ease with which many nonsense syllables may be fitted into meaningful words. For example, *bes* may fit into best, bestride, bestow, bestir, besmirch, besot, beseech, bestial; *tel,* into

A   B

FIG. 5.1. The dots in A can be perceived in a larger variety of patterns, because of their greater simplicity, than can the arrowheads in B.

tell, telephone, teleology; and *vic,* into victory, victim, vicious, victual; etc. Compare these with the more complicated units (known as paralogs), e.g., shalan, lebat, morot, zakar, which do not fit into any well-known words. Indeed, language and literature (including scientific works) represent objects of the highest order, for it is through these that the most complicated products of human activity are symbolized and so communicated from person to person.

Substitute or conditioned stimuli. The discussion of verbal and cognitive stimuli brings us naturally to consideration of symbolic stimuli, which are special cases of higher-order substitute stimuli. We now know that one stimulus can be conditioned to substitute for another stimulus within very broad limits. Not only is it possible to condition *responses* so that a sound or tactile stimulus (instead of the normal taste stimulus) evokes the salivary response, but it is also possible, as Ellson has shown (1941*a*), to evoke conditioned *sensations* by means of substitute stimuli, e.g., sensation of sound following diminution in the intensity of light. We do not need to commit ourselves to Pavlovian or more sophisticated conditioning theories to accept the fundamental truth that most higher-order behavior depends upon the ability of one stimulus to represent, evoke, or function for other stimuli. Whether by contiguity, frequency, reward, or insight, learning increases the number of stimuli that evoke a given response (stimulus generalization) and also the number of responses to a given stimulus (response generalization). This is not to deny that learning also entails discrimination and limitation of responses. Certainly speech and language are in large measure substitutes for objects, events, operations, and relations. Symbols and signs are probably the highest and broadest class of substitute stimuli since they may represent any level of abstraction and any number of objects and relations.

Aesthetic, emotional, and sexual stimuli. All stimuli are capable of arousing positive or negative affects directly or by association with other stimuli. Those that are warm and sweet seem to be naturally pleasant, whereas bitter taste, pain, and heat and cold are usually unpleasant. Similarly, stimulation of the erogenous zones of the body is pleasant but not stimulation of the cornea or the ear drum. Although everyday experience has acquainted us with effects of stimuli arousing pleasant, unpleasant, sexual, and various emotional states, little is actually known scientifically about these domains of behavior because of the difficulty in obtaining quantitative data. Kinsey and his co-workers (1948) in their measure of sexual behavior (number of orgasms per week) leave many questions unanswered, although some headway has been made with simpler affects such as color preferences (Guilford, 1934; Guilford and Smith, 1959), and aesthetic responses (Eysenck, 1940; 1942). Many of the physiological concomitants of strong emotions are known, and central nervous system loci of emotional states have been tapped (Olds, 1958; Miller, 1962). Effects of adaptation are particularly important here and much remains to be done to determine effects of background and residual stimuli as codeterminers with focal stimuli of emotional behavior—a subject to which we shall return in a later chapter.

Reduced stimulation. It is well known that objects not present to sense may excite various types of responses; e.g., the absence of a loved one may stir pleasant memories or fill one with longing, and the absence of someone disliked may yield feelings of relief and satisfaction. Complete absence of stimulation or reduction of accustomed levels of stimulation may be accompanied by positive sensory phenomena. In total darkness gray masses may be seen moving across the visual field (the "streaming phenomenon"); in complete stillness, one may hear the heart beat and slight noises from movements of the jaw and throat muscles. Thus we know that many of the stimuli bombarding the sense organs usually pass unnoticed. Not until we are deprived of them are we aware of their importance in maintaining visual, auditory, tactile, and kinesthetic levels that constitute our normal environment.

A striking example of the effect of reduction in the normal sound level was brought to my attention several years ago. Typists were unable to work following installation of sound-absorbing material in the walls and ceiling of a large office. Their complaints included pressure on the back of the head, headache, necessity for exerting abnormal pressure in order to type, and undue fatigue early in the day. The cause of these symptoms, which were reported by all the individuals in the affected area, proved to be the reduction in sound level from excessive use of sound-absorbing material, which resulted in obliteration of normal sound feedback from the machines. As a consequence, the typists hit the keys with great force, grew tense, and became painfully aware of tactile and kinesthetic sensations unnoticed when normal sound levels prevailed. Removal of some of the sound-absorbing material alleviated the symptoms immediately and subsequent adaptation to the lower-than-normal sound level made the typists happy again.

Even more striking are the effects of a nearly homogeneous environment as shown in the observations of a team of workers under Hebb reported by Heron (1957). The Ss lay in a lighted room with translucent plastic visors to cut out form vision; pillows around the head dampened transient sounds, while an air conditioner provided a constant noise background; cotton gloves and long cardboard cuffs restricted the sense of touch in hands and arms. Subjects lay on a bed for 24 hr. per day, for as many days as they cared to remain. Decreased vigilance, previously reported under monotonous conditions, made itself evident in deteriorated performance in a variety of tasks both during and following the period of isolation. Many Ss perceived images with hallucinatory clearness and seemed to have dreams while awake. The images, which at first alleviated boredom, later grew so vivid as to interfere with sleep. Electroencephalograms showed changes in brain waves after 96 hr. Perceptual distortions were also encountered: "things looked curved," "near things looked large and far things looked small" (breakdown of size constancy), "things seemed to move," and objects changed size and shape as in illusions typical of schizophrenia. In addition, the *S*s were irritable and emotional by spells.

It is evident from experiments on effects of sensory deprivation that as stimulus input is reduced or becomes too monotonous residuals in the form of illusions, hallucinations, and emotional states may come to the fore to supply dynamic vivid focal stimuli of the individual's own making. In some cases individuals simply become less vigilant and may fall asleep as reported by Flaherty, Flinn, Hauty, and Steinkamp (1960). A certain level of changing input is necessary to preserve normal behavioral functions. As a result of his studies of sensory deprivation Heron concluded that the functions of the reticular formation in the midbrain are disturbed under these conditions:

> Normal functioning of the brain depends upon a continuing arousal reaction generated in the reticular formation, which in turn depends upon constant sensory bombardment. It appears that, aside from their specific functions, sensory stimuli have the general function of maintaining this arousal, and they rapidly lose their power to do so if they are restricted to the monotonously repeated stimulation of an unchanging environment. Under these circumstances the activity of the cortex may be impaired so that the brain behaves abnormally (1957, p. 56).

The problem of reduced input from the environment looms as one of the most important in human space travel. With cramped quarters and little to do on long space journeys, ways must be found to maintain the normal sensori-motor functions and the vigilance required at critical times. One of the interesting and surprising findings from the two short space flights completed at the time of this writing was that sensori-motor coordinations of the astronauts were little affected by the state of weightlessness. However, *long-continued* absence of sensations associated with weight may have deleterious results that cannot be foreseen: muscles may become flaccid and atrophy through lack of exercise as they do when a limb is immobilized for long periods; if there is no force opposing the action of the extrinsic muscles of the eyes, they may not continue to function normally. These and many other problems will have to be faced as man leaves earth for extended flights into space.

Internal states as stimuli. The viscera, muscles, tendons, ligaments, subdural tissues, and blood vessels are fertile sources of sensory and affective experience. From what is known of the sources and end organs of such stimulation, the mode of operation of these types is no different in principle from that of external types of stimulation. Correlating highly with more or less definite types of stimulation, although their end organs are not so well known as the exteroceptors, are specific internal changes affecting interoceptors, such as the stomachic contractions associated with and partly responsible for hunger; the filling of the bladder and rectum leading to the urge to empty; the various pressure, pain, and temperature sensations felt from chest and abdominal regions; and the feelings of movement, strain, and pain from muscles, tendons, and ligaments. In addition to such more or less definitely localized sources of stimulation there are vaguer less known types of input. Central nervous mechanisms functioning more or less autonomously or as a result of the reticular activating system or perhaps as a result of hormones and other products conveyed to them by the circulation may act as primary or secondary sources of affective behavior (Olds, 1958). Such sources of stimulation may also be responsible for the extent to which the organism is vigilant (Lindsley, 1952).

Intervening variables such as *needs, tensions, motives, sets, attitudes, drives,* and so on have been invoked to deal with behavior presumably unexplainable either in terms of situational variables or in terms of receptor origins. Thus the *New Look* workers not only stressed the importance of controllable factors in perception, e.g., rewards, punishment, and food deprivation (Sanford, 1936; 1937; McClelland and Atkinson, 1948), but they also stressed the role of value systems, defense mechanisms, and other intervening variables for which external sources of stimulation cannot be specified (Bruner and Goodman, 1947; Bruner and Postman, 1948). For the latter we prefer the term *residuals* until such time as their internal or central sources are determined.

Paradoxical, illusory, and hallucinatory stimuli. When stimuli do not give rise to their usual effects, we speak of them as "paradoxical," or "illusory"; when states have the vividness of perceptions but no known external stimuli we refer to them as "hallucinations." Paradoxical stimuli might better be called paradoxical *sensations* or *perceptions* because the stimuli as such are not at fault or in error or unusual. Thus extremely cold objects like ice or dry ice may elicit a sensation of heat which is normally aroused by stimuli above 45° C. Since the experience of heat arises from simultaneous stimulation of warm and cold end organs, the paradox arises only because different regions of the temperature continuum arouse similar sensations. Sometimes lawful phenomena are called illusions because their stimuli have not been properly specified or because the concept of stimulus has been too narrowly conceived. The familiar "size-weight illusion" has nothing illusory about it when we consider that the effective stimulus for felt weight is not mass but *density:* larger objects *should* feel lighter than smaller ones having the same weight. Similarly the necessity for calling colored shadows "subjective colors" disappears if a field definition of stimulus is adopted in place of the classical definition.

Residual stimuli are sources of many hallucinations, anxieties, and other subjective states. Sometimes hallucinations can be traced to specific antecedents, such as in delirium tremens. On the other hand, many deductions supposedly based on sense data may be the result of residual contributions to perception. Thus one may perceive another as "deliberately" failing to recognize him when the other actually did not see him. In extreme cases residuals may give rise to the most vivid hallucinations. "Phantasms of the living," where one individual sees another who is a considerable distance away, undoubtedly belong in this category. The fact that such cases occur when the person seen is not even being thought about seems to point to the possibility of strong disinhibitory processes in central sensory areas similar to those in the association areas which so often give rise to "spontaneous" ideas and images. In keeping with the rule that all situational sources of stimulation should be exhausted before postulating residuals, possible focal and contextual antecedents of illusory, hallucinatory, and anxiety states should not be ruled out a priori when specific cases of such phenomena are in question.

Peripheral sources for hallucinations and illusions are continually being discovered to narrow the domain of purely centrally aroused excitations. Thus Moore (1939) believed that many hallucinations of the insane, e.g., flying through space, movement of the body when confined in bed, seeing one's body floating in air or passing through the barred windows of the hospital room, arise from disorders in the tactile-kinesthetic senses. The dependence of a stable visual world on normal tactile-kinesthetic input is now being fully appreciated. Conversely, when normal sensory input is lacking, there is greater likelihood that central processes will be augmented to "take up the slack" to preserve a balance, or to fill lacunae in perception.

Less well-defined stimuli. Thus far we have not accounted for all types of stimulation. Stimuli are responsible not only for sensory processes but also for feelings and emotions, which, even if they are classed as sensory, have dimensions of their own. When such stimuli facilitate or inhibit responses, they are said to be "reinforcers." Are reinforcing stimuli outside the classes of stimuli we have discussed, thus making another class necessary? It seems more likely that all stimuli have reinforcing properties in greater or lesser degree. Some stimuli may arouse fear or anxiety or may serve as pacifiers. The lack of specific sources of stimulation for certain fears and anxieties has led to the concept of "free-floating" anxiety, which presumably has its origins in central or other internal processes. In place of this the term "tension" is now being used both in the narrower sense of muscle tension (contraction-relaxation) and in the broader sense of fear or anxiety without definite origins. There is experimental evidence showing that tension levels may rise or fall as a function of various kinds of stimulation (Bevan and Adamson, 1960). Stimuli responsible for producing tension have been found to belong in one or another of the classes we have enumerated; but we must allow for the possibility of nonspecific sources of stimulation in mild to morbid fears, anxieties, and other abnormal states. Thus phobias arising from repressed memories are not alleviated until the original traumatic event is reinstated and clarified. In such cases the history of the individual must be known to uncover the stimulation that was initially responsible for the deviant behavior and that later acted as a powerful residual.

Still other classes of stimuli might be proposed. We speak of the "social" stimulation that one individual receives from another or from a group. One reads of "religious," "cultural," "aesthetic," and "intellectual" stimuli, and these terms are legitimate to denote the higher-order stimuli discussed earlier. Extension of the concept of stimulus to include information and meaning makes it possible to deal operationally with the higher-order stimuli that many earlier psychologists banished to the normative disciplines.

CENTRAL AND EFFERENT CONTROL OF RECEPTOR ACTIVITIES

Our survey of the main classes of stimulating situations has shown that the concept of stimulus cannot be limited to mere excitation of receptors by energies or changes in energies which impinge on individual sense organs. Likewise, the classical notion of one-way peripheral-sensory, to central, to peripheral-motor conduction must be given up in the light of modern work in which central influence often results in control of receptor functioning. The notion of sensory mechanisms functioning solely in relation to the duration and intensity of various types of stimuli has been challenged recently by physiologists as it was earlier by psychologists. Edelberg has summarized results of physiological studies in this area as follows (1961, p. 187):

Central control over the threshold of peripheral receptors or primary synapses by tonic bombardment along efferent fibers has been demonstrated in the case of muscle spindle by Granit and Kaada (1952) and by Hagbarth and Kerr (1954), in the case of the vestibular system by Gernandt and Thulin (1955), the retina by Granit (1955), olfactory receptors by Kerr and Hagbarth (1955), and by Tucker and Beidler (1956), and tactile receptors by Loewenstein (1956). Another mechanism for control of peripheral reception is exemplified in the contraction of the muscles of the middle ear, with an ensuing reduction of auditory sensitivity either in response to loud sounds (Galambos and Allen, 1958) or following reticular stimulation (Hugelin, Dumont, and Paillas, 1960).

Further evidence of the influence of central factors over sensory input is given by Edelberg:

Demonstration of selectivity as a consequence of focus of attention is described in the oft-cited experiment of Hernandez-Peon and his co-workers (1956), recently challenged in part by Hugelin et al. (1960), who showed that attention by an unanesthetized cat to mice, fish odors, and electric shocks reduced the cochlear nucleus potentials evoked by clicks (1961, p. 187).

In addition, he refers to the role of attention in the effects of warning signals on visual and auditory thresholds. To these we may add the influence of the foreperiod signal on simple reaction times. As a result of his study of the relation of GSR, vasoconstriction, and tactile sensitivity, Edelberg found evidence for involvement of the autonomic system as well as of the central mechanisms in tactile sensitivity:

. . . there is a mechanism by which the human, while in a low-level external field, in response to an alerting stimulus or to internal activation, can reduce his tactile threshold during the time of this activation; that this mechanism is prompt and readily reversible upon cessation of the arousal situation; that autonomic activity is normally associated with this sensitization in a close time relationship. A by-product of the investigation is the observation that the magnitude of these shifts in tactile sensitiviy is such that any experiment based on the assumption that there is a static tactile threshold in a given area is invalid unless the state of arousal of the organism is maintained constant in some way, or unless changes in arousal are taken into account (1961, p. 194).

That receptor mechanisms function as part of the total sensori-motor system, and not as simple passive recipients or transducers of energy as envisaged in nineteenth-century sensory physiology, is evident from Lindsley's summary of central influences on receptor activities:

. . . it appears that all sense modalities have some means of centrifugal control either at the level of the receptor itself, through reflex loops, at the first or second synapse, or more centrally located stations along the efferent pathways. The importance of this cannot be overemphasized in stimulus-response integrations of continued or sequential nature. Thus a new principle of behavioral control is added to those already known (Lindsley, 1956, p. 335).

Our survey of the situations giving rise to excitation and modification of receptor processes necessitates a broader definition of stimulus than is contained in the concept of stimulus as energy or energy change. Similarly, modern work on central and efferent control of receptor activities renders obsolete the view that sensory processes can be understood wholly in terms of peripherally aroused centripetal processes running their course without centrifugal control. We thus have a broader psychophysiological basis for higher-order, phenomenological data which we must now discuss.

PHENOMENOLOGY AND PERCEPTION

We have so far discussed types of stimuli, conditions of stimulation, and the physiological nature of perceptual processes, but these subjects are only propaedeutic to perception. Perception reveals the world about us and contains most of the stuff of our experience. Early in the history of philosophical thinking the real and the perceptual world were separated, with second place usually given to the latter because of its supposedly ephemeral and illusory nature. In their hunt for an underlying unchangeable reality the early Greek philosophers (as do many modern thinkers) forgot that we perceive, enjoy, dislike, approach, avoid; in short, they forgot that we live out our lives with phenomenal objects and activities, not with unobserved perduring substances or forces. The energies of nature are harnessed and directed to satisfy needs and desires concerned with phenomenal objects—people, food, shelter, cars, planes, works of art. Psychology, beguiled by the quest for a one-sided objectivity during the heyday of Watsonian behaviorism and Pavlovian reflexology forsook the study of perception only to return to it with renewed vigor about 20 years ago when perception was given the central position it now occupies in American psychology.

Since interest in perception has either originated from or been closely related to some type of phenomenology, let us consider the varieties of phenomenology and the problems of perception peculiar to each. Phenomenology is often used as an antonym for overt behavior; but we shall see that there is a phenomenology of behavior as well as a phenomenology of experience. At least six different phenomenological approaches are distinguished in the following sections.

The phenomenology of the man in the street. This type of phenomenology is known to us in the content of most communication. Molar characteristics of behavior, such as friendliness, beauty, meanness, and placidity, which "can be expressed in terms neither of shape and colour nor of practical use, and which are apt to exert a powerful influence on our behavior" (Koffka, 1935, p. 359), represent the type of phenomenology current in everyday life. Properties of objects and events which Koffka referred to as having "demand" or "physiognomic" character are described in everyday and sometimes in literary phenomenological terms. It has objective meaning to say that a person is clumsy or graceful in his movements, that Mischa Elman's violin playing is noted for its elegance and style, or that an athlete has good form. It is true that we perceive a face as smiling rather than as a contraction of the buccinator muscles. Difficulties with such descriptive phrases arise when we try to quantify them or to obtain agreement among observers on what is actually perceived. The progress of sciences like geology, biology, and psychology has consisted largely in analyzing and measuring molar phenomena like rocks, plants and animals, and behavior. To be sure, rocks are aggregations of minerals to the geologist, plants and animals are systems of cells to the biologist, and behavior, it is granted, is mediated by reflexes. Whether we use the analytical language of reflexes or phenomenological molar description will depend upon which is more adequate for what we wish to say. The Hindu ascetic who saw only a "bundle of bones" when the young man beside him saw a beautiful girl approaching them was right in his way, but the young man was probably not convinced of the adequacy of the other's description.

Artistic phenomenology. Closely allied with everyday phenomenology is the phenomenology of the arts—poetry, prose, music, painting, sculpture—and of all products of human artifice. Every new creation results in a new phenomenological product. Periods, styles, and national origins are revealed in written and oral communications, in artistic products, and also in the industrial artifacts of any age, group, or nation. Human products have the phenomenological stamp of the individual worker in addition to the mark of the qualities of his times. The creations of the artist, writer, scientist, and technologist are more or less new, more or less distinct from what the man in the street experiences. Thus new realities, new phenomonological objects, are created which, after sufficient exposure or through education, are accepted and perceived to be beautiful, good, useful, or normal. The manner in which writers create new phenomenological objects and relations is seen in the following selections, the first dealing with the folklore of odors, the second describing the synesthetic images aroused by vowels, presumably from the poet's own experience:

(He wondered) what there was in frankincense that made one mystical, and in ambergris that stirred one's passions, and in violets that woke the memory of dead romances, and in musk that troubled the brain, and in champak that stained the imagination; and seeking often to elaborate a real psychology of perfumes, and to estimate the several influences of sweet-smelling roots, and scented pollen-laden flowers, or aromatic balms, and of dark and fragrant woods of spikenard that sickens, of hovenia that makes men mad, and of aloes that are said to be able to expel melancholy from the soul (Oscar Wilde, *The Picture of Dorian Gray,* 1920, p. 198).

> A black, E white, I red, U green, O blue,
> Vowels; some day I shall reveal your birth:
> A, black velvet swarm of flies that over earth
> Buzz to the foulest stench, abyss of hue
> Sombre; E frank with smoke and fierce intents,
> Spears of proud glaciers, white kings, blossom-lips;
> I purple of spitting blood, laugh of fair lips
> In anger or in drunken penitence;
> U cycles, divine rhythm of the seas,
> Peace of beast-strewn pastures, of wrinkles that crease
> Brows whereon the furrow of learning lies;

O, great lightning, with strange clamors hurled
Over the quiet of angels and the world,
O omega, violet ray of her eyes.

Rimbaud, *A Season in Hell*

These two selections, taken as examples of literary phenomenology, illustrate the power of verbal symbols, to evoke images and meanings associated with odoriferous stimuli on the one hand and synesthetic sensory processes on the other. Such associations were ruled out of analytical introspective reports as not germane to the immediately given sensory processes. The images and emotions aroused by such literary passages are often as vivid and lasting as those aroused by direct sensory experiences. Music, painting, sculpture—all the products of the arts and technology—would be poor indeed if their organismic effects were limited to the sensory qualities as classically conceived. How the poet, novelist, composer, painter, and sculptor is able to produce his works is the problem of creativity; how individuals are affected by, and react to, artistic products is the problem of experimental aesthetics. Recognition of the phenomenological nature of the processes involved in artistic creation and appreciation is one of the first conditions for the psychology of art (cf. Ogden, 1938; Arnheim, 1954).

Analytical introspection. In the early days of sensory physiology and modern experimental psychology, methods had not been developed for dealing scientifically with the welter of everyday experience or with the perceptions aroused by literary, artistic, and technological products. The result was that the first experimental-quantitative studies of sensory processes were limited to determination of the adequate stimuli for arousal of specific receptors and enumeration and measurement of the sensory qualities associated with each. Studies were limited to the primary colors and the dimensions of hue, brightness, and saturation in vision; to warmth, coldness, pressure, and pain from the skin; to pitch, loudness, and volume in hearing; to what was bitter, sweet, salty, and sour in taste; to what was flowery, fruity, burned, resinous, putrid, and spicy in olfaction. The list of fundamental "sensations" was extended both by those classing themselves as introspectionists (Titchener accepted the addition of the "glassy" sensation to the roster of visual qualities) and to an even greater extent by those who rejected analytical introspection in favor of molar or phenomenological descriptions. The approach of the introspectionists belongs with phenomenology because of its emphasis on *immediate experience,* although it must be remembered that Wundt and Titchener and their followers insisted that immediate experience must be analyzed into its component sensory processes which a strict phenomological approach would not allow. Even centrally aroused processes of memory and imagination were treated as complexes of elementary "images" differing from sensations only in intensity and certain other dimensional attributes.

While almost every new and forward movement in psychology has been, in some sense, a reaction against analytical introspection, e.g., behaviorism, imageless thought, Gestalt, and the so-called "dynamic" approaches, its accomplishments have been many. To analytical introspection we owe the first catalogue of sensory qualities, early psychophysics, and later developments in the dimensional approach to consciousness (see Boring, 1933). We should, therefore, not throw out the baby with the bath in rejecting the analytical introspection of an earlier day. It may serve a useful purpose when used as a tool rather than as an end in itself.

Philosophical (Husserlian) phenomenology. The type of phenomenology that has most influenced the study of perception, furnished the basis for some clinical approaches to personality (e.g., nondirective therapy), and even served as the fundamental concept for a system of psychology (Snygg and Combs, 1949) is that of Husserl (1913) who regarded his approach as an independent philosophical discipline. I can give no better brief account of phenomenology in the strict sense than to repeat my earlier exposition which was as follows:

As advocated by Husserl phenomenology rejects such distinctions as inner-outer, real-unreal, objective-subjective, in their usual meanings. Immediately intuited experiences are taken at their face value without inquiring into their origins. Experiences are regarded as self-contained wholes. Each perception carries immediate certainty about something which Husserl called its essence. Higher mental processes are not necessary to explain meanings, values, and the objects of thought. Experience in this sense exemplifies; it does not validate since validation refers to other experiences which in turn exemplify some essence. In perceiving a tree we might reflect: "There is a tree, existing in real space and time, and here am I, a real observer, perhaps having an Ego, looking at the tree." But phenomenologically there can be no question as to whether the tree is real or imaginary, whether I am of the same stuff as the tree, or if real relations exist between the tree and myself. If the experience carries within itself marks of reality, i.e., what is meant by reality, then it can be said the tree is real. Experience is thus self-validating (Helson, 1951, p. 364).

The phenomenological approach thus relies on immediate intuition with no assumptions, deductions, or inferences to color it. Phenomenology led to acceptance and consideration of molar properties of objects and events without attempting to reduce them to elemental units or dimensions. It was also responsible, in the hands of the Gestalt psychologists, for rejection of unobservable images and sensations often invoked to explain such perceptual phenomena as phi phenomenon, color constancy, and many of the "illusions." In short, it resulted in a more direct attempt to describe and measure phenomena that analytical introspection had either refused to acknowledge by classing them as "meanings" or "values" or had analyzed in terms of sensory qualities often having little resemblance to the originally given data.

Philosophical phenomenology was neither quantitative nor experimental. Indeed, Husserl strongly objected to its inclusion in psychology, maintaining that it was an independent, philosophical branch of knowledge. For its psychological applications we must turn to the work of Katz, Rubin, Wertheimer, Koffka, Gibson, and others who have transformed phenomenology from a purely philosophical exercise into a tool for the investigation of psychological problems.

Experimental phenomenology. For lack of a better term we may refer to the phenomenology of the people mentioned above and others like them as "experimental phenomenology" as contrasted with both the philosophical approach of Husserl and the clinical approach of nondirective therapists who have made their own application of the phenomenological approach. Experimental phenomenology took molar properties of objects into the laboratory and extended the domain of sensori-perceptual phenomena. Thus Katz (1911) showed that the achromatic colors could not be described on a single or unidimensional continuum of brightness and that the chromatic colors could not be described adequately by simply adding hue and saturation to brightness. Colors also have properties of texture, liveliness, pronouncedness, transparency, volume, and gloss in varying degrees. Still other properties have been asserted to be basic in vision such as hardness, warmth, location, shape, flicker, lustre, and affective tone. Embodying both color and spatial considerations, the distinction of figure and ground by Rubin (1921) has proved of utmost importance in making possible understanding of field articulation. Gibson's work on texture gradients (1950*a* and *b*) and his classification of forms (1951) have laid the foundations for a broader attack on problems of space perception.

To understand the role of phenomenology in psychological theorizing one must go to Koffka's *Principles of Gestalt Psychology* (1935) which has its own unique flavor. The logical basis for physiological theorizing by the Gestalt psychologists was laid down by Wertheimer (1912) in his article dealing with perceived movement, where he said in effect: If there is no difference in the movement perceived from two stationary slits of light exposed in rapid succession and that from a single moving object, then physiological processes underlying them must be identical. This paved the way for the Köhler type of physiological "field" theory designed to provide a basis for extended molar attributes of perception.

Phenomenology of overt behavior. Just as sensations or attributes were considered the units out of which molar perceptual properties arise, so reflexes are often considered the functional units of overt behavior. As stated earlier, the physiologist can tell us the muscles and neural elements involved in a smile, but for some purposes the smile is more important than the reflexes by which it is mediated. In other words, molar properties of overt behavior may be interesting and important in their own right. There have been few experimental studies of what we may call the phenomenology of motor patterns of response. Time-motion studies so popular in industry several decades ago were concerned with the phenomenology of skilled acts. Photographs of the movements made by hands, fingers, and arms of skilled workers performing various tasks showed the best ways of picking up, transporting, and otherwise manipulating objects, and these molar patterns of movements were used to show the novice the kind of pattern that he should reproduce for best results.

Since most behavioral adjustments are to molar properties of the environment, the phenomenology of motor patterns of response can be used as a basis for manipulating the environment to secure optimal performance, as in the cockpits of airplanes with their numerous controls and signaling devices. For example, during the Second World War we wished to determine the optimal range of positions for manipulating handwheels on anti-aircraft fire controls. As a first step toward studying this problem we asked *S*s to draw circles of varying sizes on a large blackboard beginning with the hand positioned at the midline of the body and extending it as far as possible along eight meridians at 45° that sampled the frontal parallel plane. It was found that there was an optimal region for drawing circles, not too far from the midline of the body, beyond which it became more and more difficult to perform circular motions. The frontal plane was thus mapped for circular motions of various diameters. The figures drawn in the frontal plane could be considered as the phenomenology of such motions and they provided the information necessary for deciding where hand-wheels of various sizes could be positioned for optimal performance and comfort. The phenomenology of motor responses thus offers a rich field for further exploration.

Are phenomenal properties constitutive? To predict and control phenomena it is necessary to understand cause-effect relationships. This raises the question of whether such relationships can be inferred from the molar properties of objects and events. In other words, we may ask: Are phenomenal properties purely descriptive, or epiphenomena; or are they also constitutive? In examining this question we shall see that there is no "yes" or "no" answer as some writers have maintained who have had a bias toward one or the other side of this problem. The results of several experiments will be discussed, some in favor of an affirmative answer, some in favor of a negative answer, and a solution will be offered which seems to square with the facts.

The first example is from the area of animal behavior:

Three rats were made to jump a barrier to reach food. If the barrier was of uniform height, rats showed no preference for negotiating any particular part of the barrier. If any part of the barrier was lowered by even a small amount, the rats showed a preference for this portion. If the barrier was uniformly raised to a height which was not jumped, and then part of it was raised yet higher, the part of the barrier remaining relatively low was jumped successfully. It is concluded that if part of the barrier appears relatively low, the rat may "decide" it can jump after all . . . relative lowness is an important factor in determining a rat's jumping behavior, a factor which may override a rat's assessment of the maximal height it can jump (Mukerji, 1956, p. 140).

The second example comes from the field of stereoscopic vision. It is commonly believed that retinal factors alone determine whether images will fuse to give depth perception. To test whether *apparent* deviations from corresponding points would give depth perception, Squires (1956) presented the Zöllner figure to the left eye and the naked parallels of this figure to the right eye. Would the apparent deviation in direction of the crosshatched lines in the Zöllner figure cause the parallel lines in the combined image to appear in a different plane from the rest of the figure, and hence give depth? Observation gave an affirmative answer: Although the parallel lines fell on corresponding points of the two eyes, they appeared in a different plane from the crosshatched lines, and the resultant depth must be attributed to the phenomenal difference in the images. Even though the nonparallel appearance of the lines in the Zöllner figure may have been responsible for eye movements or faulty convergence, it is nevertheless true that an *apparent* deviation from parallelism exerted effects similar to actual deviation in the two images.

FIG. 5.2.   This figure may be seen either as a W with a line or as two tops. (After Ex and De Bruijn, 1956.)

The third example demonstrating constitutive effects from phenomenal properties of stimuli is taken from a study by Ex and De Bruijn (1956). They used ambiguous stimuli that could be perceived either as letters from the alphabet (line figures) with an added line, or as surface figures with quite different properties. Thus the start or S figure in Fig. 5.2 can be seen either as a w with a line across its top or as a surface figure denoting two tops. By means of tachistoscopic exposures, the ambiguous figures (S or start figures) were exposed first, followed by the line figures (E or end figures). If, as the authors point out, a faintly curved line is followed by a straight line, the curved line is seen to straighten itself, and the perception is one of identity. But if a circle is followed by a triangle, there is substitution and no impression of identity. If the ambiguous figures were perceived as letters, the second figure would function as an identity figure, otherwise as a substitute figure. The S figures were constructed from the E figures as a basis, so that on superposition of the S and E figures the identical elements of the two figures appeared in the same positions. When the S and E figures are exposed in succession, if the S figure is seen as a w, Ss report a growing letter w; but if it is seen as two tops, Ss report disappearance of the tops followed by the letter w.

The results present strong evidence for the effect of the perceived form of the first figure on the type of shift following exposure of the second figure. When the first figure was seen as a surface figure (i.e., not as a letter), there were 58 percent substitution perceptions, 0 percent identity perceptions, and 42 percent unclassifiable. When the first figure was seen as a letter deviate, 87.5 percent involved identity changes, 12.5 percent were unidentifiable, and there were no substitution reports. The authors conclude that phenomenal similarity determines whether an identity or a substitute perception occurs under these conditions.

This account of the phenomenal properties of visual perception is by no means complete and could be paralleled with discussions of effects of phenomenal properties in the other sense modalities. Let us consider one more example, this one in the field of lifted weights where too little attention has been paid to the *density* of the stimuli, it being assumed that only mass or weight determines perceived heaviness. A study dealing with tactile-kinesthetic density was made by Nyssen and Bourdon (1956) who used as a standard a 500-grm. block with dimensions of $21 \times 5 \times 2$ cm. and a set of series weights $21 \times 5 \times 7$ cm. ranging in weight from 500 to 1100 grm. in 50-grm. steps. Using both ascending and descending methods of limits, they determined the value of the *variable larger weight* which was equal to the *standard smaller weight*. It required a variable of 750 grm. to be judged equal to the standard of 500 grm. in the ascending order, and a weight between 850 and 800 grm. to be judged equal to the standard in the descending order. They concluded that the effective stimulus in their experiments was density, not weight, i.e., the ratio of weight to size. They refer to Van Biervliet who noted that a bottle picked up by the neck feels heavier than if it is picked up by grasping the bottom. As a result of their study Nyssen and Bourdon concluded that density is an immediate phenomenal datum and hence is a dimension in its own right, a fact confirmed by Furth (1960).

Failure to take account of the fact that perceived weight is a function of density rather than of weight per se led Brown (1953) to assume that relevance affected perceived weight when a tray weighing the same as the anchor stimulus had less effect than the anchor on the series stimuli. While this assumption may be true under some circumstances, Brown's position is open to the objection that he did not control for density as well as relevance when the tray was used in place of the anchor stimulus.

Our examples up to this point seem to set no limits on what, for want of a better term, we may call "phenomenalism." In the extreme form enunciated by Husserl, phenomenology recognizes no distinctions among presentations except such as are based on immediately intuited experiences. According to this position, for example, something contrived in a laboratory which looks like the moon in every respect (including the sky around it) is phenomenologically on a par with the celestial body if there is no basis in immediate experience by which the two may be distinguished. External validation is excluded from a purely phenomenological approach. This limitation is, of course, its weakness, for it is the very essence of scientific procedure to test concepts by as many different routes as possible. The nature of molecules, atoms, and the smaller particles—electrons, protons, positrons, and so forth—were determined not by immediate observation, for they are too small to affect our senses, but by independent sets of operations that define these entities and the properties ascribed to them.

The danger of theorizing on the basis of phenomenological properties was brought out by Knox in a test of Koffka's theory of the role of form on critical fusion frequency. Reasoning from the finding by Hartmann (1923) that the more simple two figures are, the greater is their tendency to fuse when exposed in rapid succession, Koffka concluded that stable homogeneous symmetrical figures should have a lower critical fusion frequency than irregular figures (Koffka, 1935). From the phenomenological point of view, experiential homogeneity is synonymous with fusion and experiential temporal heterogeneity is synonymous with flicker; hence the conclusion that simple regular figures should fuse at lower cff than irregularly shaped figures. To test this line of reasoning, Knox (1945) determined the critical fusion frequency for nine different figures: circle, hexagon, square, rectangle with long axis horizontal, rectangle with long axis vertical, rectangle oblique, and three nondescript irregular shapes. Measurements were made both with and without artificial pupil. No differences were found in cff between the stable symmetrical regular figures and the unstable asymmetrical irregular figures. The results demonstrated that inferences cannot be drawn merely on the basis of phenomenological resemblances when the conditions underlying phenomena are not the same. Nor did Fry and Robertson (1935) verify Hartmann's results for fusion when they controlled the hue and brightness of the stimuli and the size of pupil.

We seem to have a paradox on our hands so far as inferences from phenomenological data are concerned. On the one hand there is experimental evidence showing that phenomenal properties may have constitutive effects and do influence basic sensory dimensions; on the other hand, there is experimental evidence showing that predictions from phenomenological properties may not be verified experimentally. The resolution of the paradox is found in the distinction between phenotypical and genotypical characters. Similar phenotypes may arise from different genotypes, and in such cases they will behave differently when conditions are changed. Metamerism of colors furnishes a case in point. Thus two surfaces that are metameric (match) under one source of illumination may not be a color match under another source of illumination if their spectral reflectances are different. The necessary and sufficient conditions for two stimuli to match in color are given by the following expressions:

$$\sum_{380}^{760} E_{1\lambda} R_{1\lambda} \bar{x}_\lambda \Delta\lambda = \sum_{380}^{760} E_{2\lambda} R_{2\lambda} \bar{x}_\lambda \Delta\lambda$$

$$\sum_{380}^{760} E_{1\lambda} R_{1\lambda} \bar{y}_\lambda \Delta\lambda = \sum_{380}^{760} E_{2\lambda} R_{2\lambda} \bar{y}_\lambda \Delta\lambda$$

$$\sum_{380}^{760} E_{1\lambda} R_{1\lambda} \bar{z}_\lambda \Delta\lambda = \sum_{380}^{760} E_{2\lambda} R_{2\lambda} \bar{z}_\lambda \Delta\lambda$$

where $E_{1\lambda}$ and $E_{2\lambda}$ represent the spectral energy distributions of the sources, $R_{1\lambda}$ and $R_{2\lambda}$ represent the spectral reflectances of the surfaces, and $\bar{x}_\lambda$, $\bar{y}_\lambda$, and $\bar{z}_\lambda$, represent the red, green, and blue sensitivities of the Standard Observer. Only when these two sets of equations are equal will the two surfaces match under different types of illumination. When these equalities are satisfied, two patches of color will appear identical, even if illuminated by different sources ($E_{1\lambda}$, $E_{2\lambda}$) and even if their spectral reflectances ($R_{1\lambda}$, $R_{2\lambda}$) are different, provided they are viewed against the same background. Here prediction of phenotypical properties is possible from the genotypical constitution (to continue the argument by analogy with genetics).

It is thus apparent that immediate experience (phenomenology) unsupported by analysis is an unreliable basis for predicting behavioral outcomes. Phenomenology serves to acquaint us with what is, but it furnishes a poor guide to origins and future developments. The answer to the original problem is that phenomenal properties are constitutive when phenomenal data directly reflect their causal substrates. When two phenomena differ there is some difference in their underlying mechanisms; when they are alike the processes underlying them may be the same or different. Only analysis can determine whether phenomenological data are at bottom alike or different and the nature of the underlying mechanisms. One of the first steps in achieving an analytical, causal account of phenomena is to determine the quantitative, functional relations among the conditions responsible for their variation. In the rest of this chapter we shall be concerned primarily with a number of such determinations in various fields of perception.

PERCEPTION OF COLORS AND SPATIAL ASPECTS OF VISION

We are now ready to turn to specific problems in the sphere of perception where it has been shown that the pooling of excitations in the receptor and/or central systems results in the formation of ALs that are responsible for such perceived properties of visual objects as hue, saturation, lightness, shape, size, and direction. After discussing these we shall consider a number of phenomena in other sense modalities on which our systematic position has a bearing. Let us first consider the role of AL in determining the hue, saturation, and lightness of colors and the possibility of envisaging phenomena of constancy, contrast, and adaptation, with their attendant phenomena, within a single conceptual framework.

The data in Table 5.1 represent judgments of hue, lightness, and saturation of 17 nonselective, matt papers ranging from 3 to 80 percent reflectance as seen on daylight white, gray, and black backgrounds in strongly chromatic illumination. In daylight the papers are white, light gray, medium gray, dark gray, or black in color quality. In the strongly chromatic sources of illumination most of them are seen as having more or less saturated hues, the hue and saturation depending upon the distance of any given stimulus from the stimulus that is achromatic under the given conditions of viewing. The clue to the colors that will be seen on the three backgrounds in red, green, yellow, and blue sources of illumination proves to be the stimulus which is seen as achromatic in each case because the reflectance of the achromatic stimulus coincides with "adaptation reflectance," which is the reflectance that reveals the neutral level of the eye. In all cases, stimuli with reflectances above adaptation reflectance are tinged with the hue of the illuminant, while reflectances below adaptation reflectance are tinged with either or both components of the hue complementary to the hue of the illuminant. I called this the principle of color conversion (1958), for it expresses a general law that holds true for objects viewed in near-white and weakly chromatic sources as well as in strongly chromatic sources of light. It will be noticed from the data in Table 5.1 that adaptation reflectance depends in large measure upon the reflectance of the background: with *white* background adaptation reflectance is high; with *gray* background it is intermediate; and with *black* background it is very low. Adaptation reflectance thus tends to approximate background reflectance.

It is evident from the data in Table 5.1 and from our knowledge of individual differences in color vision that adaptation reflectance is a function of three sources of variance: (1) the reflectances of objects in the center of vision; (2) the reflectance of the background; and (3) personal factors which may affect color vision, color matching, or color naming, such as attitude, eye movements, ways of judging, eye pigmentation (if not taken into consideration), and all other factors that are not part of the situation confronting the viewer and which may be regarded as residuals. Adaptation reflectance, as seen in Table 5.1, may cover a range of values within which stimuli are seen as achromatic. We shall have to keep in mind, therefore, in making reference to adaptation level and cognate concepts, that a region embracing a number of values is meant rather than a point having a single value. The formula found adequate to predict adaptation reflectance under a variety of conditions proved to be a weighted geometric mean of the reflectances of all stimuli in the field of vision with background weighted most heavily:

$$A_r = (\overline{R}_s R_b{}^3)^{1/4} \tag{1}$$

or, more generally,

$$A_r = k_1 (\overline{R}_s R_b{}^c)^{1/1+c} \tag{1A}$$

where A_r is adaptation reflectance, k is a fractional constant, $\overline{R}_s$ is the mean of the object reflectances, and R_b is background reflectance. Background reflectance is weighted three times as heavily as the mean of the object reflectances because of its predominant area. The fractional constant, $k < 1$, was introduced to improve the fit between observed

TABLE 5.1. Hue, Lightness and Saturation of 17 Daylight Gray Samples Having Reflectances from 3 to 80 Percent Viewed in 4 Strongly Chromatic Illuminants on Daylight White, Gray, and Black Backgrounds

Reflectance	White Background	Gray Background	Black Background
	Red Illuminant		
0.80	R 9.0/2.0	YR8.0/8.0	R 8.0/8.5
.52	R 7.0/3.0	YR7.5/6.0	R 8.0/8.5
.39	R 7.0/1.0	YR7.0/4.0	R 7.0/8.0
.34	R 7.0/1.0	YR7.0/4.0	R 7.0/8.0
.27	A 5.0/0.0	yR6.5/4.0	R 6.0/7.0
.23	rB5.0/1.0	yR6.5/4.0	R 6.0/8.0
.22	rB5.0/1.0	yR6.0/3.0	R 6.0/8.0
.17	rB4.0/1.0	yR5.5/3.0	R 6.0/7.0
.16	rB4.0/1.0	yR5.5/3.0	R 5.0/7.0
.15	B 5.0/2.0	yR5.5/2.0	R 5.0/6.0
.13	B 4.0/2.0	yR4.5/2.0	R 5.0/6.0
.13	B 3.0/2.0	yR4.5/1.0	R 5.0/6.0
.11	B 3.0/2.0	yR4.0/1.0	R 5.0/6.0
.10	BG3.0/4.0	A 4.0/0.0	R 4.0/4.0
.07	BG2.0/4.0	BG3.0/2.0	R 3.0/4.0
.05	BG2.0/4.0	BG2.5/4.0	yR4.0/4.0
.03	BG0.5/4.5	BG1.0/8.0	A 0.0/0.0
	Blue Illuminant		
0.80	B 9.0/1.0	B 8.5/3.0	B 9.0/3.0
.52	rB8.0/1.0	B 8.0/2.5	B 8.0/4.0
.39	A 7.0/0.0	RB8.0/2.0	B 7.0/4.0
.34	R 6.0/1.0	RB7.0/2.0	B 7.0/4.0
.27	R 5.0/1.0	RB6.0/0.5	B 6.0/4.0
.23	yR6.0/0.5	RB5.5/0.5	B 6.0/4.0
.22	yR5.0/1.0	A 5.0/0.0	B 6.0/4.0
.17	rY5.0/1.0	A 4.0/0.0	B 5.0/3.0
.16	Y 2.0/1.0	A 4.0/0.0	rB5.0/3.0
.15	Y 2.0/2.0	A 4.0/0.0	rB6.0/4.0
.13	Y 2.0/2.0	Y 3.0/0.5	rB6.0/5.0
.13	Y 2.0/2.0	Y 3.0/0.5	rB6.0/5.0
.11	Y 2.0/2.0	Y 3.0/0.5	rB5.0/4.0
.10	RY3.0/2.0	RY2.5/1.0	RB4.0/3.0
.07	RY2.0/3.0	RY2.0/2.0	A 5.0/0.0
.05	RY1.0/3.0	RY1.5/3.0	A 3.0/0.0
.03	RY0.5/2.0	RY0.5/5.5	rY0.5/1.0

Note: Hues are given as R, G, Y, or B for red, green, yellow, or blue, with small letters indicating the minor component in binary hues. Lightness (numerator) and saturation (denominator) are in terms of a 0–10 scale.

TABLE 5.1. (Continued)

White Background	Gray Background	Black Background
Green Illuminant		
yG9.0/2.0	yG8.0/7.0	yG9.0/7.0
yG8.0/1.0	yG7.5/6.0	yG8.0/8.0
A 8.0/0.0	yG7.0/4.0	yG8.0/8.0
A 7.5/0.0	yG6.5/4.0	yG7.5/9.0
RB6.0/2.0	yG6.0/1.0	yG7.0/7.0
RB6.0/2.0	yG6.0/0.5	yG7.0/7.0
RB6.0/2.0	A 5.0/0.0	yG6.5/6.0
RB5.0/3.0	A 5.0/0.0	yG7.0/5.0
RB5.0/3.0	A 5.0/0.0	yG7.0/5.0
RB4.0/3.0	BR5.0/0.5	yG7.0/5.0
RB4.0/3.0	BR4.5/1.0	yG7.0/5.0
RB4.0/4.0	BR4.5/1.0	yG7.0/5.0
RB3.0/4.0	BR4.0/2.5	yG6.0/5.0
RB3.0/5.0	BR3.0/5.0	yG4.0/3.0
RB2.5/6.0	BR2.5/5.0	yG3.0/2.0
RB2.0/7.0	BR2.0/6.0	yG2.0/1.0
RB0.5/9.5	BR1.0/7.0	A 0.5/0.0
Yellow Illuminant		
Y 9.0/2.0	Y 8.0/7.0	Y 9.0/8.0
Y 6.0/1.0	Y 7.5/7.0	Y 9.0/8.0
A 6.0/0.0	Y 7.0/4.0	Y 8.0/6.0
RB8.0/1.0	Y 6.5/4.0	Y 8.0/6.0
RB7.0/3.0	A 6.5/0.0	Y 7.0/4.0
RB7.0/3.0	A 6.0/0.0	Y 7.0/4.0
RB6.0/4.0	A 5.0/0.0	Y 7.0/4.0
RB6.0/5.0	RB5.0/1.5	Y 6.0/4.0
RB6.0/5.0	RB5.0/1.5	Y 5.5/4.0
RB5.0/5.0	RB4.0/2.0	Y 5.5/3.5
RB5.0/4.0	RB4.0/2.5	Y 5.5/3.5
RB5.0/5.0	RB3.5/2.5	Y 5.5/3.5
RB5.0/5.0	RB3.5/3.0	Y 5.0/3.0
RB4.0/5.0	RB3.0/5.0	Y 4.0/3.0
RB3.0/8.0	RB3.0/5.0	Y 3.5/2.0
RB2.0/8.0	RB2.5/6.0	Y 3.0/2.0
RB0.5/8.5	RB1.0/7.0	A 0.0/0.0

SOURCE: From Helson, 1938. With the permission of the American Psychological Association.

and predicted values of AL. Rewriting Equation (1) in log form we have:

$$\log A_r = \log k + \frac{\log \overline{R}_s + 3.0 \log R_b}{4} \qquad (2)$$

Since only brightness adaptation is in question when the illumination is monochromatic, Equation (1) or (2) suffices to determine the achromatic point. When objects of different spectral reflectances are viewed in nonhomogeneous illumination, the achromatic point representing the chromatic adaptation level is defined as a weighted arithmetic mean of the trichromatic coefficients of the stimuli and the background. Since each color is specified by three trichromatic coefficients representing the percentages of light from three primary stimuli necessary to match the color, only two of which need to be specified as they always sum to unity, we can write an expression for the neutral or achromatic point under chromatic conditions of viewing as follows:

$$x_A = \frac{\overline{x}_s + 3.0x_b}{4}$$
$$y_A = \frac{\overline{y}_s + 3.0y_b}{4} \qquad (3)$$

where x_A and y_A are the trichromatic coefficients of the stimulus which is achromatic and which therefore specifies the chromatic adaptation level, $\overline{x}_s$ and $\overline{y}_s$ are the means of the trichromatic coefficients of the stimuli, and x_b and y_b are the trichromatic coefficients of the background.

It will be noticed that in Equations (1) to (3) we have not included a term to take account of residual sources of variance which are responsible for individual differences in color vision. Such differences exist among individuals with so-called normal color vision, as well as among color-anomalous and color-blind populations, as seen from the data in Table 5.2 for 16 individuals who judged Munsell color chips viewed in Palo daylight illumination. While about 75 per cent of the Ss reported the same hue for a given chip, the remaining Ss reported different hues, some seeing a component to one side of the predominant hue, others seeing a component on the other side of the main hue. Thus R 3/7 which was reported as unitary (pure) red by 12 of the 16 Ss was seen as a yellowish red by 3 Ss and as a bluish red by 1 S. Similarly, G 3/4 which was reported as unitary green by 11 Ss was seen as a yellowish green by 2 *S*s and as a bluish green by 3 *S*s. In the case of *P* ⅜ the 16 *S*s divided about equally into three groups, the first of which saw equal amounts of red and blue in the "purple" stimulus; the second, more blue than red; and the third, more red than blue.

TABLE 5.2. Hues of 18 Munsell Colors as Reported in Palo Daylight Illumination by 16 Observers

Stimuli	R	yR	RY	rY	Y	gY	YG	yG	G	bG	BG	gB	B	rB	RB	bR	A
R3/7	12	3														1	
R5/10	10	5														1	
R7/6	13	2														1	
YR4/5	1	4	9	2													
Y5/7					10	6											
Y7/8					15	1											
G3/4								2	11	3							
G5/7								3	13								
G7/7								4	11	1							
B3/5												6	10				
B5/6												7	9				
B7/4											1	1	14				
P3/6														6	5	5	
P5/6															10	6	
PB7/4												16					
A10/0																	16
A5/0																	16
A0/0																	16

Note: Letters indicate hues as follows: R = red; Y = yellow; G = green; B = blue; P = purple; A = achromatic. Small letters indicate minor components; for example, yR = yellowish red.
SOURCE: From Helson, 1939. With the permission of the *American Journal of Psychology.*

Individual differences in color vision have been ascribed to differences in macular pigmentation, in transmissivity of the various ocular surfaces and media, and in sensitivity of the color receptors themselves. Differences in color vision also arise from the method of observation or report or from failure of observers to employ color names in identical fashion when reporting the colors they see. Such differences among *S*s do not cease to be important under the most refined conditions of visual research as in direct color matching to a standard (cf. Halsey and Chapanis, 1954). In fact, the more refined the method of measuring color vision, the more certainly do individual differences appear. Thus the trilinear coordinates of the best white that three

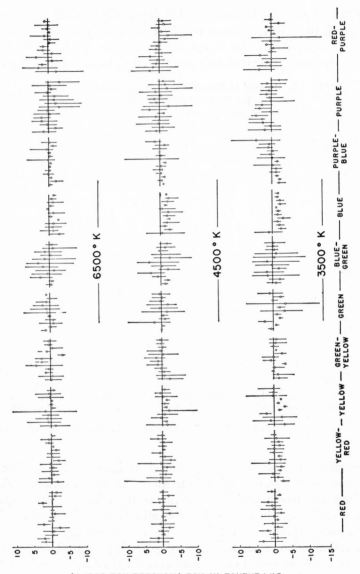

RED —— YELLOW- —— YELLOW —— GREEN- —— GREEN —— BLUE- —— BLUE —— PURPLE- —— PURPLE —— RED-
RED   YELLOW   GREEN   GREEN   BLUE   PURPLE

—— 6500° K ——

—— 4500° K ——

—— 3500° K ——

DIFFERENCE IN HUE (MUNSELL HUE STEPS)

trained observers produced by mixing the red, green, and blue primaries in a colorimeter were $x = 0.269 \pm 0.026$; $y = 0.269 \pm 0.040$; and $z = 0.462 \pm 0.057$ (Helson and Michels, 1948). The variation among Ss was thus over 10 percent of these mean values and was well above threshold for any one of the Ss.

It is necessary, therefore, to provide a term in the expressions for adaptation reflectance and for the x, y point in the C.I.E. mixture diagram representing chromatic adaptation to take account of individual differences in color vision or color responses. To do this we add a residual term, $R_r{}^r$, to Equations (1) and (2) and replace the numerical weighting coefficients by letters for purposes of greater generality giving

$$A_r = k(\overline{R}_s{}^p R_b{}^q R_r{}^r) \tag{4}$$

or, in log form:

$$\log A_r = \log k + p \log \overline{R}_s + q \log R_b + r \log R_r \tag{5}$$

where R_r is the residual factor and $p, q,$ and r are weighting factors for focal, background, and residual stimuli respectively, and the other symbols have the same meanings as in the previous equations. To simplify and normalize the weighting coefficients we let

$$p + q + r = 1 \tag{6}$$

Similarly, adding a term for the residual, r_r, and using letters for the weighting coefficients in Equations (3) for the achromatic points in the color mixture diagram, we have

$$\begin{aligned} x_A &= k(p\overline{x}_s + qx_b + rx_r) \\ y_A &= k(p\overline{y}_s + qy_b + ry_r) \end{aligned} \tag{7}$$

FIG. 5.3. Departures of the experimental means from the predicted hues of the colors perceived to belong to the 130 Munsell samples illuminated by three fluorescent sources. The circles represent the differences on the Munsell 100-hue scale between the experimentally found hues (means of five observers) and the hues predicted in accord with computations. The vertical solid lines indicate by their length the extent of the individual-observer ranges in hue estimates; and by their positions relative to the horizontal base lines (representing predicted hues), whether the predicted hues fall within the individual-observer ranges. Note that the majority of these vertical lines intersect the base line, indicating that the predicted hues do fall within the interobserver ranges. Note also that for the specimens in the blue-hue range, there is a small but regular and apparently significant exception to this general rule for all three fluorescent sources. (From Helson, Judd, and Wilson, 1956. With the permission of *Illuminating Engineering*.)

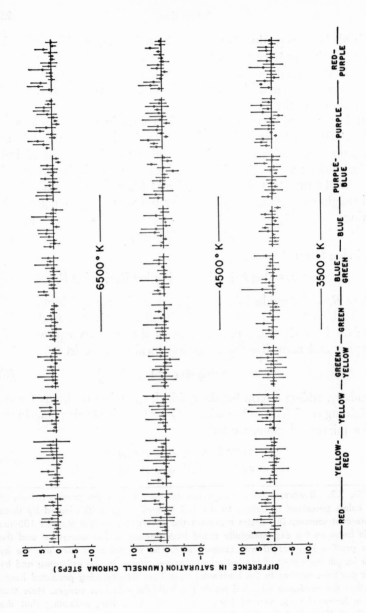

DIFFERENCE IN SATURATION (MUNSELL CHROMA STEPS)

RED —— YELLOW- —— YELLOW —— GREEN- —— GREEN —— BLUE- —— BLUE —— PURPLE- —— PURPLE —— RED-
RED   YELLOW   GREEN   BLUE   PURPLE

where the symbols have the same meanings as defined above. It should be noticed that in the definition of the coordinates of the *achromatic* point in the color mixture diagram we average the trichromatic coefficients, not their logarithms, because mixtures of colored stimuli lie on the straight line connecting the points representing the components of the mixture weighted directly by their reflectances or luminances.

A stringent test of the assumption that the colors of objects depend primarily upon the state of adaptation of the visual mechanism was made in a series of studies by the writer and his co-workers which were concerned with changes in object colors in passing from daylight to incandescent-filament illumination (Helson and Grove, 1947; Helson, Judd, and Warren, 1952) and from daylight to various types of fluorescent sources of illumination (Helson, Judd, and Wilson, 1956). The observations made in fluorescent sources of illumination provided a crucial test of the quantitative theory formulated to account for object colors perceived in incandescent-filament illumination because it was not known if a theory based on the fairly smooth spectral energy distributions of tungsten-filament lamps or daylight would hold for irregular energy distributions of fluorescent lamps. The predicted changes in hue in passing from daylight to 3500K, 4500K, and 6500K fluorescent sources of illumination were in excellent agreement with the observed hues in all parts of the spectrum except in the blue region where there was a small but significant difference between observation and prediction (Fig. 5.3). This was probably due to known deficiency of the C.I.E. Standard Observer in blue sensitivity. The predicted

---

FIG. 5.4. Departures of the experimental means from the predicted saturations of the color perceived to belong to the 130 Munsell samples illuminated by three fluorescent sources. The circles represent the differences on the Munsell chroma scales between the experimentally found saturations (means of five observers) and the saturations predicted in accord with computations. The vertical solid lines indicate by their length the extent of the individual-observer ranges in saturation estimates; and by their positions relative to the horizontal base lines (representing predicted saturations), whether the predicted saturations fall within the individual-observer ranges. Note that the majority of these vertical lines intersect the base line, indicating that the predicted saturations do fall within the individual-observer ranges. Note also that the five-observer averages of estimated saturation tend to be higher than the predicted saturations by about one Munsell step for each of the three types (6500, 4500, 3500) of fluorescent lamps studied. (From Helson, Judd, and Wilson, 1956. With the permission of *Illuminating Engineering*.)

saturations of the colors, while close, were on the whole less than the observed, showing that there was greater constancy of saturation than was expected (as shown in Fig. 5.4).

The theoretical computations were based on correction factors applied to the C.I.E. specifications of the colors in daylight to take account of the changed state of adaptation in the nondaylight sources of illumination. While no more than limited success can be claimed for the relatively simple quantitative formulation employed in these studies it is apparent that considerable progress has been made since the earlier qualitative accounts of color constancy. The more general question concerning changes in object colors when passing from daylight to other sources of illumination has been answered at least to a first degree of approximation so far as hue, lightness, and saturation are concerned. We can now say that hue and saturation remain fairly constant in spite of changes in the spectral energies of sources of illumination when the eye is able to compensate for such changes through its powers of adaptation. When this is not the case and object colors do not remain constant in sources of illumination different from daylight, the changes can be quantitatively predicted by taking into account the adaptation of the eye in the new conditions.

Colored shadows—a special case of color conversion. The principle of color conversion, according to which stimuli above adaptation reflectance are tinged with the hue of the source of illumination, stimuli below are tinged with the afterimage complementary to the hue of the source, and stimuli near adaptation reflectance are either neutral (achromatic) or weakly saturated and of uncertain hue, was formulated to cover nonselective reflectances in strongly chromatic illumination on nonselective backgrounds of high, medium, and low reflectance. The first quantitative study made of colored shadows (Self, 1959; Helson and Self, 1961) has shown that this classic color phenomenon is a special case of the principle of color conversion. Colored shadows are produced by interposing an opaque object between two sources of light which illuminate a highly reflecting, nonselective surface. While one of the two sources has usually been white or near white and the other chromatic, it is possible to use two chromatic sources. In the usual method the shadow illuminated only by the white source, which should appear achromatic if its color is determined only by the light issuing from that region, is actually perceived to have a hue complementary to the hue of the chromatic source. If two chromatic sources are employed, then the two shadows are complementary to each other, regardless of the hues of the sources. This was first noted by Goethe and later independently discovered by others, as Self (1959) has pointed out in his review of the literature dealing with this subject. The phenomenon of colored shadows produced in these ways is very striking for at least three reasons: (1) because of the high saturation of color of the shadow; (2) because of the large shadowed areas that can be perceived to be colored if the shadow caster is sufficiently far from the background; and (3) because the saturation of the shadowed color is equally great over its whole extent and does not decrease perceptibly with distance from the chromatically illuminated surround as is the case with phenomena of border contrast.

In order to specify the colors perceived to belong to colored shadows in terms of the C.I.E. system of colorimetry, the binocular matching technique was employed. Ss matched the hue, chroma, and lightness of the colored shadows as seen by one eye by choosing the appropriate chip in the *Munsell Book of Color* illuminated by Macbeth Daylight as seen by the other eye. When necessary Ss made estimates if an exact match was not possible. The method of limits was employed in making the matches, i.e., with fixed achromatic luminances, the chromatic luminance was varied in small steps in both ascending and descending orders. Since the chromatic and achromatic luminances mixed except where cut off by the chromatic shadow caster, the surround color varied in purity (saturation) as well as in luminance. The following ranges in chromatic luminances were employed:

> Red: 0.71 to 0.0059 ft.L.
> Yellow: 5.0 to 0. 0044 ft.L.
> Green. 0.52 to 0.00043 ft.L.
> Blue: 0.084 to 0.000069 ft.L.

The maximum luminances of the chromatic components were fixed by the transmissivities of the chromatic filters for light from an incandescent filament lamp having a color temperature of 2854°K. The achromatic luminances varied from 13.8 to 0.31 ft.L. Thus the chromatic luminances had a range of 1210:1.0 and the achromatic luminances a range of 44.5:1.0. With fixed chromatic luminances, the achromatic luminance was varied in small steps, first in ascending order and then in descending order as required by the method of limits. The chromaticness of the field surrounding the shadow was varied in both purity and luminance with changes in luminance of the achromatic source as well as by changing the luminance of the chromatic source of light. In this way it was possible to vary not only the ratios of chromatic to achromatic light but also the absolute amounts of light from the two sources.

The results from six Ss were consistent and may be summarized as follows:

1. The saturation of the color of the shadowed area increases as the purity of the surround increases, i.e., as less and less white light is mixed with the chromatic light; quantitatively, the chromaticness of the shadow increases as the log luminance of the chromatic light in the surround and inversely with the luminance of the achromatic component as shown by the following equation:

$$C = K_1 \log \frac{L_c}{L_a} + K_2 \qquad (8)$$

where C stands for Munsell chroma, L_c, for the luminance of the chromatic component of the surround, L_a, the achromatic component in both the surround and the shadowed area, and K_1 and K_2 are constants depending upon the hue of the surround color.

2. The chromaticness of the shadowed area does not depend upon the absolute luminances of surround and shadow but upon their ratios as shown in Equation (8).

3. Within the limits of experimental variation, the hue of the shadowed color is unaffected by the admixture of white light with the chromatic light of the surround, but its chroma (saturation) is reduced as noted above.

4. The hue of the colored shadow is *complementary* to the color of the surround as shown by the fact that the line connecting the points representing the surround colors and the points representing the shadow colors in the C.I.E. mixture diagram is a straight line passing through the white point of the diagram.

5. Colored shadows are thus seen to fall under the principle of color conversion since the less white light is mixed with the surround light, the darker is the shadow and the more saturated is its hue. The shadowed area, being below prevailing AL, takes on a hue that is the afterimage complementary to the hue of the surround.

In addition to these findings a number of interesting facts emerged from this study which will appear in due course. Among them is the greater color inducing power of blue as compared with the other three psychological primaries, red, yellow, and green.

The Land colors. Still another manifestation of color conversion is found in Land's work on two-primary-color projections (1959*a*; 1959*b*). The colors in question are produced by Land as follows: pictures of variously colored objects are taken on two black-white films, one through a filter transmitting light from 585 to 700mμ, called the long-wave record (red), and the other through a filter transmitting light from 490 to 600mμ called the medium-wave record (green). Positives are then made from these films called "separation positives" which are projected on a screen in exact register. The long-wave record is projected with light coming through the original red filter and the medium-wave record is projected directly with light from the usual incandescent-filament lamps used in projectors. Excellent reproduction of the original colors was obtained by these means. On the other hand, if the two separation positives are projected with a green filter replacing the red filter and with incandescent-lamp light through the medium-wave record as before, the colors in the original scene are reversed as would be expected from the principle of color conversion: what was red becomes green, and what was green becomes red, with corresponding changes in the other colors (cf. Walls, 1960).

Considered from the point of view of faithful rendition of object colors under changed conditions of stimulation, the Land colors may be roughly regarded as cases of color constancy (in the sense of Katz). We, however, are now in a position to give a detailed account of the object colors perceived under Land's conditions. When the original scene is photographed on black-white film through the long-wave (red) filter, colors in the region from 585 to 700mμ will affect the film to a greater extent than will colors below this region, while the scene photographed through the medium-wave (green) filter which passes light from 490 to 600mμ will emphasize colors associated with this band of wave lengths. Hence when positives are made from these two films, the long-wave positive with the red filter will reproduce the red-to-yellow colors in the original scene while the middle-wave positive passing incandescent-lamp light will reproduce the green-blue colors in near-white. Assuming an intermediate adaptation level, parts of the screen above level will then be seen as red to yellow, those near level will appear achromatic, and the parts below level will appear in varying mixtures of the afterimage complement, which is green-blue (see data in Table 5.1 with gray background). Since the afterimage complement contains a red or a blue component in addition to the color mixture complement, a wide variety of colors can be seen on the screen. The yellow-to-red colors appear because they are above adaptation luminance, the green-to-blue colors because they are below adaptation luminance. Judd has shown that essentially this qualitative account put into quantitative form successfully predicts the Land colors, spot by spot (1960).

The powerful, large areal-induction effects of relatively weak chromatic light are known to everyone acquainted with the phenomena of colored shadows. As pointed out above, when two sources of light, one chromatic and the other achromatic, are thrown on a white screen and a shadow caster is placed before the chromatic light, fully saturated complementary colors covering almost the whole area of the screen are seen where only neutral light is actually present. The color-inducing power of the relatively small area of chromatic light is far greater than would be expected from the weak chromatic contrasts achieved with gray papers on chromatic backgrounds. And contrary to the classical law of diminishing color induction with distance from borders, the shadow is equally saturated throughout its area. The variety and range of luminances present on the screen in Land's demonstrations are sufficient to yield colors that more or less faithfully reproduce the colors of the original objects, which ranged from colors of fruit and clothing to those of the human face. Various other combinations of lights were employed by Land with results that in no way conflict with the explanation offered here and by Judd (1960) and by Walls (1960).[1]

Land believed that the colors obtained with his two primaries could not be accounted for by classical factors of color vision chiefly because three primaries have usually been regarded as necessary for perceiving the full gamut of hues and saturations and also because of the immediacy with which the colors appear on projection. With regard to the first point it has been known for a long time that hue, lightness, and saturation are not in one-to-one correlation with stimulus dimensions and that vivid colors can be perceived in parts of the visual field where the usual wave-length correlates of the respective hues are missing. Simultaneous contrast colors, colored shadows, the gamut of colors seen

[1] For a more complete discussion of the Land colors the reader is referred to the articles by Judd and Walls.

in the "dimming effect," and the colors perceived in what Evans called the Helson-Judd effect (1948) are also cases where the colors cannot be accounted for in terms of the local stimulation received by the visual receptors. The data in Table 5.1 for *monochromatic red illumination* show that the usual colorimetric specification of colors in terms of local stimulation holds only for a completely dark surround where only the hue of the illuminant is seen with nonselective papers ranging from 3 to 80 percent reflectance. But on a background of intermediate reflectance, all the psychological primaries appear in various saturations. The farther the individual reflectances are *below* as well as *above* adaptation reflectance, which is usually in the neighborhood of the background reflectance, the more saturated are the colors. The organization of colors about what Land referred to as a "fulcrum" proves to be the stimulus which appears neutral in a chromatic array and hence corresponds to our adaptation reflectance or luminance. It thus appears that Land's conditions contain a superabundance of wave lengths for "jogging" the visual receptors to yield a rich assortment of chromaticities if we compare the wave lengths present in his two-primary projections with our single-primary, monochromatic stimuli that vary only in one dimension—luminance.

Land's rejection of adaptation as having any part in the production of his colors is, as already mentioned, based on the immediacy with which they appear and the fact that they do not change much in time. Some psychologists insist on limiting the concept of adaptation, including chromatic adaptation, to the desensitizing effects of durative stimulation and seem to be unfamiliar with Schouten and Ornstein's rapid (alpha) adaptation (1939) and the increase in sensitivity to afterimage complementary colors which accompanies desensitization to predominant stimulation. It is no wonder, therefore, that Land, who is not a psychologist, failed to appreciate the role of adaptation in his striking demonstrations. As Walls has said:

Land's trouble here is that . . . he shows awareness of only the long, slow, intensive sorts of adaptation which are regulated by the cold-molasses kinetics of photopigment-concentration change. The general and lateral chromatic adaptations which underlie contrast phenomena are instant upon presentation of the stimuli (which is why the contrast is *called* simultaneous). They are more akin to the alpha adaptation of Schouten and Ornstein (1939) than to the photo-chemical beta adaptation, and they are really accomplished by the exercise of inhibitions in purely chromatic pathways. . . . Since the basis of spatial induction is neural and not photo-chemical, any time consumed is hardly more than is required for a neuronic message to traverse a couple of synapses (Walls, 1960, pp. 37–38).

The vividness of the Land colors can be traced to the high ratios of luminances possible with screen projection. Added evidence that these colors are indeed manifestations of the principle of color conversion was given by Walls who reported that if the Land projections are "scanned with a slender tube, only spots of red, pink, and white can be found; all other colors vanish" (1960, p. 33), just as only illuminant colors are seen with black backgrounds in strongly chromatic light (see Table 5.1). Since a quantitative theory embodying the facts of color conversion predicts the Land colors, as Judd (1960) has shown, there is no doubt as to their origin. The Land demonstrations again bring to the fore the importance for color theory of the complementary colors that appear in various cases of color conversion. Land is correct in asserting that classical color theory is inadequate to account for such colors but he failed to appreciate the modern concept of adaptation and its relation to contrast as the source responsible for the colors seen in his demonstrations.

LIGHTNESS CONSTANCY

If the *lightness* of an object having a given reflectance is to be specified, the relation of object reflectance to adaptation reflectance must be taken into account. Whereas reflectance is a constant physical property of surfaces (barring physical changes such as fading), lightness depends upon adaptation and contrast effects. A rough approximation to lightness, L, is given by the simple expression

$$L = 10\sqrt{R} \tag{9}$$

where R is percentage of reflectance, and the constant is introduced to yield 10 as the maximal possible lightness for a surface having 100 percent reflectance. It is obvious that this formula has only a very restricted use since it does not provide for the fact that a stimulus is perceived to be darker on white background than it is on black background. The classical expression for brightness contrast is not wholly adequate, for it takes into account only the difference between object and background brightness or reflectance as shown by the formula

$$C = k \frac{R_o - R_b}{R_b} \qquad (10)$$

where C is the contrast increment or decrement which a surface having a reflectance R_o undergoes on a background having a reflectance R_b, and k is a constant depending on various factors. But the contrast of any object depends upon all other objects in the field of vision, not alone upon its relation to the immediate background so a formula is needed which embodies adaptation reflectance as the reference point for contrast effects. The following formula, devised by Judd (1940), yields excellent predictions of reports of lightness by trained observers under a wide variety of conditions provided *illuminance* is held constant:[2]

$$L = 1.03 (10R_o - 0.3) \frac{R_a + 1}{R_o + R_a} \qquad (11)$$

where the subscripts o and a denote object and adaptation reflectances, respectively, and the constants have been adjusted to yield lightness values ranging from a minimum of zero to a maximum of 10, as in the Munsell scale. Adaptation reflectance, R_a, is defined as in Equations (1) and (2). The superiority of Equation (11) over the classical formula for contrast springs from the fact that it takes into account not only contiguous areas but also all other areas in the field of view. Evans gives a striking demonstration of the need for taking into account remote areas to predict the lightness of a surface. He projects a gray on a field of white, where it is perceived as quite a dark gray; when surrounded by a darker annulus it appears lighter; when a still darker annulus is added, the infield appears still lighter; and as succeeding darker annuli are added to the annuli already present, the infield grows lighter and lighter until it ends up almost as white as the surrounding area on which it was originally projected. Replacement of R_b, background reflectance, by R_a, adaptation reflectance, makes it possible to handle the complicated field conditions in the Evans dem-

---

[2] Formulas covering the case where reflectances are held constant and illuminance is changed have been developed by Marimont (1962) using "the average illuminance . . . as in standard adaptation-level theory" (p. 800). Her formulation is given below (pp. 295–297).

onstration by a single term. In fact it is doubtful if the classical expression for contrast could handle interactions as complicated as in the case just discussed.

Let us now consider lightness constancy. Since the time of Katz it has been customary to measure constancy by matching the brightly illuminated disk to various settings of the shadowed disk in free observation, and then to match the two disks as they appear in two small apertures in a neutral screen called a reduction screen. It was not taken into account that the reflectance of the reduction screen and the illuminance falling on it could exert differential contrast effects on the brightness of the disks as they appear in the two apertures. Usually a gray (medium reflectance) screen has been used for aperture viewing, with the illuminance on the screen not specified. If the reduction screen is brighter than one of the apertures, it is darkened by contrast effects; if it is darker, it is lightened by contrast effect. Hence, any match made under reduction screen conditions is also subject to background influences that may affect the two aperture colors unequally. Furthermore, as the shadowed disk is varied, the effect of the reduction screen is not uniform, having one effect when the disk is relatively bright and another when it is dim. *Aperture measurements are therefore no more "objective" or universal than measurements made in free viewing except insofar as they define uniform surrounds for all aperture colors.*

These considerations have an important bearing on the measurements of constancy. Three values are ordinarily used in the Brunswik and Thouless formulas for measuring constancy: s, for degrees white which match the shadowed disk in free observation; p, the degrees white in the brightly illuminated disk which match the shadowed disk in the reduction screen; and w, the degrees white in the shadowed disk. These three values enter into Brunswik's formula as follows:

$$C = \frac{s - p}{w - p} \qquad (12)$$

and into Thouless' formula:

$$C = \frac{\log s - \log p}{\log w - \log p} \qquad (13)$$

We now know that the values of both s and p are affected by background conditions in aperture viewing as well as in free viewing.

Since all the values entering into these equations are in terms of degrees of white in the disks, they cannot yield comparable values in different viewing conditions, e.g., when depth of shadow or reflectance of background changes. In place of the Brunswick and Thouless measures of constancy I have proposed use of the ratio or log ratio of the luminance of the brightly illuminated disk to the luminance of the shadowed disk (1943). Either of these values shows the extent to which the eye compensates for the difference between the brightly illuminated and the shadowed disks. Since luminance is measured by light meters that provide identical (dark) surrounds for all measurements, the ratio measures are comparable for all conditions of viewing and from laboratory to laboratory. We therefore define constancy or compensation as follows:

$$C = \log \frac{L_B}{L_S} \qquad (14)$$

where L_B and L_S refer to the luminances of the brightly illuminated and shadowed disks respectively. When the two disks have the same luminance in a match, the value of the ratio is 1, and the value of C is zero, showing that the eye has not had to compensate for any difference in the amount of light coming from the two disks; if C is greater than 1, the formula yields a measure in log units of the extent to which the eye has equalized the difference between the two disks; and if C is negative ($L_B < L_S$), it means that the shadowed disk was actually sending more light to the eyes than the normally illuminated object or that a reversal of the usual constancy phenomenon has occurred. The log ratio formula never yields "superconstancy," a result sometimes obtained by the other formulas.

The ratios of the luminances of the brightly illuminated to the shadowed disks reveal that the following generalization regarding lightness constancy is true: *constancy or compensation is greater the darker the shadowed disk, no matter by what means the darkening is achieved*. The shadowed disk may be darkened by reducing its reflectance, i.e., mixing in greater amounts of black with W°, or by decreasing its illuminance (increasing the depth of shadow) or by contrast effect. Inspection of Table 5.3 shows that the ratios increase under all three of these conditions for they are higher as W° (*w* in the formulas given above) decreases, as the illuminance on the shadowed side decreases from 0.878 to 0.0009 footcandles, and as the disk

TABLE 5.3. Effect of Reflectance of Stimulus, Reflectance of Background, and Depth of Shadow on Lightness Compensation

W°	f.c.	White Background			Gray Background			Black Background		
		S°	f.c.	Ratio	S°	f.c.	Ratio	S°	f.c.	Ratio

Bright illuminance = 16.15 f.c.
Shadowed illuminance = 0.879 f.c.

W°	f.c.	S°	f.c.	Ratio	S°	f.c.	Ratio	S°	f.c.	Ratio
360	.703	322.7	11.63	16.54	208.7	7.75	11.02	184.0	6.78	9.46
270	.536	252.0	9.20	17.16	177.3	6.62	12.35	152.3	5.81	10.84
180	.360	168.3	6.30	17.50	142.0	5.33	14.80	123.7	4.68	13.00
90	.193	74.3	3.07	15.91	84.3	3.39	17.56	60.3	2.58	13.37
45	.114	33.3	1.61	14.12	43.5	1.94	17.02	31.3	1.61	14.12

Bright illuminance = 16.15 f.c.
Shadowed illuminance = 0.388 f.c.

W°	f.c.	S°	f.c.	Ratio	S°	f.c.	Ratio	S°	f.c.	Ratio
360	.310	302.7	10.98	35.42	178.3	6.62	21.35	126.7	4.84	15.61
270	.237	236.3	8.56	36.19	155.3	5.81	24.51	104.3	4.04	17.05
180	.160	156.3	5.81	36.31	126.0	4.84	30.25	85.0	3.39	21.19
90	.085	70.0	2.91	34.23	74.0	3.07	36.12	47.7	2.10	24.71
45	.050	31.0	1.61	32.20	38.3	1.78	35.60	22.0	1.29	25.80

Bright illuminance = 16.15 f.c.
Shadowed illuminance = 0.009 f.c.

W°	f.c.	S°	f.c.	Ratio	S°	f.c.	Ratio	S°	f.c.	Ratio
360	.0072	92.3	3.71	515.3	67.7	2.74	380.5	36.7	1.78	247.2
270	.0055	71.7	2.91	529.1	53.3	2.26	410.9	26.2	1.45	263.6
180	.0037	47.3	2.10	567.6	37.0	1.78	481.1	16.8	1.13	305.4
90	.0020	35.5	1.78	890.0	24.7	1.29	645.0	7.2	0.65	325.0
45	.0011	25.7	1.29	1172.7	12.8	0.97	881.8			

Note: W° = degrees white in shadowed disk
S° = degrees white in brightly illuminated disk
f.c. = apparent footcandles
SOURCE: From Helson, 1943.

in shadow is contrastively darkened by backgrounds having a higher reflectance than that of the discs. Systematic variation of the interacting conditions underlying lightness constancy yields a clear coherent picture of this phenomenon, which renders unnecessary such explanatory molar concepts as noticing or discounting the illumination and the assumption that "constancy" is mediated by central, and contrast by peripheral, processes as Katz (1935) supposed. Rather, the data point to a single visual mechanism which is responsible for constancy, contrast and adaptation. Quantitative formulations in specifying lightness, hue, and saturation (Judd, 1940; Helson, Judd, and Warren, 1952; Helson, Judd, and Wilson, 1956; Judd, 1959) argue for the under‑lying unity of constancy, contrast, and adaptation, terms that refer only to different descriptive aspects of color vision.

The decisive role of background reflectance is even more striking if the backgrounds in the shadowed and brightly illuminated regions do not have the same reflectance, e.g., white background (and disk) shadowed, black background (and disk) brightly illuminated; or white background brightly illuminated, and black background shad‑owed. The results in Table 5.4 show that generalizations regarding effects of depth of shadow and reflectance of the stimulus object on

TABLE 5.4.   Effect of a Divided Background on Lightness Constancy

A.   Shadowed White Background and Illuminated Black Background

Shadowed White Background		Illuminated Black Background		
W°	f.c.	S°	f.c.	Ratio
360	0.703	127.7	4.84	6.88
270	0.536	88.0	3.55	6.62
180	0.360	51.0	2.26	6.28
90	0.193	11.8	0.81	4.20
45	0.114	2.5	0.48	4.21

B.   Shadowed Black Background and Illuminated White Background

Shadowed Black Background		Illuminated White Background		
W°	f.c.	S°	f.c.	Ratio
360	0.703	360.0	12.92	18.38
270	0.536	334.3	11.95	22.29
180	0.360	299.0	10.82	30.05
90	0.193	223.3	8.24	42.69
45	0.114	135.0	5.17	45.35
0	0.026	21.3	1.13	43.46

Note: f.c. = apparent footcandles
Illuminance on brightly illuminated side = 16.15 f.c.
Illuminance on shadowed side = 0.879 f.c.
Reflectance of white background = 0.80
Reflectance of black background = 0.03
W° = degrees white in shadowed disk
S° = degrees white in illuminated disk matching the shadowed disk
Ratio = luminance of normal to shadowed disk
SOURCE: From Helson, 1943.

perceptual constancy cannot be made without reference to background reflectance, for what is true of one background condition may not hold for another. To the objection that variations in background have no bearing on studies of lightness constancy usually carried out against a single background condition, there are two answers. First, the use of black, gray, and white backgrounds revealed a previously unsuspected source of error in the traditional methods of measuring lightness (brightness) constancy; second, a satisfactory theory of the phenomena of constancy must account for all conditions of observation. Thus with shadowed white background and illuminated black background constancy *decreases* as the reflectance of the shadowed disk decreases. The results are opposite with shadowed black background and illuminated white background: constancy *increases* as the reflectance of the shadowed disk decreases as seen in the last column of Table 5.4. Hence background reflectance and illuminance, neglected in previous studies of brightness constancy, are seen to exercise decisive influence and must be taken into consideration in any general account of this phenomenon.

CONTRAST AND ASSIMILATION

We saw above that the extent of lightening undergone by a gray surface on a darker ground and the darkening on a lighter ground were most accurately predicted by formulas that took into account all reflectances in the field of view, not merely the reflectances of contiguous surfaces (the classical formulation of lightness contrast). The situation with respect to contrast is still further complicated by the fact that under certain conditions, as in the von Bezold "mixture" or "spread" effect, *light lines lighten* and *dark lines darken* contiguous gray areas, contrary to the usual contrast effect (cf. Evans, 1948; Burnham, 1953). Another phenomenon, the Gelb effect, has also been regarded as anomalous in that a spinning "black" Maxwell disk illuminated by a cone of light from a spotlight in an otherwise completely dark room appears white or very light gray until a very small white surface is placed in front of the disk whereupon it turns black or very dark gray. Molar explanations have been advanced for the Gelb effect which include "noticing the illumination," "differences between film and surface colors," and "structure of the visual field" (Woodworth and Schlosberg, 1954), on the supposition that the small white surface cannot exercise such a large effect by contrast alone. The Bezold and

Gelb phenomena have great systematic importance because according to most psychologists they seem to require molar concepts in addition to known visual processes for their explanation. The Bezold effect, which we shall call "assimilation," has stood opposed to contrast with no basis hitherto provided for bridging the gap between them; similarly, the Gelb effect has stood as an isolated phenomenon because the molar concepts advanced for its explanation suggested no investigations to yield quantitative data that might reveal its kinship with other known facts.

In an endeavor to bridge the gap between contrast and assimilation three studies were undertaken by my co-workers and myself (Helson and Rohles, 1959; Helson and Joy, 1962; Helson and Steger, 1963) using black and white *straight* lines on dark, medium, and light gray backgrounds in place of the Bezold black and white arabesques on chromatic grounds. The use of ruled lines made possible quantitative variations in the stimulus conditions not easily made with the artistic designs employed by Bezold, Riedel (1937), Newhall (1942), Burnham (1953), and others. With ruled lines it was possible to (1) vary the spacing between the lines, keeping line width constant (the study with Rohles); (2) vary the thickness of the lines and the spacing (the study with Joy); and (3) vary the reflectance of the intervening gray areas (the study with Steger). In all three studies, cards 7×11 in. were ruled with white lines on one half and black lines on the other half so that Ss could view the two halves simultaneously against neutral surrounds having the same reflectance as the stimulus cards. Ss judged the lightness of the intervening gray areas in terms of a rating scale ranging from very very much lighter, through equal, to very very much darker. In the first study, only lines 1 mm. in width were employed at separations ranging from 3 to 55 mm. in steps of 4 mm. In the second study, both line width and line separation were varied in a 6×6 design in which every line width was combined with every line separation. The line widths and separations were 3, 10, 20, 30, 40, and 50 mm. In the third study, a 5×6 design was used with line widths of 1, 3, 5, 11, 17, and 29 mm. and line separations of 3, 5, 11, 17, and 29 mm. In the first and second studies the intervening gray areas had a reflectance of 36 percent (approximately equal to Munsell value 6) and in the third study a near-white having a reflectance of 80 percent and a near-black with a reflectance of 14 percent were used (Munsell values 9.0 and 3.75, respectively).

In making the observations a combination of the method of paired comparisons and method of limits was used. For purposes of computation the verbal categories were translated into numbers from 1 to 9 with 5 standing for equality of the two halves of the cards. Since the judgments were in terms of white-lined or black-lined sides of the cards, they were given numerals in the first two studies such that numbers below 5 indicated assimilation (i.e., white-lined half of card judged lighter than the black-lined half or black-lined half judged darker than light-lined half) and numbers above 5 indicated contrast. In the third study, where only assimilation in varying degrees was found on the average, numbers above 5 indicated assimilation. In all cases degree of assimilation or contrast, or extent of lightening and darkening whether due to the one or the other, is determined by the difference between any given numerical value and 5, the equal judgment.

TABLE 5.5.   Mean Judgments of Stimuli Showing Continuity of Assimilation and Contrast Effects

Gray Width (mm.)		Line Width (mm.)						Total	Mean
		3	10	20	30	40	50		
3		2.73	5.59	6.31	6.40	6.68	6.86	34.57	5.76
10		3.41	4.81	5.54	5.86	6.45	6.31	32.38	5.40
20		4.09	5.40	5.68	5.90	6.13	6.40	33.60	5.60
30		3.91	5.09	5.31	5.81	6.09	6.72	32.93	5.49
40		4.36	4.90	5.04	5.72	5.95	6.13	32.10	5.35
50		4.59	4.77	5.59	5.31	6.00	6.27	32.53	5.42
	Total	23.09	30.56	33.47	35.00	37.30	38.69	198.11	
	Mean	3.85	5.10	5.58	5.83	6.22	6.45		

Note: Values below 5 indicate assimilation; above 5, contrast.
SOURCE: From Helson and Joy, 1962.

The reliability of the data is attested by the number of observations made in each: in the first study there were 10 $Ss \times 14$ stimuli $\times 4$ series, making 560 observations; in the second study there were 11 $Ss \times 36$ stimuli $\times 2$ series, making 792 observations; in the third study there were 10 $Ss \times 60$ stimuli $\times 4$ series, making 2400 observations. The three studies thus embodied a total of 3752 observations. Some of the conditions in the first study were essentially replicated in the second one so only results from the second and third studies are reported here.

The data in Table 5.5 show that as line width increases (reading across the table) assimilation gives way to contrast. Thus the numerical ratings increase from 2.73 (very much darker on the black-lined side or very much lighter on the white-lined side) with 3-mm. lines and 3-mm. line separations to 6.86 (much lighter on the black-lined side or much

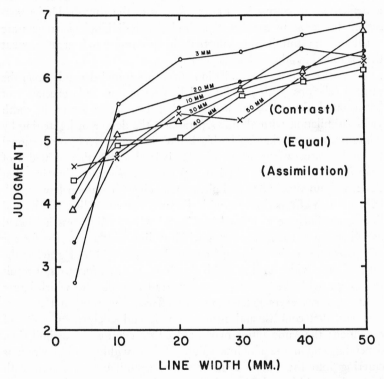

FIG. 5.5. Contrast and assimilation as a function of line width for each line separation. The parameter of the curves is line separation. (From Helson and Joy, 1962. With the permission of *Psychologische Beiträge*.)

darker on the white-lined side) with 50-mm. lines and 50-mm. line separations. Line widths in the neighborhood of 10 mm. divide the assimilation-contrast continuum into two parts separated by a region of neutrality as seen in Fig. 5.5. Contrast increases with line width (reading across the table) and decreases with line separation (reading down the table). There is, therefore, a continuum in the conditions from assimilation to contrast with a neutral zone of line widths and separations in which white and black stripes neither lighten nor darken contiguous gray areas. Because the neutral zone is narrow, as seen from the plots in Figs. 5.6, 5.7, and 5.8, and the curves are steep when crossing the neutral axis, conditions in this zone are subject to individual differences in modes of viewing which involve eye movements, fixation, and methods of comparing the two halves of the stimuli. Under conditions favorable to contrast or assimilation individual differences are small and the stimuli do not fluctuate in appearance to a greater extent than is found in other color phenomena.

Whether contrast or assimilation effects are found depends upon the mutual relations of line width and line separation and reflectance of background. From Fig. 5.6 it is seen that lines 1 and 3 mm. in width yield assimilation with all line separations, the degree of lightening by white lines and darkening by black lines being *inversely* proportional to the line separations. From Fig. 5.6 it is also seen that as width of gray *increases,* both assimilation and contrast *decrease,* showing that these two supposedly opposed phenomena obey a common law according to which effects decrease with distance. Effects of line widths and line separations are combined in Fig. 5.7 wherein lightness is plotted as a function of the *ratio* of gray width to line width, with the former the parameter in the individual curves. For each width of gray, as the ratio of gray width to line width *decreases,* contrast *increases,* a result in keeping with the classical law of contrast according to which larger inducing areas exert greater contrast effects. We must not assume, however, that contrast and assimilation depend solely upon ratios of excitation; the same ratios may yield either contrast or assimilation, depending upon the absolute values of line widths and separations entering into the ratios. Thus maximal assimilation is found with 3-mm. line width and 3-mm. line separation but maximal contrast is found with 50-mm. line width and 50-mm. line separation. The domain of assimilation includes ratios from 1:1 to 16.7:1, while the domain of contrast contains ratios from 0.06:1 to 2.5:1. Hence we must look to visual mechanisms that are affected by absolute as well as by relative amounts of stimulation in attempting to explain these phenomena.

The plot in Fig. 5.8 shows that contrast and assimilation, hitherto regarded as totally disparate phenomena, lie on a single continuum with a zone of neutrality in which a balance exists wherein there is neither effect. As remarked above, the zone of neutrality under the conditions of these studies is in the neighborhood of 10-mm. lines but there is another neutral zone, as is to be expected, beyond line separations of 50 mm., not investigated here, where areas are so large that no lightening or darkening of one by the other occurs except, perhaps, at their borders.

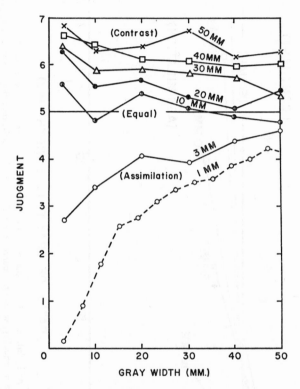

FIG. 5.6. Contrast and assimilation as a function of width of gray (line separation) for each width of line. The broken curve for 1-mm. line width is from the study by Helson and Rohles. The parameter of the curves is line width. (From Helson and Joy, 1962. With the permission of *Psychologische Beiträge*.)

We have so far discussed only the results of the second study involving medium-gray background. The third study bears out the results of the first two studies but has some interesting differences due to the fact that the intervening gray areas were almost white or almost black. The near-white and near-black backgrounds were used to determine if

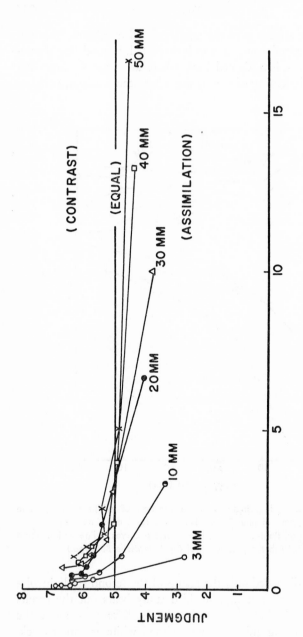

FIG. 5.7. Assimilation and contrast as a function of the ratios of gray width to line width. Note the zone of equality, where the curves cross the line of equals, and the asymptotic approach of the assimilation points to the line of equals toward the right of the figure. Gray width is the parameter in the curves. (From Helson and Joy, 1962. With the permission of *Psychologische Beiträge*.)

contrast and assimilation effects are found at the extremes of the reflectance continuum.

The results with the extreme reflectances definitely show that contrast effect is absent no matter how wide the lines and the intervening

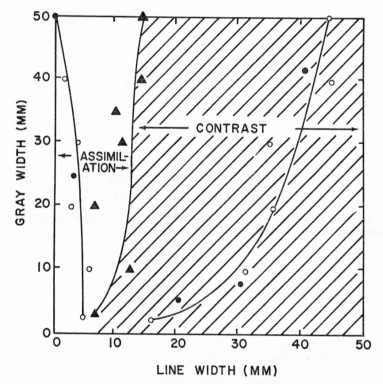

FIG. 5.8. Domains of assimilation and contrast. Each point in the plane represents the combination of line width and line separation that yields either assimilation or contrast. (From Helson and Joy, 1962. With the permission of *Psychologische Beiträge*.)

areas are. As seen from Figs. 5.9 and 5.10, assimilation effect is maximal with narrow lines and narrow intervening areas, and it decreases as either line width or area between lines increases. However, assimilation does not pass over into contrast effect with very light or very dark backgrounds, as shown by the fact that the judgments for all line widths in Figs. 5.9 and 5.10 are above the axis of equality even at the

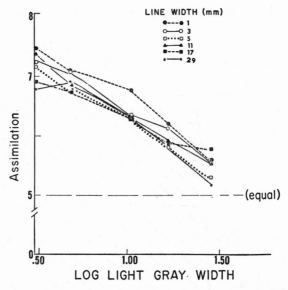

FIG. 5.9. Assimilation as a function of line separation (gray width) with background of 80 percent reflectance. (From Helson, 1963.)

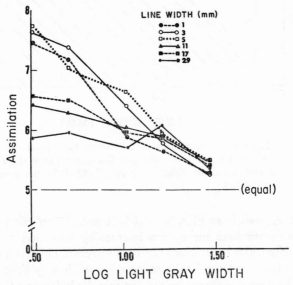

FIG. 5.10. Assimilation as a function of line separation (gray width) with background of 14 percent reflectance. (From Helson, 1963.)

widest separations. It is evident that the generalizations derived from the earlier studies with a background of intermediate reflectance must be supplemented by the findings of this study. So far reflectance of the lines has not been treated as a variable. When this is done we shall have a complete account of contrast and assimilation in terms of all reflectances in the field. Other variables, such as shape, texture, and chromaticness, are probably of importance and should be studied.

Theoretical considerations. References to the von Bezold effect as a "mixture" or "spread" phenomenon imply that it is the result of irradiation or spread of excitation on the retina or something akin to mosaic color mixture. While such mechanisms may be responsible for assimilation when line separations are no greater than can be resolved by the eye, they cannot explain assimilation with stimuli as widely separated as 57 min., the widest separation at which some assimilation was reported in the study with Rohles (50-mm. gray separation between lines viewed at a distance of 3 m.). Similarly it is doubtful that tonic eye movements are an explanation for assimilation effects with stimuli subtending relatively large visual angles. On the other hand, even if such explanations sufficed for assimilation, they would still leave contrast unexplained. In view of the fact that the conditions responsible for contrast and assimilation form a continuum in which there is a neutral zone wherein neither effect is present, it appears highly likely these phenomena are the result of opposed processes such that the predominance of one gives rise to contrast and the predominance of the other gives rise to assimilation while balance of the two processes results in neither effect. Is there a physiological mechanism sufficiently well known to support this hypothesis? Such a mechanism is provided by the concept of retinal and/or central interaction, which in some cases results in facilitation and in others inhibition of impulses from neighboring areas.

Physiological models that envisage formally similar facts of facilitation, summation, and inhibition in spinal reflexes and in retinal processes, based on spatial interaction between more or less distant neural areas, have been proposed by a number of workers, among them Sherrington (see Lloyd, 1946b), who drew a parallel between retinal function and spinal reflex activity. Polyak's histological studies have provided ample evidence for spatial interaction in the retina. In this connection he wrote that at least a "fraction of cone impulses (passes) to one or several horizontal cells from which it is distributed in all directions over the more or less distant rods and cones" by means of amacrine cells having lateral connections (Polyak, 1941, p. 395). As pointed out by Ruch (1946), the convergence of many rods and cones on bipolar cells, and of bipolar cells on ganglion cells, provides a neural substrate for interaction of streams of impulses resulting in facilitation and inhibition in vision as well as in the case of spinal reflexes. In view of the opposed nature of assimilation and contrast, we must assume that if assimilation arises from summation or facilitation of impulses of a given kind or quantity in contiguous regions, then contrast arises from inhibition of the same type of impulses in neighboring areas. We therefore assume that relatively small differences in intensity of similar processes in neighboring areas summate, or at least do not inhibit one another, thereby giving rise to assimilation; large differences, arriving at some common synapse or neural pathway, result in inhibition of less intense excitations giving rise to contrast. Ruch also points out that "convergence [provides] the neural substrate for interaction of streams of impulses resulting in facilitation and inhibition phenomena" as well as does the system of intraretinal association neurons (1946, p. 476).

To explain the assimilation and contrast effects in these studies, we need assume only that within certain limits area acts like luminance, that is, increase in area has the same effect as increase in luminance. On this basis as the width of the black and white lines increases relative to the intervening gray areas, assimilation should be replaced by contrast. Besides accounting for contrast and assimilation, this theory accounts for the neutral zone in which there is neither contrast nor assimilation as follows: If these two phenomena are mediated by a mechanism that results in summation with low, and inhibition with high, differentials of stimulation, then there should be neither summation nor inhibition at some intermediate differential in stimulation; this is actually the case. The absolute levels at which there is neither assimilation nor contrast depend upon the luminances of the lines and of the intervening areas. One prediction from this theory has been indirectly verified: if the luminance of thin lines which give assimilation is increased sufficiently, then assimilation should give way to contrast. Inspection of Fig. 5.7 shows that assimilation changes to contrast with constant line width as the ratio of gray width to line width *decreases* in accordance with the assumption that area and luminance function equivalently; the smaller gray area is equivalent to higher line luminance with resultant contrast effect. Owing to the rapid fall-off of contrast and assimilation with increasing distance from borders the area-luminance equivalence is not linear and should be treated accordingly both in qualitative and quantitative applications of the model proposed here.

The Gelb effect. When the Gelb disk is illuminated by a spotlight in a dark room, if the sudden great change from "white" to "black" as the result of the introduction of a small white surface in front of the disk is a contrast phenomenon, then the amount of darkening of the disk should be greater with larger than with smaller white surfaces in the field of view, greater when in the center of the disk than near the edge, and greater with higher than with lower reflectances. To test these assumptions, Stewart (1959) measured the degrees of black required in a black-white disk in a normally illuminated space to match a Gelb disk 12-in. in diameter, when the small white surface was either 0.5, 1.0, or 2.0-in. in diameter and when it was placed in the center and at 1, 2, 3, 4, 5, 6, and 7 in. from the center of the Gelb disk. The reflectance of the white was not varied since Koffka (1935) had already reported that the lower the reflectance of the white area, the less dark did the black disk appear. Stewart employed the binocular matching technique in which the Gelb disk was viewed by the right eye against an unlighted black ground while the matching, standard disk, composed of white and black moveable sectors, was viewed by the left eye against an illuminated black ground.

The data plotted in Fig. 5.11 from Stewart show that the Gelb disk was blackest, i.e., required the largest amount of black in the matching disk, the larger the area of the white surface and the nearer the white surface was to the center of the Gelb disk. The data plot so regularly on straight lines, except when the white surface is tangent to the disk, that there can be no doubt of the contrast origin of the Gelb phenomenon. Descriptive features of the Gelb phenomenon, as well as the quantitative data, support the contrast explanation. *S*s reported that the Gelb disk was not uniformly dark and that the greatest darkening occurred in the vicinity of the white surface, which is consonant with a contrast explanation. While there were individual differences among *S*s in the absolute amounts of black necessary to match the Gelb disk, the results for each *S* were consistent.

The Gelb effect appears to be due to a triggering action of the white surface; the effect, like the firing of a gun, is out of proportion to the immediate cause. The extent of the triggering effect can be appreciated when it is realized that the ratios of the white areas to the areas of the black disk were, in rounded percents, .02, .07, and .3 percent! Since the smallest white area gave considerable darkening of the Gelb disk,

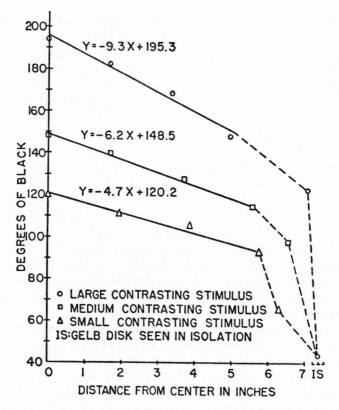

FIG. 5.11. Variations in the Gelb spotlight effect with changes in size of the contrasting stimulus and its position. (From Stewart, 1959. With the permission of the American Psychological Association.)

it is apparent that even the smallest ratio, $\frac{2}{100}$ of 1 percent to 1 does not represent the lower limit of white surface that may exercise contrast effect under the conditions of the Gelb phenomenon.

Extremely high contrast effects from very small stimuli have long been recognized in the field of vision as "glare" from small bright light sources. The Gelb phenomenon demonstrates that a very small *highly reflecting* surface as well as a small *luminous* area can give rise to large contrast effects under certain conditions. We have also found that a small white surface against a black velvet background under high illuminance appears to glow and to be self-luminous. Owing to the very low reflectance of the velvet (about one-tenth that of a good black paper), the ratio of white to black is about ten times higher than is usually experienced under ordinary conditions of viewing, with resultant high contrast effect. To us the Gelb effect is not surprising since contrast, according to the principle of color conversion, depends on the distance from level as well as on the *areas* of the two surfaces. The greater the difference in reflectance or luminance between contiguous areas, the greater will be the contrast effect. If we think in terms of the contrast of the large disk on the small white patch, rather than the other way around, then the contrast-enhanced white must be accompanied by a contrast-enhanced black disk and this is what we find in the Gelb phenomenon.

MARIMONT'S MODEL FOR COMPLEXITIES OF APPARENT BRIGHTNESS

In the earlier discussion of lightness or apparent brightness (the term used by Jameson and Hurvich, 1961) it was assumed that a number of different reflectances are viewed under a constant source of illumination. The Judd formula for lightness given in Equation (11) is based on a constant value for adaptation level. With changing illuminance not only is the weighted average of the *luminances* changed but, as Marimont (1962) pointed out, the sensitivity or gain of the entire visual system is also changed. The question arises whether a formulation in terms of adaptation-level theory can account for differential changes in high and low luminances with increases in illuminance. This question was answered in the negative by Jameson and Hurvich (1961). Their results of observations in an ingenious and complicated viewing situation parallel the paradoxical everyday observation that a bottle of india ink or a standard telephone set is perceived as blacker under bright illumination than under dim illumination. As noted by Jameson and Hurvich, the author reported this anomalous effect (1943) as the reverse aspect of "whiteness" compensation: "Compensation is just as much darkening of surfaces of low reflectance in high illuminances as it is lightening of surfaces of high reflectance in low illuminances, although the latter has received more acclaim" (p. 560). Apparently a quantitative formulation embracing phenomena found under changing illuminances as well as under constant illuminance seemed difficult to Jameson and Hurvich (as it did to Judd and Helson much earlier) because their explanation in terms of a Hering opponents-induction contrast is purely qualitative and difficult to evaluate experimentally. Before we consider Marimont's quantitative formulation, which takes a great step forward, we must describe the Jameson-Hurvich setup and chief findings.

In the Jameson-Hurvich experiment Ss viewed a fivefold pattern of squares in the form of a cross of different reflectances (hence luminances) in which each reflectance differed from its neighbor and from the background by a constant ratio. The maximal ratio of focal-area luminances was 27:1 for the brightest to the darkest of the square areas. The over-all level of illuminance of the total field was varied in three steps through a range of 1.1 log units. With the total pattern visible, Ss matched each of the square areas in random order, while varying the brightness of a standard field to the right of the squares, by shifting their eyes from one to the other. The results, briefly and in general, were that the three squares having higher luminances *increased* in apparent brightness with *increase* in the illuminance, while the darkest square *decreased* in apparent brightness, and the next to the darkest square darkened a little at the second level and lightened a little at the third level of illuminance and so may be regarded as fairly constant. By using luminances instead of reflectances, changes in illuminance are automatically incorporated into the discussion from here on. Marimont assumes that somewhere between the lowest and the third levels of illuminance there is one value for each square that would have remained constant in apparent brightness. This value she denotes by the symbol B_o, and the luminance to which it corresponds by I_o. To each B_o there is a corresponding I_o which depends upon the over-all illumination and which is related to the average value of log I over the whole viewing area. As pointed out by Marimont, the Jameson-Hurvich curves are linear in a log-log plot and their slopes increase as the illuminance is increased. Using a linear approximation, Marimont writes the equation of the family of curves for all the areas and illuminances as

$$\log B - \log B_o = k(I_o)(\log I - \log I_o) \qquad (14)$$

With the relationship between k and I_0 almost perfectly linear, we can say that

$$k(I_o) = \alpha + \beta \log I_o \qquad (15)$$

Substituting this value in Equation (14), we have

$$\log B - \log B_o = (\alpha + \beta \log I_o)(\log I - \log I_o) \qquad (16)$$

To evaluate α, β, $\log I_o$, and B_o, Marimont assumes that the value of I_0 is proportional to the luminance of any one of the squares under the three conditions. With this assumption we can solve for the unknown constants. To determine the effect of illuminance on apparent brightness of a given square, we can say that for each square, $\log I - \log I_o$ is a constant which is symbolized by c so that

$$\log B - \log B_o = c[\alpha + \beta (\log I - c)] \qquad (17)$$

From this it follows that c is positive for $\log I > \log I_o$, that is, in the case of those squares brighter than the reference level, and zero for those equal to it. As shown by Marimont this formulation yields a good fit not only to the Jameson-Hurvich data but also to the results found by Stevens (1961) for a single disk against a white surround. Further, Marimont points out, the power function found by Stevens, when units and variables are suitably transformed, is identical in form with Equation (16). By taking exponents of both sides of Equation (16) we get

$$\frac{B}{B_o} = \left(\frac{I}{I_o}\right) k(I_o) \qquad (18)$$

which represents a power law with the exponent a function of the level of illumination or the adaptation level since I_0 is the average value of $\log I$ over the whole viewing area.

For other details of Marimont's formulation, account of edge effects (Mach rings), stabilized retinal image effect, and physical model the reader should consult the publication from which this account is taken (Marimont, 1962).

BACKGROUND INFLUENCES ON FORM PERCEPTION

A study of form constancy by Nellis (1958) demonstrated that forms, no less than colors, are influenced by background and residual factors. In addition to manipulation of the usual variables in studies of form constancy (eccentricity of ellipses and orientation with respect to the line of sight) Nellis also varied the orientation of the background against which the ellipses were viewed. The additional variable of background angle of tilt makes possible a treatment of form constancy that is parallel to the variables in studies of lightness constancy as seen in Table 5.3. The analogy in Table 5.6 between form and lightness constancy is based upon functional relations rather than upon phenotypical properties. Just as increasing depth of shadow is equivalent to decreasing reflectance of object, so eccentricity of form may be varied by changing the ratio of minor to major axes of the ellipse or by changing the tilt of the ellipse out of the frontal-parallel plane. If illuminance is held constant, then there is only one way to change the lightness of the background, i.e., by changing its reflectance; similarly, only angle of tilt of background can be varied so far as modification of its spatial orientation is concerned, hence these variables are functionally analogous.

TABLE 5.6.   Parallel Variables in Form and Lightness Constancy

Lightness Constancy	Form Constancy
1. Reflectance of object	1. Eccentricity of ellipse
2. Depth of shadow	2. Tilt of ellipse
3. Reflectance of background	3. Tilt of background

The following conditions were therefore varied in Nellis' study as follows:

1. Eccentricity of the ellipses was varied by using figures with major and minor axes as follows: 6.5 × 2.5 in., 6.5 × 4.0 in., and 6.5 × 5.5 in.

2. The ellipses were turned out of the frontal-parallel plane 15°, 30°, 45°, 60°, and 75°.

3. The backgrounds were tilted either 0°, 15°, 30°, 45°, 60°, or 75° out of the frontal-parallel plane in conjunction with each of the tilts of the ellipses.

Each ellipse was thus seen at every angle of tilt against every angle of tilt of background, making a total of 90 conditions (3 × 6 × 5). Moreover, the 90 conditions were replicated with angles of tilt about the vertical axis (experiment I) and horizontal axis (experiment II) of both stimuli and backgrounds; i.e., the major axis was vertical in the first case, horizontal in the second. Form constancy was measured by matching the stimulus variable to one standard of a set consisting of 1 circle and 21 ellipses mounted on a background which was similar in appearance to the object-background variables but always in a frontal-parallel plane to the Ss. The standard ellipses varied from 6.5 × 6.0 in. to 6.5 × 0.65 in., a sufficiently wide range from perfect circularity to extreme eccentricity to provide good matches for all conditions of observation. For experiment I eight men and two women Ss were used; for experiment II three groups were used: six men and four women (college or graduate students); three boys and three girls (eight years old); and five boys and one girl (ten years old). Under the conditions of experiment II the major axes of ellipses were mounted horizontally but they and the background were tilted in the vertical dimension. Constancy was measured, by taking the ratio of the minor axis of the ellipse matching the variable to the minor axis of the "projected image" of the ellipse on the retina, and was taken to be sufficiently well approximated by the formula

$$a = b \cos \phi \qquad\qquad (19)$$

where a is the minor axis of the projected image, b is the minor axis of the ellipse, and ϕ is the angle of tilt out of the frontal-parallel plane of the ellipse. When the ratio of the minor axis of the matching stimulus to the minor axis of the variable corrected for angle of tilt is unity, there would be no compensation for angle of tilt and hence no "constancy"; if the ratio is greater than unity, then there is compensation for tilt as the variable is perceived to be "rounder" (less elliptical) than its retinal image. In Katz's terminology, there is constancy to a greater or lesser degree, depending upon how much greater than unity this ratio happens to be, but we shall refer to the effect as "compensation."

The results of Nellis's study show that the minor axes of the ellipses in the frontal-parallel plane are larger than the axes of the ellipses turned out the frontal-parallel plane 15° showing "superconstancy" (or overcompensation) of the "roundness" of the tilted ellipses for all tilts of background. With tilts of ellipses greater than 30° the matches indicate that although the ellipses are perceived to be more circular than their corresponding retinal images, they are not perceived in their true eccentricities. Furthermore, the greater the tilt of the background, the less does perceived shape approximate the actual shape of the stimuli. Three conclusions can be drawn from these results:

1. The greater the angle of tilt of the ellipses, the greater is the compensation, as shown by the ratio of the axis of the matching stimulus to that of the projected image on the retina.
2. The greater the tilt of the background, the less is the compensation defined as above.
3. The greater the angle of tilt of the ellipses, the more effective is the background tilt in reducing compensation.

Plots of the ratios of the matching to the projected image sizes (Y) against angle of tilt of the ellipses yield exponential curves which become linear when transformed as follows:

$$\log Y = me^{kx} + b \qquad (20)$$

where x is the angle of tilt of the ellipse measured in radians, m and b are the slope and y intercept determined by least-squares fit to the data, and k equals 2.5 when the tilts of ellipses and background are about the vertical axis and 1.0 when the tilts are about the horizontal axis. Thus tilt out of the horizontal plane has much greater effect in reducing shape constancy than does tilt out of the vertical plane. Furthermore, the values of m are greater for the pooled results for background tilts of 0°, 15°, and 30° than for the pooled results for background tilts of 45°, 60°, and 75°, showing that greater tilt of background reduces compensation for tilt of ellipses.

Nellis' study gives experimental-quantitative support for Koffka's concept of a "spatial level" (1935) which he did not further specify or treat analytically. Whereas Koffka was led from his concept of a spatial level to the concept of a color level, we have been led from the concept of chromatic adaptation level to the concept of a spatial level as the pooled effect of all spatial properties of objects in the field of view. The main conditions affecting lightness constancy have analogues in space perception though the analogy was not found to be complete with respect to all of the conditions in Nellis' study.

The effects of background tilt on form perception suggest analogous effects in the area of size perception. That perceived size depends upon contextual factors is a well established fact; e.g., as vision is reduced from binocular, to monocular, to pinhole vision, apparent size of objects decreases (Hermans, 1954). A circle appears smaller when it is surrounded by larger circles than when it is surrounded by smaller circles. The apparent size of any given object also depends upon the direction and slant of areas and other objects in the field of view, as shown by the Zöllner, Wundt, and Hering figures and the size-perspective illusions. Perceived spatial properties of objects, such as form, size, distance, and direction, no less than their color qualities depend upon the pooled effect of the spatial properties of all other objects in the field of vision. Spatial interactions have long been known in optical illusions, but there has been less progress in bringing order into this area than there has been in the field of color vision.

INFLUENCE OF BACKGROUND ON SIZE AND DIRECTION

The influence of contextual and background stimuli on perceived size and direction of focal parts of the visual field has long been known in illusions of extent, direction, and perspective; such influence indicates pooling of the physiological processes in mediating space perception as well as in simultaneous and successive color contrast. Let us consider experimental studies showing systematic changes in perceived size and direction of lines with variation in ancillary stimuli.

Effect of size of frame on perceived length. In a study by Künnapas (1955) a 50-mm. line in a square 7×7 cm. was taken as standard and compared with lines in squares 9, 12, 16, and 21 cm. on

TABLE 5.7. Influence of Size of Frame on Apparent Length of an Enclosed Line

Side of Square (cm.)	PSE (mm.)	Longer Limen	Shorter Limen	Interval Uncertainty
7x7[a]	50.00[a]			
9x9	51.33	52.53	49.69	2.84
12x12	52.68	54.19	51.01	3.18
16x16	54.16	55.37	52.43	2.94
21x21	55.63	57.14	53.98	3.16

[a] Standard.
SOURCE: From Künnapas, 1955. With the permission of the American Psychological Association.

a side. The lines in the larger squares were equated to the standard line with the results shown in Table 5.7. The larger the frame, the shorter the enclosed line appears to be, as evidenced by the lengths of the lines necessary to match the standard line in the different squares. The lines perceived as *shorter* than the standard (50 mm.) in the three largest squares were actually longer than the standard. The size of the frame also affected the perceived *thickness* of the enclosed lines, those in the larger squares appearing thinner as well as shorter than the lines in the smaller squares. The direction of change in this study was, as usual, away from the frame and hence is an example of repulsion from the anchoring stimulus.

From the results of the contrived experimental frame on perceived size Künnapas (1957) reasoned that the elliptical form of the visual field might be in part responsible for the illusion in which lines in the vertical direction are perceived to be longer than lines in the horizontal direction. If this reasoning is correct, then the illusion should disappear in the dark with disappearance of the frame; but owing to "force of habit" this will not occur immediately and only a reduction in the illusion should be expected. With an L-shaped stimulus consisting of two luminous lines, the vertical line was varied while the horizontal line was held at 50 mm. Under lighted conditions, the ascending length of the vertical line which matched the 50-mm. horizontal was 45.9 mm.; in the dark it was 47.0 mm.; with descending matches, the respective values were 47.0 mm. and 48.2 mm. The mean of the ascending and descending series was 46.5 mm. in light and 47.6 mm. in the dark. The vertical-horizontal illusion was thus reduced almost 33 percent in the absence of the visual frame. The decrease was significant and in the predicted direction. The differences between the ascending and descending series in the light and dark condition were also significant, showing the usual order effects characteristic of psychophysical judgments.

The finding that the shape of the visual field influences perceived extent demonstrates in striking fashion how a residual factor, though unnoticed, can significantly affect perception. Since we do not compensate for the anisotropic form of the visual field, it is evident that extents in the vertical direction are not referred solely to the vertical frame. Rather, it appears there is a common zero or origin to which extents in both dimensions are referred with the result that vertical extents are overestimated. The reduction in this effect in the absence of the visual frame also furnishes evidence for a common pool or zero which determines perception of extent in both the vertical and horizontal directions.

Contextual influences on perceived direction. The distorting effect of slanting lines cutting across parallels is well known from the Zöllner figure. Essentially this phenomenon was subjected to systematic study by Culbert (1954), who first exposed line grids for 2 min. at varying degrees of slant and then exposed test lines for only .05 sec. at $+1.5°$ to $-5°$ with respect to the horizontal in steps of 10′. He thus presented 9 test lines slanting up and to the right and 30 test lines slanting down to the right. The slants of the grids were 0°, 2.5°, 5°, 10°, 20°, and 40° down right. If the *S*s were not affected by the slant of the grid lines, their responses would be 9 up, 1 horizontal, and 30 down. The average number of "up, right" judgments was 7.9 with grid at 0°; 12.2 at 2.5°; 14.5 at 5°; 17.8 at 10°; 16.9 at 20°; and 11.9 at 40°. Since the slant of the grid lines was "down, right" and the number of judgments "up, right" exceeded the expected number (9.5) to a significant degree for all grid slants greater than 0°, the effect of the grids was to repel the test lines in the fashion typical of anchor and AL effects.

The establishment of visual spatial levels is determined almost completely by focal and background stimuli and little, if at all, by residuals, as was shown in a study by Heinemann and Marill (1954). An objectively vertical line when seen against a white background tilted 10° out of the vertical showed a tendency to become more nearly parallel to the edges of the background. But when the standard line as well as the background were both turned out of the vertical 10°, making the line parallel to the two sides of the background, there was no significant tendency for it to turn back toward the objective vertical. Thus the predominant influence on perceived slant of the line was the background rather than the previously experienced vertical norms. The authors called this an alignment effect rather than a tendency to conform to the vertical in Gibson's sense (1933; 1937*a*).

In closing this section on spatial interactions in perception of form, size, and direction which has stressed quantitative data, it should not be forgotten that everyday experience probably furnishes more potent examples of spatial pooling than do laboratory setups. Rooms and houses constructed to give distorted perspective attest the power of novel sensory data to modify our usual visual and tactile-kinesthetic frames of reference. The Ames room with abnormal tilt of floor, walls, and ceiling produces illusions of size in which size constancy completely disappears, far and near relations are reversed, and the rotating trapezoidal window with distorted perspective causes solid objects to appear to pass through other solid objects. The kind of spatial world that we take as normal and real has been built up from certain visual, tactile-kinesthetic, and movement perceptions; if these are altered, they give rise to illusions such as those in the Ames demonstrations. What we call "reality" proves to be the result of having only one frame of reference out of the many possible ones that may arise from perceptual pooling processes.

Intermodality interactions in space perception. With increasing knowledge of the importance of kinesthetic and tactile feedback in visual-motor responses and from the role of efferent impulses in receptor processes and newly discovered mechanisms in the central nervous system for intersensory interactions, it is becoming clearer that no sense modality is perfectly autonomous or functions independently of the others or apart from the motor side of the response. Qualitative observations by Kleint (1937; 1938) showed that visual autokinesis is affected by tension in the eye muscles: When S is asked to turn his eyes while fixating a spot in the dark, the spot may be perceived to move in the same or in the opposite direction to that of the eye movement, depending upon the effort exerted on the eyes. The farther the eyes are turned, the more there is perceived movement in the direction of turning: 26 percent with 10° and 91 percent with 40° turning. Conversely, vision may arouse kinesthetic perceptions: S sitting on a stool in a lighted room and turning his eyes to a point on the wall feels rotation in the direction of the fixated point. If the eyes after fixating to one side are returned to the normal position, the body seems to rotate in the opposite direction. Sometimes the point fixated appears to move; sometimes the body appears to move with respect to the fixated point. Kleint points out that under conditions in which objects in the field appear to move, one's own body acts like an object in the field and may be felt or seen to be in motion. The general rule seems to be that what is background remains stationary while objects tend to move. This rule is verified by illusions such as when the moon appears to move and the clouds remain stationary, when the banks of a flowing stream appear to move backwards if the water is fixated, and when in a ship's cabin the objects rather than the cabin appear to move. If the field around an individual is rotated, it is the body that is perceived to move, not the room.

A modified local-sign theory proposed by Bruell and Albee (1955*b*), which assumes that motor innervations to the eye muscles affect visual localization, seems to explain a number of phenomena, including the illusions of movement discussed above. Let us consider this theory in some detail by following the Bruell and Albee exposition. According to the local-sign theory each retinal point has a zero, a plus, or a minus value. The values are zero in the median plane cutting through the fovea, negative for the receptors to the right of the fovea, and positive for receptors to the left of the fovea. When the observer is looking straight ahead, objects with negative space values are thus seen to the left of the midline, those with positive values are seen to the right, and those with zero values are seen straight ahead. If the observer turns his eyes from a point C straight ahead to a point E on the right, C is still seen as straight ahead although it is now stimulating retinal receptors presumably having negative space values. Since E is seen to the right, although falling on the fovea, the foveal points act as though they now had positive space values. Bruell and Albee set up the following hypothesis to cover these facts: Whenever the dextro- or levo-rotators of the eyes receive voluntary innervation, the fovea assumes positive or negative space values accordingly as the eyes are turned to the right or left and concomitant changes occur in the space values of all retinal points. In other words, the zero (straight ahead) shifts with the fovea with voluntary changes in position of the eyes.

Bruell and Albee next consider the case where the eyes remain stationary while an object, C, is moved from the center of vision to the left. As the object moves, it stimulates retinal points with negative space values and is perceived as moving to the left. This is contrary to what happens when the eyes are voluntarily moved to the right and C stimulates negative points but still appears straight ahead. But if the eyes are turned involuntarily to the right, the object C will appear to move to the left. This result requires a second hypothesis: When the eyes move involuntarily, receptors do not change their space values. With involuntary eye movements the fovea keeps its zero values so that objects falling on it appear straight ahead and the other receptors retain their positive or negative space values.

According to the two hypotheses accounting for the opposed types of localization with voluntary and involuntary eye movements, Bruell and Albee believe it possible to predict apparent localization and movement perception from knowledge of the pattern of oculomotor innervations in a given situation. The external eye muscles, they maintain, may be voluntarily or reflexly innervated, with reflex innervation occurring either as a result of retinal stimulation or through the motor system. They point out that if a number of point sources of light to the right are lighted in a dark room, the eye tends to turn until unilateral stimulation gives way to bilateral stimulation, or, in other words, the eyes will come to rest when the fovea is on the center of the dots. The effect of asymmetrical stimulation is to cause stronger innervation of either the dextro- or levorotators. Center fixation results in equal dextro- and levorotator stimulation. What appears subjectively straight ahead tends to shift in the direction of the center of the visual field, and if this center deviates from what is objectively straight ahead of the observer, the objective and the subjective do not coincide. Usually the two do coincide because the whole visual field is filled with stimuli and thus innervation of the two sets of eye muscles (keeping to the horizontal plane) are equally innervated. Their theory therefore assumes that the space values of points on the retina depend not only on the pattern of visual stimulation but also on the types of contributions made by kinesthetic impulses from the levo- and dextrorotators. The visual field is affected by efferent as well as afferent impulses.

The authors of this theory show in detail how it explains shifts in the apparent horizontal and vertical planes, perceived movement following rotation, the autokinetic effect, apparent movement of the moon seen through clouds, and other perceptual phenomena. In agreement with Kleint and others, Bruell and Albee maintain that motor innervations to the eyes which are not sufficient to cause overt eye movements may nevertheless be sufficient to account for the autokinetic effect and other illusions of movement.

That the visual zero shifts in the manner described by Bruell and Albee cannot be doubted. Their theory that motor innervations affect visually perceived directions, positions, and movement also seems to be basically sound, but it needs to be supplemented to take into account kinesthesis and input from other sense modalities in addition to that from the extrinsic muscles of the eyes. As Müller (1917) pointed out, localization relative to the observer (egocentric localization) may be referred to the visual system (the B system), to the position of the head (the K system), or to the position of the body (the S system). Moreover, these systems are subject to various modes of functioning which affect perceived direction, position, distance, etc. (cf. the account by Fröbes, 1923, pp. 224 ff.). In other words, the visual system is affected by a larger and more varied assortment of tactile-kinesthetic impulses than is recognized in the Bruell-Albee theory which takes into account only *part* of the *B* system.

Consider the following observations that one may make quite easily: If the head is turned to right or left, what is seen straight ahead (visual zero) follows the movement of the head both when the eyes move passively with the head (contrary to the Bruell-Albee theory) and when the eyes are fixed on a given spot and assume an extreme position while the head is turned as far as possible. In such cases objects coinciding with the midline of the head tend to be seen as straight ahead although in the latter case they fall on retinal points having extreme plus or minus signs. As the head begins its movement from the normal zero position, the fixated spot remains stationary up to a certain point, after which it appears to move rapidly in a direction opposite to the movement of the head; it loses its zero values, and points in the midline of the head take over the straight-ahead position. We thus see that the *B* system is not independent of the *K* system.

An example of the influence of the *S* system (body system) is given by Bruell and Albee although they do not recognize it as such: In night driving the lights of an oncoming car may be displaced to the right, in the direction of the observer, causing him to steer further away from the oncoming car (a good example of an illusion). Quantitative evidence for the effect of the body system on visual direction was found by Werner, Wapner, and Chandler (1951) in their study of the effect of supported and unsupported body tilt on perceived verticality. These writers found that the apparent vertical shifted to a greater extent when the body was tilted without support, hence when there was greater musculature involvement, than when it was tilted with support. Moreover, the apparent vertical tilts in a direction opposite to that of body tilt, and the greater the body tilt, the greater the tilt of the apparent vertical. Since these effects are ascribed to somato- and viscerotonic processes by Werner, Wapner, and Chandler, space perception may be affected by *any* extraneous stimulation whatsoever.

This interpretation is supported by two other sets of experiments by the principal investigators and their colleagues. Wapner, Werner, and Morant (1951) reported that the apparent vertical of a rod attached to the rotating chair on which the *S* sat shifted in a direction opposite to the direction of rotation during acceleration but shifted in the direction of rotation during deceleration. Deceleration in one direction functions like acceleration in the opposite direction. Electrical stimulation applied to the sternocleidomastoid muscle of the neck and monaural stimulation caused the apparent vertical of a rod to shift in a direction opposite to the side of stimulation as reported by Wapner, Werner, and Chandler (1951).

There are also cases where the individual accepts the framework as his vertical even though it is tilted. Using a setup in which the room and the chair could be tilted in the same or in opposite direction, Witkin (1949) found that most Ss go along with the field in what they perceive to be the upright. Usually an angle between the tilt of the room and the tilt of the body serves as the perceived vertical which, in extreme cases, may be off by as much as 56°. Women accepted the room as upright at greater tilts than did men, on the average. When the room and chair were tilted to the same side, the women perceived tilts of 17.7° and the men, 11.5°. When they were tilted to opposite sides, the vertical averaged 30.3° for women and 22.9° for men. Under these and other conditions it was found that women depended more upon visual frame of reference and less upon their tactile-kinesthetic input than men did. While the reasons for them are not known these sex differences seem to be clearly established. It would be interesting, and possibly fruitful, to attempt to reduce the influence of the visual frame in the case of the women by instructing them to make greater use of their bodily sensations. In this way it might be determined if women are deficient compared with men in tactile-kinesthetic sensitivity since they were also found less able than men to maintain perfect balance while standing on a moveable platform.

Intersensory pooling in space perception also has some general implications. Nothing seems more fixed and stable than the forms, sizes, distances, and locations of objects—in short, their spatial properties— and this has given rise to the theory that perceived space is merely a copy of the "real" world. Classical introspective psychology pointed out that tridimensionality is a product and a creation of the two flat retinal images received by the eyes. Observations reported by individuals who had not achieved sight until later in life bear out this contention. Similarly the changes in color, size, and form which objects undergo when contextual stimuli are removed, as in aperture vision, also argue against a copy theory of perceived space. This theory is also wrong in implying that as long as the organism passively reflects what is impressed upon the sense organs a true picture of reality emerges but as soon as the organism becomes more than a mere registering or copying device error is introduced into perception and judgment. In the light of what is now known, space perception must be regarded as a construct, sensory in nature to be sure, but nevertheless a product in which the contributions from all sense modalities are pooled.

Our view that space perception is a product of interacting processes from all sense modalities rather than a mere copy of external reality does not imply that there is no correspondence between physical and perceived space. On the contrary, adequate adjustment to the external world requires correct or nearly correct perception of tridimensionality, distance, position, and direction, and organisms achieve this by all the means at their disposal. If perceived space were merely a copy of physical space, which is largely a matter of physical optics so far as visual perception is concerned, the approximations to constancy of size and form would be poor indeed since perception would be determined wholly by the characteristics of the images on the retina. But because there is pooling of contextual and residual factors, perception of space is, in spite of some illusory phenomena, more accurate than it would be if the organism were merely a meter or a copying device.

Effect of internal norms on recognition of forms. Illusions involving orientation of tactile forms described over 100 years ago by E. H. Weber furnish one of the most striking demonstrations of the ways in which changes in internal norms can affect space perception. Weber's description of the illusions is as follows:

We have accustomed ourselves to remember letters as they are usually given visually and as we write them. We do not recognize an L when we see it written reversed ⅃ and we recognize it just as little when we see it written upside down ⌐ or written upside down and reversed Γ . One might think that it wouldn't matter on the skin how the letter is written so far as recognizing it is concerned but this is not the case.

On the forehead L has to be written ⅃ , and on the back of the head, L, on the abdomen, ⌐ , and on the rump, Γ , in order for it to appear right and to be recognized most easily. We think of letters written on our foreheads as if we saw them from behind-forwards (von hinten nach vorn), that is, in the direction we usually look. We feel the letter as if the skin on the forehead was transparent and we read it reversed on the surface of the frontal bone. A letter inscribed on the back of the head is not read as if we read the surface turned toward the occipital bone but as if we were standing behind ourselves and were looking at the surface of the skin on the back of the head. On the abdomen it has to be written with its beginnings toward the feet and with the loop end towards the head, as if it were written on a paper laid on the abdomen in such a way that we could read best by looking downward from above (Weber, 1851, pp. 99–100).

I have demonstrated Weber's phenomenon many times by tracing letters and numbers with a blunt-pointed pencil on the forehead. The numbers 3 and 4 marked in reverse on the forehead are usually reported to be "normal" until S senses something is "wrong." Ss overcome the illusion by changing the vantage point from which they seem to be looking at the numbers. They report it makes a difference, as Weber pointed out, whether they are looking at their foreheads from behind or from in front! After some practice one can adopt either stance and see the pattern either way. I have not found it as easy as Weber implies it is to replicate the orientations of letters on other parts of the body according to his description. Fortunately the demontration works best on the forehead which is easy to stimulate and to use for demonstrational purposes.

Like the Tau effect (Helson and King, 1931), this illusion of Weber argues against a strict local-sign theory of perception of space. Whether the numbers appear to face left or right depends upon the apparent position at which the individual seems to be looking at his forehead, not solely upon the local tactile-kinesthetic signs aroused by the stimulus. The orientation of spatial patterns on the skin depends upon whether one perceives himself as looking at them from in front, behind, above, below, or even sideways. By the same token, the internal norms governing the body image are not, as some have supposed, so firmly fixed that disorientation is necessarily a sign of abnormality. Directions which depend upon the self, or, more properly, upon one's own body, such as front, back, up, down, vertical, and horizontal are by no means absolutely anchored. Relative and absolute spatial localization vary with change in position of parts of the body and of the body as a whole, with rotation, and, in general, when the usual visual, tactile, and kinesthetic relations are disturbed.

Perception of forms depends upon maintenance of normal relations between external and internal spatial frames of reference as shown by the fact that familiar plane figures may go unrecognized or may be seen as new forms if they are perceived in new orientations (Gibson and Robinson, 1935). Orientation and direction must be considered dimensions or attributes of forms as well as extensity, voluminousness, and other figural properties. Mach long ago pointed out (1886) that a square on its side changed to diamond when turned 45° so as to rest

on one of its corners. A simple experiment shows this effect arises from
the changed relations of the axes of the square to the vertical-horizontal
visual axes. If the paper on which the square has been drawn is
rotated through an angle of 45°, the square changes to diamond even
though its relations to its own frame of reference are unchanged.
According to my own observations of this phenomenon, square is
perceived almost up to 45° and then suddenly gives way to diamond.
It thus appears that coincidence of the sides of the square with the
visual vertical-horizontal axes leads to perception of square, and coincidence of the diagonals with the visual vertical-horizontal axes leads
to diamond. This effect is not found with a rectangle, e.g., one in which
the ratio of height to width is 1:3, and the reason is not hard to find;
in the case of the long rectangle the diagonals cannot be made to
coincide simultaneously with the visual vertical and horizontal axes.
Perceptions of square and of diamond depend upon conditions of symmetry or zeroing with the visual axes.

From the foregoing discussion it must not be inferred that the visual
vertical and horizontal axes are simply determined by the gravitational
vertical and horizontal. In the rod and frame test (Witkin and Asch,
1948) the perceived vertical can be made to shift with changes in the
tilt of the frame when rod and frame are the only objects visible in
an otherwise dark room. In the discussion of the Mach effect we
assume normal lighting and normal orientation of other objects in the
field of view.

ANCHOR, CONTRAST, AND PARADOXICAL
DISTANCE EFFECTS[3]

Since the publication of Gibson's work dealing with adaptation,
aftereffect, and contrast in the perception of tilted lines (1937*a*) and
Köhler and Wallach's monograph (1944) on figural aftereffects
(FAE), many studies have dealt with effects of adaptation or satiation
with spatial stimulation, chiefly in vision. In general, the phenomena
are formally similar to successive contrast, afterimages of movement,
and to what Gibson called "adaptation with negative aftereffect"
(1937*b*). FAE appears when a figure, exposed in the region affected by

[3] The following discussion is taken from Helson and Nash (1960) by permission of the American Psychological Association.

previous fixation for varying periods of time, is displaced from the adapted region. The figure to which the eye is adapted is called the inspection (I) figure and the probe figure is called the test (T) figure. Since the T figure is repelled away from the region of the I figure, T figures within I figures appear smaller while T figures outside I figures appear larger than the same figures exposed to unsatiated retinal areas. This aspect of FAE is easily envisaged as a contrast effect. A secondary aspect of FAE, found by Köhler and Wallach, seems at first to be ruled out of adaptation effects because T figures farther from satiated areas are repelled, within limits, to a greater extent than are T figures that are nearer. This is called the paradoxical distance effect (PDE) because it seems to violate the inverse distance law, according to which effects decrease with distance from a source of energy. While investigating the effects of anchoring stimuli on sets of lifted weights at various distances from the anchoring stimuli, Helson and Nash (1960) found two types of shifts in judgments, one analogous to classical anchor and contrast effects, the other analogous to PDE. Let us, therefore, consider this study in some detail since it brings FAE and PDE within the larger class of phenomena found with changes in AL.

In the lifted weights investigation Ss judged seven successive sets of stimuli formed by dropping the heaviest stimulus in the first set and adding a stimulus one step interval below the lightest to form the second set. The third and succeeding sets were formed in an analogous manner. The original set consisted of stimuli from 400 to 600 grm. with step intervals of 50 grm. and the seventh set consisted of stimuli from 100 to 300 grm. Sets formed in this way constituted the descending series. Sets formed by starting with 100–300 grm. and ending with 400–600 grm. constituted the ascending series. A week or two after Ss judged either ascending or descending series of single stimuli, which served as the control condition, the procedure was repeated with a 90-grm. or a 900-grm. stimulus as anchor or background which was lifted, but not judged, before each of the stimuli in each set. Four groups of five Ss each served in this part of the experiment. The series employing the anchor stimuli constituted the experimental condition to furnish information regarding effects of anchors, and hence of adaptation levels, at varying distances from sets of stimuli. To minimize inter-set effects and to study very large changes in AL, a control procedure was employed in which four groups of five Ss each judged the heaviest or lightest set of stimuli followed immediately by the lightest or heaviest set. Judgments were made in terms of nine categories ranging from very very heavy, through medium, to very very light and were assigned numbers from 10 for very very light, through 50 for medium, to 90 for very very heavy. Comparison of the numerical values for single stimuli and for anchor stimuli shows effects of changes in AL on members of sets (intra-set effects) and on sets as wholes (inter-set effects).

The results—in Table 5.8 for 900-grm. anchor in ascending order and 90-grm. anchor in descending order for all seven sets of stimuli and in Fig. 5.12 for 900-grm. anchor in ascending and descending orders of the lightest and heaviest sets—reveal clearly two kinds of displacements due to the anchor stimuli. The first type of displacement concerns shifts in judgments of series stimuli *within* each of the seven sets; the second concerns shifts in judgments of sets compared with sets. The first effect is seen to consist in greater displacement of stimuli nearer the anchors than farther from the anchors (within sets) and is the usual contrast or repulsion effect found with anchor stimuli. Thus with 900-grm. anchor the heavier stimuli in each set are more affected than are the lighter; with 90-grm. anchor the lighter stimuli in each set are more affected than are the heavier. But when inter-set effects are compared, an opposite effect (PDE) is found; thus, the 100–300 grm. set is displaced −145 scale points (downward) with 900-grm. anchor while the 400–600 grm. set is displaced only −67 scale points by this anchor; conversely, the 400–600 grm. set is displaced +73 scale points (upward) by the 90-grm. anchor while the 100–300 grm. set is displaced only +16 scale points by this anchor. Intra-set shifts are thus the usual anchor or contrast effects while inter-set shifts are similar to PDE effects.

The shifts in judgment are paralleled by cognate shifts in adaptation levels following introduction of the anchors. With single stimuli the AL for 100–300 grm. set is 165 grm. and with 900-grm. anchor it is 317 grm., a shift of +152 grm.; but the comparable change in the 400–600 grm. set with 900-grm. anchor is only +48 grm. since AL for this set is 361 grm. with single stimuli and 409 grm. with the anchor. Conversely, with the 90-grm. anchor, AL of the 100–300 grm. set shifts −26 grm. as compared with its value with single stimuli; but the AL of the 400–600 grm. set shifts −84 grm., or nearly three times as much. The intra- and inter-set effects appear very graphically (no pun in-

TABLE 5.8. Judgments of Seven Sets of Weights Showing Effects of Anchors on Stimuli Within Sets (Contrast) and Between Sets (Paradoxical Distance Effect)

Stimuli	100	150	200	250	300	350	400	450	500	550	600	Total
			Ascending Series Order: 900-grm. anchor									
S.S.	20	41	61	75	86							
900 B.S.	7	16	27	39	49							
Diff.	—13	—25	—34	—36	—37							—145
S.S.		34	48	62	72	80						
900 B.S.		12	24	31	41	50						
Diff.		—22	—24	—31	—31	—30						—138
S.S.			39	58	70	83	89					
900 B.S.			17	27	35	44	49					
Diff.			—22	—31	—35	—39	—40					—167
S.S.				48	64	72	81	90				
900 B.S.				29	38	44	52	60				
Diff.				—19	—26	—28	—29	—30				—132
S.S.					50	62	76	82	89			
900 B.S.					35	43	51	56	62			
Diff.					—15	—19	—25	—26	—27			—112
S.S.						55	65	77	86	88		
900 B.S.						41	45	55	62	68		
Diff.						—14	—20	—22	—24	—20		—100
S.S.							58	68	80	83	88	
900 B.S.							47	57	64	69	73	
Diff.							—11	—11	—16	—14	—15	— 67

NOTE: S.S. = single stimuli; B.S. = background stimulus; Diff. = difference.

tended) in Fig. 5.12 wherein only the shifts in judgments of individual stimuli in the heaviest and lightest sets are plotted. (For the complete data the reader is referred to the original publication, Helson and Nash, 1960.)

The greater displacing effects on AL, and hence on judgments, of anchors farther away from series stimuli follow from the definition of AL as a weighted mean of series, background, and residual stimuli. It is immediately apparent that even simple averaging of 900 grm. with a 100–300 grm. series raises level more than averaging 900 grm. with a 400–600 grm. series; conversely, the level of a 400–600 grm. series is lowered more by averaging with 90 grm. than is the level of a 100–300 grm. series. The experimental data validate this deduction since the

TABLE 5.8. (Continued)

Stimuli	100	150	200	250	300	350	400	450	500	550	600	Total
S.S.							39	50	61	74	77	
90 B.S.							65	69	77	80	83	
Diff.							+26	+19	+16	+ 6	+ 6	+73
S.S.						37	47	57	70	75		
90 B.S.						62	70	79	80	82		
Diff.						+25	+23	+22	+10	+ 7		+87
S.S.					34	46	55	65	70			
90 B.S.					57	62	69	78	80			
Diff.					+23	+16	+14	+13	+10			+76
S.S.				32	43	51	64	74				
90 B.S.				50	56	66	72	77				
Diff.				+18	+13	+15	+ 8	+ 3				+57
S.S.			26	39	54	62	71					
90 B.S.			43	53	59	69	76					
Diff.			+17	+14	+ 5	+ 7	+ 5					+48
S.S.		24	35	50	60	68						
90 B.S.		33	44	56	62	69						
Diff.		+ 9	+ 9	+ 6	+ 2	+ 1						+27
S.S.	16	29	45	54	64							
90 B.S.	24	34	46	54	66							
Diff.	+ 8	+ 5	+ 1	0	+ 2							+16

SOURCE: From Helson and Nash, 1960. With the permission of the American Psychological Association.

values of AL calculated from the data agree with predictions from the weighted mean definition regarding both direction and extent of change arising from introduction of the anchor stimuli.

Since the greater effect of anchors farther removed from series stimuli deduced from the weighted log mean definition of AL was verified in the experimental data of Table 5.8, further experimental validation of this deduction may seem superfluous. However, results of another set of experiments by Nash (1950b) provide quantitative data regarding the relative contributions of the two anchors to near and far series of stimuli and also furnish additional evidence for the pooling model underlying AL theory. In these experiments Nash bracketed each member of the series (v) with the 90- and the 900-grm.

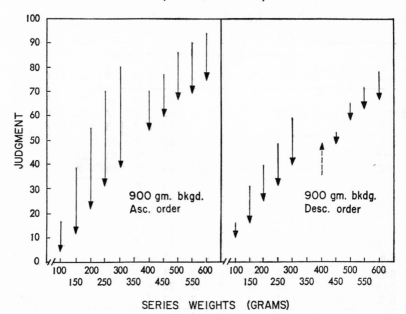

FIG. 5.12. The repulsion effect of an anchor (900 grm.) is greater on a series of stimuli farther from the anchor (100–300 grm.) than on a series nearer the anchor (400–600 grm.). The origins indicate judgments without anchor, the arrowheads judgments with anchor. (From Helson and Nash, 1960. With the permission of the American Psychological Association.)

anchors so that the series stimuli were both preceded and followed by anchor stimuli as shown in Table 5.9. As Nash pointed out, the bracketing condition provides a crucial test of AL theory because if every judgment is based on the pooled effect of all stimuli, we would expect

TABLE 5.9.   Differential Contributions of the 90-grm. and 900-grm. Anchors to the 100–300 grm. and 400–600 grm. Sets of Stimuli

Order	100–300 Series			
	AL	w_1	w_2	w_1/w_2
900,v,90	271.8	−.16	1.0	1:6
90,v,900	236.0	+.02	1.0	1:50
	400–600 Series			
900, v,90	306.9	8.21	1.0	8.2:1
90,v,900	370.2	1.50	1.0	1.5:1

SOURCE: From Nash, 1950b.

that anchors following as well as anchors preceding a stimulus would influence judgment. To evaluate the contributions of each of the anchors it is necessary to evaluate the weighting constants w_1 and w_2 in the following equation:

$$\log (A + .75d) = \frac{3.0 \, \Sigma \log X_i/n + (w_1 \log C + w_2 \log Z)/(w_1 + w_2)}{4} \quad (21)$$

where A is AL, d is the average step interval between series stimuli, X_i refers to the series stimuli, C is the 90-grm. anchor, and Z is the 900-grm. anchor. Since only relative contributions of the two anchors are in question we may let $w_2 = 1$; and rewriting Equation (21) we find that

$$w_1 = \frac{\log Z - 4.0 \log (A + .75d) + 3.0 \, \Sigma \log X_i/n}{4.0 \log (A + .75d) - 3.0 \, \Sigma \log X_i/n - \log C} \quad (22)$$

Since A can be determined from the data by least squares and all other values are known, w_1 can easily be found from Equation (22).

In Table 5.9 the ALs for the four conditions and the values of the weighting coefficients derived from Equation (22) and their ratios are given. Comparison of the ratios of the weighting coefficients for the 90-grm. anchor, w_1, with those for the 900-grm. anchor, w_2, which was assumed to be unity in all cases, shows that the 900-grm. anchor is weighted from 6 to 50 times as much as the 90-grm. anchor in determining the AL operative in the 100–300 grm. series, while in the case of the 400–600 grm. series the 90-grm. anchor is weighted 1.5 to 8.2 times as much as the 900-grm. anchor in determining the AL operative in judgments of this series. Hence the anchor farther from the series displaces AL more than does the anchor nearer the series. The values of AL and w_1 do not seem to make sense except in terms of the differential effects of the anchors on near and far sets of stimuli. Undoubtedly there are order effects; but they are masked by the pooling process since whether the anchor precedes or follows the series stimuli (v), the effect of the 900-grm. anchor is greater on the 100–300 grm. series and the effect of the 90-grm. anchor is greater on the 400–600 grm. series. These results are exactly analogous to PDE in vision, where stimuli farther from satiated areas are displaced more than are stimuli nearer such areas.

It is therefore apparent that PDE as well as the usual anchor and contrast effects can be explained in terms of the shift in level with introduction of the T figure following adaptation to the I figure. In the lifted-weight situation it follows from the weighted-mean definition of AL that introduction of an anchor outside the range of series stimuli should cause greater displacement of level in sets farther away from the anchor than in sets nearer the anchor, and this is found to be true. To explain visual PDE we need assume only that the AL resulting from the I figure (region of satiation) shifts in the direction of the T figure when it is exposed outside the region of the I figure. The new level is intermediate between the original region of adaptation and the region of the T figure, and it is to this new level that displacements are referred. It thus follows that T figures farther from the originally adapted region will be displaced more than nearer stimuli because the reference level is farther from the original level. We explain the fact that PDE is found only within a relatively limited distance from the originally stimulated region on the assumption that the T figure must be near enough to the region of the I figure to interact with it to form a new level.

Essentially the same point of view regarding the origin of PDE was put forward by Köhler in discussing the way in which I and T figures interact according to the theory of electrotonus: "If there are currents which go with I-objects, there must also be currents corresponding to T-objects. . . . To a degree, we can tell how the obstructions established by the currents of given I-objects must distort the currents of T-objects" (1951, p. 212). In other words, the physiological processes responsible for perception of T figures pool with those responsible for I figures to form a new level. Exact determination of the influence of spatial levels requires a distance function applicable to specific conditions of observation (Helson and Nash, 1960).

Direct confirmation of the adaptive nature of FAE comes from a study by Parducci (1956*b*) who employed exposure periods of 0.25, 0.75, and 5.0 sec. for the I figures and for the T figures. The interval between I and T exposures was 3 sec. for half the Ss and 10 sec. for the others. If time of exposure of the I and T figures and the time interval between them affect FAE, then we have prima-facie evidence of the adaptive nature of this phenomenon. Parducci found that the magnitude of the FAE *increased* with length of I exposure and *decreased* with length of T exposure, thus verifying the hypothesis that this phenomenon is a case of sensory adaptation.

SUBLIMINAL INFLUENCES ON PERCEPTION

In our discussion of the effects of background and contextual influences on focal stimuli we have already indicated that weak or unnoticed stimuli may change various attributes of what is perceived. The large amount of literature dating back to the *imageless thought* movement and dealing with the influence of set, attitude, *Aufgabe,* and determining tendency and the more recent work of the *New Look* group showing the influence of various inner factors on recognition thresholds, all point to the influence of subthreshold factors on perception. Still another direction in which subliminal stimuli have been shown to influence perceived attributes of stimuli is found in studies of effects of subliminal anchors on psychophysical judgments (Black and Bevan, 1960; Goldstone, Goldfarb, Strong, and Russell, 1962; Boardman and Goldstone, 1962; and Bevan and Pritchard, 1963). As noted in Chapter 4, subliminal electric shock by lowering adaptation level resulted in more highly judged intensities of supraliminal shocks (Black and Bevan, 1960). Because electric shock is unpleasant, Bevan and Pritchard (1963) decided to investigate a different sense modality. They used tone stimuli at various levels above threshold, with an anchor below threshold preceding each of the judged stimuli. A white noise was introduced to mask unwanted sounds, and it was found, contrary to expectation, that the judged intensities with anchor were lower when a subliminal stimulus was employed than they were in the control condition, without anchor. Surmising that the white noise itself acted as a supraliminal anchor, Bevan and Pritchard then omitted the masking stimulus and obtained the usual clear-cut anchor effects with tones: judged loudness was higher with the subliminal stimulus than without it. Furthermore, anchors farther below threshold (hence weaker) enhanced judged loudness more than did anchors nearer threshold.

In view of the early belief of some *New Look* psychologists in the simple direct relation between inner states and perception while using relatively complex stimulus materials, the following observation by Bevan and Pritchard regarding the complex interacting factors at work in the effects of subliminal anchors on judgments of simple sensory dimensions is pertinent:

It is appropriate to note that these subliminal anchor effects are relatively subtle and require careful manipulation of the experimental conditions in order that they be found in evidence. Consideration must be given to both the temporal and intensive proximity of the anchor to the series member, its duration, and the relative frequency of its occurrence (personal communication).

Goldstone et al. (1962) did not obtain the subliminal anchor effect with shock stimuli when the anchor was presented at the midpoint of the interval between series stimuli, but the effect was obtained when the anchor was moved nearer the series stimuli, i.e., when it preceded the series stimuli by 2 sec. instead of by 5 sec. As far as tones were concerned, however, Bevan and Pritchard found no differences among subliminal anchor presentations made early, midway, and late between series stimuli. It is not surprising that the contributions of subliminal stimuli to level are more affected than are those of supraliminal stimuli by order, frequency, duration, and other conditions of stimulation.

The effects of subliminal anchors in modifying perceived attributes of stimulation should not be confused with better-than-chance reports of subliminal stimuli that are not sensed as such. The subliminal anchor effects discussed in this section and elsewhere in this book are referable to their influence on adaptation level and are thus assumed to act much as suprathreshold stimuli do in this respect. Since the subliminal stimuli are not perceived and Ss are not asked to report in any way concerning them, they belong with the class of physiological stimuli discussed earlier in this chapter which exert physiological effects without coming to awareness. With the finding that subliminal stimuli pool with supraliminal stimuli to form level, we have added evidence of the basic physiological nature of adaptation levels underlying perceptual and judgmental processes. That shifts in judgment resulting from the introduction of background or anchor stimuli represent only semantic reformulations seems less and less credible as information on effects of subliminal anchors accumulates.

PERCEPTION OF TIME

Experienced duration offers excellent opportunities for studying series, anchor, and background effects, and in addition heteromodal interactions, because this dimension is common to all sense modalities. As far back as 1945, Postman and Miller published results in which temporal intervals ranging from 0.25 to 1.0 sec. were perceived to be longer when preceded by an anchor well below the series stimuli than when presented without this anchor. They did not symmetrize their experiment by using an anchor of longer duration than the topmost series stimulus. This was done by Behar and Bevan (1961), who found that introduction of a 9-sec. stimulus after every third series stimulus caused series stimuli of 1, 2, 3, 4 and 5 sec. to be perceived as of shorter duration than when they were presented alone. Furthermore, the long 9-sec. stimulus exerted relatively greater effects than did the short 0.2 sec. stimulus, although its lengthening effects on the series stimuli were also significant. This was probably because the series stimuli were all long relative to the short predominant stimulus. As was found in a study by Goldstone, Boardman, and Lhamon (1959), which will be discussed in the section on figure-ground effects, Behar and Bevan's results indicate that auditory durations are perceived to be about 20 percent longer than identical visual durations.

Of even greater interest is the finding by Behar and Bevan of clear-cut effects of heteromodal interactions between visual and auditory stimuli on perceived duration. With both visual and auditory stimuli the intramodal anchor effects were greater than the heteromodal effects, but the heteromodal were highly significant in their action on the intramodal. One paradoxical finding still awaits explanation: Light anchors of 10 and 20 sec. decreased apparent duration of auditory noise in the expected direction and magnitude, i.e., the 20-sec. anchor had a greater shortening effect than the 10-sec. anchor; but the noise anchors showed a reversal in the shortening effects on the lights, i.e., the 20-sec. anchor caused less shortening than did the 10-sec. anchor. Tied to this paradoxical finding was the greater effect of visual as compared with auditory anchors. Whether or not these findings are due to the fact that the anchors in this study were introduced as series stimuli, i.e., on every fourth presentation, rather than before each of the series stimuli, as is usual, must be determined by further studies.

The main finding of the study by Behar and Bevan is that modality is not a limiting factor in pooling or sensory interactions. We shall see later that cognitive materials in the form of instructions may pool with sensory dimensions to affect perceived durations, thus extending the domain of relevance for pooling to interactions between central and peripheral processes.

Background effects on the indifferent interval. We pointed out in Chapter 3 that the indifferent temporal interval, i.e., the interval neither over- nor underestimated, long thought to be less than 1 sec., is a function of the series of intervals presented for judgment and is not an absolute value independent of the conditions under which the estimates are made. A study by Hirsh, Bilger, and Deatherage (1956) shows that duration of perceived visual and auditory stimuli depends upon background stimulation as well as upon the series of stimuli being judged. They report that if *S* hears a tone or sees a light for a given temporal interval with a quiet acoustic background and reproduces the interval against a noisy background, his estimates of duration are increased compared with his estimates with constant auditory background during stimulation and response. On the other hand, if the duration is perceived against a noisy background and reproduced against a quiet background, it is underestimated compared with constant ambient conditions. The change in the indifferent interval is interesting. In the control condition, with either quiet or constant noise in both stimulation and reproduction periods, the interval correctly reproduced is about 8 sec.; it rises to 16 sec. when the interval is reproduced against a noisy background following quiet background stimulation; and it falls to 4 sec. when it is reproduced against a quiet background following stimulation with a noisy background. These results hold for both auditory and visual stimulation. In general, noisy background increases perceived duration of auditory and visual stimuli. Differences between quiet and noisy background conditions decreased as noise was introduced into the quiet conditions and approached the level of the noisy background.

Ambient light conditions did not affect the reproduced temporal intervals, contrary to the findings of Behar and Bevan, and Goldstone et al. discussed above. Hirsh and his co-workers pointed out that other types of background stimuli, which were presumably constant in their experiments, e.g., temperature and odor, may also pace *S*s' psychological clock. In addition, we must note that the affective nature of both focal and background stimuli may affect perception of duration. In these experiments the background consisted of white noise that was presumably not pleasant. What would be the effect of pleasant background auditory stimulation on temporal perception? The writer is reminded in this connection of long waits in a physician's office which were relieved by hearing soft pleasant music that made the time go faster, even though he usually occupied himself with reading.

The experiment by Hirsh et al. furnishes added evidence for our position in Chapter 3 on over- and underestimation of temporal intervals, viz., that to search for an absolute indifferent interval apart from the series and background stimuli present during the measurements is to search for a chimera. Instead we would propose that indifferent intervals be determined over a wide range of series-background conditions to discover the laws of their variation.

FIGURE AND GROUND

The distinction between focal and background stimuli is related to Rubin's distinction between figure and ground in perception (1921). Focal stimuli stand out, are figured, and are distinctive, while other stimuli in the field of view act as background. To be focal, stimuli must differ from level, in either a positive or negative direction. Thus stimuli below as well as above level, and weak as well as strong stimuli, may be focal since it is degree of difference from level that determines their distinctiveness. Stimuli become focal for a variety of reasons; among the causes are the "determinants of attention" of the older psychology, e.g., size, intensity, position, novelty, quality, movement, and internal predisposing factors such as attitude and set, which we have classified under residual stimuli. Mere instructions to "attend to" a stimulus may change it from background to focal status, while instructions to "neglect it" may change it from focal to background status.

Changing the stimuli from figure to ground affected estimations of number as shown in a study by Bevan, Maier, and Helson (1963). In this study Ss estimated the number of beans either in three large glass containers or in three small containers under figure or ground instructions. Under figure instructions they were to regard the containers as integral with the contents; under ground instructions they were to regard the containers as separate from the contents. Four groups of 75 Ss judged under four different conditions. There were 60, 230, or 410 beans in the jars filling $\frac{1}{9}$, $\frac{1}{3}$, and $\frac{2}{3}$ of the small jars and $\frac{1}{28}$, $\frac{3}{28}$, and $\frac{1}{7}$ of the large jars. The estimates were made in numbers as shown in Fig. 5.13 and Table 5.10. While all the estimates were below the actual number in each of the jars, the effects of the figure and ground instructions were unmistakable: the estimates were largest with the large jars and smallest with the small jars under figure instructions, while under ground instructions they were between the largest and the smallest. The differences under figure instructions are highly significant ($F = 6.37$, $df = \frac{1}{296}$, $P < .02$). The ground esti-mates do not differ significantly from the over-all average.

TABLE 5.10. Experimental and Fitted Values of Estimates[a]

	Large Figure		Large Ground		Small Ground		Small Figure	
Actual Number	Observed	Theoretical	Observed	Theoretical	Observed	Theoretical	Observed	Theoretical
60	46	46	39	39	36	36	32	33
230	150	153	135	136	132	130	109	120
410	267	267	240	239	228	229	212	212

[a] The theoretical values in this table were calculated from the following equations:
Large figure: $Y = .630X + 8$
Large ground: $Y = .574X + 4$
Small ground: $Y = .549X + 3$
Small figure: $Y = .514X + 2$
SOURCE: Bevan, Helson, and Maier, 1963. With the permission of the *American Journal of Psychology*.

The consistency of the estimates by each of the four groups judging under the four different conditions is shown by the closeness of the experimental data to linear plots in Fig. 5.13 and by the data in Table 5.10 derived from linear equations determined by inspection. The agreement between the values from the equations and the experimental values is remarkably close, with one exception (120 vs. 109). The y intercepts in the equations are 8, 4, 3, and 2, showing that the four groups of Ss were not basing their estimates of number on the zero of the number system. Similarly, if we determine the values at which the four curves intersect the line of unit slope, which is the locus of correct estimates, we find that they do so at 21, 9.3, 6.7, and 4.1. Hence, numbers between zero and 21, 9.3, 6.7, and 4.1 are overestimated, since they are above the line of unit slope, and numbers larger than these values are underestimated, since they are below the line of unit slope.

The question arises of how the figure and ground instructions modi-fied the responses of the four groups of Ss. Did the figure instructions cause the figure groups to perceive the jars and contents differently from the way they were perceived by the groups told to neglect the containers in making their estimates? Or were the differences among the groups merely differences in the language used to make the esti-mates? It is highly likely that the two sets of instructions influenced the ways in which the groups looked at, and hence *perceived,* the beans in the jars because the judgments were rendered in terms of

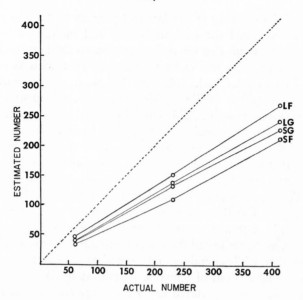

FIG. 5.13. Effects of figure-ground instructions on judgments of quantity. (From Bevan, Maier, and Helson, 1963. With the permission of the *American Journal of Psychology*.)

cardinal numbers, a judgment language that is absolute and maximally stimulus bound. Hence the type of semantic relativity claimed by Stevens (1958) to be the basis for shifts in judgment following changes in adaptation level is precluded because judgments expressed in cardinal numbers are not relative:

When *S* estimates that there are 150 beans in jar number two, he does not mean covertly or overtly that 150 is small relative to the number of beans in jar number three or large relative to the number in jar number one, or that his estimate has any other meaning except that associated with the system of natural numbers. Along with the great American mathematician, George Birkhoff, who, holding up five fingers, once remarked: "Whenever I find a collection of objects that exactly matches the fingers of my hand, I will call that collection 'five,'" our *S* was saying: "This is what I mean by 150." The argument of semantic relativity can thus have no validity for the contextual effects in this study (Bevan, Maier, and Helson, 1963, p. 469).

The manner in which the instructions affected the perception of the contents of the jars, and hence the estimates, can be envisaged in terms of differential weighting of the jars and their contents. The ground instructions weighted the contents heavily and minimized the containers with the result that the difference between the large and small jars played almost no role in these estimates. That what is focal or accented in perceptual tasks influences judgment was succinctly expressed by Woodrow (1951) in his analysis of judgments of time intervals: Ss may introduce differences in accent, some accenting the duration between the sounds bounding the intervals, others accenting the stimuli themselves; or some Ss may be active and others passive in their reception of the sound stimuli. An active attitude to the second of two sounds, Woodrow found, resulted in overestimation of its duration, while passive hearing resulted in underestimation. Instructions regarding what S shall attend to may have marked effects upon time-order "error": attending to the interval between bounding sounds gave 4.6 sec. as the estimated duration of a sound that was actually 4.0 sec. in duration, while attending to the sound gave an average estimate of 3.54 sec. The analysis of temporal judgments by Woodrow seems to fit what presumably occurred under the figure and ground instructions of this study, mutatis mutandis.

A study of temporal duration by Goldstone, Boardman, and Lhamon (1959) bears out the validity of both Woodrow's concept of accenting and the effects of figure-ground instructions in our study, which was conducted under even more stringent conditions. Goldstone and his co-workers first established that sounds of 1-sec. duration had longer perceived durations than lights: the median was 0.59 sec. for sound and 1.02 sec. for light. They used ascending and descending method of limits in which duration of a second was judged shorter, when starting from 0.10 sec. and increasing the durations, than it was when starting from 1.0 sec. and decreasing the durations. But apart from effects of starting point on judged duration, these writers found that when both sound and light were presented simultaneously, instructions to focus on sound resulted in a shorter estimated duration of one second than did instructions to focus on light. The stimulus that was figured exerted predominant weight in perceived duration. However, sensory intensity interacted with modality and instructions to affect perception of duration: in one series the sound was more intense than the light and in another the reverse was true, as determined by Ss' comparisons of the two sets of stimuli. When the auditory stimulus was more intense than the light, the perceived durations approximated auditory alone, and when the visual stimulus was more intense than the sound, the perceived durations approximated the visual alone.

There are many implications to be drawn from this fertile study by Goldstone and his colleagues. Due to lack of space we can only emphasize its validation of the point made earlier in this section, viz., that verbal instructions that *S* should figure, focus, or accent a stimulus or part of the stimulus field result in measurable effects commensurate with changes in dimensional attributes of stimulation. This finding proves again that stimulus or sensory equivalents can be found for molar, phenomenological, and cognitive or central contributions to perception, thus advancing the cause of a unitary, monistic view of the phenomena of perception.

SUMMARY

A dimensional approach is needed which provides a common frame of reference for the operation of outer and inner factors in perception. When the concept of stimulus is examined, it is found that a broader definition, including physiological, subliminal, higher-order, internal, and field stimuli, greatly reduces the number of cases for which residual sources of stimulation must be postulated. A similar examination of phenomenology discloses the strengths and weaknesses of the various types. Traditional problems of color and space perception, colored shadows, the Land colors, color constancy, contrast, assimilation, and the influence of contextual stimulation on perception of form, size, and direction were elucidated in terms of AL theory. Anchor, contrast, and paradoxical distance effects were related to adaptation-level theory as were the effects of subliminal stimuli on perception. Figure and ground function as predominating stimuli in accordance with instructions given to observers. Emphasis was upon a unified conceptualization of problems of perception.

6 *Affectivity and Motivation*

Feelings and emotions are potent inciters or inhibitors of action. Feeling states initiate, direct, and terminate almost all types of behavior and thus play a dominant role in individual modes of adjustment. The biological utility of feelings and emotions in furthering the well-being of the individual has been recognized, especially through their connection with homeostatic mechanisms (Wenger, 1950; Stagner, 1951; 1961); but their role in discriminatory and judgmental processes has often been overlooked. Feeling states inform us when stimuli are too intense or too weak and thereby influence perceptual activities. Learning and performance levels also depend to a great extent upon affective states, and the role given to reinforcement in most learning theories attests the importance of affectivity as a motivating factor. Kendrew (1935) found that even in such a neutral activity as stringing beads the performance of 17 out of 20 children was significantly lowered when they were emotionally upset over not being able to locate a toy, which had been promised them if they could find it. In short, there are probably no responses that are not influenced by affective or emotional states.

Affective and sensory processes compared. In classical introspective psychology feelings constituted a separate class of experiences, although it was granted that they were similar in some ways to sensory processes. Because all types of sensation may be pleasant, unpleasant, or neutral, and because there are no specific receptors for the affects, they were thought to be distinct from sensation until Nafe's analysis of pleasantness as "bright pressures" and unpleasantness as "dull pressures" (1924) reduced them to varieties of sensory experience. Emotions were also regarded as complexes of sensory processes, chiefly visceral in origin, strongly tinged with affect. Apart from having definite physiological loci, affects behave very much like sensory and perceptual processes. Affects have stimulus origins or may be centrally aroused. Affective adaptation resembles sensory adaptation in all important respects. Pleasantness and unpleasantness pass over into indifference and/or unpleasantness and pleasantness, respectively, with repeated or prolonged stimulation. Recovery from affective adaptation occurs after various periods of deprivation from satiated stimuli or as a result of affective contrast, e.g., when home cooking tastes better after a few bad meals out. Like complementary colors, warm and cold, strain and relaxation, pleasantness and unpleasantness are opposites although there is as yet no clear evidence that they mix to yield neutrality.

Like many sensory processes, affective states are bipolar in nature. Michotte (1950) stated the case for the bipolarity of emotions more clearly than anyone else by dividing them into two groups, integrative and segregative. The former involve approach, contact, clasp, embrace (sympathy, love, friendship); the latter involve movement away from and even breaking or destroying (apartness, segregation). He found by experiment that inanimate objects, moving along a simple path were perceived to have "approach" and "avoidance" characteristics. Movement of people and objects is polarized in that it is perceived as a property distinct from direction and distance, within certain limits.

The bipolar nature of affects is revealed, not only by their oppositional quality, but also by the existence of neutral or indifferent states which have been recognized by various workers: Transitional zones between pleasantness and unpleasantness have been incorporated in formulas embodying conditions for BCD vision (borderline between comfort and discomfort) in work tasks (Guth, 1951); domains of pleasantness, unpleasantness, and neutrality for a large number of hues as a function of lightness and saturation have been plotted (Guilford and Smith, 1959); the combinations of pitches and loudnesses that yield pleasant, unpleasant, and indifferent tones have been mapped

(Guilford, 1954*b*); and the ranges of temperatures above and below physiological zero (which is indifferent) which yield pleasantness and unpleasantness have been determined (Haber, 1958). The neutral zones between pleasantness and unpleasantness and the absence of emotion in the face of stimulation represent affective adaptation levels.

Unlike sensory processes, affective states, when once aroused, tend to persist and to be aroused more easily on subsequent occasions. Affective residuals are so strong that merely thinking about an emotional situation tends to re-instate the original feeling state. (For example, after once being made ill by canned asparagus, I was abnormally sensitive to the odor of this vegetable for years and could easily distinguish fresh from canned asparagus; the merest suggestion of the canned product aroused violent antipathy.) The effectiveness of rewards and punishments in facilitating or inhibiting responses is due both to the ease with which affective states are aroused and to the effectiveness of residuals left by them. Moreover, affects may summate over considerable intervals between reinforcements, partly due to their slow rates of decline following original stimulation.

Multidimensional objects elecit over-all affective responses because of the ease with which the affects pool. While the natural response is to objects as wholes, it is nevertheless possible in many instances to isolate the components entering into affective pooling. Just as one may learn to "hear out" the partials in a musical tone, so it is possible to isolate the components entering into affective and esthetic responses. A study by the writer and Mouton showing that such analysis is possible is discussed later in this chapter (pp. 363–366).

It has been asserted that one of the most important differences between feelings and sensations is that the former are subjective, or localized within the organism, and the latter are objective, or ascribed to objects. While this position is true to some extent, it does not consider that some sensory processes are located wholly within the organism, e.g., kinesthesis, muscular aches and pains, and sensations from the viscera; nor does it consider that some affective qualities are projected into their stimuli, e.g., the unpleasantness of bitter substances and the pleasantness of sweet substances, and especially affective qualities of such stimuli as loud tones, saturated colors, and strong odors, which are judged to belong to their sources. When adaptation has rendered pleasant objects neutral or unpleasant, the change is ascribed as much to the external objects as to the self.

Unidimensional nature of affects. In the case of stimuli that can be varied along a single dimension it has been demonstrated that the affects aroused by them lie on a single continuum, separated by neutral or indifferent zones. This is true even when the relations between stimulus magnitudes and the affects are not linear as in the findings by Haber referred to above. Works of art, musical compositions, and other complex esthetic products that cannot be ordered on unidimensional perceptual continua may nevertheless be ordered on affective continua ranging from very unpleasant, through indifference, to very pleasant.

If affects can be ordered on unidimensional continua, does it follow that all pleasant affects and all unpleasant affects are alike? The answer is obviously "No." The pleasantness of food differs from that of colors, and the unpleasantness of loud tones differs from that of losing money. Some may even argue that the pleasantness of one food is different from the pleasantness of another. Even granting that every affect is qualitatively unique (Titchener admitted that every color contains a unique component in spite of the resemblance of intermediate colors, like orange, to their primary components), it is nevertheless possible to order affects with respect to magnitude. Thus Woodworth in the first edition of *Experimental Psychology* (1938), showed that a large variety of objects can be ordered on affective continua in a chapter devoted to experimental esthetics. Indeed, some psychophysical methods have been primarily used to scale affective responses, e.g., methods of paired comparisons, order of merit, production, choice, and rating. In addition to scaling affective responses to simple sensory qualities, experimental esthetics has been concerned with the measurement of affective responses to complex objects having many dimensions and has investigated many classes of stimuli, such as forms, advertisements, personality traits, and musical compositions. Usually objects belonging to the same universe of discourse are compared, e.g., food preferences, but it is also possible to compare affective responses to different classes of objects as Stevens and his co-workers have done (1959; 1960) for sensory magnitudes in heteromodal scaling.

We thus find that affective states, like sensory processes, can be ordered with respect to magnitude, that they pool to form levels, and that they are bipolar in nature. Our discussion will include other ways in which feelings and emotions are affected by conditions of stimulation and adaptation which make it possible to envisage them within our general theory.

Order effects in affective arousal. We have already found in preceding chapters that *order* of stimuli may exert profound effects on
judgments of magnitudes and on the ways in which objects are perceived and named. Beebe-Center (1929) and Harris (1929) showed
that colors following pleasant stimuli were judged less pleasant than
colors following unpleasant stimuli. Order has also been found to be
important in affective responses to complex patterns of stimulation such
as musical compositions, Rorschach cards, stories, and humorous anecdotes. Thus in a study of ten musical selections including excerpts
from different styles of classical music as well as popular music,
Williams (1942) found that order of presentation influenced the affective ratings of some of the selections. If played in the same order two
weeks after initial presentation high consistency appeared in the ratings.
While the average ratings remained the same when the order was
changed, there was a highly significant difference between the ratings
of specific selections in the two presentations. For example, the affective
rating of Ravel's "Bolero" was higher when it followed "No Name
Jive" than when it followed a Bach "Rondeau." Williams' findings are
in accord with what musicians have long known intuitively about
effects of order on acceptance of musical compositions. When conductors arrange orchestral programs, they maximize contrast between
selections, balance styles, tempos, and contents of compositions, and
end with climactic or closure-producing works.

Are affects and emotions data of experience? In spite of the
omnipresence of affective components in behavior, a number of psychologists have taken the position that the concepts of affect and
emotion should be deleted from the psychologist's lexicon. Thus Beebe-
Center (1951) rejected the concepts of feeling and emotion as such
because he believed that failure to identify them as conscious contents
made them scientifically worthless and he maintained that such contents cannot be found. Even earlier Hunt and Flannery (1938) took
the position that many of the phenomena encountered in the field
of affectivity may more properly be interpreted as functions of secondary judgmental processes rather than as functions of primary specific
affective states because affective judgments and psychophysical judgments obeyed certain common principles. To Hunt and Flannery this
fact proved that there are no specific affective processes. Still another
reason for rejecting affective states was presented by Duffy in a number of publications (1934; 1941*a;* 1941*b;* and 1948). She maintained

that only two dimensions are needed for the explanation of all be-havior: goal direction and intensity or energy mobilization. To the writer the difficulties attendant on the specification of feelings and emotions as conscious contents are no greater than the difficulties encountered in specifying and measuring sensory and cognitive proc-esses. On the contrary, feelings and emotions are as certain, indubitable, and identifiable as are any other processes of which we are aware. In fact, it is possible to specify some emotional states with greater cer-tainty than it is to describe some sensory processes!

Early work by Guilford (1934) established the dependence of pleas-antness on hue, lightness, and saturation of colors. The quantitative relations between stimulus variables and affective values found by Guilford and his co-workers should have convinced psychologists of the psychological reality of affective states. In this connection, it should be mentioned that shortly after the publication of Guilford's work, Dashiell (1937) refused to take the position that common principles in affectivity and psychophysics ruled out affective states as such.

It is interesting that many writers who reject affective states as immediately experienced conscious contents nevertheless stress various aspects of these states which are important in our approach to this problem. Thus Carr (1925), who denied that pleasantness and un-pleasantness are experiential states that can be analytically observed, stressed the bipolar nature of feelings and emotions and the fact that they are related to approach-withdrawal reactions:

Situations that normally allow a positive reaction, i.e., one tending to enhance, maintain, or repeat the situation, are judged pleasant. Situations that arouse negative reactions, i.e., ones which minimize or rid the organism of the situation, are judged unpleasant. Situations which normally arouse neither positive nor negative reactions are regarded as lacking in affective tone (Carr's position as summarized by Beebe-Center, 1951, p. 258).

Similarly, Duffy regarded emotion as essentially a change in level resulting from demands of situations, a position akin to that of Wenger (1950) who saw emotion arising from changes in basic homeostatic (physiological) patterns of response. These two positions are very much alike in view of the fact that Duffy also speaks of emotion in terms of the way in which energy in the organism is mobilized for action. Hunt and Volkmann (1937) and their co-workers showed in a brilliant series of studies that affective judgments are subject to the effects of anchors in the same way that psychophysical judgments are influenced by predominant stimuli.

Objective operational definitions have been provided by Young (1959) which identify affects conceived as conscious contents. He defined affective processes in terms of their sign, intensity, and duration (sign refers to the presence or absence of positive or negative affect):

> What one observes in laboratory situations is that naïve animals develop approach-maintaining or avoidance-terminating patterns of behavior. If they develop the approach-maintaining pattern, I would asume that the underlying affective process is positive in sign. If they develop the avoidance-terminating pattern, I would assume that the affective process is negative in sign. If neither positive nor negative behavior develops, I would make no assumptions concerning the sign of affective arousal (p. 104).

The bare existence of approach or avoidance behavior, according to Young, is not a sufficient ground in itself for inferring affective processes. But the development of approach-maintaining or avoidance-terminating patterns by naïve animals is a criterion for the sign of affective processes. In agreement with the position taken here, he asserts that affective processes vary on a bipolar continuum. Between extremes of maximal negative and maximal positive intensity there is an indifferent or neutral zone. Also in agreement with our position is Young's belief that any theory of behavior which ignores affectivity will be found inadequate as an explanation of all the facts of behavior.

On the basis of experimental evidence, Young concluded that sensory and hedonic intensity do not lie on a single continuum, and that sensory intensity is an increasing monotonic function of concentration of solution while hedonic intensity is a nonmonotonic function of concentration since optimal concentrations are neither too strong nor too weak. (For other reasons for the independence of sensory and hedonic intensity the reader is referred to Young, 1959, pp. 106–107.) While this is in opposition to the view that there is no specific affective process apart from judgmental or other psychological processes, it does not preclude, as Young points out, the possibility of simultaneous mediation by sensory receptors of sensory and affective processes.

Basic emotional patterns. Whether or not there are hereditary instinctive patterns of behavior and what the unconditioned stimuli are for their arousal has long been a matter of dispute. Lists of unlearned emotional patterns vary from the three of Watson (fear, anger, and love) to the score or so of James and McDougall. One of the main defects of both field observation and experimental approaches to this problem has been failure to control and evaluate the contributions of background and residual factors in emotional responses. As in the case of sensory responses, effects of stimuli are neither absolute nor univocal whether in earliest infancy or in adult life. Identical stimuli may produce different responses when they appear in different contexts or when the state of the organism has altered. Especially in the field of affectivity pre-exposure to stimulation leaves residuals that modify responses to incoming stimuli. Emotional behavior has often been attributed to heredity through lack of knowledge concerning the role of situational factors. Failure to appreciate the importance of residuals in early infancy and adult behavior has led to one-sided theories of the conditioning of emotional responses. The following stimuli, activities, and states seem to arouse affective responses without having to be conditioned:

A. Generally pleasant
  1. Nourishment in the form of food and drink
  2. Sleep, rest, and relaxation
  3. Contact, both bodily and exploratory
  4. Movement of parts of the body, whole body motion, and perception of motion
  5. Optimal conditions of temperature and humidity
  6. Sex or erogenous zone contacts
  7. Absence of visceral sensations (with a few exceptions)
  8. Heterostasis
B. Generally unpleasant
  1. Intense, sudden, and strange stimuli
  2. Deprivation of oxygen and sensory input, immobilization, and, in general, deprivation of items listed in 1–6 and 8 above
  3. Pain, strain, and fatigue
  4. Internal pressures, arrhythmias in function, and abnormal visceral sensations

All of the conditions, stimuli, and responses listed above as unlearned sources of affect lead to modification of ongoing behavior and are current terms in the literature of needs, drives, reinforcement, and motivation, with the exception of the term "heterostasis," which we have taken from Davis (1958). Davis pointed to the fact that homeostasis can be maintained for a given variable only by upsetting the balance in at least one other variable. For example, "reduced variation in temperature is bought by increased variation in sweating" (1958, p. 12). We shall use this concept to cover the need for changes of *all* kinds, e.g., in perceptual, cognitive, emotional, and motor activities. Davis supports this view of heterostasis with the statement that "an organism's constancy in one aspect implies variability in another" (1958, p. 12) and with his strictures against homeostasis as a *sufficient* concept to account for all types of behavior. Behavior is governed not only by considerations of constancy, which apply mainly to the parameters governing the *milieu interieur* (Claude Bernard), but also by the need for change in stimulation and in responses. Change in activity is in itself usually pleasant and refreshing and is necessary for proper functioning of homeostatic mechanisms.

Much of the pleasure of exercise arises from changed levels of homeostatic processes: The heart beats faster, breathing is faster and deeper, muscular contractions are greater and more rapid, and practically all bodily processes are stepped up as a result of heightened action of the sympathetic nervous system. Exercise and sports also provide new experiences and new forms of response that are pleasurable in themselves. Swimming yields a tactile-kinesthetic experience of buoyancy unknown outside the water, and dancing gives rise to pleasant affect from rhythmical movements that are also at the basis of the pleasure in such sports as golf, tennis, and track events. Drama, movies, TV, music, art, sculpture, and similar types of diversion provide change in perceptual, cognitive, and feeling levels, thereby breaking the monotony of everyday experience. The importance of providing variety and change in the environment has been proved by the dire effects of long-continued sensory deprivation and bodily immobilization.

The work of the Wisconsin group showed that monkeys learn to discriminate visual stimuli for no reward other than the opportunity to explore the environment visually. Several years ago the findings of the Wisconsin workers were replicated at the United States Air Force Radiobiological Laboratory at the University of Texas. Monkeys learned to discriminate red from yellow panels only for the privilege of being able to look outside the restraining box into a hall—with no food as an incentive. As shown by Butler (1954) it was also found that objects can be ordered in value for the monkey. Monkeys were given training in opening the door to their box so that they could look at a number of stimuli outside. With one group the following response frequencies were found: another monkey outside, 189 responses; a train, 128; food, 97; an empty chamber, 70. With another group of ten monkeys, the order was the same with slightly different objectives: another monkey, 242 responses; train, 213; hearing and seeing train, 203; hearing and seeing another monkey, 159; an empty chamber (the standard condition), 161 responses. Auditory stimuli, the source of which was not seen, elicited visual exploratory responses. As a result of these and other observations, the Wisconsin workers came to regard visual exploration as a basic primary drive; but the nature of the stimulus situation seemed to be more important than inner organic states in determining the behavior of the animals. The *kind* of stimulus perceived was the primary source of visual response. It may be argued that being confined within the four walls of a cage or room is sufficiently unpleasant to furnish primary motivation for visual exploration. The results of the Wisconsin experiments as well as the results of sensory deprivation have important implications for space travel where the lack of heterostatic facilitators is accentuated because of the longer periods during which men will have to function compared with the periods of sensory and motor deprivations studied in the laboratory.

In summary, heterostasis seems to be a necessary condition for optimal perceptual, cognitive, and sensori-motor functions. Paradoxically, homeostatic mechanisms are innervated by changing demands on organisms. Organisms do not thrive as inert static automata in unchanging environments. Hence heterostasis (change) and homeostasis (constancy) must be regarded as mutually supportive and complementary processes necessary for the comfort and well-being of organisms.

Perception and affectivity. That feelings and emotions influence what we see, taste, hear, smell, and otherwise perceive and cognize is well known, although experimental psychology was slow to recognize this fundamental fact as a basic principle of sensory processes. The tendency to perceive and think in terms of one's wishes, fantasies, desires, needs, and goals has been labeled "autism" and its experimental investigation by Sanford (1936; 1937), Levine, Chein, and Murphy (1942), McClelland and Atkinson (1948), Bruner and Postman (1946–1947), Bevan and Dukes (1951), and others, was called the *New Look* psychology. This vigorous movement was reviewed and summarized by the writer in 1953 and it still has its adherents as shown by a perusal of current publications. Although the proposition that inner needs, tensions, and affects influence perception seems fairly simple and straightforward, it suggests a number of different relationships. For example, in addition to the problem of the effects of feelings on perception there is the question of the effect of perception on feelings since the relations between affects and perception are not one-way affairs. While it is true that hunger may motivate thoughts of food and influence its taste, it is also true that odor and taste of food may arouse hunger. Without perception there would be no emotions, needs, aversions, values, and goals. It is as true that the properties of perception are responsible for fear, anger, tender emotion, and desire as it is that these affect perception.

The dependence of emotion on the nature of percepts is seen most strikingly in borderline and psychotic states. Consider the following protocol from a schizophrenic girl reported by Marguerite Sechehaye (1951):

One day we were jumping rope at recess. Two little girls were turning a long rope while two others jumped in from either side to meet and cross over. When it came my turn and I saw my partner jump toward me where we were to meet and cross over, I was seized with panic; I did not recognize her. Though I saw her as she was, still, it was not she. Standing at the other end of the rope, she had seemed smaller, but the nearer we approached each other, the taller she grew, the more she swelled in size. I cried out, "Stop, Alice, you look like a lion; you frighten me" . . . but actually, I didn't see a lion at all: it was only an attempt to describe the enlarging image of my friend and the fact that I didn't recognize her (pp. 4, 5).

It is evident that the disturbance in perception (caused in some unknown way) resulted in an abnormal perception of the increase in size of her approaching friend; this abnormal perception inspired terror and led to failure to recognize the friend, i.e., it was responsible for the schizoid behavior. But even the most normal of us on occasion has reacted emotionally as a result of what we have seen or felt, e.g., been repulsed on seeing a snake or at the sight of food under the old-type fluorescent lighting with its strong green lines. Changes in context of sensory qualities, in position of objects, or in other perceptual conditions may change a pleasant object or attribute to unpleasant or vice versa.

One of the most important ways in which sensory processes are emotion producing is through feedback from muscular, visceral, and organic activities. Darrow and Henry (1949) analyzed the role of feedback from adjustive homeostatic processes in creating anxiety when the individual perceives that his physiological processes are no longer normal, for example, in oxygen deficiency, in carbon dioxide excess, in extremes of temperature, humidity, vibration, and pressure, in difficulties with breathing, and in the presence of strong odors: "All may alter the background of awareness or consciousness, and when they have acquired 'value' for the individual . . . may contribute to his 'affective state'" (p. 418). Feedback mechanisms may amplify input from dangerous situations so as to affect autonomic, humoral, and central nervous processes to an unusual degree, thus furnishing the basis for intense emotions. Such processes would be adjustive under normal circumstances when the individual can take appropriate action, e.g., by reacting with severe bodily exertion to meet the dangerous situation; but when they occur in situations that do not permit violent expenditure of energy, they result in *emotional* rather than in homeostatic responses. These writers also pointed out that perception, by permitting observation of bodily changes as they occur, provides direct and indirect control of bodily changes even though the individual has no knowledge of the physiological mechanisms by which the bodily changes come about. Under some circumstances perception may become the vehicle of anxiety by accentuating processes that would otherwise be minimal.

Frequency, intensity, recency, and other conditions of perception may have important emotional consequences. Neither very tasty foods nor distinctive actors should be experienced too frequently; otherwise they satiate. Differential susceptibility to frequency of stress was found among members of the Eighth Air Force during World War II. As reported by Hastings et al. (1944), crews joining the Eighth Air Force immediately found out that chances for survival were very slim. Some fliers requested removal from duty before making any flights. A second group did not break until after a few missions—usually by the fifth one. A third group did not develop anxiety symptoms until around the twelfth to sixteenth mission. Moreover, there were individual differences regarding the occasions when fliers exhibited anxiety symptoms, some having fear symptoms during flight, others not until after return from a mission.

The emotional impact of objects and events increases directly with their perceived nearness to us. A snake at a distance or separated from us by a barrier does not arouse as much fear as one almost underfoot. Hastings, Wright, and Glueck (1944) in their discussion of psychiatric experiences of the Eighth Air Force put it this way: closeness of a traumatic event was a large factor in determining anxiety states.

[Thus, if a flier] were hit by a 20-mm. shell, he would be more deeply affected than if he saw the man next to him hit, which would be worse than having someone hit in another part of the ship, which would be worse than hearing of someone hit in his squadron, and so on to the point where it would mean essentially nothing to him to hear of someone being hit in a B-17 over Munda (p. 132).

The effect of *nearness* holds for psychological as well as for physical distance. We are much more affected by the death of a relative than by that of a public figure, and in cases where a friend is psychologically "close" and a relative is "distant" we are more concerned about the former than the latter. As reported by Liddell (1950) the physical and, presumably, psychological nearness of the mother ewe mitigated the emotional effect of electric shock given the lamb. Every parent knows how important both physical and psychological nearness are to the infant or young child who wants to be held when in distress. Even adults desire the presence of loved ones in critical illnesses although they know this will add nothing to the actual ministrations of doctors and nurses.

Evidence that the emotions of animals as well as of humans are affected by temporal conditions of perception comes from experiments with dogs. Fredericson (1950) found greater traumatic effects in massed than in spaced periods during which dogs were confined in a box. Animals confined 10 min. straight emitted from 680 to 1822 yelps as contrasted with 21 to 916 yelps when confined for the same total period spaced in intervals of 1 min. with 1 min. of freedom. The massed group averaged 1104 yelps per puppy, the spaced group 347 yelps per puppy—a highly significant difference between the two groups.

In this discussion we have taken the position that conditions of perception were primarily responsible for arousal of emotional states, but it may be argued that the emotional states were primary and the perceptual states secondary. The latter position is the one taken by the *New Look* psychologists, at least with respect to some types of perception. So far the best evidence for the primacy of emotion on perception comes not from the laboratory but from everyday life and the psychiatric clinic. Take the following example of altered perception following a traumatic event:

> On the eighth mission . . . his tent mate and his best friend [were] shot down in flames over the target. The patient brought his own plane back uneventfully, but after his return he had an intense recurrence of anxiety with tremor, etc. but preferred to go back to flying duty after a period of hospitalization. . . . In addition, he was harassed by a specific phobic apprehension that the plane was falling off to the right—the direction in which he had seen his friend's plane fall. . . . This phobia persisted, in spite of the evidence of his senses and the instruments that the plane was in level flight. So much did this obsess the patient that he almost crashed the plane on landing, because of miscalculation. . . . (Grinker and Spiegel, 1943, pp. 122f.).

Granting that affectivity and perception interact, without attempting to decide a priori which is primary in its influence on the other, we can summarize what we have learned from this discussion in a number of propositions which may be regarded as conclusions from observed data or as assumptions underlying our interpretation of the data:

1. All experience is more or less tinged with affect.
2. Affective processes, like sensory processes, are subject to conditions of stimulation such as frequency, intensity, nearness, recency, and so on.
3. Affective behavior can be measured and ordered on bipolar continua.
4. Affective accompaniments of stimulation interact and pool to form level.
5. Affective level, like adaptation level, is a weighted mean of all present and past affective states relevant to a given class of stimuli.
6. Intensity of affect and motivating power of stimulation are functions of distance or discrepancy from *affective* levels: the greater the discrepancy from level, the more pleasant or unpleasant, and the more desired or rejected, are objects, goals, and values.
7. Affective intensity is not monotonically related to sensory or cognitive intensity, and hence one-to-one correlation between these various levels does not exist. (An achromatic color corresponding with the visual adapted state may be pleasant, unpleasant, or

neutral; work on a difficult intellectual problem may be positively or negatively toned affectively.)

8. Affects leave, in general, strong residuals that make affective arousal easier on subsequent occasions.

9. Background stimuli may modify the affective impact of focal stimuli.

10. Focal and background sources of affectivity operating in the present should be fully explored and exhausted before we attribute emotional states to genetic, infantile, or residual factors.

SITUATIONAL DETERMINANTS OF BASIC NEEDS

It is often assumed that the primary needs having to do with food, sex, and other nonlearned drives are governed by innate physiological mechanisms as contrasted with the secondary derived needs which are modified and perhaps aroused by learning. The basic needs are supposedly specific and less variable than the secondary. Variability in the satisfaction of primary needs has been attributed to "individual differences" with the implication that these are genetically determined. In general the tendency has been to stress the inner determination of primary drives and the environmental determination of psychological needs. The case for inner physiological needs has received strong support from work by Richter (quoted by Young, 1948), who found that rats deprived of the posterior lobe of the hypophysis suffer general dehydration owing to loss of antidiuretic hormone. Such rats compensate for the loss of body fluid by drinking large amounts of water. Similarly, parathyroidectomized rats develop tetany and die within a few days unless allowed access to a solution of calcium lactate, which they ingest in large quantities and which keeps them free from symptoms of tetany. Such results as these demonstrate dramatically how organic states may influence food-taking behavior although their exact basis, i.e., whether they are due to changes in peripheral or central receptive mechanisms, is not yet fully understood.

It is not necessary to interfere with body chemistry to demonstrate effects of internal factors on food preferences and amounts of food ingested. Acceptability of foods varies with amount of deprivation and the extent to which satiation has occurred. One example from controlled experimentation suffices to support this generalization which everyone knows from his own experience: Young and Falk (1956) reported that

12 nonthirsty animals, given a choice between local tap water and distilled water, selected tap water in preference to distilled in every case, but when they were thirsty this preference vanished. Even in cases where affective levels seem fairly determinate, as in this finding by Young and Falk, one combination of stimulus-frequency presentations of a substance eliciting a certain level of preferences may be replaced by another combination of stimulus-frequency presentations of another substance as shown by Young and Asdourian (1957). They gave rats a choice between a standard solution of 1 percent sodium chloride and various percentages of sugar solution to determine the number of presentations of the two necessary to establish 75 percent preference for the sugar solution over the salt solution. The results were that a 54 percent sugar solution had to be offered 17 times, an 18 percent solution 38 times, a 6 percent solution 66 times, and a 2 percent solution 122 times to reach criterion. The frequency-intensity relations found here show that the higher concentrations of sugar solution exerted greater weight in the choices of the rats than did the less concentrated solutions, a finding paralleling the equivalence of frequency and weight found by Bevan and Darby (1955) in preserving constant adaptation levels. They showed that heavy anchors needed to be presented less often than light anchors to keep adaptation level constant. However, the analogy between ALs for lifted weights and affective levels for sugar solutions breaks down beyond a certain point because the concentration-preference relation is not monotonic whereas the frequency-weight relation is monotonic.

In spite of the strong evidence for the influence of internal states on eating behavior, situational factors may affect food intake as dramatically as variations in body physiology are known to do. Young, who has stressed the importance of need as a determiner of food preferences, has also recognized the role of situational factors in the acceptability of foods (1948). He pointed out that factors other than bodily needs affect food intake, such as the spatial position of the food, e.g., for particular animals whether the food is on the right or left; the size of the food, e.g., larger grains of corn preferred to smaller grains; the quantity and accessibility of the food, e.g., the kind of container and amount of work necessary to obtain the food; and the room temperature. They found that the rate of acceptance fell as room temperature rose from 60 to 90° F, and above 90° F it fell off rapidly while rate of water intake rose sharply. Intensity of punishment has differential effects on food intake, e.g., intense electric shock prevents animals from eating while weak shocks may only retard it. Just as in psychophysical experiments where position in series influences judgments of sensory dimensions, so position in the series of concentrations of solutions may affect choice on the part of rats. Thus optimal concentration was found to be approximately 8.5 percent for sucrose and 0.7 percent for sodium chloride, but when the concentrations were above or below these amounts the rats ingested less. As Young pointed out, if the concentrations were below these amounts then bodily need could not have been involved unless the optimal amounts were above bodily needs. The quantity of fluid ingested varied markedly with the concentrations of the solution. Young found that when solution was optimal (0.7 percent) the rats ingested about 3.5 times the amount needed as judged by intake at 3 percent. Young, therefore, distinguished palatability from organic appetite:

The term palatability refers to the acceptability of food stuffs as determined by the characteristics of the food stimulus. When organic conditions are held constant, food ingestion is found to vary with the kind of food presented, with the concentration of the solution, with temperature, texture, flavor, and other properties of the food stimulus. Collectively these characteristics of the food stimulus define palatability as distinct from organic appetite (p. 301).

Eating behavior is also affected by social influences as every parent knows. Children may respond to social pressures to eat when hunger (an internal state) and aroma and flavor (the natural stimuli) apparently do not suffice to make the child eat. I know of a child who drank only one-half cup of milk and continued to drink one-half cup when the volume of the container was doubled! Chickens that have stopped eating start again in the presence of other chickens that are eating. Hence, such a basic physiological need as hunger is dependent not only upon intra-organic conditions but also on environmental conditions. If this seems to be too sweeping a conclusion, it nevertheless squares with such facts as the following: individuals have been known to starve to death rather than eat human flesh, and on the other hand, certain people devour their dead, not for lack of food, but because they are acting in accordance with religious beliefs. Situational factors may thus give rise to diametrically opposed modes of behavior even in the case of such a basic need as hunger.

The extent to which primary sex drive is influenced by environmental factors other than primary sexual objects has been documented in detail by Beach in his discussion of reproductive activities in various species of animals (1951). He showed that sexual behavior far from being simply a response to the appropriate partner as a result of an inner instinctive drive is complicated by a great variety of situational determinants. Physiological readiness for sexual responses can be influenced by such environmental conditions as length of day, temperature cycles, seasonal rainfall, or the presence and activity of other members of the same species. Still other environmental factors may affect sex behavior by their influence on circulation, central nervous system, or general systemic state by means of drugs, hormones, and diet. Even sexually ready animals often need a particular evinronmental setting to respond to potential mates as shown by the fact that male mammals often fail to respond to receptive females in strange environments. Animal breeders often take the females to the male to be bred in surroundings with which he is familiar. It is well known that wild animals often fail to reproduce in captivity; the reason for this (which often seems more mysterious than it actually is) is that their being in unfamiliar surroundings or deprived of their normal mode of life leads to inhibition of sex responses.

Background stimuli may facilitate or inhibit sex responses as shown by the following experiments cited by Beach: After being shocked on approaching a female, both rats and fish will thereafter not approach the female unless put in a new cage or tank; on the other hand, male rats that have copulated with receptive females in a particular cage often attempt to mate with males or nonreceptive females encountered in the original testing situation. Higher-order stimuli may also affect sex behavior; as recounted by Beach, roosters court and mate with hens of low social rank more often than with those whose status in the flock is high.

We have shown that situational factors can modify two of the strongest primary needs—food and sex. If reactions to stimuli in such basic modes of behavior (one concerned primarily with survival of the individual, the other with survival of the species) are modified by background or concomitant stimuli, then we must conclude that internal constitutional determinants of behavior cannot be treated apart from situational factors. While this proposition is generally accepted today by most scientific workers, it has not yet been sufficiently implemented by quantitative studies showing the extent to which focal, background, and residual components in the primary drives may be made to balance or counteract each other. The investigations of Miller, Young, and their co-workers, as well as of others, have taken into account the interplay of internal and external factors in affective behavior, but the full implications of the pooling model still remain to be explored in this area.

AFFECTIVE EQUILIBRIUM

Affective equilibrium may result either from balance of opposed pleasant-unpleasant states or approach-withdrawal tendencies, or it may denote complete absence of affect, which is so rare that we need not consider it further. Affective equilibrium resulting from opposed tendencies in approach-avoidance behavior in conflict situations has been extensively investigated by Miller and his co-workers (1959). In Miller's studies it was found that avoidance gradients were greater near a feared goal and decreased with distance from the goal, whereas approach gradients increased with nearness to the desired goal. So long as approach and avoidance gradients are linear and have different slopes, the curves of approach and avoidance must intersect at some point. As pointed out by Miller, at the crossing point of the two curves a condition of equilibrium therefore exists in which the animal stops on the way to the goal and backs up or, in general, vacillates. The distance from the goal at which approach and avoidance forces balance depends upon the relative strengths of the approach-avoidance gradients. How, then, does the animal manage to approach or retreat from the goal? This question involves the old problem posed by the ancients regarding the ass who was between two bales of hay and starved because it had no reason for turning either to the right or the left to begin eating. Such a situation does not pose a real problem because organisms do not remain in static equilibrium even when the forces impinging upon them are exactly balanced. Sooner or later one tendency (approach or withdrawal) overcomes the other so that the animal either goes to the goal or turns away from it. In the Miller model equilibrium conditions are usually, if not always, the result of presently interacting positive and negative gradients. From the point of view of AL theory this situation represents the case in which counteracting tendencies balance to yield an actual behavioral equilibrium. However, even when behavior is univocal and approach or withdrawal is observed, adaptation levels are operative: the approach or avoidance gradients are referable to equilibrium conditions that may be specified even though they are not presently acting. To explain why animals in the same situation exhibit different approach gradients, we must assume that they start with different initial adjustment levels and hence are differently affected by the same situation.

Beebe-Center's law of affective equilibrium. In 1929 as a result of experiments on affective behavior Beebe-Center formulated a "law of affective equilibrium" as follows: "The affective value of the experiential correlate of a stimulus varies inversely with the sum of the affective values of those experiences preceding this correlate which constitute with it a unitary temporal group." In support of this generalization, he cited the data presented in Table 6.1, which represent

TABLE 6.1. Changes in Affective Responses to Colors as a Result of Preceding Types of Stimulation

	Percentage of Pleasantness[a]		
S	After Pleasant Series	After Unpleasant Series	Difference
1	75%	82%	+ 9%
2	14%	33%	+19%
3	38%	65%	+27%
		Average	+18%

[a] Percentage of pleasantness is defined as the ratio of the number of pleasant judgments to the total number of judgments times 100.
SOURCE: From Beebe-Center, 1929. With the permission of the *American Journal of Psychology.*

the judgments of three Ss with respect to 21 stimuli that had not been judged to be either among the 10 most pleasant or the 10 most unpleasant of a larger set of stimuli. The 21 stimuli followed 10 of the most unpleasant members of the set first and then followed 10 of the most pleasant members of the set. From Table 6.1 it is seen that the "percentage of pleasantness" was higher following the 10 unpleasant stimuli than following the 10 pleasant stimuli in the case of each S. Essentially the same experiment was performed by Harris (1929) whose Ss judged colors on a scale ranging from −3 (most unpleasant) through 0 (neutral) to +3 (most pleasant). Harris' results are given in Table 6.2, where it is seen that the average value of 20 intermediate colors following a set of 10 pleasant colors is lower in the case of each of the four Ss than it is following a set of unpleasant colors. Both Beebe-Center and Harris maintained that these results could not be explained in terms of effects of individual stimuli on each other, especially in terms of the immediately preceding stimuli, but had to be explained in terms of the whole group of colors to which the Ss were exposed. Two additional laws were derived from these experiments: the "law of hedonic contrast," which states that an agreeable experience is heightened if immediately preceded by a disagreeable experience, and that an unpleasant experience may be felt as pleasant if a

TABLE 6.2. Effects of Preceding Stimuli on Pleasantness Ratings of Colors

| | Average Ratings of Pleasantness[a] | | |
S	After Pleasant Series	After Unpleasant Series	Differences
1	0.15	0.50	+0.35
2	−0.97	0.02	+0.99
3	0.69	1.73	+1.04
4	0.01	1.42	+1.41
		Average	+0.95

[a] The ratings were made on a scale ranging from −3 (most unpleasant to +3 (most pleasant).

SOURCE: From Harris, 1929. With the permission of the *American Journal of Psychology.*

more unpleasant state has been its immediate antecedent; the law of "mass hedonic contrast," which expresses the fact that it is the whole group of stimuli preceding a given stimulus that determines the affective state of the latter. These laws are actually restatements or corollaries of the law of affective equilibrium, according to which a stimulus following an unpleasant series of stimuli is experienced as pleasant because of a more general principle of equilibrium which requires that unpleasant states be balanced by pleasant states insofar as possible. Beebe-Center thus regarded results such as he and Harris reported as due to a compensatory mechanism, shifts in affectivity being the result of a balancing process within the organism. The balancing processes expressed in the law of affective equilibrium accounted for the effects of all preceding stimuli since the law of hedonic contrast could account only for effects of immediately preceding stimuli on succeeding stimuli. Beebe-Center pointed out that the tendency toward dynamic equilibrium is a principle common to physics and biology alike and is operative in the field of affectivity. He thus carried over a very general principle from physics and biology into psychology to explain affective responses.

In elucidating his position, Beebe-Center asserted that "the judgment 'pleasant' is obviously equivalent to the judgment 'more pleasant' than an indifferent object" (1932, p. 31). This is not the same as saying that judgments are made regarding neutral levels as weighted means of all sources of stimulation since, according to the law of affective equilibrium, judgment of affect is made with respect to the *sum* of the affective values of the experiences preceding the given stimulus. The difference in the two formulations is operationally very important, as weighted means yield quite different predictions from sums of preceding stimuli. Nor does our theory require balance of the field in the manner envisaged in the "tendency toward dynamic equilibrium" as postulated by Beebe-Center. According to adaptation-level theory there will not be a balance in the affective states aroused by simultaneous or successive contexts of stimuli unless the stimuli are such that the neutral level is near the center of the group of stimuli. This happens only in exceptional cases.

CONTEXTUAL AND BACKGROUND DETERMINANTS OF AFFECTIVITY

Influence of general surroundings on affective responses. We have already found that affective responses to stimulation may be influenced by previous affective levels (Beebe-Center, 1929; Harris, 1929). We shall now consider background and contextual influences on the affective quality of focal stimuli. Affective and emotional responses are so much the result of previous experience and ancillary stimulation that it is hardly possible to speak of the pleasant or unpleasant quality of objects considered in isolation from their residual and contextual accompaniments. It is a matter of everyday experience that individuals are influenced by the surroundings in which they live, work, and play. Maslow and Mintz (1956) demonstrated that judgments of the energy and well-being of individuals in photographs were greatly influenced by the aesthetic characteristics of the rooms in which the judgments

were made. The photographs were alternately male and female. The
Ss were allowed to define the terms "energy" and "well-being" for
themselves. Maslow and Mintz stressed the fact that Ss must be allowed
to "soak" in the room in order for its esthetic quality to be experimentally effective. Ss judged the photographs in (1) a "beautiful"
room that impressed them as attractive, comfortable, and pleasant;
(2) a room that impressed them as ugly, repulsive, and disgusting;
and (3) an office that seemed to be an average room. The ugly room
was a janitor's storeroom in dishevelled condition, and the beautiful
room was attractively furnished and decorated. The photographs were
10 negative prints of faces to bring out "bone structure." Judgments
were made in terms of a rating scale from 1 to 6 so that total scores
for the 10 photographs could range from 10 to 60. The scores were
treated to yield an average value for each S on the dimension of energy
and well-being. The results given in Table 6.3 show that in the beautiful room the judgments were higher than in the ugly room to a
significant degree, 37.99 as against 31.81. The difference of 3.99 between the average room and the beautiful room was also statistically
significant, but that between the ugly room and the average room was
not significant although in the expected direction. Since the center of
the scale was 35 for the 10 photographs, values below 35 are on the
fatigue, displeased side of the scale and those above 35 are on the ener-
getic, well side. In Table 6.3 it is seen that the average room gave

TABLE 6.3.   Effects of Beautiful (BR), Average (AR), and Ugly (UR)
Surroundings on Judgments of Energy and Well-being

	Averages	Differences	t	P
UR	31.81	AR–UR = 2.19	1.12	<.30
AR	34.00	BR–AR = 3.99	2.04	<.05
BR	37.99	BR–UR = 6.18	3.54	<.001

SOURCE: From Maslow and Mintz, 1956. With the permission of the *Journal of Psychology.*

results near the average; the ugly room, below average; and the
beautiful room, above average. The authors pointed out that the results
were not due to suggestion or role playing and that all properties of
the room were acting upon the Ss: color, size, neatness, and cleanliness
(the ugly room was the smallest).

In a subsequent study, Mintz (1956) investigated the effects of prolonged exposure to the beautiful and ugly rooms. In the first experiment Ss were in the rooms a relatively short time—only 15–20 minutes. It was to be determined whether the effects of the rooms were short-term effects or whether Ss on prolonged exposure would adapt to the rooms so that the initial differences between them would be negated. In the second experiment the Es in the previous experiment were Ss without knowing that they were being studied! Es spent six sessions testing a total of 32 Ss. They were in the rooms twice for one hour in the first week, twice for two hours during the next week, and twice for one hour during the third week. The Es were thus in the rooms a total of eight hours. The time spent by the Es in the two rooms was also noted and it was found to be significantly higher in the beautiful room than in the ugly room. They left the ugly room sooner than the beautiful room. Comments of the Es revealed their feelings toward the two rooms: they wanted to quit the unpleasant room and complained of headache and sleepiness while waiting for the test Ss in it, whereas they felt like working and remaining in the pleasant room. The shorter times spent by Es in the unpleasant room may have been because Ss worked faster here than in the pleasant room, but this is not the only explanation for the findings of this study.

Surroundings also influenced expressed liking for school subjects in a study by Phares and Rotter (1956). Judgments were significantly affected by the kinds of rooms in which the questions were asked. School children read statements concerned with athletics, academic work, and manual training in the gym, in a classroom, and in the manual training room. As seen in Table 6.4 significant differences were found between athletic and academic replies given in the classroom

TABLE 6.4. Influence of Environment on Preference Ratings of Three Types of Subject Matter

Subject Matter	Test Room				p
	Academic	Athletic	Manual Training		
Academic	9.54	10.21	9.26	Ac–Ath	<.001
Athletic	9.83	8.40	9.90	Ath–Man	<.001
Manual training	9.12	9.82	9.28	Man–Ac	>.10

SOURCE: From Phares and Rotter, 1956. With the permission of the American Psychological Association.

and in the gym, and between athletic and manual replies given in the gym and in the manual training room. There was no significant difference between academic and manual replies in the classroom and in the manual training room, possibly because the situations were too much alike (the benches in the manual training room may have been reminiscent of desks in the classroom).

The studies by Maslow and Mintz and Phares and Rotter explain, for example, why people pay higher prices in restaurants where the decor is pleasing, even though the food may not be superior. Aesthetic factors play a large part in almost everything that people do because of their effects on affective levels.

Affective responses to object colors on colored backgrounds. Nowhere are the effects of surroundings on perception and affectivity greater than in the field of color preferences yet investigations of the affective value of colors have been concerned only with colors viewed against achromatic backgrounds and illuminated by sources having spectral energy distributions more or less close to average daylight. In studying affective responses to colors it is necessary to take into account not only the spectral reflectance of the objects, but also the spectral energy distribution of the light source and the spectral reflectances of the background and of other objects in the field of view. Since the light sent by objects to the eyes is the product of spectral energy of the source multiplied by the spectral reflectance of the object, it follows that colors of objects vary with changes in spectral quality of the light falling on them. In addition, object colors are affected by contrast with neighboring surfaces and by the chromatic adaptation of the eye. Colors of objects, therefore, change more or less with any change in viewing conditions and these changes are accompanied by variations in affective tone. Often the "real" colors of objects are assumed to be the colors observed under daylight sources against neutral backgrounds. If there is a large variety of colors in the field of view, with no large area of surrounding color, and the illuminance does not depart too widely from the spectral energy of average daylight, this assumption does not introduce large errors. But if objects are viewed against chromatic backgrounds, or if the source departs widely from average daylight, object colors may change radically. Since the pleasantness of colors depends upon the way they are perceived, actual conditions of viewing must always be taken into account when color preferences are in question.

The effects of spectral energy distributions of sources and of the spectral reflectances of background colors on the affective ratings of object colors were studied by the writer under a grant from the Illuminating Engineering Research Institute. The stimuli, 125 Munsell chips, were viewed on 25 backgrounds in 5 different sources of illumination by five men and five women. The number of observations totaled 156,250, of which 31,250 were made in each of the 5 illuminants. The colors were rated for pleasantness according to the following categories which were assigned the numbers in parentheses for purposes of computation: very very pleasant (9); very pleasant (8); pleasant (7); mildly pleasant (6); neutral or indifferent (5), mildly unpleasant (4); unpleasant (3); very unpleasant (2); and very very unpleasant (1). About 12 chips were exposed at a time on one of the backgrounds both to expedite the observations and to provide a variety of colors to facilitate the judgments. The *S*s were graduate and undergraduate men and women at the University of Texas, some married, and one or two with more than average interest in art. All *S*s were paid but expressed an interest in taking part in the experiment which required many hours from each one. The colors were presented in booths illuminated by each of the five sources: three were fluorescent lamps, 4500K, 6500K, and 3000K, and two were incandescent lamps, 2854K (illuminant A) and 6500K (approximation to daylight). Because of the large number of observations, very small differences between means are highly significant statistically in this investigation.

Effects of light sources on ratings of pleasantness. Upon going into a room, hall, or auditorium we are almost immediately aware of the color and luminance of the source of illumination even though it is not seen directly. With indirect lighting we may not be able to decide whether ceiling and walls are pink and illuminated by white light or white and illuminated by pink light, but such cases are rare because the quality of the illumination is usually unmistakable. Usually interiors have a predominating color that is largely determined by the spectral energy of the source of light and by the colors of large areas in the field of view. Since the source tinges all objects more or less with its own color, its spectral energy is of prime importance in determining the colors that are seen and their esthetic effects. Strong red, orange, and yellow components in sources of light arouse feelings of warmth (in an emotional sense) and nearness, while strong green, greenish-blue, and blue components arouse feelings of coldness and distance.

The spectral composition of light sources is particularly important for the colors of foods and complexions because most individuals react strongly to small changes in the color of these everyday stimuli. The data in Table 6.5 show how butter, raw beef, apple, lettuce, and

TABLE 6.5. Pleasantness Ratings of Foods and Complexions in Five Sources of Illumination by Four Women and Six Men Ss

	6500K Incandescent		2854K Incandescent		3000K Fluorescent		4500K Fluorescent		6500K Fluorescent	
	M	W	M	W	M	W	M	W	M	W
Butter	7.1	5.5—	7.0	7.0	5.5—	5.7	6.6	7.2+	7.5+	6.8
Beef, raw	4.8—	4.7—	7.3+	6.1	4.6	5.0	6.5	6.5+	6.1	5.0
Apple	7.8	7.5	8.5+	7.8	7.5—	5.5—	7.9	8.2+	8.1	8.0
Lettuce	6.1—	5.5—	7.5+	7.5+	7.0	6.0	6.6	7.0	6.4	6.2
Tomato	6.1	6.8	8.1+	7.2+	6.0—	5.0—	7.6	7.0	7.2	7.0
Faces	5.4—	6.2	6.7+	7.8+	6.0	6.0—	6.4	6.8	6.1	6.3
Average	6.2	6.0	7.5+	7.1*	6.1—	5.6—	6.8	7.1*	6.9	6.6

Note: + = most preferred
— = least preferred
* = tie

tomato and the complexions of two individuals were rated in five different sources of illumination by men and women. Since a change of one-tenth of a category step is highly significant, it is seen that all items are significantly affected by the sources in which they were seen. Raw beef was rated unpleasant-to-indifferent in 6500K incandescent filament light and in 3000K fluorescent light but was definitely on the pleasant size in 2854K incandescent light. Similarly, tomato was rated very pleasant in 2854K incandescent light and just above indifference in 3000K fluorescent light. Complexions were rated pleasant-to-very-pleasant in 2854K incandescent light and only mildly pleasant in the four other sources. Taking all foods and complexions together, the highest ratings of pleasantness were made in 2854K incandescent filament light and the lowest were made in 3000K fluorescent light.

The average ratings of the pleasantness of the 125 Munsell chips on the 25 backgrounds by the 10 Ss reveal significant differences between several of the sources in their over-all esthetic effects as shown by the data in Table 6.6. Looking first at the average ratings of all colors on all backgrounds, we find the order of sources and their ratings from best to worst to be 4500K fluorescent light, 5.94; 2854K incandescent lamp light, 5.90; 6500K fluorescent light, 5.85; 3000K fluorescent light, 5.78; and 6500K incandescent lamp light, 5.69. Since a difference as small as 0.10 is highly significant, 7 out of the 10 differences between sources are highly significant and one or two others are significant statistically, if not for practical considerations.

TABLE 6.6.   Ratings of 125 Munsell Chips on 25 Different
Backgrounds in 5 Sources of Illumination

Source	Ratings
4500K Fluorescent	5.94
2854K Incandescent	5.90
6500K Fluorescent	5.85
3000K Fluorescent	5.78
6500K Incandescent	5.69

Note: Order is from best to least liked sources.

That the quality of sources of light may enhance or diminish affective responses to object colors is shown by the data in Table 6.7, where the 25 backgrounds are ordered in each source of light according to the average ratings of the 125 Munsell colors. Considering the top eight backgrounds we find that in three of the five sources certain background colors are missing. Thus in 2854K incandescent light not one of the blue or purple-blue backgrounds appears. This yellowish source of light "kills" the blue background, making it a poor background for most of the object colors. This source favors red, yellow, and green backgrounds. Similarly, in 6500K fluorescent light, no green background is found among the top eight, with red and yellow backgrounds favored above purple-blue. The situation is even more striking in 6500K filament light where no red or blue backgrounds are found among the top eight backgrounds. In the best source, 4500K fluorescent light, all the psychological primaries including white and medium gray are among the best backgrounds. In this light, green and yellow are favored over the red and purple-blue backgrounds. While it is fairly safe to say that a source that does not enhance all the psychological primaries is not the best source, we can not say that all sources in which the psychological primaries appear among the top colors will necessarily be good sources because with the 3000K fluorescent light all the psychological primaries are present

TABLE. 6.7. Background Colors Ordered According to Pleasantness Ratings of 125 Munsell Chips in 5 Different Sources of Illumination

	4500K Fluorescent			2854K Incandescent			6500K Fluorescent			3000K Fluorescent			6500K Filament		
	H	L/S	Ra	H	L/S	Ra	H	L/S	Ra	H	L/S	Ra	H	L/S	Ra
1.	N	10/0	6.37	N	10/0	6.46	5.0 R	8/2	6.22	N	10/0	6.18	N	10/0	6.05
2.	5.0 G	2/2	6.34	5.0 G	8/2	6.15	5.0 Y	9/12	6.17	5.0 R	8/2	6.05	5.0 G	2/2	5.96
3.	5.0 Y	8/2	6.24	5.0 YR	5/14	6.12	N	10/0	6.13	5.0 Y	9/12	6.05	N	1/0	5.96
4.	5.0 Y	9/12	6.22	5.0 Y	8/2	6.11	5.0 Y	8/2	6.04	2.5 PB	8/2	6.01	5.0 Y	8/2	5.93
5.	5.0 G	8/2	6.20	5.0 R	8/2	6.04	2.5 PB	8/2	5.92	5.0 Y	8/2	5.89	5.0 Y	9/12	5.89
6.	5.0 R	8/2	6.12	5.0 Y	9/12	6.03	5.0 R	2/2	5.91	5.0 G	8/2	5.89	5.0 G	8/2	5.86
7.	2.5 PB	8/2	6.00	5.0 G	5/4	5.96	N	5/0	5.89	2.5 PB	2/2	5.84	5.0 Y	2/2	5.84
8.	N	5/0	6.00	N	2/2	5.94	5.0 R	4/14	5.87	N	1/0	5.83	5.0 GY	7/10	5.78
9.	5.0 R	2/2	5.96	N	5/0	5.92	2.5 PB	5/2	5.87	5.0 G	5/2	5.83	2.5 PB	5/2	5.74
10.	N	1/0	5.93	2.5 PB	8/2	5.91	N	1/0	5.85	N	5/0	5.82	5.0 YR	5/14	5.73
11.	2.5 PB	5/2	5.89	5.0 G	5/2	5.89	5.0 G	8/2	5.85	5.0 G	2/2	5.80	2.5 PB	8/2	5.72
12.	5.0 R	5/2	5.88	5.0 R	4/14	5.87	5.0 YR	5/14	5.84	5.0 YR	5/14	5.76	5.0 R	8/2	5.72
13.	5.0 GY	7/10	5.87	N	1/0	5.87	5.0 G	5/4	5.83	5.0 R	2/2	5.75	5.0 G	5/2	5.70
14.	5.0 Y	5/4	5.86	2.5 PB	5/2	5.86	5.0 Y	2/2	5.83	5.0 G	5/4	5.72	N	5/0	5.69
15.	5.0 Y	5/2	5.85	2.5 PB	5/4	5.86	5.0 R	5/2	5.82	5.0 R	4/14	5.69	5.0 R	2/2	5.64
16.	2.5 PB	2/2	5.85	5.0 GY	7/10	5.86	5.0 GY	7/10	5.82	10.0 PB	3/10	5.69	5.0 G	5/4	5.63
17.	5.0 G	5/2	5.85	2.5 PB	2/2	5.85	5.0 G	2/2	5.82	5.0 GY	7/10	5.69	10.0 PB	3/10	5.61
18.	10.0 PB	3/10	5.83	5.0 R	5/2	5.82	5.0 G	5/2	5.78	2.5 PB	5/2	5.66	5.0 Y	5/4	5.56
19.	10.0 RP	4/12	5.82	5.0 R	5/4	5.82	2.5 PB	5/4	5.77	5.0 R	5/4	5.66	2.5 PB	2/2	5.56
20.	5.0 Y	2/2	5.80	5.0 Y	2/2	5.76	5.0 R	5/4	5.77	5.0 R	5/2	5.66	5.0 R	5/4	5.53
21.	5.0 R	4/14	5.79	5.0 Y	5/2	5.76	5.0 Y	5/2	5.72	10.0 RP	4/12	5.63	2.5 PB	5/4	5.52
22.	5.0 R	5/4	5.77	5.0 Y	5/4	5.76	2.5 PB	2/2	5.66	5.0 Y	5/2	5.63	10.0 RP	4/12	5.49
23.	5.0 YR	5/14	5.74	10.0 PB	3/10	5.68	10.0 PB	3/10	5.66	5.0 Y	2/2	5.63	5.0 R	5/2	5.49
24.	5.0 G	5/4	5.74	5.0 R	2/2	5.66	5.0 Y	5/4	5.64	5.0 Y	5/4	5.61	5.0 Y	5/2	5.41
25.	2.5 PB	5/4	5.65	10.0 RP	4/12	5.58	10.0 RP	4/12	5.60	2.5 PB	5/4	5.59	5.0 R	4/14	5.34

Note: H = hue; L/S = lightness/saturation; Ra = rating; N = neutral; R = red; Y = yellow; G = green; PB = purple-blue.

among the top eight backgrounds but the average ratings of the chips in this source are low.

Color of background and affective responses to object colors. Backgrounds influence object colors in two ways: (1) by modifying object colors through simultaneous contrast or assimilation and (2) by the kinds of combinations they make with the object colors. So great is the effect of contrast that object colors may be perceptibly changed in lightness and chromaticness as a result of the presence of other colors in their neighborhood. One literally perceives a different object color in such cases with resultant changes in affective value of the new color. Object colors that are acceptable in one context may be unacceptable in another; since object colors are never seen in isolation, the esthetic impression made by any color depends as much upon neighboring colors as on the light sent by the object to the eye.

Examination of the top five backgrounds in each source of illumination (Table 6.7), evaluated by the average ratings of 125 different colors on each, shows that certain background colors appear again and again: white background is rated first four times in four sources of illumination and third in the fifth source; green is rated second three times; yellow and yellow-red are rated third three times; and yellow is rated fourth in four of the five sources. Surprisingly, black rated third in one source (6500K filament). Since colors of backgrounds are the predominating colors in the field of view they exercise predominant influence on the affective responses to interiors as wholes and also to specific colors. Through simultaneous contrast, object colors are profoundly modified in hue, saturation, and lightness by the colors of neighboring areas with resultant effects on their affective value. Color preferences are therefore always dependent upon background or contextual colors and, in addition, upon functional considerations such as type of object, use to which it is put, and many other practical considerations. Owing to the importance of the eyes, hair, and face, their colors are most important in the choice of colors for hats and other wearing apparel. Not only must the colors of articles of clothing harmonize with each other, but they must also harmonize with complexion and hair colors.

The extent to which the pleasantness of an object color may vary from background to background appears strikingly in Fig. 6.1, where the average judgments of five men and five women of Munsell 5R 4/4 on 25 different backgrounds is plotted for two sources of illumina-

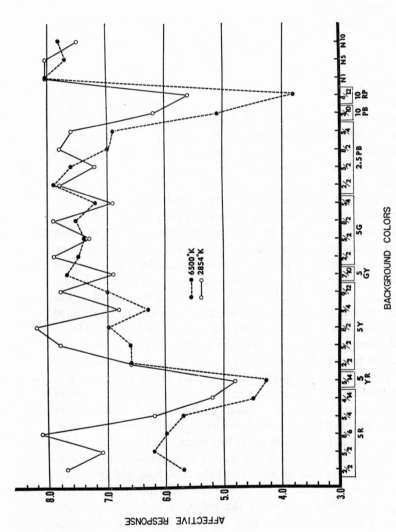

FIG. 6.1. Effects of 25 different background colors on the pleasantness ratings of Munsell 5R 4/4 in 6500° K filament and in 2854° K filament illumination. From the closeness of the plots in the two sources of illumination it is apparent that color of background is of greater importance than spectral energy of source in determining affective responses to object colors.

tion, 6500K and 2854K incandescent filament lamps. On most back-grounds this red of medium saturation and medium lightness is judged mildly to very pleasant, but it nosedives to mildly unpleasant when viewed on 2.5 YR 5/14 (a very saturated yellow-red of medium lightness) and on 10 RP 4/12 (a very saturated red-purple of medium lightness). On the other hand, contrary to the common view that similar hues do not go well together, we find that 5R 4/4 is rated very pleasant on 5R 8/6 background, which is very light desaturated red, and also on a very light desaturated yellow background, 5Y 8/2. The very pleasant ratings given this color on black and medium gray backgrounds may come as a surprise to many. From a comparison of the curves for 2854K and 6500K incandescent-light sources in Fig. 6.1 it appears that backgrounds may have greater influence on affective responses to colors than do sources of light. The differences in ratings between the two curves are much less than are the differences due to the backgrounds. However, if two sources with greater differences in spectral energies were compared, differences in ratings of pleasant-ness would be much greater and the importance of sources would show up to a greater extent. The similarity of the two curves in Fig. 6.1 attests the reliability, and perhaps the validity, of the affective ratings in this study since the ratings were made independently under the two sources of illumination.

Having considered the relations of object and background colors to spectral energy of sources and color of background, let us turn to the role of lightness and saturation of backgrounds on affective ratings of object colors. From Table 6.7 it is seen that the backgrounds receiv-ing the eight highest ratings are for the most part very light (8, 9, or 10) and have very low saturations (2 or 0), with the exception of backgrounds having a yellow component. Unsaturated backgrounds induce minimal color contrast and are least pronounced and, therefore, cause less change in object colors than do saturated background colors. This explains why the neutral (N) grounds, 10, 5, and 1 are con-spicuous among the top eight backgrounds. While practical considera-tions may rule against the use of white for walls, drapes, and other large areas in homes, white can be an advantage in museums and other public places where it is desired to enhance colors of paintings or industrial products as much as possible.

Lightness and saturation of object colors. Most of our discussion has been confined to the pleasantness of backgrounds as evaluated by reference to the average pleasantness ratings of object colors. Some generalizations can be drawn regarding the role of lightness and saturation of the colors themselves on ratings of pleasantness. From Table 6.8 it is seen that the lightest colors are most preferred, with a grand mean of 5.90. This is significantly higher than the grand mean of the colors of medium lightness, 5.77. The darkest colors, with a grand mean of 5.83, are preferred to the medium colors, in general, although not to a significant degree. The role of saturation is even clearer than that of lightness as seen from Table 6.8: the most saturated colors have the highest grand mean, 6.19, the least saturated colors have the lowest grand mean, 5.43, and the colors of medium saturation lie between with a grand mean of 6.08. While these grand averages are significantly different from each other, there are exceptions to this generalization for in some cases dark and weakly saturated colors may be rated higher than the lighter and more saturated colors.

TABLE 6.8.   Pleasantness of 125 Munsell Colors in 5 Illuminants as a Function of Lightness and Saturation

Lightness:	Grand Mean
Darkest Colors	5.83
Medium Colors	5.77
Lightest Colors	5.90
Saturation:	
Least Saturated Colors	5.43
Medium Saturated Colors	6.08
Most Saturated Colors	6.19

Pleasantness of hues.   Up to the time of writing, the data in this study on the effect of hue on ratings of pleasantness had not been analyzed, but there is no doubt of the importance of this dimension of colors in affective responses. Extensive data regarding the pleasantness of hues viewed against neutral backgrounds have been published by Guilford and his co-workers (1934, 1939, 1940, 1949). As we know from Guilford's studies, hue cannot be treated apart from saturation and lightness; and our own study showed that pleasantness of object colors cannot be treated apart from color of background (see Fig. 6.1). Of great interest are the isohedonic curves recently published by Guil-

FIG. 6.2.   Isohedonic contours for red, yellow-red, and yellow as a function of their saturation and "brightness." (From Guilford and Smith, 1959. With the permission of the *American Journal of Psychology*.)

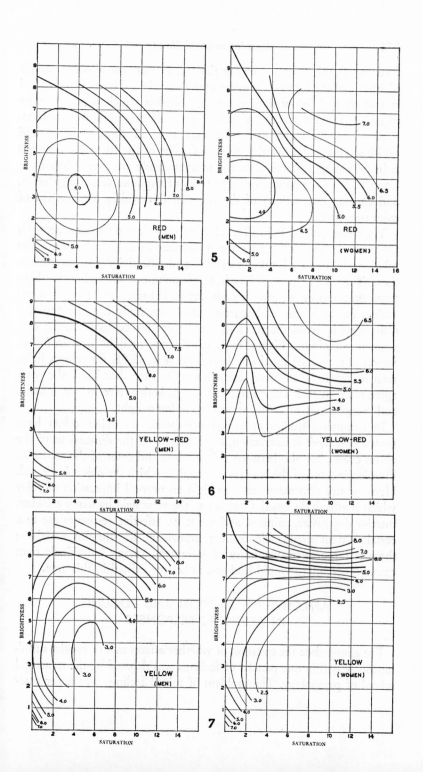

ford and Smith (1959) showing the loci of uniform affective ratings of hues as functions of lightness and saturation. The isohedonic loci run above and below the indifferent isohedon which divides the *x-y* plane into regions of pleasant, indifferent, and unpleasant hues as functions of lightness and saturation (see Fig. 6.2 from Guilford and Smith). They point out that the chief value of the ishedonic contours is in providing predictions of the most probable affective values from knowledge of the Munsell designations of the hue, value (lightness), and chroma (saturation) of the chips in this widely used system of color standards.

The isohedonic plots in Fig. 6.2 show very clear differences between the sexes in the preferences for a number of colors. Although the relations between stimulus variables and affectivity are curvilinear, there is a regular progression from pleasantness, through neutral, to unpleasantness in the case of each hue as lightness and saturation are varied, for both men and women. Our own study has also revealed differences between the sexes in preferences for colors of foods; e.g., women rated butter highest in 4500K fluorescent light, men in 6500K fluorescent; women rated raw beef highest in 4500K fluorescent light, men in 2854K incandescent-lamp light. On the other hand, the sexes agree often in their color preferences, e.g., both prefer lettuce, tomato, and complexions in 2854K incandescent-lamp light.

In summary, studies of affective responses to object colors have shown that there is interaction, not only among the dimensions of the object colors, but also between object colors and color of the source of illumination and of the background against which the object is viewed. Here sensory dimensions pool to yield an over-all impression of color which is affectively toned. Contrary to the view held by many colorists, interior decorators, painters, and scientists, affective responses are to a certain extent predictable from a knowledge of stimulus variables; there is far greater unanimity of judgment among individuals than casual observations would lead one to believe existed in this area.

AFFECTIVE INTERACTION AND POOLING IN AESTHETIC RESPONSES

For a long time the question of whether affects mix or coexist simultaneously within one pattern of feelings was debated by the structural school of psychology. The problem of mixed feelings was never completely resolved; the final verdict seemed to be that feelings do not completely coalesce—especially when they are of opposite kinds like pleasantness and unpleasantness—but are experienced successively by rapid shifts of attention from one to the other. This solution is not fully satisfactory because it does not explain how different dimensions of complex objects, each with its own affective value, pool to yield a single affective response; nor does it explain how a mood may color or dominate reactions to whole classes of stimuli. If an unpleasant mood could be negated merely by shifting attention to other objects, the advice to forget about troublesome matters would be an easy solution to many problems. The dilemma faced by introspectionist psychologists in trying to deal with affective interaction arose from their failure to recognize that feelings, like sensory processes, may pool to form affective levels while retaining some of their individuality. The independence of the components of affective responses ensures the separateness of specific feelings; the tendency on the part of the organism to pool incoming impulses with residuals from past experience results in the formation of affective levels.

We have already seen how stimulation that is predominantly pleasant or unpleasant may influence affective reactions to subsequent incoming stimuli. The pooling of different dimensions of stimulation and their affects yields a total impression that is emotionally toned. Over 25 years ago Guilford (1934) succeeded in showing the relative contributions of hue, lightness, and saturation to the total affective responses to pairs of colors viewed against neutral surrounds thus demonstrating that affective pooling occurred and could be predicted quantitatively. That the complex dimensions of art objects pool to yield over-all affective responses was shown in a study by Mouton and Helson (1956). Reproductions of 20 paintings representing different periods and styles and consisting of landscapes, still lifes, action scenes, and portraits were employed as stimuli. Modernistic pictures requiring training in art or artistic sophistication were purposefully excluded. The reproductions varied in size but were sufficiently large for details to be plainly visible from any position in a classroom seating 25 people.

Fifty college students, 26 men and 24 women, served as *S*s and made judgments in terms of a 10-step rating scale ranging from "like extremely" through "neutral" to "dislike extremely" with plus 25 assigned to the topmost category, 0 to neutral, and —25 to the bottom category. The pictures were first rated on general impression or over-all liking and then on each of four dimensions: (1) color and texture, (2) content, (3) dynamic quality, and (4) space. The dimensions were explained as follows: Color and texture include such aspects of the painting as the hues and saturation of the colors, the composition of light and shadow, color contrast, and the texture of the surfaces as represented by the painter; content was defined as the subject matter of the painting and what the artist was trying to express; dynamic quality was described as the action or tension aroused by the picture; and space was defined in terms of the balance and proportion of the whole configuration and use of form and space. In order to ensure independence of the judgments, Ss judged only one dimension at a time after the first judgment of over-all liking. Each judgment was recorded and placed in an envelope.

The order of presentation of the stimuli was determined by first arranging the pictures in alphabetical order and then assigning a position to each on the basis of a table of random numbers. For the first presentation, ratings were in terms of the general impression of liking by all Ss. In order to control for order effects, Ss were then divided into four groups with each group judging the dimensions in a different sequence. As shown in Table 6.9, a balanced Latin-square design was

TABLE 6.9.   Latin-square Design for Order of Judging
Dimensions of Paintings

Group	Order of Judging			
	I	II	III	IV
A	Color	Content	Dynamic quality	Space
B	Content	Space	Color	Dynamic quality
C	Dynamic quality	Color	Space	Content
D	Space	Dynamic quality	Content	Color

SOURCE: From Helson and Mouton, 1956.

used to determine the sequence for rating the specific dimensions so that each dimension preceded and followed every other dimension once.

The results of the experiment are given in Table 6.10, where average ratings of the 20 pictures by the 50 Ss and the SDs of the distributions of judgments are given. From the averages in this table it is seen that the pictures were rated predominantly on the pleasant side with the spatial dimension (as defined above) receiving the highest rating (+2.95) and the dynamic quality the lowest rating (+0.85). The SDs

TABLE 6.10. Average Ratings of 20 Paintings by 50 Ss on a Scale Ranging from —25 to +25

Dimension	Mean Rating	Standard Deviation
Total Impression	+1.86	12.23
Color	+1.83	14.14
Content	+1.98	14.17
Dynamic quality	+0.85	13.71
Space	+2.95	13.86

SOURCE: From Helson and Mouton, 1956.

are large, 1 SD including about half the judgment scale. While the pictures elicited a wide range of judgments, individual differences in the judgments of Ss tend to equalize the averages. Another factor contributing to the small differences between the average judgments is the wide range of pictures employed. If only one style of picture had been used instead of a variety of styles, the mean judgments might have been far above or below the mean of the scale. The data, nevertheless, yield information regarding the pooled effect of the four dimensions in determining the total impression. The intercorrelations among the five sets of ratings are given in Table 6.11, and from these correlations beta coefficients were calculated. All the correlations were significantly different from zero, indicating that each of the dimen-

TABLE 6.11. Intercorrelations between Judgments of General Impression and 4 Dimensions of 20 Paintings by 50 Ss

	Color	Content	Dynamic Quality	Space
Total impression	.664	.772	.688	.616
Color		.677	.709	.582
Content			.763	.723
Dynamic quality				.612

SOURCE: From Helson and Mouton, 1956.

sions was related to the others and that all were related to the general impression. The highest correlation, .77, was between content and over-all impression. This finding is what one would expect from a relatively naïve group of judges who are more influenced by subject matter and objective references than are artistically sophisticated individuals, especially in view of the fact that the pictures were all representative in character. The spatial factor appears in three of the four lowest correlations, as seen from Table 6.11, probably because it is the least defined and most abstract of the four criteria.

The degrees of importance of the four dimensions to the over-all esthetic impression are given by the constants of the regression equation as determined by the Wherry method:

Total impression = .4197 content + .1727 color
$$+ .1213 \text{ dynamic quality} + .0567 \text{ space} + .42$$

The relative importance of the four dimensions is given by the beta coefficients which were: content, .4863; color, .1997; dynamic quality, .1371; and space, .0643.

Both the regression weights and the beta coefficients indicate that content was most important in determining general impression, with color second, dynamic quality third, and spatial dimension last. The relative importance of the contributions of the four dimensions is obtained by taking the ratio of each beta coefficient to the sum of the beta coefficients. This procedure shows the contribution of content to be 54.8 percent, color 22.5 percent, dynamic quality 15.4 percent, and space 7.3 percent. It is not surprising that content or subject matter contributed most to over-all liking since all the paintings represented landscapes, human figures, or faces. If modernistic paintings had been employed, the results would undoubtedly have been different because in modern abstract painting content counts for little while color and composition are important. This conclusion is supported by a factor analysis made by Eysenck (1940), which showed a bipolar factor in paintings that could be called formal vs. representational. The multiple correlation for all dimensions with general impression was found to be .801 (uncorrected R). This value indicates that a better prediction of the over-all impression can be obtained by combining the dimensions with one another than by considering any of the dimensions separately, and we are justified in assuming that the over-all judgment was the result of a pooling process.

The additivity paradox. In using a linear multiple-regression equation to predict the dependent variable from values of a number of independent variables we assumed that the contributions of the independent variables were additive. However, the additivity assumption does not hold in many cases, as pointed out by Johnson (1955). Two examples used by Johnson help concretize the problem: will employees be happier with $4000 yearly salary and a bonus at Christmas of $200 than with a yearly salary of $4200? Is the merchandizer correct in assuming that a customer would rather pay $X for a pound of coffee containing a prize worth $A than to pay $X — $A for the coffee? If the former is true, it would mean mathematically that $X — $A + $A is greater than $X, whereas if the additivity principle holds, $X — $A + $A = $X. If the additivity principle does not hold in such cases as these, how can it serve as the basis for predictions by means of linear regression equations? Let us consider these examples in relation to the state of the organism as well as to the stimulus situations. The employee who receives the bonus at the end of the year has a large increment added to prevailing level, whereas the same amount distributed over the year is neutralized as level rises from month to month. Similarly the housewife who does not stop to think that she is paying more for the coffee when a prize is given with the purchase feels that she is getting something in addition to the coffee, but the wise buyer realizes she is paying for the prize and would rather pay less for the coffee and do without a prize that is not of her own choosing.

We are now in a position to venture a guess as to when the additivity principle is valid and when it is not. If the adjustment levels underlying responses to components of a complex situation are not too different from the adjustment level underlying the response to the total situation, then the additivity principle is not seriously in question and linear multiple-regression equations may be employed for predictive purposes. If, however, two or more situations evoke quite different sets or adjustments, then the additivity principle may be seriously in error. In the case of our study of paintings, if Ss judged the four dimensions of the pictures separately and there was no pooling in the total impression, the ALs would have been so different in the several judging situations as to vitiate predictions made on the basis of the additive model. Such a model is valid only when similar adjustment levels can be assumed to underlie responses. Fortunately conserving tendencies in the organism, expressed in the assumption that AL is the result of an averaging mechanism, tend to restrict changes in AL within fairly narrow limits, so that the assumption of additivity introduces no serious errors when this is true.

The additivity principle is in question in the treatment of sensory dimensions no less than in the sphere of affectivity. MacAdam (1950) found that the law of additivity of luminosities did not apply to the brightness of color mixtures: if a white mixture was kept unchanged in the comparison half of a field and the red component of an equally bright white mixture was *reduced* in intensity, the resulting bluishgreen color was *brighter* than the white. Attneave (1950) found in predictions of total similarity or difference of colors from the similarity or difference of their separate dimensions that where the range of variation was not too great, judgments were amenable to metric treatment but not on a Euclidean or simple additive basis. Judged differences were approximately proportional to the difference between the logs of the dimensions of the stimuli; hence the additive principle did not hold. It thus appears that the quantitative laws governing pooling of dimensions, whether in the domain of sensory or affective phenomena, must be determined for the specific conditions under which the responses are made.

AESTHETIC ADAPTATION LEVELS

It is often assumed that aesthetic responses are the result of higher psychological processes, or that they demand special training and knowledge. Although it is true that the appreciation of art is facilitated by knowledge of the work and life of the artist and his times and the history of art as a whole, it is also true, as Arnheim has shown in his monumental book, *Art and Visual Perception* (1954), that the good painting, sculpture, or musical composition, must be constructed in accordance with fundamental principles of perception. While Arnheim's emphasis is predominantly on the importance of salient structural features in the work of art (in line with the Gestalt tradition), he also recognized the importance of the adjustment level with which the individual approaches a work of art. Arnheim pointed out that just as one adapts to the odors, surrounding temperatures, and noises in a room, so one perceives the pictorial representations of one's own cultural environment as "styleless"—that is, as natural and correct. To be considered good or great, an artistic production must not fall within the individual's adapted zone or depart too far from established adaptation levels. Art that is different but not too far from prevailing levels is accepted. If it coincides with prevailing level, it is not considered creative, fresh, or novel but is regarded as stale, imitative, and repetitive. If it departs too far from established level, it will not be understood or perceptually acceptable. To denote acceptable level, Arnheim said there is an "artistic reality level" which prevails in a given period. Most individuals are not aware of the highly complicated and specific style of many works of art produced in their own period or in preceding periods with which they are familiar. Unfamiliar works of art from any period strike us with their unusual features. We accept Cézannes and Renoirs today, but only a few decades ago they looked offensively unreal to the people of that generation. Arnheim ventured the following prediction in line with this analysis:

Probably only a further shift of the artistic reality level is needed to make the Picassos, the Braques, or the Klees look exactly like the things they represent. Anybody who is concerned with modern art will find it increasingly difficult to remain aware of the deviations from realistic rendition that strike the newcomer so forcefully. Even though our daily life is being permeated with all the devices of modern art by designers who use them for wallpapers, store windows, book covers, posters, and wrappers, the man in the street has hardly gone beyond the reality level of 1850 in painting and sculpture. I must emphasize that I am not referring here to matters of taste, but to the much more elementary experience of perception. When confronted with a still life by van Gogh, a modern critic actually sees a different object than his colleague saw in 1890 (1954, p. 93).

Change in level thus accounts readily for the well-known fact that many pictures were at first disliked and then were accepted by more and more of the public. The opposite may also occur. A picture that is very, very pleasant at first sight may soon cloy and become extremely distasteful. The connoisseur realizes that this may happen and he evaluates works of art on the basis of qualities that will be acceptable over a long period of time. The work of art as a pattern of stimuli does not, of course, change. Only the adaptation level of the individual, the era, or the culture changes. As Arnheim pointed out, what looks strange to us may look all right to our descendants.

New styles in art, whether or not they are liked, may affect both feeling and perceptual levels and thus influence succeeding reactions. Personal experiences occur to me in this connection: after an exhibition of "natural sculpture," which consisted of elongated pieces of driftwood and branches of trees, I was driving home through a park and was startled to see that the individuals sitting and lying on the grass and on benches were distorted into long angular forms like those I had just seen. Similarly, ever since seeing a painting depicting the leaves on trees as *masses* responding to wind and gravity, I have perceived them in this manner. In addition, my exposure to modern music, most of which I do not particularly like, has had the effect of making some of the older classical music sound too simple and monotonous!

It is not hard to understand how the preferences for their own musical scales arose in various cultures and epochs: the diatonic and equally tempered scales in Western music and the pentatonic scale in Eastern music were the result of adaptation to continued stimulation with such scales over long periods of time (cf. Ogden, 1938). Similarly, the liking for visual forms differs from country to country and from era to era; the general public usually rejects the products of the avant-garde. Time and repeated exposure to works of art are needed to change adjustment levels to the point where they are accepted by the majority. After adjustments to new art forms are made the new ways of seeing and hearing seem normal, perhaps natural. But it must be remembered that new appreciations involve new phenomenological data as a result of changes in level. Often cognition and learning help change ways of perceiving and thereby lead to new affective experiences. Thus, I did not appreciate Debussy's compositions until I learned to listen to his music in long-section rather than in cross-section, thereby perceiving its dynamic quality to a far greater extent than before.

What we have referred to as adjustment or adaptation level in connection with appreciation of art Koffka referred to as a class schema: "The class schema . . . forms a sort of framework, or standard, and what does not conform to the standard appears inferior" (1935, p. 349). He goes on to say that schemata are not immutable for the more new works are produced, the more will they contribute to the picture schemata. He also recognized that different schemata are not unrelated to each other and may indeed interact in the sense that architecture, music, and other schemata may influence picture schemata. Koffka went even further toward our position when he said: "Style, fashion, manners, frequently enough, even morals, are all manifestations of the same fundamental principle, the development of class schemas with their particular 'levels.' These class levels play a part perfectly comparable to the spatial framework, inasmuch as they also 'Put things in their places' " (1935, p. 350). The reason we accept Van Gogh while his contemporaries rejected him, Koffka pointed out, is not because we are better critics, but because our picture schemata are different from theirs and admit his pictures, whereas their schemata did not.

Changes in level of aesthetic responses under laboratory conditions were demonstrated in the early work of Beebe-Center (1929), Hunt and Volkmann (1937), and others. Thus the effects of residuals, which are most difficult to demonstrate under experimental conditions, were shown in a study by Hunt and Volkmann (1937) dealing with affective values of colors. The same set of colors was judged under two sets of instructions. At the first session Ss were asked to judge the pleasantness of 10 Milton Bradley colors on a 7-point scale in which the higher numbers were for pleasantness and the lower for unpleasantness. In a second session Ss were to think of the most pleasant color they could imagine and to let 7 define this "mental" color. The results for the two sessions were different: the second judgments were lower, showing that the very high anchor exerted decisive effects on the pleasantness of the series of colors in much the same way that an actually presented extremely pleasant color would be expected to do. Moreover, the stimuli at the upper end of the series shifted down more than did the stimuli at the lower end of the series, as is usually the case with actual anchors when sensory dimensions of stimuli are judged. This laboratory demonstration of the effectiveness of a mental anchor shows how powerful may be the influence of residual stimuli on affective responses. It should be pointed out that residuals had more influence in the Hunt and Volkmann study than was found with lifted weights when Ss imagined a very heavy weight as anchor in an unpublished study by the writer. The difference between the two studies is in keeping with what we know from everyday experience: sensory processes are usually less subject to the influence of residuals from past experience and imagination than are affective and cognitive processes.

Stimuli merely accompanying focal stimuli may exert effects similar to the effects of explicitly given anchors even when Ss are not instructed to take them into consideration in making their judgments. So potent is the influence of a very pleasant or very unpleasant stimulus in the field of view when judging the affective value of stimuli that it has been used in a "sure-fire" experiment by the writer for some years in his classes. Typical results were obtained as follows: Nine Ss were first asked to judge a set of 40 advertisements cut at random from a popular magazine in terms of a scale with values of extremely unpleasant (10), very unpleasant (20), unpleasant (30), mildly unpleasant (40), neutral (50), mildly pleasant (60), pleasant (70), very pleasant (80), and extremely pleasant (90), with the numbers in parentheses assigned to the judgments. Then eight advertisements with a mean of 58.6 were picked from among the pleasant choices, and the Ss rated the eight stimuli again with one of the most pleasant advertisements casually placed in their field of view. No instructions were given to take the added stimulus into account in making their judgments. The mean judgment of the eight stimuli then dropped from 58.6 to 37.7. Similarly, eight advertisements were picked from among the less pleasant group having a mean of 36.5 and were judged with one of the most unpleasant advertisements in the field of view. The mean judgment then showed a rise from 36.5 to 50.9. The same experiment performed with musical chords gave the following results: when the chords were preceded by a very pleasant chord, the mean judgment of the set dropped from 51.1 to 46.2, but when preceded by a very unpleasant chord, the mean judgment of the set rose to 53.5. Thus, whether or not explicit instructions were given to take background stimuli into consideration, affective level changed to a significant degree when extreme anchors were present.

Changes in affective level as a result of repeated stimulation or habituation have also been demonstrated under laboratory conditions. In a study by Culbert and Posner (1960), Ss were required to equate jet- and propeller-airplane noises for equal-annoyance level. In general, owing to the greater annoyance of the jet noise, its SPL (sound pressure level) had to be reduced for two groups of Ss by 14.1 db. and 13.3 db. to be equally objectionable to a given propeller noise during the first set of trials. On the second trials, the penalty imposed on the jet noise by the two groups of Ss dropped by 10.6 db., and in the third session by 8.6 db. and 8.7 db. One group of Ss equated jet to propeller as standard, the other equated propeller to jet as standard with the similar results just noted. Decrease in annoyance as a result of habituation was found, the difference between the first and second sessions and that between the first and third sessions being significant well beyond the 1 percent level. The authors interpreted their results in terms of adaptation. On a priori grounds, the jet noise should become less annoying in line with the usual effects of repeated stimulation. Movement of the adaptation level in the direction of stimulation serves to normalize stimuli which would otherwise retain their extreme character.

Our explanation of effects of habituation differs from classical theories of this process. Classical theories of habituation can account only for movement of affective value toward neutrality since they regard adaptation as a process by which effectiveness of stimulation is always reduced, never enhanced. According to our view, adaptation may cause stimuli to change from pleasant to indifferent to unpleasant or from unpleasant to indifferent to pleasant. Our view accounts both for reduction in affective value to the point of neutralization of stimuli and also for reversal of affect with continued repetition, something which the classical concept of adaptation does not do.

Changes in affectivity of stimulation are not solely due to movement of neutral level toward or away from given stimuli. As a result of repeated exposures to stimuli, changes in affectivity arise because new dimensions or aspects of the stimuli are perceived which act as new sources of stimulation. Stimuli arousing affective states do not impinge upon purely passive organisms. The visual object of art is explored by the eyes, music is listened to differently each time it is heard, and objects used in play and in pursuit of hobbies elicit new reactions leading to new sources of enjoyment. A ball may be thrown on the floor or up in the air; it may be bounced or thrown to be retrieved by the household pet; it may be retrieved by a child crawling under or over furniture; and it can be manipulated with the hands or by means of clubs, sticks, paddles, bats, or rackets, each mode of response giving rise to its own mode of enjoyment. No wonder the ball is one of the most universal and best liked toys by children and adults alike. Only on the premise that objects and events have exactly the same properties with repetition do we conclude that the effect of repetition is always to diminish affective value. It is only when all possibilities of new experience and new reactions to objects have been exhausted that we become indifferent to them or bored by them (cf. McClelland *et al.*, 1953).

Humans as predominant affective stimuli. The emotional impact of things human is shown, not only in interpersonal face-to-face interactions, but also through human surrogates such as pictures of faces and forms, personal anecdotes, names, works of art and drama, and mass media of communication. It is trite but true that the greatest interest of the human is in other human beings. We have already seen that monkeys in enclosures worked harder for the privilege of being able to see one of their own species than for the privilege of looking at other objects in an adjoining room. Both humor and tragedy are almost entirely concerned with what befalls human beings. It is funnier to see a person lose his dignity than to watch a kitten chase its tail and most of us are affected more by human misery than by that of animals or by the loss of property. In a factor-analysis study of humor, Eysenck (1942) found three bipolar factors in a large variety of jokes, two of them having human reference: thus, sexual were preferred to nonsexual, complex were preferred to simple, and personal were preferred to impersonal jokes. The personal qualities most often furnishing sources of humor were found by Cattell and Luborsky (1947) to be good-natured self-assertion, easygoing sensuality, sex-repressed aggressiveness, and rebellious dominance.

Mere reference to persons, whether by names or by pictures, has power to influence behavior. In a study of the melodious quality of poetry, Philip (1951) found that poetic selections were rated higher when the names of the authors were given than when only the period in which the poetry was written appeared. To add interest to pictures of scenes, monuments, and travel, a person is included even though he or she may be unknown to most of those who will see the picture. Advertisers use pictures of individuals to help carry their message, and the human representation has been used for centuries in religious paintings, stained glass windows, and sculpture. God, in Michelangelo's painting of the Creation on the ceiling of the Sistine Chapel, is depicted as a huge, powerful man. Had early pictures of the mushroom cloud following explosion of the atomic bomb been made to incorporate its power and ghastliness in the form of a human face, more people would realize more vividly what lies in store for the world in an atomic war.

MOTIVATION, INTERVENING VARIABLES, AND AFFECTIVITY

It is generally recognized that motivation depends greatly on affective states for there is little or no motivated behavior that is not affectively toned and aroused. Before we can develop a positive concept of inner stimuli as motivators, let us consider some of the criticisms of the use of intervening variables in psychology. In the past few years, there have been increasing signs of dissatisfaction with intervening variables and hypothetical constructs which postulate unobservable entities, relations, and processes to explain behavior. Without attempting to give a complete history of these criticisms, let us follow the mounting resistance to such constructs, beginning with Hunt's study of the ambiguity of descriptive terms for feeling and emotion (1935). Upon asking a large number of women in an introductory course in psychology to define fear, pleasantness, unpleasantness, esthetic feeling, and beauty, Hunt obtained the results given in Table 6.12. While there is considerable agreement among *S*s regarding the objective nature of the term beauty, the other terms do not fare as well. Aesthetic feeling shows the largest dispersion among the four definitional types, with pleasantness, unpleasantness, and fear next in order. The objection that the judging group could not be expected to show high agreement regarding the meanings of the terms does not hold water since there is just as much disagreement among professional psychologists as there is among laymen.

TABLE 6.12. Dispersions of Terms Denoting Feeling and Emotion

| Terms | Definitional Types | | | |
	Sensory	Relational	Objective	Subjective
Fear	80	42	5	0
Pleasantness-unpleasantness	22	37	20	0
Esthetic feeling	25	46	13	38
Beauty	22	4	121	4

SOURCE: From Hunt, 1935. With the permission of the *American Journal of Psychology*.

In the same year that Hunt's data appeared showing the ambiguity of feeling terms, Skinner's book *The Behavior of Organisms* was published deprecating the use of the concept of drives. He maintained that it is better to say "Eating salty hors d'oeuvres leads to drinking" than to say "Eating salty hors d'oeuvres makes people thirsty, and the thirst drive leads them to drink." Skinner felt that it would be better to stick to observed behavior than to postulate inner drives as sources of responses.

By 1950 we find an increase in the number and intensity of criticisms of inner states as explanations of behavioral phenomena. Wolpe (1950) pointed out that if the physiological correlates of the various needs are compared, there seems to be no characteristic common to all of them except that they are all antecedents of neuro-effector responses. Furthermore, needs cannot be distinguished from ordinary sensory stimuli, for if "the stimulating effects of 'primary needs' stand out in any way from those of other stimuli, it is only that they tend more often to be strong as measured by strength and extent of effector sysems" (p. 21). Similarly, drives become strong stimuli that impel to action, and, conversely, any stimulus may become a drive! The same may be said for motive.

A different attack on the concepts used in motivational theory was made by Koch (1951). Motivational processes vary with writers and psychological systems. Said Koch:

> They vary in level of analysis, from assorted degrees of the molar in behavioral theories, to assorted degrees of the molecular in physiological theories. They vary in generality from Freud's *libido* and McDougall's *horme,* to tension systems which Lewin correlates with his quasi-needs and intentions. To these concepts may be imputed the most widely divergent properties: in some theories they may represent a class of persisting stimuli, in others an energy source, in still others a class of regulating and directing mechanisms (p. 148).

As an antidote to what he called the disorientation in motivational theory, Koch recommended a return to the facts even though they consist of "a ridiculously meager set of scattered experimental findings and empirical observations [which prove] on close analysis, to be ambiguous, unreliable, of indeterminate generality, or downright trivial" (p. 149).

Irwin's assessment (1951) of inner constructs was no higher than Koch's and holds little more promise. Like Koch, Irwin found that each author has his own intervening variables and that definitions of such terms seem to be private. Lewin's tensions, for example, are hard to define and localize and are not meant to be physiological or to have an anatomical localization. Speaking of Freud's concept of libido, Irwin wrote:

> There is nothing more Freudian in quality than the devious, amebic, and subterranean wanderings of the "libido" in search of an outlet. At the same time, the nature of the libido and its relation to sexuality are left dim and

uncertain with even the closest attention to Freud's words. He himself has called the theory of instincts [another subjective term!] the "mythology" of psychoanalysis (1951, p. 209).

We have chosen only two or three of the intervening variables Irwin subjected to critical analysis in his review of the concept of motivation but the story is much the same for the others.

Both Allport's concept of functional autonomy and Hull's "residual drives" came in for criticism by Datel and Seward (1953) in attempting to explain the persistence of scratching by rats following application of collodion to the ears. The collodion was applied from the fifth through the ninth days of the observations, and the ear scratching dropped sharply after the ninth day; but some scratching continued for 25 days even though signs of skin irritation and sensitization had disappeared 5 or 6 days after withholding application of the irritant. The persistence of a form of behavior induced by known stimulation does not seem to be explained by reference to hypothetical inner states. Harlow, in his work with animal subjects, has also rejected hypothetical inner states as explanations of learning and discriminative behavior. He wrote: "Regrettably, these motivating processes were defined in terms of pain and pleasure, and it is probably best for us to dispense with such lax, ill-defined terms as pain, pleasure, anxiety, frustration, and hypotheses—particularly in descriptive and theoretical rodentology" (1953, p. 23). Instead, Harlow stressed the importance of *stimuli* as sources of motivation and he presented evidence against the theory that learning is dependent upon drive reduction. He concluded that internal drive as such is a variable of little importance, especially as we ascend the phyletic scale where learning increases in complexity. Monkeys learn to respond when there is no reward in the sense of reducing internal drives other than the desire to look out of an enclosure. Indeed, the monkey may reward himself on both *correct* and *incorrect* responses by swallowing a little of the food he has collected and stored in his buccal cavities!

The postulation of inner variables to account for observed behavior is not limited to animal or personality psychology, according to Payne and Hauty (1954). They pointed out that it is conventional to suppose that subjective dispositions or biases affect performances involving work decrement and fatigue. It is often assumed that feelings, emotional states, and task attitudes help determine task proficiency, but "such factors are merely inferred as intervening variables to account for differences in task proficiency" (p. 267). Using different sets of instructions to investigate effects of attitudinal factors on work decrement, they found no significant effects attributable to this source. General conclusions cannot be drawn from negative findings since under different conditions instructions may affect performace; nevertheless, we must agree with the admonition of Payne and Hauty that work-decrement phenomena should not be explained by attitudinal constructs in the absence of supporting experimental evidence.

The veritable gobbledygook of terminology in which intervening variables has been clothed can be seen in Ausubel's review of the concept of drive (1956) and associated terms. His own attempted clarification of drive as a "multiple determined, summated threshold state affecting a selectively generalized group of reaction potentials" (p. 220) makes use of intervening variables which are open to the same objections as the ones he criticized.

The multiplicity of inner factors, the difficulty of separating and identifying them, the tacit assumption that inner determinants have an existence more or less independent of situational factors, the impossibility of defining many of them operationally, and other difficulties cast doubt on the usefulness of inner constructs divorced from situational defining operations. One solution for the difficulties inherent in postulating internal unobservable inciters of behavior is to group them into the class of stimuli that we have called "residuals." When known situational and organic sources of stimulation do not fully account for observed behavior, we propose that remaining sources of variance be labeled "residuals," until more specific information is available concerning them. This position has a number of positive consequences for an experimental approach to motivation. First, it turns attention back to situational factors for an explanation of many responses now thought to be the result of inner determinants. Mounting evidence shows that properties of stimulus situations may account for many responses attributed to such inner factors as drives, needs, motives and the like. The search for situational determinants of affective, emotional, evaluative, and cognitive responses should be continued in order to narrow the domain of residuals wherever possible.

We may illustrate what we mean by the search for situational determinants of behavior with two examples, one from psychophysics, the other from the field of interpersonal behavior. The first example concerns an S in a large group of subjects who judged a set of lifted weights ranging from 200 to 400 grm. The responses of this S did not distribute normally over the category scale, which ranged from very very light, to very very heavy, whereas the other Ss used almost all nine categories of the scale. This S judged all the weights to be light, using only one or two of the nine categories. Calculation of the adaptation level of this S showed that in addition to the series weights a residual factor operated to raise his neutral level to 2000 grm. as compared with neutral levels of about 250 grm. in the case of the other Ss. Questioning revealed that previous manipulation of weights much heavier than any used in the experiment (rather than an innate personal factor) was responsible for his judgments, and we were able to obtain a stimulus equivalent in place of an intervening variable to explain this Ss' "deviant" responses.

Our second example concerns a woman who, upon being asked, contributed a dollar toward a gift for a secretary who was leaving the psychology department, when most other persons contributed only 50 cents. All the individuals were shown a clip sheet that indicated the amounts others had presumably contributed. Whereas the other Ss gave amounts approximating the average of the amounts on the clip sheet, this S, seeing 10 cents as one of the entries, felt that she should make up for this low contribution. It would have been in harmony with current trait approaches to personality to assume that a trait of generosity or kindliness was operative to a greater extent in this S than in the others. This interpretation may be true, but had she noticed the modal contributions (another situational factor) she would, by her own admission, have made a smaller contribution. We are thus relieved of the necessity of postulating an inner factor to account for this S's response.

A second consequence of our position is that it makes possible substitution of stimulus or situational for inner determinants of behavior. Everyday usage predisposes us to explain behavior by means of inner factors even when it can be explained by situational factors. We speak of a couple as having a community of "interests," thus placing the emphasis on inner states; but it would be more correct operationally to speak of a community of "stimuli" since it is their willingness to experience similar types of stimuli that forms the basis of their common behavior. Stimuli, rather than subjective states, serve to bind individuals together, for people do not remain together silently enjoying similar inner states! Take, for example, the actual case of a woman who watched her neighbor's television and remained on friendly terms with her until she obtained a set of her own. Thereafter her visits to the neighbor's house ceased, and she began to find many things to criticize in her neighbor's behavior. So long as there was a *situation* to bind them together, their friendship continued; when the situation changed, their interpersonal relations changed. Objects, goals, and situations arouse, maintain, and satisfy so-called needs, interests, and drives just as much as inner states lead or drive us to objects, goals, and situations. Since situational determinants of responses are easier to localize, isolate, and measure than are inner states, they are more fruitful for conceptualizing problems of behavior. We are therefore inclined to a *stimulus* theory of motivation and action.

Stimulus theories of motive and affect. Two conceptualizations of motivation have been prominent: one regards motivation as an intervening variable or as internal states that initiate, direct, maintain, and terminate courses of action; the other regards motivation as essentially any condition of stimulation, external as well as internal, that instigates behavior. Among the proponents of the latter view is Miller who takes the position that "all drives are strong stimuli . . . any stimulus becomes a drive if intense enough" (1959, p. 253). Bunch (1958) has also argued that all motivation is a matter of stimulation whether from peripheral or central sources. In line with the division of sources of variance of behavior into focal, contextual, and residual stimuli, it is our view that the stimulus theory of motivation is essentially correct, although it is in need of supplementation. The stimulus theory of motivation is operationally sound because motivation has been studied by varying stimulus conditions, even in the case of motives that arise from stimulus deprivations such as hunger and sex.

We may take Bunch's theory as typical of stimulus theories of motivation for purposes of exposition. According to Bunch, weak stimuli are nonmotivating and strong stimuli are motivating. Intensity of stimulation is reckoned from "starting threshold" (1958), which appears to be the absolute threshold or something akin to it. Changes in motivating power of stimuli, as when weak stimuli acquire and strong stimuli lose motivating power, are said to occur through "learning." There are several difficulties with this formulation of the stimulus theory of motivation. First, if effective intensity is taken as distance from absolute threshold, and motivating power is originally assigned only to intense stimuli, it is not clear how stimuli *near threshold* may have motivating power without learning, as is often the case. Second, change in motivating power of a constant stimulus in different contexts cannot be explained by recourse to learning because often there is neither time nor occasion for learning to occur with change in context. And third, a stimulus-intensity theory of motivation runs into difficulties in explaining how *absence* of stimulation may build up tensions and excite action.

Most of the difficulties of stimulus theories of motivation vanish if we take as the zero of intensity not the absolute threshold but the adaptation level. It then follows that stimuli below level as well as above level may possess motivating power because it is discrepancy from level in either direction that determines distinctiveness. Changes in level, whether due primarily to changes in contextual or focal stimuli, can account for changes in effectiveness of stimulation without the necessity of invoking learning mechanisms. Very weak as well as strong stimuli may motivate turning, approaching, or fleeing responses when they are unusual or are otherwise discrepant from established sensory or affective levels. But a more difficult problem for stimulus theories of motivation to solve is that affectivity is not a monotonic function of stimulus intensity, and motivation, in turn, is not a monotonic function of affectivity. The curvilinear nature of these relationships does not rule out a stimulus theory of motivation; it only means that motivation must be plotted as a nonmonotonic function of both stimulus intensity and affectivity.

To act as motivators, stimuli, regardless of their origin, must activate central neural centers. Differences between motives, such as peripheral vs. central, external vs. internal, refer to the original or primary locus of excitation: if a loud sound elicits a startle reaction, perhaps leading to flight, or if the acquisition of wealth is a prime interest, then the motivation is said to be peripheral or external; if stomachic contractions arouse pain and hunger or if endocrine glands are hyper- or hypoactive, with resulting modifications in behavior, then the motive is said to be internal; and finally, if stimulation starts within the central nervous system, say in the reticular activating system or in the hypothalamus, then the motivating stimulus is said to be central. But in every case central mechanisms must be activated for motivated behavior to be observed. A stimulus theory of motivation does not exclude internal and central neural sources of motivation; at the same time it has an advantage over other theories in making possible a dimensional approach to problems of motivation.

The McClelland-Clark theory of affect and motivation. A theory of the relations between strength of affect and intensity of sensory excitation has been presented by McClelland and Clark (1953) who have also worked out its implications for motivation. The theory assumes that pleasantness is the result of small discrepancies from sensory adaptation levels while negative affect (unpleasantness) is the result of larger discrepancies from adaptation levels as diagramed in Fig. 6.3. Affect is thus regarded not simply as a function of increasing intensity of stimulation but in terms of discrepancy of stimulation from adaptation level. McClelland and Clark also assume that "natural" adaptation

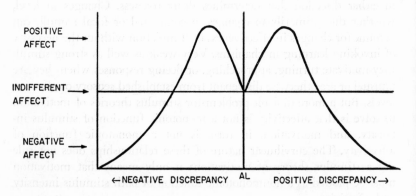

FIG. 6.3. The McClelland-Clark "discrepancy-from-level" theory of affect: small variations from level are pleasant; large variations are unpleasant. (From Haber, 1958. With the permission of the American Psychological Association.)

levels of sensory receptors differ from one another. This is related in part to the differences in thresholds of the various receptors (e.g., sweet vs. bitter). A given discrepancy will not be as effective when threshold is high as it is when threshold is low. Threshold is taken as cognate with adaptation level since nothing is sensed within threshold limits. Hedonic thresholds generally require a larger variation from level than do sensory thresholds, and therefore hedonic states may require time or persistence of stimulation to be aroused. Discrepancies from adaptation level give rise to a positive-negative affect function in both directions along a continuum although some functions may be unidirectional.

After publication this theory received considerable support from a study by Haber (1958) dealing with affective responses to warm and cold stimuli as a function of distance from the temperature to which the skin was adapted. Hands of Ss were first adapted to various temperatures of water and then transferred to water of different temperatures. The number of times each temperature was preferred over the adapted temperature was taken as a measure of affect. Haber found for temperatures in the vicinity of 33° C that the maximum number of preferences came within discrepancies of ±1° although some chose discrepancies as much as 3° on the plus side. There were also a number of other exceptions, e.g., one S preferred zero discrepancy at 36° while another S preferred zero discrepancy from adaptation level at 38°, and still a third S did not prefer zero discrepancy until 40° adaptation was reached, a value that would be considered high for most Ss. From Fig. 6.3 it is seen that as the discrepancy from adaptation level increases, the preference curve at first rises and then falls rapidly to cross over to the side of negative affect. Haber's results are in line with what we often observe in everyday experience: stimuli that are too intense or too weak are less pleasant than stimuli of intermediate intensity. Thus, a very weak sound may be disagreeable because of the strain necessary to hear it while a very loud sound is also disliked but for different reasons.

Let us consider some of the implications of the McClelland-Clark theory. McClelland and Clark maintain that increases or decreases in stimulus intensity can be related to motivation only if adaptation level and learning are also taken into account. This point of view differs from the pure stimulus theory of motivation in two ways: first, the effect of changes in stimulus intensity must always be taken with respect to adaptation level, not on an absolute basis; and second, it is assumed that such changes produce affective states immediately but that motives become effective only through learning. Thus while adaptation levels may be affected by learning and experience, the affective reaction to discrepancies from adaptation level is immediate. Once the adaptation level is given, affect depends only upon discrepancy from level.

These writers also included expectation levels in their application of the concept of adaptation level to affectivity and motivation. If expectations are considered to be adaptation levels, then changes in patterns of stimulation may be involved in hedonic effects just as differences in sensory stimulation may give rise to hedonic states. Differences from expectation, if they are not too large, are pleasant. Thus rats that take *different* paths leading to the reward may eat the food where it is or carry it elsewhere to eat. In other words, after learning where the food is the animal introduces variation to relieve the monotony of exactly the same series of acts. If expectations are of low probability, confirmation produces negative affect as in fear of the strange; if of moderate probability, they produce pleasure, as in reading a detective story; and if they are of high probability, precise confirmation produces boredom with a tendency to discontinue the act, as in rereading a detective story one has finished. On the other hand, if one begins with no expectations, there is no affect, as in the case of the child that begins to play with a new toy. As he plays with it he develops certain expectations having varying probabilities that will be confirmed or not confirmed. After the expectations become certainties, the fun of playing with the toy is lost and boredom results.

The McClelland-Clark theory has also received support from studies of affective responses to the color cards in the Rorschach test and from responses to other types of visual stimuli. That so-called "color shock," exhibited by some individuals when the colored inkblots of the Rorschach test are shown, arises from the unexpected change from achromatic to chromatic presentations and hence is an effect of order, has been documented by George and Bonney in a review and interpretation of the relevant literature (1956*a*) and in results of their own studies (1956*b*, and Bonney and George, 1959). Among the studies they cite is that of Siipola (1935) who showed that it is not color as such that is unpleasant when visual materials are presented, but the perception of color *inappropriate* to the form, such as a *green face*. In accordance with the McClelland-Clark formulation small departures from expectation are pleasant but radical wholly unexpected departures are unpleasant. George and Bonney found that a sample of college students who ranked the Rorschach cards in order of preference preferred the color cards to the achromatic cards presumably because they were novel. Wallen (1948), they reported, found that when the Rorschach color cards followed achromatic cards they were less pleasant than when they followed other color cards. The percentages of normal *S*s who liked the color cards were very different in normal and reverse orders of presentation, as shown by the data in Table 6.13 from Wallen.

Further tests of the influence of order of presentation and appropriateness of colors to the objects depicted were made by George and Bonney. In the first study (1956*b*) they presented *S*s with 12 slides in a standard order. The slides consisted of four stimulus forms: apple, pear, flower, and fir tree. Each form appeared as an achromatic outline figure (O), as appropriately colored (A), or as inappropriately colored (I). The same hue was used for both the appropriate and inappropriate

TABLE 6.13.   Positive Responses of Two Groups of Normal Men to Rorschach Cards in Standard and Reverse Orders of Presentation

	Positive Responses (Percent)	
Card Number	Standard Order	Reverse Order
I	15	43
II	23	37
III	23	35
IV	34	23
V	58	52
VI	49	54
VII	26	14
VIII	72	54
IX	62	38
X	69	23

SOURCE: After Wallen, 1948. With the permission of the American Psychological Association.

color, e.g., red apple and red pear. Four groups of Ss made judgments of the pleasantness of the materials in different standard orders on an affective rating scale. Three hypotheses were tested:

1. Appropriately colored forms (A) would be preferred to inappropriately colored forms (I).
2. Outline or achromatic forms (O) would become more unpleasant as Ss become bored on seeing them repeated.
3. Inappropriate forms would tend to become progressively less unpleasant with repetition.

The first two hypotheses were verified but the third one was not verified as shown in Fig. 6.4. While there was no adaptation to the inappropriately colored objects, there were marked preferences for the A over the I figures while the O figures were less preferred as more were presented.

In a subsequent study Bonney and George (1959) found trends in affective responses by presenting two groups of college undergraduates a series of alternating A and I colored slides. Each group judged 12 slides that were similar to the ones used in the first study but with some

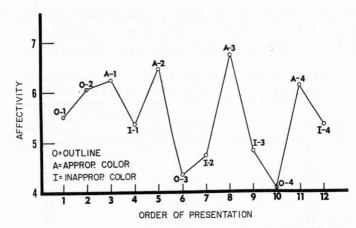

FIG. 6.4. Effects of order of presentation on affective responses to appropriately colored (A) and inappropriately colored (I) figures. (From an unpublished study by George and Bonney. With the permission of the authors.)

substitution of objects. It was hypothesized that *A* figures would be judged increasingly more pleasant as they followed more *I* figures, and conversely it was hypothesized that *I* figures would be judged increasingly less pleasant later in the series. The results in Table 6.14 partially

TABLE 6.14. Pleasantness Ratings of Appropriately Colored (A) and Inappropriately Colored (I) Slides of 6 Objects by 40 Ss

	Pleasantness Ratings						
	Order of Presentation						Type
Type	1	2	3	4	5	6	Mean
A	6.30	5.42	5.25	5.57	5.37	6.97	5.82
I	5.57	5.70	5.22	4.82	4.07	3.07	4.75

Note: Higher values denote more pleasant responses.
SOURCE: From Bonney and George, 1959.

support these hypotheses: the *A* figures start with high ratings, then drop somewhat, and finally end high, whereas the *I* figures tended on the whole to decrease in affective rating throughout the series of presentations. It appears that expectancy functions vary as envisaged in the McClelland-Clark formulation.

Returning to the role of motive formation in the McClelland-Clark theory, we find that "A motive is formed by pairing cues with affective arousal over the conditions that produce affective arousal" (p. 67). Cognitive expectation levels or structures may lead to action in direct opposition to simple sensory pleasures and pain. It is in this way that learning enters into motivation for motive is the result of pairing cues with affect, or the conditions which produce affect, to influence behavior. This assumption leads to the conclusion that all drives (motives) are learned but that affective arousal, on which motives are based, is essentially unlearned, depending only upon discrepancy from adaptation level. However, since learning and experience may influence adaptation levels, motives may be affected indirectly through the effects of learning on levels.

The McClelland-Clark theory seems to account for hedonic tone of sensory stimulation, and it receives support from many phenomena of cognitive behavior where expectancy levels are operative. It is difficult, however, to agree that motives are entirely a matter of learning since, in accordance with the position taken above, any stimulation that departs sufficiently from level may serve to facilitate or inhibit action and thereby may be classed as a motive. Since stimuli may immediately facilitate or inhibit behavior, with or without affective arousal, as in the startle reactions elicited by extremely intense sudden stimuli, the McClelland-Clark formulation should include among motivating stimuli those which evoke unlearned reactions to stimulation as well as those which are conditioned by learning. Furthermore, we need to take into account affective levels that are not directly dependent on intensive aspects of stimulation. Thus, objects can be ordered with respect to affective or esthetic considerations from least pleasant through indifferent to most pleasant on affect continua. In such cases the greater the discrepancy from affective adaptation level the greater is the hedonic tone whether positive or negative. While it is true that in the field of sensory stimulation large departures from level are usually disliked, it is not true that large departures from neutrality, when objects are ordered on an affect continuum, are unpleasant on the *positive* side of the continuum. The fact that affective adaptation levels may be independent of sensory and cognitive levels explains how positive affect as well as negative affect can theoretically increase in intensity without limit, something which is not so patent in the McClelland-Clark formulation, where only negative affect increases without limit.

A number of earlier writers formulated discrepancy-from-level theories of incentives and motivation that are similar to our formulation and that of McClelland and Clark. Crespi, whose work on incentives and reinforcement will be discussed in the chapter on learning, formulated a principle that he regarded as similar but not identical to the principle of expectancy of Hilgard and Marquis (1940):

Incentive-value is profitably viewed as proportional to the distance between *level of expectation* (both of quantity and quality) and *level of attainment*. The attainment of the incentive-amounts and qualities below the level of expectation, this thesis holds, is frustrating in proportion to the degree of positive deviation" (Crespi, 1942, p. 513).

It is apparent that levels of expectation and attainment are important for theories of motivation, reinforcement, and incentive and that they are cognate with our concept of adaptation level.

Disparity from level in attention and cognition. Peak (1955) has employed the principle of disparity from level to explain attention-compelling stimuli in both the sensory and cognitive spheres: "the disparity between an AL for intensity of a sound and an incoming sound may be the motivational source for attending to the stimulus . . . if the stimulus is difficult to categorize or compare with the existing AL attention will tend to continue until it is so categorized" (1955, p. 164). At the perceptual level the disparity from AL covers the well-known conditions of attention and suggests quantitative approaches to the problem of the determinants of attention (cf. the concept of "distinctiveness" in Chapter 7). Size, quality, intensity, novelty, etc. attract attention to the extent that they depart from the average of the attribute in question. Thus a red figure stands out among a group of black figures exposed tachistoscopically; a number among a group of nonsense syllables or a nonsense syllable having a different color from the rest is remembered better than the others even when it is given the poorest position in the series as shown by Van Buskirk (1932) and by Köhler and von Restorff (1935). Since stimuli that coincide with level are neutral, it is departure from level that determines degree of distinctiveness.

As illustrated by Peak disparities in cognition also lead to perceptual and intellectual search. I may not be sure of something that I see, e.g., whether it is a bird or a plane, and as long as the doubt or disparity exists, I continue to search and explore. The inability to match existing categories with what is perceived may be the basis for the drive to know if this inability arouses sufficient affect to result in action. Similarly, cognitive-affective systems are involved when there is a disparity between the feelings aroused by a job and the job one wants. In her use of the disparity from AL principle, Peak, like the writer, restricts it to stimuli belonging to a common universe of discourse or to stimuli that enter into a single system. Her illustration in this connection is also very apt. She says that the disparity between her athletic ability and Babe Zaharias' ability does not trouble her but the disparity between her old car and a new model may furnish the motive to buy a new one. Superlative athletic accomplishment is so far outside her aspirations that an outstanding woman athlete excites no feelings of emulation or envy, but the means to buy a new car are within her power and so there is a felt disparity that may motivate her.

Importance of minimal stimuli in emotion. It was stated above that affective thresholds are higher than sensory thresholds, and this is usually true so far as the hedonic tone of sensory stimulation is concerned. Stimulus intensities must exceed certain limits beyond sensory threshold to be pleasant or unpleasant. But when sensory thresholds are exceeded and where meanings, goals, and intentions are concerned there may be little relation between sensory intensity and emotional reaction. Thus, failure to keep an appointment or an insult or a compliment uttered in a soft tone or in a subtle way may arouse emotions that are not commensurate with the actual intensities of the stimuli. Moreover, situations that arouse little emotion the first time may elicit violent emotional reactions when repeated. As emotional level "drops" it requires less stimulation to arouse affects, and hence emotions can be conditioned more easily and permanently than sensory or cognitive processes. Due to this fact the relation between intensity of affect and intensity of stimulation often becomes inverse; with repetition, less and less of the same or similar stimulation is required so that minimal cues suffice to trigger strong emotional responses. Neurotic, hypochondriac, and psychotic individuals are often taken out of their normal environments and given a change of scene to relieve them from the slight but potent annoyances to which they have become oversensitive. The blush of shame, the blanch of fear, and explosive reactions are not always aroused by intense stimulation or extraordinary situations; the merest suggestion of a situation, a word, or a memory may evoke strong affect as a result of residuals from previous emotionally laden experiences.

SUMMARY

Affective processes are similar in basic ways to sensory processes; i.e., they are bipolar and subject to order, intensitive, series, and background effects and have similar relations to neutral or equilibrium points. Affective and emotional levels are established even more easily and quickly through pooling and interaction than are sensory levels. A modified stimulus theory of motivation was proposed; disparity-from-level theories of affect and motivation were discussed and their bearing on attention and cognition were pointed out.

7 Learning and Performance

Despite the advanced state of experimentation and theorizing, the field of learning presents a bewildering array of facts and theories which as yet fit no single conceptual frame of reference. Conditions such as frequency and contiguity, which are considered all-important by some learning theorists, are asserted to be without significance by others, and reinforcement (reward or punishment), which looms large in some theories, finds no place in others. Many of the basic facts are also in dispute as shown by controversies concerning the existence of latent learning, discontinuous learning, and learning by understanding or insight. While a great deal of research has been devoted to some questions, other equally important ones, such as the nature of inner resistances to learning, have received little or no attention in work inspired by current theories. In view of recent attempts to understand borderline and psychotic states in terms of learning theory (Mednick, 1958; Bandura, 1961) and to develop a rationale for psychotherapy, it is important to achieve a systematization of the facts and laws of learning to understand deviant as well as normal behavior. Learning conceived as a kind of adaptation seems to offer a promising lead in this and other directions.

All types of learning, from the simplest conditioned reflex to social learning, have been regarded by various workers as adaptive in nature. We have already quoted Piéron (1950) on the adaptive nature of reflexes (Chapter 2). Yerkes (1934), dealing with the complexities of primate learning, used as the title of his definitive work on chimpanzees "Modes of *behavioral adaptation* in chimpanzee to multiple-choice problems" (italics ours). Throughout this monograph Yerkes spoke of "adaptation" where other psychologists usually speak of learning, as in the following excerpt: "Reinforcement, inhibition, conflict, attention, are manifestly important in connection with the appearance, functioning, and disappearance of systematizations or transient modes of response, and upon them depend the rate and perfection of *adaptation*" (italics ours) (p. 56). Humphrey, in discussing extinction of the jumping response by frogs to repeated tapping on their cage, envisaged negative adaptation "as an organic adjustment involving the establishment of equilibrium to a temporally discrete four-dimensional situation, this result being effected by conservative processes initiated by the living system" (1930*b,* p. 504; 1930*a,* 1930*c*). More recently, Smith (1952) defined learning curves as "a development, and adaptation to a special learning situation" (p. 364). On analyzing individual curves of mirror learning, he found that some fell rapidly, others slowly, some in discontinuous steps, and others in continuous declines. Such characteristics, if studied in conjunction with other aspects of individual behavior, might reveal individual modes of adaptation and furnish a new avenue of approach to personality study and theory according to Smith. Tolman (1942), defined social learning as a "reasonable activity which tends to keep the individual well-adjusted to the actual environmental realities" (quoted by Hilgard, 1948, p. 277). Quotations from other eminent workers who have held to the position that learning is a form of adjustment or adaptation are not needed in support of our position that this concept in its broad biological sense is basic and general enough to encompass the numerous facts and theories now covered by the concept of learning.

Learning as process vs. learning as accomplishment. Failure to distinguish between the process of learning and criteria of learning has resulted in much confusion. Often the manner of learning is treated as though the conditions, method, or route by which learning occurs constitute learning in the sense of what is accomplished. By learning it is generally understood that an individual is able to do something at time t_1 that he was not able to do at an earlier time t_0. Learning implies that a criterion, skill, or goal which has been set by or for the individual has been reached. Learning usually implies a higher level of performance in a task than the individual was capable of before. Once the criterion has been met, learning has occurred. The *process* of learning may be fast or slow, good or bad, gradual or sudden, and may be facilitated or hindered by means of primary or secondary reinforcement and so on. Many controversies could have been avoided in the area of learning if the difference between the *how* and the *what* of learning had been explicitly recognized. (This situation is like confusing the *fact* that a man is a millionaire with the *manner* in which he acquired his money.) The conditions known to facilitate or hinder learning are concerned with the process by which learning occurs. The criteria, goals, standards, and ideals reached as a result of practice, insight, perceptual restructuration, and other modifications of behavior define learning or what is learned.

Disregarding for the moment the conditions under which the result is achieved, we find that the most salient feature of that which is learned is accomplishment or an adaptation to some criterion, level, or norm of performance; hence we may regard learning as a process of matching performance with predetermined norms. When material is memorized, when a rat learns a maze, when a skill or ability is developed, when a method for solving problems is acquired, behavior satisfies some criterion. Just as organisms adjust their levels of response in accordance with levels of stimulation where sensory processes are concerned, so learning consists in responses signifying an adaptation to criterion. Learning as an achievement of an isomorphism between the demands of a task and behavior has been nicely described by White, who takes learning to play a new piece on the piano as his paradigm.

On the sheet of music there are marks standing for tones of different pitches and durations and intensities. Marks indicate combinations of tones, phrasing, rests, tempos, etc. There is an isomorphism between the notes on the page and white and black keys of the piano keyboard. This isomorphism must be established in a functional manner by the player.

At first the responses on both the sensory and motor sides are slow, piecemeal, and painful. Each note is separately observed and the required movements of hands and fingers and feet (to manipulate the loudness pedals) are likewise uncoordinated and executed in part-wise, painful fashion. As the learning progresses the responses flow more easily, one into the other, both on the sensory and the motor sides and from the afferent to the efferent systems, the one being translated into the other. The eyes begin to travel ahead of the hands and feet. Practice has resulted in an adaptation wherein the behavior meets the requirements of the composer as set forth in the music. With sufficient learning the adaptation proceeds almost automatically, at least certain portions of the responses are automatic, leaving the attention free to concentrate on the finer aspects of the playing known as expression, interpretaiton, and the like (modified from White, 1916).

The concept of learning as an adaptive, matching process brings a number of facts and theories together under a single rubric. The Gestalt psychologists emphasized perceptual restructuration as an essential condition of learning, as in the discovery of hidden figures in puzzle pictures. Their contention that solution of a problem consists in the achievement of an isomorphism between factual (*sachliche*) and perceptual or thought processes finds a place in our concept of learning as a matching process. Similarly, rote memory and probability learning, often stressed in S-R theories, can also be viewed as instances of matching stimulus patterns with appropriate response patterns.

Innate vs. acquired behavior. Some adaptations are said to be native, others learned. The position is often taken that if something is native the mechanism of its operation cannot be known; contrariwise, it is often assumed that because something is learned its mechanism is thereby known. Both positions are partly correct and partly in error, for it is possible to discover the *modus operandi* of innate modes of response and to remain in ignorance about the way in which learned acts come about. In most cases we know as little about the neural mechanisms underlying learned behavior as we do about reflex and instinctive activities. It is, however, highly probable that similar modes of behavior, whether innate or learned, involve similar, if not identical, neurophysiological mechanisms. We assume that pooling mechanisms operative in the formation of learned activities are similar to those operative in native patterns of behavior. We have already seen (Chapter 5) that instructions to treat sensory input as either figure or as ground ("learned" behavior) resulted in modification of what was perceived in much the same manner that assimilation and contrast (innate visual mechanisms) affect perception. Hence the crucial question for us is not whether a given type of behavior is native or acquired but what its adaptive nature is and what the conditions of its arousal and modification are.

LEVEL OF ASPIRATION AND AL

Among the many factors which have been found to influence performance requiring skill, knowledge, or practice, in the attainment of goals, level of aspiration is unodubtedly one of the most important. It has been the object of numerous researches from many angles as shown by reviews of the literature dealing with this concept (Frank, 1941; Lewin, Dembo, Festinger, and Sears, 1944; and Heim, 1957). Level of aspiration is not a simple concept; it has varied meanings and manifold relations. Whereas Frank defined level of aspiration as the "level of future performance in a familiar task which an individual knowing his level of past performance in that task, explicitly undertakes to reach" (quoted by Heim, 1957, p. 194), Lewin, Dembo, Festinger, and Sears preferred to give an operational definition in terms of a sequence of events as follows: "A person has scored six in shooting at a target with ring 10 at the center. He decides the next time to try for eight. He attains five, is much disappointed, and decides to try the next time to reach six once more" (1944, p. 334). This example contains many of the basic ingredients of behavior involving level of aspiration: setting of a goal; goal attainment or discrepancy; relative success or failure; knowledge of past performance with hope, expectation, or desire for future performance; and manner of reacting to actual performance. The paradigm can be extended to include other determinants or aspects of level of aspiration, e.g., social norms, reinforcement, difficulty of task, effects of performance in one task upon another, correlation with other modes of behavior.

From the variety of conditions found to affect level of aspiration it is obvious that it cannot be restricted to attainment of goals. We must regard aspiration level as one of many factors that influence performance levels. Not until recently have workers in this area recognized that level of aspiration is subsidiary to the *adjustment level* underlying each activity and that it has importance only to the extent that it influences general level. We are thus able to account for the fact that aspiration level is sometimes of paramount importance and at other times of negligible importance. Thus Lewin, Dembo, Festinger, and Sears formulated a theory of aspiration level which involved pooling positive and negative valences stemming from choice of level, probabilities of success or failure based on considerations of past experiences, wishes, fears, expectations, and group standards. But these writers did not include in their analysis factors that contribute so importantly to the *adjustment level* underlying the activity as a whole. In other words, in common with most other workers in this field, they considered only factors relevant to *aspiration level* which is only one of many components of *adjustment levels*.

Essentially the same criticism of aspiration level has been made by Heim (1957). She pointed out that aspiration level does not account for the unwitting adaptation of Ss to level of difficulty of intelligence test items when they are not aware of doing better with difficult items in difficult context than in easy context. Performance levels shift up or down in accordance with difficulty of tasks as well as with intensity of stimulation in psychophysical situations. In this connection Heim stated: "The adaptation results point the moral once again against any theories which assume that levels of difficulty or ability are static and may be treated *in vacuo*" (p. 206).

The investigation of interaction between situational factors and level of aspiration is exemplified in studies of tracking behavior made during World War II (Helson, 1949). Observation of many Ss during practice runs in which they were required to align a moving pointer with a stationary marker by means of handwheel controls convinced us that different Ss had different standards of excellence or "par" that played an important part in their performance. Some operators seemed to be satisfied with a noticeable discrepancy between the moving pointer and the stationary index, while others tolerated no more than the barest perceptible deviation. Ideally, Ss should have been satisfied only with the smallest perceptible deviation from perfect alignment, but it was obvious that tolerance limits varied between individuals although they were fairly constant for one individual. Under the assumption that our Ss had consciously or unconsciously adopted given standards of excellence which were primarily a function of *apparent* tracking error, we resorted to visual magnification of pointer motion with results shown in Fig. 7.1. The gain in accuracy was unmistakable and amounted to 200–300 percent with all values of aiding-time constants (cf. the 1:1 curve with the 4:1 curve in Fig. 7.1). Presumably when an individual whose visual tolerance limit is 0.375 in. perceives a deviation (on the average) of four times this amount, or 1.50 in., he improves his performance to bring the perceived error nearer his limit. Even operators whose standards are high and whose tracking performance is so good

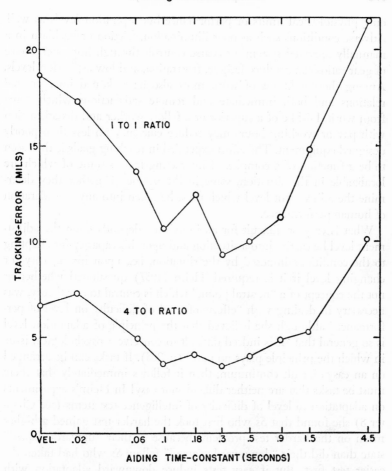

FIG. 7.1. Reduction of tracking error with increased (4:1) magnification of operator performance. The beneficial effects of higher magnification are seen at all values of aiding time-constants and in the case of velocity control. (From Helson, 1949. With the permission of the *American Journal of Psychology*.)

that they keep the moving pointer close to the target with hardly any perceptible deviation improve their performance when the error becomes noticeable through visual magnification.

Whether or not individuals perform at their optimal levels depends only partly upon their standards of excellence and the goals which they set themselves to reach. The tools and conditions of work affect not only physiological limits of performance but aspiration levels as well. Adverse conditions such as poor illumination, friction or backlash in a manually operated system, or coarse controls through improper choice of gear ratios can produce fatigue, frustration, and low aspiration levels. Among the conditions of work must also be reckoned interpersonal relations and both immediate and remote satisfactions which come from work. Dislike of a superior or a fellow worker and dissatisfaction with pay or working hours may reduce efficiency no less than poorly designed equipment. The effort expended in reaching goals is thus seen to be a function of a complex of interacting factors some of which are localizable in the situation, some in the person. Together they determine the adjustment level which must be taken into any consideration of human performance.

What is easy or difficult for an individual depends upon the adjustment level he carries into a situation and upon his capacity for adapting to the conditions imposed by the situation, i.e., upon his capacity for changing level if it is required. Heim (1957) questioned whether or not the concept of a "neutral point," which is central to our theory, was necessary in dealing with "effects of level of difficulty on level of performance" although she believed that the principle of adaptation level is so general that "it is indeed difficult to conceive a psychological issue in which the principle plays no part" (p. 208). If tasks can be arranged on an easy-difficult continuum, then it follows immediately that there must be tasks that are neither difficult nor easy! In Heim's experiments on adaptation to level of difficulty of intelligence test items (see Chapter 8) she found that Ss who first took the harder test gained a higher mean on the harder test problems because of their "upward-adapted" state than did their "downward-adapted" fellow Ss who had taken the easier test first. But if easy tests induce downward adaptation with resultant lower test scores on difficult items and hard tests result in upward adaptation with higher test scores on difficult items, then it is *theoretically* possible to devise tests that are neither easy nor difficult and which require neither upward nor downward adaptation and hence should have little or no effect on subsequent tests. This deduction from theory has been verified in the domain of psychophysical judgments (Helson, 1947) and is required by Heim's results on adaptation to level of difficulty as well as by experiments dealing with transfer from tasks of one level of difficulty to tasks of another level of difficulty (cf. Gibbs, 1951 and other experiments referred to by Heim, 1957). The concept of a "neutral point" is necessary, therefore, to render a complete account of adaptation to levels of difficulty, just as it is necessary to understand adaptation to intensity levels. The same argument applies *mutatis mutandis* when considering effects of previous performance on succeeding performance in level-of-aspiration experiments.

That the concept of aspiration level and the evaluation of skilled performances require the concept of neutral levels or points was long ago recognized by Mace (1931) when he investigated the influence of "implicit standards" on level of performance. He pointed out that individuals evaluate their performances in terms of good, fair, or poor, and of adequacy and inadequacy. He defined implicit standards in terms of *the central point in the neutral zone between the limen of disappointment and the limen of satisfaction* over one's performance and also as the point of transition from variability to stabilization of performance. The assumption was that so long as performance does not come up to the standard set by S, there will be trial and error behavior until the behavior pattern becomes stable. Mace thus recognized that there may actually be a number of neutral points or adaptation levels in the performance of tasks because his neutral points refer to different aspects of performance such as satisfaction (affectivity) and variability. Presumably, results on various dimensions should correlate highly since optimal performance yields maximum satisfaction and maximum stability of pattern. Nevertheless, performance must be related to each dimension and measured in terms appropriate to each.

Mace also appreciated the importance of sensory input for the development of skills. He reasoned that a modification in the design of the target in an aiming test would entail a corresponding modification in the Ss standard of performance and thereby influence the practice curve, and he regarded influences of this kind as "indirect incentives." In one of his experiments, Mace required Ss to spear targets with a pencil (Muscio's aiming test), and he found that the group which worked with a target consisting of four concentric rings spaced 1 mm. apart did much better than did the group which worked with a target consisting of only two rings spaced 5 and 10 mm. from the bull's eye. His graphs show that performance of the first group was better initially, all during the practice trials, and at the end of the practice than the performance of the second group. There are probably other effects in addition to the figure-ground effect which Mace believed responsible for the superiority of the finer target; but the importance of his work lies in his demonstration of stimulus properties as a source of incentive and determiner of level of performance.

In spite of an occasional study such as Mace's, it is noteworthy that investigations of level of aspiration have rarely been concerned with the influence of stimulus input on actual performance, attention being rather on inner factors. Lewin, Dembo, Festinger, and Sears gave the following list of determinants of level of aspiration: reference scales; situational factors, such as success and failure; transfer from one task to another; range of difficulty of tasks; group standards; socio-economic background; habitual success and failure; reality levels; individual differences; and so on. But there is no reference, in their otherwise excellent summary, to conditions of stimulation and to the potentialities of this source for raising or lowering performance through its influence on adaptation levels in general and on level of aspiration in particular. It is beyond question that the conditions of stimulation profoundly affect performance level and individuals' estimates of what they can and cannot do when faced with various tasks. For it is through perception that we literally see what and how well we are doing. In tracking tasks magnification of target motion and positioning errors result in improved performance by enabling the operator to see better, to appreciate his errors better, and to perceive the results of his own manipulations. Similarly the feedback from his own hands, arms, legs, head, and whatever parts of the body are involved in the accomplishment of a task, tells the pilot, the operator of a machine, the golfer, or the musician whether he is performing smoothly, efficiently, and comfortably. Our senses convey not only *what* we must do, but just as important, how we are doing; and this information guides responses and contributes to the over-all excellence of performance of all kinds.

BACKGROUND AND CONTEXTUAL FACTORS IN LEARNING

The importance of nonfocal stimuli was perhaps first realized in studies of animal learning where a variety of background factors were explored by early workers. Watson (1907) found that after rats had learned to run a maze, the number of errors and the time increased significantly if the maze was rotated. The fact that the relation of the maze to the larger surrounding spatial environment was important was verified with birds as animal subjects by both Porter (1906) and Hunter (1911). A more extensive investigation including nonspatial background conditions was made by Carr (1917) who found, among other things, that change in illumination and change in position of the maze or the experimenter affected most of the rats. While some background conditions did not affect learning, Carr came to the conclusion that "any sensori-motor act cannot be regarded as an isolated independent function; the act was learned with a wider sensory environment, and it never ceases to be wholly free from those conditions during or after its development" (1917, p. 291). Since these early studies, there have been other investigations of contextual determinants of learning in animals; but learning theorists have not systematically incorporated background factors in their theories.

Turning from animal to human learning let us look briefly at experiments showing the influence of contextual and background stimuli on recall and problem solving. Wong and Brown (1923), working with Yerkes' multiple-choice problems, found that aesthetic factors affected efficiency in problem solving. Ss working in a poorly lighted, dusty, disordered attic room solved 5.6 problems per individual with an average of 230 trials, while Ss working in a well-lighted, well-furnished room solved 7.8 problems per individual with an average of 243 trials. Smith and Guthrie (1921) reported that relearning was more economical when surroundings were the same as the original, even when the contextual variable was only odor of oil of peppermint!

One of the most exhaustive empirical studies concerning effects of context on the learning and recall of paired associates was made by Pan (1926). Ss had to reproduce the second member of the pair on seeing the first. The conditions of presentation of the stimuli in the learning and recall sessions were as follows:

Context Conditions	*Stimuli*
No context	HALF–DEW
	lock
Unrelated context	BEST–CHILL
	brown
	match
Context related to	ZOO–SMOKE
response word	pipe
	fire
Context related to	GUN–PRINT
stimulus word	hunting

Context Conditions	*Stimuli*
Context related to	cane
both stimulus and	LAME–SUGAR
response words	cloth
Number context for	1
words	RIOT–MELON

Under these conditions Pan found that three kinds of context aided learning: (1) a word context that was *logically* related to the *response* member of the paired associates, (2) context related to both the stimulus and response words, and (3) variable context related to the response word. In the case of the variable context, the background word was changed during the learning trials. Conditions detrimental to learning were found to be: (1) contextual words related to the *stimulus* member of the paired associates, (2) number context, and (3) word contexts logically unrelated to both members of the pair. Tests of recall showed that removal of context accompanying the original learning was detrimental when it was logically related to the response word but not if it was related to the stimulus word. Removal of unrelated context had a slightly beneficial effect on recall. In general, introduction of a context logically related to the response word proved beneficial; change of context was distinctly unfavorable to recall.

Background and contextual influences on learning and recall have again become of interest as shown by a number of studies dealing with this problem during the past few years. In the earlier studies, especially with animals, little attention was paid to the question of whether or not background stimuli were "noticed." Because of interest in the problems of latent learning, secondary reinforcement, need and drive reduction, and awareness of relations, recent studies have been concerned with the effect of degree of relevance of background to focal stimuli and with the problem of whether or not contextual stimuli need to be attended to, perceived, or cognized to be effective. Whereas Pan's study showed definite influence of logically related contexts upon ease of learning and recall and little or no influence of unrelated contextual materials, later studies have shown that purely fortuitous background conditions may exercise significant effects on focal items and are themselves learned even though there is no conscious intention on the part of *S*s to remember them. Thus Weiss and Margolius (1954) found that relearning required fewer trials with more items recalled in a paired-associates experiment when the color of the background was the same in the learning and relearning trials than when it was different. This finding confirmed and extended a similar result reported by Dulsky (1935) and was later confirmed by Peterson and Peterson (1957). Dulsky found that if the color of the background on which paired nonsense syllables were presented during recall was different from the color of the background during learning, both the number of syllables recalled and the number correctly recalled decreased and the number of trials necessary for relearning increased. The response syllable was thus linked with the color of background as well as with the stimulus syllable though not quite so strongly. Such results point to interaction and pooling in learning and recall as well as in sensataion and perception. Why arbitrarily chosen background colors accompanying both nonsense and meaningful material should be remembered is inexplicable unless we assume that background stimuli pool with focal stimuli during learning and function later in recall. During examinations, students report recalling the room, the book, and other objects present while studying even though they are totally unrelated to the material in the examination.

Conditions which affect learning and recall of focal stimuli seem to affect stimuli of all degrees of marginality in much the same way that they affect the primary stimuli. Thus Peterson and Peterson (1957) found that a colored background presented very frequently with a given word (e.g., a red background with the word salt) served to reinstate a high-frequency word rather than a low-frequency word (e.g., red background with the word food) when the colored background was presented alone. Transfer also was greater in new paired-associates learning when the same background color was employed with the response member of the pair in the learning and transfer trials. Similarly, Goldstein and Solomon (1955) found that serial position affected recall of nonfocal as well as of focal stimuli in a simple task. In their experiment Ss traced a path connecting a set of numbers from 1 to 25. Letters were placed in the path which were not germane to the task, yet frequency of recall of the letters depended on position in the usual fashion. Thus the letter in first position was later recalled most frequently, the one in second position next, and so on with minimal recall of the letter in eighth position after which the curve of recall rose sharply for the letters in ninth and tenth positions. These results are all the more striking when we consider that the focal and contextual stimuli were different (numbers vs. letters). Even stimuli that are completely below the threshold of verbal report have been found to affect problem solving of a simple sort (Kolers, 1957), thus bearing out the early experiments of Miller (1939) and later ones showing that stimuli may be effective in recall which were originally not perceived as such.

An experiment by Pratt performed nearly 30 years ago (1935) demonstrated the interaction of focal and fringe or background stimuli in what is recalled. One hundred two-digit numbers were read to 193 Ss: sixty-five numbers appeared only once, one was repeated three times, another five times, another seven times, another nine times, and still another eleven times. With no specific instructions regarding the series 55 percent of the Ss remembered the number that was heard most frequently. When the experiment was repeated with another group of 60 Ss, who were told to note all digits containing a zero, the number of Ss who were able to identify the number repeated the largest number of times dropped from 55 to 37 percent. But when a third group of 135 Ss was instructed to be ready to identify the number that appeared most often in the series, 78 percent of the group were able to do so. Memory thus depends upon stimulus-background-residual interactions and is not merely a reproduction of impressions of isolated stimuli or even of stimuli in such-and-such series, as might be inferred from Ebbinghaus types of learning situations. Recall depends on the instructions, conceived either as focal or background stimuli; on more or less nonfocal incidental accompanying stimuli; and on residual factors, such as sets, attitudes and mode of attending. While residuals are usually personal in origin they may be induced by the instructions or by secondary sources of stimulation as in Pratt's instructions to attend to numbers containing a zero.

It is also now well established that stimuli of which Ss are unaware may influence learning and recall. Studies in which Ss are required to gauge their responses to the probabilities of occurrence of stimuli show that they are able to do so even though they are not aware of the relative frequencies of the stimuli or that the problem is one of probability discrimination (Goodnow and Postman, 1955; Estes, Burke, Atkinson, and Frankmann, 1957). In such cases response frequencies quickly match stimulus frequencies. Thus in a class experiment in which Ss had to anticipate whether the next letter would be T or X and T was correct in 75 percent of the trials, Ss averaged 47.5 percent in the first 20 trials, 68 percent in the second set of 20 trials, and thereafter guessed approximately 75 percent in the next five sets of 20 trials each. After trial 140, T was never presented and the averages dropped to 33 percent in the first 20 extinction trials and to 8 percent in the second set of 20 extinction trials.[1] Nowhere is learning as output-input matching or adjustment to level of stimulation better exemplified than in such "probability-learning" situations.

PROBABILITY LEARNING

We have seen that Ss adjust to levels of stimulation without being consciously aware of the actual frequencies to which they are responding under laboratory conditions. Few events in life occur with perfect regularity, and much of our behavior is predicated on the probabilities that we have learned to assign to various occurrences. To be exact, the probabilities do not refer to events in themselves so much as to relations between different occurrences. Thus we assume that thunder will follow lightning or that it is very likely that the postman will bring a letter today which did not arrive yesterday. Hopes and expectations are not always in accord with knowledge, for when our emotions are involved we do not go entirely by facts and figures. The significance and affective value of objects and events bias our judgments and expectations. Everyone who has played bridge, bought stocks, played the horses, or taken any sort of risk knows that his actions are governed by emotional as well as by rational considerations. Insofar as response tendencies are based on *expectations* we must take into account not only mathematical probabilities but personal factors which influence decisions.

In recent years there have been many studies of behavior in situations where events occur with less than 100 percent and more than 0 percent frequency. As pointed out by Estes, Burke, Atkinson, and Frankmann (1957) traditional discrimination experiments have been limited to cases in which two situations differ with respect to at least one component or cue and in which the probability of reinforcement is 0 or 1.00; but it is more generally possible to give differential reinforcement to various cues and to study learning as a function of problematic situations. Thus a light and tone may be presented with probabilities of 0.7 for tone and 0.3 for light when the left door is correct and with probabilities of the same two stimuli reversed when the right door is correct

[1] These data were obtained by Dr. D. A. Grant who kindly made them available to the writer.

(i.e., 0.3 for tone and 0.7 for light). This procedure broadens the base of learning theory and makes possible a common set of principles for learning, perception, judgment, decision making, and related types of behavior. Brunswik was one of the first to emphasize that simple perceptions of size, distance, and perspective are not univocally determined because real-life situations are ambiguous in that they contain many cues leading to different goals. "One of the . . . tasks of a molar environmental psychology is to find out the extent to which environmental hierarchies of probabilities of object-cue as well as of means-end relationships find a counterpart in similar evaluations by the organism" (1943, p. 259). This position led Brunswik to design a new type of experiment in animal learning wherein reinforcement for the two sides in a simple T maze was 100 and 0 percent; 75 and 25 percent; 67 and 33 percent; 100 and 50 percent; or 50 and 0 percent. One of the combinations, 67 and 33 percent, proved to be below threshold; but the other combinations gave increasing frequency of choices of the more highly rewarded side in the following order: 100–50, 75–25, 50–0, and 100–0 percent (Brunswik, 1939). This type of experiment was also performed in studies of psychophysical judgment by Brunswik and Herma (1951) who showed that when weights were lifted more times with one hand than with the other, contrast effect was greater on the side that lifted more frequently. Contrast is thus affected by probability of occurrence as well as by the usual gradient-difference relation. This experiment was later repeated by Levin who showed that the effect was not merely a result of the relative frequencies of lifting with the two hands but was a function of the summated effects of weights and frequency of lifting. Both serve to establish adaptation levels or indifference points such that judgment of weights presented to each side will be

. . . determined by the difference between the weights and the indifference point existing for each side . . . the bimanual comparison of each pair of weights is . . . not a comparison of the weights presented at the moment but rather a comparison of the differences between each one and the indifference point, or "adaptation level," corresponding to its side (Levin, 1952, p. 532).

The classical experiment linking probability learning and partial reinforcement was performed by Humphreys (1939) as follows: Ss saw two lights, one on the left, the other on the right, and after the left light came on they were asked to guess whether or not the right light would go on. For one group of Ss the right light always came on after the left light, while for another group of Ss the right light came on only half the time in random order following the left light. Following initial trials the right light never came on after the left light. The two groups responded very differently in the extinction trials. The first group needed only one or two omissions of the second light to conclude that it would not be lit, but the second group needed many trials to reach this conclusion. This experiment was the first in a long series of studies continuing into the present. Goodnow and Postman (1955) found that Ss who believed they were behaving in accordance with a principle in matching a key design actually learned to act in accordance with the probabilities underlying addition or subtraction of lines from designs without being aware that the problem was one of probability discrimination. The probabilities in this experiment ranged from 100:0 through 90:10 down to 50:50 in steps of 10.

The question arises if a pure frequency theory can explain results of experiments such as those of Brunswik and Herma, Goodnow and Postman, and Humphreys which we have cited as examples of probability learning and perception. We have seen that Levin, who made a test of the frequency hypothesis, concluded that mere frequency of presentations of the lifted-weight stimuli would not explain the contrasts found in bimanual lifting without taking into account the adaptation levels which are established in the liftings. Is it not also true that the two groups of Ss in Humphreys' experiment had different levels as a result of the different frequencies to which they were exposed with resultant differences in their extinction curves? The omission came with far greater force to the first group, with its 100 percent level established in the initial trials, than to the second group, with its 50 percent expectancy level established initially. Hence the first group reached the decision that the light on the right would not appear more rapidly than the second group did.

That effects of partial reinforcement must be referred to level receives strong support from experiments in which it has been found that *distribution* of reinforcements as well as *frequency* is an important factor in extinction. Sheffield (1949) was able to obtain very different extinction results through variation in spacing of the partially or completely reinforcing stimuli. Using two groups of rats divided into two subgroups, Sheffield gave massed and spaced reinforcement training and massed and spaced extinction trials. She found that with massed training, 50 percent reinforcement gave greater resistance to extinction than 100 percent reinforcement, but after spaced training (15 min. between starts as against ½ to 2 min. for massed animals) the groups receiving 100 and 50 percent reinforcement showed no differences in resistance to extinction. Jenkins and Rigby (1950) found partial reinforcement yielded about 40 percent more responses in extinction trials than did continuous reinforcement, but they regarded their data as contrary to Humphreys' results, perhaps because they stress that partial reinforcement may be given in various patterns, i.e., after a given number of trials, after a fixed length of time, randomly, and so on. They point out that extinction results depend upon the patterns of reinforcement; but this is precisely what the opponents of frequency theories assert!

Residual effects in probability learning. Under laboratory conditions it is possible to vary the amount of reinforcement at will, and there can be no doubt that conditions of daily life also provide various degrees of reinforcement to individuals. Under both conditions reinforcement presumably arouses differential expectancies. Stevenson and Zigler (1958) have hypothesized that the expectancies aroused by partial reinforcement administered and tested in a laboratory setting may be a function, not only of the experimental conditions, but also of the expectancy levels of *S*s *prior* to exposure in the laboratory. They investigated the effects of discrepancies between expected and obtained reinforcement with special attention to the influence of such discrepancies upon variability of responses in the test trials. They tested the hypothesis that variability would increase as the obtained frequency of reinforcement decreased below the expected level of reinforcement. By using groups of *S*s whose expectancy levels differed before entering into the test situation, they were able to determine the effects of given amounts of partial reinforcement in the laboratory as related to level of reinforcement in the daily life of the individuals. The *S*s in the Stevenson and Zigler experiments were groups of normal and feeble-minded children equated for mental age but differing in chronological age. The normal group averaged 5.5 years with MAs of around 6 years and the feeble-minded group averaged 12.8 years with MAs around 6.1 years. The task which was partially reinforced in the learning trials required the *S*s to push one of three knobs, right, middle, or left, which dispensed marbles through a slot. A red light served as signal to push the knob and made possible measurement of the latency of responses. The positions of the correct knobs were randomized among *S*s though one position was always correct for each *S*. In the case of the 66- and

33-percent groups random schedules of reinforcement were employed. After 80 acquisition trials *S*s were given 40 extinction trials during which no reinforcement was employed. Three sets of experiments were therefore performed as follows:

Experiment I. In the initial experiment three groups of normal children were given positive reinforcement in a task involving position discrimination 100, 66, and 33 percent of the time, respectively. On the assumption that normal children come into the experimental situation with high expectancy levels (perhaps around 100 percent) because of the high positive reinforcement they have received at home, it was predicted that the 66- and 33-percent groups would manifest greatest variability and hence give fewer correct responses in the learning trials.

Experiment II. As a check on the first experiment, groups of feeble-minded children were given 66 and 33 percent reinforcement. Since their expectancy level prior to the experiment was lower than that of the normal groups (they came from an institutionalized environment where positive reinforcement can be presumed to be less than in the case of the children from normal homes), it was predicted that the discrepancy between the experimental (learning) situation and their residual levels would be lower than that of the normals, who were given the same partial reinforcement, and that they would therefore perform better than the normals. No difference was expected between the 100-percent reinforced normal groups and the feeble-minded groups.

Experiment III. Here an attempt was made to alter the expectancies with which normal children came into the experimental situation (after learning trials with partial reinforcement) by giving two groups 100 and 33 percent reinforcement on nonlearning tasks, after which both groups were tested on a discrimination problem with 66 percent reinforcement. It was predicted that fewer correct responses would be made by the group which received 100 percent reinforcement in the pretraining sessions than by the 33 percent group. In the case of the 100 percent group, 66 percent reinforcement is a negative discrepancy from the pretraining level, while for the 33 percent group it is a positive discrepancy from their pretraining level; hence more variable behavior was expected from the first than from the second group.

The results fully confirmed the predictions made by Stevenson and Zigler: the 33 percent group in the first experiment never responded even at the chance level; the 100 percent group learned more rapidly than did the 66 percent group; both groups showed negatively accelerated learning curves as a function of trials. Differences in latency and in extinction also appeared between these two groups. The feeble-minded groups, however, showed no significant differences in their learning, no matter how much they were reinforced, a marked contrast with the normal groups. But the 66 and 33 percent feeble-minded groups did better than the normal groups receiving the same degrees of reinforcement. The 100 percent reinforced feeble-minded groups did not differ from the normal 100 percent group as predicted, the difference between 67.5 for the former and 70.1 for the latter being insignificant. Finally, the groups given varying amounts of reinforcement in the pretraining trials were significantly different following the initial 10 learning trials: the 100 percent group chose the correct knob in the learning trials less often than did the 33 percent group, the negative discrepancy from expectation in the learning trials proving to be detrimental to learning, the positive discrepancy proving to be favorable to learning.

We thus find that expectancies established *prior* to the experiments may alter the effects of partial reinforcement. Residuals must therefore be taken into account in dealing with probability learning as well as with classical all-or-none types of reinforcement.

TRANSFER OF LEARNING

One of the most important problems in learning theory is to account for transfer of training from one situation or activity to other more or less similar situations or activities. Theories of transfer have emphasized (1) responses to specific stimuli or (2) responses to the relations between stimuli or to patterns of stimulation. The former are generally called "element" theories and the latter "pattern" theories. Among the element theories which have been influential we may cite those of Pavlov (1927), Thorndike (1911), and Spence (1937). While very different from each other in some respects, element theories are alike in assuming that learning consists in the establishment of specific responses to specific stimuli (cf. Hunter, 1952) and that carry-over effects depend upon some type of "spread" from neural centers activated by these stimuli to other centers activated by similar stimuli. Theories of stimulus or response generalization are of this type.

The model for most pattern theories is Köhler's structure-function concept (1925) according to which learning is not a matter of establishing responses to particular stimuli but rather consists in the apprehension of the structural or functional aspects of the stimulus situation. According to this view transfer of training occurs to new situations whether or not identical or similar elements are present, provided that functional relations are perceived in the new stimulus configurations which are the same as, or similar to, the ones in the original learning.

Different as element and pattern theories are, they are very much alike in what they fail to take into account. Neither makes provision for contextual or background effects and the interaction of these with focal stimuli (elements, relations, patterns) during learning and transfer trials. A test of the element and pattern theories was made in a study by Kaplan and Helson (1950) as follows: Ss were shown five gray squares mounted on black background arranged in random order and were asked to choose one. They were then informed whether their choice was right or wrong. The grays had reflectances of 15, 20, 28, 50, and 62 percent. The reflectance of 28 percent was called the correct stimulus, and after Ss made five correct choices in succession, the same stimuli were then presented on white background. The first choice of the correct stimulus on the new background constituted the test of transfer of training. According to element theories, the gray having 28 percent reflectance should have been chosen from among the five grays on the white background because it was identical with the training stimulus; and according to pattern theories it should have been chosen because it occupied the same position in the lightness pattern or scale on white background as it did on the black background. If, however, transfer is based on similarity, i.e., the same gradient of excitation taken with respect to AL, then the stimulus of 50 or 62 percent reflectance should be chosen on the white background since these stimuli had approximately the same lightness on the white background that the training stimulus had on the black background as calculated by Judd's lightness formula given on p. 277. Of the 62 Ss, 53 percent chose the stimulus having 50 percent reflectance; 8 percent chose the stimulus having 62 percent reflectance; 32 percent chose the stimulus having 28 percent reflectance; and the remaining 7 percent chose the stimulus having 20 percent reflectance. Hence 61 percent of the Ss chose in accordance with similarity of the stimuli in the learning and transfer trials, 32 chose the identical (element) or middle (pattern) stimulus, and the remaining 7 percent chose in accordance with none of the theories discussed here.

The experiment just described was done independently by Campbell and Kral (1958) using parakeets as subjects. They also found that a shift in background produced a shift in response away from a familiar card which had been rewarded to a familiar card which had never been rewarded. Six birds were taught to eat from a food dish over which a card was placed having a lightness value of 3 and to avoid a dish with cards having lightness values of 1 and 5.[2] Training was given with background lightness of value 4. After 20 correct choices in the training period, food dishes with covers of values 1 and 3 were presented on background having a lightness value of 2. In the 20 transposition trials the birds chose the dish with the card of value 1 rather than the card of value 3, the frequencies being 17, 16, 14, 17, 18, and 9 for the six birds. Campbell and Kral maintained that the animals transferred by similarity since the card of value 1 on background of value 2 was most nearly equivalent to the card of value 3 on background of value 4. In view of the choices made by *S*s in our study we can say that transfer depends on similarity of quality as well as on similarity of relations or structure, depending upon the conditions of training and test trials.

It is becoming recognized by students of animal learning that absolute intensity of stimulation per se is not sufficient to account for the learning of discrimination (Bragiel and Perkins, 1954; Perkins, 1953; Johnsgard, 1957; Riley, 1958). In visual discrimination the contrast between the stimulus and the background against which it appears may serve to enhance stimulus value. Thus, rats responding to white on black background exhibit shorter latencies than rats responding to black on white background. Hull (1951), quoted by Johnsgard (1957), referred to results similar to those of Bragiel and Perkins in support of his stimulus-dynamism concept. Bragiel and Perkins found that rats responded significantly more rapidly to a black stimulus on white background than to a white stimulus on black background. Johnsgard repeated their study, employing backgrounds of intermediate reflectance (gray) and stimuli that were higher, lower, or near the background reflectance. He found that stimulus dynamism operates in accordance with *contrast* relations rather than in terms of absolute intensity. Johnsgard also interpreted the conflicting results in the literature as springing

[2] The authors refer to the reflectances of their stimuli and backgrounds by ordinal number as follows:

Ordinal number	1	2	3	4	5
Reflectance	.32	.41	.61	.73	.83

from the fact that workers investigated only limited ranges of the lightness continuum with stimuli either very near or rather distant from background reflectance. Johnsgard concluded that both his results and those of Bragiel and Perkins support a contrast interpretation of stimulus intensity dynamism. What Johnsgard regards as a contrast phenomenon is essentially what we have referred to as similarity of gradients from level.

Although identical stimuli were employed by Kaplan and Helson in the training and transfer trials, with background as the variable, it is more usual to employ different stimuli with the same background in the learning and critical sessions. In our study the stimuli were perceived differently as a result of change in background reflectance even though the relations among the stimuli and their physical properties were maintained the same in the learning and transfer trials. James (1953) has dealt with the problem of transfer of training when the stimuli are different in the transfer situation from what they were in the training conditions. In applying the concept of adaptation level to explain the findings of several investigators he made the following assumptions:

1. In the process of training there is established in the subject a neutral level corresponding to the adaptation level when one of two stimuli is reinforced.
2. The subject learns to avoid stimuli which are more intense and to approach those which are less intense than the neutral or vice versa.
3. The process of establishing a neutral point is independent of reward and punishment although these may affect the character of the responses on either side of the adaptation level.
4. When new stimuli are presented to the subject, they will produce a gradual change in the position of the adaptation level, and the rate of shift will depend upon such factors as number of trials, distribution of practice, and intelligence.

From these assumptions James pointed out that if the critical stimuli fall one on either side of the adaptation level, perfect transfer will result. If both stimuli fall on the same side of the adaptation level responses will be random with respect to the critical cue until continued experience with the test stimuli has shifted the adaptation level in the appropriate direction. The critical test of this formulation of the transfer problem was made by James in using the weighted log mean formula in Equation (2) below to calculate the neutral points for the conditions obtaining in a number of studies. James thus accounted for both positive and negative cases of transfer found by previous investigators.

In proposing the adaptation level approach to problems of learning and transfer James criticized both Gestalt and S-R theories of stimulus equivalence as lacking a step-by-step account of the successive coordinations and differentiations which lift behavior above the level of the schematic reflex. It is important to know, according to James, how the organism may be influenced by general states and yet respond to a particular stimulus in a particular way; and he pointed out that the psychophysical relations necessary for the study of similarity within the framework of, for example, Hull's theory cannot be determined (1953, p. 345). A step-by-step account of learning and transfer behavior was made by Smith (1956) in a study of background effects on learning and transposition of lightness discriminations. The subjects were 24 groups of high school students and 24 groups of second-grade children, with 4 in each group. Smith presented two grays on either a black, gray, or white background in 10 successive trials until one was correctly chosen, after which the same two grays were presented on one of the two other backgrounds and the number of correct choices in 10 critical presentations was noted. The stimuli, presented in pairs to the various groups, were Munsell gray papers with Munsell values of 2.5–3.0, 3.5–6.0, 4.5–5.0, and 8.5–9.0 on backgrounds of 2.0 (black), 4.75 (gray), or 9.2 (white). The stimuli were chosen so as to be above or below the background in lightness or to straddle the background lightness. The stimuli were 2×2 in. mounted on white, gray, or black backgrounds of 12×12 in.

In Smith's study, as in that by Kaplan and Helson, the stimuli were the same in both learning and transfer trials, but owing to change of background they were *perceptually* different on the new backgrounds. If Ss did not reach the criterion of 10 consecutive correct choices in the learning trials within 50 exposures, the learning was terminated and a score of 50 was assigned. Six sequences of learning-transfer backgrounds were employed: black to gray, gray to black, gray to white, white to gray, white to black, and black to white. Transfer was assumed to occur if at least 8 of the 10 responses in the critical trials were to the positive stimulus of the learning trials. Since there were only two stimuli, the positive stimulus bore the same relation to the negative stimulus in the transfer trials that it had in the learning trials, and it should have been chosen according to element and pattern theories, in which choice of the positive stimulus depends only on identity of stimulus or on the relation between the stimuli. But according to AL theory the differential contrast effects of the three backgrounds must also be taken into account in the learning and transfer situations. Such effects may lead to quite different predictions of which stimulus will be chosen in the transfer trials.

Two important factors are operative in both learning and transfer: (1) ease of discriminating the stimuli, one of which is positive and the other negative; (2) relation of the stimuli to the levels operative in learning and in the transfer conditions. Smith made the following assumptions regarding ease of learning to choose the positive stimulus: the number of trials to reach criterion is directly related to the difference between the average lightness of the stimuli being discriminated and the adaptation level based on all objects in the field of view, and it is inversely related to the difference between the stimuli. Symbolically,

$$N_r = f\left[\frac{A - \overline{S}}{S_2 - S_1}\right] \tag{1}$$

where N_r is trials to learn the positive stimulus, f is "function of," A is adaptation reflectance, $\overline{S}$ is the average reflectance of S_1 and S_2, the stimuli to be discriminated. The value of A is taken to be a weighted log mean as defined in Chapter 4:

$$\log A = \frac{\sum_1^n \log X_i/n + 3.0 \log B}{4} \tag{2}$$

where X_i refers to the reflectances of the stimuli on background reflectance B, and n is the number of stimuli. Since the number of trials to learn must be a positive number, values of the numerator and denominator in Equation (1) are always taken as positive.

The numerator in Equation (1) is based on the assumption that the greater the difference between the average reflectance of the stimuli and adaptation reflectance, the larger will be the number of trials to learn to choose the positive stimulus. Since A is largely determined by B, especially with only two stimuli in the field, the numerator of Equation (1) really embodies the common finding that it is more difficult to establish a positive response to one of a pair of reflectances far from background reflectance than to members of pairs that straddle background reflectance, e.g., one gray lighter than the background, the other darker.

The denominator in Equation (1) is based on the assumption that the greater the difference between the stimuli, the easier it is to discriminate between them and hence to establish a positive response to one. Values of N_r yield only rank order or relative difficulty of learning the correct stimulus if the function, f, is not determined. Since individuals of widely different ages served as Ss, there is also an age factor which influences the results. It was assumed that the second-grade Ss would require a larger number of trials than high school Ss to reach learning criterion, and this assumption was found to be true in 7 of the 12 learning conditions; in 3 of the conditions the high school Ss required more learning trials than the second graders but only by insignificant amounts.

It should be noted that small values of N_r may arise either from small values of the numerator or large values of the denominator of Equation (1). The learning situations involving small values of the numerator and large values of the denominator were expected to be easy for both the young and adult groups. Conditions involving moderately large values of the numerator and small values of the denominator (0.5 Munsell value difference) were expected to be moderately difficult for the second-grade Ss and easy for high school Ss. Large values of the numerator with small values of the denominator were expected to be very difficult for the young Ss and moderately difficult for the high school Ss. As shown in Table 7.1, for the young group the designations were as follows: easy for six conditions with N_r values ranging from 0.02 to 1.22; moderately difficult for four conditions, N_r values 2.9 to 6.1; and difficult for two conditions, N_r values 8.5 to 11.3. In the case of the high school group they were: easy for ten conditions, N_r values 0.02 to 6.3; moderately difficult for two conditions, Nr values 8.5 to 11.3; with none designated as difficult. These assessments of the difficulty of learning the stimulus combinations on the various backgrounds were based in part upon some preliminary results in a pilot study made with the two age groups. However, no pilot observations were made with the 2.5 and 3.0 stimuli or with the 8.5 and 9.0 stimuli, and the predictions of these discriminations was based solely upon the N_r values.

From Table 7.1 it is seen that the difficulty ranking of the various

TABLE 7.1. Predicted Difficulty and Observed Trials to Learn Correct Stimulus under Various Stimulus-Background Conditions by Two Groups of Ss

N_r	Stimulus-Background Conditions	Second-grade Ss		High School Ss	
		Prediction	Trials to Learn	Prediction	Trials to Learn
0.82	3.5 and 6.0 on Black	Easy	14.6	Easy	15.1
0.02	3.5 and 6.0 on Gray		12.2		16.5
1.22	3.5 and 6.0 on White		13.1		13.7
0.10	4.5 and 5.0 on Gray		12.7		12.5
1.10	2.5 and 3.0 on Black		17.1		11.4
0.70	8.5 and 9.0 on White		14.5		16.2
4.30	4.5 and 5.0 on Black	Moderately Difficult	28.3		20.6
6.10	4.5 and 5.0 on White		30.0		18.2
2.90	2.5 and 3.0 on Gray		50.0		43.0
6.30	8.5 and 9.0 on Gray		34.0		16.3
8.50	2.5 and 3.0 on White	Difficult	50.0	Moderately Difficult	33.5
11.30	8.5 and 9.0 on Black		50.0		43.4

SOURCE: From Smith, 1956.

stimulus-background combinations, derived from Equation (1), are in high agreement with the actual number of trials required to learn the correct response. The notable exception is the 2.5 and 3.0 stimuli on gray background, which could not be learned by the second-grade group and was moderately difficult instead of easy for the high school group. It was later found that these stimuli were not discriminable, when a test was made with four high school students who had not been *S*s in the main experiment. These *S*s were asked to report any perceived difference between the two stimuli as they advanced from a distance toward the apparatus. Three of the four *S*s could not consistently indicate the darker of these two stimuli and the fourth *S* could do so only after considerable study. Only by holding the stimuli in their hands and examining them closely could the 2.5 and 3.0 lightness values be consistently discriminated. It therefore appears that the half-lightness step between 2.5 and 3.0 in these Munsell papers was not as large as the half-steps between 4.5 and 5.0 and between 8.5 and 9.0 (also used in this experiment).

We now have to formulate an expression for the conditions governing transfer by taking into account the relations of the stimuli to both the learning and the transposition conditions. To account for the results found in the transfer trials Smith assumed that the number of incorrect choices with the stimuli presented on the new background would be a direct function of the magnitude of the *difference* between the adaptation level established during the training trials and the adaptation level in the transfer trials, and an inverse function of the difference between the stimuli. Symbolically,

$$E_r = f\left[\frac{A_L - A_T}{S_1 - S_2}\right] \tag{3}$$

where E_r represents the relative number of incorrect choices in the transfer situations, A_L is the adaptation level established during the learning trials, A_T is the adaptation level in the transfer trials, S_1 and S_2 are the stimuli, and f stands for "is function of." Again, the adaptation level is calculated according to Equation (2), using the reflectance of the new background; both numerator and denominator are again taken as positive.

It is evident that the numerator of Equation (3) expresses the assumption that the AL established during the training trials would act as a residual during the transposition trials. The further assumption was also made that the greater the difference between the training and transposition levels, the less likelihood there would be that the correct stimulus would be chosen in the critical trials. Since the correct choices in the critical trials were not rewarded and no comment was made to indicate whether or not responses were correct or satisfactory to the experimenter, the critical trials served only to determine the relative difficulties of the various training and transposition conditions. A condition that helps to differentiate the stimuli, for example, 2.5 and 3.0 on black background, is easier both to learn and to transpose than a condition which diminishes discriminability, for example, 2.5 and 3.0 on white background. The denominator in the equation for transposition, Equation (3), is the same as the denominator in Equation (1) and so needs no discussion.

Smith's study has made clear that not all learning and transposition conditions are equally easy and that both practice and critical tests depend in large measure upon the difficulty of the task. In the pilot study it was found, in accordance with expectations, that all Ss in both age groups would be able to transpose a discrimination involving stimuli with lightness values of 4.5 and 5.0 from a black background to a gray background; but they were not able to transpose correctly when the same stimuli were learned on a gray background and the critical trials were made on a white background. Hence contextual factors are as important in determining transfer of training as are the focal stimuli.

Let us now return to the actual transposition results. The transposition-difficulty scores yielded by Equation (3) are given in Table 7.2 along with the average number of errors made by the various groups of Ss in the two age levels. Since the criterion of transposition was at least 8 out of 10 correct choices in the critical trials (a criterion that was adopted *before* the experimental Ss were run), values of less than 2 mean that transposition occurred. The agreement of theory with experimental data can be seen by comparing the values in the columns headed "Errors" with the E_r values and with the predictions given in parenthese (T and NT). E_r values of 4.40 or less were expected to yield transposition, those above 5.0 were not.

From Table 7.2 it is seen that transposition, or failure to transfer the correct response to the new background, was correctly predicted for 10 of the 12 stimulus-background conditions in the case of both age groups. It should be noted that three of the four incorrect predictions involved stimuli (2.5 and 3.0) which were later found to be below threshold of discrimination for *S*s tested at the viewing distance used in the experiments.

TABLE 7.2.   Average Number of Errors in Critical Trials and
Predictions of Transposition

Stimulus-Background Training and Critical Conditions	E_r	Errors	
		High School Subjects	Second-grade Subjects
3.5–6.0			
B to G; G to B	0.88	0.00 (T)	2.00 (T)
G to W; W to G	1.20	0.25 (T)	1.88 (T)
B to W; W to B	2.08	0.00 (T)	3.88 (T)[a]
4.5–5.0			
B to G; G to B	4.40	0.75 (T)	1.57(T)
G to W; W to G	6.00	3.38 (NT)	4.38 (NT)
B to W; W to B	10.40	3.63 (NT)	5.83 (NT)
2.5–3.0			
B to G; G to B	4.00	5.25 (T)[a]	5.25 (T)[a]
G to W; W to G	5.60	4.50 (NT)	
B to W; W to B	9.60	1.57 (NT)[a]	3.50 (NT)
8.5–9.0			
B to G; G to B	5.00	3.00 (NT)	5.00 (NT)
G to W; W to G	7.00	6.75 (NT)	5.86 (NT)
B to W; W to B	12.00	3.33 (NT)	3.25 (NT)

Note: B = black; G = gray; W = white; T = transposition predicted; NT = transposition not predicted.
[a] Contrary to prediction.
SOURCE: From Smith, 1956.

The data confound learning-transfer orders of backgrounds, i.e., learning on gray background followed by transfer trials on white background is not distinguished from learning on white background followed by critical trials on gray background. Breakdown of the performance of each of 192 *S*s (96 in each age group) reveals individual differences both in number of trials to learn and in number of errors made in the critical transfer trials. Smith's assumption that there would be significant differences between the two age groups in the number of trials to learn but not in the transfer trials was borne out by statistical analysis of the results. It thus appears that once a discrimination is learned, transfer depends solely upon the new conditions rather than on developmental level in this particular type of task.

Smith reported a number of cases of "negative transfer" wherein Ss trained to respond to the lighter of the two stimuli consistently chose the darker member of the pair on the new background and conversely, those trained in darker chose the lighter. Whether or not this type of "error" was due to adoption of explicitly formulated hypotheses, such as "Now I must pick the other one," or was due to reversal of classical contrast effect must be settled by research directed specifically to this question.

Transfer as a function of differences in tasks. Problems of transfer of training have generally been envisaged in terms of degrees of *similarity* of elements, relations, techniques, or methods in the original and new learning situations; but as Szafran and Welford (1950) point out, this is only one approach. Another is to determine how performance on one task alters performance on another task. The two tasks may differ in difficulty (Szafran and Welford, 1950; Heim, 1957), in familiarity (Gibbs, 1951), in use of optimal or nonoptimal manipulanda (Helson, 1949), in conditions of practice, as in variation of intertrial intervals (Adams, 1954), and in other attributes of tasks and learning conditions. In the experiment by Szafran and Welford the same task was varied by introducing features that made performance more difficult. Their Ss threw loops of light-weight chain at a target 8 ft. away under three conditions: (1) directly; (2) over a horizontal bar 32 in. above the ground and 5.5 ft. away, with the target visible under the bar; and (3) with the target visible in a mirror placed behind a screen at the same height and distance as the bar. Groups of Ss practiced throwing at the target under the three conditions in different orders. It was found that practice with bar and screen first resulted in positive transfer to the easiest, direct condition while there was small negative transfer from direct and far to screen. Thus there was positive transfer from the harder to the easier task and slight negative transfer from the easier to the harder tasks. As the authors pointed out, these results are not explainable in terms of stimulus or response similarity since these concepts would predict results different from the ones actually found.

Evidence supporting the thesis that transfer is greater from more difficult to less difficult tasks than from easy to difficult tasks was also provided by Gibbs (1951) who studied tracking performance. Initial practice with opposed motions of handwheel control and target (unfamiliar arrangement) speeded learning the familiar, direct relation between handwheel and target motions. Gibbs interpreted his findings in terms of levels of ability required for the initial and subsequent tasks and pointed out that practice on easy tasks does not necessarily develop abilities to deal with difficult tasks, level of ability being limited by the content of the initial task.

A study by Bevan and Saugstad (1955) utilized a psychophysical setup to study transfer from tasks requiring discriminations of large or small step intervals between stimuli to a task requiring discrimination of very small step intervals. In this study groups judged series of stimuli in the 200–400 grm. range which differed by 40, 10, or 7.5 grm. and then transferred to a series differing by only 4 grm. in the 84–116 grm. range. The group judging the 40-grm. intervals in the pretraining trials did better on the finer discriminations required in the test series than did three other groups that judged series in which the step intervals were much nearer those of the critical series. Moreover, the control group, which had no pretraining, was next to the best group in two of the three criterion measures. In view of similar findings by Lawrence (1952) of visual discrimination in animals, it seems certain that the superiority of practice with wide step intervals between stimuli was not an artifact arising from the type of materials employed (lifted weights), the nature of the discrimination, or the use of human *S*s.

It thus appears that no generalization can be made regarding superiority of transfer from easy-to-difficult or difficult-to-easy tasks. Indeed, Gibbs, in the study just discussed, showed that when measures other than performance measures on the individual tasks are used as the criteria, we cannot say that it is best to begin with harder and proceed to easier tasks. If total learning time or rate of learning is taken as the criterion, easy-to-difficult order may be as good as difficult-to-easy order of learning. Where fine discriminations are required, it may be better to begin learning with coarse or large differences rather than with fine differences that are difficult because *S*s may become frustrated or despair of achieving the required level of performance and may give up early in their training. The task must be sufficiently difficult to interest and engage the subject but not so difficult as to frustrate and thwart him (cf. Lewin, Dembo, Festinger, and Sears who pointed out that individuals set goals within upper and lower bounds of difficulty, 1944).

Influence of context on generalization gradients. Closely related to transfer of learning, and perhaps a special case of transfer, are the twin phenomena of stimulus and response generalization. When a response to a stimulus is learned it is found that stimuli more or less like the conditioned stimulus (CS) are responded to in varying degrees. In terms of such measures as number of choices of new stimuli, drops of saliva secreted, response latency, or running time, the maximal or optimal values are elicited by CS with diminished responses to other stimuli the less they resemble CS. That maximal response is not made to CS in cases of "relational" transfer has been known since the work of Köhler (1925) and others; but the fact that generalization gradients depend upon the context of stimulation has only recently been shown by Thomas and Jones (1962). In their study, five groups of ten Ss each were shown a standard visual stimulus of 525 μm (middle green) for 60 sec. and then were asked to identify this stimulus when it appeared among a series of five stimuli randomly presented. In each of the series this stimulus occupied different positions, as seen from the composition of the five series: for group I the series consisted of 485–525 μm in 10 μm steps; for group II, 495–535 μm; for group III, 505–545 μm; for group IV, 515–555 μm; and for group V, 525–565 μm. The critical stimulus, therefore, was at or near the bottom, middle, and top of the series. The results appear in Fig. 7.2, where it is seen that the maximal frequency with which a stimulus was identified as the standard stimulus depended upon the context of stimuli presented each group. In the lowest series, where the standard was the topmost stimulus, it was not the modal choice, which was one step below, viz., 515 μm. Similarly, in the next series, 515 μm, not 525 μm, was identified most often as the stimulus previously exposed for 60 sec. Only where 525 μm was at the center of the series or displaced one step above center did it receive the modal number of choices. Finally, in the highest series (group V) the modal choice moved up to 535 μm. For all groups the modal response was displaced toward the center of the distribution of test stimuli. As pointed out by Thomas and Jones, this experiment was concerned with Ss' ability to identify a previously experienced stimulus in a new context and thus involved the type of response typical of generalization experiments. From these results (Fig. 7.2) it is apparent that the stimulus-generalization curve does not necessarily reach its peak with the training stimulus but rather depends on the properties each stimulus has by virtue of its relation to prevailing level.

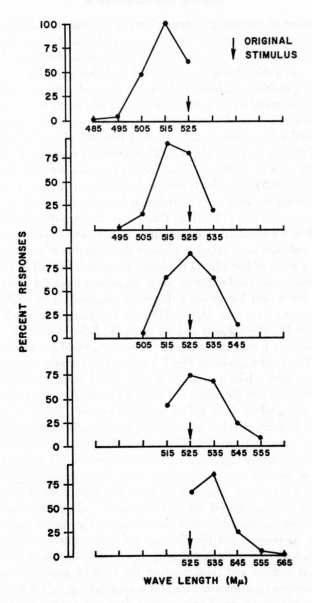

FIG. 7.2. Generalization gradients as a function of the series of stimuli used to determine frequencies of responses. (From Thomas and Jones, 1961. With the permission of the American Psychological Association.)

The results of Thomas and Jones are striking because they cannot be explained by simultaneous or successive contrast or by Pavlovian "irradiation." It has long been known that the hues of spectral stimuli vary as the colors adjacent to them are changed, a phenomenon usually thought to involve simultaneous contrast; but in their experiment, the stimuli were exposed successively in random order so this explanation must be ruled out. Similarly, displacement of the maximum of the generalization gradient away from CS and toward the center of the series stimuli also rules out Pavlovian irradiation and theories based on similar assumptions. Rather, we must assume that stimulus generalization depends, not only upon specific properties of individual stimuli, but also upon their relations to other stimuli and the state of the organism. This is only a roundabout way of saying that transfer and generalization gradients depend upon prevailing AL.

The classical generalization curve must be regarded as a special case which appears when CS is repeated without variation. It is not found in non-Pavlovian types of learning, e.g., in the Harlow type of learning situation, where Ss are presented with a variety of problems of the same level of difficulty during each stage of the learning process. From this type of study Harlow concluded:

The behavior of the human being is not to be understood in terms of the results of single learning situations but rather in terms of the changes which are effected through multiple though comparable learning problems. . . . Training on several hundred specific problems has not turned the monkey into an automaton exhibiting forced, stereotyped, reflex responses to specific stimuli. These several hundred habits have, instead, made the monkey an adjustable creature with *increased capacity* to adapt to ever-changing demands of a psychology laboratory environment (1949, pp. 51, 59).

In everyday life as well as in many present-day laboratory situations Ss are faced with *classes* of stimuli, not with a single stimulus repeated without variation. When the same stimulus qua stimulus reappears it usually comes in a new context of stimulation under natural conditions of learning. In such cases generalization gradients do not maximize at specific stimulus values and then decrease monotonically on either side of the modal values. Rather, ranges of stimuli are responded to "maximally" or with equal probabilities as in the Harlow learning situation. Stimuli that do not belong to the given class elicit chance responses or no responses as long as other features of the situation are the same. This interpretation covers results of the experiments of Harlow and Thomas and Jones and the special case of Pavlovian conditioning; it calls for more study of learning situations involving ranges of stimuli and contextual effects rather than study of acquisition of responses to specific stimuli as in classical learning and conditioning.

As examples of learning involving responses to a range of conditions let us consider two types of what has been called "psychomotor" learning, one studied by Adams (1954) and the other by Helson (unpublished Foxboro work). In the latter, Ss aligned a moving constant-speed pointer with a stationary index by putting in an opposing motion by means of a rotary handwheel control. The amount or rate of movement required to align the two elements was 10.1, 20.3, 39.9, 80.4, or 140.0 rpm. Deviation, or tracking error, was assessed in terms of the time in msec. necessary to align the pointer and the stationary index if no additional movement were imparted to the pointer. In other words, space error was translated into time error (for a fuller discussion of this point see Helson, 1949). The rate of turning necessary for perfect performance was governed by the gear ratios in the handwheel-pointer linkages. Turning speeds were randomized so that Ss received practice with all five turning rates in each practice hour.

The results, shown in Fig. 7.3, represent averages of four Ss for 8 hr. of practice, each hour on a different day. The parameter for the five curves is turning speed. It is seen that tracking error decreases at all turning speeds with successive hours of practice and that performance in each practice hour is better, the higher up the required turning rates are toward the breaking rates (not shown) of individual Ss (usually between 150 and 200 rpm). Comparison of Fig. 7.3 with Fig. 3.8 shows that whether turning speeds or practice hours are considered, the respective shapes of the error curves are much the same, being concave upward in general. The slopes of the performance curves depend upon turning rate as well as upon amount of practice, each independent variable having its own slope.

Of great practical importance is the finding from these studies that performance is better with little or no practice in the case of optimal turning rates than after hours of practice with the poorer (slower) rates. Thus the average time error during the *first* hour of practice with 140.0 rpm is 17.1 msec., while after the *eighth* hour of practice

with 10.1 rpm the error is 22.9 msec. If we compare performance having
the best with that having the poorest turning rate during the first hour,
the error with 140.0 rpm is, as just stated, 17.1 msec.; but with 10.1
rpm. it is 61.8 msec. or about 350 percent poorer! Moreover, comparison
of individual results shows that the poorer operators profit more by
the optimal turning speeds than do the better operators, a fact verified
in a tracking study by Gibbs (1951).

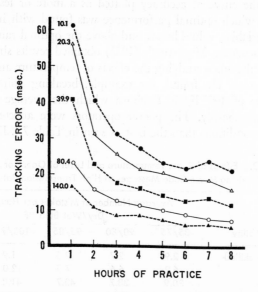

FIG. 7.3. Showing decrease in tracking error in successive hours of practice
with all rates of turning. Performance with optimal handwheel speeds (80.4 to
140.0 rpm) is better during the first hour of practice than with a poor condition
(10.1 rpm) after eight hours of practice.

In the study by Adams (1954) we find that the slope and final level
of tracking curves depend upon intertrial rest interval, each interval
giving its own characteristic curve. While all curves are similar in
shape, being negatively accelerated as a function of successive trials,
the curves derived from the longer intertrial rest intervals are steeper
and have higher time-on-target asymptotes than those embodying data
with the shorter intertrial intervals. Performance level is thus related
to the spacing between the practice intervals.

While Adams found increasing accuracy as intertrial rest intervals increased from 0 to 30 sec. this study does not tell us whether or not there is a limit to the beneficial effects of lengthened intertrial interval. With respect to speed of handwheel turning and other conditions of manipulanda, we found in the Foxboro studies (Helson, 1949) that increases in size, weight, and other characteristics of handwheels aided performance up to certain points, after which there were more or less sharp breaks, usually because physiological limits were exceeded. In such cases the curve of accuracy plotted as a more or less U-shaped function in which optimal performance was found with intermediate values of variables, values below and above the optimal range yielding poorer performance. Mackworth (1952) obtained results similar to the Foxboro results when studying the effects of temperature and humidity on performance. He found, for example, breaking points at room temperatures of 100° F/90° F above which the average number of mistakes rose sharply. The poorer operators were affected more by the adverse conditions than the best as seen in Table 7.3. Data are not

TABLE 7.3.   Effects of Room Temperature and Level of Operator Ability on Receiving Morse Code Messages at High Transmission Rates

Operator Ability	Average Number of Mistakes per Hour per Man Dry/Wet Bulb °F				
	85/75	90/80	95/85	100/90	105/95
Exceptionally skilled	2.9	2.7	2.5	1.9	6.2
Very good	6.2	6.6	7.9	12.0	99.8
Competent	30.9	28.7	40.7	41.8	174.9

SOURCE: From Mackworth, 1952. With the permission of the author.

given for the low end of the temperature-humidity range, where we would expect performance to break sharply. It is highly probable that there may be conditions that do not yield U-shaped functions. Curves of this type are so often found, however, that it is natural to assume that the U-shaped function holds until disproved under specific conditions of performance.

It is evident from studies of tracking and various other types of performance (Payne and Hauty, 1954, 1955a, 1955b) that both outer and inner factors affecting learning and skills do not result in acquisition of specific stimulus-response units. Rather it appears that characteristics of manipulanda, ambient conditions like temperature, humidity, and oxygen tension, drugs, spacing of trials, and attitudinal and motivational factors determine levels of activity with respect to kinds or classes of stimulus-response relationships.

Latent learning. The discussion of background factors in learning leads us to questions of latent learning, secondary reinforcement, and other facets of the role played by nonfocal stimuli in behavior. The problem of latent learning has aroused considerable controversy among learning theorists largely because proponents and antagonists alike have tended to take an all-or-none position about whether there is such a thing. In accordance with our assumption that *all* stimuli confronting the organism in any stimulus-response situation have some effect on the *organism* and that the state of the organism is of fundamental importance in all behavior, it follows that the existence or efficacy of latent learning cannot be decided on a "yes" or "no" basis for all situations. Since latent learning concerns the effects of nonfocal, secondary stimuli, we must ask in each case: To what extent do nonfocal stimuli affect given types of behavior? In some cases background stimuli may be of minor, perhaps negligible importance compared with focal stimuli; in other cases background stimuli may be very important in perception and learning either through their effect on focal stimuli or more directly by acting as signs, cues, signals, or orienting elements in complex situations. A very young child often cries in strange surroundings but is less likely to do so if held in the mother's arms. In the latter case it might be assumed that the child is unaffected by the surroundings, and some might go so far as to assert that the child does not perceive the environment. But let the mother leave and crying starts, not merely because of the absence of the mother, since the child does not cry every time he is left alone in familiar circumstances, but rather because of the novel situation. In emergencies domestic animals often resort to short cuts which they have never before used but which they have learned indirectly in travels around their neighborhoods.

In humans *verbalization* may be an important factor in latent learning and may act as a secondary (self) reinforcer. Thus Postman, Adams, and Phillips (1955) found that cue words nearer in meaning to a memorized list of words exerted greater effect on recall than did words farther removed from the learned list. Often verbalization is accompanied by, or indicative of, a correct grasp of problems, and it has sometimes been made the differentiating factor between insightful and trial-and-error learning. Stevenson and Iscoe (1954) found in one study that the *amount* of transfer in learning size discriminations was related to the extent to which young subjects verbalized the stimulus relationships; but in a subsequent study (1955) they found that defective children who could not verbalize the relation were also able to transfer in the critical trials. Verbalization may furnish short cuts in learning and problem solving by focalizing cues, relations, and properties of stimuli, thereby increasing their effectiveness. So-called "thought experiments" (*Denkexperimente*) carried on by means of verbalization enable Ss to attempt various solutions without the necessity for manipulating objects, and solutions may thus be found in less time and with fewer errors.

Some light is thrown on this problem in a study by Philbrick and Postman (1955). Ss were given words to which they responded with a number, responses being called "right" or "wrong." The stimulus words varied in length from 2 to 10 letters, and the correct response consisted in giving a number that was less by one than the number of letters in the stimulus word. The problem was considered learned when Ss gave 18 correct responses. The results of the experiment were presented separately to Ss who learned the principle underlying the correct responses and to Ss who did not. Although both groups showed significant learning, the striking finding was that the Ss who verbalized the correct principle had a marked rise in the average number right on the trial preceding the verbalization since the verbalization came *after* the discovery. Philbrick and Postman regarded *the awareness of the principle as equivalent to favorable variation in the stimulus complex.* Verbalization thus functioned as a surrogate for stimulus and/or response variation.

The results of the experiments we have just discussed support the assumption that effects of incoming stimuli pool more or less automatically in learning and recall in very much the same fashion that they do in sensory and judgmental phenomena. Just as in psychophysical experiments Ss do not need to be consciously occupied with background and anchor stimuli to be affected by them, so in learning and recall it is not necessary for stimuli to be focal or for Ss to be specifically motivated. Estes (1956) expressed a similar view:

> . . . it is becoming clear that the behavior of human subjects in learning experiments may be modified in predictable ways by such operations as reinforcement or variation of stimulus conditions regardless of whether the subjects are aware of the purpose of the experiment, of what they are learning, or of the variables to which they are responding (p. 21).

CONDITIONING, HABITUATION, AND EXTINCTION

Much mystery has attached to the phenomena of habituation (negative adaptation) and dehabituation (recovery of conditioned responses). In the usual sequence in which these phenomena appear an organism pursuing its daily round of activities is more or less suddenly subjected to conditioning procedures. A dog held in a harness hears a sound of brief duration followed by a bit of meat powder on its tongue. After a number of trials the sound alone is sufficient to bring saliva to the dog's mouth. If the sound is repeated without the meat powder the amount of saliva secreted diminishes until there is none and extinction is said to have occurred. The latter phase is also referred to as negative adaptation or habituation, and it is supposed to appear when conditioned stimuli are not reinforced. A slightly different example of habituation, apparently not a result of conditioning was given in an earlier chapter: "The cage containing a number of frogs is tapped at intervals of about two seconds. The frogs at first react by jumping but if the tapping is continued reaction soon ceases" (Humphrey, 1930*b*, p. 503). While negative adaptation and extinction in the Pavlovian sense can not be completely equated, they are very similar. Dehabituation or spontaneous recovery is the reappearance of a conditioned response that has been extinguished. Again Humphrey gives an easily remembered example: "If the hands are clapped at intervals of 2 or 3 seconds behind an *S*'s back until the wink reflex has disappeared (an example of an unconditioned response that becomes habituated) after a sharp blow on the shoulder, which ordinarily calls out a pronounced wink, the clap of the hands will again elicit the wink reflex" (1930*a*, p. 361).

Although it is usually asserted that extinction occurs because CS is not reinforced, daily life furnishes many examples of constantly reinforced responses that nevertheless extinguish! Consider the soda fountain clerk who is told on beginning his duties that he is free to drink all the chocolate malts he likes. After a few days he consumes less and less and finally hates the sight of a chocolate malted milk. If the reader says, "But ah, satiation enters in," he is perfectly correct! Why has *affective adaptation* been forgotten in reinforcement theory? Why do reinforcers that were originally positive become neutral and then negative? The phenomenon of *affective extinction* followed by reversal of positive to negative affect has received little or no emphasis in learning theories that make reinforcement primary. The importance of affective habituation or negative affective adaptation extends to the most basic needs and drives. Except for a few "neutral" foods, such as potatoes and bread in our western culture and rice in eastern cultures, repeated ingestion of a given food leads to satiation and, if continued, to repulsion. Staple foods do not satiate quickly because being neutral they serve as backgrounds for the tasty viands; but too much of anything, even of the fundamental satisfiers, leads to reversal of affect.

Extinction of responses may be followed by spontaneous recovery or faster conditioning than the original. Organisms are more or less suddenly taken from their "normal" activities and subjected to conditioning procedures. Without reinforcement the learned responses may grow weaker and finally fail to appear. What has happened? Obviously the organism has reverted to the condition it was in with respect to the CS and CR prior to the conditioning. To use Zubin's suggestive term (1958), the organism has reverted to its "idling state." Only when learning involves *vitally* instrumental responses, or full insight into the arousal situation, or profound emotional effects, does extinction fail to occur and can response be said to be fixed.

The artificial nature of Pavlovian conditioning and hence the ease with which it is extinguished can be seen from the following account of the difficulties Brogden had in conditioning his first animal:

I had some serious difficulties with the first dog I tried to condition. I was shown how, I was told how, and I had read how. At the end of several training sessions the dog was not giving any conditioned responses, so at the next session I increased the intensity of the shock. There were still no conditioned responses, so I again increased the intensity of the unconditioned stimulus. On a given trial, the animal struggled, and chewed through the strap that provided for attachment of a lever to the right foot, the foot that was being shocked and that was to be conditioned to the bell-conditioned stimulus. I got some leather, cut it, and riveted it together to make a new strap. When this was attached to the lever and to the dog's foot, I continued the training session. It was not many trials before the animal responded to the bell again by chewing the strap in two. Shortly thereafter my career as a psychologist was giving way to that of a harness maker, and the dog had a stable conditioned response of chewing a strap in two at the sound of a bell. When I sought advice, it was pointed out to me that I was using a shock of too great intensity, the lever strap was too long, the head stock was too high, a collar clip was not being used, and the belly strap was adjusted too loosely. Too much shock produces struggling and disuse activity. A long strap facilitates its being chewed in half. The adjustments of the head stock and belly strap force a posture on the dog from which fore limb flexion can be made only with great difficulty. With the appropriate changes in these experimental conditions, further application of the training procedure resulted in elimination of the conditioned chewing response and quick establishment of a stable, clearly defined conditioned flexion response to the sound of the bell (1951 b, pp. 227–228).

Compare the difficulty of establishing Pavlovian CRs with the ease of conditioning in everyday life and under favorable laboratory conditions. It takes only one strong emotional experience to make one afraid of the dark for the rest of his life or to condition him against a particular food for many years. In such cases nonreinforcement of the response does not lead to extinction. Solomon and Wynne (1954), discussing the results of studies of massive pain-fear reactions instilled by a few intense shocks, found that dogs gave as many as 650 avoidance reactions following termination of shock when the CS appeared, without showing any signs of extinction. Extinction in Pavlovian conditioning procedures follows nonreinforcement because the CRs are essentially nonvital or nonadaptive. Avoidance responses seem to condition more readily and to extinguish less readily than do responses associated with pleasant affect. Since situations eliciting strong avoidance behavior are painful or threatening to the organism their biological utility is readily apparent. This phenomenon has many implications for anxiety arousal and anxiety reduction. Solomon and Wynne explain it in terms of the principle of partial irreversibility of classical conditioning, which has a physical analogue in hysteresis, and which neurophysiologically "might be the permanent reorganization of central nervous system networks" (p. 361). This position is readily translatable into AL terms.

We thus see that current reinforcement theories have difficulty both in accounting for persistence of responses when reinforcement has long since ceased in cases of massive pain-fear reactions and in accounting for the converse phenomenon of habituation or satiation with continued reinforcement. We have suggested that these difficulties largely disappear if account is taken of *affective* adaptation and affective stimulation, especially of negative affect amounting to trauma, as a cause of more or less permanent shifts in level. Ordinary reinforcers change level only temporarily. We can thus understand the phenomena of extinction in ordinary Pavlovian conditioning and the inadequacy of the milder therapeutic measures for alleviation of deep-seated anxieties and depressions. There appears to be a common element here even though the two cases are very different; i.e., the organism reverts to its previous state in that CR extinguishes in the former case and fails to be extinguished in the latter. Recognition of an affective dimension that may vary more or less *independently* of other dimensions may help to clear up the paradoxes of opposed effects of repetition, phenomena of extinction, and the results of intense fear and pain stimulation.

The nonhabituation (nonextinction) of responses associated with unpleasant situations occurs much more frequently both in everyday life and in laboratory studies than is the case with responses associated with pleasantness. If this is generally true, then such an asymmetry should be incorporated in discrepancy-from-level theories of affectivity (Hebb, 1949; McClelland et al., 1953; and Haber, 1958). Hebb's discussion of emotion seems to stress the greater effects of painful, unpleasant stimuli on learning and habituation. According to Hebb the facts of emotional disturbance suggest that in familiar environments conflicts in phase sequences do not occur, but with unfamiliar painful stimuli and in absence of customary stimulation there may be conflicting sequences resulting in cortical disorganization: "up to a certain point, lack of correspondence between expectancy and perception may simply have a stimulating (or 'pleasurable') effect; beyond this point, a disruptive (or unpleasant) effect" (1949, p. 149). If the strange is repeated, there will be a reorganization of assemblies; and change of interassembly facilitation can re-establish the stability of the phase sequences concerned. "With a varied experience, the animal will become less and less dependent on any particular stimulation that is not a constant feature of his environment. This is an effect of learning on emotion, a mechanism of adaptation to the strange" (p. 150). Here Hebb is dealing mainly with disruptive (unpleasant) emotional effects on learning and habituation.

Concerning the failure to neutralize unpleasant stimuli or to make them pleasant by continued exposure, Hunt and Quay (1961) found that although rats reared on vibrating platforms from before birth to 56 days of age pressed a bar to stop the vibration less often than did controls, they did not press the bar more often to restore vibration— in other words to restore their normal environmental conditions. They cite the work of Warren and Pfaffmann (1958) showing that rats raised on drinking water containing a harmless bitter substance rejected it less than did controls when allowed a choice between it and ordinary water, although they preferred the ordinary water. Hunt and Quay also refer to the work of Meier et al. (1960) in which rats weaned at 25 days and exposed to flickering illumination for 65 to 79 days thereafter preferred steady illumination, as did the controls, when allowed to make a choice. There thus seem to be stimuli having positive or negative "innate reinforcement value" according to Hunt and Quay. There are actually two considerations in their presentation: (1) innate affective or reinforcing value of stimuli and (2) asymmetry in the positive-negative discrepancy from level and associated effects. To establish the latter these workers should have subjected animals to positive reinforcement paralleling the negative-reinforcement condition. Their claim that there is an asymmetry in the discrepancy from level of positive and negative affect which invalidates the "butterfly" curve of Haber was not experimentally demonstrated although there is a high probability that it is correct. One can only agree with their conclusion that further investigation of receptor inputs having innate reinforcement is needed.

THE ROLE OF DISTINCTIVENESS IN LEARNING

Focal stimuli are, by definition, in the center of attention and therefore stand out in perception and are responded to more readily than nonfocal stimuli. As we pointed out earlier, stimuli may be focal because of intensity, size, position, frequency, and so on. Generally, stimuli are focal or distinctive to the extent that they differ from the average level of stimulation. Distinctiveness is as important in learning and performance as it is in perception, but it has not figured prominently in most theories of learning. Before a problem or task can be mastered, the relevant stimuli or relations must become focal. With most adult humans verbal instructions are sufficient to activate and direct behavior, as pointed out by Dollard and Miller (1950). (Their concept of "the acquired distinctiveness of cues" was a result of attaching verbal labels to stimuli.) But with children and subhumans it is usually necessary to reinforce responses by other than verbal means to make relevant stimuli focal. The difficulties encountered by reinforcement theories of learning in attempting to deal with effects of negative reinforcement, particularly with the fact that it may facilitate responses as well as inhibit them, are largely obviated once it is recognized that the role of reinforcement is to make stimuli focal as well as to satisfy needs and drives.

A number of studies have shown that distinctiveness, conceived as departure from level, is a potent factor in memory and learning. A quantitative theory of distinctiveness (Murdock, 1960) has succeeded admirably in making possible the prediction of a number of findings in both learning and discrimination. Before taking up the theoretical study let us consider two experimental studies showing that distinctiveness influences the recall of different types of materials.

In the first study Maxwell (1936) found that the greater the departure from social norms or the greater the incongruity of an event with established norms, the more often it was recalled. The common features of everyday experiences, as everyone knows, serve to establish perceptual and behavioral norms usually taken for granted and hence not noticed as such. Departures from such norms, including socially accepted forms of behavior, stand out and are remembered. In Maxwell's experiment *S*s were told a story containing six malapropisms that ranged from subtle to strongly incongruous. The *S*s repeated the story 24 hr. later. The full list of errors and the types of norms which were violated in the story were as follows:

Religion: Father Malone hurried from mass at 7:30 P.M. to attend the dinner party. (Mass is celebrated only in the morning.)

Sports: Sir John was tired from bowling two "overs" in succession. (This is not possible in cricket.)

Social: Sir John's wife was called "Mrs. Tribe." (She should be referred to as "Lady Tribe.")

Everyday life: The electric lights were turned on at 7:30 P.M. although the day was clear. (In Britain the lights would not be turned on this early at the time of year of the experiment.)

Domestic: Dinner began with apple pie. (This is not customary.)

Logical: While eating, one of the guests uttered a shriek and fell over dead with a bullet wound in her head. Sir John rushed to her side and pulled a knife from her heart. (Both the murder and the inconsistent account of how she died were unusual.)

The results showed that small departures from accepted norms were mostly forgotten or omitted in the retelling of the story (e.g., calling Lady Tribe "Mrs. Tribe"), while the widest departures were most often remembered (e.g., eating apple pie first at dinner and the account of the murder).

Frequency *serves to establish norms,* but, contrary to the commonly accepted view, it may not be particularly effective in recall. Stimuli coinciding with level have minimal distinctiveness and hence are remembered less well than stimuli that deviate from established norms or levels of expectancy. The lack of distinctiveness in memory may often be traced back to a lack of distinctiveness in perception, a fact that receives support from the Köhler-von Restorff segregation effect and from other phenomena to which we now turn.

In a study by Nachmias (1958) the items in lists of nonsense syllables varied in size, as shown in Table 7.4, and were presented in

TABLE 7.4. Design of Experiment and Size of Letters

	Height of Letters (cm.)									
Group	0.50	0.63	0.70	0.98	1.22	1.53	1.90	2.38	3.00	3.72	4.66
A–S	CEF	JYZ	MEQ	TOV	WUB	YIL	GAX				
A–L					CEF	JYZ	MEQ	TOV	WUB	YIL	GAX
B–S		WUB	YIL	GAX	CEF	JYZ	MEQ	TOV			
B–L					WUB	YIL	GAX	CEF	JYZ	MEQ	TOV

SOURCE: From Nachmias, 1958. With the permission of the *American Journal of Psychology.*

planned random order to eliminate effects of position. The distinctiveness of the items was taken to be a function of their distance (in either direction) from the adaptation level of the list. The syllables differed in size by 25 percent from one another thus forming a geometric series in which the middle syllable approximated AL. Hence the farther from the middle stimulus any syllable was, the more distinctive it was presumed to be and the easier it should be recalled. As seen from the design of the experiment as given in Table 7.4, the size of the syllables was varied as a whole keeping individual items the same relative to other members of the list (groups A-S vs. A-L and B-L vs. B-S) and also by changing the sizes of items relative to each other (groups A-S vs. B-S and A-L vs. B-L). Fifty-six *S*s, divided into four groups, read the lists aloud six times as the syllables were exposed in random order. They then engaged in a digit-symbol matching task for 45 sec. following which they were given about 60 sec. to recall the syllables learned in the first part of the experiment.

The results, shown in Table 7.5, support the hypothesis that recall depends, at least in part, on the distinctiveness of items: taking the four groups as a whole, the average order of recall of items was lowest for the syllable at AL, next lowest for the syllables on either side of AL, and highest for both the largest and smallest syllables and their

TABLE 7.5.   Mean Order of Recall as a Function of Position in Series

| | Size-rank of Syllables Recalled | | | | | | |
	1	2	3	4	5	6	7
A–L	3.07	4.18	4.21	4.75	4.93	3.56	3.32
A–S	3.71	3.68	3.71	4.57	4.29	4.50	3.54
B–L	3.64	3.86	5.32	5.11	3.79	2.71	3.64
B–S	3.64	3.61	4.71	4.46	4.36	3.29	3.86
Mean	3.51	3.83	4.49	4.72	4.34	3.52	3.59

SOURCE: From Nachmias, 1958. With the permission of the *American Journal of Psychology*.

immediate neighbors. Since the positions of the syllables were varied these effects are not effects of spatial or temporal position but of position in the size hierarchy. Classical serial-position effects are thus seen to be special cases of the more basic and general phenomenon of departure from level.

In a second experiment Nachmias presented a list of words differing in frequency of usage according to the Thorndike-Lorge count. The T-L log frequencies of usage were checked by having Ss rate the words for familiarity; results given in Table 7.6 show a high correla-

TABLE 7.6.   Mean Order of Recall as a Function of Thorndike-Lorge Frequency and Familiarity

| | Stimulus Words | | | | | | | | |
	gasket	mayhem	hanker	sentry	treble	forage	extend	reveal	profit
Log *f*	−0.36	−0.36	−0.26	0.7	0.7	0.7	1.7 to 2.0		
Rating	1.44	1.56	1.78	2.33	1.67	1.78	2.89	3.00	3.00
Recall	3.7	4.1	4.7	6.2	7.8	5.8	4.8	3.8	4.2

SOURCE: From Nachmias, 1958. With the permission of the *American Journal of Psychology*.

tion between the two measures. To establish an AL *S*s read the words aloud six times, were given a digit-symbol matching test for 45 sec., and then were asked to recall. The assumption made by Nachmias was that if the AL was in the central region of frequencies, recall of words after a number of presentations would be poorest for the middle items and better for those at a distance form AL. As seen from the data in Table 7.6, words at and near the log mean of the series rated lowest in order of recall while words at the *low* as well as the high ends rated high in order of recall.

The results of this study are of far-reaching importance. If recall depends upon the state of the organism as well as upon frequency or familiarity, then it is erroneous to assume, as has been done in interpreting results of experiments with meaningful materials, that ease of recall always varies directly with frequency or familiarity regardless of context. Thus much of the controversy over recognition thresholds for words having strong emotional connotations has hinged on the question of degree of the familiarity of the words. Although familiarity is an important determinant of recognition and recall, the study by Nachmias shows that less familiar items may be more distinctive and hence recalled more readily. Once again it has been shown that degree of familiarity and frequency of usage by themselevs do not wholly determine associative processes. At first sight it might seem that we are here dealing merely with another example of set, *Aufgabe,* or *Einstellung,* but further consideration shows this is not so. Terms like *set* and *Aufgabe* imply singleness of task or universe of discourse, but the words in Nachmias' experiment—*gasket, mayhem, hanker, sentry, treble, forage, extend, reveal,* and *profit*—belong to no single domain, induce no particular set, and arouse no single train of associations. The explanation in terms of distinctiveness not only has the advantage of being the simplest and most easily tested operationally but also relates similar effects in perception and recall under a single concept.

That distinctiveness can be given a quantitative measure and correlates highly with learning and ease of discrimination has been shown by Murdock (1960), who defined distinctiveness in terms of degree of difference of any item from all other items in the same (unidimensional) universe of discourse. In accordance with the Weber-Fechner law, Murdock takes the differences in the logs of stimulus values, be they energy or serial position, in computing total difference of any stimulus from other members of a set. Thus if 2, 4, 6, and 8 are the logs of the energies of a set of stimuli, then the total difference of the first (2) is 12 $(2 + 4 + 6)$, that of 4 is 8 $(2 + 2 + 4)$, that of 6 is likewise 8, and that of 8 is 12. The percent difference, D percent, of any stimulus is the total difference divided by the sum of the total differences. In the example above the total difference is 40 $(12 + 8 + 8 + 12)$, and the D percent for the four stimuli are 30, 20, 20, and 30 percent. It is thus seen that items near the middle have minimal distinctiveness and items near the ends have maximal distinctiveness. Owing to the log function, the D-percent scale is not symmetrical. In the case of longer series, where taking logs is felt to a greater extent than in shorter series, items at the beginning of a series have higher D percent than do end items equally far from the center (cf. Table 5 in Murdock, 1960, p. 25). The assumptions underlying the D scale, as Murdock points out, are similar to those made in AL theory where the difference (in logs) between any stimulus and adaptation level is the measure of distinctiveness.

Murdock's formulation successfully predicted experimental results for accuracy of learning to identify different types of stimuli by method of absolute judgment, by effects of serial position on recall (the "bowing" effect), and by paired-associate learning (weights and color names in one experiment and temporal intervals and letters of the alphabet in another). The empirical justification for choice of the Weber-Fechner function is that the log function gave consistently lower standard errors of estimate than either the power function or rectangular (chance) distributions. While space does not permit a detailed resumé of Murdock's discussion of the D scale its power is immediately evident in (1) the impossibility of achieving a scale in which all stimuli, even when equally discriminable, have the same D percent; and (2) constancy of the *shape* of the serial position learning curve "despite variations in the distribution of practice, rate of presentation, familiarity of items, individual differences, meaningfulness of material, and interitem and intertrial intervals, which affect such measures of learning as number of trials to criterion." An alternative theory of the influence of serial position on learning has been proposed by Feigenbaum and Simon (1961) which they call an "anchor point" theory, but they do not claim the generality for it that Murdock has shown for the D scale. Indeed, Murdock's formulation provides another bridge between psychophysics and learning theory, a desideratum that Estes (1956) asserted was necessary for the further development of the latter.

The concept of distinctiveness of stimuli leads immediately to the problem of differential reinforcement or contrast effects in learning, a problem that has attracted more and more workers since Crespi's classic study (1944) of amount of reinforcement and level of performance. The conflicting results in this area show the need for a more adequate and inclusive theory to deal with effects of reinforcement. Such a theory has been offered by Bevan and Adamson (1960) and is discussed in the following section.

REINFORCEMENT AND PERFORMANCE

During the last 20 years evidence has accumulated that, as Bower has put it, "Contrary to the interests of parsimony in theory construction . . . the reinforcing effect of a given amount of reward is not a static parameter; rather, the conception that emerges from these studies is that the reinforcing effect depends upon the context in which the reward quantity occurs" (1961, p. 196). If we interpret "context" to include all conditions of reinforcement, not only magnitude and frequency, but also temporal spacing and interactions among the diverse conditions of reinforcement, then Bower's statement is eminently correct. In addition, it is necessary to distinguish between stimulus agent, usually taken as the reinforcer, and process, as Bevan and Adamson (1960) pointed out, if shifts in effectiveness of reinforcers arising from contrast, adaptation to repeated rewards, the retroactive paradox, the superiority of partial reinforcement, and other factors are to be brought under a single rubric. Since the classic findings of Crespi (1942)—in which rats indulged in more peering, scurrying, head jerking, biting, jumping, grooming, face washing, and fitful retracing forms of behavior after being reduced from 16 to 4 or 1 unit of food reward—there has been considerable controversy regarding the effects of differential reinforcement.

The need for a theory to embrace a variety of results that appear conflicting or contradictory is shown by even a cursory review of a few salient studies in which reinforcement is the independent variable. In Crespi's study data, such as those in Table 7.7, clearly show that running speed is a function of absolute amount of reward and, just as important though not so frequently noted, that individual differences are, in general, less with higher than with lower magnitudes of reinforcement. But contrary to these apparently clear-cut findings are those of Meyer

(1951) and Schrier and Harlow (1956), working with monkeys, and Lawson (1957) working with rats, as pointed out by Bower:

> . . . rate of error elimination in a series of visual discrimination problems was not significantly related to the amount of reward when S received the same amount (large or small) on every problem . . . [but] if S received different amounts of reward for performing correctly on different problems of the learning series, learning rate on a given problem varied directly with the amount of reward for that problem (1961, p. 196).

TABLE 7.7.   Running Speed as a Function of Amount of Incentive

Incentive	Number of Rats	Average Mean Speed in Feet per Second						Mean	σ
1	6	0.95	0.76	0.45	0.32	0.30	0.22	0.50	.078
4	4	1.33	0.95	0.80	0.73			0.95	.070
16	4	2.06	1.90	1.56	1.08			1.65	.190
64	4	3.88	3.74	3.51	3.33			3.62	.057

Note: Incentives are given in $\frac{1}{50}$ grm. of food. N = number of rats.
SOURCE: From Crespi, 1942. With the permission of the *American Journal of Psychology*.

The most striking result of Crespi's study was the paradoxical finding, from the point of view of absolutist theories, that rats given no food reward had a mean running rate of 1.22 ft. per sec. as against mean rates of 0.50 and 0.95 ft. per sec. for rats given 1 and 4 units of reward. Moreover, the coefficients of variation were greater for the two latter groups than for the zero group!

These last results, usually referred to as the "Crespi" or "contrast" effect were verified by Zeaman (1949) but subsequent findings, as pointed out by Hall (1961) have been controversial. As detailed by Hall, some have found "elation" (greater effect of a larger reward following a smaller), others have found no elation but some "depression" (smaller effect of a smaller reward following a larger), and some have found neither effect. The situation is even further complicated by Logan's findings (1960) that variations in reward behave differently around small and large average amounts. With constant differentials in rewards in two alleys, Bower (1961) found clear-cut evidence of contrast effects: rats that alternated between eight pellets of food in one alley and one pellet in a second alley asymptoted in the highly rewarded alley at about the same running speed as a constant eight-pellet group but at a significantly lower running speed than rats given constant one-pellet reward. Hence there was a "downward" contrast effect but not an "upward" contrast effect, which, as Bower recognized, might have been due to the ceiling inherent in the running-speed measure in the case of the very large reward.

Contrary to the view that differential reinforcement involves contrast or interaction between the two rewards is the position expressed by Goldstein and Spence (1963) that only the absolute magnitudes of the rewards are operative in determining the running speed of rat Ss from start to goal. While Goldstein and Spence make out a good case for the effects of the absolute magnitudes of their rewards, something known for a long time, further consideration of their data shows that the effects of specific rewards also depend upon the magnitudes of other rewards received by Ss. In their study four groups of rats were given either ten and zero, ten and one, ten and five, or five and one pellets as a reward in each of two alleys. If there is a contrast effect we would expect the ratios of running speeds to parallel the ratios of rewards. This is actually the case as we see from Table 7.8 based on

TABLE 7.8. Comparison of Mean Asymptotic Response Speeds to Differentially Reinforced Discriminanda for Groups with Different Combinations of Reward Magnitudes

Response Measure	Speed in Feet per Second							
	Groups Designated by Number of Pellets to Each Discriminandum							
	10 vs. 0		10 vs. 1		5 vs. 1		10 vs. 5	
Starting	1.44	.83	1.39	.90	1.45	1.18	1.50	1.35
	(1.73)		(1.54)		(1.23)		(1.11)	
Running	3.26	1.54	3.10	1.98	3.30	2.57	3.28	3.07
	(2.11)		(1.57)		(1.28)		(1.07)	
Goal	2.51	.97	2.34	1.89	2.60	2.12	2.70	2.61
	(2.58)		(1.23)		(1.24)		(1.03)	

Note: Values in parentheses are ratios of the running speeds under the two conditions in each case.
SOURCE: From Goldstein and Spence, 1963. With the permission of the American Psychological Association.

Table 1 from Goldstein and Spence. Taking the three measures of running speeds, (1) starting, (2) running from start to beginning of path chosen to represent the goal run, and (3) the goal running speed, there are twelve ratios involving running speeds to match with the magnitude ratios in Table 7.8. In every case but one, higher reward ratios are paralleled by higher running ratios thus showing the existence of contrast or relative effects of the rewards as well as of the absolute effects claimed by Goldstein and Spence to be the only factors operative. Actually, the correspondence of eleven of the twelve ratios with the reward ratios carries no more weight than the correspondence of four ratios based on one of the measures, since the three measures of speed are admittedly correlated. While the fact that the ten-pellet rewards elicit about the same running speeds in all cases argues against the operation of contrast, the fact that the five-pellet reward elicits the same running speed as the ten-pellet rewards argues against the Goldstein and Spence theory. Also arguing against the absolute theory are the slower running speeds to the one-pellet rewards in the ten vs. one as against the five vs. one conditions and the slightly faster speeds to the five pellets when they are the more highly rewarded condition in two of the three running measures. The differences referred to here, although not always statistically significant, are all in the direction predicted by contrast theory. Most important of all, the larger the difference in rewards, the sooner the differentiation in the running speeds for large and small rewards develops, a fact noted by Goldstein and Spence. We therefore conclude that the results of the study by Goldstein and Spence furnish evidence for contrast effects as well as for absolute effects of magnitude of reinforcement.

It would be strange if well-established facts found in everyday life were not replicated under laboratory conditions, even when rats are used as Ss. How often are individuals disappointed and unhappy when a gift, reward, or salary raise, though sizable, does not come up to expectations or is less than that received in the past. Unfortunately, Crespi and many workers after him who found interactions between rewards of different magnitudes have imputed to their rat Ss such anthropomorphic states as "elation, frustration, emotional tension, eagerness, anticipatory excitement" (Crespi, 1942) or "anticipation of reward and anticipation of frustration" (Bower, 1961). Such constructs have little operational value and tend to bring the concept of internal referents or norms into disrepute. On the other hand it is true that effects of reinforcing stimuli must be evaluated with reference to the state of the organism in the light of numerous experimental results. Just as pitch and frequency, intensity and loudness, luminance and lightness, wave length and hue, and other sensory stimuli and their experiential correlates must be distinguished, so must reinforcers as stimuli be distinguished from reinforcers as processes. However, the way to do this is not by invoking such intervening variables or hypothetical constructs as frustration, anticipatory excitement, conflict between anticipation of reward and anticipation of frustration, and the like, which are sufficiently ambiguous when used to interpret human behavior, let alone rat behavior. Instead one must determine the stimulus equivalents of internal norms and evaluate the effectiveness of reinforcers in terms of their relations to such norms. Let us consider an auspicious start in this direction.

The Bevan-Adamson reinforcement model. If it is permissible to assume a reinforcement analogue to sensory adaptation levels, then, Bevan and Adamson (1960) reasoned, three basic conditions should be met with reinforcing stimuli: (1) Different distributions of stimuli should yield different indifference points (IPs) or ALs for shock and hence different psychophysical scale values. (2) Pretest differences in shock levels should be manifested in different evaluations of experimental intensities of shock. (3) Shock inputs should act as weighted averages over *time.* Accordingly three sets of experiments were performed. In general, the experiments followed the determination of the IPs and involved human maze learning with a common intensity of shock after pretest adaptation to various intensities applied outside the context of the learning situation. Without attempting to give the various refinements in experimental procedure, different IPs were found —using a rating scale from very weak, through medium, to very strong —with three sets of shocks employing one rectilinear and two positively skewed frequency distributions. With equal frequencies of five shocks ranging from 1300 to 3300 μamp., the IP was 2287 μamp.; with a positively skewed series in which weakest to strongest shocks were presented 30, 25, 20, 15, and 10 times respectively, IP was 2087 μamp.; and with a still more positively skewed series in which the shocks were presented 35, 30, 20, 10, and 5 times respectively, IP was 1900 μamp. In other words, as the lower intensities were presented more often, the shocks judged medium went down in intensity with resultant higher judgments of intensities for the series as a whole. Hence judgmental responses to shock are affected by internal norms and are scalable.

After the psychophysical or behaviorally effective values of the shock intensities were determined, a second experiment was performed in which one group of 17 Ss was given 30 shocks of 1300 μamp. at 10-sec.

intervals, a second group 30 shocks of 2300 μamp., and a third group 30 shocks of 3300 μamp. to judge. Following the judging series, all Ss were given a 28-unit 2-choice bolthead maze problem in which contact with the incorrect bolthead of each pair resulted in the delivery of a single 2300 μamp. shock lasting 200 msec. If the effective intensity of shock is a function of prevailing ALs, then the three groups should have been differentially affected by the identical shock stimulus during the learning trials. This was found to be the case. Performance in the maze differed with the *apparent* intensity of shock which was a function of shock level established in the pre-experimental trials. In the initial trials three groups performed at chance level, but in subsequent trials the curves diverged indicating different rates of learning. Learning was most rapid in the first group (1300 μamp.) for whom the experimental reinforcement was strong relative to the magnitude of the pre-experimental adapting shock. Performance was poorest in the case of the third group (3300 μamp.), for whom the experimental reinforcement was relatively weak, and intermediate in the case of the second group (2300 μamp). The results thus clearly indicated that the effects of reinforcement depend upon residual adaptation levels brought to the experiment as the result of the prior experiences of the Ss.

The third experiment was performed to test the postulate that effects of varying inputs are weighted averages over time. Evidence already in the literature supported this assumption. Logan, Beier, and Ellis (1955) found that the average running speed was the same for a group reinforced with five pellets on each trial as it was for a group that received nine pellets on one-half of the trials and one on the alternate trials. Leventhal, Morrell, Morgan, and Perkins (1959) found there was no preference for an alley reinforced on every trial over one reinforced with double the amount on half of the trials. In the third experiment of Bevan and Adamson the maze performance of a control group of Ss receiving a fixed magnitude of shock for every error was compared with that of (1) a group receiving a symmetrical distribution of shocks having the same mean intensity, and (2) groups receiving positively and negatively skewed distributions of shocks. It was expected that the first experimental group would not differ significantly from the control while those receiving greater and less shock on the average would perform with different efficiencies from the other groups. Using five shock intensities employed in the first experiment, four groups were tested as follows: Group *A* received on incorrect trials a positively skewed, random distribution of 70 shocks as follows: 31, 26, 22, 14, and 7 percent of weakest to strongest shocks, the mean intensity being 2000 μamp. Group *B* received a negatively skewed distribution mirroring that of group *A* with a mean intensity of 2600 μamp. Group *C* received a symmetrical distribution, 7, 22, 42, 22, and 7 percent, about a mean intensity of 2300 μamp. Group *C'* received a shock of 2300 μamp. for all errors. The use of a more difficult task than that in the previous experiments ensured a specified minimum of reinforced trials and equalized the number for all *S*s.

The results of this third experiment gave evidence of the pooled effects of the various stimulus distributions. Group *A*, which received the lowest mean intensity of shock, gave the poorest performance, and group *B*, which received the highest mean intensity, while differing reliably from group *A*, gave the next poorest performance. The best performances were made by groups *C* and *C'* which received the same average shocks of intermediate average intensity. Groups *C* and *C'*, as expected, did not differ significantly from each other. Hence performance level relates reliably to average reinforcement level, with best performance resulting from intermediate intensities of *negative* reinforcer. Whether averaging effect is tantamount to pooling reinforcement over time is still unclear from these experiments, as the authors point out. The establishment of this relationship is necessary to extend the pooling model of AL theory to the area of reinforcement. For this purpose a definitive demonstration would require, they believe, a quantitative prediction of performance (associated with some designated average level) from performance levels associated with each of the component intensities that contribute to the average. In a subsequent experiment, using rat *S*s, the effects of pretest shock ALs on running speeds were, in the main, confirmed by Black, Adamson, and Bevan (1961). *S*s given shocks of 600 μamp. in a pretest series in a shuttle box ran slowest to escape shock of 450 μamp. (relatively weak) in a straightaway, while *S*s given shocks of 300 μamp. in the shuttle box ran fastest to escape shock of 450 μamp. (relatively strong) in the straightaway. *S*s given 450-μamp. shock in the shuttle box ran at a slightly faster than the 600-μamp. group and slower than the 300-μamp. group with a shock of 450 μamp. in the straightaway; while the control group, which had no pretest shuttle-box trials, ran faster in the straightaway than did the medium pretest group. The authors point out that the superiority of the control over the group given medium shock is predicted by the pooling hypothesis since the group with shuttle-box training received twice as many shocks per day and therefore its reinforcement norm during straightaway trials should have been closer to asymptotic value. For the medium group the intensity of shock in the straightaway was no different from that in the shuttle box, and hence it had been adapted to more than the shock of the control animals starting out in the straightaway. Thus the results with both human and animal Ss confirm the pooling model and the effects of level on performance.

With the three basic conditions satisfied for carrying over the sensory adaptation-level model to reinforcement, we may now turn to the quantitative formulation of the Bevan-Adamson model (Bevan, 1963a, b):

1. Organisms differentiate between primary (s_p) and background (s_b) stimuli.
2. Organisms create norms $(\bar{s})$, by averaging stimuli over time:

$$(\bar{s}) = \frac{(s_{b1} + s_{b2} + \cdots s_{bn})^x}{N_b} \frac{(s_{p1} + s_{p2} \cdots s_{pn})^y}{N_p} \qquad (4)$$

where N_b and N_p refer to the number of background (s_{bi}) and primary (s_{pj}) stimuli respectively, and x and y are weighting coefficients denoting the relative contributions of the s_{pj} and s_{bi} to the internal norm.
3. Magnitude of reinforcement, R_{ji}, must be distinguished from magnitude of the reinforcing agent, S, the former depending upon the distance of the reinforcing stimulus from the already established norm, $\bar{s}$, and equal to $s_p - \bar{s}$ which may be symbolized Δs. This differential may be large, denoting strong reinforcement, small, denoting weak reinforcement, or zero.
4. In addition to the effects of reinforcement as such, the tension level (i) must be taken into consideration in assessing the effects of reinforcement and this, like $\bar{s}$, has temporal continuity and is affected by many factors, e.g., physiological state and amount of deprivation. The relation between i and performance is curvilinear, performance being best at intermediate levels, and poorer at both low and high levels, of i.
5. The effectiveness of reinforcers is thus a function of both Δs and i concurrently.

The implications of these assumptions for nine classes of phenomena associated with reinforcement are as follows:

1. *Reinforcing agents as psychophysical stimuli.* The evidence shows that reinforcing agents behave like psychophysical stimuli in being

scalable on continua having neutral or indifferent regions and in being subject to both series and anchor effects. The pooling model is therefore applicable on the basis of experimental as well as a priori considerations.

2. *Effective intensity of reinforcement and performance efficiency.* From the definition of Δs it follows that the effectiveness of a reinforcing stimulus is not a fixed value. This value changes with variations in $\bar{s}$ as new stimuli are added, as effects of old stimuli diminish, and with changes in internal norm as a result of other factors. Like sensory stimuli, reinforcing stimuli derive their effectiveness from their relation to prevailing levels: if the reinforcing agent is above its background level, it will appear intense; if below level, it will appear weak; and if it is near or at level, it will be medium or neutral. Performance efficiency will vary in accordance with some function of reinforcing effectiveness.

3. *Effectiveness of reinforcement and distinctiveness of the reinforcing agent.* From the above it follows that the greater the difference between a reinforcer and the general level, the more distinctive it will be and the greater will be its effectiveness as a reinforcer.

4. *Adaptation to repeated reinforcement.* The loss with repetition in the effectiveness of stimuli as reinforcers may be accounted for by the assumption, supported by evidence from sensory adaptation, that reinforcing stimuli pull level in their own direction, thus reducing the differential between s and $\bar{s}$ with resultant loss in reinforcing power. The loss in effectiveness can presumably be counteracted by changing the intensity of the reinforcer to preserve the same differential between s_p and $\bar{s}$ during successive presentations of reinforcing stimuli.

5. *Patterns of intermittent reinforcement and performance efficiency.* From what has been said it follows that certain patterns of intermittent reinforcement have a greater effect upon performance than continuous stimulation. If nonreinforced trials can be viewed as having zero intensity, then such trials should have the effect of reducing $\bar{s}$ and thus of enhancing the magnitude of Δs. In addition to the intensive level, the tension level must also be taken into account in evaluating effects of reinforcement as shown in the study by Bevan and Adamson (1960) discussed above and in studies such as that by Grant and Schipper (1952) in which the largest number of CRs per reinforcement in eyeblink conditioning was found with 50 and 75 percent schedules and a lower number with 25 and 100 percent schedules. Still other phe-

nomena, such as nonrandom programs of reinforcement and the relation of extinction performance to reinforcement schedules, are also capable of explanation in terms of the present model as shown by Bevan (1963).

6. *Temporal spacing of reinforced trials.* Since each application of a fixed value of reinforcement is assumed to bring its effective value nearer to the indifference level, rapid repetition should be accompanied by relatively rapid neutralization of stimulation with consequent decrement in performance. In accordance with the assumption of a curvilinear relationship between tension level and performance, it follows that spacing of reinforcements that is too wide will also result in poorer performance. Extended periods of zero reinforcement cannot support optimal tension levels for performance. For experimental evidence of these assumptions the reader is referred to the original publications (Bevan, 1963).

7. *Performance with shifts in reinforcement magnitude.* The Crespi or contrast effects discussed earlier in this section lend support to the assumption that Ss integrate reinforcements over time and/or trials, resulting in establishment of level such that the effectiveness of succeeding reinforcers depends on their relation to prevailing levels. It is thus possible to account for differential responses to differences in magnitude of reinforcing stimuli without recourse to terms referring to supposed inner states, particularly of animal Ss. Undoubtedly more quantitative data are needed to determine the exact relationships between stimulus differentials and response differentials. The model proposed here has the advantage of accounting for effects of absolute as well as relative contrasting magnitudes of reinforcement.

8. *Performance with combinations of different types of reinforcement.* In this discussion no distinction has been made between types of reinforcers, e.g., rewards vs. punishments, since they may act as either positive or negative reinforcers, depending upon the specific conditions of their use. As Bevan points out, both may be scaled in terms of their effectiveness and while their respective ranges of influence may not coincide, they overlap to a marked degree. We assume that it is their intensity relative to the norm, not their bene- or nociceptive quality, that determines effectiveness in altering behavior. Since rewards and punishments lie on opposite sides of the neutral point of affective continua this fact must be taken into consideration when they are used in combination, e.g., a positive reinforcer may be enhanced if employed following a negative one, and vice versa.

On the assumption that effectiveness depends upon the arousal value of reinforcers or their ability to change tension level, it follows that whether correct responses or errors are reinforced makes little theoretical difference. This conclusion is supported by experimental evidence, e.g., Muenzinger's study (1946) showing that when shock was given on correct turn in a brightness-discrimination problem, 49 trials were required to criterion, and when it was given for both correct and incorrect responses, 40 trials were required to criterion. Again, it should be pointed out that further work is necessary to determine the exact relations between positive and negative reinforcers on the one hand and performance on the other.

9. *Resistance to extinction and reinforced performance following extinction*. Bevan states that if the period of extinction is considered a sequence of zero or minimum reinforcements, then tension may be expected to return toward its initial level, with a consequent reduction in performance efficiency. On the other hand, the usual period of deprivation between extinction sessions should enhance tension level and thus make possible spontaneous recovery and the disinhibitory effect of "irrelevant" stimuli. Other implications of this model regarding reinforcement levels and extinction and effect of number of extinction trials on subsequent reinforcement are also discussed by Bevan (1963).

It is clear that the Bevan-Adamson model is applicable to the great variety of complex reinforcing situations. In its insistence on scaling and evaluating reinforcing stimuli with reference to internal norms, reinforcement theory is brought nearer to psychophysical theory, with resultant implications for learning and performance both in the laboratory and under conditions of everyday living.

SUMMARY

Learning is regarded as a form of adaptation in which behavior matches or is in some sense isomorphic with a norm, criterion, or goal. We are not interested in the time-honored problems regarding innate and learned behavior, so much as in the kinds of adaptations individuals make and the possibility of modifying behavior in various ways. Level of aspiration is only one of the many factors that influence accomplishment. Background factors may be as important as the focal stimuli to which individuals respond in the process of learning. Transfer of learning, influence of contextual stimuli on generalization gradients, latent learning, habituation, and extinction are discussed from the point of view of AL theory. The concept of distinctiveness is important for learning and judgment. Phenomena of reinforcement—such as contrast effects, effects of patterns and intensities of intermittent reinforcements, and performance with combinations of different types of reinforcement—and extinction phenomena are accounted for in terms of the Bevan-Adamson pooling model which transfers basic assumptions from psychophysics to learning theory with considerable success.

8 *Cognition and Thinking*

The brain is an extraordinarily effective instrument for adapting the organism to its environment and for altering the environment to suit the organism. A comparative neurologist, surveying the development of the central nervous system, would point to the tremendous growth of the cerebrum in higher animals, particularly in primates, as evidence of the way in which evolutionary mechanisms have enabled organisms to extend the range and complexity of their adaptations to the world in which they live. Dempsey says in this connection that "the phylogenetic ascent may be regarded as an increasingly successful effort by animals to free themselves from the limitations of their environments" (1951, p. 230). Because his unaided bodily structures are not adapted for life under conditions such as are found in the arctic, under the sea, in the air, or in outer space, and because he has only limited ability to resist the onslaughts of disease and epidemics, the intelligence of man has devised shelters, clothing, ships, airplanes, and medicines to counteract the deficiencies and weaknesses of his organism as originally fashioned by nature. Today we are on the threshold of the time when man's intelligence may make possible alterations in bodily structures and functions after birth, and perhaps even during embryonic development, to achieve more perfect adaptations to the hazards confronting him. Every invention, every product of culture, every extension of man's activities and powers represents the product of creative thinking. Even accidental discoveries prove valuable when someone is able to use them creatively to solve old problems or to adapt them to new uses. Thinking is thus responsible for the most subtle and complex adaptations achieved by organisms. Thinking is far from being the "flow of ideas" running their course according to the laws of association; it is the prime behavioral instrument of adaptation.

It has been traditional to regard thought processes as higher than sensory and manipulative activities, thereby creating a gulf between them. The common phrase "higher thought processes" implies that the other psychological processes belong to a lower class of activities. The distinction has also been made between concrete and abstract behavior, with the position taken that the capacity for abstraction may be lost, while the concrete attitude remains, e.g., after brain injuries and in certain types of schizophrenia (Goldstein and Scheerer, 1941). Thus, a patient who may be able to throw balls into boxes at different distances but unable to report which box is farthest away is said to have lost the capacity for abstract thinking. After considering a number of studies Cameron (1944) concluded:

> There is good reason for doubting the usefulness, to say nothing of the validity, of these determined efforts to maintain separate categories of "abstract" and "concrete" behavior. The notion is based upon an equally hypothetical differentiation betwen "perceptual" and "conceptual" thinking; and upon inspection this will be found to reduce to little more than the ancient narcissistic flattery that granted rationality to adult human thought but denied it to children and animals—some stoutly denied it to women also. The current form of this dichotomy is grounded in certain nineteenth century evolutionary doctrines of ontogeny and phylogeny which, paradoxically enough, were originally designed to establish, not such breaks or chasms between species but an essential *continuity* between the structure-functions of human beings and other animals (1944, p. 904).

Stressing the same point in somewhat different fashion, Hayakawa pointed to the similarity between the simpler physiological processes and cognitive processes as adaptive mechanisms:

> Mr. Smith's body automatically adjusts itself, within certain limits, to changes in climate or atmosphere, from cold to warm, from dry to moist, from fresh to foul; no conscious effort on his part is required to make these adjustments. . . . Mr. Smith . . . also adjusts himself automatically to changes in the verbal climate, from one type of discourse to another, from one set of terms to another, without conscious effort (1941, p. ix).

The position that so-called higher thought processes as well as sensory processes are adaptive in nature has gained acceptance among physiologists, chief among them being Cannon (1939) and Dempsey (1951):

. . . voluntary activity, instinctive reactions, and even intellectual behavior of a high order cannot be excluded from consideration [of homeostatic processes]. . . . The suggestion that homeostatic principles govern sociological as well as physiological forces implies that parallel or analogous mechanisms should be demonstrable in both fields (Dempsey, 1951, p. 233).

Our position regarding the adaptive nature of cognition and thought processes implies (1) that these processes aid in the adaptation of the organism to the environment and (2) that cognitive processes obey laws that are formally similar to the laws governing sensory, perceptual, and judgmental phenomena.

COGNITION AND ACTION

Most contemporary psychologists would agree that cognition, perception, thinking, memory, and imagination are forms of behavior, just as much as the easily observed motor activities are. The question arises of what the relation is between cognition, logic, and sensorimotor behavior. There are two opposed views of this question: (1) the laws of logic are the laws of thinking and (2) the laws of thinking are the laws of logic. In both views, thinking is divorced from other forms of behavior and is regarded as a type of activity in a class by itself. Wertheimer (1945) expressed the relation between logic and behavior as follows:

Some . . . think that traditional logic has no connection with actual *behavior*. This is a mistake. For application to behavior merely presupposes a connecting axiom, approximately as follows: behavior will be unreasonable, will fail of achievement, will run into trouble, if it is determined by factors parallel to mistakes in the sense of traditional logic (1945, p. 7).

We would turn Wertheimer's statement around and make behavior primary and logic derivative from action. Propositions which imply contradictory or inconsistent modes of behavior cannot be logically correct, for it is as impossible to think contradictorily as it is to act contradictorily, since thinking is itself a form of action.

The dependence of knowledge on behavior has never been expressed better than by Santayana:

The question what is knowable and what unknowable to any animal is . . . easily answered by one enjoying the requisite facilities for observation. If an animal possesses organs capable of . . . response to a determinate thing, that animal can know this thing; if on the contrary the presence of this thing in influencing the animal materially does not stimulate any reaction focused upon that thing—any turning, or visible contemplation, or defensive movement, or pursuit—then the thing in question is unknowable to that particular animal and can never become an object of his thought, action, or desire (1941, pp. 227–228).

Whether or not Santayana would be willing to include abstract philosophical types of thinking in his account of knowledge as a behavioral phenomenon, I do not know; but according to the position taken here, his description should ultimately be applicable to all types of thinking.

The ancient logical paradoxes show how impossible it is to "live" with logical contradiction because of the opposed types of behavior that they demand. Take, for example, the logical paradox "Every generalization is false." If this generalization is true, then it must be false, for it asserts the falsity of all generalizations. But if it is false, then it exemplifies its own truth. Better still is the paradox involving the student and the teacher of law. The latter agreed to wait for payment of his teaching fees until the student won his first case at law. The student, failing to begin practice of law, was sued by the teacher. Each argued as follows before the judge:

TEACHER: If I win this case, the student should pay according to the judgment of the court; if I lose this case, he wins, and he should pay because he agreed to pay after winning his first case.

STUDENT: If I win this case, I should not pay according to the judgment of the court; if I lose this case, I should not pay because I have not yet won my first case.

It is obvious that the two contestants are making use of two distinct and contradictory principles: the judgment of the court and the action required by the contract. These lead to contradictory results and cannot both be employed. When the contestants went into court they tacitly agreed to abide by the decision of the judge. It is the judge who interprets the meaning of the contract, and subsequent action depends no longer on the contract, but on the decision of the judge as to what the contract means. Paradoxes of this type have perplexed logicians since ancient times, and many solutions have been offered, one of the most famous being that of Bertrand Russell. His position was embodied in his theory of types which states that we must not confuse different types of logical statements. Thus, to ask if the class of all classes is a member of itself, is meaningless, for two levels of abstraction are being confused. (Russell, 1920, pp. 135, 185). Russell asserts that we must stay at one level of abstraction; in our words, we must abide by one principle to avoid contradiction. Just as a limb remains motionless when extensors and flexors are stimulated simultaneously, so thought is paralyzed by contradiction. The laws of logic therefore rest on actual and possible forms of behavior, the latter occurring only in thought.

This view of the nature of logic does not commit us to the fallacious doctrine that *all* laws of thought are also laws of logic.

PERCEPTION AND THINKING COMPARED

Having taken the position that thought is a form of action and subject to the same basic laws that govern other activities, we must not overlook the differences between thinking and other types of activities, particularly between perception and thought. It has been customary to regard perception as the meeting ground of sensation and thought in the belief that the pure deliverances of the senses lack a meaning which must be supplied by past experiences. Whether or not sensory qualities are ever experienced in pure or isolated form, it is operationally difficult to separate sensation from perception and perception from thinking. There is, however, a basic difference between perception and thinking which is largely responsible for the other differences between them and for their different roles in adapting the organism to various features of the environment. In perception peripheral sensory components are predominant, while in thinking central components predominate.

Perception is always tied to particular objects, relations, and events in the here and now, whereas thinking can be concerned with the past, present, or future and operates with surrogates or symbols. Perception may be regarded as the means whereby organisms adjust to what immediately confronts them, whereas thinking may be regarded as the means whereby organisms adjust to what will be or may be or has been. To concretize the difference, I perceive a book which has a definite shape, color, weight, and even more or less predetermined subject matter. But the *thought of book* is not restricted to this or that book and may range over the entire domain of books that I have experienced and extend to purely imaginary books. Thus I may *think* of a book that is triangular or circular, has any size, any content, and even of a book that exists only as a tape recording or in Braille.

Language, considered for the moment as a part of thought, illustrates why thinking is so much richer than actual experience. Single words as well as phrases, sentences, paragraphs, and larger units of discourse may connote a wealth of meanings and possible experiences. Compare such words as kind, run, terror, seem, cosmos. Any of these can be elaborated indefinitely. The world of language—including logical, philosophical, scientific, and literary language—contains more potentialities for experience than does the actual world itself because it encompasses the imaginary, the ideal, and the possible, as well as the real. Taken from the purely atomistic point of view, the number of words that can be united to form meaningful sentences, paragraphs, and books is even greater than the number of units of which they are composed. Miller (1959) pointed out that the more highly developed central processes are due to the "potentialities of compounding more similarly functioning units rather than to a completely new type of function" (p. 244). He also wrote as follows:

> One of the factors which make the mental processes of man so much "higher" than those of animals may be a greater capacity to respond selectively to more subtle aspects of the environment as cues—especially to aspects such as triangularity, numerosity, and other relations and patterns which are commonly referred to as "abstract." Another factor may be a capacity to make a greater variety of distinctive central cue-producing responses, and especially a greater capacity to respond with a number of different cue-producing responses simultaneously, so that further responses may be elicited on the basis of a pattern of cues representing several different units of experience (p. 247).

It follows from its origin that perception is limited to a two-valued logic: a thing either is or is not, since there are no intermediate stages between perceiving and not perceiving. This type of logic came down to us from Aristotle but it has proved inadequate for modern logic, which is based on the possibilities of thinking rather than the properties of perception. In thinking we may employ a logic which has many values or many possibilities with their own degrees of probability. Thought may be concerned with objects and relations that do not exist or even with mutually exclusive concepts and their implications. Perception is limited to what is, but thinking can include contingencies. Many experiments would not have to be performed if psychology had a sufficient body of knowledge to provide material for *Denkexperimente* that could yield the right answers by the operations of thinking. The implications of assumptions can be traced in thinking without the restraints imposed by the concreteness and limitations of perception.

The creative aspects of thinking appear in what has traditionally been called "inductive" and "deductive" reasoning. In the former, thought proceeds from the particular to the general; and in the latter, from the general to the particular. Thus, from the fact that we have never seen persons over a certain age alive, we conclude that *all men are mortal;* if we assume the proposition that all men are mortal as a valid generalization, we can deduce from it that Socrates, being a man, must be mortal. Both types of thinking yield new information.

A final difference between perception and thinking is in their structuration. Perception is usually structured, a fact made the basis of their system by the Gestalt psychologists. Thought patterns, on the other hand, are labile and undergo many modifications before becoming fixed, although there are cases where creative ideas appear suddenly, completely structured.

The following sets of propositions summarize what we have said concerning perception and thinking:

Perception	Thinking
1. Aroused by external objects and has predominantly sensory components	1. May be aroused by external or internal stimulation but has predominantly central components
2. Concerned with here-now presentations	2. Concerned with past, present, or future and is symbolic or surrogative
3. Singly determined and nonsubstitutive	3. Multiply determined, labile, and substitutive
4. Reaction to "what is"	4. Deals with contingencies and possibilities
5. Concerned with the "real"	5. May be concerned with real or imaginary
6. Its logic is two-valued and governed by law of excluded middle	6. Its logic is many-valued and operates with probabilities
7. Order is imposed from without and usually well structured	7. Order is derived from within and is dynamic
8. Supplemented by cognition	8. Returns to perception for validation

The differences outlined above must not be regarded as absolute or sharp since perception and thinking partake of each other in some degree, there being an element of both in each. Perception of an object as a member of a class, e.g., in the statement, "This is an orange," involves some thought element, and all thinking has some perceptual reference or content. Perhaps the most distinctive feature of thought is that it makes possible a release from the here and now, whereby the world of experience is extended beyond the confines of sensory contacts.

THE COMPLEXITY OF THOUGHT PROCESSES

We have discussed cognition and thinking as if they were simple and coordinate processes, when, as a matter of fact, they are neither simple nor, if we accept Guilford's analysis, coordinate. According to Guilford (1957b) thinking is one of the two main components or manifestations of *intellect*, the other being memory (see Fig. 8.1).

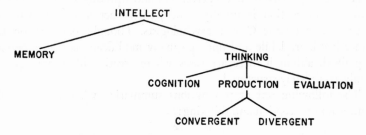

FIG. 8.1. The structure of intellect. (From Guilford, 1957b. With the permission of the author.)

Thinking involves cognition or awareness of what confronts us, production of a solution in response to our awareness, and evaluation of the products of thought. Furthermore, the act of production can proceed either toward a single solution, as in cases where only one answer or solution is correct (convergent thinking) or it may proceed in several directions toward any one of a number of solutions, as in cases in which there are no right or wrong solutions (divergent thinking). According to Guilford, scientists usually employ convergent thinking because their problems usually require unique or true solutions and artists, writers, and composers employ divergent thinking because they are not bound to come out with a single result. Guilford's analysis of intellect has clearly shown that a number of different activities are involved in thinking. In addition, economical efficient solutions to problems often require change of "set," or flexibility, which has been extensively investigated by a number of workers, particularly Luchins and Luchins (1942, 1950, 1959). Guilford and his co-workers (Frick, Guilford, Christensen, and Merrifield, 1959) have distinguished between spontaneous and adaptive flexibility. The former is responsible for variety or diversity of ideas, the latter for the restructuring of interpretations and approaches employed in problem solving. These types of flexibility, they point out, may be capable of division into subtypes whose nature and number depend upon the particular conditions of thinking. Factor-analysis approaches to cognitive processes by Guilford and his co-workers have yielded factors which throw light on the adaptive nature of the intellectual processes, something which was lacking in the associationistic accounts of thinking.

Although as a result of Guilford's work we are aware of the complexities of thought processes, we shall discuss cognition and thinking as if they were cognate terms and shall not attempt to disentangle or identify their components. Our discussion follows the model we have used for perception and judgment, which is consonant with other approaches such as that of Guilford and his co-workers.

COGNITIVE ANALOGUES OF FOCAL, BACKGROUND, AND RESIDUAL STIMULI

In considering the problems of sensory processes, judgment, and learning, the division of sources of variance into focal, background, and residual stimuli was useful. Can this paradigm be fruitfully applied in the consideration of cognitive processes? Even though cognition is largely a central process, our paradigm is applicable because it refers not so much to origin or locus of stimulation, i.e., whether inside or outside the organism, as to the importance or primacy of stimuli in the causal constellation of conditions responsible for any type of behavior. Ideas, as well as external stimuli, may function as focal or contextual determinants of thinking. In discussing cognitive, imaginative, and problem-solving processes, a change in terminology is indicated but the new terms are analogous to the terms we have used in previous chapters. In discussing cognition and thinking, we shall refer to the *predominating idea* instead of to the focal stimulus. Predominant ideas may consist essentially either of a single concept like kindness, the speed of light, the law of gravitation, the law of association, and the concept of adaptation level, or of a system of ideas having a central focus. Style, motif, thread, plan, pattern, central thought, hypothesis, assumption, and postulate may serve as predominant ideas in writing, in composing music, and in other kinds of creative activity. Murphy (1958) has gone so far as to say "Most of the great periods can be characterized by a word or phrase representing the great ideas which they sought to realize. . . . A dominant idea thus provided in each case an explicit meaning for the creativeness of the age" (p. 149).

The predominating idea in thinking is set by the task, problem, question to be solved, or goal to be reached. Strictly speaking, we mean by the predominating idea its denotation, i.e., the object to which the thought refers or its meaning. This is to be contrasted with its connotation. Corresponding to background or contextual stimuli in perception are the associations aroused by the predominating idea in cognitive processes. The context of ideas aroused by a central idea is known as its connotation and such ideas are the analogue of background stimuli. Contextual ideas are as important for predominating ideas as background stimuli are in influencing focal stimuli in perception. Finally, corresponding to residual stimuli in perception are all other factors that affect the predominating idea and its connotations. We shall mean by residuals, when speaking of thought processes, all determinants of thinking which are not included under dominant or contextual cognitive processes. Residuals may be physiological (organic) or emotional, or they may be other ideas of which the individual is not fully aware. The cognitive analogues of focal, background, and residual stimuli are therefore as follows:

Perception	Cognition and Thinking
1. Focal stimuli	1. Predominant ideas or concepts
2. Background stimuli	2. Associations; connotations
3. Residual stimuli	3. Remote and "spontaneous" associations; affective, physiological, and other determinants of thought processes

Characteristics of predominant ideas. Practically all of the conditions or properties which tend to make stimuli distinctive or focal also operate to make ideas or concepts dominant in thinking. Predominant ideas have the following characteristics in purposeful productive thinking:

1. They are characterized by vividness, intensity, and persistence. They may be so vivid and intense and persistent as to be obsessive, and they may or may not be correct and fruitful.

2. They appear after an intense or long period of concern and considerable acquaintance with a given topic or area. While they often seem spontaneous (*freisteigende Vorstellungen*), they actually come from a matrix of thoughts having a common denotation.

3. They may be regarded as the analogue of predominant or anchor stimuli in perception and judgment. They exercise predominant weight in directing thinking.

4. They not only have more or less specific referents, but they also arouse many other ideas that furnish their connotation or background, and hence they are rich in connotation as well as in denotation. They are implicative and entail or imply other ideas. As a rule, the context of ideas is consistent with the core idea and when context and core ideas are not consistent, thinking is impeded and solutions cannot be found to problems.

5. They are subject to the constraints of their denotations and, to a lesser extent, of their connotations.

6. They facilitate thinking about problems and suggest certain approaches to problems which may or may not be fruitful. What is thought about a problem and what is attempted in its solution depend upon the lines of thought suggested by the predominant idea.

7. Fruitful predominant ideas suggest new problems in addition to solving old ones.

8. If our view is correct, that the extent to which thinking is creative depends upon the fruitfulness of the predominating idea, then the predominating idea must be original in some sense. It is often claimed that there is nothing new under the sun and this implies that not even the products of thinking are ever original. Without attempting to argue this question, we take the position that there really are new things under the sun, whether they are merely new configurations of old elements or new products never before experienced. Thinking fills lacunae, supplies answers, *adds something to the given*.

It is sometimes asserted that a problem contains all that is needed to solve it. While this may be true in a sense, something must be supplied by the individual or *thinking* would not be required to reach a solution. Thinking is thus distinguished from mere recognition and recall and from the performance of learned skilled acts. The individual *contributes* something as a result of his thinking, and hence thinking is a creative process par excellence. On the other hand a well-known concept *may* lead to new results if it is emphasized, if its sphere of application is enlarged, or if it is put in a new context. Every idea has potentialities but only the ones that are nurtured will bloom. And just as object colors change on backgrounds of different colors so ideas are modified by the contexts in which they are presented. Hence the fruitfulness of predominating ideas may reside in their originality, in their being emphasized, or in their being placed in new contexts.

These characteristics of fruitful predominating ideas are supported by considerable evidence. Consider how some of the greatest names in science, philosophy, and art are associated with a single predominating idea or style, e.g., Darwin and evolution; Einstein and relativity; Wertheimer and Gestalt. It is not sufficient simply to be obsessed by an idea to be creative. The paranoiac individual has predominant ideas but they lead nowhere except to the psychopathic hospital because they are completely idiosyncratic and false. They do not fit with the common body of knowledge, and they do not help the individual to adapt either to his problems or to his environment. While devotion is usually a necessary, it is not a sufficient condition for an idea to prosper. When there is no realization of the full importance of an idea, a necessary condition for its development is lacking. Few people are able and willing to follow the ramifications of a single idea or to trust the full implications of an important fact. Of the vast number of people before Pavlov and Bechterew who observed that the mouth waters at the sight of food, how many saw the significance of this isolated fact? Association was known to the ancient Greeks but only in a casual way. It was not until the British associationists, centuries later, made it the basic principle of all mental processes that its importance was fully realized, although many now reject it as an all-embracing concept.

The way in which a predominating idea in a young lad revolutionized modern physics was recounted by Wertheimer (1945). Einstein's obsession with problems of time and the speed of light led to the theory of relativity. According to Wertheimer, the problem started when Einstein was only 16 years old and occupied him for seven years, but it took him only five weeks to write his first paper on relativity after he came to question the customary concept of time. Let us follow

Wertheimer in his presentation of the manner in which Einstein was led step by step to the formulation of the doctrine of relativity. As a young man Einstein was puzzled about light and asked himself questions: What if one were to run after a ray of light? What if one were riding on the beam? What is the speed of light? Would its velocity in relation to one thing hold for another thing in motion? Many such questions concerning the speed of light led Einstein to wonder if light could not be used to determine if one were in a moving system. How measure the movement of the earth? He knew the velocity of light in relation to a system, but its consequences for other systems were puzzling. How does one know he is in a moving system? Light does not seem to know systems in absolute motion or at absolute rest. Such considerations then led to Maxwell's electromagnetic theory and to problems of classical mechanics. From these he came to see that time measurement involved the notion of simultaneity. What does simultaneity mean for events in different places? This proved to be more complicated than it seemed at first sight; one needs a set of operations to determine simultaneity if it is to have any physical meaning. The relative motion of objects affects measurements or statements about simultaneity. Then events which are simultaneous for a stationary object are not simultaneous for a moving object and vice versa. Conversely, every statement about time has meaning only if its frame of reference is stated. Similarly, the measurement of space (length) presupposed that there is no movement of the object relative to the observer. Einstein formulated the equations by which time and space measured in one (moving) system could be translated into time and space measurements in another (moving) system. He saw that an invariant was needed and he found it in the constancy of the speed of light for all moving systems. Thus it was that his early preoccupation with the speed of light resulted in the discovery of the invariant that forms the basis for the special theory of relativity.

Einstein's preoccupation with the consequences of a single idea is an example of one of the greatest accomplishments in the history of man's thinking. Thanks to Wertheimer, who was able to question Einstein about his thought processes over the years in which the theory of relativity was being developed, we have some notion of the nature of this momentous discovery from a psychological point of view. How enlightening it would be to us if there had been a Wertheimer to question Newton on his discovery of the universal law of gravitation!

Let us see how individuals solve problems of a very small order compared to those solved by Newton and Einstein. The following accounts by two students showing how they solved a problem (Woodworth and Schlosberg 1954, p. 834) also illustrate the role of the predominating idea in thinking. The problem is stated as follows:

A man stopping at a hotel ran out of money and would have no more for 23 days. The landlord would not trust him, but as he had a heavy gold chain of 23 links, the landlord agreed to accept one link in payment on each successive day and to restore the chain on the receipt of the money. Problem: how many links does the owner have to cut in order to fulfill his engagement? The answer is: two links.

The problem is which two links if removed will yield all combinations from 1 to 23. The first solution is given in the following protocol:

I asked myself how divide 23 units into five groups which are created by taking out two units. These five groups must yield all the numbers from one to 23. I first tried taking links 12 and 3 out on the assumption the problem involves symmetry, i.e., if I could create groups yielding numbers 1–12, then I could build to 23. I then found that although the problem does involve a certain symmetry relation the 12 and 3 groups proved to be wrong because they do not yield one of the numbers between one and 12. After trying other numbers I suddenly realized I only have to build to 11 not 12 because if I can construct a group that contains the numbers 1–11 then I have 12 left in the rest of the chain with which to make the other numbers required to build to 23. Since 3 and 12 gave most of the numbers between 1–12 and I needed a small number of links, I tried taking out links 4 and 11 and these proved to be correct.

Analysis of this protocol reveals what happened in solving the problem:

1. The problem when rephrased presented itself as one involving symmetry as the essential condition of a solution. This suggested the idea to divide 23 into groups which when combined would yield all numbers from 1 to 23.

2. Constraining conditions: He had to get a group as small as 1 and as large as 11 (first erroneously believed to be 12). The symmetry condition told him that he did not have to worry about half of the numbers because if he could build to some number near the middle, he could add to what was given from then on.

3. He followed out what is given in 1 and 2. This did not work because 12 was chosen for the dividing point and he could not get 6 and the other numbers adding to 12.

4. He tried various other combinations.

5. No luck until he saw that if he divided at link 11, there would be 12 remaining for the symmetry condition. After he rejected division at 12, the outlook for getting a small number to yield the missing number 6 seemed much more promising.

6. He then tried 4 and found it yielded all numbers required between 1 and 11, and with the 12 links in the rest of the chain, the problem was solved by the amended symmetry condition.

7. Concrete aids to solution: The student drew circles to represent links and indicated breaks in the links to help concretize his thinking and manipulations. He also wrote down the number of elements in each group and added them to be sure that he was making no mistakes in his subvocal arithmetic. The correct groups then proved to be 1, 3, 6, 1, 12. Since they add to 23 in various combinations, this proved to be the correct solution. It is seen that there was an interplay of concrete and abstract procedures in this solution. Even the abstract principle expressed in the predominant idea was capable of concretization because it mirrored the conditions laid down in the problem, that is, to take only two links out of a chain of 23 so as to yield groups of links containing all the numbers from one to 23. The predominant idea arose from the "must" of the problem and it was then followed to the end.

A solution by another student is given in the following protocol:

I realized that if I had to take out two links that these two links immediately gave me the numbers 1 and 2, so it would not be necessary to cut the third link because this would give me a group of two duplicating the two single links, which I could not afford to do. I then saw that it was necessary to get a group of three and since there was no other way to do it, I knew that I would have to cut link four. This would give me 1 and 3 and the other one would come when I cut the other link. These would give me altogether 1, 2, 3, 4, and 5. I then knew that I needed to get six, so if I cut the fourth link I would need a group containing six and this I could get by cutting the eleventh link. By combining the links which I had cut with the groups left I now had all the numbers from 1 to 11 and the problem was solved, because I would then build with 12 links on up to 23.

It is obvious from reading this protocol that the predominant idea which this student utilized involved a principle of minimization, i.e., using the fewest number of links and groups to obtain the required combinations up to 23. At each step of the solution, it is seen that he was guided by considerations which proved to yield a much shorter and more direct solution than was the case with the first student's solution which was governed by the principle of symmetry.

We have used the term *predominating idea* where other writers have used *set, expectation, expectancy, attitude, goal, Aufgabe,* or *Einstellung.* We prefer the term *predominant idea* because it is analogous to the focal stimulus in perception and because it points to actual properties of the concepts around which systems of thinking develop. Results of a study by Cofer (1951) illustrate how the focal concept determines a whole system. Lists of words were presented to Ss with the request to indicate the one which did not belong with the others, e.g., *skyscraper, temple, cathedral, prayer.* In the order given, *prayer* was rejected, but in the order *prayer, temple, skyscraper, cathedral, skyscraper* was more apt to be rejected. When the list began with *skyscraper,* the idea of a building of some sort was aroused; when it began with *prayer,* the idea of religion was aroused, with resultant choices in each case. The first word thus served as the focal stimulus and determined which words belonged and which should have been excluded.

C. Day Lewis, an outstanding British poet, has made the *predominating idea* central in his account of poetic creativity (1961). The poet, he maintains, like the scientist, is an *explorer* who is not sure of what he will eventually come up with in his search. First, there is emotional stir—partly feeling, partly excitement, partly apprehension—which "throws up" a line of poetry: "I brood upon this line, trying to discover in what direction it is pointing, to what experience it refers, and to what sort of poem it is a clue" (p. 67). Sometimes a single word or a phrase serves as the "clue" not only to the content of a poem but also to its meter. Once something is given, other phrases, images, and associations attach themselves to the bait and are carefully reeled in. What we have called the "predominating idea" Day refers to as "clue," "donnée," "theme," "meaning."

Just as stimuli are more effective the more they are figured or structured against their backgrounds, so ideas have been found to be more effective the better structured or the more specific are their denotations. This has been shown in a number of studies, particularly of the anagram type. Thus, Hunter (1956) showed that anagrams are solved more quickly and there are less failures when the task is specific (e.g., to make words meaning animals, trees, and parts of the body) than when the task is general (e.g., to make words, without further specification). The results of Hunter's experiments were as follows:

Median time to solve anagrams in specified lists $= 3$ sec.
Median time to solve anagrams in unspecified lists $= 12.5$ sec.
Total number of anagrams failed in specified list $= 35$ (8.1 percent)
Total number of anagrams failed in unspecified list
$$= 129 \text{ (29.86 percent)}$$

The more specific the predominant idea, the easier it was to solve the problems in Hunter's study. A study by Helson and Cover (1956) showed similar results for the general vs. specific information given Ss in the task of recalling famous names. The specific categories were British movie actor, playwright, opera composer, revolutionary leader, physicist, and portrait painter. The general categories were actor, writer, musician, statesman, scientist, and artist. First, 24 names were given the Ss to classify. The group of Ss given the general categories made 1.76 errors and the group given the specific categories made 1.66 errors in classifying the names. Hence the names were about equally well known to the two groups. After classifying, all Ss did something else for 20 min. and then were asked to write down as many of the names as they could remember of the 24 given them. If they could not recall the categories, they were allowed to see the list of categories again. The general-category group recalled a mean of 11.08 names out of the 24, whereas the specific-category group recalled a mean of 14.30 names, the difference between the groups being significant beyond the .001 level. Of the 24 names, 23 were recalled by a larger percentage of Ss given the specific categories than by Ss given the general categories.

The results of this study are also borne out by the results of studies having to do with single vs. multiple set or direction of thinking. Problems that give rise to more than one dominant idea may be more difficult to solve than are problems which arouse only one predominant idea. Of the following examples from Woodworth and Schlosberg (1954, p. 843) the first is more difficult than the second:

Edith is fairer than Olive, but she is darker than Lily. Who is darker, Olive or Lily?

Lily is fairer than Edith; Edith is fairer than Olive. Who is the fairest, Lily or Olive?

The first form was answered correctly by 46 percent of an eight-year-old group, the second form by 72 percent. The two forms of the problem are equivalent logically, but they are not equivalent psychologically because the first suggests two directions of thought (fairer, darker) and the second suggests a single direction (fairer).

Postman and Bruner (1949) investigated the effect of single vs. multiple sets on perceptual recognition thresholds under the following conditions: Under single set, Ss saw two words tachistoscopically exposed at a 45° angle. One was always a color word, the other a neutral word. The task of Ss was to see the color word as fast as he could and report it as well as everything else he saw in the field. In the multiple set condition, Ss were presented either with a color word and a neutral word or with a food word and a neutral word. Ss had to report either the color word or the food word. It was found that the mean recognition time under multiple determination was 228 msec. and under single determination, it was 191 msec. They also found that multiple determination inhibited the effects of practice, as shown by failure of the Ss to improve in the second half of the experiment when the multiple set was given after the first. When the single set condition came second, Ss showed improvement in recognition time over the multiple determination condition.

We must not confuse multiplicity of cues, which may aid in solving problems, with arousal of competing dominant ideas that may hinder thinking. Polya (1948) pointed out that often complicated problems in mathematics are solved more easily than simple problems because the former offer more cues to solutions than do the latter. Eriksen and Hake (1955) found experimentally that as the number of dimensions increased, the percentage of correct judgments went up in judging size, hue, and brightness of colors. As shown in Table 8.1, when size alone was judged, the number of correct judgments was 47.5 percent; when hue alone was judged, 53.4 percent; and when brightness alone was judged, 41.3 percent. But when size-hue was judged the number correct went up to 76.2 percent; when size-brightness was judged it was 59.8 percent; and when hue-brightness was judged, it reached 84.2 percent. Finally, when size-hue-brightness was judged, the number of correct judgments rose to 96.5 percent. These experimental findings are in direct contradiction to the assumption made by Descartes that the simpler his perceptions were the more certain he could be that they were true! Here the more complicated the situation, the more correct was the judgment.

TABLE 8.1. Correct Judgments as a Function of the Amount of
Information in the Stimulus

Stimulus	Information (Bits)	Percent Correct
Size	2.84	47.5
Hue	3.08	53.4
Brightness	2.34	41.3
Size-hue	3.55	76.2
Size-brightness	2.98	59.8
Hue-brightness	3.76	84.2
Size-hue-brightness	4.11	96.5

SOURCE: From Eriksen and Hake, 1955. With the permission of the American Psychological Association.

Cognitive data may supplement perception and have stimulating value as shown by Kurtz and Hovland (1953). These workers found that fifth-, sixth-, and seventh-grade children showed better retention scores when the name of the object was pronounced in addition to being circled on a printed sheet, as against merely circling the picture of the object when it was presented. Verbalizers were also found to be superior on verbalization and picture identification of the objects one week after exposure. On recall tests, the verbalization group was superior to a control group who were only visualizers.

Although multiplicity of cues may aid judgment, thinking, and recall, the presence of more than one predominating idea may lead to difficulty in the solution of problems. The difficulties may be of the following sorts: (1) some of the ideas may lead to wrong solutions; (2) the ideas may be incompatible, and a decision must be reached regarding which ones to pursue; (3) a fruitful idea may not be explored because the presence of other ideas may lead to its abandonment before it has actually been proved unfruitful.

It is evident that thinking does not proceed in a straightforward progression even in working out elegant theoretical systems. Finding proofs in mathematics, presenting evidence in law, and interpreting scientific data are backward and forward processes of trying out hunches, guesses, hypotheses, and conclusions and then working back to their justification. The attainment of simple structure (to borrow a term from factor analysis) is usually the end result of thinking, not its beginning. Generally, more ideas are rejected than are accepted in good thinking. For a long time the process of finding solutions to problems was known as "trial and error"; but the process is more one of fitting, adapting, rearranging, or adjusting thinking to meet the demands of problems. Sometimes only the keystone of the arch must be supplied to support a whole structure because when this is found everything else fits into place. But only very rarely does a whole musical composition, a complete painting, or a final theory spring suddenly into mind. Structures, whether made of brick and mortar or of ideas, must be *built,* even though the builder has an idea of the whole which governs the process of creation.

Modes of thinking. It has long been a matter of debate whether imagery is necessary to carry on thinking, whether animals that have no language can think, and whether thinking and verbalization (overt or covert) are synonymous. Instead of trying to settle these very general questions let us consider only the question of symbolic vs. representational thinking.

Not all thinking occurs by means of symbols, and to the extent that it does not, it is subject to the limitations of perception or actual manipulation. Some types of problems are solved by the majority of *S*s through representation of all their concrete features. An example of this type of thinking is given in the following problem: Imagine a cube, 3 in. on a side, painted red all over; imagine this cube broken up into smaller cubes, 1 in. on a side. How many of the smaller cubes have paint on three sides? How many have paint on two sides? How many have no paint at all? A mathematician or an amateur geometer would probably solve this problem without recourse to imagery in which an actual cube is reinstated; but the average individual duplicates in visual, tactile, and kinesthetic imagery what he would do if he had the cube and performed the indicated operations. Another standard problem that has been used to demonstrate imagery to classes in psychology is the following: A squirrel moves around the trunk of a tree always facing the center. A man walks around the tree always keeping the trunk of the tree between himself and the squirrel. Does the man go around the squirrel in the sense of being east, north, south, and west of him? Does the man go around the squirrel in the sense of being in front, behind, and to the side of him? To answer these questions the vast majority of individuals must duplicate the tree-squirrel situation in imagery.

If the conditions of a problem can be translated into symbolic form, then its solution may be much easier because symbols are superior to concrete objects and operations in several respects. For those trained in the use of symbols it is found that:

1. Symbols are easier to manipulate than objects.
2. Many more operations can be kept in mind if they are symbolized than if they are represented concretely.
3. Relationships appear more clearly.
4. Concrete properties not essential for solution are more easily disregarded.
5. The operations of thinking are reduced to a minimum when they are carried by means of symbols.

The manner in which a concrete problem was managed more easily by being treated symbolically was shown in a study by Helson and Helson (1946). The problem was as follows: A certain moving picture theater admits men for 30 cents, women for 20 cents, and children for 1 cent. On a certain day there were 100 people in the theater, and the receipts totaled $10.00. How many men, women, and children were in the theater? By translating the given conditions into algebraic form the problem is easily and logically solved. Symbolic substitution used to clarify thinking should not be confused with the images and secondary sensory processes found in memory processes. These latter have little or no value in productive thinking because they do not free thought processes from the constraints of the concrete situation. Symbols in productive thinking function as true substitutes for the originally given relations and are full of meaning for the problem. They may reveal new or more general aspects of problems which were not evident in the original.

Concrete representations or operations may often be an aid to abstract thinking provided they are of the proper kind. Such representations as Euler diagrams aid considerably in solving problems involving syllogistic reasoning and have been known for centuries. It is very easy to show by Euler diagrams that no valid conclusion can be drawn from the two premises "no X's are Y's" and "no Y's are Z's" because three possibilities are open, any one of which may be true. If the X's are denoted by one circle and the Y's by another circle they do not overlap because no X's are Y's; and the Z circle does not overlap with the Y circle because no Y's are Z's. It is seen immediately that the Z circle may overlap the X circle or may even be wholly contained within the X circle without violating the two premises, so that the conclusion that some Z's are X's, all Z's are X's, or no Z's are X's are all possible and hence no single conclusion can be drawn from the premises. Here a concrete representation of the conditions stated in the premises leads quickly and correctly to the proper conclusion. However, there are individuals who solve even complicated geometric problems without recourse to concrete representations. In the case of a mathematician known to the writer this ability was developed by translating geometric concepts and relations into verbal meanings or definitions. All his thought processes utilized symbolic rather than concrete representations of problems.

BACKGROUND AND CONTEXTUAL INFLUENCES IN COGNITIVE PROCESSES

Nowhere is the influence of context more evident than in language, where the meanings of single words may be completely modified by adjectival and adverbial modifiers and by the phrases, sentences, and paragraphs in which they are embedded. The meanings of spoken words and statements are greatly affected by subsidiary factors such as accompanying intonation, gestures, and emotional expressions. Often statements must be understood in the light of social, economic, or artistic norms that are taken for granted. The society matron who asserts that nobody attended a party given by a rival does not mean that no single person attended or even that the number of guests was small, but that no one of social importance or from her set attended. When strong emotional biases are operative or expressed in language, even quantitative terms may be greatly altered in meaning. The information conveyed by language depends upon more than the individual words, phrases, or even sentences. Studies by Mosier (1941) and by Jones and Thurstone (1955) showed that intensitive modifiers shift the scale positions of terms away from the center of the scale toward the extremes. Words have a denotation that represents their average or common meaning, and this is modified by the context in which they appear.

A study by Helson, Dworkin, and Michels (1956) showed that words which are regarded as practically synonymous behave very differently in different contexts. In this study, Ss were presented with 26 common words and phrases having quantitative denotations, with different numbers serving as backgrounds. Some of the words employed were *few, some, many, nobody, everybody, hardly anybody, practically everybody, most, a minority*. Four groups of 75 Ss selected at random from classes in various courses at a university were given the 26 terms and asked to indicate the number denoted by each, while keeping a background number in mind. The background numbers were 100, 1,232, 1,444,690, and 1,728,583. The background numbers were chosen with two ends in view: first, the numbers ranged from small to very large; and second, except for 100, they were chosen to prevent rounding or an easy way of answering by taking percentages of the background number. The subsequent results showed that the differences in estimates made with the two lower background numbers were not significant, nor were those between the two largest numbers. Results are in terms of the averages of the estimates made, with the two smaller and the two larger numbers translated into percentages of the background numbers ("derived percentages").

It was hypothesized that the higher the background number against which the quantitative terms were judged, the higher the resultant adaptation level would be and the smaller the percentages denoted by the terms would be. The results bear out the hypothesis completely. The grand mean of the quantities with the two lower backgrounds was 44.5 percent and that for the two larger backgrounds was 39.6 percent, a difference which is highly significant. Moreover, 23 of the 26 terms yielded lower estimates with the higher background numbers than with the lower background numbers in accordance with the hypothesis underlying the study (see Table 8.2). The standard deviations of the items show that there is considerable variation between Ss in the quantitative denotations of the words and phrases. Thus, *all* may denote from 90 to 100 percent of the background number, while *nobody* and *none* may range from 0 to about 4 percent. While some of the variation may be due to the difficulty of making exact estimations, e.g., 51 percent of the three higher background numbers in the case of *majority,* this does not explain the variance of such words as *nobody* and *none,* which could easily have been zero with all backgrounds if this term meant literally the same thing to all Ss. The wide range of values reported for such words as *generally* and *majority* shows that people do not stick to dictionary meanings of common terms; for example, *generally* may denote as little as 50 percent of the background number or as much as 99 percent, depending upon the individual estimator. Likewise,

TABLE 8.2.   Classification of Terms on the Basis of Background Number

Terms	Percentage Change (D)	SD of Change $\sigma_{\text{diff.}}$	$D/\sigma_{\text{diff.}}$	Class
1. All	− 0.5	0.9	0.6	R
2. Everybody	+ 1.0	1.7	0.6	R
3. Practically everybody	− 1.0	1.9	0.5	R
4. Almost all	− 1.0	1.7	0.6	R
5. Almost everybody	+ 3.5	2.5	1.4	R
6. Most	+ 2.5	2.2	1.1	R
7. Generally	− 0.5	2.6	0.2	R
8. A majority	− 2.0	2.2	0.9	R
9. Too many	− 9.0	3.4	2.6	I
10. A lot	−13.5	2.6	5.2	A
11. Many	−12.5	3.0	4.2	A
12. A considerable number	− 9.5	2.5	3.8	A
13. Fairly common	− 2.5	3.0	0.8	R
14. Quite a few	− 8.5	3.0	2.8	I
15. A minority	− 7.0	2.0	3.5	I
16. Too few	− 2.0	2.1	1.0	R
17. Some	− 9.0	1.8	5.0	A
18. Several	− 7.0	1.6	4.4	A
19. Few	− 7.5	1.0	7.5	A
20. Uncommon	− 5.5	1.4	4.0	I
21. Hardly anybody	− 7.0	1.1	6.4	A
22. Scarcely anybody	− 3.0	0.9	3.3	I
23. Practically nobody	− 4.0	1.6	2.5	I
24. Almost no one	− 2.0	0.9	2.2	I
25. Nobody	− 0.5	0.4	1.2	R
26. None	0.0	0.2	0.0	R

Note: Percentage changes are differences of the mean derived percentages for the two large and for the two small background numbers.
SOURCE: From Helson, Dworkin, and Michels, 1956. With the permission of the *American Journal of Psychology.*

majority may vary from 40 percent to 83 percent of the background numbers in spite of the fact that the dictionary meaning of the term is univocally 51 percent or more.

Inspection of the data in Table 8.2 also reveals that the 26 terms divide into three functional classes: some change greatly with background number, others change little, and the rest hardly or not at all. Items 1 to 8, which do not change significantly percentagewise with large changes in the background numbers, were called relative (R) terms. Other items, for example, 10 to 12 and 17 to 19, show large and highly significant variation from the lower to the higher backgrounds and were called absolute (A) terms. Other items which did not change as much as items 10 to 12 were called intermediate (I) terms. We are dealing functionally with (1) terms that change with background in such a manner as to yield fairly constant percentages (R); (2) terms that show a highly significant change in the numbers which they denote as the background numbers changes (A); and (3) terms between the first and second classes which change from background to background but not as much as do the second class of terms. Grouping the items into the three classes is based on the significance of the difference between the percentage estimate with the two lower backgrounds and the two higher backgrounds. Terms in which $D/\sigma_{\text{diff.}}$ is greater than 4 are placed in the absolute category, those in which $D/\sigma_{\text{diff.}}$ is between 2 and 4 are placed in the intermediate category, and those in which $D/\sigma_{\text{diff.}}$ is less than 2 are placed in the relative category.

The constancy of some of the words at the top and bottom of the list, such as *all, everybody, practically everybody,* and *none,* might seem at first to contradict the hypothesis that changes in adaptation level affect the quantitative denotations of the terms. Closer consideration, however, shows that this result supports the hypothesis since it has been previously shown (Helson and Michels, 1948) that stimuli farthest from adaptation level tend to be less affected by changes in it. Grand means of the estimates may be taken to represent the adaptation levels, viz., 44.5 for the lower and 39.6 for the higher background. The greatest change in quantitative denotations of the words should be found with the intermediate terms, and this was found to be the case.

The extent to which words, phrases, concepts, and ideas are *products* of their contexts is often overlooked because meanings are apprehended so quickly they appear to be self-contained independent units. But novel or strange words remind us how dependent every cognitive unit is upon its frame of reference. All have meaning only within a specified universe of discourse. A large farm in New England would be a small ranch in Texas, and what passes for well-to-do in a small town would hardly be considered affluent in a big city. Failures in communication between individuals, groups, and nations spring from the lack of common contexts from which word units derive much of their meaning. For the Christian the calendar zero is the birth of Christ, but for the Moslem, the Hindu, and the Hebrew, the calendar has origins in other events. Among primitive peoples there is no single universal event by which age is reckoned, the age of a man being of interest only in relation to that of his fellows, i.e., older or younger than so-and-so. As long as points of reference are known and understood, almost any system of counting, dating, and comparing will work, although some systems may be more convenient than others. Interpersonal communication depends upon common norms or referents which are metaverbal and often they must be sought in the larger contexts of history, social customs, or personal attitudes.

We have shown how predominant ideas arouse connotations or contexts of ideas. The process may also act in reverse: a number of ideas may act as background to give rise to a new concept or theory. Often a great idea emerges against an accumulated fund of knowledge, and intellectual problems are epitomized, as it were, in the predominating idea—a phenomenon that Boring called the *Zeitgeist* (1942). Dyson (1958) has argued that as a general rule every great innovation in physics, with some notable exceptions, is "merely the decisive moment in a gradual growth of understanding which extends over about 60 years. Thirty years commonly pass between the recognition of a puzzling phenomenon and the birth of the idea that will explain it. Another 30 pass between the birth of the idea and the working out of its major consequences" (1958, p. 81). The emergence of a new basic idea may not be possible until thinkers in a given area have divested themselves of previous notions. How completely they must do this is illustrated by the following story from Dyson:

A few months ago, Werner Heisenberg and Wolfgang Pauli believed that they had made an essential step forward in the direction of a theory of elementary particles. Pauli . . . was prevailed upon to give a lecture explaining the new ideas to an audience which included Niels Bohr. After Pauli's lecture there was a general discussion during which he was criticized rather sharply by the younger generation of physicists present. Finally Bohr was called upon to sum up the argument. He said: "We are all agreed that your theory is crazy. The question which divides us is whether it is crazy enough to have a chance of being correct. My own feeling is that it is not crazy enough." (1958, pp. 79, 80).

Present-day physics has reached the point where in order to make progress it must resort to bold and radical conceptions and theories that must account for an unseen world in which space, time, and energy relations are quite different from those experienced in ordinary perception. Times as short as 10^{-10} sec. and even less encompass the lives of some particles, and the energies of subatomic processes are so enormous that they stagger the imagination of individuals accustomed to thinking in terms of kilowatts and horsepower.

It would appear that the fruitfulness and importance of ideas depend upon the extent to which they emerge from the background or stereotype of prevailing modes of thinking. Ideas that arouse only the usual or stereotyped contexts are not figured against prevailing backgrounds and hence they do not excite contemporaries, nor will they have any interest for future thinkers. This brings us to the role of residuals or more remote determiners of thinking.

RESIDUAL FACTORS IN THINKING

As already indicated, there are many residual factors in cognitive processes, some causal in nature, others only manifestations of underlying mechanisms. The following example of a residual determiner of thought processes, due to a temporary organic state, was reported to me in a letter from a psychologist friend:

After a dose of too much sun, I almost fell over from dizziness as I got out of bed the next morning. I managed to get some breakfast down and as I lay on the couch the inspiration for the beginning of Chapter One came, and I could almost hear the first three paragraphs. The idea for a new test technique also came, solving an old problem of mine. During the night I woke two or three times. One time I had a most beautiful parade of colored forms, like an animated motion picture. If I have ever wanted to paint, it was then. Today I saw my doctor and he accounted for my symptoms on the basis of deficiency of sodium.

Something akin to thought processes goes on at levels below the level of awareness. A mathematician suddenly saw the solution to a problem in one area of mathematics while he was lecturing on a topic in another area! Here the solution to an old problem broke into an ongoing thought process while the individual was concerned with an entirely different topic. Such occurrences are usually interpreted as evidence for subconscious mentation or purely spontaneous ideas.

The results of an experiment by Essenberg (1955) on "the deterioration of intelligence" of albino rats, chronically poisoned by nicotine, point to the influence of physiological conditions on retention and discriminative behavior. Two groups of rats, an experimental and a control, were trained in a Hebb-Williams closed field maze until comparable initial levels had been established. The experimental animals were then injected, and both groups were given weekly refresher runs in the maze. After six months the performances of the two groups were compared; the results are seen in Table 8.3. The experimental animals required over twice as long to run the maze and made almost twice as many errors as the control animals. It was also found by Essenberg that growth and weight were lower for the experimental animals than for the controls.

TABLE 8.3.   Mean Scores of Rats Chronically Poisoned by
Nicotine Compared with Normals

	Initial Scores		After Six Months	
	Time	Errors	Time	Errors
Experimentals	76	11	200	18
Controls	75	12	94	10

Note: The time is in seconds and the runs were made in the Hebb-Williams closed field maze.
SOURCE: From Essenberg, 1955. With the permission of the *Journal of Psychology*.

Feeling states are also residual determiners of cognitive processes, as anyone knows who has tried to write, solve problems, or engage in any kind of productive thinking. The interaction of feeling states and cognitive processes has been well stated by William Gibson, the playwright, in an address before the American Psychological Association (1959):

. . . writing, when it goes well, is no trouble at all and hardly deserves the name of work. It is one of life's chief delights, and enhances my capacity to take delight in the rest of life, however insipid, and is so indistinguishable from play that often, in the midst of it, I stop and wonder at how I was born so lucky that the citizenry supplies me with food, clothing, and shelter, simply for building with my colored blocks. . . . When it goes badly, my experience is precisely the opposite: it is one of life's chief burdens, diminishes my capacity to enjoy anything, however delectable, and is so indistinguishable from cesspool-cleaning that I often wish I had taken that up instead.

It is hard to determine from this account whether the feeling tone impedes the writing or the difficulty in writing arouses the unpleasant feeling states; but there can be no doubt that the two interact.

DIMENSIONAL ATTRIBUTES OF COGNITIVE STIMULI

Just as physical stimuli can be ordered and measured on a number of different continua, so cognitive processes can be ordered and measured on a number of different dimensions. Since cognitive processes and language are so closely related, we may discuss the quantitative aspects of thinking with respect to the quantification of verbal symbols and meanings. Examples of intensity, frequency, and order effects in language and cognitive processes are legion; we shall restrict ourselves to illustrations of quantitative determinations of such effects.

Role of frequency in levels of meaningfulness. One of the earliest methods of quantifying cognitive materials was to determine the frequency of associations to individual words and nonsense syllables. For a long time the early Kent-Rosanoff frequencies of associations to 100 common words were used as indexes of idiosyncratic behavior. According to the hypothesis on which this test was based, individuals who gave too many unique responses to common words were considered deviant. The meaningful associations to nonsense syllables were determined as long ago as 1928 by Glaze and have since been redetermined by other workers (Archer, 1960). The lists given in Table 8.4 show how difficult it is to construct trigrams which are absolutely devoid

TABLE 8.4.   Meaningfulness of CVC Trigrams

0–10 Percent	20–30 Percent	40–50 Percent	60–70 Percent	80–90 Percent
XYH	TEF	BEW	GAN	BOL
XOJ	VIQ	FIP	CEZ	WAM
XUY	ZUR	YAN	KEM	NOV
KYJ	CYF	DYZ	LEP	GEN
ZIJ	BYM	JYB	SYP	REB
XEH	QUM	QAC	WOK	LUV
QYG	YUN	WUP	GUR	VIP
XOS	DYQ	CUK	VOY	GEL
BYW	VED	MUW	HOD	CAF
VIJ	NIR	HYL	HUS	JUT

SOURCE: From Archer, 1960. With the permission of the American Psychological Association.

of meaning. Even syllables arranged to have no meaningful associations have meaning for some individuals.

The more frequently words are used the more frequently they are associated with other words. The role of associative frequency in the attainment of concepts has been made the basis of a theory by Underwood (1952) and Underwood and Richardson (1956a and 1956b). This theory assumes that the attainment of a concept requires perception of the relationship between the concept and its instances. This perception is chiefly dependent on the contiguity and probability of relevant associative responses to the concept instances. The probability determines response dominance, and the mean response dominance of the concept instances is termed *dominance level*. Response dominance is determined by taking the percentage of the total number of responses to a stimulus that falls in a given response category. Thus, 76 percent response dominance of "small" for the word "gnat" means that 76 percent of the responses given to the word "gnat" by a number of *S*s fell in the category of "small." Underwood and Richardson have shown that the ease of attainment of a concept is directly related to dominance level (i.e., mean response dominance). Freedman and Mednick (1958) studied the variance of the instances making up the mean response dominance to determine the effects of high and low variance of the instances on the attainment of concepts. The material used by them is shown in Table 8.5, where the variance of instances making up the

TABLE 8.5. Terms Used in Study of Ease of Attainment of Concepts Having the Same Dominance Level but Differences in Variance of the Instances Comprising the Dominance Level

Variance Level	Noun	Response Dominance (Percent)	Mean Dominance of Concept	Noun	Response Dominance (Percent)	Mean Dominance of Concept
High	gnat	76	"small" 24%	garlic	58	"smelly" 24%
	needle	9		vinegar	14	
	stone	7		daffodil	12	
	canary	5		coffee	12	
Low	sauerkraut	24	"smelly" 23%	cradle	24	"small" 24%
	hospital	23		closet	24	
	tobacco	23		rice	24	
	gym	21		pin	22	

SOURCE: From Freedman and Mednick, 1958. With the permission of the American Psychological Association.

mean dominance of the concept "small" in one case is high, going from 76 percent for *gnat* to 5 percent for *canary* and in the other case is low, being 24 percent for each of the words listed. The variances of the terms associated with the concept "smelly" were similar. *S*s were given these sets of terms and a set of buffer terms to categorize, the buffer terms being introduced to make the task more difficult. The concept for the buffer term was "round." The terms were presented in random order with instructions to find three terms to apply to all 12 words (they were *smelly, small,* and *round*). Two groups of *S*s received the high- and low-variance lists and the buffer list. Freedman and Mednick assumed that high-variance lists would be learned more easily than low-variance lists. This assumption was verified by all measures, e.g., by the number of *S*s who attained the correct concepts for the lists and the time spent in attaining the concepts. Since the lists had equal levels of dominance, it was shown that variance as well as dominance level is important in determining the ease of attainment of concepts.

That frequency of usage may affect recognition thresholds of words was shown in several of the *New Look* studies, although they were primarily concerned with the effect of needs and values on perception. Howes and Solomon (1950) showed that frequent words had mean duration thresholds of .129 sec. as against thresholds of .213 sec. for infrequent words. This result was substantiated in a study by Postman and Schneider (1951) although the differences they found in thresholds were not as large: .109 for frequent words as against .118 for infrequent words. The duration thresholds in the Postman-Schneider study were affected by the differences in the value status of the words, which cut across the differences in frequency of usage. In a study of the role of frequency in verbalization, Cofer and Shevitz (1952) reported a larger number of associations with high-frequency words than with low-frequency words. We must conclude that frequency of usage has important effects on the meaning of verbal materials.

Intensity indicators of levels. Concepts may also be ordered on an intensive continuum as shown by the following list of words, which, most people would agree, increase in intensity as one considers them from left to right:

neutral	strong	stronger	strongest
odor	smell	stink	putrid

The intensity of words can also be changed by adjectival or adverbial modifiers, as was shown by Mosier (1941). First, let us consider Mosier's determination of the affective ratings of a number of common words. Ss were asked to rate 296 words (selected from Thorndike's word list) that were considered suitable for scaling along an unfavorable-neutral-favorable continuum. Ss were given a rating scale in which 6 was neutral, 11 was most favorable, and 1 was most unfavorable and were allowed to assign zero to a word which they did not understand or which they felt they could not scale. From the frequency distributions of the ratings and from the equal-appearing intervals (modified Thurstone method), the words were scaled and measures of ambiguity were determined for each word. Table 8.6 shows the frequencies of

TABLE 8.6. Frequencies of Responses to Words, Median Category, and Q Values

Stimulus Word	Rating											Median	Q
	1	2	3	4	5	6	7	8	9	10	11		
Disgusting	43	51	32	16	3							1.6	1.6
Unsatisfactory	14	39	47	31	17							2.5	1.8
Neutral				1	6	133	5		1			5.5	0.6
Normal	1			1		104	15	5	12	7	1	5.7	0.9
Desirable						3	9	29	57	43	8	8.6	1.6
Excellent							2	3	14	33	96	10.2	0.9

SOURCE: From Mosier, 1941. With the permission of the *Journal of Social Psychology*.

category ratings of six words, the median category rating, and the interquartile range (Q) of the ratings. It is seen that the words can be ordered along an intensitive-affective continuum. We may also compare the favorableness of the words by considering the median category rating assigned to each: *Disgusting* is given the lowest median ranking, 1.6; as would be expected, *excellent* is given the highest ranking, 10.2; and *neutral* and *normal* are almost at the center of the scale with median values of 5.5 and 5.7, showing that they are rated in accordance with their usual meanings. The Q values give an indication of the ambiguity of the terms: terms with larger scatters must be considered to be more ambiguous than terms with smaller variances.

The effects of adverbial modifiers are shown in Table 8.7 for four terms. It is seen that the effect of an intensive is to shift the meaning away from the neutral region of the scale toward one of the extremes.

For example, *desirable* has a median rating of 4.5 when it is unmodified; but when modified by *quite,* it has 4.76; by *very,* 4.96; by *unusually,* 5.23; and by *very very,* 5.66. As pointed out by Mosier, certain intensives are weak, for example, *quite, very,* and *unusually* shift the terms only a small amount from their unmodified positions.

TABLE 8.7.   Effect of Adverbial Modifiers on Ratings of Adjectives

Modifier	Desirable	Agreeable	Poor	Unsatisfactory
Unmodified	4.50	4.19	1.60	1.47
Quite	4.76	4.45	1.30	1.00
Very	4.96	4.82	1.18	0.75
Unusually	5.23	4.86	0.95	0.75
Completely	5.38	4.96	0.92	0.00
Highly	5.35	5.02	*	0.71
Extremely	5.42	5.10	0.95	0.10
Very very	5.66	5.34	0.55	0.25

SOURCE: From Mosier, 1941. With the permission of the *Journal of Social Psychology.*

A study very similar to Mosier's was made by Jones and Thurstone under the suggestive title "The Psychophysics of Semantics" (1955). Fifty-one descriptive words and phrases for rating the meaning of terms designed to denote the affective values of foods were given to 905 enlisted persons. The scale ranged from —4, through zero, to +4; zero was for *neutral,* —4 for *dislike,* and +4 for *like.* There are points of agreement and disagreement between this study and Mosier's. This study reconfirmed two basic hypotheses of Mosier's work: (1) The meaning of a word may be considered to have two parts—one constant, its social meaning, and one variable, its individual meaning. (2) Frequency of responses to a word can be made to project a normal distribution along a scale and words which do not have a normal distribution (bimodal words) yield interesting semantic implications. Mosier found a break in the continuum, the precipice effect, for a number of the words which he presented. There was an apparent end effect at the middle category, as if his *S*s used two continua, unfavorable-to-neutral and neutral-to-favorable, or in terms of his scale, 1–6, and 6–11. This was not found by Jones and Thurstone, who attributed the difference to the instructions which Mosier gave: "Try to keep the steps between 1 and 6, 6 and 11 equal so far as differences of favorableness are concerned." Mosier himself considered this a possibility. Their demonstration that the method of successive intervals was applicable in scaling semantic materials adds evidence to our thesis that cognitive stimuli may be ordered on dimensional continua which have neutral or zero regions with respect to their intensity and affective aspects.

THE CONCEPT OF LEVEL IN COGNITIVE PROCESSES

We have stressed the adaptive nature of thinking and cognition, and it may be asked if the concept of level also applies to thinking, imagination, and creativity. There are, it is generally agreed, continua of cognitive abilities involving various dimensions of intellectual performance on which individuals may be ordered. Thus, IQ has long served as an index of cognitive level. Level may be defined in terms of the quality or degree of difficulty which an individual can attain in tests of intellectual capacity. It may be measured in terms of the transition point from easy to hard, or as the best an individual can do in tests graded for difficulty. Cognitive level may be also measured in terms of work, i.e., either by the rate at which individuals perform tasks, or by the total amount accomplished with or without set time limits. The measure of level may be based on one or all of a variety of dimensions of intellect, e.g., information, memory, span of apprehension, insight, originality, creativity, capacity for abstraction, ability to use symbols, and flexibility of thinking. The concept of adaptation level when applied to intellectual functions represents the intellectual adjustment to a specific task on a specific occasion with whatever means the individual has been able to mobilize.

The stability of intellectual levels, in spite of their tremendous complexity is one of the most remarkable features of organismic behavior. The constancy of the IQ, while not as independent of environmental conditions as formerly believed, nevertheless attests the stability of higher intellectual functions. Let us consider some recent work bearing on the problem of the constancy of intellectual functions.

Constancy of intellectual output. In a study involving successive counts of connected words used by individuals Baker (1955*a*) found that the number of new words in successive units of 2,000 up to a total of 10,000 gave a negatively accelerated curve. Material which he studied consisted of letters written to the editor of a newspaper by a woman over a period of years. In units of 10,000 (with a total of 40,000) words, it was found that the number of different words was constant, i.e., about 1,400 in each 10,000. But the number of new or different words in the four blocks of 10,000 was as follows: 1,400 in the first; 700 in the second; 500 in the third; and 500 in the fourth. The number of new words seemed to approach an asymptote of 500 new words per 10,000. In a study of the protocols of words used by patients in psychiatric interviews, Baker found a similar falling off in successive sessions. In another study (1955b) he analyzed writings of ten service men and found that in groups of 500 connected words there was a fairly constant number of different words: Subject A used 255 different words in the first 500 words; 264 in the second; 263 in the third; and 256 in the fourth. Taking only the first 1000 words in groups of 500, subject E used 232 words in his first 500 and 233 in the second; subject F used 225 in the first and 224 in the second; subject J used 208 in the first and 209 in the second. Thus, in writing there seems to be a typical level of performance in the use of different words, the number being fairly constant for each individual. Baker's conclusions regarding the constancy of word usage, both in the individual and from individual to individual, were verified by Smith (1955) in a study of the diaries and journals which two women kept for many years. However, the constancy of usage may be upset by a particular subject matter and also with advancing age.

If the findings of Baker and Smith are generally correct, it would appear that individuals have a certain amount or level of linguistic material upon which they may draw for certain types of intellectual performance. Does this mean that performance is limited by the total number of words which an individual is capable of using? The same question may be asked about specialized abilities in various areas: How many different ideas do great mathematicians have as compared with average mathematicians? How many different ideas do great philosophers develop as compared with mediocre philosophers? How many different ideas do great statesmen have as compared with average politicians? There can be no question that leaders in the history of thought have varied very widely with respect to the number of their original contributions. For example, Einstein is noted for many first-rate ideas in the field of physics, but Mendel is known for only one great contribution to the field of genetics. Leonardo da Vinci is probably unsurpassed in the number and variety of his contributions to painting, science, engineering, and almost every other field of human activity known in his day; but usually creative activity is limited to single areas and even to specialties within areas. Robert Browning, for example, is a poet of the first order, but his plays do not rank with the plays of the great dramatists. With notable exceptions, including Shakespeare, dramatists have not been poets and poets have not produced great drama.

Experimental results bearing on these and other questions are now beginning to appear. Christensen, Guilford, and Wilson (1957) have investigated and found differences between the rate of production of creative responses and the rate of production of items requiring only simple recall. They used a variety of tasks involving various types of creative thinking to determine the amount produced in various periods of time. Fluency and originality were tested by requiring individuals to give titles to stories, *clever* titles, names of United States cities, pleasant associations, friends whose names begin with *S,* names of birds, etc. Originality was measured by means of three criteria: (1) uncommon responses, (2) remoteness of associations, and (3) cleverness of responses. They found a rather uniform rate of production for creative and for clever responses, in contrast to a negatively accelerated rate of production for items requiring simple recall. Two of the three aspects of originality—uncommonness and remoteness of associations—increased with time; but the third, cleverness, was found to be independent of time. This study is also important in showing that level of intellectual performance depends very greatly upon what is being measured and also upon the portion of the work curve that is taken as an index of the level of performance.

With the increasing number of older people in the population, the decline of intellectual abilities with advancing age is of considerable importance. After surveying the literature on aging, Miles came to the following conclusion:

> Closest to the age trend of decrement of physiological processes are the psychophysiological, the motor functions of activity, and those of sensory perceptions. As function becomes more complex psychologically, the decrement appears less significant until in the highest processes of interpretation and imagination unconstrained by limitations of speed and amount, measurable performance continues with relatively little decline in quality or persistence to the very end of the life span (1942, p. 757).

However, from a number of studies since Miles' survey it appears that there is some decline in mental capacity with advancing age. While soundness of judgment and creativity may persist at levels characteristic of the individual almost to the end of life, it is nevertheless true that there is a decline in ability to shift from one aspect of a situation to another, or to respond selectively to one quality of a situation by abstracting it from all others in the situation. A study by Esta Berg (1948) bears on this point. She used 60 cards on each of which were one to four figures of the same shape and of a single color. The four figures were stars, crosses, triangles, and circles, and the four colors were yellow, red, green, and blue, so that a single card had four green triangles or two yellow circles, etc. Each card could be categorized according to the number, form, or color of the figures. Four stimulus cards were presented: (1) a red triangle, (2) two green stars, (3) three yellow crosses, and (4) four blue circles. Reproductions of these stimulus cards appeared in the response cards. The four stimulus cards were laid down before S from left to right. The response cards were given to S with the instructions, "I want you to put these cards into four groups, underneath the ones lying on the table. I will tell you whether you are right or wrong." The initial correct category was arbitrarily determined to be either number, color, or form. After S sorted five successive cards correctly, the sorting category was shifted to one of the unused categories; after five correct sortings, again the category was shifted, and so on. After the three categories were used up, another cycle of three was used, and still another making nine in all. If S used the whole pack before the complete series was used up, the pack was reshuffled and used again.

On the basis of performance, the 51 Ss were divided into three groups: (1) those who went through the nine categories successfully, discovering early that E was changing the correct category; (2) those who went through the nine categories but had only a vague notion of what E was doing and were not able to state precisely what the shift entailed; (3) those who could not complete the nine categories and had no notion of what went on. Groups 1 and 2 improved toward the end, reducing their errors; but the differences between the groups were significant at the 1-percent level. An older age group, ranging from 58 to 73 years, with a mean of 66, never got beyond the first shift (reported by Berg from an unpublished thesis by Marrow). This group had an incomparably greater tendency to perseverate than did any of the younger groups. They continued to sort for the first spontaneous category, without changing, until the experiment had to be stopped.

Clay (1954) denied that mental power stays constant with age, even when the speed factor is canceled out by using untimed tasks. He employed a test in which *S*s were allowed all the time they wished, although the time was recorded. The test consisted of rows and columns of squares on which counters with numbers had to be placed to make row and column totals. The first row and the first column totals were the same, the second row and second column totals were the same, and so on. The easiest and hardest tasks are shown in Figure 8.2. A given number of counters of various denominations were given to *S*s to fill

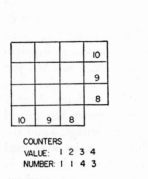

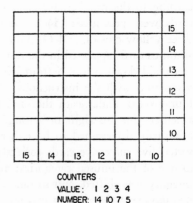

COUNTERS
VALUE: 1 2 3 4
NUMBER: 1 1 4 3

COUNTERS
VALUE: 1 2 3 4
NUMBER: 14 10 7 5

FIG. 8.2. Problems given young and old age groups requiring the column and row totals through use of counters having the values given above. (From Clay, 1954. With the permission of *British Journal of Psychology*.)

the squares to make the required row and column totals. Two groups of *S*s were employed: 64 naval men from 18 to 24 years, with a mean of 20.9 years, and 64 pensioners, from 55 to 78 years, with a mean of 67.5 years.

The older and younger groups were approximately equal on the easiest problem. The number of *S*s solving the problems decreased as the problems grew more difficult, but the decrease was greater in the older group. The older group spent about the same amount of time as the younger group, except on the second problem. Hence, the results of other workers showing that older individuals take a longer time to perform intellectual tasks was not borne out here. The increased amount of material was more difficult for the oldsters than for the younger group. The amount of data that had to be organized to solve the problems was the chief difficulty. The older group could perceive and understand what they had to do, but they could not correct their errors and they became muddled more often; the younger ones were more methodical in correcting errors.

How far the results of the Berg and Clay studies can be generalized regarding the intellectual capacities of older individuals is problematical. The tasks in both studies were somewhat mechanical and arbitrary and may easily fail to interest an older group. Some of the tasks used by Guilford and his co-workers, such as finding clever titles and giving uncommon responses, seem more promising for investigating differences in intellectual performance among age groups than the mechanical tasks of the earlier studies.

Adaptation to levels of difficulty. Clear effects of adaptation levels were demonstrated by Heim (1955) in performances on intelligence tests. She showed that adaptation to level of difficulty and to rate of work has important consequences for measurement of intelligence and her work and conclusions deserve the following rather lengthy summary.

She found that a group tends to maintain a certain constant relation between performance and characteristics of the task, although the absolute level of performance may be less constant than is often supposed. This can hold only within certain limits because an impossible task can scarcely evoke upward adaptation and because limits may shift as Ss become upwardly or downwardly adapted in taking intelligence tests. Successive adaptation was apparent in that the time limits on a first test influenced the rate of work on a second test: a short time limit on the first test produced an increased rate of work on the second test, and a relatively long time limit on the first produced a slower rate of work on the second test. Rate of work carried over as a residual from the first test to influence rate of work on the second test. Hence there is an artificial element in designating tests as speed tests and groups as fast or slow without considering the instructions and the total test situation. In Heim's study, Ss were given easy tests of intelligence in which hard items were included, and hard tests in which easy items were included. She was thus able to study the effect of level of difficulty or context on test performance. She distinguished between immediate adaptation to level of difficulty and successive adaptation, which represents the effect of previous adaptation on succeeding performance. Ss obtain lower scores on hard items that are embedded in an easy set of items because they become attuned or adapted to the level of difficulty as they work through a test. Hard questions tend to be answered more correctly in a hard context than in an easy context. These effects, then, represent effects of immediate adaptation to level of difficulty.

Successive adaptation was found in the performances of Ss who took a hard test first and an easy test second: they did better with hard items in the second context than did equated Ss who took the easy test first and the hard test second. Her explanation of this result was that a subject who takes a hard test first has adapted to a high difficulty level and he will embark on his second test in an "upwardly adapted" state. One of the consequences of these findings is given by Heim:

> It would follow that the notion of one intelligence scale along which the total population can be distributed is untenable. Such a notion implies that every individual possesses a constant amount of a static quality, measurable by standard tests of intelligence. In the writer's opinion, there are objections to this view, many of which are not easily susceptible to experimentation. But the findings of this paper, if convincing and if confirmed by other investigators, would suggest that the subject's response to the same test problems will vary; he will sometimes do himself less than justice (still on the *test* criterion) and he will sometimes do "surprisingly well." Experimental evidence has been adduced in favor of one possible reason for such "test unreliability" (1955, p. 221).

Other considerations follow from the concept of adaptation to level of difficulty:

> It would impose, for instance, far greater care than is usually exercised in the earlier stages of testing: before administering an intelligence test to a group, the intellectual level and homogeneity of the group, and the level of the test, would be considered in relation to one another. The aim would be to allow scope to the maximum possible upward adaptation to a level of difficulty, that is, the test chosen would be as difficult for the subjects as is consistent with their understanding of the problems set. This suggestion is made in the belief that it is more valuable when testing to determine the subject's upper limits than to determine—albeit unreliably—what he *cannot* do.

The phenomenon would have not only practical consequences. If proved conclusively, it might have some effect on the theory of intelligence and intelligence testing since it would throw doubt on the existence of a static entity measurable and expressible in purely quantitative terms, and isolable from other characteristics, notably those usually subsumed under "personality" (1955, p. 221).

From this study, it is evident that the measure of cognitive power depends upon the conditions determining the adaptation or adjustment of the organism to the measuring instrument, as well as upon other factors within the organism.

Generalizations are not valid concerning whether there is more transfer from a difficult to an easy task or more transfer from an easy to a difficult task. Each has been found to be true in different areas. Baker and Osgood (1954) found that the judgments of groups beginning with easy pitch discriminations deteriorated with practice. Repeated practice with large discriminanda made detection of small differences difficult. Their explanation of this result was that the discriminations in the more difficult test were made against the previous level of expectancy and were thus erroneous. These workers found that a gradual transition from easy to difficult was the best regimen for achieving upward adaptation to level of difficulty. This finding was substantiated by Lawrence with animals that did better when approaching a difficult discrimination through a series of gradual discriminations than by other methods of training (1952). On the other hand, Green (1955) found no statistically significant differences between training on easy tracking tasks or hard tracking tasks and subsequent performance on easy or hard tasks. He found that all four targets, small and large, developed the same skills so that the transfer effects were equally good. Green might have found different results in his experiments had he intermingled a few easy tracking trials with the hard trials instead of transferring directly from hard to easy and if he had intermingled a few hard trials among the easy trials before transferring to the difficult ones. In other words, if Green had duplicated Heim's design, his results might have shown differences in transfer from hard to easy as against easy to hard tasks.

In this area, we can only conclude that owing to the interplay of cognitive with situational factors, generalizations regarding transfer of training involving upward or downward adaptation to level of difficulty must at present be clearly restricted to the specific conditions under which results are obtained. However, this does not invalidate the general position that the level of adaptation is an important factor in determining quality of performance in specific activities.

TEMPORAL POOLING IN COGNITION AND THINKING

We have found that order of presentation is important in psychophysical judgments and in sensory and perceptual processes. Order
involves both spatial and temporal conditions of pooling and hence
affects level. In the field of thinking, spatial and temporal order effects
were handled by the Gestalt psychologists by the assumption that there
was an isomorphism between stimulus complexes and thought processes. Koffka envisaged problem solving essentially as an act designed
to achieve an isomorphism between thinking and reality: "Cognition
arises through the occurrence of a psychophysical process similar to the
real process" (1935, p. 368). According to Koffka, if there is a real
solution to a problem, the act of thinking is directed toward finding
a symbolic or verbal pattern isomorphic with the true nature of the
problem and its solution. But the problem of order or patterning of
thought processes is broader than the manner in which Koffka conceived it, for cognitive processes, especially in productive thinking, are
concerned with the formation of systems or solutions, the elements of
which have not been given in a nicely ordered series for the organism
to duplicate according to the principle of isomorphism. What we need
is a *functional* isomorphism to account for the formation of correct
Gestalten when order is not given and has to be achieved. Order may
be given, discovered, or invented and imposed on experience. The
principle of representational isomorphism applies only to cases where
stimulus order already exists. A truly functional isomorphism must
account for order which is achieved through a synthesis of discrete
items, no matter how presented, and which leads to correct solutions.

As Hearnshaw has pointed out, temporal integration is perhaps the
most necessary condition for adequate intellectual adjustments. Such
adjustments are highly dependent on temporal patterning. The importance of temporal patterning is best appreciated when it is absent, as
in cases of patients suffering from word or motor aphasia. In aphasia,
there is not only an inability to recall or to use the correct words to
denote objects and activities, but there is also an inability to assemble
articles requiring an ordered series of moves, to play games like cards
or chess, and to reproduce the plan of a building which cannot be
viewed all at once and/or comprehensively. Hence, the defect in

aphasia can be regarded as an inability to integrate units in serial order or in temporal succession.

We are constantly having to summate our experiences, evaluate them, and make predictions as to the future on the strength of them, and in doing this we necessarily have to integrate temporally separated events. . . . The behavior of the normal human adult takes place in an extended temporal framework (Hearnshaw, 1956, p. 9).

Hebb (1949) and other writers have also stressed the great importance of temporal integration in behavior. Temporal integration, like sensory pooling, may occur very swiftly, automatically, and without conscious intervention; or it may be a slow painful process of deliberate synthesis in order to achieve a required solution to a problem. With repeated or continued effort, conscious awareness of elements entering into a task fades out and may finally disappear altogether. The dropping of conscious elements occurs not only in tasks involving recall of known materials, i.e., in simple association and in solutions of easy problems, but also in sensori-motor tasks and in tasks involving the most abstract and difficult types of thinking. Titchener (1910) admitted that meaning which has been firmly established may be carried by nonconscious physiological processes. In the famous Würzburg experiments on thinking it was found that frequently Ss could identify neither the conscious elements responsible for their solutions to problems nor how they reached their decisions. Later work on cognitive processes went even further than the earlier studies in demonstrating that "complex guiding processes can be formed, retained, and used without the person's being aware of the process at any step" (Leeper, 1951, p. 732). In view of the appropriateness of solutions achieved without conscious intervention in the final stages, it appears that pooling occurs at subconscious levels and in ordered meaningful ways. In other words, not only are old systems activated in thinking, but new systems may be formed *automatically* to yield creative solutions below the level of awareness.

Evidence of the importance of temporal pooling in intellectual activity comes both from everyday experience and from experiments in judgment, cognition, decision making, and other complex types of behavior with which we are familiar. In an example from everyday life, Hearnshaw pointed out that the question "Did you do a good day's work today?" requires temporal integration in order that a proper answer be given. Our everyday estimates of quantity, quality, composition and other characteristics of collections or groups of objects require pooling of many different dimensions and properties of stimulus situations. It is a remarkable fact, as I have pointed out previously, that over-all judgments of complex objects like works of art and political and social issues may be made sometimes without a moment's hesitation, although they are based upon many experiences with many different objects. One may define an expert or an authority as one who can give a snap judgment about a matter and later can substantiate it after deliberate reflection.

Experiments also bear out our contention that cognitive pooling occurs and may lead to quite accurate results even though it is automatic and unpremeditated. In an experiment by Blake and Holtzman, Ss were given four sets of eighteen two-digit numbers spoken at two-second intervals through a tape recorder in various types of distributions (rectangular, normal, and Poisson). The sets of numbers had different ranges and also differed in absolute size, i.e., in the 10's, 40's, or 70's. The estimated averages by the Ss were not significantly different from the arithmetic means of the sets of numbers (reported in Blake, Rosenbaum, and Duryea, 1955). Shuford has reported that Ss are able to give good approximations for the probability of joint occurrences of two independent events, even when they are unable to compute the mathematical expectations and when they are apparently unable to describe how they derived the probability (1959, p. 14). He also found that Ss, in approximating the objective probability of compound events, tended to overestimate small probabilities and to underestimate high probabilities, thus showing a decentered equilibrium point comparable to decentered PSE in psychophysical judgments. Since little or no learning occurs when Ss play betting games and otherwise take part in decision experiments, we must assume that there is an automatic adjustment to the level of stimulation through an averaging mechanism which operates below the level of conscious awareness and which is similar to that operative in other types of behavior.

Time and temporal pooling influence processes in which there is cognitive participation, as in the comprehension of spoken words and phrases. The normal individual understands written and spoken language so readily that its temporal character is often overlooked. Studies have shown that the most easily understood verbal communications require a certain amount of time to be understood. Speech can be understood even though changes are made in the wave pattern, e.g., by deleting higher frequencies, by peak-clipping (cf. Licklider, 1951), or by increasing the rate and keeping the frequency spectrum of the sounds unchanged. In a study by Garvey accelerations up to twice the original rate of speech left the intelligibility of the speech at 95 percent or better. At two and a half times the normal rate there was still at least 90 percent intelligibility. An acceleration of three times the original was accompanied by a drop to 75 percent of normal intelligibility. Not until the speed was three and a half times the normal rate did the intelligibility drop to 50 percent, while accelerations of four times normal resulted in a drop below 50 percent level. Garvey concluded that with discrete, spondaic test words like sunset and baseball, the critical speed for intelligibility is two and a half times the normal speed. This study also showed that *what* is pooled is as important as the rate at which the material is given, for the intelligibility dropped considerably more when the accelerations were accompanied by frequency shifts in the spectrum of the speech than it did when there was only an increase in acceleration. Thus with an acceleration of 1.75, the intelligibility was 95 percent, but with frequency shift (using the same materials and identical procedures otherwise) it dropped to 90 percent. At two and a half times normal speed, a mean intelligibility score of less than 10 percent was obtained with a frequency shift, but one of 93 percent was found with the chop-slice method, which did not involve frequency shift (Garvey, 1953).

Hearnshaw (1956) was able to show how uninterrupted pooling is necessary for understanding printed communications. He inserted nonsense material or words having no relevance into connected discourse, for example, "Cotton goods SUGID cannot be LOCOL made everywhere RULEB for spinning CUMOZ and weaving." For the sentence to make sense, the extraneous material must be disregarded. Extraneous meaningful material was equally effective in disturbing the reading, for example, "Cotton goods DEVOTE cannot be FAULTY. . . ." Hearnshaw found significant differences in the extent to which Ss were disturbed by such interpolations, and he suggested that this might be used as a differentiating test of abstract ability and temporal integration. On the other hand, if a pattern of elements is introduced rhythmically among a random sequence of letters, then the pattern becomes structured very rapidly and separates out in perception and recall from the random materials, as in the following examples (Hearnshaw, 1956): Random

sequences of letters were presented on a continuously moving tape at
the rate of one hundred letters a minute, the aperture being large
enough to expose five letters at a time. *FFR* was the only repeated
sequence of letters with either long or short interpolated series of
letters. The long series first consisted of six letters, and the short of
three letters; these were gradually changed to eight for the long and
five for the short series. For example, the following series contains
the repeated pattern:

G K A S F F R L P X Q F F R Z O Y B F F R L

All *S*s rapidly structured the various series. The letters *FFR* always
separated out and were perceived quite differently from the other
letters. Repetition here facilitated grouping of temporally extended
series of units to aid in recognition.

Miller, Bruner, and Postman (1954) furnished experimental proof
that many visual patterns which were thought to be nontemporal in
nature require time for apprehension and recall. These workers constructed patterns of letters with four orders of approximation to
English, such that zero order was pure nonsense and the fourth order
approached English meaning, for example:

> Zero order: YRULPZOC; VQWBVIFX; EAPMZCEN
> First order: STANUGOP; IYDEWAKN; YWDNMIIE
> Second order: WALLYLOF; CHEBADNE; HEFLINYC
> Fourth order: IRCANING; ATEDITOL; LYMISTIC

Each pattern was constructed according to definite rules from tables
of random numbers and using English prose, and each contained 8
letters. There were 15 patterns in each order, giving 60 pseudowords
which were exposed for 10, then 20, 40, 100, and 500 msec. The patterns were exposed in random order at each of the exposure times in
ascending series beginning with 10 and ending with 500 msec. The
number of correct letters regardless of position and also the number in
the correct position were taken into account. Hence, there were two
measures of correctness of reproduction: total letter score and placement score, the latter being in parentheses in Table 8.8. The data in
Table 8.8 show that both total number correct and placement scores are
a function of the order of approximation to English and the length of
exposure. It is seen that the closer the order of the letters is to English,
the larger is the percentage of letters correct whether or not position

of letters is taken into account. It is also seen that with both methods of evaluating the results, as the exposure time increases, the percentage correct also increases.

TABLE 8.8. Letter Scores and Placement Scores (in Parentheses) as Functions of Order of Approximation to English and Exposure Time

Exposure (msec.)	Percentage of Correct Letters				
	Order of Approximation to English				
	Zero	First	Second	Fourth	Fourth/Zero
10	15.8	23.5	19.4	22.7	1.44
	(5.5)	(10.8)	(10.7)	(12.6)	(2.23)
20	32.9	43.5	46.0	55.8	1.66
	(19.6)	(25.7)	(27.3)	(37.1)	(1.90)
40	50.2	61.2	69.0	73.0	1.45
	(31.6)	(37.8)	(46.6)	(57.4)	(1.81)
100	52.8	69.2	77.6	87.1	1.65
	(36.9)	(43.0)	(59.5)	(70.1)	(1.90)
200	62.5	73.5	83.2	91.2	1.46
	(41.0)	(47.5)	(67.5)	(79.2)	(1.93)
500	66.0	85.0	90.5	96.0	1.45
	(49.0)	(66.2)	(76.2)	(91.0)	(1.85)
500/10	4.2	3.6	4.6	4.2	
	(8.9)	(6.1)	(7.1)	(7.2)	

SOURCE: From Miller, Bruner, and Postman, 1954. With the permission of the *Journal of General Psychology.*

Hence, there are two factors at work here, redundancy, or approximation to English, and exposure time; and the question is which one is more important in reproduction. An answer is provided by the ratio of percent correct at fourth order to percent correct at zero order approximation to English at each time of exposure and also by the ratio of the percent correct at 500 msec. to percent correct at 10 msec. exposure at each order of approximation to English. From the last column in Table 8.8 it is seen that the ratios of percents correct at each exposure between fourth order and zero order approximation to English are practically constant, averaging 1.52 for letter scores and 1.94 with position taken into account. These ratios show the influence of familiarity in perception and recall of letter patterns. However, if we compare the ratios for percent correct at 500 msec. to 10 msec. without regard to position, we find that they are much greater than the ratios at each of the orders of approximation to English with exposure time constant. The ratios for time are also very constant and average 4.15 as against the average ratio of 1.52 for familiarity. Similarly, we find that if we take position into consideration, the time ratios are higher than are the ratios for familiarity, averaging 7.3 against 1.94. *It thus appears that exposure time is about three times as effective as familiarity in determining the number of letters recalled with or without regard to position.* These results show again that perception and understanding of language depend upon temporal pooling. It is surprising but true that both perception and recall are more affected by *time* than by *familiarity* or redundancy. If the ratios of correct placements at the longest and shortest times are considered, it is apparent that temporal integration is more important for spatial patterning than it is for recall, which does not require correct order. *The results of this study show the influence of temporal pooling not only for apprehension of meaning but also for formation of simple linear patterns of elements.*

Pooling is also of importance in cognitive processes in the temporal spacing of practice and recall periods. The effects of temporal spacing have long been known from facts of retroactive inhibition, as summarized in Jost's well-known law. Retroactive inhibition has generally been investigated in memory processes. It appears from a study by Kendler, Greenberg, and Richman (1952) that temporal spacing may influence insightful behavior. These workers employed Luchins' well-known water-jar problem as follows: Ss were presented with an empty 29-cu. in. container, an empty 3-cu. in. container, and a large third container; the task was to get 20 cu. in. of beans into one of the jars. Of the problems given to the Ss the second through the ninth could be solved by a set procedure, which in algebraic form was $b - a - 2c$. Problem 10, the critical problem, could be solved by this method or in a more direct way. Two groups of Ss were employed, one having a zero interval between the first nine problems and the tenth problem (massed group), the other having a 3-min. interval (spaced group). The results showed a definite superiority of the spaced group in that 48 percent of the spaced group as against 26 percent of the massed group used the direct method in solving the critical problem. The difference between these two percentages is significant at the 2-percent level. Moreover, the habitual method required a longer time for solution of the critical problem than the shorter direct method.

Hence, distribution of practice is important in tasks requiring thinking as well as in simple memorization.

Temporal integration may depend upon spatial patterning. Tinker (1955) presented Ss with reading material in the vertical instead of in the usual horizontal fashion. Initial vertical material took 74.1 sec. to read; after a total of 42 readings it took 60.9 sec. Arranged in the usual horizontal manner, the material was read initially in 49.4 sec. and finally in 50.0 sec. Although the horizontal was faster than the vertical reading, as would be expected, the improvement of 17.8 percent in the vertical was surprising since Ss had always known horizontal reading.

An even more radical type of presentation, called "square-span" reading was made by Andrews (1949) to get the advantages of both horizontal and vertical grouping of reading materials. An example of square-span reading is as follows:

| Thinking consists | making use | has been |
| partly in | of what | learned before |

In this form of presentation, the words are grouped in *thought units* rather than by linear spacing. Acting on Andrews' proposal, North and Jenkins (1951) compared square-span grouping with normal horizontal printing that was modified by spacing to achieve thought units called "spaced units." The hypothesis was confirmed, says Tinker, when they found that the spaced-unit printing was superior to the square-span printing and also to the normal horizontal arrangement. Actually, square-span presentation was found to be only slightly less efficient than normal horizontal printing.

Lest square-span reading seem to be completely novel, let us recall its use in reading music. For example, pianists must read the bass and treble clefs simultaneously in what amounts to square-span reading and conductors of symphony orchestras must be able to utilize even larger square-span units to see at a glance all the different instrumental parts in the orchestra. Spacing reading material according to thought units, whether in square-span or horizontal form, will probably prove to be superior to conventional spacing. Our conventional method of spacing words linearly provides word units which are smaller than are necessary for efficient reading and comprehension.

It is as easy to adjust to larger meaningful units, within limits, as it is to adjust to smaller units as shown in the comprehension of tachistoscopically exposed letters, words, and short sentences. Sentences may be perceived correctly at shorter times than are short words or individual letters. We have here an example of the fact that wherever stimulus presentations are already ordered, work can be saved by avoiding the necessity for the organism to create the patterns necessary for most efficient perception and recall.

Another example of the interaction of spatial and temporal factors in the creation of cognitive patterns is found in reduced sentences taken from Schonell (1946):

1. Thx pxxdxxtxxx xf pxppxt plxyx txkxx thx xdxx dxxxlxpxd xx thx pxxxxdxxg xhxptxx x xtxgx fxxthxx.
2. X xurxxer exaxoraxion ix xo xisxrixute xaxers anx xrayons so xxax a xacxxrounx can xe maxe.

In the first reduced sentence there are 81 letters of which 35, or 43 percent, furnish cues for making the original words. Moreover, most of the letters left in this sentence project above or below the line; *p, d,* and *f,* thus provide greater differentiation than do the *x*'s for forming word patterns. The greater difficulty of the second sentence, which contains 75 letters, of which 49 or 65 percent furnish cues for completing the words, arises from the fact that the cue letters do not provide the pattern differentiation which aids recognition of words. Thus in spite of the fact that sentence 1 contains 23 percent more cue letters than sentence 2, the latter is much more easily read than the former. We see that spatial patterning interacts with temporal patterning in the efficiency with which meaningful wholes are created in perception with consequent results on understanding verbal materials.

Pooling, or integration, depends upon stimulus conditions and also upon the extent to which the organism is able to accomplish temporal patterning in the face of adverse stimulus conditions, as shown in a study by Chapanis (1954) dealing with reconstruction of abbreviated printed messages. This study was based upon assumptions of information theory as follows: Owing to the frequency with which various letter combinations occur (the structure of the language), we expect certain letters to follow others. Thus, *u* usually follows *q* in English, and *th* usually is followed by a vowel. Certain letters, for example, *E, T, O, I,* and *N* are often used, whereas *Z, J, Q, K,* and *X* are relatively rare. From the point of view of information theory, common usage, which means high probability, leads to high expectations, which in turn means a high degree of redundancy. Chapanis referred to Shannon's estimate of English redundancy, which is about 50 percent, on the ground that it is possible to reconstruct English when 50 percent of the material has been deleted. Chapanis' study was concerned with the extent to which the average person can dispense with redundancy in reconstructing English and, on the other hand, with how redundancy may help in certain ambiguous situations. In addition, the experiment was to discover how well a heterogeneous sample of Ss could reconstruct English texts when various amounts had been deleted from them.

The material in Chapanis' study consisted of 13 prose passages varying widely in difficulty. Deletions were made in these passages either in random or in regular fashion. Six amounts of text were deleted: 10, 20, 25, 33.3, 50, and 66.7 percent. Letters, spaces and punctuation marks were counted as units to be deleted, there being 300 units in each passage. The positions of the deletions were varied from passage to passage. The Ss were asked to rewrite in full the deleted material and to guess if they did not know what the words should be.

The results showed that for passages up to 25 percent deletion there was an almost linear increase in the number of items supplied, either right or wrong. But when 33.3 percent had been deleted, the total amount of material supplied decreased, until with 67 percent deleted, the median S attempted to supply very few items. Up to 25 percent, Ss usually supplied the right amount of material; but for amounts greater than 25 percent, little material was added. For example, when 50 percent, had been deleted, the median amount supplied was less than 25 percent. Furthermore, the inserted material was not correct. When only 10 percent was deleted, scarcely 80 percent inserted was correct, and as the amount deleted increased, the correct material markedly decreased. When 10 percent was deleted, Ss were able to restore 90 percent; when 30 percent was deleted, about half could be correctly restored; with 50 percent deleted, the median S restored about 10 percent correctly. More was restored with regular deletions because random deletions occasionally resulted in the omission of entire words, which made the task harder. Chapanis concluded that Shannon's estimate of redundancy was too low when more difficult passages were used, when knowledge of the material was lacking, and when other conditions were not optimal for Ss. Of considerable importance is his incidental observation that material which is easy to read according to the Flesch count is not necessarily easy to reconstruct because the deletion of too many short words makes it much more difficult to reconstruct the passage.

We have spoken of temporal integration as if it only carried the past into the present, but it also involves projection into the future. The ability to project into the future is one of the most important human capacities. Animals, when not completely welded to the present, have very limited powers of extrapolation into the future as compared with those of man. We possess the power of projecting far into the future, treating the future as if it were the present. Temporal integration thus has a double aspect, the first involving a recapitulation or mobilization of relevant past experiences or residuals, the second involving projection into the future with present acts adjusted to future contingencies.

Temporal projection into the future is possible because of the rich connotative power of verbal units. Words possess all the connotations of language because a single word may connote as much as a phrase, sentence, or paragraph does. Collocations of words according to the rules of grammar and syntax have possibly more potentialities of experience than the actual world has. Every combination of words conveys its own shade of meaning, nuance, or type of information. Since cognitive processes depend largely upon the use of language or symbols having the properties of language, it is seen that thinking has almost infinite variation and this provides the basis for extrapolation into the future.

To be fruitful, cognitive processes, must, as Shakespeare said of the imagination, "body forth the form of things unseen, and give to airy nothingness a local habitation and a name." In other words, cognitive processes must spring from reality or be referable back to reality, or else they must form a coherent consistent system in their own right. Non-Euclidean geometries furnish a beautiful example of consistent theoretical systems which at first did not seem to have any real counterparts but which are now thought to mirror the universe.

EMOTIONAL DETERMINANTS OF COGNITIVE PROCESSES

Since Pascal pointed to the emotional source of much of our thinking in his famous epigram, "The head finds reasons to support the heart's desire," and since the work of Freud, laymen as well as psychologists have been aware of the influence of emotional states on cognitive processes. The term rationalization was coined to cover phenomena of this kind. Affective determinants of thought processes have been classed as residual factors in cognition because they are extraneous to the logic of the thought process and also because they are usually not under the control of the experimenter. This classification must not, however, be construed as de-emphasizing the role of feeling in the thought processes. Affects may be made focal, however, by designing experiments in which the emotional content of cognitive stimuli is systematically varied as was done by the *New Look* psychologists in their studies on the effects of needs and values on perception (cf. reviews by Helson, 1953; Jenkin, 1957; and Adams, 1957).

Feelings and emotions have also been shown to influence cognitive processes involved in aspirations and hopes. Preston, Spiers, and Trasoff (1947) distinguished between realistic aspirations "based on an appraisal of the extent to which an individual is capable of meeting the demands of the situation with which he is confronted" and unrealistic aspirations, i.e., hopes which are functionally independent of actual performance and often of the actual probabilities of attaining goals. Previous to the study by these writers, Irwin and Mintzer (1942) found that *S*s reported different numerical values for aspirations based on expectations and those based on hopes. In their study, Preston, Spiers, and Trasoff varied the difficulty of the task (throwing darts at various distances from the target) and also varied the motivation by giving or witholding prizes. The *S*s were required to give a statement of their level of aspiration and what they hoped to achieve under the conditions of the experiment and after varying amounts of preliminary practice. While level of aspiration decreased with the difficulty of the task, "hope" did not depend upon the realities of the situation for up to 50 trials of preliminary practice. Furthermore, *S*s hoped for higher final scores than they actually expected after a considerable amount of practice. For the two experimenters who handled the *S*s the hoped-for scores were 82.5 and 80.0. However, the actualities of the situation finally made themselves felt in the last 20 percent of the trials because by then the hoped-for and expected scores became firmly anchored to the scores which had been actually achieved, i.e., both the hoped-for and expected scores were more realistic.

Preston and his co-workers made the following distinctions in levels of reality of aspired-to or hoped-for goals: (1) goals in accordance with fact or "reality," (2) goals expected, (3) hoped-for goals, (4) wished-for goals, and (5) goals only achieved in fantasy. Each of these is based upon a different level of probability. If the office worker is expecting an increase in salary from an across the board raise and is also hoping for somewhat more on the basis of merit, he is at level two. If he hopes for possible promotion and wishes to become a departmental head or president of the concern, he is at levels three and four. If his fantasy is a clean-up in the stock market or a fortune left to him by a distant, perhaps unknown relative that will enable him to satisfy every desire, he is at level five. As one's strivings are directed toward these various goals one is considered normal or abnormal depending upon the time and energy spent thinking of their attainment. The individual who spends an inordinate amount of time on improbable or impossible goals, or who is dominated by them to the extent that attainable goals suffer, is regarded as maladjusted. On the other hand, depending upon one's success in attaining impossible goals, one may be called a dreamer, a crackpot, a man of vision, or a genius. The genius is one who has succeeded in attaining goals which to the ordinary individual, sometimes even to individuals expert in the area, appear to be impossible.

The extent to which ideas dominate thinking is not only a function of their logic and practicality but also a matter of their emotional content. Cold concepts do not incite to any kind of action. We have already seen that the importance of ideas is usually not manifested unless the ideas are fully investigated and their implications are followed through. For this to happen, ideas must have strong emotional appeal. Feelings as well as logic are the ultimate determiners of the fate of concepts, theories and hypotheses.

COGNITIVE PROCESSES AS SYSTEMS

The concept of predominating ideas entails the concept of cognitive systems since predominating ideas immediately imply other ideas having a connection with them. Just as anchors, standards, and background stimuli exert preponderant influence on perception and judgment, so predominant ideas facilitate related ideas and inhibit others. Systems of ideas are utilized in reasoning, the syllogism being the oldest and simplest model. Studies of syllogistic reasoning have revealed important psychological sources of error and stimulus factors which turn thinking into right or wrong channels. One of the chief sources of error in syllogistic reasoning was called the "atmosphere effect" by Woodworth and Sells (1935). The premises of a syllogism may have one of four possible forms: positive, negative, universal, or particular. The form of the premises creates a sense of validity for the corresponding conclusion: a positive premise predisposes toward a positive conclusion; a particular premise predisposes toward a particular conclusion, even though the other premise is universal; and a negative premise creates a predisposition to give a negative conclusion, even though the other premise is affirmative. Another source of error, as pointed out by Woodworth and Sells, springs from the ambiguity of language, e.g., "some" in the premise "some x is y" may mean at least some, perhaps all, or it may mean some but not all. Any one of these interpretations may be adopted with resultant valid or invalid conclusions. A system of ideas may thus be colored or biased by a single facet of the whole or by one aspect of the system, particularly by the form or meaning of the first premise.

Atmosphere effect and ambiguity of language have their locus largely in stimulus sources and may be obviated through use of symbols, defining terms, etc. There are, however, residual or organismic factors in invalid inferences. One of these, pointed out by Woodworth and Sells, is the caution or wariness with which S draws conclusions: it is more incautious to accept a universal than a particular, and more incautious to accept an affirmative than a negative proposition. A larger percentage of invalid particulars is accepted than of universals, and a larger percentage of negative propositions is accepted than of affirmative ones. Another important residual determinant of invalid reasoning is found in emotional factors. Osgood and Stagner (1941) found that in rating occupations Ss tended to rate esteemed occupations high in all characteristics. They concluded from their study, in which occupations were ranked on a number of traits, "that the mere presentation of a set of occupational stereotypes for a series of judgments caused Ss spontaneously to establish a prestige framework which then determined in a highly reliable manner judgments on the specific traits listed" (p. 289).

Lefford (1946) demonstrated the influence of emotional factors in reasoning by presenting to Ss syllogisms with emotional content and syllogisms of the same mood with neutral content. The Ss judged the validity of the syllogisms, i.e., whether conclusions followed validly from the premises, and also stated their agreement or disagreement with the content of the syllogisms. Neutral or nonemotional (nE) syllogisms gave either unimodal or normal distributions of judgments of validity, whereas the emotional (E) syllogisms gave a J curve in which judgments piled up at the low end of the distribution. Moreover, there were residual effects from syllogisms given earlier: if E syllogisms were given first, the nE curves were skewed toward the low end compared with the responses of the total population of *S*s some of whom were given nE syllogisms first. With E first the *S*s were less able to judge correctly the validity of conclusions. If nE preceded E, the distribution of E was bimodal as against the J curves when E came first. Hence the same process was at work in the opposite direction. Even when nE and E syllogisms were randomly distributed, the E syllogisms gave a J distribution and the nE syllogisms gave a unimodal distribution of responses. This study clearly demonstrated that, contrary to the logician's assumption that reasoning is independent of the content of propositions, the majority of naïve individuals are affected both by the meaning and by the emotional impact of propositions.

Properties of good cognitive systems.   Ideal cognitive structures are best approximated by the postulational systems of logic and mathematics. While everyday thinking is not perfectly logical in character and cannot always be derived from explicitly formulated postulates, nevertheless consideration of the properties of postulational systems furnishes us with yardsticks by which to gauge cognitive processes. A good system of postulates possesses the following characteristics:

1. It must be as *simple* as possible, and its postulates must be as few in number as possible. Simplicity in the fundamental assumptions helps preserve the simplicity of the system as a whole. "The supreme criterion of scientific theory is *simplicity*" said the English physicist Whyte (quoted by Klüver, 1958). Systems that are not based on simple assumptions may become hopelessly complicated in attempting to deal with complex phenomena.

2. The assumptions or postulates upon which a system of ideas rests must be *consistent*. This requirement is self-evident and although Emerson relegated consistency to the hobgoblins of little minds, no logical or scientific system that contains contradictions has any hope of being accepted by anyone but its creator. To test the consistency of an abstract system there is only one known method: it must be given a real interpretation. If an abstract system has a real interpretation, or an interpretation in terms of real entities and relations, and no inconsistency appears, it can be regarded as a consistent abstract system.

3. The postulates of a system should be *independent* of each other. A lack of independence means that some of the postulates can be de-

rived from the others and the system is tautologous. This violates the postulate of simplicity.

4. The postulates of a system must be *complete,* i.e., the entities, relations, and operations must be adequate to yield all the theorems in the system without the necessity for new or additional postulates.

All these characteristics of logical systems can perhaps be comprehended under the single principle of economy of thought. In the case of scientific systems having concrete content, or application to the world we know, there is another requirement: scientific systems must not contradict one another. As stated at the beginning of this book, scientific knowledge consists of interrelated propositions that are consistent. Consequently, ideas in one domain of science should fit with ideas in other domains, or at least they should not be inconsistent with them. Thus physicists have not been happy having to assume that light consists of waves to explain some phenomena and that it consists of particles to explain other phenomena. Much effort has been expended to bridge the gap between the two theories. Consistency of all theories within a science is but another aspect of the operation of the principle of economy. So long as there are opposed interpretations of a phenomenon, opposed adjustments are necessary in dealing with it, and thinking is more complicated than it needs to be.

The nature and consequences of contradiction. Contradiction involves a clash of two or more objects or relations that entail opposed consequences or modes of action. Things are what they are, in and for themselves, just as each perception is consistent within itself. Only when ideas are put into context does inconsistency or conflict arise. Absurd propositions may be believed so long as they are not tested by reference to other propositions. A patient I once saw in a mental hospital believed that he was the Savior and fancied himself related to the great religious leaders of all time through a complicated set of family relationships he had worked out for himself. Anything conflicting with this system of relationships was rejected. Thus the paranoiac achieves consistency at the expense of reality. Some psychiatric textbooks describe the thinking of the paranoiac as logic-tight, but a system of ideas that can be maintained only by excluding contrary, relevant facts cannot be called logical. Good thinking must stand up against the demands of reality and by this is meant the context of all other ideas logically related to any predominant thought. Failure to resolve contradiction results in confusion and paralyzes action.

A number of writers have investigated the mechanics and consequences of incompatible cognitive processes, notably Bateson and his co-workers (1956) and Festinger (1961). Bateson, et al., have formulated a theory, based on the incompatibilities of various levels of communication, which throws light on play, fantasy, and schizophrenic thinking. Their theory has much in common with some of the basic ideas expressed in our treatment of thinking. For example, they also assume that contradiction makes a single adjustment to a situation impossible because it signals or calls for opposed modes of action. Bateson and his co-workers have called this the "double bind." They find the seeds of schizophrenia in the persistence of situations that require contradictory responses on the part of the individual. The individual is caught in a squeeze from which there is no escape save by splitting the psyche. But the schizophrenic's difficulties may also spring in large part from his own distortion of signals—a possibility which is not given sufficient weight by Bateson and his co-workers in their treatment of the double bind. They point out that the patient resorts to many subterfuges to get out of the double bind: he pretends he is somebody else or that he is somewhere else or was somewhere else; his disorientation can be interpreted as a way of defending himself against the situation he is in. Still other reactions may be manifested by patients caught in the double bind. If the patient does not know what kind of message he is getting he may defend himself in paranoid, hebephrenic, or catatonic ways. "The human being is like any self-correcting system that has lost its governor; it spirals into never-ending, but always systematic, distortions." The patient may even distort his internal messages in order to support his outside distortions. The schizophrenic is unable to talk about his difficulties, and this further increases the strain. "The ability to communicate about communication, to comment upon the meaningful actions of oneself and others is essential for successful social intercourse" (Bateson, Jackson, Haley, and Weakland, 1956, p. 258).

Bateson has extended this theory to include play and fantasy. It is based essentially upon the fact that language may communicate information concerning objects or concerning language itself, in which case it is a metalinguistic statement. There are also metacommunicative messages where the subject of discourse is the relationship between the speakers. Here one individual sends signals to another, by way of language, gestures, etc., to indicate the nature of the behavior in progress. Many metacommunicative messages are not verbalized, e.g., those of animals. These are interpreted as "mood signs," or signals. Individuals recognize signals that may be trusted, distrusted, falsified, denied, amplified, corrected, etc. We often respond to signals automatically, as if they were direct objective indications of events in our environment instead of signals concocted by others like ourselves. The play of animals, and indeed of humans, remains play only so long as the signals are interpreted as play and not combat. Other forms of behavior also involve signals, e.g., a threat denotes other actions. Acting denotes life at the same time that it is known to be only a representation. Such instances point to the establishment of what Bateson calls a frame or context: things mean certain things within certain frames. When contradictory communications are placed within a single frame we are caught in a double bind as long as we attempt to stay within the frame. An example given by Bateson is as follows:

> All statements within this frame are untrue.
> I love you.
> I hate you.

The first statement is self-contradictory about itself since if it is true, it must be untrue at the same time. It carries with it all the others in the frame by its reference to them. If it is true, then all the others are false; if it is untrue then the others must be true! This example belongs among the famous logical paradoxes which have come down to us from the ancient Greeks and which, as we have seen, boil down to the requirement of opposed adjustments to a situation. We have something of this sort at the perceptual level if we are required to match a set of grays on a white background with a set of grays on a black background: the darkest grays on the white background cannot be matched by any grays on black background and the lightest grays on the black background cannot be matched by any grays on the white background.

Bateson conceives frames as psychologically determined and defines frame as a "class or a set of messages or meaningful actions." Words such as *play, movie, interview, job,* and *language* denote frames. This list could be indefinitely extended. Frames are further delineated by adjectives, adverbs, verbs, phrases, and may be elaborated in sentences, paragraphs, and whole books. Their characteristics are listed by Bateson as follows:

1. Frames are exclusive and by excluding certain messages or meaningful actions they include others.

2. They are inclusive and by including certain things they exclude others.

3. Frames are related to premises. A picture frame tells the observer not to use the same sort of thinking in interpreting the picture that he might use in interpreting the wallpaper outside the frame; similarly statements must be interpreted within the frames in which they appear.

4. Frames are metacommunicative because they define explicitly or implicitly the set of messages about which they communicate. Conversely, every message defines a frame.

5. Frames are within larger frames in the sense that they are desired, even for backgrounds, to set a limit or to prevent infinite regression.

6. Outside the focal stimuli within frames there is a background which in turn is limited by the outline of another frame. Bateson points out that this double framing is not merely a matter of frames within frames but an indication that mental processes require an outer frame to delimit the ground against which the figures in the frame are perceived. In our terms this means that stimuli requiring different adjustments define different frames.

The normal individual usually makes a more or less sharp division between frames that are "real" and frames involving unreal, fantasied, or imagined objects. The flight of the schizophrenic to his world of dreams is but an exaggeration of the behavior of children or superstitious adults. Such adults accept contradictory signals at face value or resort to the world of the supernatural in their thinking as soon as they are presented with phenomena that are apparently at variance with the usual laws of nature or that are outside their ken. This form of behavior is manifested in the reactions of many adults to the tricks of magicians, to strange coincidences, or to sudden unexplained natural or human events. Consider the following trick in which a broken match is apparently mended instantaneously:

I take a handkerchief from my pocket and open it, shaking it well to show there is nothing concealed in it. I then place a wooden match in the center of the handkerchief and let it rest in the palm of my left hand. After folding the corners of the handkerchief over the match, I present it to someone to break through the handkerchief. I ask for silence so that the sound of the breaking match can be heard by all. After the match is broken I unfold the handkerchief for all to see and there, in the center of the hand-kerchief, lies the unbroken match. I then take the handkerchief by one corner and shake it well to show there is nothing concealed within it. I also bare my hands and arms to show there is nothing concealed in them. This trick was repeated several times for a graduate student who came from a foreign country; he declared solemnly, "There is no physical explanation of this phenomenon."

The hardheaded skeptic, however, stays within the reality frame and knows there is a broken match *somewhere*. He refuses to believe that the match he felt and heard break was mended in a second or two while the handkerchief was being unfolded. He asks himself where can the broken match be? How is it concealed? How is it disposed of? If we lived in a world where scientists believed rabbits came out of hats simply by tapping them with wands, we would undoubtedly have foun-dations donating millions to find out why this occurs! The late Harry Houdini, perhaps the greatest magician who ever lived, claimed no supernatural powers and wagered that he could duplicate the feats of any other magician or any "spirit" medium with his own methods. In spite of his denials, many thousands of people who saw him perform came away with the belief that he did possess supernatural powers.

The world of the average man consists of a system based almost completely on his immediate perceptions. The world looks flat and was so regarded for untold generations. The first geometry, Euclidean, was the geometry of a flat universe. Its later extension to three dimensions was also a geometry of lines derived from an essentially flat world. Only a few Greeks and only a few moderns at the time of Columbus came to the conviction, based on certain observations and deductions therefrom, that the world was actually a sphere and not a finite flat plane. Today the majority of people, including many who have gradu-ated from college, believe it is *always* true that 6×4 is equal to 4×6 because that is what they were taught in school. They are unaware of the fact that the commutative law of ordinary algebra in which $a + b = b + a$ and $a \times b = b \times a$ need not hold in other algebras. Similarly, in the arithmetic of finite classes it is not true that n equals $n + 1$ but with transfinite cardinal numbers not only is n equal to $n + 1$ but n equals $2n$. Of course "equal" has a new meaning in transfinite cardinal number theory, one which is not used in ordinary arithmetic. It should not be forgotten that strange algebras, non-Euclidean geometries, and

other systems of mathematics have some roots in perception and may
even be represented by real objects, relations, and operations. For example, the breakdown in the ordinary commutative law has a real,
everyday analogue. Ordinarily we assume that the distance from A to B
is the same as the distance from B to A but consider the following situation: the road from A to B has a bridge on which traffic is blocked to
those traveling from B to A. In returning from B to A, because of the
blocking of the bridge, it is necessary to take a roundabout route to
cross the river. Hence the distance from B to A is greater than that
from A to B. Although they operate within an abstract system, the
logician, philosopher, mathematician, and theoretical physicist have
their "feet" (or at least one foot!) planted in "reality"; they constantly
check deductions, not only for consistency within the system, but also
with respect to other systems. Similarly the normal individual acts in
accordance with perceived physical and social norms, not merely in
accordance with his private cognitive frames.

ABSTRACT THINKING: A RESULT OF DEVELOPMENT AND LEARNING

The ability to manipulate symbols and to think in abstract terms is
often assumed to be the result of genetic endowment and not a matter
of learning and experience. However, there is much evidence to support
the contrary view, viz., that abstract behavior is, like almost all other
abilities, a matter of learning. Jahoda (1956) found that the Goldstein-
Scheerer Cube Test (GSCT) was subject to environmental and cultural
influences no less than various intelligence tests. Jahoda found that Gold
Coast African boys 13–18 years of age deemed the use of four blocks
strange and often used only one block. They also tended to ignore
spatial orientation, 0°, 45°, and 90° being judged equally correct. More
significant perhaps was the finding that home background was important: the average score for boys from literate homes was 84.9 and from
illiterate homes it was 65.1 (.02 level of significance). That these findings were not due to a deficiency in ability for abstract thinking but to
a lack of perceptual skills was proved when these Ss improved with
practice.

The possibilities for developing capacities for abstract thinking early
in life have hardly been realized, chiefly because of the widespread
prejudice that this type of behavior is innate. Due to the weight of

tradition, children are still introduced to mathematics through the most difficult and unpleasant route, viz., through the memorization of numbers and arithmetical operations, such as addition, subtraction, and multiplication. We have not taken advantage of the fact that children quickly learn the rules of games and readily act in accordance with the constraints imposed by these rules. Mathematics also requires action in accordance with set rules and if it were taught essentially as a game in which the abstractions were concretized by means of operations with tangible objects, such as blocks, diagrams, and figures, many more children would develop mathematical modes of thinking. I know that this procedure is possible because I taught a child who was not yet five years old the rudiments of algebra in a game with blocks. The child was taught to change the signs from plus to minus or from minus to plus when moving blocks from one side of the equality sign to the other. One of the greatest obstacles to learning algebra was absent in this young child because it did not occur to him to ask what numbers the letters represented; he had not learned arithmetic! The letters and their signs were manipulated for their own sake as a game played according to the prescribed rules. Similarly, when the child learned arithmetic the numbers were taught as parts of an ordered system with recurrent properties. When this child found that numbers larger than 100 were obtained by simply utilizing the numbers that he originally learned, difficulty with large numbers was never encountered. Before the age of seven, this child was introduced to logarithms as a short cut for multiplying and dividing. Paradoxically, by concretizing the abstract, it was possible to advance this child very rapidly in mathematical thinking.

The reader may question whether all children can learn mathematics at an early age or if special mathematical aptitude is needed. There are individual differences in interest and aptitude for abstract thinking but it must be granted that we have been slow in exploring this area. Considering the dry memory work required of children learning the multiplication tables and the uninteresting methods employed in teaching both rudimentary and higher mathematics, it is not surprising that many children develop a distaste for mathematics and for other types of strict thinking as well. So much of mathematics is concerned with elements and operations that are defined by relations that the teaching of mathematics should begin with relations. There is no reason why the child's attention should not be focused on mathematical relations and operations rather than on the acquisition of numbers through the exercise of memory. Many of the most fundamental relations in mathematics are immediately perceptible. For example, greater, less, between, similar, equal, matching, and many other relationships are appreciated by young children, in some cases before they can be verbalized. My belief that children can be taught fundamental mathematical concepts and operations at a much earlier age than is now being done is based on the assumption that contrary to the beliefs held by many, so-called abstract thinking is not necessarily more difficult than are rote memory processes. Since much abstract thinking has its roots in immediate experience, what is required to teach children mathematics is not so much a break in their usual modes of thinking as a break with traditional approaches to the education of the children.

Cognitive processes are subject to certain restraints, but at the same time they allow great freedom for the imagination. Abstract systems are determined by the assumptions or postulates on which they rest, and once these are chosen, if they are consistent, all deductions follow with absolute certainty. This is why rational deductions are favored over empirical findings in scientific work. Since one is not free to accommodate deductions to fit untoward findings, conclusions reached on purely rational grounds, when verified, have a force that is much greater than empirical findings. The rigor of deduction in theoretical systems is ameliorated by the fact that we can exercise the greatest freedom in choosing the postulates with which we begin. Different abstract systems may be built by altering only a single postulate, as in the case of Euclidean and non-Euclidean geometries where the definition of "parallel" determines the type of geometry one obtains from the postulates.

Reasoning proceeds within a frame (context, background) of permissible operations and relations. While the rules governing permissibility may be freely chosen, as in choice of the fundamental postulates of a deductive system, once they are chosen they become as independent of individual whim as so-called objective fact. The logician, mathematician, and theoretical scientist adopt or create frames which determine the content and direction of their thinking. Both internal and external desiderata govern the choice of postulates and these, in turn, govern the system or frame within which thinking proceeds.

The elegance, economy of thinking, and power of mathematics can be conveyed to young minds if its various branches are properly taught. To do this, it is necessary to know how best to present the subject from a psychological as well as from a mathematical point of view. There is room here for co-operation between psychologists and mathematicians just as co-operation between psychologists and engineers has paid off in improved designs and equipment for optimal human operation.

CREATIVE THINKING

One of the chief problems confronting the psychologist interested in cognitive processes is that of creativity. Creativity and words allied to it such as creator, creation, imply something new, something novel, bringing into existence something that did not exist before, be it ever so little. It is often asserted there is nothing new in the world because the ingredients entering into every creation have been in existence so only the configuration or pattern is new. This view of creativity is defended by pointing to syllogistic reasoning, where conclusions supposedly contain nothing that is not already known in the premises. For example, take the time-worn syllogism: all men are mortal; Socrates is a man; therefore Socrates is mortal. Since Socrates is contained within the class of men any property accruing to the class belongs to the members of the class and therefore nothing new is learned in the conclusion that Socrates is mortal. What is overlooked in this argument is the difference between what is *logically* novel and what is *psychologically* novel. Although Socrates is contained within the class of men and mortals and therefore logically partakes of the properties of both, the information contained in the conclusion that Socrates is mortal may be quite new in a psychological sense. An illustration taken from the philosopher Royce is logically identical with the syllogism we have just discussed, but since the conclusion does not follow as obviously from the prior information, it demonstrates the difference between logical and psychological novelty. The story told by Royce in this connection was as follows:

A dinner was given to honor a priest who had served in the same town for 50 years. In responding to the eulogies bestowed upon him, he stated that this was a very happy occasion indeed, but it reminded him that his first confessor in this town was a young man who had committed a murder. As he engaged in further reminiscences, the richest and most influential man in town arrived and took his place at the head table which had been reserved for him. After the priest had finished, the leading citizen was called upon to make the remarks that he would have made had he arrived earlier. He rose and said, "This is indeed a most auspicious occasion, and I am most happy to be here, especially in view of the fact that I was Father O'Brien's first penitent in this city."

This story reduces to the following syllogism: First confessor was a murderer; leading citizen was first confessor; therefore leading citizen was murderer. While no new information is conveyed logically in the syllogism, psychologically there is something new in the conclusion. The way in which most people react upon hearing this story leaves no doubt of the novelty of putting, so to speak, two and two together and coming out with four. Although no one would deny that in mathematics new concepts, relations, theorems, numbers, and systems are constantly being discovered or created, Bertrand Russell defined mathematics "as the system of all possible tautologies." From the point of view of logic this definition may be correct, but from other points of view it is not.

Originality and novelty are the essence of creativity. Creative products are also useful in some sense—theoretically, practically, aesthetically, economically, or morally. The truly creative product may be considered a system or miniature world in its own right. This is true of such creative products as novels, plays, symphonies, paintings, theories, and many operations and methods which revolutionize traditional ways of doing things. It is also true of lesser creations such as short stories, musical compositions, and new empirical findings. A creative product must have the properties of a meaningful, coherent whole, or Gestalt, even though its ingredients are purely fanciful as, for example, Shakespeare's *Midsummer Night's Dream*. Every part must contribute to every other part and the whole must have a characteristic property which is none other than its predominating or anchoring idea. The predominating idea defines or delimits the world that the creative individual tries to concretize in a systematic whole.

Imaginative products, as we pointed out earlier, must have some connection with reality. Although Wordsworth defined the poet's task as one in which he makes the real seem unreal and the unreal seem real, note that in both cases the connection with the real must be maintained. Fruitful creative products must prove interesting to others as well as to their originators. In this connection William Gibson (1959) pointed out how the creator faces in two directions as he works:

I am aware at the moment of writing that I am gazing in two directions at once, into myself and out to an audience, and what I put down on paper must satisfy standards in both directions or it will not put down. The standards facing out are concerned entirely with those aspects of form in part enumerated—logical sense, sound, image, structure—as a means of making the unit largely intelligible to the mind of whatever audience I am aiming at, but impactful upon its physique; they are intended to insure . . . that the audience shall not only comprehend what I said, but feel what I imagined. The standards facing in partake in the same aspects of form, but their sine qua non is discovery. The moment of inspiration is a moment of discovering something new and unwritten in myself. . . . Such discoveries may range from a minute turn of phrase to the overall concept of a large piece . . . this discovery inward, and formulation outward, happen simultaneously, or so close thereto that I often cannot say which has come first (1959).

In other words, there is a community of attitudes, feelings, ideas, and expectations on the part of the audience, which the creator must to some extent satisfy if his creation is to be appreciated by others. At the same time the creator must also satisfy certain internal norms which depend upon his goals and the nature of the material with which he is working.

We have by no means exhausted the various problems and possibilities of creative thinking. The concept of the predominating idea is not a variant of association theory for associationism does not furnish a satisfactory basis for originality and creativity.[1] The creative worker is not the individual who has the largest number of associations in his field of endeavor; he generates new ideas and systems of thinking.

Why is thinking distasteful to so many people? Thinking is difficult, and it is accompanied by considerable negative affect when it does not "go." It usually requries many readjustments before closure occurs or a problem is solved. The thinker must create new worlds and "live" in them to determine if they are self-consistent and if they make sense in other respects. Perhaps an even more potent reason for the unpopularity of thinking is that it requires the individual to shut out his immediate environment in order to devote himself fully to the objects of thought. To most people this is not pleasant. Thinking requires that "one absent himself from felicity" for a while, or from ordinary satisfactions, to achieve more or less remote goals. Abstract thought is, moreover, farther removed from tissue needs than any other type of

---

[1] Wundt postulated a class of "logical associations" to remedy this defect in associationism but it is at best an *ad hoc* postulate designed to fill a gap in association theory.

activity and is therefore not reinforced by ordinary satisfiers. To those who have learned the delights of intellectual accomplishment, ordinary satisfactions are pale by comparison. Perhaps if intellectual activities were encouraged at earlier stages in the educational process there would be more superior individuals in the world and less stereotypy in thought and action.

SUMMARY

Cognition and thinking are conceived as forms of action, with the laws of logic regarded as derivative from possibilities of action. When thinking and perception are compared, it is found that the paradigm of focal, background, and residual stimuli may be applied to thought processes with certain modifications. Characteristics of fruitful predominating ideas were listed, and the advantages of concrete and abstract modes of thinking were discussed. Since thought processes are amenable to dimensional approaches, it is permissible and fruitful to use the concept of level here as well as in other types of behavior. The importance of temporal pooling is recognized as well as the emotional determinants of thinking. Good cognitive systems have certain properties, and contradiction has its own nature and consequences, particularly with reference to Bateson's theory of play, fantasy, and schizophrenic thinking. Ability for abstract and creative thinking is regarded as capable of development under appropriate stimulation, particularly during the early formative years.

9 *Personality*

Up to this point we have been concerned with the functioning of the organism in more or less specific ways, e.g., in perception, judgment, memory and learning, and thinking. All our studies of these activities have been conducted for the most part on intact, total organisms. In the case of human studies we have not yet employed the term *personality* in accounting for what we have found. How and why, it may be asked, did the concept of "personality" come to be used in psychology, first as a descriptive term and later as an explanatory concept? Antedating the introduction of the term was an interest in the ways and extent to which individuals differed from each other in speed of reaction, in memory ability, in types of imagery employed in remembering, in intelligence, and in such physical characteristics as rates of bodily growth and types of physical constitution. The interest in differences among individuals as opposed to the formulation of general laws and principles applicable to all organisms was called the "psychology of individual differences" by William Stern in 1900, although Francis Galton as early as 1869 must perhaps be given the credit for having explicitly recognized variation or departure from the norm as a problem in its own right (cf. Murphy, 1949, p. 117 ff.).

APPROACHES TO PERSONALITY

The various approaches to personality are legion (cf. Guilford, 1959), and it is not within the scope of this book to treat or even mention them all. Instead let us consider some of the more important attempts to deal with the concept of personality, especially as they have a bearing on the theory developed in this book.

From the beginnings of studies of individual differences through to modern conceptions of personality there has always been present, either implicitly or explicitly, a belief in inner powers, dispositions, or tendencies which, through variations in strength and manner of combination, make a given individual unique. Indeed, we may almost equate personality with uniqueness since personality refers to the ways in which one individual is different from another.

Individual behavior patterns persist over long periods of time and are more or less consistent, giving each person a uniqueness. The persistence and uniqueness of complex as well as simple response patterns have been responsible for the belief in more or less fixed inner determiners of behavior. It is argued that when individuals respond identically in different situations it is because the same *inner* factor has been tapped to call forth the same response. Personality, in line with this belief, is then defined as the sum total of *inner* determinants of behavior; and the task of the psychologist is to isolate and measure the amount or strength of internal factors so as to be able to understand and predict individual reactions in life situations. The quest for inner determinants of behavior has passed through a number of phases differing more or less from each other but having in common the belief that the mainsprings of behavior, the unique features of individual behavior, have their locus inside the organism rather than outside. Indeed, the term *personality* carries the implication that the individual is largely to be understood in what he brings to situations, personality being the *species* to the *genus* environment.

We may distinguish five approaches to personality as follows: (1) instinct theory, (2) typology, (3) trait theory and its variants, (4) S-R and environmental theories, and (5) eclectic approaches.

Instinct theory. During the early part of this century and due largely to the influence of Darwinism, the doctrine of instincts dominated thinking about the mainsprings of individual and group behavior (McDougall, 1908; Freud, 1933). The intensity and kind of response an individual makes in any given situation depends upon the strength and interplay of his instinctual endowments. Individuals possess different amounts of self-assertiveness or self-abasement, sexuality, acquisitiveness, maternal instinct, and so on through lists varying among authors and with the same author from time to time (cf. Murphy, 1949). Situations might arouse instinctual activities, or situations might be sought or created by the individual when his instinctual drives became sufficiently intense. In general, the stronger the instinct the less stimulation was presumably required to trigger it into action. While the theory of instincts served a useful purpose by furnishing names and global descriptions of patterns of behavior supposedly common to all men, and in McDougall's definition shared by the higher animals as well, it was soon superseded by concepts derived from experimental-quantitative approaches to animal, child, and social behavior (Pavlov, 1927; Watson, 1926; Allport, 1924; and many others) and also by the typological approach of such men as Jung, Spranger, and others.

A list of McDougall's instincts would have to include the emotion that accompanies the behavioral expression, the natural stimulus or condition in which the instinct is aroused, and its abnormal or exaggerated forms. Here is one list of instincts with their associated emotions (in parentheses) as given by McDougall in 1908: flight (fear); repulsion (disgust); curiosity (wonder); pugnacity (anger); self-abasement (negative self-feeling); self-assertion (elation); parental (tender emotion); reproduction (lust); gregariousness (restlessness when alone); acquisition (?); construction (?); hunting (?); feeding (appetite, hunger); sleep (?). The last six instincts were admitted by McDougall to have no well-defined emotional accompaniments.

Instinct theory as such cannot account for cultural influences on the expression of emotions and on their behavioral counterparts, the instincts. Indeed, the personalities of individuals, although differing between cultures, may be so similar within a culture that some writers, particularly Watsonian behaviorists and some neobehaviorists, deny there are any instincts whatsoever (Kuo, 1924), or reduce them to a few "drives" which are channeled or conditioned according to the conditions of life of the individual. Many an elementary text has recounted how the Arapesh of the South Seas are a kindly, noncompetitive race of people because infants are treated with warmth and affection, are suckled whenever they cry, sleep with the mother, are carried by her wherever she goes, and are continuously fondled and caressed. On the other hand, the Mundugumor are a tough, warlike people whose children are treated harshly, kept in uncomfortable baskets, not suckled unless clearly in need, not caressed or fondled, and made to fend for themselves as early as possible. Even the so-called instinct of pugnacity, which might be expected to lead always to physical combat, expresses itself in relatively pacific ways among some people: Eskimos sing songs abusing each other in public, and Kwakiutl Indians fight by giving away or destroying as much of *their own* property as may be necessary to outdo their rivals. Hardly anything seems left of supposed inner instinctive drives when we consider the extent to which behavior may be modified by situational and cultural forces.

Typology. From ancient times, beginning with Heraclitus, who described the "good man" as containing a preponderance of warm and dry elements and the "bad man" as containing a preponderance of wet and sodden elements, through Hippocrates, Theophrastus, and Galen, to modern times, philosophers, psychiatrists, and latterly psychologists have attempted to classify human beings into easily identifiable types. The motives for typing are succinctly stated by Guilford (1959) as follows:

> The classification of persons into type categories is a most natural approach for the beginner in personality studies. It is the method of the "man on the street," who indulges in the popular pastime of pigeon-holing the people whom he knows. It is an effort toward economical evaluation and recognition of persons. The individual finds it expedient to classify people so that he can react one way to persons in one class and a different way to persons in another class. He predicts and controls the behavior of others from what he thinks their classifications or types to be (p. 89).

We have had morphological typologies in which various aspects of physical constitution (body build, relative sizes of parts of the body—limbs, trunk, neck, facial features, skull conformations) have been correlated with temperaments or specific behavior patterns (Kretschmer, 1926; Paterson, 1930; Sheldon, 1940; 1942; and for still more examples, cf. Guilford, 1959). On the other side we have also had purely psychological typologies formulated without regard to possible constitutional or physiological correlates: the value types of Spranger (1928); the tough- and tender-minded types of James (1890); the objective vs. subjective types of Binet (based on observations of only his own two children!); the analytic vs. synthetic types of Benussi (1914); the oral, anal, and phallic types of Freud (1920); the introversive and extraversive types of Jung (1923); the ascendant and submissive types of Allport and Allport (1928); and, to make an end of a list that can be pursued indefinitely, the authoritarian type of Adorno, Frenkel-Brunswik, Levinson, and Sanford (1950).

Typologies differ from author to author and have undergone successive changes in the direction of greater complexity and scalability, but they have in common the quest for determiners of behavior having their locus entirely within the organism. Insofar as situations affect persons they only furnish occasions for the manifestations of inner characteristics. The ineffability of the individual in terms of typologies was shown by Allport and Odbert's list (1936) of 18,000 dictionary terms that could be used to describe personality, a list that was not deemed sufficient to furnish a *complete* description of the uniqueness that characterizes each and every individual! As Guilford (1959) showed, all that would be needed to describe 10 billion unique individuals would be 10 scalable traits each with only 10 distinct steps (giving 10^{10} unique values, if no two individuals were alike in all respects). It is apparent that typologies can serve no better than instincts to furnish concrete predictions of how individuals will behave in various situations for they do not result in the establishment of functional relations between manipulable variables.

The trait approach to personality. Perhaps the most radical, clearcut statement of the doctrine of traits as inner determinants of personality was made by Carr and Kingsbury (1938), who defined traits as concepts describing the "reactive nature of an individual." According to their views, modes of action adapted to the exigencies of a situation "cannot be regarded as an expression of the constitutional nature of the individual" and hence do not reveal traits. On the contrary, the maladaptiveness of a response reveals its trait character, e.g., rude behavior on the part of a host towards his guests reveals that he is a rude person because the trait manifests itself in a very unlikely situation. Since traits are supposed to change slowly and persist for long periods, situational factors are excluded from the definition as well as temporary organic states and behavior arising from special conditions like fatigue. Carr and Kingsbury strongly implied that traits are only the result of inherited capacities in their statement that the "observed modes of conduct [are] functions of the constitutional nature of the individual," but modern trait theorists admit that inner dispositions may be products of learning as well as of inheritance. Burt expressed the view that factors or traits "are principles of classification described by selective operators. *The operand on which these* *operators operate is not the 'mind,' but the sum total of the relations between minds and their environments"* (quoted by MacKinnon, 1944, p. 34). In spite of this formal recognition of the role of the environment in the manifestation of traits Burt's definition provides no operational way of investigating the interactions that yield persons manifesting traits in specific situations!

Granting that traits are manifested in specific situations and represent the contribution made by the organism to behavior, trait theory as yet fails to account for interactions among traits, the extent to which a trait will be manifested in specific conditions, or which trait, among different traits possessed by an individual, will be manifested on any particular occasion. So far trait theorists have not established correlations between degrees of stimulation and intensity of response, a basic requirement for control and prediction of behavior patterns. Nor does trait theory account for the suppression of a tendency in one situation and its strong manifestation in another, e.g., the fact that a man may be overbearing with his family and submissive to his boss. In short, while trait theory provides a taxonomy of behavior patterns and thus furnishes a structural concept of personality, it has so far failed to provide a correlated taxonomy of situations and the functional dependencies which relate the two. This lack seems to be inherent in test approaches to traits and can be remedied only by supplementing them with experimental-quantitative procedures involving situational as well as organismic variables.

Factor-analysis approaches. Factor-analysis approaches to personality are, in general, refinements over simple trait theories because they employ mathematical methods to obtain the fewest number of concepts that will account for the results of (relatively) large numbers of tests. While the end result is the discovery of personality traits, or factors, a number of advantages accrue to factor analyses which are not found as a result of simple scaling of traits. If traits represent common modes of behavior of individuals in different situations then factors may be said to represent traits common to different tests. Like simple trait theory, factor analysis yields components of the structure of personality or of particular aspects of personality like intelligence, cognition, or aptitudes. Depending upon the kinds of test materials on which factor analyses are based, they may yield static or dynamic dimensions of personality. Thus if the tests are of the inventory type wherein the testee is called upon to report on his activities, attitudes, or preferences, no amount of analysis can supply information regarding functional relations of variables, a necessary condition for development of a theory as well as a science of personality. If, on the other hand, the tests are miniature work situations or call upon the testee to show what he can do by solving problems, reasoning, manipulating geometric figures, giving definitions of terms, etc., then the results of tests and factor analyses may yield information having the power of experimental approaches.

S-R and environmental theories. One of the most extreme positions with respect to the environmental origins of personality traits has been expressed by Stephenson (1956) who maintained that the factors obtained by factor analyzing personality ratings are not in the individuals being judged but in the judges themselves. According to Stephenson, *X*'s (judges) rate *Y*'s (subjects) by way of a system of modes of regard which are in the *X*'s, not in the *Y*'s. Hence the factors also must be in the *X*'s rather than in the *Y*'s. Many S-R theorists who regard personality traits as learned modes of behavior ameliorate the extreme- environmental position by assuming that conditioning and learning are ultimately based on innate drives such as hunger, sex, and fear, with their positive or negative reinforcing properties. But the great importance of the conditions under which innate drives are manifested, according to S-R theorists, tends to land them in the pure environmentalist camp.

The eclectic approach. While recognizing the presence of both situational and personal determinants in the expression of personality patterns, the eclectic approaches usually end up considering the two independently because they have lacked a systematic basis for bringing them together. Even when both sets of determinants are put into such formulas as $B = f(E,O)$ (behavior is a function of environment and organism), the eclectic position has usually not provided a way of assessing the interactions of E and O operationally. But not all attempts to bring outer and inner determinants of personality are eclectic or suffer from the inchoateness of eclecticism. Sakoda (1952) and Guilford (1959) take positions close to ours and envisage all behavior as the product of levels determined by the interaction of outer and inner sources of stimulation. Sakoda maintained that "a trait is not meaningful unless it is considered in the context of a kind of situation" (p. 849), although some traits may not require consideration of situations, presumably if they are sufficiently general in character. Sakoda proposed that studies be made to discover general situations correlative with general traits so that traits may be defined within the context of situations *ipso facto*. Individuals would be assessed with respect to their behavior in kinds of situations. It would then be possible to answer questions such as the following: "In what kinds of situations does he possess ability?" "What is the extent of his social adjustment in different kinds of social situations?" Sakoda says, "In every instance the general trait of an individual would be defined in the context of a kind of situation" (p. 851). Adopting a position close to our own, Guilford (1959) stated that "a trait is regarded as a kind of predisposition, and in this sense it is in a class with the residual that helps to determine the adaptation level" (p. 51).

PERSONALITY AS PRODUCT OF FOCAL, BACKGROUND, AND RESIDUAL STIMULI

Let us now turn to a consideration of personality within the framework of AL theory by first considering stimulus sources of variance in personality traits.

The three sources of variance found operative in sensory processes, judgment, affectivity, learning, and cognition are also operative when the sources of stimulation are other persons as is the case in personal interactions. In social situations we find that some persons are focal, others exercise lesser claims on attention and form the social background for ongoing interpersonal responses, and others, like residual stimuli, add their contribution to individual reaction patterns. While social psychologists often speak as if they believed that interpersonal relations involve only total personalities, it is obvious that social intercourse is mediated by audio-visual and other sensory processes. Indeed social situations have their substrate in physical conditions and often the peculiar quale of a social situation depends upon some physical feature of which we may be totally unaware, e.g., the quality and level of illumination or the decor of a room. Individuals communicate their thoughts, attitudes, hopes, expectations, memories, and sentiments by means of speech, gestures, facial expressions, and by other signals which are called "social stimuli" because they serve as mediators of interpersonal relations. Among social stimuli must be included the arts, theater, movies, television, literature, and other cultural artifacts since these also convey messages from person to person. Among stimulus determinants of personality patterns let us first consider the individual's own bodily processes.

Bodily sources of personality patterns. There are persistent bases *within* the individual for consistent action, among which must be reckoned genetic inheritance, body chemistry, and sensory input of all kinds. The role of genetics in *behavior* is far from being proved or understood, although the genetic determination of physical characteristics seems well established, provided the role of environmental factors, such as diet, climate, birth injuries, childhood diseases, exercise, and a host of others, is not overlooked. [Lord Bryce in *The American Commonwealth* pointed out that children of brachycepahlic immigrants have longer heads (dolichocephalic) than their parents which he attributed to the American diet.] Similarly body chemistry may be responsible for both physical and mental well-being or disease and thus can exert profound influence on behavior (Williams, 1957). But it should be remembered that internal factors also depend upon forces impinging upon the organism and upon such external materials as food, drink, drugs, and the air that is breathed.

The most important stimuli determining personality come from our own bodies! Our bodies and bodily processes are a constant source of stimulation and remain more or less in awareness as focal, background or residual stimuli. In this connection consider the results of some studies by Jourard and Secord:

Sixty-two male undergraduates answered a questionnaire regarding parts of the body using a five-category scale ranging from "strong negative feelings" through "neutral" to "strong positive feelings." Pearson r's were determined between body cathexis and parts that could be measured easily such as height, weight, shoulders, chest girth, and muscular strength. Except for weight the correlations were positive between size of parts and body cathexis, showing that large size was associated with positive feelings and small size with negative feelings. This finding was in contrast to the finding for women: women's desires were for small size of all body parts except for bust (Jourard and Secord, 1953; 1954). So far as the women are concerned we can be quite sure that the reactions to their bodies in the year 1954 A.D. were largely culturally determined with present overemphasis on large bosoms in movies, television, dress styles, and in devices designed to accentuate the bosom, just as the bustle of a former era accentuated the behind. The cultural determination of body cathexis, especially as regards the ideal or desirable female type, is found in histories of dress, the stage, sculpture, and art. Thus our bodies, largely fashioned by genetic factors, are cathected in accordance with social pressures.

Feelings of satisfaction or dissatisfaction regarding one's body were found by Secord and Jourard (1953) to carry over to feelings about the self, conceived chiefly in terms of various patterns of behavior, e.g., morals, artistic talents, imagination, popularity, self-confidence, manual skill, handwriting, manners, intelligence, conscience. Attitudes toward body parts are carried over to a moderate degree and in the same direction, as shown by r's of 0.58 for men and 0.66 for women, to evaluations regarding the self. Secord and Jourard studied normal, if not superior, groups of men and women. How much more important does the body become as an ever-present determinant of personality when one is afflicted with a deformity, is abnormally short or tall, has an extremely large or upturned nose, is markedly overweight, or with a physical appearance that betrays him as belonging to a minority racial group? Jourard and Secord (1955) found that deviation from the ideal or cultural stereotype of size of parts of the body was more important to women than men (cf. the r's given above) because, they surmised, one of the most significant factors in a woman's general adjustment is how attractive she feels she is to men. "If she does not feel or appear 'beautiful' she feels a loss of self-esteem" (p. 246). The changes in patterns of behavior, commonly called personality changes, to compensate for or to adjust to felt inferiority arising from small size, bad looks, inferior bodily strength, etc., impressed Adler to such an extent that the concept of compensation became central in his system of psychology. While he and others following him may have over-emphasized the importance of inferiority complexes in determining one's outlook on the world (life style) or in choosing a career or in the decision to excel along certain lines, there can be no doubt that bodily characteristics are most intimately related to one's self-concept. Since the body is an ever-present object of awareness it must be regarded as one of the most important determinants of personality and of social modes of adjustment.

Finally, in any consideration of the body as a source of stimulation we must not omit sensory input from intero- and proprioceptors which provide feedback from muscles, tendons, joints, glands, and viscera. Such feedback tells us not only what we are doing but *how* we are faring. Many important differences in personality often attributed to innate factors or to acquired traits may be the result of hyper- or hypo-sensitivity to pain, to visceral impulses, or to somatic input in general. Darrow and Henry (1949) pointed out how dangerous situations that arouse abnormal physiological processes, e.g., such as arise from carbon dioxide excess, extremes of temperature, humidity, vibration, pressure, or strong odors, may alter the background of awareness by feedback from autonomic, humoral, and other sources. Under such conditions many individuals react "emotionally" rather than adjustively, especially when, as in the case of the submariner or flier, there is no opportunity to escape or to work off the energies aroused by the abnormal situations. Under normal conditions of living some individuals are more sensitive than others to aches, pains, buzzing in the ears, and defects in refraction which are not exactly compensated by proper lenses, so that they are classed as neurotic, nervous, finicky, or plain oversensitive. Any dentist or doctor can testify that differences in sensitivity to pain are so great that what one patient regards as painless or only as a mild pain another may report as unbearable, a fact borne out by the marked differences among *S*s in pain and heat thresholds (Burnett and Dallenbach, 1927). The present popularity of tranquilizing drugs among medical men attests the fact that reduction of sensitivity to sensory input, particularly from the viscera, helps reduce anxiety even when it does not actually abolish pain or other unpleasant sensations.

In pointing to bodily sources of individual differences in response patterns we do not imply that these patterns are not learned. On the contrary, the degree of awareness of bodily signals and the response are just as much a matter of conditioning and learning as a matter of sensory thresholds. In fact we have here a reasonable basis for the learned character of many traits which are often thought to be innate because their sensory basis is overlooked.

Hallucinations, commonly thought to spring from purely internal sources, may arise from external stimulation. Riss (1959) found that seven psychotic *S*s who were actively delusional and hallucinating, reported hallucinations when stimulated by sounds above threshold, and one of the seven reported sounds at threshold or when no sound was present. The sharp line between hallucinations as internally aroused and delusions as externally caused seems on the verge of disappearing. Riss' experimental findings do not, of course, imply that it is not possible for hallucinations in the old sense to occur; they do cast doubt, however, on the supposition that extreme distortions of reality are entirely independent of stimulus origins.

Moore (1939) also has stressed the role of peripheral sources of hallucinatory and delusional symptoms, especially exaggerated or disturbed tactile-kinesthetic sensations. The author recalls a woman patient in a mental hospital who maintained that her body floated out the window every night after she retired and that on these excursions she had various experiences, chiefly of a sexual nature. In her case it seems probable that when visual stimulation was not present to mask her tactile-kinesthetic impulses, which may have been exaggerated in the prone position, she had experiences of movement and floating with secondary elaborations of places, persons, and events that were not real. In accordance with this interpretation therapy might begin with, or at least include, measures to alleviate or correct the abnormal tactile-kinesthetic input which furnished the sensory basis for the patient's hallucinations and delusions.

Each individual's body has more or less constant features embracing structure, appearance, function, and feedback, providing him with more or less continuous stimulation. The complex of bodily sensory impulses may furnish a unique and sufficient basis for each personality but these are by no means the sole sources of individual differences in behavior. Extero-, bene- and nociceptors as well as proprio- and interoceptors bring the individual information concerning objects other than his own body, and these too play an important part in traits often regarded as constitutionally determined. Each individual lives in a more or less constant physical and social environment which contributes to the constancy of behavior attributed to traits. Individual X has a certain occupation or profession which brings him into contact with certain kinds of people almost every day of his life. He is a member of a family in which he occupies a certain position and carries out certain functions as parent, spouse, uncle, or other relation. He is a member of various groups or organizations; habitually reads certain kinds of literature—professional, financial, fictional, historical; watches certain TV programs; and goes to certain plays and movies. In short, the "life style" of an individual (to borrow Adler's concept, 1924) exposes him to recurrent types of stimulation, with the result that he reacts in characteristic ways. While no two individuals react identically to the same stimulation, each reacts in ways representing his mode of adjustment to the situations he confronts.

It is remarkable, in view of the constancy of physical and social stimulation, that differences among individuals are perceived to be as great as they are. Lest we overlook the importance of constant social, cultural, and physical forces in shaping individual behavior, it is well to remember how hard it is to perceive individual differences among people of a culture different from our own. Until we become well acquainted with a foreign civilization, the similarities among its members strike us much more forcibly than do their individual differences.

Anchoring of personality in the here and now. In the light of the foregoing discussion it follows that personality is the functional unity of an organism that is located in a given space and time and is acted upon and reacting to external and internal forces and meanings which range from simple sensory stimuli to complex social situations and higher-order concepts and symbols. We conceive the self-stimulation of the organism to be as important as stimulation by others, both as it affects others and the individual himself. Personality characteristics often attributed to hypothetical inner factors may be traced to the manner in which the individual reacts, not only to external stimulation, but also to feedback from his own activities, physiological as well as behavioral. We have here a basis for the anchoring of normal individuals in the here and now (cf. Schilder, 1942). Because our bodies are always at a determinate place in space and time, each individual has a unique perspective. The normal outlook, while anchored in the present, stretches toward both the past and future, with greatest weight given to the here and now, which serves as the reference point both for on-going behavior and for projections in memory into the past and in plans or aspirations for the future. The system of perceptions, memories, imaginations and overt responses that constitute personality has its origin or point de repère in the present.

Differential weighting of past, present, and future characterizes the changing life perspective with aging, as Charlotte Bühler has noted (personal communication). In childhood and early youth there is little or no past and the future (temporal reference here being taken to include outlook on both time and life's activities) stretches out in ever widening vistas with no closure in sight (Fig. 9.1). As one enters maturity and middle age, the accumulation of experiences broadens the outlook on the past and the future begins to lose its indefinite expansiveness; past and future assume about equal areas in the total life perspective. Then as old age draws on, there is greater accumulation from the past and the future constricts toward the point that marks the cessation of activity. This description fits, of course, only the composite or average individual. There are marked individual differences in weighting past, present, and future. In psychotic conditions we find extremes in this respect: the patient suffering from senile

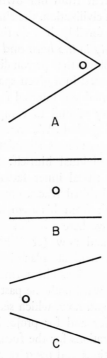

FIG. 9.1. The life perspectives: (A) in early youth; (B) in full manhood and middle age; (C) in later life. The past is to the right and the future to the left of the here and now, denoted by O. (Based on a personal communication from Dr. Charlotte Bühler.)

dementia may regress to childhood with little awareness of the present and no outlook on the future; in schizophrenia the present may lose its normal feeling tone so that normal anchoring in the here and now is lost with its attendant complications; and in the early euphoric excited state of general paralysis of the insane the patient is full of grandiose schemes for the future. On the other hand some outstanding individuals at very advanced ages may not give the impression of ever entertaining the thought of diminution of activity or of death, so that for such individuals life is always open, expanding, and pregnant with the possibility of further work and enjoyment. For them the future is as heavily weighted as it is for much younger people. In cases where individuals brood over the past or fail to see anything worth living for in the future, re-emphasis on the present and what life offers here and now may be the key to a healthier outlook. The paradigm of adaptation levels as weighted means of present and residual stimulation furnishes a rationale for counterbalancing situational or personal factors responsible for maladjustment insofar as psychotherapeutic measures can be effective in such cases.

ASSESSING PERSONALITY

Tests of personality may be roughly ordered along a subjective-objective continuum, depending upon the latitude allowed the individual to reveal his "inner" self. At the one extreme are the *projective* tests, best represented by the amorphous Rorschach ink blots, which supposedly allow full play to inner determinants of perception, memory, and imagination; while at the other extreme are *action* studies in which situations are so firmly structured as to reduce personality differences to a minimum. Between these two poles of the subjectivity-objectivity continuum fall instruments designed to measure personality traits by allowing both inner and outer determinants of personality to function. Thus the Thematic Apperception Test (TAT) of Murray (1943) utilizes pictures of individuals in various situations which are sufficiently ambiguous to allow for considerable play of the subject's imagination in constructing a story. A step away from the subjective pole are the questionnaires and interviews in which questions regarding the subject's past and present behavior, attitudes, fears, anxieties, likes, dislikes, hopes, and ideals, must be answered. Depending upon how the questions are loaded and how the interview is conducted, such methods of obtaining information are, on the whole, nearer the subjective than the objective pole of personality evaluation for reasons we shall give later.

Finally, in our rough scheme, there are situational tests of personality which are nearer the objective end of the continuum. These tests were explicitly introduced during the Second World War for the purpose of selecting candidates for extrahazardous duties behind enemy lines (OSS Assessment Staff, 1948). Even among situational approaches to personality there are, however, important differences as revealed by a comparison of the OSS tests and the Texas action studies, which may also be classed with situational tests. In the former the purpose of the tests was *selection* and hence their main function was to act as a screening device for the armed forces. The latter were for establishing functional relations between controlled variables, the interest being in the laws governing the relation between the variables isolated for study. An exact parallel exists in the field of sensory processes where dark-adaptation thresholds which are determined to select pilots for night flights are contrasted with those determined to establish functional relations between stimulus variables and visual sensitivity. We do not expect to formulate scientific laws from screening devices but knowledge of scientific laws may make it possible to devise useful tests for screening, diagnosis, and other purposes.

Projective approaches to personality. Consideration of the rationale underlying the use of various personality tests reveals different, often diametrically opposed, assumptions regarding the best way of obtaining knowledge concerning residual sources of action. At the one extreme is the view underlying projective tests such as the Rorschach, TAT, and Szondi tests that the less structured the stimulus materials are in a personality test the greater is the likelihood that inner deep drives and tendencies will find expression and reveal the core of personality. As Holtzman has put it, "In clinical practice it is customary to assume that the subject's associations to a series of ink-blots may be considered a representative sample of his 'true' personality and that skillful interpretation is all that is required to delineate at least the major features of it" (personal communication). Three corollaries follow from such assumptions as these, according to Macfarlane and Tuddenham (1951): (1) belief that a protocol is a sufficiently extensive sampling of the subject's personality to warrant formulating judgments about it; (2) belief that the psychological determinants of each and every response are basic and general; (3) belief that projective tests tap the durable essence of personality equally in different individuals. To these assumptions we may add that it is also implicitly assumed that the individual reveals himself best when he is approached as indirectly as possible regarding his own springs of action. This assumption is contrary to the one underlying questionnaires and inventories, which is that the individual is perfectly able to report on his own present, past, and future behavior when questioned directly. Both points of view seem equally open to objection as objective valid ways of determining how individuals behave in various situations.

It is apparent that projective tests suffer because the testee is allowed so many degrees of freedom in his responses that it is impossible to establish functional relations between the inkblots and the responses to them. The common belief that responses to projective materials refer to deep-seated dynamisms is without any proof whatsoever. In this connection a review of the relationships between personality and performance in small groups by Mann (1959) contains an interesting finding. Mann found that he could assign about 350 aspects of personality to one or more of the following 7 traits frequently revealed by factor-analysis techniques: adjustment, extraversion, introversion, dominance, masculinity-femininity, conservatism, and interpersonal sensitivity. But about 150 variables could not be fitted into any one of these 7 categories, the majority of them coming from projective tests! He concluded that "both the titles and the known correlations with the other personality measures (of these other variables) combined to mystify this reviewer as to what meaning they might have outside the language system of the particular technique" (Mann, 1959, p. 244).

Situational factors in personality testing. While supposedly designed to understand the *individual,* the meanings assigned to Rorschach responses are actually based upon *classes* of responses given by particular *classes* of individuals, e.g., the number, percentage, and comparative frequency of responses based on wholes, details, movement, colors, etc., relating to humans, animals, anatomy, or lifeless objects (cf. Shaffer, 1936). Koffka, in an unpublished study reported at a conference of Rorschach workers in 1939, found that an individual taking the Rorschach test under two sets of instructions which induced opposite moods gave protocols which were interpreted as two different personalities by a skilled interpreter who was unaware of the circumstances under which the protocols were obtained. Since this report by Koffka, workers have become increasingly skeptical concerning the inner determination of responses to projective materials of all sorts and have stressed the role of a multitude of situational factors as determinants of responses in personality tests. In this connection Henry and Rotter (1956) commented:

A growing body of literature demonstrates that many factors other than an individual's basic personality structure are operating in any test situation, and that these factors are important determiners of the types of responses given. . . . *individuals adapt their behavior to the total environment in which they find themselves,* and external stimuli as well as inner motivations and dynamics shape behavior at any given time (p. 457, italics not in original; cf. also Miller, 1953; and Sarason, 1954).

Henry and Rotter reported that an experimental group of testees who were told that the Rorschach test was designed to discover emotional disturbances of a serious nature in mental patients, gave, in accordance with predictions, an increased number of F (forms) and D (details) responses and a decreased number of W (wholes) responses as compared with a control group given the Klopfer instructions. In other words, the experimental group were more cautious and conforming in their responses than the control group as a result of the instructions given before the test was taken, thus confirming Koffka's finding that sets or attitudes induced by the examiner may importantly influence responses to the Rorschach materials.

A number of different workers have shown that bodily and behavioral characteristics of the examiner also influence responses to inkblots. Lord (1950) found that thirty-six males given the Rorschach test by three different females, one adopting a neutral attitude, the second an accepting, and the third a rejecting manner, gave significantly different types of responses under the three conditions and also that the response categories varied significantly with repetition of the test. Sells (1952) reported that Rorschach responses appeared quite uninhibited in a group test with relative absence of the examiner but that emotional responses seemed to be controlled in individual testing with the examiner constantly present. Acting on this observation of Sells, Bernstein (1956) gave the TAT test to sixty-eight women college students in a school of nursing. They were randomized into four groups as follows: (1) oral, with examiner absent and testee speaking into a dictating machine; (2) oral, examiner present; (3) written, examiner absent; and (4) written, examiner present. In each case the results with examiner present were significantly different from those with examiner absent, the presence of the examiner acting, as Sells had stated, as an inhibiting factor for highly emotional material. When the examiner was absent the TAT stories were sadder, had sadder outcomes, and showed greater involvement on the part of the Ss.

Examiner attitudes and the minor (background) reinforcements given by the examiner in the testing situation can not only influence response or judgment but can also modify the content of the testee's sensory and cognitive processes. A study by Solley and Long (1958) indicated that interpersonal relations in an experimental situation may affect both perception and learning. They found that verbal reinforcement in a perceptual learning task in which *E* said "uh-huh" when *S* saw one aspect of the Necker cube, and withheld comment at the appearance of the other aspect, was not as effective in the case of one *E* as in the case of another *E*. It was observed that one spoke softly while the other spoke loudly, the former being more effective than the latter. Only when both *E*s spoke at about the same level were results from the two comparable. Another background factor was also found to be important, viz., if *E* took time to chat with *S* in friendly fashion before the experiment proper then an "uh-huh" reinforcement was effective, otherwise it was not. The learning curves of perception of the reinforced aspect of the Necker cube leave no doubt as to the effectiveness of the verbal reinforcement when there is a positive social relationship between *E* and *S*. While the actual manner in which such higher-order factors as "positive social relationship" and verbal reinforcement influence perception is not known, there can be little doubt that they can do so. It may be by way of increased vigilance, by a closer approach to physiological threshold, by modifying the way the eyes are fixated, or by the many other ways in which attitudinal factors influence sensory processes. In the case of such complicated stimuli as inkblots it is conceivable that a friendly atmosphere may facilitate cognitive and memorial processes to the point where testees see more than they would under less favorable circumstances.

Perhaps the most important study of examiner influence on Rorschach protocols from a practical point of view is that of Wickes (1956), who showed that responses of which the examiners themselves are wholly unaware may influence the kinds of responses made by *S*s. The mannerisms controlled in this study were (1) perfunctory verbal comments such as "good," "fine," and "all right," and (2) nonverbal responses such as smiling, nodding the head, and leaning forward in chair. With one group of *S*s the examiner made one of the verbal responses to *S*s' *M* responses, and with the other group he made one of the bodily responses to the first 15 cards and no responses to the second 15 cards. With the control group the examiner made no overt responses of any kind. The results showed that the examiner's reactions, both verbal and nonverbal, affected the number of M responses significantly.

Intelligence has been considered to be the most fixed and unalterable trait that an individual may possess, and yet measures of intelligence depend upon the rapport established between examiner and child. Sacks (1952) tested three groups of three-year-old nursery children, ten in each group, under the three conditions shown in Table 9.1. In the

TABLE 9.1. Effect of Type of Personal Relationships between Examiner and Three Groups of Three-year-old Nursery Children

Groups	Pre-experimental IQ	Postexperimental Relationship	Postexperimental IQ	P
A	125.4	Warm, friendly	139.9	.01
B	123.6	Cool, detached	128.6	.05
C	123.1	Control	124.7	.70

SOURCE: From Sacks, 1952. With the permission of the American Psychological Association.

pre-experimental test all groups were given the 1937 Revision of the Stanford Binet Form L; and Form M was given in the postexperimental test after the experimenter worked as an assistant teacher for one hour with each group. From the P values in Table 9.1 it is seen that there was a significant increase in IQ in the case of the two experimental groups (14.5 points in group A and 5.0 points in group B) but none in the control group. The increase in group B where none was presumably expected is attributed by Sacks to familiarity with the examiner gained during the experimental treatment.

That the general environment in which a projective test is taken may influence testees' protocols was brought out in a study by Kimble (1945) in which Ss took the Rorschach test in two different sets of surroundings. The standard situation for taking the test was the laboratory office of the examiner while the "social" situation was a cafeteria in which at least two other people were present at the time of the test. Fourteen Ss were involved; nine took the test first in the social situation and then in the standard situation, and five took the test in the reverse order. Composite records were made for the fourteen Ss in each of the two situations. The most significant difference was found in the experience balance (E/B) measure. The social situation produced a rise in the color sum of eleven of the fourteen Ss, the other three showing no difference, but in no case was it less. Of the three Ss two were diagnosed as psychopathic, hence the rigidity displayed was not unexpected. The Rorschach test thus proves to be sensitive to differences in testing situations. Kimble, on the basis of these results, concluded that "the view that personality is an entity operating entirely independently of situational variables is illusory" (p. 92).

The discussion showing that situational factors influence scores on personality tests, although somewhat lengthy, by no means exhausts the ever-growing literature on this subject (cf. Guilford, 1959; and Baughman, 1958). Yet in spite of mounting evidence against the *mystique* of purely inner determinants of personality, which are supposedly revealed by means of projective and other tests, many workers still seem to proceed on the assumption that personality consists of tendencies, traits, or dispositions independent of the situations in which they are manifested. From an *operational* point of view, since inner factors do not appear *in vacuo,* a definition of situation-free personality factors is meaningless. Personality, in our view, is *the person in the situation,* and only what is not accounted for in terms of focal, contextual, and background stimuli may be ascribed to personal or inner factors.

Masling (1960) gave expression to the most extreme, if not optimistic, assumption regarding the earlier uncritical attitude toward projective tests as follows:

> . . . the asumption was made that a projective test was as single-minded as the X-ray revealing information only about the patient without in any way being influenced by the person who administered the test, the method of administration, or the situation in which it was used (p. 65).

After reviewing the extentive literature dealing with situational and interpersonal factors which influence the outcomes of projective testing Masling said:

> . . . the procedure that many clinicians hoped would serve as an X-ray proves, on close examination, to function also as a mirror, reflecting impartially S (subject), E (examiner), the situation and their interactions. . . . *These influences are not sources of error, however, but indications of adaptation to the task* (p. 81, italics ours).

Test responses conceived as modes of adaptation should be investigated and evaluated to gain fuller knowledge of projective testing according to this writer.

Inventory-questionnaire approach to personality. We have seen that the projective tests more or less tacitly assume that the individual reveals himself best when he is not asked to report directly concerning his own motivations and inner states. Inventories and questionnaires which require the individual to report on his own behavior apparently proceed on the contrary assumption, i.e., that he not only knows his own responses but knows *why* he makes them. Apart from its limitations, which are usually granted, this approach suffers from two serious inherent defects, which can neither be remedied through application of more refined statistical treatments of test results nor by attempting to construct better tests by methods currently employed in test construction. The first shortcoming springs from the assumption that the testee is *able* to report his own behavior correctly. In questioning this assumption we do not question the testee's honesty, willingness to cooperate, etc. Focal responses, which are all that are usually available for report, depend so much upon contextual and residual factors that protocols regarding them cannot be taken at face value unless the accompanying determinants are also known. A "yes" answer to the simple question, "Do you often have wakeful spells at night?" may mean many different things, depending upon the background conditions associated with the wakefulness. Even when an individual replies to 100 such items and is then classified by cutting scores which place him in a given category (neurotic, paranoid, or whatnot), the danger of incorrect classification and diagnosis is great. Something other than more tests and more formulas is needed, as Meehl, among others, has pointed out in papers bearing the appropriate titles: "Wanted—a Good Cookbook" (1956*a*), and "When Shall We Use Our Heads Instead of the Formula?" (1956*b*).

The second serious defect in inventory and questionnaire tests lies in the fact that they are based essentially on intuitive judgments regarding various patterns of behavior rather than on experimentally determined correlations between critical variables. To put the matter crudely, one might ask how the maker of a personality test knows what to ask. The method of intuition, no matter how well buttressed by statistical devices applied to global data, cannot rise above its source and cannot be a substitute for procedures based, as Meehl also points out (1956), on scientific data, laws, and principles. The advantage of experimentation over intuition as a source of information is that it offers far greater promise for revealing previously unknown facts that are *causally* rather than *casually* related.

Effects of test variables on responses of Ss. That the traits uncovered by personality tests are to a large extent functions of the nature of the tests themselves has been demonstrated in a number of studies concerned with such traits as aggressiveness (extra- and intrapunitiveness) and rigidity. A study of the influence of word changes upon responses to picture-frustration situations by McQueen and Pearson (1959) casts doubt on the purely internal origin of aggression. From a total of 97 students given the Rosenzweig Picture-Frustration (P-F) test, 30 were chosen who received the highest extrapunitive (*E*) scores and 30 who had received the highest impunitive (*M*) scores. None scoring high in intrapunitiveness were selected for the second part of the study. It will be remembered that in the Rosenzweig P-F test one individual is shown saying something to another and a blank space is left for *S* to supply what the answer of the second individual is to the first. The statements accompanying the pictures express various forms and degrees of aggression. The answers supplied by *S*s are taken as indications of their own aggressive tendencies. Three sets of cartoons were drawn and provided with statements which were neutral (*N*) in one set, extrapunitive (*E*) in another, and impunitive (*M*) in the third. One-third of the extrapunitive and intrapunitive *S*s, as determined by the original version of the P-F test, were given either the *N*, *E*, or *M* sets of pictures and were then scored for extrapunitiveness and impunitiveness according to the responses made to the three modified versions of the P-F test.

The results in Table 9.2 show that degree and direction of aggression in P-F situations can be largely determined by salient features in the

TABLE 9.2. Extrapunitive and Impunitive Scores as a Function of Stimulus Conditions

	Word-type Statements[a]		
	N	E	M
Mean extrapunitive scores of extrapunitive Ss	8.3	13.6	6.4
Mean impunitive scores of impunitive Ss	14.2	6.2	16.7

[a] N = neutral; E = extrapunitive; M = impunitive.

SOURCE: From McQueen and Pearson, 1959. With the permission of *Perceptual and Motor Skills*.

test situation, e.g., by the content of the word messages accompanying the pictures. The number of extrapunitive responses by *S*s deemed extrapunitive according to the original P-F test depended to a significant extent upon the types of word stimuli accompanying the pictures. As seen from Table 9.2 the average extrapunitive means of *S*s rated extrapunitive on the Rosenzweig P-F test are highest with *E*, next with *N*, and lowest with *M* word stimuli; similarly the average impunitive means of *S*s rated impunitive on the original P-F test are highest with *M*, next with *N*, and lowest with *E* word stimuli accompanying the pictures. Conversely, the supposedly impunitive *S*s give a relatively high number (11.3) of extrapunitive responses when extrapunitive word stimuli accompany the pictures and supposedly extrapunitive *S*s give a relatively high number of impunitive responses (14.3) when presented with impunitive word stimuli. The authors therefore conclude as follows:

. . . word-stimuli in the P-F situations were more influential in determining the degree and/or direction of aggression than were the presumed aggressiveness traits as measured by the Rosenzweig P-F test [and the results cast] some doubt upon the practice of presuming that the aggression shown at one time by an individual is a more or less stable trait (pp. 409–410).

In line with the above findings a much earlier study by Schroder and Rotter (1952) showed that what has been regarded as the inborn trait of "rigidity" is instead a failure to learn something presented under certain stimulus conditions. Flexibility appears to be a learned type of response in which *S*s look for and expect alternative pathways for the solution of problems. Rigid behavior, according to these authors, is typified by absence of such learning or by the expectancy of a simple correct solution. A similar view of rigidity as inability to learn a new discrimination in response to changing circumstances was also held by Buss (1952).

Since it is easier to modify learned behavior patterns than it is to change supposedly inborn traits, the view that recurrent behavior patterns are more or less situationally determined leads to important practical consequences. Situations can be manipulated and modified, conditions of learning can be altered, habits can be changed, and patterns of behavior need not be unalterably fixed if the doctrine of traits as hereditary forms of response is given up. Traits would remain only as residuals after situational determinants of behavior had been exhausted. There would always be the possibility that situational factors would be found to override the personal factors operative in behavior. Such was found to be the case in Benedetti's study (1956), where the number of jars in the water-jar problem was increased beyond the three usually used to study rigidity. When four, five, or six jars were used, Benedetti found fewer than half as many solutions governed by sets established by previous solutions as in the three-jar problems of Luchins. He found that if the situation allowed greater freedom of choice in the critical trials, there was less evidence of *Einstellungseffect*. Benedetti therefore questioned whether there is even a low-order generalized trait of rigidity. Instead of starting with *S*s suspected of being rigid, Benedetti suggested that we first find stimulus variables which lead to consistent individual differences with respect to mechanization of behavior in different contexts and then explore the personality structures of the relevant persons. If some individuals are then found to be more rigid than others their behavior could be described in terms of the situation (task) rather than in terms of unobservable inner traits.

It was shown in a study by Dollin and Sakota (1962) that the responses to projective tests may be influenced by the simplest of all stimulus variables, order of presentation. TAT pictures were rated sadder when they followed less sad or neutral pictures than when they were presented first, and "happy" pictures were rated happier when they followed sad or neutral pictures than when they were presented first. The conclusion was as follows:

The perceived mood of a picture depends not only upon its stimulus quality and the personality characteristics of the subject. The total experience represented by an array of cards ought also to be considered. The subject's evaluation of the stimulus, in other words, is not an isolated event; it is influenced by preceding experience with related stimuli (p. 343).

Every method of assessing, measuring, and evaluating personality is essentially a situational tapping of the individual at a particular time, in a particular place, at a particular moment of his life's history, by means of a particular set of stimuli. The test instrument itself consists of a set of stimuli designed to evoke various patterns of responses symptomatic of the individual. The extent to which tests and the interpretation of test results reveal basic underlying predispositons to act in certain ways in certain classes of situations depends upon the extent to which the test reveals the operation of residual sources of variance attributable to the individual as distinct from sources of variance attributable to the test and the conditions prevailing at the time of taking it. Since only the test, certain features of the test situation, and the individual's responses are known, although imperfectly, the extent to which variance is properly divided between situational and personal sources is a matter of inference based on more or less highly sophisticated statistical and mathematical considerations. Realization of this fact should act against reifying the performances and functions revealed in behavior patterns into inner traits, tendencies, or dispositions independent of the conditons under which they are observed.

We are now in a position to appreciate the essential difference between inferences from tests and inferences from experiments. In experiments conclusions are in the form "Y is such and such a function of X," so that for any value of X the value of Y is given (assuming continuous functions). The interdependence of X and Y expressed in the function makes them practically a unity and the prediction of Y presupposes that the original conditions under which X and Y were observed are again in operation. With tests, on the other hand, inferences are drawn concerning abilities, traits, tendencies, and dispositions which are presumably located in the individual and are therefore independent of the test which merely serves to tap or trigger the latent factor in the individual. Having knowledge about the individual, predictions are then made concerning what the individual will supposedly do in certain situations. If the analogy between conclusions from experiments and from tests were complete then we would predict only from one performance on the test to another performance on the same test, but not from the test to behavior in other situations. In the case of an experiment the variables are each ordered along unidimensional continua, whereas in test situations, as well as in the situations for which the test is a predictor, many variables are ordered along many dimensions. We thus see why predictions from test results to life situations are so poor in most cases. Tests represent types of situations, and only insofar as the conditions of life have properties in common with the test situations will prediction be good from the one to the other.

PROJICIENCE

Long ago James (1890) pointed out how the self grows to include all that a man can call his own:

[This includes] not only his body and his psychic powers but his clothes, and his house, his wife and children, his ancestors and friends, his reputation and works, his lands and houses, and yacht and bank-acount. All these things give him the same emotions. If they wax and prosper, he feels triumphant; if they dwindle and die away, he feels cast down (Vol. 1, p. 291).

We have seen that in our encounters with objects, situations, and events there is a feeling either of projecting ourselves outward or being hemmed in by them. Much as an amoeba extends its pseudopodia along the line of its motion or withdraws them from noxious stimuli, so we project ourselves outward and toward positive, wanted goals and withdraw from unwanted ones. We have already referred to the phenomenological aspects of approach-withdrawal behavior as described by Buytendijk (1950). Let us refer to this dynamic quality of behavior as *projicience,* which is broader than the concept of projection and does not carry the connotation of wish fulfillment so often associated with the latter. There is an element of projicience in every response, from the simplest perceptions to the most abstract types of thinking. Let us first consider some simple cases of projicience and then proceed to its more complex manifestations.

Foremost among the components of experience are the impressions received from our bodies and their ongoing activities as pointed out earlier in this chapter. While all awareness is of our own neural states, as recognized by Johannes Müller in his famous laws of specific nervous energies, only certain experiences are referred to the self, the others are projected to form the objects and events of the external world (cf. Sherrington's chapter, "Two Ways of One Mind," 1941). In normal individuals predominant weight is given to the here and now, and projicience is outward rather than inward. From the here and now one projects into the past and into the future, and from here to there—*there* extending in all directions away from the body, with the body as center of each one's spatial coordinate system (Koffka, 1935, p. 332). Placing and dating start from the here and now, which serves as the center of the spatiotemporal frame in which behavioral as well as physical objects and events are ordered. Always entering into the act of projicience is an accompanying positive, negative, or indifferent affective tone. Because the origin of the projicience vector is a here and now that is unique for each individual, it is the basis for the *ego* and the *self*.

Projicience occurs at the simplest perceptual levels: one not only *sees,* one also *looks.* Similarly, we not merely receive auditory, tactile, gustatory, olfactory and kinesthetic stimulation but we hear, touch, taste, smell and move objects in order to focalize some stimuli and to relegate others to background status. The extent to which focalization is directed by interests and feelings determines in large measure the significance and importance of what we experience. Even in cases of primary, involuntary attention, where stimuli are focal because of their intensity, suddenness, size, or quality, there is reaching out or withdrawal on the part of the organism. In health we are usually not aware of the extent to which we react to the simplest sensory stimuli; but in severe illness, when ordinary stimuli and even normally pleasant stimuli like music and visitors cannot be endured, it is borne in on us how the simplest responses require our active participation. Just as in Newtonian mechanics every action is accompanied by an equal and opposite reaction, so every impingement upon the organism calls forth a response that is more than a passive reflex.[1]

The affective, emotional aspect of projicience has been vividly described by Buytendijk:

> Feeling and emotions are the affirmations of our attitudes toward situations, and the pure phenomenon of feeling reveals the human being always projecting it (feeling) and always projecting the world. The pure description of a feeling is the description of an existing human being in his well-defined attitude toward a situation. The projection is the signification of the act of feeling, a spontaneous movement (s'éclater vers—ejecting himself toward), which implies a totality of relations and their development. Feeling is the mode of replying to a situation and transforming it as a projected new world, in which unknown qualities are categorically experienced. There are as many feelings as there are situations, and the situation is created by the mode in which I have accepted it, that is, by my chosen projection. Of course this projection is not the result of reasoning and my choice is not arbitrary. I choose my emotional attitude in the same unreflective, non-considering (thematic, not thetic) mode of consciousness as I choose my words in speaking or writing (1950, p. 130).

> Conscious existing contains (in its own limitation) the possibility of feeling in its original signification of close relationship to the act of touching (p. 131). When I admire something or hate someone, I, in *one* intentional act of feeling, project both myself as admiring or hating and the qualitative structure of the object or person. The created situation is not a static pattern, but an animated, vivid, lively unit that appeals to me by the claims of its qualities, provoked by my feelings (1950, p. 132).

[1] In accordance with this view there is projicience in *respondent* as well as in *emitted* behavior.

Buytendijk thus gives a description of the way in which objects, persons, and events become endowed with value, significance, and meaning by pointing to their ultimate basis in the feelings and emotions accompanying the act of projicience. We have already discussed (Chapter 6) in some detail the modes of feelings aroused in our encounters with the world. We might add to Buytendijk's excellent phenomenological analysis, however, by indicating how specific conditions affect the feelings and emotions, the interests, and the value systems which are often regarded as symptomatic of personality types or traits.

Behavior patterns as functions of dimensional variables. Factors operative in perception, judgment, and learning, i.e., frequency, intensity, nearness in actual or psychological space and time, order, and other conditons of stimulation, affect patterns of responses ascribed to personality factors. Thus Hastings et al. (1944) reported that the closeness of the traumatic event to the individual was a large factor in determining anxiety states:

If he [a flier] were hit by a 20 mm. shell he would be more deeply affected than if he saw the man next to him hit, which would be worse than having someone hit in another part of the same ship, which would be worse than hearing of someone hit in his squadron, and so on to the point where it would mean essentially nothing to him to hear of someone being hit in a B-17 over Munda [thousands of miles away] (p. 132).

Frequency of exposure (flights in enemy terirtory) was a predominant factor in the emotional breaking points of many fliers. Crews joining the Eighth Air Force immediately found out that their chances of survival were very slim, with the result that marked differences were found in the "amount" that various men could take. Some fliers requested removal from flying duties before actually making any flights; a second group did not break until after a few missions, usually by the fifth; a third group did not develop anxiety symptoms until after the twelfth to sixteenth mission.

The dimensions of frequency and duration have been found to play a role in the traumatizing effects of electroconvulsive shock. Stone (1947) found a gradual lowering of maximal cognitive level with as many as fifteen to twenty repeated convulsive shocks. Worchel and Narciso (1950) reported that a single electroconvulsive shock does not obliterate traces of material learned immediately prior to shock, but after five shocks in a period of eight days Ss were not able to learn a series of ten nonsense syllables to criterion of one perfect repetition in forty-five trials. The effects of shock were cumulative but they were reversible in that memory ability five to nine days after the last shock was equal to that prior to the first shock. The theory of the general adaptation syndrome proposed by Selye (1950) suggests that frequency, intensity, spacing, and other dimensions of stressful situations affect physiological levels of functioning in the way envisaged behaviorally in the theory of adaptation level.

Animals as well as humans are influenced by spatiotemporal conditions of stimulation. Fredericson (1950) found greater traumatic effects in dogs when they were confined for unbroken periods than when they were confined for the same length of time in spaced intervals. Dogs confined for 10 min. straight in a box emitted from 680 to 1822 yelps, whereas dogs confined for 1 min. and given 1 min. of freedom for a total of 10 min. emitted from 21 to 916 yelps for the same total period of confinement. The averages for the two groups were even more striking: the massed group averaged 1104 yelps per puppy; the spaced group, 347 yelps.

The arousal of chronic states of anxiety by conditioning procedures demonstrates the efficacy and importance of conditions of stimulation in the establishment of personal modes of behavior. Liddell (1950) reported that a classically conditioned flection of fore limb in the sheep and goat from mild electric shock persisted for three years without reinforcement. A chronic unrelieved tension aroused by conditioning may alter behavior for years or life, not only in the laboratory, but also in pasture and barn. Liddell emphasized that in the conditioning procedure of the classical Pavlovian type monotony is the underlying factor in creation of anxiety. A seemingly innocuous training procedure can be made traumatic by rigid constancy of all time values. Thus if ten-second signals inevitably reinforced by mild electric shock to the foreleg follow one another at constant intervals of two to seven minutes, experimental neurosis will ensue. This procedure is simpler than Pavlov's difficult sensory discriminations for producing neurosis, and it is even more effective.

Consider the differences in behavior following variation in the conditions of simple conditioning as described by Liddell:

With 5-minute intervals between the 10-second signals for shock, a type of experimental neurosis develops in which overreaction and chronic agitation are observed. At first, the sheep reacts precisely to each signal, remaining calm and alert in the intervals. Respiration is regular and pulse slow. But with the onset, usually sudden, of neurosis, overreaction replaces the skilled flexion of forelimb at the signal and diffuse agitation with rapid pulse and respiration replace the former quiet and poise.

The animal's disabling responsivenes in pasture and barn is shown by its exaggerated vigilance both by day and by night. If one approaches the neurotic animal in the flock, it at once takes alarm and, losing its normal gregariousness, may escape by itself. At night in the barn its heart is sensitively responsive to the familiar nocturnal sounds, accelerating at the bleating of a lamb or the creaking of a windmill. While the normal sheep rests during the hours of darkness, the neurotic animal is ceaselessly active at night.

By altering the equal temporal spacing of signals for shock, we can change at will the frequency (or "wavelength") of the rhythmical rising and falling tension within the nervous system (p. 183).

Liddell pointed out that different spacing of stimuli leads to different neurotic patterns, such as tonic immobility, in which there seems to be a preponderance of parasympathetic activity. Realization of the role played by simple dimensional conditions of stimulation led Liddell to the following conclusion:

. . . perhaps reward, punishment, and even motivation will soon be largely discarded in psychological . . . research for the same reason that we have discarded them in our own limited investigation, viz., that they have no operational significance in actual experimentation (p. 18).

Since tension builds up in the intervals *between* shocks, shock per se cannot be regarded, according to Liddell, as either punishment or reward. These now appear to be value judgments rather than statements of conditions producing anxiety in animals.

Spatial as well as temporal conditions were found by Liddell to play a part in the arousal and persistence of neurotic responses. Thus, the presence and nearness of the mother to a female goat shocked in a dark room resulted in entirely different behavior paterns from those developed by another female goat shocked in a room by itself. The second animal developed rigid stereotyped responses to the shocks, backing into a corner of the room and precisely flexing its foreleg, as if confined by an actual Pavlov restraining harness. The animal in the room with the mother showed much more spontaneity and variability of behavior in response to the rigid regimen of conditioning to darkness followed by shock. This animal responded to darkness by going to its mother and gave no precise flection of the forelimb to shock.

During the 2 min. between dark periods it would lie down beside the mother, rising, when the lights went out, to receive the shock that followed 10 sec. later. After the shock, and when the lights came on, it again lay down beside the mother. Thus, complex behavior patterns involving strong emotions and often leading to neuroses may have their origins in very simple environmental conditions, e.g., in repeated stress (shock) at regular intervals, requiring precise response.

It is our thesis that individual bases of action are referable to intra-organismic norms which are the joint product of stimuli impinging upon the organism and residual effects of previous stimuli. Such norms are established and operate in a fashion that is *formally* similar to the operation of adaptation levels in perception and judgment. Since most types of reaction are not based on deliberate assessment of all present and past stimuli, intra-organismic norms are formed quite automatically and unconsciously. Sherif has stressed this fact so far as it relates to social norms: "Men incorporate in themselves a set of norms or standards from their social surroundings. Whether they wish to or not, whether they are conscious of the fact or not, makes no difference" (1936, p. 25). As an example Sherif points out the child's attitude toward a minority group may not be the result of actual contact with that group but the result of being exposed to prevailing attitudes toward the group held by people with whom the child is associated. Opinions, expressive movements, facial expressions, and the reinforcement of responses by parents and playmates pool to form levels or norms which govern the behavior of the growing child.

It is now generally agreed that many behavior patterns are fixed very early in life, some before the first and second year. Because they are laid down so early and because their sources in the environment are overlooked they are often attributed to inner factors. Parents often complain that they are unable to find reasons for attitudes, habits, and unwanted types of responses in their children although the causes may often be traced to minimal cues in their own behavior patterns to which the children respond. Lois Murphy (1946) has shown how children may automatically adopt the attitudes of their mothers. Charlotte Bühler gave the following example of how a child picked up almost imperceptible signals from its mother in developing a fearful pattern of behavior:

A little girl of 18 months could never be persuaded to play alone in her well protected back yard. She cried until allowed to stay inside the house close to her mother. Examination showed that the mother herself was extremely afraid to be alone anywhere and that she had pangs of fright whenever she put the child outside in the yard to play. To the degree that the mother adjusted during therapy, the child was gradually willing and later even happy to play alone outside (1951, p. 204).

We must, therefore, look to fringe as well as to focal stimuli to discover the source of many behavior patterns often mistaken for innate dispositions. Small differences in the way infants and children are treated may have important consequences for future behavior.

Personal norms in judgments of physical and behavioral aspects of personality. In nearly all interpersonal relations individuals judge themselves and others according to personal characteristics ranging from bodily appearance to habits, abilities, temperament, intellectual capacity, and specific or general accomplishments. Whether we are making up a list of guests for a dinner party or considering individuals for jobs, raises, or various kinds of honors, we act in accordance with supposedly relevant norms. Even in "objective" tests individual norms play a part, as shown by Guilford (1954), who listed the "errors" in psychophysical judgments which have their parallels in measurements of attitudes, personality traits, etc. To us this result is not surprising because individual norms or standards are the pooled effects of situational and personal factors, and hence they represent the operation of adaptation levels in the making, giving, and evaluation of personality tests and in our conclusions regarding the testees. A number of studies, some now classical, throw light on the formation and operation of individual norms as they affect judgments of one's self and of others.

The way in which an individual's norms are largely determined by his own characteristics and the "corrective" influence exerted by very distinctive characteristics on level were shown in Marks' (1943) investigation of judgments of skin color by Negro college students. Although this study is now well known to every student of social psychology it has so much systematic importance that it bears repetition at this point. Ratings were obtained from three groups of colored students who rated skin color and five other characteristics of their fellows: energy, personal charm, intelligence, stoutness, and intimacy. Marks' findings were as follows:

. . . each judge establishes his own reference scale and . . . this scale is independent of the subjects rated but not of the rater's own past experience. . . . each judge's rating scale tends to be egocentric, i.e., a subject is seen as darker or lighter than the rater and judgments are made accordingly. . . . The egocentricity of the reference scale of skin color judgments may well apply to the judgments of any characteristic to which social value is attached (p. 375).

On the other hand, the skin color of the group does contribute to the individual norm because the very dark individual cannot see himself as neutral and must compromise with his tendency to put himself at his neutral point and "objective" reality.

Marks hypothesized that "one strives in many situations to put himself at the average," and in accordance with this assumption asserted that the 65-in. man does not see himself as short but instead sees the 68-in. man as tall. This inference was verified experimentally eight years later by Hinckley and Rethlingshafer (1951) in a study wherein 521 men were asked to rate 28 heights ranging from 4 ft. 8 in. to 6 ft. 11 in. on a 9-point scale of very very short, very short, short, medium short, neither tall nor short, medium tall, tall, very tall, and very very tall. It was found that 118 short judges (5 ft. 8 in. and under) regarded 68.56 in. as medium height and 152 tall judges (6 ft. and above) regarded 69.56 in. as medium. The curves for the two groups based on median scale values are distinct at every height as shown in Fig. 9.2. *Each height was judged greater by the short men than by the tall men.* Further confirmation of the hypothesis that one's own characteristics act as anchor or background stimuli in setting individual norms was found by Rethlingshafer and Hinckley (1954) in a study of judgments of age by individuals ranging from about 10 to 77 years: The older the individual, the higher is the age that he judges to be old—as every college teacher knows who perceives his students as younger and younger with his own advancing years.

The results of the studies by Marks, and by Hinckley and Rethlingshafer, attest the importance of the individual's own characteristics, status, or position in the establishment of his norms and hence in his judgments of himself and others. On the other hand, as pointed out above, individuals' estimates of themselves are also influenced by what they perceive to be current around them. We refer again to a study which is now classical: Chapman and Volkmann's investigation of the influence of social norms on individual level of aspiration (1939). Three groups of college students were informed of the supposed scores made by experts (authors and literary critics), peers (college students), and inferiors (WPA workers), and then were asked to estimate what

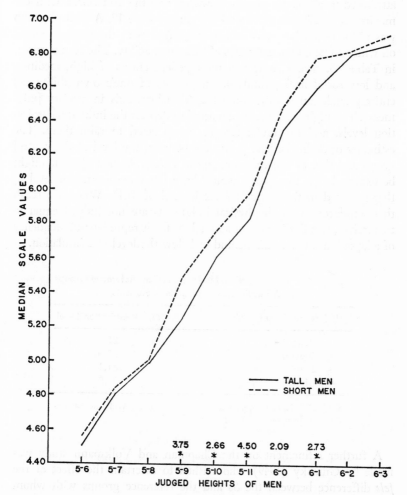

FIG. 9.2. The median scale values assigned to heights of men on a nine-point rating scale ranging from very very short to very very tall. (The judged heights are in feet and inches.) The quotient of the difference between the judgments of tall and short men and the probable error of this difference is shown above the heights of 5–9 through 6–1. (From Hinckley and Rethlingshafer, 1951. With the permission of *Journal of Psychology*.)

they thought they would make in a test of literary ability. The score attributed to all of the groups, however, was the same, 37.2, with the maximum possible score 50 and the chance score 17. A control group was given no background information other than the extreme scores on which to base their estimates of their own ability. The results, given in Table 9.3, clearly show that the repellent effects of high, medium, and low social backgrounds on judgments of one's own ability are entirely analogous to the influence of backgrounds in sensory judgments. The high reference group acted to depress the individual aspiration levels, and the low reference group acted to raise them. The estimates of Ss in the peer group fell between the level of the control group and that of the reference group (37.2). At first sight it might be expected that this group would have the same aspiration level as that imputed to their equals (37.2 instead of 31.1). When we recall that standards in psychophysical judgments are not judged equal to themselves, this finding is not anomalous for it represents the tendency of adaptation levels to lag behind or below the level of stimulation.

TABLE 9.3.   Effects of High, Medium, and Low Reference Groups on Aspiration Levels of College Students

Reference Group	Mean Aspiration Level
None	27.0
Superior	23.0
Equal	31.1
Inferior	33.0

SOURCE: From Chapman and Volkmann, 1939. With the permission of the American Psychological Association.

A further refinement on the Chapman and Volkmann study was made by Gilinsky (1949) who wished to ascertain the effect of the *felt* difference between the Ss and the reference groups with whom they were supposedly in competition. One hundred college students divided into 10 groups of 10 each were told that other groups with IQs of 170, 160, 150, 140, 130, 120, 110, 100, 90, and 80 had all made scores of 18 on a vocabulary test which they were to take, and on which they could obtain any score from 0 to 36. The three highest reference groups were said to be educators; the next four, college students; and the three lowest, laborers. Before taking the test the Ss were asked to estimate their own IQs. The results, given in Table 9.4, show that the level of aspiration, or their own predicted score, almost doubles as the supposed IQ of the reference group falls from 170 to 80. Moreover, the level of aspiration is significantly related to the perceived difference in ability between the Ss and the reference groups, as shown in the right half of the table. With positive differences, i.e., where Ss rated their own IQs above those of the reference groups, the estimated scores are higher than with negative differences where they rated themselves below the reference groups in intelligence; and in the case of the Ss who rated themselves near the reference group, the average predicted score is close to the score given for the reference group (19.6 as against 18).

TABLE 9.4. Mean Levels of Aspiration (LA) and Mean Estimates of Own IQs for 10 Experimental Groups in Conjunction with the Supposed IQs of the Reference Group and Felt Difference from Them

Reference Group	Imputed IQ	Mean Estimates of Own IQs	Mean LA	Own IQ Minus Reference-Group IQ	Mean LA	N
1	170	122.5	14.5	61–71	34.0	1
2	160	130.0	16.4	50–60	30.4	5
3	150	119.0	12.9	39–49	25.6	7
4	140	121.6	17.6	28–38	26.0	5
5	130	133.3	19.4	17–27	23.4	15
6	120	125.0	19.3	6–16	20.0	8
7	110	121.3	20.1	− 5–+ 5	19.6	17
8	100	121.7	24.6	−16– − 6	17.2	4
9	90	123.5	26.4	−27– −17	15.2	15
10	80	126.4	27.2	−38– −28	16.2	5
				−49– −39	13.8	10
				−60– −50	12.9	7
				−71– −61	12.0	1

SOURCE: From Gilinsky, 1949. With the permission of the American Psychological Association.

Returning to Chapman and Volkmann's interpretation of the results of their study, we find that they envisaged the various factors in their situation much as we do. They assumed that Ss are acted upon by (1) the minimum and maximum scores possible in the test; (2) knowledge of the reference groups or what people of given levels of ability were able to make in the test; and (3) their own estimates of their ability, although this third factor, as Gilinsky pointed out, was not explicitly controlled or investigated. In Gilinsky's study the third variable was explicitly introduced and controlled, with the result that a factor which has to be treated as a "residual" in the Chapman and Volkmann study emerges as a background condition in the study by Gilinsky. Unfortunately the number of class intervals for felt difference between own IQ and reference group IQ is not the same as the number of scale intervals into which this measure and its associated aspiration levels are paired; so it is not possible, except by making some broad assumptions regarding this distribution, to evaluate the relative contributions of presumed performance of another group and *Ss*' estimates of the scores which they would make in the test.

Let us now take up the second part of the Chapman and Volkmann study in which no significant effects were found as a result of information given *Ss* regarding the performance of a high and a low reference group. In this part of the experiment *Ss* took four forms of the Otis self-administering tests of mental ability on four successive days. On the first day all *Ss* had the same instructions; on the second day all were told the first day's score and were asked what they expected in the second test (aspiration level); on the third day *Ss* were divided into two matched groups, *A* and *B*, and were told the scores of the two previous days; in addition, half of the *A* group were told that WPA workers made an average 0.9 points above their scores and half were told that the WPA workers made a score 0.9 points below their scores. Group *B* was also divided in half and given these scores, but they were told that the reference group consisted of New York members of the National Academy of Sciences. On the fourth day *Ss* were told their scores for the preceding three days and, in addition, the members of group *A* were told that the average of the class was 5.2 points below their own average and the members of group *B* were told that the class average was 5.2 points above theirs. The results on the third and fourth days showed no significant change in aspiration levels as a result of "knowledge" of the different reference groups. We believe that this negative result was found because the factual information regarding their own achievement on the first two days acted as a strong residual regarding what they could do and thus affected their aspiration levels.[2]

[2] Another factor, referred to by Chapman and Volkmann, which militated against changes in aspiration level of scores on the third and fourth days' tests, was the fact that *Ss* probably had already worked up to their limit and could not work harder. This supposition may well account for failure of ALs to *rise* in

In a study by Blake, Helson, and Mouton (1957), which is referred to below, it was also found that objective factual knowledge is more difficult to change through social pressures than are matters of opinion and attitude, which are capable of a variety of interpretations. Stated differently, when an individual's evaluation of himself is based on objective factual information, it is difficult to dislodge him from his position. Under these circumstances the weight of the reference group diminishes and AL is almost wholly determined by the factual information given to Ss.

The second part of the Chapman and Volkmann study is especially instructive because it demonstrates very clearly the importance of the nature of the task or situtation confronting the individual in determining aspiration level and self-evaluation, as well as the importance of the reference group relative to the individual. In fact it should not be difficult to show experimentally that a given reference group or model may function as a superior norm with respect to one type of task and as an inferior norm with respect to another, or even, as happened in this study, that it may exert no effect.

The studies by Chapman and Volkmann and by Gilinsky have analogues in many life situations. Merton and Lazarsfeld (1950) pointed out that there was far more criticism of chances of promotion by men in the Air Corps, where there was a conspicuously high rate of promotion, than by members of the Military Police, where chances of promotion were about the worst in any branch of the service and where the men complained less. Similarly, the attitude of a married soldier toward his induction into the armed forces depended on whether his judgment was determined by reference to drafted married men, to unmarried associates, or to married civilian friends. The individual assessed his position very differently against the various groups with which he compared himself.

Behavior patterns of the "complainer," the "sour puss," the "trouble maker," etc., which are ascribed to traits, are often the result of situational factors such as continued association with disliked colleagues, an unhappy home life, or chronic illness. Since in such cases the behavior

---

the case of Ss informed of inferior reference-group score, but it does not account for failure of ALs to *drop* in the case of Ss informed of the score of the superior reference group. The difference between the first and second parts of this study may be traced to differences in the contents of the tests or type of task employed in the two cases, though this also is only a guess.

patterns disappear when the situation is changed, they are not said to fall under the definition of personality traits; but what is then the criterion of a trait? Even patterns of behavior common to different situations may still be situationally determined if the situational factors have common properties. Residuals may be activated by situations to call forth recurring types of behavior attributed to traits. It has been found that family troubles lead to more automobile accidents than do psychoses, and the importance of such situational factors as family life, friends, and immediate working colleagues has been recognized in industry where special clinics for workers and "retreats" for executives have been set up to determine if changes in situational factors may not reduce tensions and improve performance.

Influence of background on ratings of personality traits. A pioneer, qualitative study was made by Asch (1946) showing effects of background terms on interpretations of adjectives denoting personality traits. In this study two lists of words containing *calm* and *strong* were given two groups of Ss as follows: group *A* were given the words *kind, wise, honest, calm,* and *strong;* group *B* were given *cruel, shrewd, unscrupulous, calm,* and *strong.* Each group was asked to describe the person denoted by the words in each list but by using other terms. From the Ss' descriptions it was evident that *calm* and *strong* had different meanings in the two lists: in the second list *calm* meant cold, cool, frigid, icy, scheming, while in the first list it meant soothing, gentle, and tolerant. The meaning of *strong* underwent similar changes in the two contexts. That the connotations of words depend greatly on the contexts in which they appear has long been known, but Asch's study served to show the importance of this fact in the use and interpretation of personality ratings.

If the initial list of traits in the Asch study is regarded as background and the two critical items are considered focal stimuli, and if the words have been scaled on some continuum, then the relative influences of the two classes of stimuli may be determined. This was done by Podell (1961) in a study that considerably advances the pioneer study by Asch. Seventy-eight terms denoting favorable, neutral, and unfavorable personality traits were scaled by Thurstone's method of equal-appearing intervals, and a list of thirty-one words was selected, ranging from 1.2 (most favorable) to 6.6 (most unfavorable) in approximately 0.2 step intervals. From this list three terms having an average scale value of 1.80 (favorable) and three terms having an average scale value of 5.33

(unfavorable) were employed as the initial background list. *S*s were given either the favorable background words (capable, informed, considerate) or the unfavorable background words (mediocre, smug, harsh) and asked to choose four words from the remaining twenty-five words in the list "to be most likely to describe the kind of person denoted by the background terms." The mean scale value of the check list was 3.6. On the basis of AL theory, Podell reasoned that "the average favorableness of the traits chosen should fall somewhere between that of the initial list and that of the check list" (1961, p. 594). The results bear out this expectation from theory: the average of the median scale values of the words chosen on the favorable side of the scale was 1.89, slightly but not significantly above that of the background words (1.80), and the average of the median scale values on the unfavorable side of the scale was 5.12, highly significantly below that of the background words (5.33).

To determine the relative influences of the background and check lists on the choice of terms, Podell assumed:

$$AL = \frac{(\Sigma X_i / n_i) w_i + (\Sigma X_j / n_j) w_j}{w_i + w_j}$$

$$w_i + w_j = 1 \tag{1}$$

where X_i and X_j refer to the scale values of the traits in the initial and final lists respectively, n_i and n_j refer to the number of traits in each list, and w_i and w_j are the weighting factors denoting the relative contributions of the initial and final lists.[3] The values of AL were assumed to be equal to the mean median responses under the two experimental conditions, that is, 1.9 and 5.1. The values of the weighting factors for the check list calculated according to Equation (1) were found to be 0.05 and 0.16 with corresponding weights for the initial lists of 0.95 and 0.84. The influence of the initial lists thus proved to be from 5 to 19 times greater than that of the check list, a result in keep-

---

[3] It should be noted that in Equation (1) the arithmetic means of the lists are employed rather than the geometric means because the words were positioned on a psychological scale, not on a physical dimension requiring a log transformation to yield psychological values. The *d* factor, for size of step interval between stimuli, was omitted as "too refined for an exploratory study." However, since the values of AL were derived independently from the data of the experiment it was only necessary, as Podell did, to use the equation to determine the values of the weighting coefficients, w_i and w_j.

ing with the qualitative findings regarding the importance of the initial terms in the Asch study.

The final study we shall discuss showing the influence of context on personality ratings is one by Young, Holtzman, and Bryant, (1954) who sought answers to the following questions:

1. What effect does an unfavorable context of items have upon favorable and unfavorable items in rating scales?
2. What effect does a favorable context of items have upon favorable and unfavorable items?
3. What effect does a mixed context of items have upon favorable and unfavorable items?
4. What is the effect of order of items in a personality test involving multiple ratings?

The "items" consisted of 180 statements, approximately half of which were positive and half negative. The 180 statements were presented in 8 different forms according to the design given in Table 9.5.

TABLE 9.5. Design of Study Investigating Effects of Content, Position, and Order of Rating Scale Items

Form	Content Favorable	Content Unfavorable	Order
1	90+		Random
2	90+		Reverse of 1
3		90−	Random
4		90−	Reverse of 3
5	45+(a)	45−(a)	Random
6	45+(a)	45−(a)	Reverse of 5
7	45+(b)	45−(b)	Random
8	45+(b)	45−(b)	Reverse of 7

Note: (a) Taken from forms 1 and 3.
(b) Items from forms 1 and 3 not used in forms 5 and 6.
SOURCE: From Young, Holtzman, and Bryant, 1954. With the permission of *Educational and Psychological Measurement*.

The items were chosen from 800 adjectives in the Allport-Odbert list of personality traits and were included in short statements such as "is clumsy," "is nosey," "thinks everyone has it in for him," "has many friends," "is masculine," "is careful with the property of others." Space does not permit discussion of the criteria and procedures by which the 90 positive and 90 negative items (later reduced to 89) were finally chosen. Seven hundred and forty-two airmen undergoing basic training at Lackland Air Force Base were given the forms to fill out. Special precautions were taken to make certain that every rater knew well the individual whom he rated and that every rater was rated by at least one other individual. The men who rated each other lived in the same barracks and occupied adjoining bunks for at least six weeks preceding the ratings. For other details concerned with matters of design, such as replication of the forms, the reader is referred to the original study. The ratings were made on this five-point scale:

A. Completely or always characteristic
B. Usually or largely characteristic
C. Sometimes or moderately characteristic
D. Seldom or slightly characteristic
E. Never or not at all characteristic

Indexes of response shift due to context, position, and order of the items were computed so as to yield frequency distributions across the 5 steps of the rating scale for each of the 89 items on each rating form. The effect of order was studied by comparing item responses in one order with item responses in reverse order.

While effects of position and order of items were significant with only 6 of the 89 positive items in positive context and 6 of the 89 negative items in negative context, the results for context were found to be strikingly significant. All but 3 of the negative items were found to shift toward the upper end of the scale ("completely or always characteristic," category *A*) when judged in mixed as compared with negative context and of these shifts, 44 were significant at or beyond the .05 level (forms 3 and 4 vs. forms 5 and 6; and forms 3 and 4 vs. forms 7 and 8). Similarly the overwhelming majority of the positive items shifted toward the lower end of the scale ("never or not at all characteristic," category *E*) when moved from a purely positive to a mixed context. Of these shifts, 22 were significant at or beyond the .05 level. While 49 percent of the negative items changed significantly with context, only 25 percent of the positive items changed significantly, a difference which is significant. It therefore appears that rating-scale items that are descriptive of undesirable traits are more sensitive to changes in context than are items having to do with favorable traits.

The authors explain their results within the framework of adaptation-level theory as follows:

Considering the task of judging a large number of personality traits from the point of view of adaptation-level theory, the Adaptation Level of an individual at a given moment would be the result of three factors: (*a*) the particular trait being judged at a given moment; (*b*) the judgments made on the traits preceding the given one in the series; and (*c*) the past experience of the rater in appraising others. For a given trait in the present study, only the second factor provides an explanation of the striking shifts in the average Adaptation Level from one experimental group of airmen to the next.

From adaptation-level theory one would expect an item reflecting a desirable trait to appear more positive when embedded in a mixed context than when in a context of positive items only. The contrast of negative and positive items in the same context would accentuate the desirability of the trait in question. Similarly, a negative item should appear more negative in a mixed context than in a purely negative one.

Because in the mixed context an approximately equal number of both positive and negative items precede a particular item in the series, the mean Adaptation Level of a large number of raters for that item would be near the center of the scale. Assuming that, in general a positive halo effect is operating, the mean Adaptation Level for a positive item in a mixed context would probably be slightly away from center toward the "completely characteristic" end of the five-point scale. The mean Adaptation Level for the same item in a positive context would shift to a position on the scale farther away from center toward the "A" category, since the "A" end of the scale is used more frequently in responding to items in a positive context. To maintain the same relative degree of "positiveness," responses to a positive item would have to shift in the same manner as the Adaptation Level when the item context is changed. This is exactly what happens in every case where the degree of response shift due to change in context is statistically significant.

Again, assuming a positive halo effect, the mean Adaptation Level for a negative item in a mixed context would be close to the junction of the "C" and "D" categories of the scale. For the same item in a negative context, the Adaptation Level would be closer to the "not at all characteristic" end of the scale, perhaps even slightly inside category "E." With change in item context, responses to a given negative item would also have to shift in the same manner as the Adaptation Level if the item is to have the same relative meaning for the individual rater. Similarly, in order to maintain the same degree of negativeness of rating when items are made more neutral by moving them from the mixed to the all negative context, the rating should shift toward the "A" end of the scale. This however is opposed by the effect of establishing an Adaptation Level toward "E" since responses for items in an all negative context occur more frequently toward that end of the scale.

In Figure [9.3] a schematic diagram of shifts in Adaptation Level to be expected with change in context is presented for each of the above situations. A concrete example may make the analysis clearer. Suppose that in judging Individual S on the positive trait, "is generous," the rater, R, decides that S is slightly more generous than the average airman, say, one step above the rater's indifference point for this item at the moment. If this particular item has been preceded by positive items only, R's Adaptation Level or indifference point will be near category "A," say at the position in

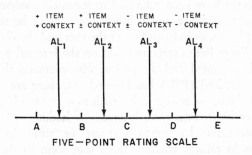

FIG. 9.3. Schematic diagram of shifts in AL due to changes in item context, as predicted for a hypothetical positive item reflecting a desirable trait (AL$_1$ and AL$_2$) and for a hypothetical negative item referring to an undesirable trait (AL$_3$ and AL$_4$). (From Young, Holtzman, and Bryant, 1954. With the permission of *Educational and Psychological Measurement*.)

Figure [9.3] marked by AL$_1$. To record a judgment one step above his Adaptation Level for this item, R would give S a rating of A. Suppose instead that R is using a rating form on which roughly half the items preceding this particular one are positive and the remainder are negative. The Adaptation Level of R for this item would now be somewhere in the center of the scale, say at the point in Figure [9.3] marked AL$_2$. To assign S an equivalent amount of the trait, R would give S a rating of B.

Although presumably a positive halo operates in most of the ratings, the difference in negative and positive items is of interest. While 82 of the 89 negative items had approximately median splits with categories A, B, C, D, in one half of the distribution and category E in the other, only 29 of the 89 positive items had comparable splits with categories B, C, D, E, in one half and category A in the other. This implies, as would be expected, that a "slight" amount (category D) of an undesirable trait is less enhancing than a "large" amount (category B) of a desirable trait. For this reason, fewer significant response shifts would be expected for positive than for negative items, in moving from a pure to a mixed context. This is borne out by the present data in which significantly more negative than positive items showed appreciable response shifts due to change in context (Young, Holtzman, and Bryant, 1954, pp. 513–515).

We thus see from the studies in this section dealing with effects of order and composition of items in rating scales that judgments of personality traits may be influenced to a significant extent by internal norms. These norms, in turn, are affected by factors in the scales which depend upon the composition and patterning of items in the scales. Even after items have been subjected to statistical analyses and culled to ensure their reliability and validity, they cannot be regarded, like the units of physics, as independent of the user and the objects they are to measure. Every item exerts an effect on the internal norms of both the person being rated and the person who evaluates the ratings. In addition, as Guilford (1959) has pointed out, there are other sources of "error" in the use of rating scales, such as rating too high or too low (general rater bias), rater-ratee interactions leading to "halo" effects, rater-trait interactions leading to "contrast" or "similarity" errors, and logical errors in ratings wherein traits that seem to the rater to be similar or logically related are given similar ratings. All of these so-called errors or biases point to the importance of internal norms in the use of scaling instruments no matter how "objectively" they may be constructed and administered.

Residual factors in use of scales. The manner in which individual norms affect judgment can be seen from Fig. 9.4 depicting the scales employed by two individuals. The neutral region in *B*'s scale is higher than that in *A*'s scale with the result that acts, traits, abilities, skills, or performances ordered on these scales will be judged quite differently by *A* and *B*. The position and width of the neutral regions in the two scales determine the "cut-off" points for "good," "bad," and "indifferent." Suppose *A* and *B* are asked to judge individual *X* with respect to some trait. According to the scales in Fig. 9.4, *X* would receive a favorable rating from *A* and an unfavorable rating from *B*. This conclusion follows merely from the difference in the neutral regions of *A*'s and *B*'s scales on the assumption that they are judging exactly the same trait. Suppose, however, that *A* and *B* focus on somewhat different aspects of *X* as shown in Fig. 9.5. In such a case even though their scales are identical, their judgments of X will be very different, as Bjerstedt has pointed out, because they are using "aspect-different scales" (1956). Actually A and B are judging X on different dimensions. Aspect-different scales may arise from various sources, such as failure to interpret instructions in the same way, thus leading to a lack of interpersonal synonymity on the part of the judges; or a judge may choose another

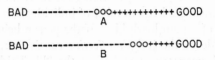

FIG. 9.4. Showing how some items may be rated differently by two individuals when their neutral points do not coincide. (Modified from Bjerstedt, 1956.)

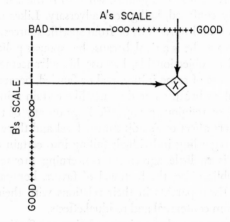

FIG. 9.5. Showing how "aspect different" scales may result in different evaluations of the same individual by two raters. (From Bjerstedt, 1956. With the permission of CWK Gleerup.)

dimension because it seems more important to him than the one he was asked to scale; or he may introduce an emphasis not intended by the examiner, e.g., "Is so-and-so a good workman?" may be taken as, "How will he work with *me,* or how will his promotion affect my chances for advancement?" (Bjerstedt, 1956).

Important consequences follow from aspect-different scales in judging personality. It is often taken for granted when a judge is furnished with scales containing specific sets of characteristics describing personality, especially after the scales have been standardized according to the meticulous sampling and statistical methods now available, that the judge will rate each individual solely on the items and in terms of the units provided him. But if the judge knows the individual he is rating, he already has certain thoughts, attitudes, likes, or dislikes, which enter into his responses to the scale items. In rating an individual, say, for intellectual competence, he may be rating the individual on an affective continuum embracing a large number of individuals, some of whom he likes and some of whom he dislikes. If the person being rated falls on the "dislike" side of the judge's *affective continuum,* he will under-rate intellectual competence; and if on the "like" side, he will over-rate this trait. It would be hard to deny that strong likes and dislikes affect every conceivable trait on which an individual can be judged. Thus to *A* individual *X* is a genius, while to *B* the same individual is an intellectually confused, belligerent adversary. Likes or dislikes can spring from over-all impressions or from specific sources. One may dis-like another because he is a rival, because he espouses policies or theories that seem bad or objectionable, because his advancement may block one's own, because of some injury, real or fancied, because he has been more successful, or because one does not like certain minority national, racial, political, or religious groups. Feelings on any of these or count-less other matters affect one's adjustment level and these in turn affect all judgments regarding individuals falling into certain categories. No wonder there is so little agreement concerning promotions, awards, elections to public office, the bestowal of favors, honors, emoluments, and penalties. Even parents in their relations with their children are not immune from contextual and residual effects.

There are many everyday sayings pointing to affective bias, e.g., "It depends upon whose cat's tail is in the door whether or not you shut it." Phrases such as "fair-haired boy," "protégé," "favorite student," and "outstanding disciple" all denote strong personal involvements which bias judgment of specific traits. The most refined and objective tests and scales for evaluating individuals do not guarantee that the measur-ing instruments will be used free from the operation of individual norms.

Judgments made by superiors, peers and subordinates of the per-formance, habits, traits, and abilities of individuals are biased by residuals of various kinds, especially those having to do with national and racial origins, politics, religion, economic status, looks, names, blemishes, disabilities, family connections, and other factors which may have no significant relation to an individual on the job, in his profession, or in his social relations. Perhaps it was because of his own humble origins that the poet Robert Burns insisted, "A man's a man for a' that!"

Since all stimuli pool to form level it is inevitable that extraneous factors enter into evaluations of all personal qualities. Objective as well as subjective methods of evaluating personality are influenced by background and residual stimuli of which we may be totally unaware. The so-called halo effect is said by Guilford (1954) "to force the rating of any trait in the direction of the general impression of the individuals rated." Thus we tend to overrate individuals whom we know and like and to underrate those whom we do not know and especially those whom we dislike. The halo effect may influence judgments of relatively impersonal factors, such as efficiency, rate, and quality of work, and other characteristics of individual behavior. Levine and Butler (1952) reported that 29 foremen who rated workers on accuracy, effective use of working time, output, application of job knowledge, and cooperation tended to *overrate* people in the higher-grade jobs and to *underrate* those in the lower-grade jobs. Since the sum of the ratings on the five scales determined over-all performance and wage rate, these biases had important practical consequences for the workers.

So important is it to place everyone in some frame of reference that in all societies, civilized and primitive alike, people want to know, not only such facts as age, occupation, and marital status, but also where a person came from, what his national or racial origin is, where he was born, the church he attends, and other facts concerned with his immediate or remote past. Interest may also extend to his relatives and their occupations and domiciles. In some cultures it is not deemed rude to ask a man about his income in order to be sure to treat him with proper respect! Such placing of individuals in frames of reference is fraught with the danger of evaluating them with respect to national, racial, occupational, and other stereotypes which may be extraneous to their ways of behaving in specific situations. Characterizations of individuals in the large may be misleading when it comes to assessing their character, abilities, and responses in work and interpersonal situations. A Frenchman, German, or Englishman has characteristics that identify him as such, but he responds in accordance with the types of situations in which he finds himself in a new culture as well as in accordance with residuals from his past experiences. From what we know of the influence of situational factors in behavior, it would probably be wiser to concentrate on the types of situations in which individuals will be called upon to work in than on their supposed inner traits and dispositions.

Social suggestion: an instance of adaptation. It is generally agreed that food preferences of children are among the most difficult responses to change yet Duncker (1938) showed that a predominant situational factor such as behavior of a model could significantly alter the food choices of children ranging from two years and eight months to five years and two months of age. This study is of interest not only because of its findings but even more because of Duncker's interpretation. The children first indicated their preferences for six foods by choosing the first liked, second liked, etc. After the first choice, the food was removed and the second choice was made from the remaining five foods, and so on through the six. It was found that the second child, observing a first child, chose what the first child did in 81 percent of the cases. Since 25.6 percent of the choices were the same when the children were tested alone as they were in the group situation, the difference of 55.4 percent gives the proper base for the actual influence of the model—a highly significant percentage.

In the second part of this study the children were told a story in which the "hero" expressed great dislike for one food and great liking for another food. The two foods in the story were chosen so that the disliked food (chocolate taste) was actually preferred by the children to the one the hero supposedly liked (valerian on sugar). After hearing the story, the children usually reversed their preferences, and the effect persisted for several days as shown in Table 9.6. Duncker regarded the results as astounding in view of the weakness of the social stimulation, which was merely a story, and the disillusioning effect when the children found chocolate to be the hero's *nonpreferred* food. Moreover, the aftereffects of the story were remarkable in that 47 percent of the children still chose the nonpreferred food two days after hearing it, while as many as 10 percent of the children still showed effects after an interval of 12 days. When the story was retold on the thirteenth day, only 30 percent of the Ss (as opposed to the original 67 percent) chose the hero's food. Part of the drop in the choices prior to the thirteenth day may have been due to some forgetting of the story by some of the children.

TABLE 9.6.   Children Who Preferred the Hero's Food at
Varying Intervals after Hearing Story

Interval in Days	Percentage of Children
Immediately	67
2	47
6	36
12	10
13	30
15	20

SOURCE: From Duncker, 1938. With the permission of the
American Psychological Association.

Duncker's interpretation of these findings has special significance for us. After considering the possibility that change of context due to the story may have changed the meaning of the food and also the attitude of the children, he concluded that the results were primarily due to "modification of the subject" as a result of *adaptation:*

In all cases of *adaptation* it is not primarily the object but the subject that is changed. If an organism is compelled to cope repeatedly with a certain type of food, it does not remain quite the same organism, but rather it tends apparently to adjust itself to the new task by mobilizing suitable conditions of reception and assimilation. A conspicuous example is the ease of drug addiction in which a person becomes so accustomed to the object that he would break down if suddenly forced to go without it. . . . Since adaptation is a function of repetition, and repetition is the most immediate outcome of imitation and suggestion, adaptation must be one of the major processes exploited by social suggestion (1938, p. 507).

Social suggestion, then, in Duncker's view is an instance of adaptation.[4]
Rubenfeld, Lowenfeld, and Guthrie have suggested that social climate has its origins in subception, on the basis of an experiment in which twelve geometric figures were projected eight times in random order, each figure twice at each of two exposure speeds. Eight of the figures were variants of an essentially basic rectangular form and four of them

[4] A comment is in order concerning the close approach to AL theory of Duncker's account of social suggestion. It shows that application of AL theory to social phenomena, far from resting on analogical reasoning, is a natural extension of the theory from the field of psychophysics and judgment to interpersonal relations.

were variations of a basically triangular form. Some of the figures were accompanied by shock and GSR was recorded. Subception was said to occur if a significantly greater number of high GSRs were elicited by misreported square figures accompanied by shock than by misreported triangular figures not accompanied by shock. Subception in this sense occurred. The authors concluded that "individuals may constantly be subceiving events to which they are not attending fully at a given moment. Stimulation may be impinging, yet not be sufficiently defined for the individual to verbalize it. . . . The subtle yet powerful effects of what are called social climates suggest this kind of subceiving" (1956, pp. 180–181). Facts of everyday life lend support to this experimental finding. Groups and cultures impress us not only by their outstanding focal qualities but also by accents, inflections, and nuances that are hard to identify. These, along with the salient characteristics determine the social climate in which individuals live.

NORMS AND SUPERNORMS IN BEHAVIOR

Individual modes of behavior, we have found, issue from the adjustment levels developed for meeting demands of self, family, friends, and society. Actions in accordance with norms established by social custom and legal pressures represent, as a rule, the minimum requirements of society. Cahn (1956) called this type of action "parvanimity" as contrasted with magnanimity which represents the operation of supernorms in individual behavior. He pointed out that often group pressures force the individual to behave magnanimously, but since "under identical group pressures, individuals differ as to degree of magnanimity, and since some act magnanimously when there is no group pressure in operation, we are justified in seeking individual as well as social explanations for especially generous behavior" (1956, p. 209). Hence, individuals may, under certain conditions, act in accordance with supernorms in the eyes of the law, and legal decisions may be made in accordance with supernorms rather than in accordance with prevailing norms. Among such conditions Cahn lists the following:

1. When an individual is in a more advantageous position, he is in a position to give or yield more and, indeed, is often expected to do so. One who has more can be more generous than one who has less.

2. If one pays another to perform a special service, he expects a certain standard to be maintained which may well be above the ordinary

call of duty or of custom. Under these circumstances one expects action in accordance with supernorms by having paid for them.

3. If one assumes an obligation either for some benefit or because someone else may suffer if the obligation is not fulfilled, then one may be forced to act in accordance with supernorms in fulfilling the commitment.

4. The norm rises when there is some special relation between individuals, e.g., the confidential relation between a lawyer and a client and between a doctor and a patient. In relations like these, as Cahn points out, conduct that would be ordinarily permissible may become an illegal abuse of confidence.

5. When one is at the mercy of another because the latter is the only one who can supply or render certain services, then supernorms come into question because the ordinary usages of a society may not be fair or just. The restraints imposed on public utilities by regulatory bodies and on innkeepers by law are examples of the operation of supernorms that are invoked when individuals or groups are in a position to exercise extraordinary powers over others.

6. If one has performed a magnanimous act and thereby holds himself out as "fit for the level of a supernorm," he "will not be allowed to sink below the level he has shaped *for himself*" (1956, p. 213). The more often one acts in accordance with supernorms, the more he is expected to behave in accordance with them, and if a supernorm has been attained only once, "it will leave an ineradicable vision of that which he can reach and below which there must remain a feeling of falling short" (1956, p. 214).

There are also special occasions in which individuals act in accordance with supernorms to rise above their habitual levels of behavior. Times of danger or catastrophe, occasions when individuals are in dire need of food, shelter, or a job, an accident on the highway, and many other situations may call forth magnanimous actions on the part of people. Sometimes magnanimous sentiments take strange turns, as in the outcry against executing a murderer who was rendered completely helpless by a policeman's shot after the killing, and in the legal provision that a man must not be insane at the time he suffers the death penalty even though he was sane at the time of committing the crime and during his trial and conviction.

Acting in accordance with established norms may give the individual a sense of well-being but acting in accordance with supernorms may have tremendous feedback that persists for long periods. Cahn has described what happens in such cases (1956):

There is a distinct sense of augmented power that comes from a magnanimous deed and, like other accesses of power, inspires a pervasive euphoria. One feels, as it were, elevated, literally buoyant. And the reason for this delightful sensation is not far to seek: it is that the magnanimous act constitutes an assertion of command over destiny. It masters destiny by proclaiming in the teeth of prescribed, usual consequences that these need not ensue, that one has willed that they shall not and therefore they do not (p. 209).

Emergencies do the work of moral revelation. Suddenly and without forewarning, the rhythm a man is accustomed to in his daily life will break into a wild clangor like an alarm bell, beat out a frantic summons to action, and then—just as quickly—subside to its normal, regular tempo. When the emergency has passed, he is likely to know something entirely new about his latent capacities or incapacities. He may discover with gratification or shame, what kind of moral being he has made of himself and what care he really feels for other human selves that move about him (pp. 184–185).

That an individual's status and his relations to certain other individuals, etc., impose special norms of conduct peculiar to each of his functions is recognized not only by society but also by the law. As Cahn points out, "a surgeon will be judged like a layman when he drives his car but not when he performs an operation" (1956, p. 219). We expect certain minimum standards of conduct of parents toward children and of persons claiming to have special knowledge who perform services for us, e.g., plumbers, roofers, and appliance repairmen. Within each sphere of human activity there are norms of performance to which we hold others and also ourselves. These may require minimum levels of efficiency, courtesy, kindliness, honesty, and all the other virtues recognized by our society or they may require actions pointing to the operation of supernorms in human conduct.

From the preceding discussion it might be inferred that individuals act in accordance with supernorms only when subjected to extraordinary circumstances, when situations become so demanding that they *impel* to magnanimous actions. We have already noted that there are individual differences in this respect, as there are in all matters affecting human behavior. In addition, individuals do not always act in accordance with exactly the same norms, and they differ in the extent to which they must be forced into acts of magnanimity. Some individuals act in accordance with what are to them their ordinary norms but which for others represent supernorms. Philanthropists give to worthy causes far beyond what is expected of them; religious leaders may give their lives for moral principles; writers, artists, and scientists habitually perform at extraordinary levels in their respective areas; and thousands of unhonored and unsung individuals follow "the paths of rectitude" beyond the requirements of custom or law.

Internal norms and supernorms do not come into being from purely internal sources. They have their origin and develop through the interplay of both external and internal forces and hence depend, like all adjustment levels, upon the total constellation of stimuli affecting the individual. Our emphasis on past and present situational determinants of norms has been termed "the principle of the route" by Cahn in his discussion of the bases of the moral choices individuals are called upon to make at various times:

In our times it is customary to discuss the problems of moral choice as though they presented themselves in some vast and formless nowhere, as though moral decisions were taken in a sort of impersonal void. Although we have learned to allow for the indirect influence of social and cultural factors on the decisions that are made, we give little or no consideration to the one special causative factor that most directly shapes our individual responses. The missing factor may be called "the principle of the route."

According to "the principle of the route," a moral choice is made only at some presented time and place by some specific person or persons, who have previously lived lives that appear to them, at any rate, as unique. The choice is conditioned and restricted not only by previous social and external circumstances in the chooser's biography but also by his own previous commitments of a voluntary nature and by the general objectives he has thereby imposed on the course of his life. He chooses *now* and *here,* because *now* he has brought himself *here* on his way to *there* (1956, p. 113).

We thus find that even the highest moral decisions are based upon standards that develop from the experiences of the organism over more or less extended periods of time. As Duncker has phrased it, "Life is, of course, among other things, a sum total of solution-processes which refer to innumerable problems, great and small. It goes without saying that of these only a small fraction emerge into consciousness. Character, so far as it is shaped by living, is of the type of a resultant solution" (1945, p. 13). The predominant role of education, reading, travel, exposure to the highest products of a culture, and the contagion of inter-personal relations whether in the family, the university, at work, or in recreative pursuits, must be recognized in the formation of individual norms and supernorms. Realization of the specific, often mundane, origins of personality patterns may lead to better understanding and control of the forces shaping the behavior of individuals and societies.

NONCONFORMING INDIVIDUALS

Behavior may deviate from established norms on either the good or bad side. Extreme or unusual departures from socially current norms, even when on the *good* side, are regarded as eccentric, abnormal, or bad. In our society when an individual gives away all of a large inheritance, especially if he gives it to destitute individuals rather than to founda-tions or institutions, he is judged to be abnormal, often to the point where family or friends will go to court to prevent him from indulging his excess of charity.[5]

In almost every type of behavior, the golden mean, as Aristotle called it, constitutes the norm. The good may become bad when it exceeds the norm: thrift may become stinginess or miserliness; virtue may become prudishness; anxiety may become neurosis; philanthropy may become profligacy; curiosity, collecting, sexuality, and vigilance may become mania. The limits are set overtly and covertly both by society as a whole and by each individual for himself. Since individual norms are so largely determined by social norms we are apt to take for granted that acceptable practices in our culture are the best or the only permissible ones. Our own norms *feel* right to us and determine our scale of values. Marks, in the study we discussed above, pointed out that the 65-in. man does not regard himself as short; he regards the 68-in. man as tall! In extreme cases, the world seems wrong while the individual alone seems to himself to be right. In this connection Bur-row remarked:

In respect to evaluations of individual conduct, everyone feels that *his* opinion is correct. . . . And where this assumption of mine is participated in by others, those so participating are regarded by *me,* by every *"me"* as also right. Contrariwise, those who fail to agree with me are not right (1950, p. 468).

[5] Such a case was reported in the newspapers some years ago.

A poet has expressed it this way:

> *Points of View*
> Within a world where dissonances rule
>   A Mozart's grace would seem cacophony.
> And where goose-wisdom finds its apogee,
>   Plato or Socrates would look a fool.
> Amid the kingdoms of the color-blind,
>   Renoir or Rubens would appear inane.
> And in a land of feather-heads, the brain
>   Would be despised—a mark of sub-mankind.
>
> To worms, the bees are crazed with sun and flight;
>   To tortoises, the deer are mad with speed;
> To crows, the swan is ludicrously white;
>   And frogs may hold the toads an upstart breed.
> Thus each, though twisted as a wind-blown weed,
>   Sees his own curves as straight, his clouds as light.[6]
>   *Stanton A. Coblentz*

The effects of holding extreme positions are well known in everyday life and have been replicated under experimental conditions. The farther an individual's position is from the center of monotonic scales ordered intensively, the narrower is the region of acceptable difference from his own position and the more apt he is to magnify differences (Sherif and Hovland, 1961). Extreme positions constrict judgment and

TABLE 9.7.   Number of Ranks Assigned by Each of Two Subjects, One a Radical, the Other a Conservative

	Radical S	Conservative S
Radical	7.5	8.5
Conservative	10.0	5.2

SOURCE: From Cartwright, 1941.

blunt discrimination: gradations in other positions are not recognized, and anyone who differs at all from the extremist is *ipso facto* in the opposite camp. In a study by Cartwright (1941*b*) a radical *S* and a conservative *S* rated 20 well-known people on a scale of radicalism-conservatism. Each extremist perceived more people as belonging to the opposition than to his own group as shown in Table 9.7. The radical *S*

---

[6] With the permission of the *Kansas City Star*.

used 7.5 scale positions to classify individuals he regarded as radical but 10 positions for those whom he considered conservative; the conservative used 8.5 positions for those he regarded as radical and only 5.2 positions for those he regarded as conservative. In this case the conservative appears to be more conservative than the radical was radical for the former employed a total of 13.7 ranks against 17.5 ranks employed by the radical in making his judgments.

The following simple diagram illustrates the ways in which others may differ from "me" and still be thought right:

WRONG   **RIGHT**   WRONG

· · · · · · · · · · · · · · · · ·(·)· · · · · · · · · · · · · · · ·

Self

Everyone on my side is right, provided he does not go too far. Almost everyone on the other side is wrong. Those who are on my side may deviate more from me and still be regarded as right (or with favor) than those on the other side. The best I can grant is that those who are on the other side *a little, may be* right, but not those who differ a lot from me! The parentheses indicate the limits within which others may be different from me and still be regarded as right. Sometimes we tolerate no difference from our position, especially if ours is an extreme one.

Burrow pointed out that systematized affect and prejudice may exist in normal as well as neurotic *S*s and may infect a whole society:

[An example was] the early malaria-infected communities whose daily proved experience was a state of habitual malaria and who therefore possessed no standard of comparison whereby to distinguish a known condition of disease from an unknown state of health. From their constant experience these confirmed sufferers were led to conclude that malaria was a normal condition (1950, p. 476).

Scientists who were not victims of *Plasmodium malariae* had to come upon the scene and introduce "a wholly new basis of reference" to establish a standard of health.

This example points to the need for some nonconformists or deviants in our political, economic, and social affairs if progress is to be made. If all individuals and communities are afflicted with a disorder, how or where, asked Burrow, are we to find a standard for comparison by which to differentiate between healthy and unhealthy human adaptations? Social psychologists also recognize this tendency of society to be satisfied with its own norms when they point out that every nation is taught to use its own character as the norm by which to judge others (Sherif and Sherif, 1953). Whyte (1957) has inveighed against the tendency of modern industry to choose conforming individuals for executive positions and to reject individuals who depart even minimally from pre-established norms. He maintained that many psychological tests of personality for selecting personnel in industry are designed to exclude deviates who may be the creative individuals while favoring the "well-adjusted" mediocre personalities. Scientists entrusted with the task of perfecting instruments for selecting people for key as well as routine positions and industrial and government executives who must make choices for important positions—indeed, society as a whole—are faced with a dilemma: as long as many people are involved and must interact to keep modern industry, government, and other large-scale projects going, it is necessary to have a certain amount of teamwork. Individuals must be chosen who will conform more or less to certain organizational requirements. On the other hand, progress comes from creative individuals who are not necessarily conforming individuals, and they too must be encouraged and allowed to function within organizations that would stagnate without them. As industry, government, and military services have to depend more and more upon trained, often creative, personnel, ways will have to be found to accommodate the nonconformists who function best under least restraint.

Conformity and nonconformity, like all other states, are relative and are found in various degrees. We have special words for extremes of nonconformity, such as *renegade, apostate, turncoat, traitor, heretic, backslider,* each with its own shade of meaning but all denoting deviation from some group norm. Various degrees of opprobrium attach to individuals falling in these various categories, as pointed out by Coser (1956). The renegade is one who deserts to the opposition and is hated more than ordinary members of the opposition. The renegade, unable to return to the group he has deserted, is more loyal to the new group than are those who have belonged to it all along. The heretic, on the other hand, may appear worse to a group than the apostate. "The latter deserts the group to go over to the enemy while the heretic presents a more insidious danger for while upholding the group's central values and goals, he threatens to split it into factions that will differ as to the means for implementing its goal" (Coser,

1956). Such social phenomena are analogous to the well-known repulsion effects of backgrounds or anchors which are greater the nearer stimuli are to the anchors: the apostate and the heretic are rejected more violently than are bona fide members of the opposition because of their nearness, past or present, to the group! Coser also pointed out that the more frequent as well as the closer the interactions of groups, or members of groups, the more occasion there is for hostility toward deviant members.

When is an individual regarded merely as a nonconformist, and at what point is he called traitor, renegade, or apostate? An individual may be with, ahead of, or behind the group with respect to various issues. A person may be ahead of his party on one issue and with or behind his party on other issues and still be considered a loyal party member. Thus "Mr. Republican" himself, the late Senator Taft, stood practically with the Democrats on the matter of public housing, but was never accused of heresy or backsliding by his Republican colleagues. But the Democratic Governor who threw his support to a Republican candidate for President and the Republican Senator who switched in mid-term to the Democratic Party were labeled heretics or something worse by the members of their erstwhile parties. Groups serve as backgrounds for their members and a Republican in the Democratic camp or a Democrat in the Republican camp stand out in sharper contrast than the party member who deviates on a single issue, particularly if it is not crucial. Most important of all in identifying the traitor is *change of label*. For one who has been identified with one group to openly identify himself with the opposition by taking its name constitutes the height of injury to the other group.

The abnormal personality. While every deviate from the so-called normal personality differs in some respect from every other deviate as well as from the norm, the adaptations of abnormal individuals are characterized by a lack of stable frames of reference and by the predominant weight given to inner as opposed to outer (i.e., situational or reality) factors. That maintenance of stable norms is necessary for consistent objective responses was shown in the results of a weight-lifting study by Kaplan and the writer (1950) with pre- and post-lobotomized psychotics. It was found that these Ss differed in their judgments from normal Ss in the following ways: (1) They confused the focal with background or anchor stimuli, judging the latter when the instructions called for them to respond to the former. (2) They frequently judged heavier stimuli to be lighter than stimuli weighing less; i.e., inversions in their judgments were common. (3) Their range of responses was smaller than that employed by the normal controls in that they used only half as many scale categories as did the normals. (4) Responses of the psychotic *S*s showed little or no effects of anchors on series stimuli. The psychotic *S*s thus seemed unable to establish the stable frames of reference necessary for ordered discriminations involving a graded series of stimuli which were subject to context effects.

With regard to "reality centering," the normal individual is anchored in the here and now while cognizant of past and future. Present stimuli are weighted sufficiently to maintain orientation in time and space. Psychotics, on the other hand, are typically disoriented with respect to time or place or both, and their affective-cognitive balance is also upset due to the greater weight of inner as opposed to outer sources of stimulation. Overweighting of stimuli, having their origin within the organism, of past or imaginary happenings, of "things that can't be helped," of events removed in time or which the individual cannot change by his own efforts all lead to anxiety, frustration, and, in the extreme cases, may be manifestations of abnormality. The normal individual adapts to extreme stimuli and to repeated frustrations in such a way as to ameliorate their severity and to maintain his balance. Just as physiological homeostatic mechanisms are directed toward maintenance of normal values of body temperature and pH content of the blood, so at the behavioral level, but with much greater latitude in permissible range of normal values, there is a psychological homeostasis governing stimulus-response relationships. Paradoxically, the normal individual's frames of reference are varied and shift in accordance with changing conditions, but they remain stable because they are anchored in the here and now; whereas those of the abnormal individual are narrow in range, are not modified in accordance with altered circumstances, and do not remain stable with constant input because of the preponderant influence of fortuitous residuals that mask, distort, and otherwise render ineffective environmental stimuli.

In short, the abnormal individual is unable to put present stimuli, situations, and persons in normal perspective because he overweights some stimuli and residuals to the exclusion of others and he cannot maintain stable frames of reference with changing configurations of stimulation. As a result he is easily confused, cannot manage his affairs, and becomes divorced from reality. The anxious person overweights consequences of present situations, the guilty or remorseful individual is unable to shake off memories of past actions, and the psychotic patient has retreated to his own private world. The task of the counselor, the psychotherapist, and the psychiatrist consists in counteracting the predominant influence of disturbing focal or residual stimuli by every means at his command. Whether one attacks abnormality by means of drugs or surgical procedures, by altering the environment, or by "talking-out" methods, the aim is to create frames of reference enabling the individual to adjust more adequately to the world about him.

SUMMARY

Adaptation-level theory by combining inner and outer determinants of personality within a single frame of reference avoids the extremes of the pure environmental theories and the pure typological and trait theories. Personality is envisaged as the product of external and internal forces, acting at specific times, in specific situations, and having specific outcomes characteristic of the individual. What one does on a test, whether it be structured or unstructured, depends upon the nature of the test, the background against which the test is given (including the characteristics of the tester), and upon transient as well as steady personal adjustment levels. This point of view requires a shift from thinking in terms of generalized traits, types, or attitudes to thinking in terms of specifiable variables in concrete situations and leads to a taxonomy of traits in situations rather than one of traits in persons. Personality patterns are seen to be constructs arising from the *functional* dependencies between situational and response variables, thus bridging the gap between outer and inner determinants of behavior. This approach should aid in identification of variables selected for study and in the integration of personality variables with phenomena found under controlled laboratory conditions. A critical problem for personality theory is to understand how residuals interact with present stimulation, how they become fixed, and how they may be modified or counteracted by appropriate control of the environment to change conduct.

10 *Interpersonal Behavior*

To the layman, as well as to many psychologists, social psychology appears to be more humanly oriented and more practical than other areas of psychological investigation. It is felt that people should know as much as possible about this area in order to get along with each other at all levels, international as well as personal. The need for solidly based information regarding personality and interpersonal relations has stimulated the invention of personality tests and scales for measuring group opinions and attitudes on a wide variety of issues. In spite of considerable success along these lines, the *science,* as distinguished from the *technology,* of interpersonal relations has lagged because of a lack of theoretical models to guide research. As a result social psychologists have turned to principles and models derived from studies of judgment, perception, and learning to guide their investigations of personal and interpersonal behavior. In this chapter we are concerned mainly with applications of one such model to the study of interpersonal relations, in an endeavor to see if lawful, functional dependencies exist in social phenomena which are formally similar to the kinds of relations found in perception and learning. We shall first try to clarify a number of issues in order to make the presuppositions underlying our approach explicit, in the hope that it may carry us a step nearer to a *science* of social relations.

THE NATURE OF GROUPS

It is often assumed that the study of group behavior requires new concepts in addition to those applied to individual behavior in order to account for phenomena of interpersonal relations. Early social psychologists and sociologists were responsible for the introduction of such concepts as group mind, collective consciousness, collective unconsciousness, *Volksgeist,* and collective representations (cf. Allport, 1954) to deal with group phenomena as opposed to individual behavior. Later writers have used other terms such as "social medium" and "social frames of reference" for group behavior. While the earlier terms have fallen into disuse other concepts similar to them are being used because, as Allport points out, the same problems remain (Allport, 1954; Cattell, 1948). In recent years there has been a tendency to ascribe to groups global characteristics such as "fascistic," "totalitarian," and "democratic." In this connection, Cattell points out that the use of large terms for small variables will result in an embarrassing harvest of muddle "when no proof is offered that these are unitary patterns or when the variables actually measured are perhaps the least important for defining the total pattern" (1948, p. 50). Since groups are composed of individuals, it has also been customary to postulate special tendencies in the individual, such as the herd or gregarious instincts and various personality traits, to account for individual readiness to fraternize and to participate in group activities of all sorts. It is apparent that neither the earlier nor the later global approaches to individuals as members of groups and to groups as such have been wholly satisfactory.

That groups exhibit Gestalt properties seems to be a generally accepted fact even by some who believe that an analytic approach is necessary for a proper understanding of group behavior (see Cattell, 1948). Concepts like "group mind" seem to have arisen from the recognition that while groups possess properties similar to certain properties of the individuals composing them, they also have properties over and above those of their constituent units, i.e., they are true Gestalten. Groups possess two of the three fundamental properties laid down by von Ehrenfels for *Gestaltqualitäten* plus two additional properties of Gestalten: (1) The actions and goals of groups are more than the sum of the actions and goals of the individuals composing them (postulate of super-summative properties). (2) Groups persist although their individual units change (postulate of transposability of whole properties or independence of wholes from parts). (3) There is interaction among the members of groups, the degree of which determines the strength or cohesion of the whole. (4) Groups respond as wholes to stimuli directed to their parts.

But one of the necessary conditions laid down by von Ehrenfels for the existence of Gestalten is lacking in groups. He said that every Gestalt must have a "common carrier." Thus if n individuals each hear one of n tones they do not hear the melody because there is no common carrier for the n units. In the case of the individual who hears n tones there is a common carrier in nervous substance to mediate the melody. Groups have Gestalt properties, properly speaking, only as long as there is *communication* between the members of the group when a common carrier may be assumed to exist. Concepts like "group mind" were obviously meant to supply an enduring substrate which groups as such simply do not have. Groups exist only as long as there is interaction or communication among their members or as residuals in the behavior of individuals.

We see, therefore, that groups are constituted by and through the interactions of individuals who communicate with one another by various means. When individuals are not in communication, the group exists only as a residual that affects overt behavior of its members. Thus while groups cannot be said to have a common substrate or carrier, they depend upon *sets* of carriers, *viz,* their members. There are also inanimate carriers of group products: written records, works of art, shrines, monuments, buildings, and all the visible evidences of cultures and subcultures which act as focal or background stimuli and thereby function as surrogates for the individuals who once functioned as members of groups.

The paradigm of focal, background, and residual stimuli is useful in dealing with group behavior as well as in dealing with individual responses though there are differences in content and complexity. The view that groups may be conceptualized in terms of interactions of individuals makes concepts like the group mind, group medium, and collective consciousness superfluous. It is consonant with the definition of social psychology usually accepted by workers in the area: "With few exceptions social psychologists regard their discipline as *an attempt to understand and explain how the thought, feeling, and behavior of individuals are influenced by the actual, imagined, or implied presence of other human beings"* (Allport, 1954, p. 5).

Conceptualization of group activities and products in terms of the actions of the individuals comprising the group does not involve a bad kind of reductionism. Just as the natural sciences have made tremendous strides through the discovery and manipulation of the natural units comprising molar phenomena, so social psychology, sociology, and anthropology can make progress through better understanding of their natural units. Interaction in groups is both horizontal and vertical: one individual acts upon another and thereby upon the group and the group also acts upon its members. In face-to-face conditions groups act immediately as focal or background stimuli; in other circumstances they may act as residual stimuli to influence individual behavior when the individual is not actually with the group, e.g., the church member who does not drink because his religion forbids taking alcoholic beverages. Conversely, leaders and persons occupying special positions in groups may influence the members of the group even though there is no physical meeting of persons, e.g., when the members of a union or of a political party are swayed by the dicta of a union leader or the head of the party. There is no case of group behavior or properties of groups which are not referable, ultimately, to individuals. We therefore face no special problems in envisaging interpersonal relations in the same formal terms that we have applied to individual behavior.

By conceiving group products as the result of interaction and pooling of individual responses the greatest impediment to an experimental approach to group behavior is removed. Cobliner, a sociologist, takes an even stronger position in favor of treating groups from the standpoint of the behaviors of the individuals composing them. He argued (1955) that if we take the individual level of integration rather than the group level we can understand the *dynamics* of the situation rather than the end result that is the group action.

One of the main difficulties with social psychology has been a plethora of concepts characterizing properties of groups and group behaviors and a dearth of dimensions for ordering them. Of the number and variety of concepts in social psychology, the following constitute but a partial list: reference group; membership group; cohesiveness; leadership; group opinion, organization, solidarity, motives, and goals;

minority groups; group involvement; power structure; morale; propaganda; scape-goating; social distance; shared frame of reference; reference group; social status; stereotype; and even group "traits." Various writers have called attention to the complexity, ambiguity, and global character of such concepts (Cattell, 1948) and have pointed out that even such an apparently simple individual trait as "leadership" has proved to be anything but unitary (Guilford, 1959). The call for analysis, hence for simplification, of social concepts is not only in the interests of economy of thought but also to achieve a more general, basic approach to problems of interpersonal relations.

Designation of group levels. We have seen how the concept of adaptation or adjustment levels has proved applicable to the study of judgment, perception, and learning. The question now facing us is whether this concept can be fruitfully applied to the understanding of group behavior. It is frequently assumed that the concept of adaptation level can be applied only to sensory and psychophysical data or to areas where stimuli or situations can be specified in physical units (cf. Allport, 1955). This concept is often referred to as "dimensional" because of its origins in psychophysics and perception and because of its emphasis upon quantifiable aspects of behavior. That the theory is not restricted to sensory phenomena and can be fruitfully applied to such areas as personality and interpersonal relations has been shown in a number of studies which are discussed in this chapter. In considering problems in social psychology three fundamental facets of adaptation-level theory should be kept in mind: (1) emphasis upon adjustment or adaptation as a fundamental fact of social as well as individual behavior; (2) the three-fold division of sources of stimulation, hence of variance, into focal, background, and residual stimuli; and (3) the definition of adaptation level as a pooled effect and its employment as a parameter in quantitative formulations of social behavior.

The first of these three aspects of AL theory, adaptation, is not new or foreign to social psychology since the adaptive nature of group activities has often been stressed both by social psychologists and biologists. Physiological adaptation to the environment determines whether or not groups survive; and politico-economic actions of groups are important in the adjustments of some or all members of a society. Groups are thus responsible for many behavioral adaptations, so the concept of adaptation in a broad sense applies to group as well as to individual behavior.

The three-fold division of sources of variance in behavior holds for individuals in groups as well as in solitary situations. The concept of stimulus, however, must not be interpreted merely as energy imping-ing upon the organism without regard to its meaning and the infor-mation it conveys. Nor must stimuli be identified only with local stimuli. People affect others not only as visual or auditory stimuli but, perhaps far more importantly, as stimuli having physiognomic and demand characters; individuals are friendly or hostile, cooperative or uncooperative, interesting or boring, likable or repulsive, leaders or followers, rich or poor, and so on through the whole gamut of char-acteristics of individuals which are of importance in their interpersonal relations. Individuals act upon other individuals as focal stimuli in the broad sense here indicated, and as background and as residual stimuli also.

Let us pause for a moment to consider the large part played by residuals (memories, habits of action, biases, sets, phantasies, and even imaginative products) in group behavior. Whereas residuals often play a small part in sensory, perceptual, and simple judgmental proc-esses, they may be all important in social interactions. The individual carries with him many residuals that influence his behavior—residuals from his family, his church, his union, his political party, his business or professional colleagues, in short, from the *class* to which he belongs. So strong are residuals in interpersonal relations that it seems as if the usual laws of memory based on laboratory learning experiments do not hold, and the memory of a loss, an injury, an insult, may grow rather than diminish with time. Someone has said that families forget a murder sooner than they do a property loss. In everyday affairs past events may be more potent at a later time than when they originally occurred. An experiment by Hovland, Lumsdaine, and Sheffield (1949) furnishes experimental evidence for the greater impact of older resid-uals: During the war a pro-British film was shown to a large audience of randomly selected American soldiers. It was found that the effects of the film were, on the whole, greater nine weeks after the showing than five days afterwards. These writers called this anomalous effect the "sleeper effect." Everyday experience furnishes countless examples of the failure of the classical curve of retention, especially of the emo-tional impact of stimuli, to drop with time. Hence, the lasting residual effects of social influences must be recognized.

The third aspect of adaptation-level theory is its insistence on quantitative functional measures of all behavioral data. If group behavior or interpersonal interactions can be specified in terms of operationally quantifiable concepts, then there is no bar to the full use of the theory in this area as well as in the areas in which it originated. Measurement of group levels is essentially a heuristic matter and offers no special methodological difficulties in view of the many modern psychometric methods for measuring all aspects of individual behavior. In general, it is customary, when dealing with sets of data, to take values that are representative of the set, such as the mean, median, or mode. By current methods of measurement, groups can be compared with respect to responses made to stimuli that are not physically measurable as well as with respect to stimuli that are measurable in physical units. Thus one may compare groups with respect to such diverse characteristics as intelligence, generosity, or radicalism. If it is possible to measure or score *individuals,* it is *ipso facto* possible to specify group level. Coombs (1948) pointed out that if the position of an individual relative to other individuals can be determined on tests, questionnaires, etc., a status score for a group would be merely the average of the status scores of the individuals comprising the group. In addition, measures of the dispersion of individuals within a group must also be taken into account to determine whether or not the group presents a unified front on a given issue. This characteristic of groups can be derived from the status scores of the individuals comprising the group (Thurstone, 1945; McNemar, 1946; Coombs, 1948). In this connection Thurstone suggested:

It may even be possible to *define the morale of a group in terms of the sum of the affective dispersions of all its debatable issues.* . . . Measurement of the seriousness of crimes can be made by psychophysical methods in which the dispersions are signs of heterogeneity or lack of unity in the group and its code (Thurstone, 1945, p. 248, quoted by Coombs, 1948).

The question now arises: How may we formulate the concept of adaptation level to make it meaningful for group as well as for individual behavior? We may do this by specifying the conditions under which groups divide equally or remain neutral or indifferent with respect to various alternatives. If there were only two choices, accept or reject, a 50-50 division would indicate that the conditions were, as a whole, neutral so far as the group was concerned. With three choices available, a 33-33-33 division would signify an essentially neutral group.

Similarly, conditions which produce equal division of the members can be characterized as representing the adaptation level of the group. But just as psychophysical thresholds are often defined in terms of 75 percent response or some other arbitrary measure, so it is possible to set arbitrary criteria in defining levels of group attitudes. Thus Birch (1945) found that in a group asked to state their agreement or disagreement with two opposed statements regarding the attitude of the state toward the individual with respect to treatment of unemployed, the ill, etc., 97 percent of 177 members of the group agreed more or less with the "liberal" position and only 3 percent with the opposite point of view. This group could, therefore, be said to be very liberal. Birch also found that the *extent* of agreement was markedly affected by labeling the statements as "communistic," "fascistic," "liberal." The group can therefore be further characterized in terms of such additional parameters as degree of agreement and, as indicated above, in terms of dispersion of responses to each of the statements. The origin with respect to which levels are said to be high or low is, like all origins, more or less arbitrary. Origins at equilibrium points have, however, special significance: they provide natural origins on bipolar and multi-dimensional continua. For example, if a moderate request to contribute money for a gift elicits a 50 percent favorable response from a group, then we know that a stronger request would probably result in more than a 50 percent favorable response and contrariwise, that a weaker request would result in less than a 50 percent favorable response (cf. Rosenbaum, 1956). We find, thus, that levels of group behavior are specified in terms of the *conditions* under which members of the group meet certain criteria, just as ALs, thresholds, and other psychophysical parameters are specified in terms of conditions under which responses meet criterion.

For the mean of the attitudes, opinions, or points of view of individuals comprising a group as the value representing level of group attitude or opinion, it is assumed that each individual counts as one and only one unit. In other words, it is assumed that an unweighted mean adequately represents group level. In many cases this value is adequate, e.g., to compare amounts donated by various groups for some purpose. But in the case of the sentiments of a political party before election the opinions of leaders will carry far more weight in influencing the vote than will those of the average citizen. In predicting group levels it is therefore often necessary to weight the opinions of leaders more heavily than those of rank and file members. Similarly, conditions affecting groups must also be differentially weighted. A more general measure, therefore, of group level would be a weighted mean in which all factors, external as well as internal, affecting the group would be weighted in accordance with their influence. Thus if we wished to define conditions under which the largest possible amount of money for a given cause could be raised we would have to weight differentially the strength of the request, the conditions under which it is made, and the ability of individuals to contribute.

Requirements for an experimental approach to interpersonal relations. To meet the requirements of scientific rigor while at the same time preserving verisimilitude to life conditions is, perhaps, the most difficult problem facing the social psychologist. One may conduct an experiment in psychophysics or learning without having to make provision for a "reality" dimension; but if we are to perform meaningful experiments in the field of interpersonal relations, they must be carried out under realistic conditions having truly social qualities. It is more difficult to create personal interactions while controlling the situation in an experiment in social psychology than it is to exclude unwanted personal or social factors from a psychophysical experiment. If experiments in social psychology are to yield results that have any meaning beyond the particular situations in which they are made, it is necessary that experimental Ss feel that the experiments represent bona fide situations, viz., that the situations are what they purport to be. Thus if the purpose of an experiment is to determine what the effect of group opinion is upon an individual's responses, then the individual must believe that the responses of the group are bona fide reactions to the situation. For example, if Ss are required to respond after hearing members of the group make palpably wrong or distorted judgments, control of the experimental situation has largely been lost because it is then not possible to relate Ss' responses to univocal elements in the stimulus situation. Have the distorted judgments of the group modified Ss perception? Or does S interpret his task as one of agreeing with the group? Or does S adopt a role to meet the bizarre responses in still another way unnkown to E? Luchins (1944) found that 100 percent agreement was easily obtained on the part of children when the stooge gave correct reports of comparative lengths of lines, but when the stooge gave incorrect reports 100 percent agreement was not reached. In repeated trials, however, either large increases in the number of agreements were obtained or else a complete lack of agreement was easily reached! According to Luchins, children try to square themselves when they are driven to "senseless" responses, saying, "He [the stooge] means longer when he says shorter," or "I am blind." In such situations one does not know to what extent each set of stimuli (lines to be judged or judgments of the stooge, in the case above) is responsible for Ss' responses. Social psychology must define and control its stimulus situations no less than is required in other areas in order that the *effective* stimulus shall be known.

A second requirement of experiments in social behavior is that stimulus conditions be varied in graded systematic fashion. It is not enough to sample behavior with respect to a variable or condition at a single point on a continuum or merely at the extremes as is too often done. We can illustrate the point at issue concretely by reference to one of the earliest and, for its time, one of the most important experiments performed in social psychology. Investigating the comparative influence of majority and expert opinion on attitudes, Moore (1921) required 95 Ss to make 18 paired comparisons for linguistic, ethical, and musical stimuli. In the linguistic set, Ss checked each of the more offensive grammatical errors in pairs of items; in the ethical set they checked the more offensive of two traits of character; and in the musical set they expressed their preference for one of two resolutions of chords. Two days later the experiment was repeated to obtain a control percentage of reversals in judgment. After two and a half months the experiment was repeated but this time the Ss were told the majority choices, and two days later the experiment was again repeated, and the Ss were told the experts' choices. Taking the original percents as base (Table 10.1A) the percentage of reversals in judgments were found to be five times

TABLE 10.1A. Percentage of Reversals in Judgments of Linguistic, Ethical, and Musical Stimuli as a Result of Influence of Majority and Expert Opinion

| | Percentage of Reversals | | |
	Linguistic	Ethical	Musical
Control	13.5	10.3	25.1
Majority influence	62.2	50.1	48.2
Expert influence	48.0	47.8	46.2

SOURCE: From Moore, 1921. With the permission of the *American Journal of Psychology.*

above chance for linguistic and ethical stimuli and a little less than twice above chance for musical stimuli. Majority and expert opinion had about the same effects on ethical and musical materials but majority opinion was more potent than expert opinion with linguistic materials.

This experiment of Moore's was the forerunner of many more investigations showing the influence of social pressures on judgments of many different types of material. It is an excellent empirical study giving clear-cut results for *spot values of the independent variables.* The amount or strength of majority and expert opinions was not varied, consequently it cannot be regarded as a systematic study since it does not reveal the relation between variation in the independent variables (majority and expert opinion) and the dependent variable (influence on judgments as measured by reversals). To be sure, majority and expert opinion were compared on three different types of materials, but we do not know from this study what the influence is of a bare majority (51 percent) as compared with that of 10 percent or 90 percent of the population or whether the effect of a few experts is as great as that of many experts or the extent to which degree of expertness influences attitudes. In short, though this study by Moore was a landmark 40 years ago, it is not a systematic, quantitative investigation. These criticisms of an early important study are not made in a caviling spirit but for the purpose of furthering systematic investigations in interpersonal relations.

Different results were in fact obtained by other investigators 20 years after the Moore study, perhaps because their stimuli fell on another part of the stimulus continuum. Burtt and Falkenburg (1941) studied the influence of majority vs. expert opinion on religious attitudes of church groups. A Likert-type scale covering several phases of religious beliefs was administered on two different occasions to a sample of churchgoers. The second time the scale was administered, some statements were said to indicate beliefs of a majority and others beliefs of experts (clergymen). A third group was given the statements without background information. While the experimental groups were influenced by both majority and expert opinion, there was no significant difference in the influence exerted by these two prestige sources. Contrary to Moore's findings, expert opinion carried as much weight as did majority opinion. It is therefore not sufficient to compare the influence of two variables without having first established the functional relation between number of experts or degrees of expertness and attitude change and that between number of individuals (including the "majority"), from almost nobody to almost everybody, and attitude change. So long as only spot checks are made in social psychology, no basic understanding or interpersonal relations is possible.

By way of contrast with these studies is one by Marple (1933) which was also concerned with the effects of majority and expert influence on attitudes but with control of the independent variable, age of Ss. In this study the attitudes of 300 high school seniors, 300 college students, and 300 representatives of Iowa adults toward policies in education, politics, and economics were determined before and after Ss were told the supposed opinions of a majority and of experts. One hundred Ss in each group responded to 75 questions in a test that was repeated a month later as a control and then after informing them of majority and expert opinions regarding the issues. The responses were in terms of a three-category scale, "yes," "uncertain," or "no." The results show that (1) majority opinion exercised greater influence than did expert opinion on all age groups; and (2) with increasing age of Ss, both majority and expert influence declined and the differences between the two became less (Table 10.1B). The regularity of the decline in suggestibility and of the differences between majority and expert opinions with increasing age is impressive because of the dimensional nature of the independent variable.

TABLE 10.1B.   Susceptibility of Three Age Groups to Majority and Expert Opinion

| | Changes in Attitudes Following Social Pressure | |
	Toward Majority	Toward Experts
High school seniors	64.2	51.2
College seniors	55.2	45.0
Older Iowans	39.8	34.0

SOURCE: From Marple, 1933. With the permission of the *Journal of Social Psychology.*

The results of the three studies concerning influence of majority vs. expert opinion are by no means univocal. Two agree regarding the greater effect of majority opinion, but we have seen that the difference between majority and expert opinions diminished with advancing age. Replication of the dimensional variable, age, is easy and if suggestibility is found to decline with age over a wide variety of situations, then a solid fact will have been established on which to build in the field of social psychology.

The remainder of this chapter deals with a number of experiments in which several values of the independent variable were used in order to determine the type of function relating the independent and dependent variables. We shall show that it is possible in this way to discover relations formally similar to learning and sensory functions in the field of interpersonal behavior. The power gained from knowledge of functional relations between independent and dependent variables is attested in all fields of science and technology. What has been lacking in approaches to personality and interpersonal relations is precisely the kind of information contained in statements of functional dependencies. The uses and advantages of such relations are many. Given the functional relation between two scaled or dimensional variables, the amount of one variable associated with a given amount of the other is known. The form of the relation, when plotted or stated analytically in an equation, may give an indication of the type of process involved and the degree of similarity to related phenomena. Rates of change of one variable as a function of change in the other variable can be determined, and the limits of generalizations may be established. In addition, quantitative relations make possible interpolation between and extrapolation beyond observed values, and hence predictions are possible both for purposes of validation of hypotheses and for control of phenomena. Not the least of the advantages of knowledge of functional relations between variables is that only by this means can laws, hypotheses, and theories be formulated and tested with precision.

STIMULUS AND RESIDUAL DETERMINERS OF ATTITUDES

The first study in the area of interpersonal interactions explicitly undertaken within the framework of AL theory was made by Schein (1949) under the writer's direction. We were interested in determining if, and to what extent, social stimulation could modify psychophysical judgments. The amount or intensity of social stimulation was varied by varying the size of the group to which each test S was exposed. The experiments were conducted as follows: Ss judged a set of stimuli, weighing 200, 250, 300, 350, and 400 grm. and presented in random order, by calling them very very heavy, very heavy, heavy, medium heavy, medium, medium light, light, very light, or very very light. In the solitary situation no background or anchor stimulus was employed since it was necessary to establish a baseline for the effects of both anchor stimuli and social influences, which were introduced later. Upon completion of the preliminary experiments the Ss were told that in order to speed up collection of data several Ss would be taken together. Six groups of four, three, and two Ss were then formed with one in each group randomly chosen to be the test S. There were thus eighteen groups, with a test S in each who judged the stimuli *after* hearing the other members of the group. In the group situation Ss lifted a background weight of either 90 or 900 grm. before each of the series stimuli with the exception of the test Ss who were given a 300-grm. weight as the background stimulus. Since the stimuli were not visible the test Ss had no reason to believe they were not exposed to exactly the same anchors as the other Ss. The choice of the 300-grm. background was made for two reasons: (1) so that the test Ss would lift two stimuli in succession as the control Ss were doing, and (2) because judgments of the series stimuli were known not to be affected much by an anchor near the center of the series. Since the adaptation level with stimuli 200–400 grm. is only a little lower than adaptation level with these stimuli and a 300 grm. anchor, upward or downward shifts in judgments of the test Ss in the group situation would then be due to the influence exerted by the judgments of the control Ss. On the other hand, the judgments of the control Ss should shift upward toward the "heavy" side of the category scale with 90-grm. background and downward toward the "light" side of the scale with 900-grm. background. Since we were interested in the absolute amount of displacement in the judgments of test Ss, the judgments have been pooled regardless of direction of shift.

From Table 10.2 it is seen that the 900 and 90-grm. background stimuli caused a shift of 2.6 category steps in the case of the control Ss, and shifts of 1.03, 0.38, and 0.23 category steps in the case of the test Ss. While shifts of less than half a category step are probably not statistically significant, the displacements in the judgments of the test Ss were almost without exception in the direction of the group shift (up with the 90-grm. groups and down with the 900-grm. groups). Furthermore, the results show that size of group determines the extent of group influence: the four-member group exerts most influence on the test Ss, the three-member group next, and the two-member group practically none at all. Amount of social pressure is differentially effective in determining judgments of the test *Ss*. However, the greatest amount of social pressure was not as effective as actual change in the physical conditions of stimulation, for the control *Ss* shifted their judgments to a greater extent than did the test *Ss*.

TABLE 10.2. Average Shift in Judgment of Eighteen Ss as a Result of Hearing the Judgments of Other Ss in Groups of Four, Three, or Two Persons

Stimuli (grm.)	Control Ss (90- or 900-grm. Background)	Test Ss		
		Group of Four	Group of Three	Group of Two
200	2.40	0.80	.75	.55
250	2.80	1.15	.00	—.20[a]
300	2.80	1.05	.35	.30
350	2.60	1.20	.60	.35
400	4.60	1.95	.20	.15
Mean	2.60	1.03	.38	.23

[a] The minus sign indicates that the average shift in this case was in a direction opposite to that of the control Ss.
SOURCE: From Schein, 1949.

The results of the Schein experiment were important in that they lent support to two basic assumptions which were necessary for further applications of the AL paradigm to the study of interpersonal behavior. First, they showed that social stimulation can be varied in intensity with the possibility of obtaining functional relations between independent and dependent variables in social situations; and second, they showed that pooling may occur not only within sense modalities or between cognitive systems (something shown much earlier by such studies as McGarvey's, 1942) but also between sensory and cognitive processes. This study thus served to establish the fact that effects of focal physical stimuli pool with social background and also with individual residuals and thus influence the judgments of test *Ss*.

The next investigation of the pooling model in attitude change was made by Fehrer (1952). Three groups of *Ss* were each given a set of statements to rank on a militarism-pacifism continuum on which 1 denoted extreme pacifistic content, 5 denoted neutrality or about equal pacifistic-militaristic content, and 9 denoted extreme militaristic content. The control group was given the *C* scale consisting of 55 regularly spaced items, that is, 5 items from each of the Thurstone scale values from 0 through 10 and constituting an equally balanced set of stimuli. The second group received the M scale (militaristic) which was weighted toward the militaristic side by omitting most pacifistic statements. It contained 6 items at each scale value from 3 through 10, making a total of 48 in all, and with mean scale value of 6.99. The third group received the P scale which was weighted toward the pacifistic end and contained 48 items, 6 at each scale value from 0 through 7, with a mean of 3.95. In addition the scales were so constructed that 25 items were common to all three, 40 items were common to the C and M scales, 40 items were common to the C and P scales, and 30 items were common to the M and P scales. Fehrer thus depended upon differences in composition of the scale items to produce changes in AL. Since the changes in series stimuli are not nearly as effective as changes in background stimuli, so far as AL is concerned, and the use of numerical categories tends to anchor judgments in accordance with the solidly established "number" system that most college Ss have acquired, and also because the large percentage of items common to the three scales tends to obliterate differences in ALs, Fehrer's study must be regarded as furnishing strong support to AL theory so far as the over-all results are concerned which are given in Table 10.3.

TABLE 10.3. Means and Differences between Mean Scale Values of the 25 Common Items on Scales C, M, and P

Scale	Mean	Difference		t
C	5.494	(C–M)	.326	3.492[a]
M	5.168	(C–P)	−.094	1.043
P	5.588	(P–M)	.420	4.795[b]

[a] Significant between the .01 and .001 levels.
[b] Significant beyond the .001 level.
SOURCE: From Fehrer, 1952. With the permission of the American Psychological Association.

In accordance with deductions from AL theory the average scale value of P items was highest (5.6), showing that the items were scaled more toward the militaristic side in pacifistic context while the average of the C scale items was 5.5, exactly in the middle of the equally balanced scale, and the average of the M scale items was lowest (5.2), showing that in militaristic context the items were scaled more toward the pacifistic side. Two of the expected three differences are statistically significant; the one which is not significant is that between the C and P series. The common items in the three scales are displaced according to expectation with the exception of items with extreme scale values which Fehrer interpreted as evidence against AL theory. But this result is consistent with our theory when it is remembered that displacements of stimuli are less the greater their distance from AL. If stimuli are sufficiently intense or far from level they may be unaffected by other stimuli or changes in background as found by Helson and Michels (1948). The differential displacements in one direction in the M scale and in the opposite direction in the P scale of items common to the three scales furnish striking confirmation of AL theory.

We must now consider items near the middle of the scales. The results are conflicting, depending upon the items supposed to represent the center. Taking the broadest band, which includes nine items, we find that these have average values of 5.7 on the P scale, 5.5 on the M scale, and 5.8 on the C scale, which Fehrer interpreted as showing that "A-L does not shift systematically and significantly with a change in the composition of the three scales." We need make no new assumptions to account for these findings since principles previously established apply here. It is obvious that the small and statistically insignificant movement of the middle items in Fehrer's three scales springs from the fact that AL is not a *point* but a *region* (Helson, 1948). The middle items were not affected significantly because of the small changes in AL with changes only in *composition* of the stimuli. AL must move well above or below a given neutral region if all the items in that region are to be displaced. The fact, found by Fehrer, that moderately pacifistic and moderately militaristic items shifted significantly with changes only in composition of scale items is very striking and her supposedly negative findings prove not to be so, on closer examination.

A replication and extension of Fehrer's study was undertaken by Ball (1953) who varied background or anchor stimuli, leaving the scale items constant. In addition, Ball studied the residual effects of previously experienced anchors thus making an even more stringent test of AL theory than did Fehrer. Some issues left hanging by Fehrer's work were also clarified by Ball and will be discussed subsequently. Ball chose 38 statements from the Droba "Attitude Toward War" scale (1931), ranging from moderately pacifistic, through neutral, to moderately militaristic. While the Droba scale contains statements having scale values from 0 through 11, Ball used statements from 2 to 9.5 to avoid the extremes of the scale. This is one of the important differences between Ball's and Fehrer's study to which we shall return later. Of the 38 statements, 9 were rephrased so as to be ambiguous, self-contradictory, or meaningless if carefully considered. This was done to test the hypothesis advanced by several workers that ambiguous statements are shifted more easily than are clearly structured propositions.

Three background conditions were provided by introducing the first 19 statements either with the phrase "Most people think that" or the phrase "Few people think that" or by omitting the background material. The three groups of Ss were designated by the phrase serving as background for the first 19 statements: group M (most), consisting of 61 men and 37 women, was given statements 1–19 with "Most people think that" background first ($M1$) and statements 20–38 with "Few people think that" background second ($F2$); group F (few) consisting of 60 men and 37 women, was given statements 1–19 with "Few people think that" background first ($F1$) and statements 20–38 with "Most people think that" second ($M2$); the control group C, consisting of 65 men and 35 women, was given the 38 statements without any background statement.

Extent of agreement or disagreement was indicated by placing an X on a line underneath each statement. The right end of the line was marked "strongly agree," the middle "indifferent," and the left end "strongly disagree." Instructions were for Ss to "place an X at that position on the line which you think best fits the degree of your own agreement or disagreement with the issue." The position of the X was measured in eighths of an inch. Since the line was 45/8 in. long, values below 22.5 indicate disagreement and values above indicate agreement in varying degrees.

The following specific hypotheses were tested in this design:

1. Statements expressive of attitudes toward war and peace should elicit higher agreement when accompanied by favorable background and lower agreement when accompanied by unfavorable background. Group M was thus expected to rate statements 1–19 higher than were groups F or C. Conversely, group F was expected to rate statements 1–19 lower than either groups M or C were. Hence the ratings of group C should lie between those of groups M and F.

2. A second background having an effect opposite to the first background should be less effective than if it were not preceded by the latter owing to the residual effects of the latter. Hence statements 20–38 were not expected to be rated as low by group M as by group F, or conversely, as high by group F as by group M, with the result that the ratings of group C should fall between those of groups M and F.

3. If the acceptability level of the Ss for the statements is sufficiently raised or lowered then neutral statements should shift along with other statements in the scale.

The results, given in Tables 10.4 and 10.5, show that the three hypotheses were verified. Ratings of statements accompanied by "Most people believe that" were significantly higher (24.78) than ratings of

TABLE 10.4. Mean Ratings of Two Sets of Statements by Three Groups with Three Background Conditions

Group	Background	Mean Rating of Statements 1–19	20–38
I	"Most"	24.78	
	"Few"		21.43
II	None	23.96	22.75
III	"Few"	20.35	
	"Most"		23.46

SOURCE: From Ball, 1953.

TABLE 10.5. Comparison of Ambiguous and Unaltered Items under Three Background Conditions

Statements	Background "Most"	None	"Few"
Unambiguous	24.9	24.1	21.7
Ambiguous	21.7	20.9	18.3
Difference	3.2	3.2	3.4
t	1.1	.94	2.2[a]

[a] Significant at the 5 percent level.
SOURCE: From Ball, 1953.

statements accompanied by "Few people believe that" (21.43). Similarly, $M1$ statements were rated significantly higher than $F1$ statements (24.78 as against 20.35), the former being rated highest and the latter lowest among the six background conditions. Just as there was a sig-

nificant drop in ratings when going from the $M1$ to the $F2$ condition
so there was a significant rise in going from the $F1$ to the $M2$ condition
(20.35 to 23.46). Hypothesis I concerning effect of backgrounds on
attitudinal levels was thus strongly supported by the results from the
two experimental groups.

Comparison of the $F2$ with the $M1$ condition, and the $M2$ with the
$F1$ condition shows the residual effect of the first backgrounds on the
second sets of judgments. We expect, in accordance with hypothesis II,
the $M2$ ratings to be lower than the $M1$ ratings because of residual
effects of the $F1$ background, and $F2$ ratings to be higher than $F1$
ratings because of the residual effects of $M1$ condition. These expectations are borne out by the data in Table 10.4. While the difference
between the $M1$ and $M2$ conditions on the one hand and that between
the $F1$ and $F2$ conditions on the other are not statistically significant,
showing that presently operating background is more potent than
residuals from past experience, it is noteworthy that the pulling effects
of the previous backgrounds are both in the expected directions. The
plots in Fig. 10.1, in spite of the lack of significant differences between
the first and second sets of 19 statements show clear regressions in the
$F2$ ratings toward the $M1$ ratings and in the $M2$ ratings toward the $F1$
ratings. If the average ratings of the groups can be taken as representative of group level of opinion, then the two groups are seen to approach
each other and the control group in the second half of the experiment,
due to the residual influences of the background preceding the second
ratings.

The Ball study was also designed to throw light on the assumption
that statements at or near the center of attitude scales are more labile
and shift more easily than statements farther from the center. Edwards
(1946) seems to have been responsible for the belief that greater displacement of items near the middle of attitude scales is due to the
fact that they "are more ambiguous and less well structured, and hence
more readily subject to the personal interpretations of the judges"
(Hovland and Sherif, 1952, p. 830). Hovland and Sherif (1952) and
Sherif and Hovland (1953) found that neutral items were displaced
more than were extreme items in attitude scales. But Fehrer (1952)
found that neutral items common to three scales made up from the
four forms of the Thurstone "Attitude Toward War" scales (two by
Droba and two by Peterson) did not shift *significantly* as a result of
being in different *contexts*. However, the neutral items in Fehrer's

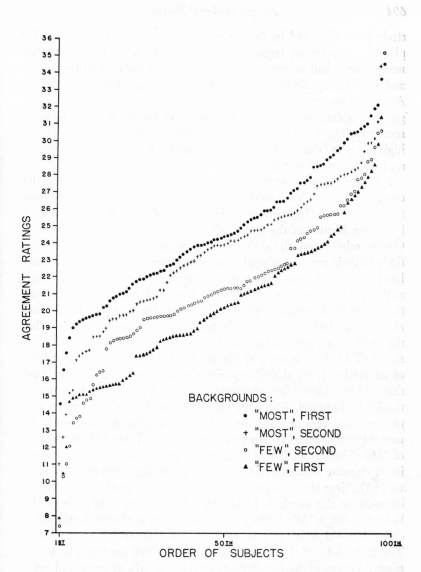

FIG. 10.1. Interactions of residuals with background stimuli in determining response to statements in an "Attitude Toward War" scale. (From Ball, 1953. With the permission of the author.)

study were displaced in the expected direction even though the displacements were not large enough to be statistically significant: the neutral items had average scale values of 5.53 in the militaristic context and 5.74 in the pacifistic context as would be expected from AL theory. As often happens with group data, the average value for the control group was exceptionally high, 5.77. Most of the difficulty in Fehrer's results springs from the fact that her control group gave abnormally high ratings to the neutral items, if the results for the other two groups are to be taken at face value.

Ball's data bearing on the question of displacement of items near the center of the scale leave no doubt that items *near the center of the scale* are subject to displacement with shifts in adaptation level, a fact denied by Fehrer because of the abnormally high control means in her study. On the other hand, the shifts of these items cannot be attributed entirely to their greater ambiguity because statements deliberately formulated to be ambiguous, even contradictory, were not displaced as much as the neutral items or as much as many of the statements farther from the center of the scale. *Distinguishing, then, between statements from the middle of the scale and truly ambiguous statements,* we find that the shifts in ratings are in accordance with our third assumption, as seen in Table 10.5: Items near the middle of the scale, or in the vicinity of adaptation level, shifted significantly more with changes in level than did the stimuli farther removed only in the case of "Few people think" background. But with all background conditions there was greater disagreement with the ambiguous statements than with the unambiguous ones as shown by the averages in Table 10.5. In the case of "Most" background the ratings of the ambiguous statements moved in an opposite direction to that of the unambiguous statements (21.7 vs. 24.9). Since these statements were deliberately made ambiguous or inconsistent this result is highly logical. The small shifts found by Fehrer in her middle items must therefore be attributed to the small changes in AL arising from varying only composition of the items. The large shifts of the center items found by Ball are traceable to the greater effects of background statements on AL as compared with effects of changes in composition of statements comprising the scale.

Our position is as follows: Movement of the items near the center of attitude scales with changes in context or background arises from their proximity to level. This position has the advantage of separating the effects of ambiguity or inconsistency on judgment from the effects

due to changes in adjustment level from other causes. Statements near
the center of attitude scales need not be ambiguous even though they
may express more or less neutral opinions. A proposition expressing
a neutral attitude may be as well structured as one expressing an extreme position. We can thus account for movement of unambiguous
items in the middle of scales as well as for the shifts of truly ambiguous
statements.

Sex differences and background influence. The differences between the men and women *S*s are of interest in view of studies in the
literature showing women to be more suggestible than men in a number of different situations. The data in Table 10.6 indicate that the
women rated the items significantly higher with "most" background
and significantly lower with "few" background than did the control
group, while the men rated the items significantly lower than the
control *S*s only with the "few" background. The women also differed
significantly from the men in the ratings with "most" background.
It thus appears that the failure of "most" background to yield a significantly higher rating for the group as a whole is due to the ratings
of the men under this condition. As in Fehrer's study the control group
made higher ratings than were to be expected on the basis of the two
experimental groups.

TABLE 10.6. Differences in Responses of Men and Women to
Three Background Conditions of Rating Items

Background	Women	Difference		t	Men	Difference		t
Most	24.9	(M–C)	1.3	2.4[a]	23.6	(M–C)	0.4	0.8
Control	23.6	(C–F)	2.3	3.0[b]	23.2	(C–F)	2.6	3.2[b]
Few	21.3	(M–F)	3.6	4.4[b]	20.6	(M–F)	3.0	3.7

[a] Significant beyond the 5-percent level.
[b] Significant beyond the 1-percent level.
SOURCE: From Ball, 1953.

Social vs. personal norms in expressions of attitudes. An extended
study of effects of contextual or background stimuli on ratings of
social desirability (social norms) and judgments of *S*s' own behavior
patterns (personal norms) was made by Buss (1959). Ten statements
descriptive of aggressive behavior patterns—such as *I sometimes get
into fights* and *I tend to use strong language*—were presented for judgment under seven background conditions. The ten statements were

unelaborated in condition I; then the ten statements were modified grammatically to fit each of the introductory phrases listed below in conditions II–VII:

I have trouble controlling (*my tendency to*) . . .
I can't help . . .
I am tempted to . . .
I am guilty about . . . or alternately *I am concerned about* . . .
Like most people . . .
I must admit . . .

The items were ranked by 70 college men and 92 college women for social desirability on a 9-point scale with maximum desirability at 9 and minimum desirability at 1. Then the 70 items were divided into seven 10-item inventories with no content repeated within a single set. A group of 714 college men and women were asked to answer whether or not an item was true of their own behavior. The number of times an item was answered "true" was taken as the frequency of "endorsement." Each S answered only one 10-item inventory so that N for each of the seven inventories was about 100 with a range of 95 to 106.

From Table 10.7 it is seen that the unelaborated items and "Can't help" background items were rated lowest for social desirability (2.8)

TABLE 10.7.   Mean Social Desirability Ratings and Frequency of Endorsement of Inventory Items as a Function of Seven Background Conditions

	Trouble Control-ling	Must Admit	Can't Help	Guilty	Like Most	Tempted	Unelab-orated
Desirability	3.3	3.2	2.8	5.5	3.1	3.3	2.8
Endorsement (Percent)	32.0	48.2	25.6	34.5	47.8	47.8	36.5

SOURCE: From Buss, 1959. With the permission of the American Psychological Association.

with "Like most" background slightly but insignificantly higher (3.1). The same items given with the other four backgrounds were all rated significantly higher than the three just discussed. Strangely enough, the average rating with "Guilt" or "Concerned about" background was slightly above (5.5), the dividing line between social desirability and undesirability. Turning to the results for "endorsing" we find that background effects are just as pronounced as they were in the ratings for social desirability: in the case of the former the range was from 25.6 to 48.2 percent endorsement, or nearly 2:1, while the range in the means of the latter was from 2.8 to 5.5, again nearly 2:1. Significant increases in number of endorsements were found with backgrounds of "Must admit," "Like most people," and "Tempted"; and a significant decrease was found with "Can't help." We thus find that context may significantly modify responses to statements which *S*s are called upon to judge under very different conditions from (1) the study by Ball of attitudes toward war and peace and from (2) this study by Buss of social desirability of aggressive acts and patterns of *S*s' own behavior.

Perhaps the most interesting result of Buss' study is that certain of the ten items differentiated significantly across backgrounds when the task required the *S*s to rate themselves with respect to the modes of behavior denoted by the items, but there was practically no differentiation among the means of the ten items in the ratings for social desirability. The lack of differentiation may be partly attributed to the fact that the ratings of social desirability were made by the same *S*s against all seven background conditions while different *S*s were employed with each of the background conditions in the self-ratings. Also, the range of frequencies of endorsement is inflated because the lowest frequency, 12.7 percent, occurs with an item that refers to a type of behavior that is more rare, at least among college students, than other forms of aggression. Without this item, the range of endorsements drops from 5:1 to 3.5:1. Even with these considerations in mind, the differences among items are far greater in the self-endorsements than in the ratings of social desirability. It appears that social-desirability ratings are based on quite different frames of reference from those of self-ratings. Since the ten items came from a single universe of discourse, aggressive behavior, and were therefore fairly homogeneous, personality variables (residuals), as Buss points out, must have been strongly operative when the judgments involved self-reference. Residuals were thus more effective in differentiating item content than were the background conditions, although the latter produced significant effects when all the items together are evaluated.

A more direct comparison of the difference between social norms and personal norms could be made by having *S*s rate self-behavior on the same nine-point scale that was used in rating social desirability. If each *S* rated both social desirability and his own behavior on comparable scales, then the relation of personal to social norms might appear more clearly than it did in this study.

The studies we have reviewed in this section dealing with effects of composition of items and contextual materials on responses to attitude scales all show the operation and importance of adaptation levels. Cognitive and emotional systems aroused by focal and background stimuli as well as personal sets, preformed attitudes, and biases pool to influence responses to specific items of the scale. Measurements of attitudes are relative to prevailing adjustment levels. This fact should not be interpreted as an argument against the possibility of measuring attitudes, for we have seen that all measurements of behavior are subject to the same limitation. On the positive side, it provides a basis for prediction and control of attitudes in that responses may be modified by changes in focal and background stimulation. That this can be done is shown in the next section dealing with experimental studies of conforming behavior.

FOCAL, BACKGROUND, AND RESIDUAL STIMULI IN CONFORMING BEHAVIOR

One of the most important problems in social psychology, and in a systematic approach to behavior, is that of conforming behavior because the adequacy of most social adjustments is measured by the extent to which individuals obey (conform to) laws, precepts, and the customs of the societies in which they live. This type of behavior has been studied in expressions of attitudes toward various issues. While the term "attitude" derives from the concept of posture or mood, pointing to inner, personal origins, it is also recognized that attitudes are a function of situational factors. In recent years there has been increasing criticism of organizations, institutions, and cultural patterns which force individuals to adopt attitudes characteristic of "the organization man" (Whyte, 1957), to adopt prevailing stereotypes regarding social and economic issues, or to react according to the class in which one's profession, income, or inheritance has put him. To the psychologist an understanding of how and why individuals conform is of importance because without a certain measure of conformity there could be no family, no society, and no social, economic, political, and cultural interactions among individuals and groups. On the other hand, an understanding of the ways in which groups force individuals to conform may furnish a basis for countermeasures necessary to combat overconformity that leads to stagnation and loss of individual initiative, creativity, and spontaneity.

To test the hypothesis that formation of attitudes is the result of interactions between focal, background and residual stimuli, Helson, Blake, Mouton, and Olmstead (1956) devised the following experiment: 45 college men students were asked to rate their agreement or disagreement with 18 statements taken from the Thurstone-Chave "Attitudes Toward War" scale (Thurstone, 1930; 1931) by means of seven categories assigned numerical values as follows: strongly disagree (1); disagree (2); mildly disagree (3); neutral (4); mildly agree (5); agree (6); and strongly agree (7). The Ss first made their judgments while alone in a room and some days later made them a second time as the last member of a group. The "group" actually consisted of the tape-recorded responses of four individuals which the test Ss heard over earphones. The Ss believed themselves to be the fifth members of the group. The eighteen statements were chosen so that six came from the promilitaristic side of the scale, six from the antimilitaristic side, and six from the central region of the scale. The simulated group expressed strong agreement with two promilitaristic, two antimilitaristic, and two neutral statements; expressed neutral attitudes toward two statements from each part of the scale; and expressed strong disagreement with two statements from the three parts of the scale. It was thus possible to determine the effect of group opinion on test Ss when the simulated group expressed agreement, disagreement, or neutral attitudes toward representative statements from the promilitaristic, antimilitaristic, and neutral regions of the Thurstone-Chave scale. For verisimilitude, one of the simulated group expressed somewhat less-strong agreement or disagreement with the statements, and in the case of the neutral items, one of the simulated group expressed mild agreement, one mild disagreement, and two gave neutral responses. Each test S served as his own control in that judgments made under the simulated group condition could be compared with judgments made previously under the solitary condition.

The residual factor chosen for study was position on an ascendant-submissive continuum on the supposition that ascendant individuals would be influenced less than submissive individuals by the opinions of others, and that average individuals would fall between the other two groups. Accordingly Ss were given the Allport-Allport ascendance-submission test (1928), and on the basis of the scores on this test 45 Ss were chosen to be divided equally among the three classes as follows: those with A-S decile scores from 1 to 4 were classed as ascendant; those with scores of 5 and 6 were classed as average; and those with scores from 6 to 10 were classed as submissive individuals. Since the simulated group furnished a standardized background of opinions for all Ss by being tape-recorded, differences among the three classes of test Ss most probably arose from residual or personal sources of variance. It is obvious that other residuals might have been chosen for study—e.g., father-mother or other family relationships, economic status, college standing or major subject—but none seemed as natural and sensible as tendency toward conformity (ascendance-submission) in this study.

Three predictions from the general hypothesis stated above were tested:

1. In line with the results of the study by Ball (1953), which we have already discussed, it was expected that test Ss hearing strong expressions of agreement or disagreement on the part of other individuals would be influenced to shift their private judgments in the direction of the sentiments expressed by the background Ss.

2. Submissive individuals were expected to be influenced by group opinion to a greater extent than either ascendant or average individuals, as measured by the Allport and Allport A-S scale.

3. With neutral background opinions it was expected that there would be no significant differences between ascendant, average, and submissive Ss in the amount of influence exerted by the background group.

The results in Table 10.8 and the analysis of variance (not reproduced here)[1] fully support both the general hypothesis and the three predictions based upon it. Attitudes are the results of interactions between focal, background, and residual stimuli, as shown by the fact that when the background Ss strongly agreed or disagreed with statements, the test Ss moved toward greater agreement or disagreement, respectively, whether the statements expressed promilitaristic, antimilitaristic, or neutral attitudes. Ascendant Ss were influenced least by the group, average Ss next, and submissive Ss most.

That the submissive Ss were influenced more by background opinion

---

[1] For details regarding results of analysis of variance and certain other findings in this study, the reader is referred to the original publication.

TABLE 10.8. Attitudes of Test Ss (Means) as a Function of Content of Statements, Background Opinions, and Ascendance-Submission Classification[a]

Mean Attitude of Test Ss

Background Opinion	A-S Classification	Content of Statement			
		Promilitaristic	Neutral	Antimilitaristic	Total Mean
Agree (7, 7, 6, 7)	Ascendant	5.67 (1.08)	4.73 (2.02)	4.13 (2.62)	4.84 (1.91)
	Average	5.97 (0.78)	5.33 (1.42)	5.30 (1.45)	5.53 (1.22)
	Submissive	6.00 (0.75)	5.77 (0.98)	5.37 (1.38)	5.71 (1.04)
	Mean	5.88 (0.87)	5.28 (1.47)	4.93 (1.82)	5.36 (1.39)
Neutral (5, 4, 4, 3)	Ascendant	4.07 (0.07)	4.57 (0.57)	4.50 (0.50)	4.38 (0.38)
	Average	3.33 (0.67)	4.53 (0.53)	4.97 (0.97)	4.28 (0.28)
	Submissive	3.40 (0.60)	4.60 (0.60)	5.00 (1.00)	4.33 (0.73)
	Mean	3.60 (0.40)	4.57 (0.57)	4.82 (0.82)	4.33 (0.46)
Disagree (1, 1, 2, 1)	Ascendant	4.67 (3.42)	2.33 (1.08)	3.33 (2.08)	3.44 (2.19)
	Average	3.40 (2.15)	1.87 (0.62)	2.37 (1.12)	2.54 (1.29)
	Submissive	3.13 (1.88)	2.00 (0.75)	2.27 (1.02)	2.47 (1.22)
	Mean	3.73 (2.48)	2.07 (0.82)	2.66 (1.41)	2.82 (1.57)

	.01	.05
Row means	1.131	.859
Column submeans	.652	.495

Note: Values in parentheses refer, in column I, to responses of the four members of the background group; and in the other columns, to the extent, in category steps, to which the average test S differed with the average opinion of the background Ss.

[a] The differences between any two means necessary for significance at or beyond the .05 and .01 levels of confidence are as follows:

SOURCE: From Helson, Blake, Mouton, and Olmstead, 1956. With the permission of the American Psychological Association.

than both the ascendant and the average *S*s is shown by the values in parentheses in Table 10.8 which represent the differences between the means of the three groups of *S*s from the mean of the background opinions. The submissive *S*s deviate *less* from background judgments than do the ascendant and average *S*s when the pressure is on, viz., with strongly agreeing and strongly disagreeing responses on the part of the simulated *S*s. With background opinion neutral, the submissive *S*s differ slightly, but not significantly, more than do the average *S*s from the simulated group as seen in the last column of Table 10.8 for the neutral background reports. The differences in extent of influence exerted by the simulated group upon the ascendant, average, and submissive *S*s are brought out even more clearly when comparisons are made in terms of the shifts in total number of category steps *toward* the group opinions by each of the three classes of *S*s (Table 10.9). The difference between the means of the ascendant and submissive *S*s (6.6 category steps *toward* group) is significant beyond the 1 percent level. While the shift of the ascendant group *away* from the simulated group is largest and in the expected direction, it is not significantly different from that of the average and submissive groups.

TABLE 10.9. Changes in Attitudes by Ascendant, Average, and Submissive Ss as Shown by Movement Toward or Away from Background Group in Terms of Number of Category Steps

Subject Type	Steps Toward Group	Steps Away from Group
Ascendant	10.5	2.2
Average	15.5	1.3
Submissive	17.1	1.7

SOURCE: From Helson, Blake, Mouton, and Olmstead, 1956. With the permission of the American Psychological Association.

As is not uncommon with experimental approaches to problems, this study also yielded some completely unexpected findings. The first is that the movement *away* from private opinion toward background opinion is a *positively* accelerated function of the *number* of changes made by the test *S*s. Since there were eighteen statements, *S*s could modify their privately stated opinions a maximum of eighteen times when exposed to the opinions of the simulated group. Actually the maximum number of changes from private opinion was eleven made by two *S*s, with the modal number, thirteen *S*s, making six changes, and the minimum number, two *S*s, making two changes. The plot in Fig. 10.2 shows that while the *average S* moved from about two to nearly three category steps toward the group each time he changed from his private expression of attitude, the docile *S*s tended to move

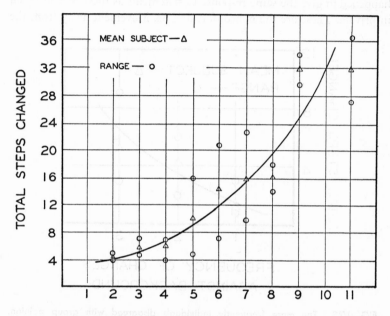

FREQUENCY OF CHANGES TOWARD BACKGROUND

FIG. 10.2. The more frequently individuals shifted in the direction of group opinion, the more they changed from views expressed in private. (From Helson, Blake, Mouton, and Olmstead, 1956. With the permission of the American Psychological Association.)

more toward the group the more frequently they changed from their privately expressed convictions. Thus the individual in Fig. 10.2 who modified his opinion twice moved a total of four category steps, but the individuals who modified their opinions nine and eleven times moved a total of thirty-two category steps, or about twice as much each time as the first individual. This accounts for the positively accelerated curve in Fig. 10.2. Hence magnitude of change in the direction of group opinion is a positively accelerated function of frequency—an unexpected finding.

An even more surprising result is that the plot of *Ss* who moved *against* the group is also a positively accelerated curve, as seen in Fig. 10.3. These *Ss* voiced opinions contrary to the background group, sometimes at the expense of consistency when the simulated group happened to give the same response to statements as these *Ss* had given in private. These are the nonconforming *Ss*. Movement away from the

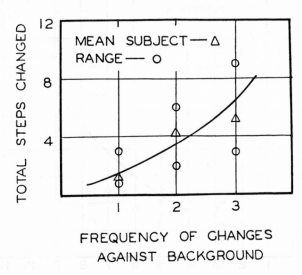

FIG. 10.3. The more frequently individuals disagreed with group opinion, the greater was their disagreement with the group. (From Helson, Blake, Mouton, and Olmstead, 1956. With the permission of the American Psychological Association.)

group was far less common than movement toward the group (Tables 3 and 4 in the original publication, Helson, Blake, Mouton, and Olmstead, 1956, pp. 319–320).

Among the important issues raised by this study, as well as by a number of other studies, are two which have been investigated by various workers as separate questions. The first concerns the generality of conforming behavior in individuals: Do individuals who conform in one situation also yield to group norms in other situations? This question immediately raises another: Does not the type of situation, task, or demand made on the individual have something to do with whether or not he will be influenced by the opinions of others? Ferguson (1944) found consistency in responses by Ss to group opinion on three attitudinal scales dealing with religion, humanitarianism, and nationalism, but since the materials in this study were all concerned with opinions it provides no basis for assessing conformity tendencies in individuals when factual tasks are involved. On the other hand, Crutchfield (1955) found significant split-half correlations indicating a significant degree of generality of conformity with a test containing 21 items involving 7 different tasks. But difficulty of the task and the degree to which the group differed from the test Ss were not systematically varied, though both are known to affect conformity behavior (see Coffin, 1941). Hence a study was made by Helson, Blake, and Mouton (1957) to determine the degree of consistency in individual responses to tasks varying in content and in difficulty as group opinions ranged from agreement to wide disagreement with the individual's position. Generality of conforming behavior was thus studied as a function of nature and difficulty of the task and also with respect to the kinds of pressures exerted on the test Ss by the group.

The simulated-group technique employed in previous studies was again used with ninety test Ss who heard the responses of four individuals to the various tasks through earphones under the impression that the members of the group were in adjoining rooms. Again the background group was a tape recording made by Ss who were instructed in what to say. Three tasks were given in the order listed: (1) reporting number of metronome clicks; (2) expressing attitudes with respect to statements about war and peace from the Thurstone-Chave militarism-pacifism scale; and (3) solving arithmetic problems "mentally." Each task consisted of nine items each, making a total of twenty-seven responses on the part of each test S. The simulated group, acting as a background stimulus, gave three correct and six incorrect responses regarding the number of metronome clicks and in answers to the arithmetic problems. In the case of the Thurstone-Chave statements, the background group gave three responses identical with the modal responses of a college population similar to the experimental Ss and serving as a standardizing group, and six other responses, of which two differed from the modal responses of the standard group by two, by four, and by six category steps. The statements were chosen from the two extremes of the scale to allow large as well as small and medium variations on the part of the background group from the position of the test Ss, on the assumption that the attitudes of the latter were, on the average, similar to those of the standardizing group. Attitudes were expressed on a seven-category scale ranging from "strongly agree," with a value of seven, through neutral, with a value of four, to strongly disagree, with a value of one.

The factual tasks varied in difficulty, and the background group responded with answers which were more or less discrepant from the true answers. The difficulty of the arithmetic problems was determined by reference to a standardizing group, the easy problems being those which were answered by at least 75 percent, the items of medium difficulty by 25 to 75 percent, and the difficult items by less than 25 percent. The metronome clicks ranged from 23 to 27 and were given at 140, 170, or 200 per minute. The background group responded with judgments differing from the true number by 0, 1, and 3. Unfortunately the metronome clicks were not standardized prior to being given to the test Ss with the result that the rates employed did not provide sufficient differences in difficulty to yield as clear-cut effects as did the other tasks.

The responses of the test Ss, when analyzed, fell into five categories, which must be distinguished in order to make a proper evaluation of the extent to which conformity occurs across tasks, as a function of difficulty within tasks, and as a function of discrepancy of the background responses from "objectivity." The five types of responses and their designations were: (1) C responses, which were identical with those made by the background group; (2) O responses, which differed from the background group but in opposite direction, e.g., when background group made a plus error the test S made a minus error; (3) I responses, which fell between the "objective" answer and the background judgment; (4) B responses, which were more incorrect than, but in the same direction as, those of the background group; and (5) S responses, which were correct or identical with the modal response of the standardizing group.

The results are given in Tables 10.10 and 10.11. While the percentages of all five possible types of responses made with the three types of materials are given (Table 10.10), only the C responses were considered in evaluating generality of conforming behavior. From Table 10.10 it is seen that test Ss were far more subject to background opinion in the case of the Thurstone-Chave statements (41.5 percent) than in the case of the more objective, factual type of material represented by the metro-

TABLE 10.10. Percentages of S, C, I, B, and O Responses on Critical
Trials with Metronome, Attitudes, and Arithmetic Tasks

Type of Response	Percentage of Responses		
	Metronome Task	Attitude Task	Arithmetic Task
S	56.85	20.19	63.15
	(88.89)	(60.00)	(95.56)
C	30.19	41.48	27.41
	(62.22)	(94.44)	(62.22)
I	7.04	34.81	2.96
	(31.11)	(91.11)	(16.67)
B	1.48	3.15	1.85
	(6.67)	(13.33)	(10.00)
O	4.26		3.52
	(18.89)		(18.89)
N	0.18	0.37	1.11
	(0.01)	(0.02)	(0.07)

Note: Values in parentheses indicate percentage of Ss giving one or more of each
type of response.
Key: S = correct or identical with modal response of standardizing group
          C = identical with responses of background group
          I = fall between "objective" answer and background judgment
          B = more incorrect but in same direction as responses of background group
          O = differed in opposite direction from responses of background group
          N = no response given
SOURCE: From Blake, Helson, and Mouton, 1957. With the permission of the *Journal
of Personality*.

TABLE 10.11. Frequency of Conforming Responses as a Function of
Stimulus and Background Factors in the Attitude Task

Background Discrepancy	Modal Value		
	1	7	Total
Small (2)	63	60	123
Moderate (4)	21	24	45
Large (6)	21	36	57
Total	105	120	225

SOURCE: From Blake, Helson, and Mouton, 1957. With the permission of the *Journal
of Personality*.

nome clicks (30.2 percent) and the arithmetic problems (27.4 percent). Furthermore the number of Ss making conforming responses shows how much more amenable individuals were to group suggestion in matters of opinion than in matters of fact; 94.4 percent of Ss conformed with group opinion on one or more of the six possible occasions in the case of the Thurstone-Chave statements, but only 62.2 percent of the Ss agreed with the group in both the metronome and arithmetic tasks.

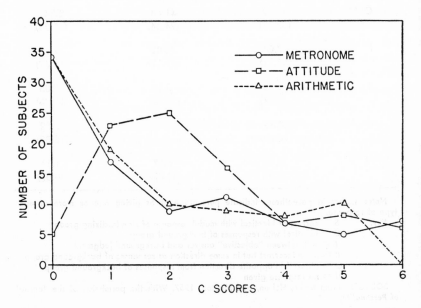

FIG. 10.4. Frequency of distribution of C scores for the metronome, arithmetic, and attitude judgments. (From Blake, Helson, and Mouton, 1957. With the permission of the *Journal of Personality*.)

Only 5 percent of the test Ss were never influenced by the group in the attitude study.

The number of Ss who made identical responses with those of the background group on some or all of the six items of the three types of tasks is given in Fig. 10.4, which also shows clearly the difference between the attitude responses and the factual responses. The factual curves are almost identical both in shape and absolute values. The modal number of Ss falls at zero C scores in the arithmetic and metronome tasks but at two in the attitude task. The curve for attitudes has some semblance of normality, though skewed, while the curves for arithmetic and metronome are decidedly not normal. A more normal distribution of *S* scores for the factually oriented tasks could probably be obtained either by increasing the background pressures or by increasing the difficulty of the arithmetic and metronome items.

There are two other factors in the stimulus situation which determine the extent to which individuals conform with group opinion: difficulty of the task and the position taken by the group vis-à-vis the individual. The effects of these two variables appear in Tables 10.11, 10.12, and 10.13. Since there was no variation in difficulty of items in the expression of attitudes, we have to consider only the effect of the group's attitude on that of the test *S*s in this part of the study. In general, individuals conformed to a greater extent to group opinion when the background group differed from the presumed position of the test *S*s by a small amount, as shown in the three tables. When the group deviated by two category steps from the standardizing *S*s, there were 123 instances of complete conformity on the part of the test *S*s, but when the group deviated by four category steps, the number dropped to 45, and with six category steps it rose to 57 which is still significantly lower than with the smallest deviation (Table 10.11). Similar results were found with the factual materials. There were 100 instances of complete conformity when the background *S*s were off by one click in the metronome study but only 63 instances of conforming when they were off by 3 clicks (Table 10.12). With small discrepancy from correct re-

TABLE 10.12. Frequency of Conforming Responses as a Function of Stimulus and Background Factors in the Metronome Task

| Background Discrepancy | Click Rate | | | |
	140 (Easy	170 (Moderate)	200 (Difficult)	Total
Small (1)	28	37	35	100
Large (3)	23	18	22	63
Total	51	55	57	163

SOURCE: From Blake, Helson, and Mouton, 1957. With the permission of the *Journal of Personality*.

sponse in the arithmetic study there were 91 instances where test *S*s agreed with the group, but with large discrepancy the number dropped to 57 (Table 10.13).

The results so far point to the environing conditions as the determiner of conforming behavior for each of the conditions under study. But it would be a mistake to conclude that inner personal factors do not also influence individual responses even in the face of strongly compelling outside influences. Indeed, as Bridgman long ago pointed out (1928), a condition must not be assumed to be without influence until it has been measured and found to be ineffective. It devolves upon us to determine whether or not there is any evidence for the operation of personal factors in this set of studies. If there is consistency on the part of Ss in yielding to group influence in these three different tasks, then we have evidence for *some* generality in conforming behavior and thus for the operation of personal as well as situational factors.

TABLE 10.13   Frequency of Conforming Responses as a Function
of Stimulus and Background Factors in the Arithmetic Task

Background Discrepancy	Easy Items	Moderate Items	Difficult Items	Total
Small	16	37	38	91
Large	0	23	34	57
Total	16	60	72	148

SOURCE: From Blake, Helson, and Mouton, 1957. With the permission of the *Journal of Personality*.

The evidence for generality in the behavior of test Ss comes from three different statistical criteria. Split-half reliability of items grouped into equivalent halves matched for item position, item difficulty, and for degree of background discrepancy yielded coefficients of .78 (corrected for double length = .87) in the metronome and the arithmetic tasks, which by chance came out the same, and .68 (corrected = .82) for the expressions of attitudes. These coefficients indicate that the conformity responses were highly consistent within tasks throughout variations in content and difficulty of items as well as in magnitude of discrepancy from true responses. To assess conformity in the three different tasks, conforming responses on each of the tasks were totaled by Ss, and the frequency distribution of Ss having composite conforming scores was found to range from zero to seventeen, the largest for any S being one less than the maximum number possible, eighteen. The three factors deemed important for dividing the composite C scores to balance various effects in the two halves of the split-half test were item difficulty, order of presentation, and degree of background deviation from true or modal responses. The resulting split-half reliability co-efficient, .87 (corrected = .93), also indicates high consistency of conforming when the three studies are treated on a combined basis.

In addition to the split-half reliabilities, chi-square tests were made between the total C scores from each of the three possible combinations of tasks, on an individual-by-individual basis, with the conformity distribution for each task dichotomized as closely as possible to the median. The resultant chi squares were: 18.56 for the metronome and attitude tasks, which, with 1df, is significant at the 1 percent level; 14.80 for metronome and arithmetic tasks, which, with 1df, is also significant at the 1 percent level; and 4.31 for the attitude and arithmetic tasks, which, with 1df, is significant at the 5 percent level. Finally, approximate measures of association are possible in spite of the skewness of the distributions through product-moment correlations which were: metronome and attitude, .59; metronome and arithmetic, .51; and arithmetic and attitude, .38, which are all significant beyond the 1 percent level. All measures, therefore, agree and point to the operation of conforming tendencies within Ss over tasks. Personal factors are thus seen to interact with situational factors in determining conforming behavior.

From the finding that conforming responses are more frequent with difficult tasks than with easy ones, and when background opinion is not too far from either the truth (in the case of tasks involving factual materials) or from the position of the Ss, we are led to the following question: Are conforming responses a simple monotonically decreasing function of deviation of group attitudes from attitudes of test Ss, or are there some finer points in the relation between shifts of test Ss toward a group and the position of the group vis-à-vis the S? The technique of the "Big Lie" used in political propaganda and in advertising are workaday examples of one kind of social pressure by which groups are influenced. "Truths" which are far from the truth and even far from the beliefs of the majority of those to whom they are directed may nevertheless influence many people. Thus the denial of any guilt on the part of the German nation for World War I, and the broad accusations against the Allies for Germany's postwar plight by the Nazis, converted enough Germans to bring Hitler to power with all the tragic results of World War II. On a smaller scale, but utilizing the same principle by which to convert people, the unscrupulous businessman advertises that a saucepan having a value of $7.50 may be obtained for $1.00 by dealing directly with his firm (a case known to the writer), when actually similar pans were found in neighborhood stores for the same price.

In what does the effectiveness of the Big Lie consist? How does it succeed in swaying so many people when the majority of those influenced cannot be supposed to be sufficiently gullible to believe what is being told them? Some insight into these questions was provided in an experimental study by Helson, Blake, and Mouton (1958a). The experiment was conducted with 230 male college students, 50 acting as a standardizing group, and 180 acting as Ss in two independent groups of 90 each. The statements regarding war and peace from the Thurstone-Chave scale (Thurstone, 1930; 1931) were again employed as stimuli. The 50 Ss serving as norm for the experimental Ss judged the statements on a seven-category verbal scale with numerical values assigned as follows for purposes of computation; strongly disagree, 1; disagree, 2; mildly disagree, 3; neutral, 4; mildly agree, 5; agree, 6; and strongly agree, 7. From the responses of this group, statements with modal responses of either 1 or 7 were employed to provide the greatest possible range for the test Ss to shift as a result of hearing the opinions of the background Ss. They were also chosen because extreme statements are most strongly anchored and least subject to modification by social pressures. Shifts toward the extreme statements on the part of the test Ss would thus provide significant evidence for the influence of the group on individual opinion. Since the Ss in the two experimental groups were drawn from the same population as the standardizing group, it was assumed that they would have given the same modal responses had they judged the statements under solitary conditions, free from background influence.

The test Ss heard, through earphones, the opinions of four other individuals, presumably in adjoining rooms but actually recorded on tape and giving predetermined, essentially uniform, opinions which differed from the modal responses of the standardizing group by zero, two, four, and six category steps as shown in Table 10.14. Since responses to the statements had modal values at the extremes of the category scale (either 1 or 7) test Ss could give either the modal response or responses differing from it by as many as six category steps, e.g., a statement having a modal value of 1 could elicit responses all the way from 1 to 7, and one having a modal value of 7 could elicit responses

TABLE 10.14. Statements, Modal Values, Order of Statements, Background Opinions, and Background Discrepancy from Modal Responses for Groups I and II

Statements and Modal Opinions of Standardizing Group		Order of Presentation		Background Opinions and Discrepancy from Modal Values	
		Group I	Group II	Group I	Group II
War brings out both good and bad qualities in men.	7	1	1	3, 2, 3, 3 (4)	3, 2, 3, 3 (4)
War is the only means of preserving national honor.	1	11	2	5, 5, 6, 5 (4)	5, 5, 6, 5 (4)
There is no progress without war.	1	6	3	5, 5, 6, 5 (4)	1, 1, 1, 1 (0)
If war were abolished, civilization might disappear because of the loss of fighting energy.	1	4	4	7, 6, 7, 7 (6)	7, 6, 7, 7 (6)
It is our duty to serve in a defensive war.	7	5	5	3, 2, 3, 3 (4)	5, 6, 5, 5 (2)
Only a coward opposes war.	1	7	6	1, 1, 1, 1 (0)	1, 1, 1, 1 (0)
The benefits of war outweigh its attendant evils.	1	8	7	7, 6, 7, 7 (6)	3, 3, 2, 3 (2)
Those military units should be retained which afford training to body and mind.	7	9	8	1, 2, 1, 1 (6)	1, 2, 1, 1 (6)
War is ennobling and stimulating to our highest and best qualities.	1	10	9	1, 1, 1, 1 (0)	1, 1, 1, 1 (0)
We should have some military training in our schools.	7	2		1, 2, 1, 1 (6)	
Might is right.	1	3		1, 2, 1, 1 (0)	

SOURCE: From Helson, Blake, and Mouton, 1958a. With the permission of the *Journal of Social Psychology*.

all the way from 7 to 1. Other conditions of the experiment are also shown in Table 10.14: orders of statements as given to the two groups of Ss, judgments of the background Ss, and the magnitude of the discrepancy between the modal responses of the standardizing and background groups. Discrepancies of four and six category steps were employed with experimental group I and discrepancies of two, four, and six category steps with group II. The simulated group also made responses identical with the modal responses (zero discrepancy) with some sentences having a modal value of 1 (strong disagreement) but not with any having modal values of 7 because of the difficulty of obtaining a sufficient number of statements producing this modal response (strong agreement) in the standardizing group. This accounts for the unfilled cells in Tables 10.14 to 10.17.

TABLE 10.15. Percentage of Ss Responding in Various Categories as Function of Discrepancy of Simulated Group from Opinions of Test Ss

Category Intervals	Discrepancy in Category Steps				Average
	0	2	4	6	
			Group I[a]		
1–2	80.00		68.89	60.00	69.63
3–4–5	19.44		27.22	22.22	22.96
6–7	00.56		3.89	17.78	7.41
			Group II		
1–2	92.22	83.33	56.67	56.67	72.22
3–4–5	5.56	15.56	41.11	20.00	20.56
6–7	2.22	1.11	2.22	23.33	7.22

Note: Modal response was strong disagreement (1).
[a] For explanation of empty cells see text.
SOURCE: From Helson, Blake, and Mouton, 1958a. With the permission of the *Journal of Social Psychology.*

The results of the study appear in Tables 10.15 and 10.16. The responses of the test Ss have been grouped in category intervals on the assumption that 1 and 2 represent different degrees of disagreement; 3, 4, and 5 represent neutral or nearly neutral attitudes; and 6 and 7 represent degrees of agreement. The percentages of Ss responding within these intervals are shown in Tables 10.15 and 10.16 against the degree to which the expressed attitudes of the background group differed from the standardizing group and hence, presumably, from the test *S*s. In Tables 10.15 and 10.16 all values outside the first row represent responses different from the modal opinions of the standardizing group and hence show the influence of the background group on the test *S*s. From these tables we see that as the opinions of the background group depart from those of the standardizing group, more and more test *S*s also depart from the modal responses and move toward the background group. Not only do the test *S*s give fewer modal responses as the background group deviates more from the standardizing group, but the number of responses in the more discrepant categories increases markedly. The results are statistically significant far beyond the 1 percent level as shown by the appropriate chi-square tests for both tables.

TABLE 10.16. Percentage of *S*s Responding in Various Categories as Function of Discrepancy of Simulated Group from Opinions of Test *S*s

Category Intervals	Discrepancy in Category Steps				Average
	0	2	4	6	
Group I[a]					
6–7			60.00	38.33	49.17
3–4–5			32.78	16.67	34.72
1–2			7.22	25.00	16.11
Group II[a]					
6–7		71.11	32.22	24.44	42.59
3–4–5		27.78	51.11	35.56	38.15
1–2		1.11	16.67	40.00	19.26

Note: Modal response of standardizing group was strong agreement (7).
[a] For explanation of empty cells see text.
SOURCE: From Helson, Blake, and Mouton, 1958a. With the permission of the *Journal of Social Psychology*.

That the results are not due to the fact that the test *S*s could be easily moved away from statements with which they strongly disagreed appears from a comparison of the data in Tables 10.15 and 10.16, the former for statements with which the standardizing group disagreed for the most part, the latter for statements with which they agreed. In both cases test *S*s moved away from the side of the scale which they would have employed if not subjected to group pressures.

The data in these tables are summarized in Table 10.17 in order to make them comparable in deriving new information from the results as a whole. That the influence of background opinion is not a simple linear function of degree of discrepancy from the attitudes of the test Ss is shown by the differences between the average percents in Table 10.17 which are not constant. Although the absolute number of Ss influenced by background opinion increases up to the maximal background discrepancy, the differences in the percentages first increase and then decrease (an average difference of 9 percent between zero and two cate-

TABLE 10.17. Percentage of Ss Responding in Various Categories Different from the Standardizing Group When the Simulated Group Differed from the Standardizing Group (and Presumably the Test Ss) by 0, 2, 4, and 6 Category Steps

Opinions of Test Ss	Group	Discrepancy from Test Ss in Category Steps[a]			
		0	2	4	6
1	I	20.00		31.11	40.00
1	II	7.78	16.67	43.33	43.33
7	I			40.00	61.67
7	II		28.89	67.78	75.56
Average		13.89	22.78	45.56	55.14

Note: Combined results for groups I and II for all conditions.
[a] See text for explanation of empty cells.
SOURCE: From Helson, Blake, and Mouton, 1958a. With the permission of the *Journal of Social Psychology.*

gory steps of discrepancy, followed by one of 23 percent between two and four category steps, which, in turn, is followed by one of 10 percent between four and six category steps). The differences show that the pulling power of background opinion either approaches a limit or may even reverse so far as the number of individuals who may be affected is concerned. The largest difference between numbers of Ss influenced by background is found between two and four category steps of discrepancy, and this appears to be the maximum region of efficiency. Linear interpolation between the two highest average percentages in Table 10.17 gives about five category steps of discrepancy from modal responses as the deviation from test Ss' views to pull 50 percent of them away from their private expressions of attitude.

The results of this study stand in sharp contrast with the results of the earlier study, where the number of test Ss agreeing with background opinion declined sharply as the latter deviated to a greater extent from objective fact (Blake, Helson, and Mouton, 1957) The difference between the two studies arises from the difference in content to which the test Ss were called upon to respond: with factual materials, where large departures from objectivity can be more or less easily detected, test Ss are not so much influenced by social pressures. The Big Lie works better in areas concerned with attitudes than in areas concerned with "facts, knowledge, or beliefs arising from testable experience. . . . Such results provide a systematic basis for understanding both Hitler's success in using the 'Big Lie' to controvert established attitudes and Russia's (later) failure to reconstruct attitudes concerning the factual history of scientific discovery and knowledge" (Helson, Blake, and Mouton, 1958*a*, p. 58). It is sad but true that propaganda is more effective in the realm of attitudes that are governed by feelings and emotions and where facts are harder to come by than the realm of scientific inquiry. Coupled with a residual "will to believe" the Big Lies does its work.

It is not suggested that even in matters of sentiment and belief (as opposed to knowledge), individuals swallow whole what they are told or what is drummed into them incessantly. Indeed, the data of this study show that most individuals do not accept majority opinion when it deviates too much from their own position. But the data indicate that the more extreme the views to which he is exposed, the more often does the individual move away from his own position, though he may not move all the way to the extreme position. In other words, to elicit complete agreement with a position, it must not be too far from the views of those who are to be won; but to dislodge individuals from their position toward another point of view, the more extreme the point of view the more individuals will change at least a small amount, from their previously held views (see Fig. 10.5). This phenomenon finds expression in the adage, "Where there is smoke there must be [some] fire." Thus, although one may not accept Russian propaganda regarding the capitalistic system, exposure to such propaganda may well shift one away from complacency—something that is admitted by most capitalists who fortunately are allowed in this country to hear all shades of opinion.

Extreme statements in social, political, artistic, and other areas where facts are hard to determine provide strong stimulation whether or not they are believed as such. They exert their effects as predominant stimuli, pulling levels in their direction, with resultant effects on sentiments, beliefs, and attitudes. Furthermore they leave residuals which

also affect levels in important ways. Iago's reiterated hints that Desde-
mona was unfaithful finally changed a loving husband into a frenzied
murderer. The housewife does not have to be convinced that a saucepan is worth $7.50 as advertised in order to be persuaded to buy it for
$1.00. She disbelieves the actual claim but concludes that even if it is
worth half or one-third the advertised value, it is still a good bargain;

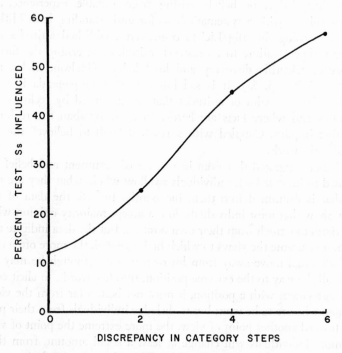

FIG. 10.5. The more extreme is the expression of an attitude, the more individuals are influenced by it. (From Helson, Blake, and Mouton, 1958a. With
the permission of *Journal of Social Psychology*.)

and she responds accordingly. Almost everyone in postwar Germany
now denies ever having believed Nazi propaganda, but many were
sufficiently influenced by it to countenance acts of barbarism against
their own people and against neighboring nations. In our own country
the smear campaign has been used effectively to win elections even
though the majority of the voters did not fully believe the statements
that nevertheless decided their votes.

In the studies of conforming behavior we have seen how various intensitive factors in situations and in the person pool, with the resultant balance of forces determining the behavioral outcome. The general paradigm underlying the studies of conformity and the action studies we shall now discuss can be symbolized in terms of the combined strengths of the three interacting classes of variables. Letting + symbolize a strong incitement to positive response; 0, a mild or indifferent incitement; and —, a weak incitement or a stimulus to contrary action, there are twenty-seven combinations of the three classes of stimuli with only these three degrees of intensity. By omitting residuals and taking into account only focal and background stimuli the number of combinations is reduced to the nine given in Table 10.18. The intensitive

TABLE 10.18. Paradigm of Strengths of Focal and Background Stimuli
Acting upon Ss in the Texas Action Studies

Background Stimulus	Focal Stimulus		
	Strong	Moderate	Weak
	Combinations		
Positive +	++	0+	—+
Neutral 0	+0	00	—0
Negative —	+—	0—	——

Key: + = strong condition
0 = neutral condition
— = weak or negative condition

variations of stimulation are balanced around the neutral condition. In general we expect a preponderance of positive responses under the conditions of the upper left-hand corner of the table and a preponderance of negative responses under the conditions of the lower right-hand corner of the table, with equal numbers of positive, negative, and neutral responses in the center of the table and with the other cells yielding frequencies according to their respective positions. The Texas action studies, involving a number of everyday acts, such as signing petitions, obeying signs, volunteering, were explicitly designed in accordance with the combinations of intensity conditions given in Table 10.18. The extent to which observed frequencies of positive, negative and, where conditions allow, indifferent responses conform to the expectations symbolized in Table 10.18 will depend upon many factors, among them, the degree to which the situational factors were correctly evalu-

ated or calibrated to function as strong, neutral, weak, or negative
stimuli and the degree to which uncontrolled residuals were or were
not operative.

STUDIES OF EVERYDAY ACTIONS

Violation of a prohibition.   The interplay of conditions determining
behavior toward a prohibited act appears clearly in a study of sign
violation by Freed, Chandler, Mouton, and Blake (1955). Under the
conditions of this study one of three signs was posted denying entrance
to a college building. The signs which varied from strong through
moderate to weak, were as follows: "Absolutely No Admittance—Use
Another Entrance"; "You Are requested to Enter by Another Entrance"; "Absolutely No Admittance." Each of these focal conditions
was employed with a positive, neutral, and negative background condition. A planted individual, upon seeing someone approaching the
door, either violated the sign and entered just ahead of the individual
being tested or, seeing the sign, turned and entered through another
door of the building. The neutral background condition simply consisted of omitting the planted *S*.

The combinations of three degrees of strength of the prohibition and
the three of the background condition yielded results shown in Table
10.19. Under the strong positive condition, where the model obeyed the

TABLE 10.19.   Reactions of Groups to Nine Combinations of Stimulus-sign
Strength and Social Backgrounds

Model	Strong Stimulus		Moderate Stimulus		Weak Stimulus	
	Conform	Violate	Conform	Violate	Conform	Violate
Conforms	10	0	5	5	6	4
Absent	7	3	5	5	0	10
Violates	1	9	2	8	0	10

SOURCE: From Freed, Chandler, Mouton, and Blake, 1955. With the permission of the
Journal of Personality.

strongest sign, all test *S*s also obeyed. Where the prohibition was weak
and the model violated, all test *S*s also violated the prohibition. In the
neutral condition, in which the prohibition was expressed mildly and
there was no model, *S*s split 50–50, half the *S*s violating, the other half
obeying the injunction not to use the entrance. But even with the ex-

ample of a conforming model, only 50 percent of the test Ss obeyed the moderate sign, which merely requested use of another entrance and did not explicitly deny admission by the door in question. The same focal stimulus thus exerts quite different effects with different contextual stimuli in an everyday situation. Situational determinants may outweigh inner tendencies to conform or to abide by explicit or implicit social codes that require cooperation and a willingness to respect the needs or convenience of others as well as one's own.

While intermediate external conditions do not always yield frequencies exactly halfway between the frequencies found under extreme conditions, the results, in general, support the thesis that strong focal and background stimuli impinging upon the organism may be more important in what people do in social contexts than are inner factors. We find in this study, as in others, the greater power of the negative stimulus to arouse negative reactions as compared with the power of strong or positive stimuli to arouse positive responses. Thus nine of the ten individuals violated the strongest prohibition when the model violated, but only six of the ten conformed to the weak sign when the model conformed. This result is not surprising when it is remembered that most of the individuals in the experiment were students who were in the habit of using the prohibited entrance and therefore had strong residual forces operating to violate the prohibition. The fact that there were, on the whole, more violations (60 percent) than there were obedient reactions (40 percent) shows that residual factors were operative in unbalancing the frequencies in the intermediate conditions. The great strength of residuals in favor of using the prohibited entrance appears in the results with the weakest sign, where all ten Ss violated the prohibition without perceiving a violation by another person. The finding that there were no violations of the strongest sign when the model obeyed shows how compelling situational forces may be in counteracting strong residuals.

Petition signing. Like the other types of acts in the studies we are discussing, the act of signing a petition is a response that can be dichotomized into "yes" or "no" and thus quantified; and the conditions under which individuals are called upon to sign can also be rigorously controlled. Among the factors influencing this type of response, the following were chosen for study by Helson, Blake, and Mouton (1958b): (1) the nature of the request made in the petition, *i.e.,* its appeal to potential petitioners; (2) the influence exerted by the example of another who either signs or refuses to sign the petition; and (3) the effects of a combination of positive with positive, positive with negative, and negative with negative factors in the petition-signing situation. In addition, the residual factor of personal susceptibility to accede to a request of this kind was also determined independently. In terms of the AL paradigm, the request to sign and the subject matter of the petition constituted focal stimuli, the positive or negative action of a planted model furnished the background stimulus, and the individuals' tendencies toward conformity acted as residual stimuli. All three classes of stimuli varied from strongly negative, through neutral or average, to strongly positive. The outcomes from the extreme conditions, all factors strongly positive or strongly negative, were so close to expectations that they prove to be of less interest than the conditions in which the three classes of factors were of different strengths.

The conditions under which test Ss were approached to sign petitions were as follows: (1) The petition concerned a proposal which had previously been found to elicit 96 percent positive response on the part of Texas students, viz., to floodlight a fountain on the University of Texas campus; Ss were approached while seeing another person accede to the request to sign. (2) The same proposal was presented while Ss saw another person refuse to sign. (3) The petition concerned a proposal to remove the soft-drink dispensers from University of Texas buildings, a proposal that elicited only 15 percent as signers in a pre-experimental group; Ss were approached while seeing another person signing. (4) Ss were approached while the other person refused to sign the soft-drink petition.

The design is shown in Table 10.20. The exact manner in which the test Ss were approached was as follows: Students who had volunteered to take part in another experiment and were being conducted by a guide to the experimental room were accosted by the experimenter, who first requested the guide to sign the petition. After the guide responded positively or negatively according to pre-arranged plan, the test S was requested to sign. None of the test Ss knew that their reactions in the petition situation were being studied or that there was any connection with the experiment for which they had consented to act as Ss. The petition-signing situation was quite natural and was in line with what occurs not infrequently on college campuses.

The results of this experiment confirmed our expectations and also yielded new information regarding net effects of situations containing

TABLE 10.20. Stimulus and Background Conditions under Which Ss Were Asked to Sign a Petition

Petition	Percent Signing in Standardizing Groups of 29	Background-model Response
1. We, students at the University of Texas, petition for the addition of floodlights to Littlefield Fountain.	96	"Sure, I'll sign it." "No, I'd rather not."
2. We, students at the University of Texas, petition to remove all soft-drink dispensing machines from University buildings.	15	"Sure, I'll sign it." "No, I'd rather not."

SOURCE: From Helson, Blake, and Mouton, 1958b. With the permission of the *Journal of Social Psychology.*

opposed elements. As shown by the data in Table 10.21 when the proposal was agreeable and another was seen to sign it the number signing reached 93 percent. Since the number signing in the pre-experimental, standardizing group was 96 percent without a planted signer, the positive background stimulus did not increase the pulling power of the

TABLE 10.21. Frequency of Petition Signing as a Function of Nature of Proposal and Action of a Planted Model

	Social Background			
	Model Signs		Model Refuses	
Proposal	Ss Sign	Ss Refuse	Ss Sign	Ss Refuse
Positive	14	1	9	21
	93%	7%	30%	70%
Negative	10	20	0	15
	33%	67%	0%	100%

SOURCE: From Helson, Blake, and Mouton, 1958b. With the permission of the *Journal of Social Psychology.*

proposal which, by the way, had been in effect for some years. Not a single one of the 45 students asked to sign the petition indicated that he knew the fountain was already being floodlighted. High desirability of a proposal which appealed to inner convictions sufficed to elicit overwhelming positive reactions on the part of those approached. But with the same proposal, when another individual was seen refusing to sign, the percentage of signers dropped from 93 to 30 percent!

Considering the negative proposal, which was signed by only 15 percent of the standardizing group, we find that 33 percent of the students signed when they saw another do so, but none signed when the guide refused. The accompanying positive background stimulus resulted in doubling the number signing an unpopular petition over the number who signed without social facilitation in the pre-experimental conditions. Again the power of negative influence in a situation is shown by the results for both the popular and unpopular proposals. The number of signers when the model refused to sign the popular proposal dropped from 93 to 30 percent while the number of signers of the unpopular proposal dropped from 33 percent to 0. The differences between all values for all conditions, as well as their interactions (Table 10.21) are significant beyond the 1 percent level of confidence. We can therefore assert that the test *S*s were affected differently by the content of the petitions and that they were also significantly affected by seeing another person sign or refuse to sign the petitions.

The results from the extreme conditions, *i.e.,* both focal and background stimuli positive or both negative, show that individual differences among members of a fairly homogeneous population can be practically wiped out: 93 percent signed in the one case, and 100 percent refused in the other case. Differences in personality do not, perhaps cannot, appear when situational forces are sufficiently compelling. But when situational forces are weak or conflicting, personality factors make themselves manifest. We expected under the conditions of this study that in situations involving both positive and negative factors, individuals with stronger tendencies toward conformity would sign more often than individuals with weaker conforming tendencies. Conforming tendencies of the *S*s were evaluated by their performance in a simulated group experiment where they were called upon to state their attitudes toward statements taken from the Thurstone-Chave scale for militarism-pacifism, to report on the number of clicks of a metronome, and to give answers to arithmetic problems after hearing four other individuals give their judgments first, as described in the discussion of the generality of conforming behavior (p. 646). Since the responses of the background group departed in various degrees from truth in the case of the metronome and arithmetic tasks and from the modal responses regarding attitudes of a standardizing group similar to the test

*S*s, it was possible to determine the extent to which the test *S*s in the petition-signing experiment were susceptible to interpersonal pressures. In addition, they were also given the Allport A-S Reaction Study so that we had information concerning their position on an ascendance-submission continuum. Complete conformance with the background group on any task would be denoted by the maximum possible score of six since there were six stimuli in each test. Similarly, higher scores on the A-S reaction study would indicate higher susceptibility to group pressures.

The scores of the test *S*s in these four tests, fractionated on the basis of those who signed and those who refused to sign the two petitions, as shown in Table 10.22 leave no doubt as to the operation of inner

TABLE 10.22. Mean Conformity Scores of *S*s on A-S Reaction Study and on Three Tasks Dichotomized on Basis of Petition-signing Responses

| | Negative Proposal | | Positive Proposal | |
Tests	Signers	Nonsigners	Signers	Nonsigners
A-S Reaction	5.30	4.65	6.00	4.76
Metronome	2.60	1.75	2.33	1.71
Attitude	2.50	2.75	2.67	2.52
Arithmetic	2.10	1.30	2.00	1.72

SOURCE: From Helson, Blake, and Mouton, 1958b. With the permission of the *Journal of Social Psychology*.

factors in the petition-signing situation: seven of the eight comparisons between mean conformity scores of the two groups are in the expected direction, *viz.*, those signing had higher conformity scores than did those refusing to sign, and they also had higher scores in the A-S reaction test, a sign of greater submissiveness. The differences between the two groups are significant beyond the 1 percent level. We thus find that the responses made in any situation are the outcome of the interplay of situational and personal factors. Which will predominate depends upon the strengths of each. In the petition-signing study we were able to create extreme conditions, which almost completely negated inner convictions and tendencies. Even in the case of a proposal that went counter to the convictions of most *S*s, one-third followed the example of a model in signing the petition.

It should be noted that inner factors may find expression in well-structured as well as in unstructured situations: in the petition-signing situation even the conditions in which there were conflicting forces at work were well structured. Situations involving balance or cancellation of opposing forces may be well structured as well as situations heavily loaded toward a given outcome.

According to commonsense views and in line with some approaches to personality, the ways in which individuals react to various situations are referable to the kind of people they are, *i.e.,* to the nature and strength of their characters, traits, drives, propensities, temperaments, or dispositions. On this basis the same situation may elicit quite different responses from different individuals either because their inner springs of action vary in strength or because environmental forces trigger different inner determinants of action. Thus a request for a donation, to serve as a member of a committee, or to sign a petition, may bring forth positive, negative, or indifferent responses on the part of various individuals. We have used the phrase "same situation" on the premise that is often made that a situation is the same for all individuals when it is presented under similar or identical conditions. This premise we know is at best only approximately true because no two individuals *perceive* a given situation in exactly the same way. One individual may regard a request for a donation as an opportunity for giving to a worthy cause, another as just one more attempt to obtain money from gullible givers, and another as an occasion where refusal would mean loss of social prestige and acquiescence would satisfy social or personal norms. On the other hand, the "same situation" may not actually be the same situation if even minor (not to mention major) details are not kept constant. There are many ways of raising money, getting out the vote, and enlisting sympathy and aid for various causes, and many differences in face-to-face approaches. Situations thus possess as many different degrees of freedom as do individuals, and the question arises whether situations possess taxonomic properties that determine the way individuals will react to them.

The action studies that follow were particularly directed toward the question just asked either because they concern situations in which traits or inner predispositions are usually assumed to be more important in determining behavior than are the conditions of stimulation or because they have distinctive features that challenge Ss to make decisions that really matter to them. Such situations can be said to have decisive taxonomic features.

The dynamics of volunteering responses. Volunteering is commonly defined as offering to do or undertake something in accordance with one's own choice or, as the dictionary puts it, "in accordance with one's own 'free will.' " In most situations, however, one does not offer to do something unless he knows what to do or what is wanted, so even acts of volunteering usually occur in response to requests for aid, services, or cooperation by one person from another. Considering the frequency with which most individuals are asked to act in various ways, volunteering is probably one of the most common forms of social response. Yet apart from a study by Schachter and Hall (1952) there were no studies of this fundamental type of behavior until studies appeared by Rosenbaum and Blake (1955), Rosenbaum (1956), and Blake, Berkowitz, Bellamy, and Mouton (1956). With systematic variation of conditions under which requests for aid were made, these workers found that volunteering is far from being a spontaneous act of free will but, on the contrary, it can be predicted quite accurately in many cases from the circumstances surrounding invitations to actions. More important than recognition of the fact that there are individual differences in responses to requests for aid is knowledge concerning the specific conditions under which people will or will not respond to pleas for help. Studies of volunteering throw considerable light on a number of basic questions in this area.

The two studies by Rosenbaum and Blake (1955) and by Rosenbaum (1956) were carried out in such a way as to have all the earmarks of a perfectly natural situation. None of the individuals realized that while being asked to give some time as subjects in a psychological experiment, they were, by acceding or refusing, *ipso facto* being subjects in an experiment! Students studying in the education and psychology library at the University of Texas were approached by the experimenter (*E*) with the request to take part in a psychological experiment. In the experiments by Rosenbaum (1956) the requests were framed to have three degrees of strength: "Will you please assist in a psychological experiment?" (weak); "I need subjects to take part in my experiment. Won't you please help out by being a subject for me?" (moderate); and "I have to finish my thesis by [here a date was given] and I am desperate for subjects now. Won't you please help out by being a subject?" (strong). In addition, a positive or negative social background was employed by planting an assistant next to the individuals about to be asked to participate in the experiment. In half the cases the assistant readily agreed, and in the other half the assistant refused to cooperate, whereupon E turned to the unwitting test S and made the request of him. Three groups of fifteen Ss were subjected to the three strengths of request with positive social reinforcement and three groups of fifteen each were subjected to the three strengths of request with negative social reinforcement. In addition three groups of fifteen each served as controls with the three strengths of request but with no model present. The combinations of stimulus (request) and background (action of model) conditions yielded nine degrees of pressure on the test Ss which varied from negative, to neutral, to strong, in various degrees.

The results in Table 10.23 show that frequency of volunteering is largely determined by the conditions under which the requests for

TABLE 10.23.   Number of Volunteers as a Function of Strength
of Request and Social Pressure

Action of Model	Strength of Request			Mean
	Strong	Moderate	Weak	
Agrees	12 (80)	12 (80)	6 (40)	10 (67)
Absent	12 (80)	7 (47)	0 (0)	6 (41)
Refuses	11 (73)	1 (7)	1 (7)	4 (29)
Mean	12 (78)	7 (48)	2 (16)	7 (47)

Note: Values in parentheses are percents. Percents and means are rounded to the first digit.
SOURCE: From Rosenbaum, 1956. With the permission of the American Psychological Association.

help are made. Wherever there is a preponderance of positive forces, the great majority of individuals accede, and wherever there is a preponderance of negative forces in the situation, the great majority of individuals refuse to help. Between the extremes where the forces for and against volunteering are more nearly balanced, the number who cooperate is in more or less direct relation to the strength and direction of the forces acting on the test Ss. The situation designed to be neutral yielded as near a 50–50 division as is possible with an odd number of individuals in a group, seven of the fifteen having volunteered under this condition. The operation of inner or residual factors is seen in the cases where some individuals refused to participate when the conditions were strongly compelling and in cases where individuals acceded to the request even when the conditions were weak or loaded against volunteering. The interactions between focal, background, and residual stimuli in this experiment are not as simple as they presumably are in psychophysical or sensory experiments; nevertheless the number of positive responses increases from the weakest to the most compelling conditions in accordance with expectations.

The impact of the nine experimental conditions was assessed by Rosenbaum not only by the number of individuals agreeing or refusing under each of the stimulus-background conditions but also by the estimates made by Ss, of their *willingness* to take part in the experiment. They were asked, after responding to E's request, to indicate how willing (or unwilling) they were to participate in terms of a scale ranging from extremely willing (15), to extremely unwilling (0), through indifferent (7). The data labeled observed in Table 10.24 can

TABLE 10.24.   Observed and Theoretical Measures of Willingness to Volunteer under Nine Stimulus-Background Conditions

	s_1		s_2		s_3	
	Theoretical	Observed	Theoretical	Observed	Theoretical	Observed
b_1	10.3	9.4	8.7	9.1	8.1	7.5
b_2	8.6	9.1	7.0	7.4	6.4	4.6
b_3	7.1	8.6	5.5	5.5	4.9	5.3

SOURCE: From Rosenbaum, 1956. With the permission of the American Psychological Association.

be considered the products of pairs of nine stimulus-background conditions which can be put into simultaneous equations of the form

$$W = s_i + b_j$$

where W stands for willingness, s_i stimulus strength, and b_j background strength. A least-squares solution of these nine simultaneous equations[2] yields the relative strengths on an interval scale of the stimulus and the background conditions as given in Table 10.25. Combining the appropriate s_i, b_j for each stimulus-background condition actually employed yields the theoretical values given in Table 10.24 which can be compared with the averages of the estimates made by the fifteen Ss under each condition. It is seen that the theoretical and reported measures of willingness agree quite closely, being within one

[2] The least-squares solution was furnished by Dr. Henry Helson, University of California, Berkeley.

category step in all cases except for s_3b_2. Comparison of the actual frequencies of volunteering with the measures of willingness shows that the two are highly correlated and hence that there was a real connection between the intensitive situational conditions and the "motivation" of the Ss.

TABLE 10.25. Least-squares Solution of Relative Strengths of Stimuli and Backgrounds in the Volunteering Study

s_1	s_2	s_3
5.12	3.49	2.92
b_1	b_2	b_3
5.19	3.49	1.98

Note: Normalized to yield equal strengths for the neutral stimulus and background conditions, s_2 b_2.
SOURCE: Based on data from Rosenbaum, 1956.

The conditions of the volunteering experiment simply called for "yes" or "no" responses in essentially a singly determined situation so far as the Ss were concerned. The action of the model may have created some conflict in the individual, *e.g.*, when test Ss who did not volunteer saw the model go willingly and when test Ss felt they would like to take part in a psychological experiment but the refusal of the model raised doubts in their minds. The alternative after refusal in this experiment was simply to turn back to the task which was occupying S before he was approached by E. The question arises what happens when the alternative is something one would prefer not to do. Such cases arise when refusal to accede to a request means social censure or even worse. One may hate to steal but might do so to avoid facing hungry dependents. This type of behavior involves the choice of the lesser of two evils. Blake, Berkowitz, Bellamy, and Mouton (1956) showed under the controlled conditions of an experiment that seemingly positive acts may really be acts of avoidance. There are, in the light of their findings, at least two kinds of positive acts: those which represent a response to a desired goal which is wanted in its own right and those which are made to avoid an undesirable and unwanted goal or a worse alternative. The individual himself may not always be cognizant of his own motivation. While the second type of response has long been known and referred to as "flight from reality" it has only recently been subjected to systematic variation and measurement.

The experiment, as in the case of all the action studies, was conducted in a natural, everyday situation: An instructor dismissed his class, and as he was leaving E entered and called for volunteers to take part in a psychological experiment. Under these circumstances the alternative to volunteering was the very attractive one offered of getting out of class with the possibility of going for a walk, smoking, talking with one's friends, etc. In the second condition, which also served as a control, E entered a class and called for volunteers. The instructor agreed to excuse those who took part in the experiment. In this condition the alternative to volunteering was continuance in the class with whatever feelings the students might have about remaining in class. For the majority of students, we can be sure the alternative to volunteering in this condition was not as attractive as in the first condition. In the third condition, the instructor had announced a "pop" quiz and was engaged in writing the questions on the board when E entered and called for volunteers. The instructor agreed to excuse any students who cared to leave and participate in the psychological experiment. Here the alternative to volunteering was unpleasant, or must be judged so in the light of the results which are given in Table 10.26. In addition, two ways of stating willingness to volunteer were employed with different groups of Ss: privately, by signing names on slips of paper; publicly, by a raising of hands. The variations in conditions required six groups and there were thirty-four to eighty-five Ss in each.

TABLE 10.26. Frequency of Volunteering as a Function of Attractiveness of Alternatives

	Alternative	Attractiveness	Total Number of Ss	Volunteers Number	Percent
		Private Expression			
1.	Dismissal from class	++	67	18	26.8
2.	Remain in class	0	83	38	45.7
3.	Take "pop" quiz	——	85	84	99.0
		Public Expression			
1.	Dismissal from class	++	34	4	11.0
2.	Remain in class	0	39	12	30.7
3.	Take "pop" quiz	——	54	54	100.0

SOURCE: From Blake, Berkowitz, Bellamy, and Mouton, 1956. With the permission of the American Psychological Association.

The results show that increasing numbers of individuals agreed to participate in the psychological experiment as the alternatives to volunteering became more distasteful. Since less than half the class volunteered when the alternative was to remain and finish the class hour, participation in the experiment must be regarded as a less pleasant prospect than attending the particular classes involved in this study. Yet when the alternative was sufficiently distasteful, as was the case when it meant taking an unexpected examination for which they were probably unprepared, almost everybody in the two classes subjected to this condition preferred to volunteer. If avoidance of the unpleasant is escape from reality, then this investigation shows that individuals who have never resorted to this form of behavior have been lucky in having not only strong constitutions but very favorable environments as well! Again we find that extreme conditions practically wipe out individual differences attributable to inner personality factors.

One result, which is not discussed by the authors, appears clearly in Table 10.26 and merits some speculation. There were more volunteers with private expression of willingness than with public expression, in two of the three conditions. Were not residual factors responsible for these differences? Did willingness to volunteer carry some felt opprobrium, i.e., in the first case the presumed hostility of the class toward anyone who set an example of doing work when it was possible not to work and in the second case the feared displeasure of the instructor for those leaving his lecture to do something else no matter how meritorious it might be? We are suggesting that other factors presenting other alternatives may also have been at work to influence some individuals in the situations studied here.

Another type of volunteering was investigated by Blake, Rosenbaum, and Duryea (1955) which involved gift giving. Since requests for donations for various causes are frequently made, it seemed natural for two graduate students to go among their fellow students asking for contributions to be used to purchase a gift for a departmental secretary who had announced her resignation. As each individual was asked to contribute, *E* permitted him (or her) to see a sheet of paper on a clipboard that ostensibly contained the amounts donated by other individuals. Nothing was said about what others had given or the amount that was expected. Five different sheets were used on the clipboard, one for each of the conditions being tested. In one condition, nothing appeared on the sheet so that the amount given was simply a function of the strength of the request and the attitude of the individual. Under the second and third conditions the average amount was 25 cents, but in the former the variation about the mean was small, in the latter it was large. Similarly under the fourth and fifth conditions the average amount was 75 cents, but the variation was small in the former and large in the latter condition.

Two different individuals acted as *E*s under each of the five conditions, with very much the same results across *E*s (pooled in Table 10.27). A surprising finding was that the condition producing the

TABLE 10.27. Average Amounts Contributed by Five Groups of Ten Ss under Five Different Background Conditions

Condition	Background Condition		Amount Contributed	
	Norm	Variation	Average	Average Deviation
I	No external norm		80.0	25.0
II	25 cents	small	28.5	5.6
III	25 cents	large	35.0	12.0
IV	75 cents	small	63.5	15.8
V	75 cents	large	63.0	17.0

SOURCE: After Blake, Rosenbaum, and Duryea, 1955. With the permission of *Human Relations.*

largest average contribution was the first, in which no information was supplied to *S*s! This result can only mean that individual norms already established for donations of this sort were higher than the ones set in the experiment. Since in seven of the remaining eight cases (two groups in each of the remaining four conditions) the average amounts contributed were not significantly different from the means of the amounts shown on the sheets, we conclude that the *S*s were influenced to act in accordance with external norms when they were provided rather than in accordance with previously established norms. It is also noteworthy that the responses of two groups solicited independently by two different *E*s under the first condition were definitely bimodal, all donations being either 50 cents or 1 dollar. This result shows that individuals act in accordance with already established norms in situations that do not provide norms for their guidance.

As is to be expected, the variability was greatest under the first condition, where no standards were provided for the amount that should be given. The average deviations of the donations, shown in Table 10.27, increase as the amounts presumably given by others become more variable about their means. While the *S*s in the groups tested under conditions II, III, IV, and V tended to approximate the means of the amounts shown on the clip sheet, individual *S*s were influenced to donate more or less than the average by specific amounts perceived on the clip sheets, thus contributing to the variability under each of the conditions. When *S*s cast their eyes over the clip sheet, some numbers may have stood out thereby exerting greater influence than the mean of the set on some of the responses.

It seems reasonable that there should be greater variability in responses when there are no explicitly defined norms and when the components entering into norms are more variable. In the former case, variability in individual norms becomes manifest because there are no constraining or counteracting norms, and in the second case, the situation provides what is essentially a larger range of norms from which individuals may choose in making their decisions. There are many practical implications of this finding. For example, we expect far less variability in driving speeds where speed limits are posted than in areas where only the top legal limit applies. In some states the legal limit is defined not only in terms of maximum allowable speed but also with respect to actual traffic conditions, weather, road hazards, and other environmental contingencies. The individual is thus not permitted to drive at the legal limit unless road conditions warrant it. More and more the law requires the individual to conform to norms which are held to be reasonable in the light of all the known facts and not merely with respect to statutes that lay down no constraining conditions for concrete situations.

The study of gift giving which we have reviewed here demonstrates that the act of giving a gift to an individual, to a charity, or even to an educational institution is much more than the expression of a trait of generosity or the magnanimous response of a kind soul or both. It is an adjustive act which results from all the forces, outer as well as inner, bearing on the individual. The weaker the internal forces favoring an act, the stronger must be the external forces to bring it about. According to the view presented here, traits of generosity, honesty, and conformity are *created* by situations and by people as well as by sources within the individual.

An action study involving honesty. There is probably no characteristic of behavior which is presumed to be more firmly established by the time individuals reach college age than the so-called trait of honesty. For honesty seems to be an expression of all the years of training and upbringing and perhaps of the "inheritance" of individuals. Can honesty be created in part by the conditions in which individuals find themselves? A study by McQueen (1957) bears on this question by showing how powerful situational and interpersonal factors may be in determining whether individuals are honest or not. Twelve groups, each composed of twenty-five members of sections of general psychology at the University of Texas, were either upgraded or downgraded two or six points in an objective-type examination. The examinations were returned under one of the following conditions:

Condition I: Students were asked to report *any* errors in grading by returning their papers with appropriate notation to the instructor at the end of the hour; if no errors were noted, they were to retain the papers.

Condition II: The papers were returned with the same instructions as in Condition I but after all the items had been checked, one of the students who had been instructed to do so beforehand, reported that he had been given *more* or *fewer* points than he had earned. In response to this remark the instructor merely nodded his head and referred the student to the directions he had given earlier regarding reporting errors in grading.

Condition III: This condition was like II in all respects except for the fact that when upgrading was reported, the instructor thanked the student profusely for his fine show of honesty and personal integrity and ended by saying that he felt the student should be commended for his action.

The results leave no doubt as to the efficacy of situational and interpersonal determinants in honest behavior. As shown by the data in Table 10.28, only 4 percent reported errors of upgrading in the first

TABLE 10.28.   Percentage of Ss in 12 Groups of 25 Each Who Reported Errors in Grading under 12 Stimulus-Background Conditions

	Percentage of Ss Reporting Errors			
Conditions	+6 Error	+2 Error	−2 Error	−6 Error
I. Merely asked to report	4	4	96	100
II. Model reports upgrading or downgrading	60	56	92	96
III. Model reports and is thanked by instructor	80	92	100	100

SOURCE: From McQueen, 1957. With the permission of the *Journal of Personality.*

condition while 98 percent reported downgrading under the same condition. Apparently no environmental fillips were necessary to incite the students to report errors of downgrading! In Condition II 58 percent reported upgrading, an almost 15-fold increase as a result of the example set by the instructed student. The number who reported downgrading was slightly lower in Condition II (94 percent) than in Condition I, for unknown reasons. In Condition III (where the student was profusely thanked for being so honest and forthright) 86 percent in the two upgraded groups reported being upgraded, while 100 percent reported being downgraded. Even under the strongest pressures to be honest, 7 of the 50 individuals in the two upgraded groups preferred higher marks to the satisfactions that come from being honest. It is to be hoped that the 14 percent who failed to report being upgraded will not be exposed to too much temptation following their graduation from college! Apparently the magnitude of the upgrading error, whether two or six points, played no statistically significant role in the results according to the over-all analysis of variance of the data; but the fact that 23 out of 25 Ss reported upgrading of two points under Condition III while only 20 in 25 reported upgrading of six points under this same condition suggests that a wider variation in grade errors may reveal some interesting information regarding tolerance levels and breaking points where honesty is concerned.

Implications of the studies for generality of behavior patterns. Our conclusions regarding the generality of conforming behavior represent a position between those who maintain that there is no general trait of suggestibility or conformity and those who maintain that traits are manifestations of personalities and not of situations. Goldberg (1954), from his study of situational determinants of social norms, concluded, "It would appear that investigations of the acquisition of social norms would more fruitfully concentrate upon the analysis of the immediate situation rather than on stable personality characteristics of S" (p. 329). Our studies showed even stronger situational determinants of conformity than Goldberg's study did; nevertheless they also showed significant effects attributable to consistency in conforming behavior in different tasks. Also we found greater frequency of yielding on the part of Ss who received higher conformity scores on the Allport A-S Reaction Study. Hence our position is based on both theoretical and empirical grounds. We assume that every act involves, to a greater or lesser extent, both situational and personal determinants; results of both the conforming and the action studies (gift giving, volunteering, violation of a prohibited act, petition-signing behavior, etc.) have given evidence supporting the validity of this assumption. That Goldberg failed to find evidence for any generality in conforming behavior due to personal factors must be attributed to the nature of the task given his *S*s (judgment of intelligence from photographs) and the manner in which social pressure was applied (actual size of group was not varied since *S*s were merely told by *E* that groups of either two or four had judged IQs to be at variance with *S*s judgments). Furthermore the low intercorrelations between the nine experimental conditions on which he based his argument cannot be interpreted against some generality in conformity behavior because the experimental conditions were actually variants of a single type of task. In the Texas studies, tasks differing in type as well as in difficulty were employed and yielded evidence of generality.

Evidence for generality of conforming behavior comes from Beloff (1958) whose study employed the experimental procedures of the Helson, Blake, Mouton, and Olmstead investigation (1957). He found that *acquiescence,* defined as agreement with expressed group opinion in a situation involving pressures from others, and *conventionality,* defined as concurrence with tenets, attitudes, and mores of a culture or subculture, were correlated; and hence, he concluded there is a generalized tendency toward or away from conformity in individuals. Beloff found (as Ball did) significant differences between men and women, the former being more conforming with respect to politico-social issues, the latter with respect to aesthetic issues.

The opponents of generality of any type of behavior can still argue that similarity of responses in various situations is not evidence for the operation of general factors in personality because similarity in responses may be due to common factors in the different situations. Thus it is defensible to take the position that all tasks in the Texas studies were more or less similar in requiring *S*s to respond under social pressures or after seeing or hearing models taking certain courses of action. Certainly this argument has some validity, but it assumes that properties of situations are independent of the persons in the situations, and this position is as one-sided as the view which it opposes, i.e., that traits are independent of situations. Rather, as in the controversy over heredity vs. environment, which occupied psychologists several generations ago, both situational and personal factors must be conceived as interacting in every expression of personality with neither inner factors nor environmental factors having meaning apart from the other.

ASSIMILATION AND CONTRAST IN JUDGMENTS OF SOCIAL, CLINICAL, AND PERSONALITY MATERIALS

The concepts of contrast and assimilation which are now being used as descriptive terms in social psychology (Hovland, Harvey, and Sherif, 1957), clinical psychology (Campbell, Hunt, and Lewis, 1957), and in personality theory (Berkowitz, 1960; Sears, 1936; Goldings, 1954) have much the same meanings that they have in sensory psychology. When differences in judgments of scale items are enhanced, *contrast* is said to be operative; and when they are reduced, *assimilation* is said to be operative. Contrast denotes difference, repulsion, complementarism, and movement away from an object's attributes or position, whereas assimilation denotes likeness, attraction, and movement toward objects and qualities. Thus, assimilation appears in the judgments of individuals in favor of dry laws who regard any statement somewhat on the "wet" side of prohibition as "dry" and in the responses of kind individuals who perceive others as kind whether or not they are. Contrast appears in the judgments of dry individuals who regard any position differing slightly from their own as wet and in the responses of generous persons who perceive others as stingy (cf. Berkowitz, 1960).

Descriptively, the principles of contrast and assimilation are simple and straightforward enough and point to functional differences in such diverse areas as sensory processes, psychophysical judgments, reactions to communication and social pressures, and in evaluations of self and others. Thus it has been found that individuals accept statements representing positions near their own position and reject statements which diverge greatly from their own position (Hovland, Harvey, and Sherif, 1957). Judgments of items in the central region of attitude scales tend to be displaced more by changes in context than are items at the extremes, a fact we have already discussed in some detail (pp. 602 ff.); and an individual's position on a continuum, e.g., skin color or height, affects his judgments of others (pp. 553 ff.). These and many other phenomena may be regarded as cases of contrast or assimilation. The diversity of conditions under which contrast and assimilation occur leaves us with a plurality of phenomena requiring explanation. We have already seen (Chapter 4) that assimilation as well as contrast depends upon the relation of stimuli to AL in the study by Parducci and Marshall (1962). The following question now arises: Is this theory of assimilation and contrast also valid for judgmental phenomena in the fields of social, clinical, and personality psychology?

In dealing with this question we shall make use of a modification of the model proposed by Hovland, Harvey, and Sherif (1957) in their study dealing with effects of communication on attitude change. In this investigation attitudes toward prohibition were determined by requiring Ss to indicate which one of nine statements came *closest* to their own position on the question and which one was *most* objectionable. In addition, Ss also indicated which statements were acceptable and which were objectionable. Unmarked statements were taken to be indifferent or neutral. The nine statements ranged from extremely dry (*A*) through neutral (*E*) to extremely wet (*I*). The following three statements represent the two most extreme items and a neutral item on the scale:

(*A*) Since alcohol is the curse of mankind, the sale and use of alcohol, including light beer, should be completely abolished (extremely dry).

(*E*) The arguments in favor and against the sale and use of alcohol are nearly equal (neutral).

(*I*) It has become evident that man cannot get along without alcohol; therefore, there should be no restriction whatsoever on its sale and use (extremely wet).

Statements *A, B, C,* and *D* were on the dry side of the scale and statements *F, G, H,* and *I* were on the wet side. Latitudes of acceptance and of rejection were given by the distributions of acceptable and objectionable responses and the latitude of indifference was given by the statements which were neither acceptable nor objectionable. Following the determination of Ss' attitudes, wet and dry communications were presented to selected groups of Ss and latitudes of acceptance and rejection were again determined to test the effects of the content of the communications on the attitudes of Ss regarding like-dislike, reasonable-unreasonable, biased-unbiased, and propaganda-fact dimensions of the statements.

The results showed that communications "diverging widely" from Ss' positions were pereceived as farther removed than they actually were (contrast effect), whereas communications close to Ss' own position were judged to be closer than they actually were (assimilation effect). Positions close to *S*s' were judged to be fair, factual, and reasonable as contrasted with positions at some distance which were judged to be propagandistic and unfair. Latitudes of acceptance, rejection, and neutrality were formalized by Hovland, Harvey, and Sherif in a hypothetical model (Table 10.29) which closely approximated

TABLE 10.29. Hypothetical Latitudes of Acceptance and Rejection and Indifference of Ss Holding Each Position

Rating Positions	Own Position								
	A	B	C	D	E	F	G	H	I
A	++	+	0	—	—	——	——	——	——
B	+	++	+	0	—	—	—	—	—
C	0	+	++	+	0	—	—	—	—
D	—	0	+	++	+	0	—	—	—
E	—	—	0	+	++	+	0	—	—
F	—	—	—	0	+	++	+	0	—
G	—	—	—	—	0	+	++	+	0
H	—	—	—	—	—	0	+	++	+
I	——	——	——	——	—	—	0	+	++

Key: + = acceptance
— = rejection
0 = indifference
++ = strong acceptance
—— = strong objection
SOURCE: From Hovland, Harvey, and Sherif, 1957. With the permission of the American Psychological Association.

actual distributions where there were sufficient numbers of *S*s for the scale positions. The plus signs indicate acceptance, the minus signs indicate rejection, and the zeros indicate indifference toward the scale items. The double plus signs stands for the most acceptable statement, and this is taken as representative of *S*'s own stand; the double minus sign represents items to which *S*s strongly objected. The distributions of favorable, neutral, and unfavorable responses of *S*s holding each of the nine positions of the wet-dry scale have a symmetry which suggests that there is an underlying basic principle at work.

The distributions in Table 10.29 are ordered according to the order of the scale items, from extreme dry to extreme wet, with the result that they are not monotonic in the case of *S*s holding intermediate positions *C, D, E, F,* and *G.* In this order individuals holding the intermediate positions appear to have two regions of indifference (indicated by the two zeros in their distributions). While it is possible to interpret the model in this form in terms of our theory, we would have to assume, in the case of Ss holding the intermediate positions, that the wet-dry issue involves two separate continua, each with its own neutral region or adaptation level. For our purposes it is simpler to re-order the distributions so that all acceptable items are at one end (left) of the distribution and all objectionable items at the other end (right) with the neutral items falling together, as shown in Table 10.30. In the new order all the distributions are monotonic and have a single zone of indifference. I have also taken the liberty of assuming that items more than two steps removed from the neutral positions are either very objectionable (double minus signs) or very acceptable (double plus signs) following Hovland, Harvey, and Sherif's treatment of the *A* and *I* distributions (Table 10.29).

With Table 10.30 before us the following deductions can immediately be made from the distributions of judgments relative to the positions

TABLE 10.30. Hypothetical Latitudes of Acceptance, Indifference, and Rejection of the Ss Holding Each of the Nine Possible Positions

A	B	C	D	E	F	G	H	I
++	+	0	—	—	——	——	——	——
B	A	C	D	E	F	G	H	I
++	+	+	0	—	—	——	——	——
C	B	D	A	E	F	G	H	I
++	+	+	0	0	—	—	——	——
D	C	E	B	F	A	G	H	I
++	+	+	0	0	—	—	——	——
E	D	F	C	G	B	H	A	I
++	+	+	0	0	—	—	——	——
F	E	G	D	H	C	I	B	A
++	+	+	0	0	—	—	——	——
G	F	H	I	E	D	C	B	A
++	+	+	0	0	—	—	——	——
H	G	I	F	E	D	C	B	A
++	+	+	0	—	—	——	——	——
I	H	G	F	E	D	C	B	A
++	+	0	—	—	——	——	——	——

Note: Revised from table 10.29 to yield monotonic distributions in rows.
Key: ++ = most acceptable
     + = acceptable
     0 = neutral or indifferent
     — = objectionable
     —— = strongly objectionable
SOURCE: Modified from Hovland, Harvey, and Sherif, 1957.

of the indifferent scale items. Considering the contrast effect first, we find that there are two cases which should be distinguished.

Case I: Inspection of the hypothetical distribution of judgments reveals that positions or statements on one side of the neutral region are acceptable, those on the other side are rejected *Hence items on opposite sides of the neutral region are ipso facto contrasting items even though they are close together*. Items on one side of the neutral region may be shifted to the opposite side if the adaptation level changes, as shown by comparing the positions of items *E* and *A* in the first and fourth rows. Items in the vicinity of the neutral region are more affected by changes in adaptation level and so exhibit greater contrast effect than do items farther away from level, e.g., items *B, C,* and *D* in the first, second, and third rows. We see that items close together on a scale may contrast since, if the neutral region happens to move between them, they will elicit opposite responses. This can happen when anchors or standards are introduced which change level.

Case II: Contrast may also be manifested in the divergence of items on the same side of the scale. Scale items undergo differential displacements with changes in adaptation level, a fact that is as true of social and clinical judgments as it is of psychophysical judgments. Items on one side of a scale may diverge as a result of changes in level because of introduction of anchors, changes in context of items, etc., as Podell (1961) has shown in a study of personality traits.

Let us now consider phenomena of assimilation. Consider the scale positions of the stimuli in Fig. 10.6. From this figure it is apparent that contrast and assimilation are *complementary* processes, not independent processes as is often assumed. As a matter of logic, *if the scale is finite, items that move away from each other must at the same time move closer to other items on the scale*. Separation of items in one part can be accomplished only through bunching in other parts of finite scales. The complementary nature of contrast and assimilation is borne out by experimental data from attitude and psychophysical scaling. Because of their greater simplicity, let us first consider the lifted-weight data presented in Fig. 10.6 which were obtained (Helson, 1948) under the following conditions: Ss judged a set of weights ranging from 200 to 400 grm. in steps of 50 grm. in terms of a nine-category scale by method of single stimuli and also with a 900-grm. or a 90-grm. anchor preceding the series stimuli. The categories and the values assigned them for purposes of computation were: very very heavy, 9; very heavy, 8; heavy, 7; medium-heavy, 6; medium, 5; medium-light, 4; light, 3; very light, 2; and very very light, 1. Since the judgments by method of single stimuli are most evenly spaced, they may be taken as the standard against which to gauge shifts in judgments following introduction of the anchors. With a 900-grm. anchor the judgments of the stimuli are displaced downward, the heaviest members of the series being affected more than the lightest; with a 90-grm. anchor the judgments are displaced upward, the lightest members of the series being affected more than the heaviest. In both cases the displacements are away from the adaptation levels which are close to the stimuli eliciting a judgment of 5. Contrast and

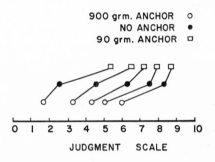

FIG. 10.6. Shifts in judgments of lifted weights showing contrast and assimilation effects associated with large changes in AL due to the introduction of anchors outside the series stimuli. These results are analogous to the contrast and assimilation effects found in expressions of attitudes when individuals hold extreme positions on issues, as shown in Fig. 10.7.

assimilation effects are greatest with respect to stimuli in the vicinity of changed levels since it is judgments of these stimuli which shift most from their previous positions in the judgment scale (contrast). The judgments of these stimuli are also crowded together more than are the judgments of stimuli farther removed from level (assimilation). Exactly the same phenomena appear in scaled values of statements concerned with the social position of Negroes by average Ss, pro-Negro Ss, anti-Negro Ss, and Negro Ss (cf. Fig. 10.6 with Fig. 10.7 which is taken from Hovland and Sherif, 1952). In the case of two of the extreme groups, pro-Negro whites and Negroes, all but two of the eleven statements are bunched on the unfavorable side of the scale with most scale values unused; in the case of the third extreme group, anti-Negro whites, all but four of the eleven statements are rated favorable to the

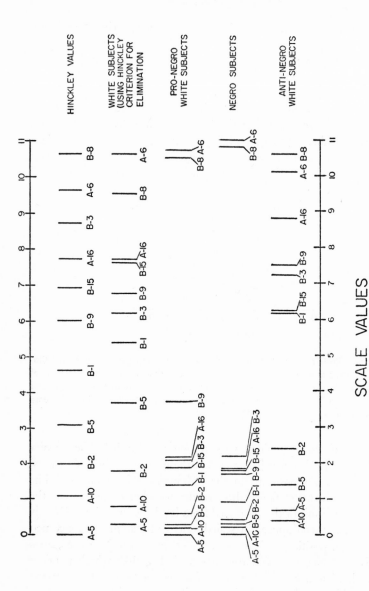

FIG. 10.7. Contrast and assimilation effects in social judgments of individuals holding extreme positions. (From Hovland and Sherif, 1952. With the permission of the American Psychological Association.)

Negro with several values unused in rating the items. Effects of extreme positions in attitude scaling are exactly analogous to effects of extreme anchors in psychophysical judgments as shown by comparing the data in Figs. 10.6 and 10.7. In both cases the distribution of judgments depends upon the adjustment levels of the respondents.

It appears from Fig. 10.7 that the more extreme an individual's position is with respect to an issue, the more his neutral zone will be displaced from the center of the scale, and the larger the number of items or positions which he will reject. Reverting to the data in Table 10.30, we see that an individual who holds to the extreme dry position, *A,* finds only position *B* acceptable in additon to his own, is indifferent to *C,* and finds all the other positions on the scale unacceptable. Similarly, an individual who is extremely wet, as in the last row in Table 10.30, finds only position *H* acceptable in addition to his own, is indifferent to *G,* and finds all others unacceptable. As the neutral region moves away from the extremes of the scale, latitudes of acceptance, rejection, and indifference become more nearly balanced (Hovland, Harvey, and Sherif, 1957). A similar result is found in the psychophysical judgments in Fig. 10.6. Thus the findings in the two studies concerned with attitude scaling and the study concerned with effects of anchors in psychophysical scaling are explicable in terms of shifts in level.

There are other implications of our account of contrast and assimilation, but further quantification is needed for them to be precise. Thus the discriminability of, or differential reactivity of *S*s to, scale items depends upon the form of the function relating stimulus conditions and responses. As pointed out in Chapter 4, various types of spreading (contrast) or bunching (assimilation) of scale values can be described by S-R functions for specific conditions of judging.

Before closing this discussion of contrast and assimilation, we must consider the position that AL theory accounts for contrast effects in judgment but not for assimilation effects (Campbell, Hunt, and Lewis, 1957). These writers believe that assimilation is a "new" phenomenon not anticipated by current theories of judgment and that it cannot be formulated in terms of monotonic functions. Although AL theory is not restricted to monotonic quantitative relations (cf. McClelland and Clark, 1953; Haber, 1958) we have just shown that contrast and assimilation can be handled by a monotonic ordering of judged scale items.

The study by Campbell, Hunt, and Lewis was inspired by an observation of Hunt's that during World War II psychiatrists with a *background* of private practice tended to consider examinees to be more disturbed psychiatrically than did psychiatrists with a *background* of state hospital experience. Accordingly an experiment was devised in which normal *S*s were asked to rate definitons devised to represent various degrees of abnormality. The scale ranged from 1 to 9, with 1 denoting normal, and 9 most disturbed (schizophrenic). The following are definitons from the normal, intermediate, and most disturbed portions of the scale: *gamble:* to take a chance, risk (1); *brim:* outside diameter with a margin (5); and *state:* that's before, that's long before not happiness (9). Items with scale values of 5 were the main object of concern since only shifts in scale values of these items were considered as indicators of contrast or assimilation effects. Definitions having ratings of 5 were presented in five contexts, i.e., in sets of five, with definitions rated as follows in the five sets: 1–5, 2–6, 3–7, 4–8, and 5–9. Thus definitions with values of 5 appeared in all five positions in the five sets. The sets were presented in two different orders, one group of *S*s judging the sets in ascending order (1–5 to 5–9) and the other in descending order (5–9 to 1–5). Thus the high-to-low group began with item 5 at the bottom of the 5–9 set and ended with it as the top of the 1–5 set. Conversely, the low-to-high group began with item 5 at the top of the 1–5 set and ended with it at the bottom of the 5–9 set. In other words, one group began with the more disturbed and ended with the less disturbed definitions while the other began with the less disturbed and ended with the most disturbed definitions.

Significant contrast effects were found only in the high-to-low order, i.e., the definitions with values of 5 were rated less disturbed when in high (more disturbed) context than when in low (less disturbed) context. Contrast, in this sense, was also found in one of the sets in the ascending (low-to-high) order, but assimilation was a more common finding (at least with *some S*s): item 5 was rated *higher* in higher contexts than in lower contexts. Campbell, Hunt, and Lewis offered a variety of explanations to account for the assimilation effect, some of which are compatible with, if not directly deduced from, the theory espoused here. For example, they say that if the items were in the severe range, some *S*s had a tendency to make severe ratings—hence assimilation. To us this statement can only mean that residuals from the preceding low sets were sufficiently strong in the case of these *S*s to keep AL *low* relative to the high sets, thus resulting in higher ratings for the definitions with values of 5 in the more disturbed sets. Furthermore, the fact that there was much more evidence of assimilation in the ascending order than in the descending order of presentation favors our interpretation and argues against assimilation as an independent and "new" type of judgmental process; for if assimilation is a distinct process it should have appeared as often in the *descending* order as in the *ascending* order. Campbell, Hunt, and Lewis have no explanation for the asymmetry of these effects. Finally, it should be pointed out that effects of level would have emerged more clearly with qualitative categories than with the numerical ratings employed in this study. We have found that the firm properties of the number system can mask changes in perceived characters of stimuli, and therefore we prefer category to numerical scales for showing shifts in adaptation levels.

The assimilation effects found in part of the Campbell, Hunt, and Lewis study may have been an artifact since a replication of their experiment by Miller and Engen (1960) showed only the usual effects of context and little evidence of assimilation. Nor were the judgments influenced by the semantics of the response system. Miller and Engen used line lengths in groups of five varying from 0.75 to 15.25 in. Ss judged the lines either beginning with a set of five lines from 0.75 to 6.75 in. and changing gradually to a set containing lines from 6.75 to 15.25 in., or judged in the reverse order. The results of 20 Ss for the short-to-long groups show overestimation of the 6.75-in. line in the first phase (i.e., when it was the longest line in the set) and progressive underestimation as this line was presented in contexts of longer lines. The results of 20 Ss with the long-to-short group were, in the main, opposite: in the context of long lines the 6.75-in. line was underestimated and, as the context lines decreased, the 6.75-in. line was overestimated. Changes in context affected the other lines in each of the sets in a manner similar to the 6.75-in. line chosen for discussion.

ATTITUDES AS POOLED EFFECTS OF PERCEPTUAL, COGNITIVE, AND EMOTIONAL COMPONENTS

Less has been done with the emotional than with the cognitive aspects of attitude formation in psychological investigations and theorizing. Attitudes have at least three distinguishable components that must be taken into consideration. Attitudes are directed toward or away from *objects* that may be concrete or abstract. One may have a set toward a food, an event, a political issue, or an intellectual problem, and the way it is perceived determines its perceptual character. How one thinks about objects determines their cognitive character, and how one feels about objects indicates their emotional impact. Usually the term "attitude" refers to the emotional aspect of responses to objects. To understand the development and expression of attitudes, we must know how objects are perceived and what their relation is to sensory and emotional levels as well as what their cognitive frames of reference are. Attitudes are thus pooled effects of perceptual, cognitive, and emotional components which determine levels of acceptance or rejection. Explicit recogniton of the complex pooled nature of attitudes has been expressed in a quantitative model by Peak (1955). In her model Peak employed only two components, cognitive and emotional; but her example shows that the perceptual component was not missing from her analysis since it must have played a part in evaluating responses to situations in the manner she proposed.

Let us consider Peak's application of her model to a concrete case (Table 10.31). She presented a hypothetical case of an individual faced

TABLE 10.31.   A Model for Evaluating Cognitive-Affective Components of Attitudes

Considerations	Probability	Feeling Loading	Derived Affect Load
Property values	.5	—6	—3.0
Equal opportunity	.6	+6	+3.6
Lowered status	.8	—8	—6.4
		Total affective loading	—5.8

SOURCE: From Peak, 1955. With the permission of the Nebraska University Press.

with the sale of a home, in his neighborhood, to a non-white buyer. His attitude is based on the probabilities (as he evaluates them) that desegregation (1) will lead to changes in property values in the neighborhood; (2) that it will, however, contribute to greater progress toward equal opportunity for the minority group; and (3) that it will lower the status of the whites in a neighborhood in which non-whites can buy property. Each of these considerations is weighted by its attendant probability and also by its affect loading which may be positive or negative, to yield a derived affect load. The total affective loading is calculated as the algebraic sum of the derived affect loads. For the case assumed in Table 10.31 the net affective loading is negative in spite of the fairly strong positive component contributed by the "equality of opportunity" consideration. This model recognizes the complex nature of attitudes and the fact that the various components (cognitive, affective, perceptual) are differentially weighted as they pool to yield a net effect. Since the model is based on linear additive assumptions, it can be formulated in terms of multiple regression equations or otherwise made to yield quantitative functional relations.

SUMMARY

One must consider the nature of groups and the criteria for evaluating group behavior before discussing the requirements for a science of interpersonal relations. Situational and personal factors are found operative in conforming behavior and in various types of everyday actions investigated under laboratory conditions. Strong social stimulation may be made to outweigh personal factors in predictable ways in many types of behavior. The presence of conforming tendencies in a variety of tasks argues for some generality in behavior patterns of individuals. Certain phenomena in judgments expressive of attitudes, such as contrast and assimilation, are functions of individual adjustment levels and do not require separate mechanisms for their explanation. Cognitive and emotional components pool with perceptual data in determining social adaptations.

Appendix

TABLE A. Computations for Deriving the Best Fitting Value of A and b and Scale Values of Stimuli for Lifted-weight Data Obtained by Category Ratings Translated into a Scale from 1–10 According to Equation (41) in Chapter 4 Through the Use of Transformed (Y) Values of J Given in Table B.

X	J	Y (From Table B)	X' (Coded X)	X'Y	X'²	J_t
200	3.4	0.7241	−2	−1.4482	4	3.3
250	5.0	1.0000	−1	−1.0000	1	5.1
300	6.3	1.2989	0	0.0000	0	6.4
350	7.4	1.6316	1	1.6316	1	7.4
400	8.2	1.9412	2	3.8824	4	8.2
		$M_y = 1.3192$	$M_x' = 0$	$\Sigma X'Y = 3.0658$	$\Sigma X'^2 = 10$	

$1/A' = (3.0658/10)/50 = 0.0061316$

$b = 1.31916 - (0.0061316 \times 300) = -0.52032$

$A = A' - bA' = 163.09 - (-84.86) = 247.95$

$J_t = 10(X - A)/[X + (1 + b)/(1 - b)A] + 0.5K$

$\quad = 10(X - 247.95)/(X + 78.24) + 5.0$

SOURCE: From Helson and Himelstein, 1955. By permission of the *American Journal of Psychology*.

TABLE B. Tabulated Values of $Y = (0.5K + J)/(1.5K - J)$ as a Function of J

J	Y	J	Y	J	Y	J	Y
0.00	0.3333	2.50	0.6000	5.00	1.0000	7.50	1.6667
0.05	0.3378	2.55	0.6064	5.05	1.0101	7.55	1.6846
0.10	0.3423	2.60	0.6129	5.10	1.0202	7.60	1.7027
0.15	0.3468	2.65	0.6194	5.15	1.0305	7.65	1.7211
0.20	0.3514	2.70	0.6260	5.20	1.0408	7.70	1.7397
0.25	0.3559	2.75	0.6327	5.25	1.0513	7.75	1.7586
0.30	0.3605	2.80	0.6393	5.30	1.0619	7.80	1.7778
0.35	0.3652	2.85	0.6461	5.35	1.0725	7.85	1.7972
0.40	0.3699	2.90	0.6529	5.40	1.0833	7.90	1.8169
0.45	0.3746	2.95	0.6598	5.45	1.0942	7.95	1.8369
0.50	0.3793	3.00	0.6667	5.50	1.1053	8.00	1.8571
0.55	0.3841	3.05	0.6736	5.55	1.1164	8.05	1.8777
0.60	0.3889	3.10	0.6807	5.60	1.1276	8.10	1.8986
0.65	0.3937	3.15	0.6878	5.65	1.1390	8.15	1.9197
0.70	0.3986	3.20	0.6949	5.70	1.1505	8.20	1.9412
0.75	0.4035	3.25	0.7021	5.75	1.1622	8.25	1.9629
0.80	0.4085	3.30	0.7094	5.80	1.1739	8.30	1.9851
0.85	0.4134	3.35	0.7167	5.85	1.1858	8.35	2.0075
0.90	0.4185	3.40	0.7241	5.90	1.1978	8.40	2.0303
0.95	0.4235	3.45	0.7316	5.95	1.2099	8.45	2.0534
1.00	0.4286	3.50	0.7391	6.00	1.2222	8.50	2.0796
1.05	0.4337	3.55	0.7467	6.05	1.2346	8.55	2.1008
1.10	0.4388	3.60	0.7544	6.10	1.2472	8.60	2.1250
1.15	0.4440	3.65	0.7621	6.15	1.2599	8.65	2.1496
1.20	0.4493	3.70	0.7699	6.20	1.2727	8.70	2.1746
1.25	0.4545	3.75	0.7778	6.25	1.2857	8.75	2.2000
1.30	0.4599	3.80	0.7857	6.30	1.2989	8.80	2.2258
1.35	0.4652	3.85	0.7937	6.35	1.3121	8.85	2.2520
1.40	0.4706	3.90	0.8018	6.40	1.3256	8.90	2.2787
1.45	0.4760	3.95	0.8099	6.45	1.3392	8.95	2.3058
1.50	0.4815	4.00	0.8182	6.50	1.3529	9.00	2.3333
1.55	0.4870	4.05	0.8265	6.55	1.3669	9.05	2.3613
1.60	0.4925	4.10	0.8349	6.60	1.3809	9.10	2.3898
1.65	0.4981	4.15	0.8433	6.65	1.3952	9.15	2.4188
1.70	0.5038	4.20	0.8518	6.70	1.4096	9.20	2.4483
1.75	0.5094	4.25	0.8605	6.75	1.4242	9.25	2.4783
1.80	0.5152	4.30	0.8692	6.80	1.4390	9.30	2.5088
1.85	0.5209	4.35	0.8779	6.85	1.4540	9.35	2.5398
1.90	0.5267	4.40	0.8868	6.90	1.4691	9.40	2.5714
1.95	0.5326	4.45	0.8957	6.95	1.4845	9.45	2.6036
2.00	0.5385	4.50	0.9048	7.00	1.5000	9.50	2.6364
2.05	0.5444	4.55	0.9139	7.05	1.5157	9.55	2.6697
2.10	0.5504	4.60	0.9231	7.10	1.5316	9.60	2.7037
2.15	0.5564	4.65	0.9324	7.15	1.5478	9.65	2.7383
2.20	0.5625	4.70	0.9417	7.20	1.5641	9.70	2.7736
2.25	0.5686	4.75	0.9512	7.25	1.5806	9.75	2.8095
2.30	0.5748	4.80	0.9608	7.30	1.5974	9.80	2.8462
2.35	0.5810	4.85	0.9704	7.35	1.6144	9.85	2.8835
2.40	0.5873	4.90	0.9802	7.40	1.6316	9.90	2.9216
2.45	0.5936	4.95	0.9900	7.45	1.6490	9.95	2.9604

SOURCE: From Helson and Himelstein by permission of the *American Journal of Psychology*.

References[1]

Abe, S. Experimental study on the co-relation between time and space. *Tohoku Psychologica Folia*, 1935, **3**, 53–68.

Adams, J. A. Psychomotor performance as a function of intertrial rest interval. *J. exp. Psychol.*, 1954, **48**, 131–133.

Adams, J. A. Human tracking behavior. *Psychol. Bull.*, 1961, **58**, 55–79.

Adams, J. K. Laboratory studies of behavior without awareness. *Psychol. Bull.*, 1957, **54**, 383–405.

Adler, A. Study of organ inferiority and its psychical compensation. *Nerv. ment. Dis. Monogr.*, Ser. 1917a, No. 24.

Adler, A. *The Neurotic Constitution*. New York: Moffat, Yard & Co., 1917b.

Adler, A. *The Practice and Theory of Individual Psychology*. New York: Harcourt, Brace & World, 1924.

Adler, A. *The Problems of Neurosis*. New York: Cosmopolitan Book, 1939.

Adorno, T. W., Frenkel-Brunswik, E., Levinson, D. J., & Sanford, R. N. *The Authoritarian Personality*. New York: Harper & Row, 1950.

Allport, F. H. *Social Psychology*. Boston: Houghton Mifflin, 1924.

Allport, F. H. *Theories of Perception and the Concept of Structure*. New York: Wiley, 1955.

Allport, G. W. The historical background of modern social psychology. In G. Lindzey (Ed.), *Handbook of Social Psychology*. Cambridge, Mass.: Addison-Wesley, 1954.

[1] Discussion of some of the references cited here had to be omitted from the final version of this book. They are included because they are germane to various problems discussed in the text.

Allport, G. W., & Allport, F. H. *A-S Reaction Study*. Houghton Mifflin, 1928.

Allport, G. W., & Odbert, H. S. Trait-names: a psycholexical study. *Psychol. Monogr.*, 1936, **47** (Whole No. 211).

Anastasi, A. The estimation of area. *J. gen. Psychol.*, 1936, **14**, 201–225.

Anderson, N. S., & Klemmer, E. T. A review of stimulus variables of patterns. Symposium on pattern recognition sponsored by Project Michigan, Ann Arbor, October 21–23, 1957.

Andrews, R. B. Reading power unlimited. *Texas Outlook*, 1949, **33**, 20-21.

Archer, E. J. Re-evaluation of the meaningfulness of all possible CVC trigrams. *Psychol. Monogr.*, 1960, **74** (Whole No. 497).

Arnheim, R. *Art and Visual Perception*. Berkeley: University of California Press, 1954.

Asch, S. E. Studies in the principles of judgments and atitudes: Determination of judgments by group and by ego standards. *J. soc. Psychol.*, 1940, **12**, 433–465.

Asch, S. E. Forming impressions of personality. *J. abnorm. soc. Psychol.*, 1946, **41**, 258–290.

Asch, S. E. The doctrine of suggestion, prestige, and imitation in social psychology. *Psychol. Rev.*, 1948, **55**, 250–276.

Asch, S. E. *Social Psychology*. New York: Prentice-Hall, 1952.

Atkinson, J. W., & McClelland, D. C. The projective expression of needs. II. The effect of different intensitites of the hunger drive on thematic apperception. *J. exp. Psychol.*, 1948, **38**, 643–658.

Attneave, F. Dimensions of similarity. *Amer. J. Psychol.*, 1950, **63**, 516–556.

Attneave, F. Psychological probability as a function of experienced frequency. *J. exp. Psychol.*, 1953, **46**, 81–86.

Attneave, F., & Arnoult, M. D. The quantitative study of shape and pattern perception. *Psychol. Bull.*, 1956, **53**, 452–471.

Ausubel, D. P. Introduction to a threshold concept of primary drives. *J. gen. Psychol.*, 1956, **54**, 209–229.

Ausubel, D. P. The use of advance organizers in the learning and retention of meaningful verbal material. *J. educ. Psychol.*, 1960, **51**, 267–272.

Bagchi, B. K. The adaptation and variability of response of the human brain rhythm. *J. Psychol.*, 1936, **3**, 463–485.

Baker, K. E., & Dudek, F. J. Weight scales from ratio judgments and comparisons of existent weight scales. *J. exp. Psychol.*, 1955, **50**, 293–308.

Baker, L. E. The influence of subliminal stimuli upon verbal behavior. *J. exp. Psychol.*, 1937, **20**, 84–100.

Baker, R. A., & Osgood, S. W. Discrimination transfer along a pitch continuum. *J. exp. Psychol.*, 1954, **48**, 241–246.

Baker, S. J. Constancy factors in language: introduction to the language of thought. *J. gen. Psychol.*, 1955a, **52**, 255–283.

Baker, S. J. The theory of silences. *J. gen. Psychol.*, 1955*b*, **53**, 145–167.

Ball, J. H. The influence of background and residual stimuli upon the measurement of attitudes. M.A. thesis, University of Texas, Austin, 1953.

Bandura, A. Psychotherapy as a learning process. *Psychol. Bull.*, 1961, **58**, 143–159.

Bartley, S. H. The psychophysiology of vision. In S. S. Stevens (Ed.), *Handbook of Experimental Psychology*. New York: Wiley, 1951.

Bartley, S. H., & Chute, Eloise. *Fatigue and Impairment in Man*. New York: McGraw-Hill, 1947.

Bass, B. M., Wurster, C. R., Doll, E. A., & Clair, D. J. Situational and personality factors in leadership among sorority women. *Psychol. Monogr.*, 1953, **67** (Whole No. 366).

Bateson, G. Cultural determinants of personality. In J. McV. Hunt (Ed.), *Personality and the Behavior Disorders*. New York: Ronald, 1944.

Bateson, G. A theory of play and fantasy. *Psychiat. Res. Rep.*, 1955, **2**, 39–51.

Bateson, G., Jackson, D. D., Haley, J., & Weakland, J. Toward a theory of schizophrenia. *Behavioral Sci.*, 1956, **1**, 251–264.

Battersby, W. S., Krieger, H. P., & Bender, M. B. Visual and tactile discriminative learning in patients with cerebral tumors. *Amer. J. Psychol.*, 1955, **68**, 562–574.

Battig, W. F., Nagel, E. H., & Brogden, W. J. The effects of error magnification and marker size on bidimensional compensatory tracking. *Amer. J. Psychol.*, 1955, **68**, 585–594.

Baughman, E. E. The role of the stimulus in Rorschach responses. *Psychol. Bull.*, 1958, **55**, 121–147.

Beach, F. A. Instinctive behavior: reproductive activities. In S. S. Stevens (Ed.), *Handbook of Experimental Psychology*. New York: Wiley, 1951.

Beebe-Center, J. G. The law of affective equilibrium. *Amer. J. Psychol.*, 1929, **41**, 54–69.

Beebe-Center, J. G. *Pleasantness and Unpleasantness*. New York: Van Nostrand, 1932.

Beebe-Center, J. G. Feeling and Emotion. In H. Helson (Ed.), *Theoretical Foundations of Psychology*. New York: Van Nostrand, 1951.

Beebe-Center, J. G., & Waddell, D. A general psychological scale of taste. *J. Psychol.*, 1948, **26**, 517–524.

Behar, I., & Bevan, W. The perceived duration of auditory and visual intervals: cross-modal comparison and interaction. *Amer. J. Psychol.*, 1961, **74**, 17–26.

Beloff, H. Two forms of social conformity: acquiescence and conventionality. *J. abnorm. soc. Psychol.*, 1958, **56**, 99–104.

Benedetti, D. T. A situational determiner of the Einstellungs-effect. *J. gen. Psychol.*, 1956, **54**, 271–278.

Benussi, V. Versuche zur Bestimmung der Gestaltzeit. *VI Kongr. f. exptl. Psychol.,* Göttingen, 1914.

Berg, E. A. A simple objective technique for measuring flexibility in thinking. *J. gen. Psychol.,* 1948, **39,** 15–22.

Berkowitz, L. The judgmental process in personality functioning. *Psychol. Rev.,* 1960, **67,** 130–142.

Bernstein, L. The examiner as an inhibiting factor in clinical testing. *J. consult. Psychol.,* 1956, **20,** 287–290.

Bevan, W. Perception: evolution of a concept. *Psychol. Rev.,* 1958, **65,** 34–55.

Bevan, W. The pooling mechanism and the phenomena of reinforcement. In O. J. Harvey (Ed.), *Motivation and Social Interaction.* New York: Ronald, 1963.

Bevan, W. The concept of adaptation in modern psychology. In M. A. Goodsky (Ed.), *The Application of Biological Principles to the Development of Physical Systems.* New York: Prentice-Hall, 1963*b.*

Bevan, W., & Adamson, R. Reinforcers and reinforcement: Their relation to maze performance. *J. exp. Psychol.,* 1960, **59,** 226–232.

Bevan, W., & Adamson, R. Internal referents and the concept of reinforcement. In N. F. Washburne (Ed.), *Decisions, Values, and Groups,* Vol. 2. New York: Pergamon, 1963.

Bevan, W., Barker, H., & Pritchard, Joan F. The Newhall scaling method, psychophysical bowing, and adaptation level. *J. gen. Psychol.,* 1963, **69,** 95–111.

Bevan, W., & Darby, C. L. Patterns of experience and the constancy of an indifference point for perceived weight. *Amer. J. Psychol.,* 1955, **68,** 575–584.

Bevan, W., & Dukes, W. F. Value and the Weber constant in the perception of distance. *Amer. J. Psychol.,* 1951, **64,** 580–584.

Bevan, W., Maier, R. A., & Helson, H. The influence of context upon the estimation of number. *Amer. J. Psychol.,* 1963, **76,** 464–469.

Bevan, W., & Pritchard, Joan F. The effect of subliminal tones upon the judgment of loudness. *J. exp. Psychol.,* 1963, **66,** 23–29.

Bevan, W., & Saugstad, P. Breadth of experience, ease of discrimination, and efficiency of generalization. *Brit. J. Psychol.,* 1955, **46,** 13–19.

Bevan, W., & Zener, K. Some influences of past experience upon the perceptual thresholds of visual form. *Amer. J. Psychol.,* 1952, **65,** 434–442.

Birch, H. G. The effect of socially disapproved labelling upon a well-structured attitude. *J. abnorm. soc. Psychol.,* 1945, **40,** 301–310.

Bishop, R. Points of neutrality in social attitudes of delinquents and non-delinquents. *Psychometrika,* 1940, **5,** 35–45.

Bjerstedt, Å. *Interpretations of Sociometric Choice Status.* Lund (Sweden): CWK Gleerup, 1956.

Bjorkman, M. Some relationships between psychophysical parameters. *Rep. psychol. Lab.,* University of Stockholm, 1958, No. 65.

Black, R., Adamson, R., & Bevan, W. Runway behavior as a function of apparent intensity of shock. *J. comp. physiol. Psychol.,* 1961, **54**, 270–274.

Black, R. W., & Bevan, W. The effect of subliminal shock upon judged intensity of weak shock. *Amer. J. Psychol.,* 1960, **73**, 262–267.

Blackwell, H. R. The influence of data collection procedures upon psychophysical measurements of two sensory functions. *J. exp. Psychol.,* 1952, **44**, 306–315.

Blake, R. R., Berkowitz, H., Bellamy, R. Q., & Mouton, J. S. Volunteering as an avoidance act. *J. abnorm. soc. Psychol.,* 1956, **53**, 154–156.

Blake, R. R., Helson, H., & Mouton, J. S. The generality of conforming behavior as a function of factual anchorage, difficulty of task, and amount of social pressure. *J. Pers.,* 1957, **25**, 294–305.

Blake, R. R., & Mouton, J. S. Present and future implications of social psychology for law and lawyers. *J. pub. Law,* 1955, **3**, 352–369.

Blake, R. R., & Mouton, J. S. Evaluation of the simulated group technic for studying social behavior. In R. R. Blake and H. Helson (Eds.), *Situational and Personal Factors in Conforming Behavior.* Air University, School of Aviation Medicine Report No. 56–86. Randolph AFB, Texas, 1956.

Blake, R. R., Rosenbaum, M., & Duryea, R. A. Gift-giving as a function of group standards. *Human Relations,* 1955, **8**, 61–73.

Block, W. E. Adaptation-level theory: paradigmatic application to projective testing. *J. clin. Psychol.,* 1962, **18**, 466–468.

Boardman, W. K., & Goldstone, S. Effects of subliminal anchors upon judgments of size. *Percept. mot. Skills,* 1962, **14**, 475–482.

Bonney, W. C., & George, C. E. Adaptive behavior and adaptation-level theory. *Tech. Rep. No. 3,* Office of Naval Research Project NR 174-054, Contract Nonr 2119 (01), September, 1959.

Boring, E. G. Urban's tables and the method of constant stimuli. *Amer. J. Psychol.,* 1917, **28**, 280–292.

Boring, E. G. *The Physical Dimensions of Consciousness.* New York: Appleton-Century-Crofts, 1933.

Boring, E. G. Koffka's "Principles of Gestalt Psychology." *Psychol. Bull.,* 1936, **33**, 59–69.

Boring, E. G. *Sensation and Perception in the History of Experimental Psychology.* New York: Appleton-Century-Crofts, 1942.

Boring, E. G. The moon illusion. *Amer. J. Physics,* 1943, **11**, 55–60.

Boring, E. G. Dual role of the Zeitgeist in scientific creativity. *Sci. mon.,* 1955, **80**, 103–106.

Bower, G. H. A contrast effect in differential conditioning. *J. exp. Psychol.,* 1961, **62**, 196–199.

Bower, G. H. The influence of graded reductions in reward and prior frustrating events upon the magnitude of the frustration effect. *J. comp. physiol. Psychol.*, 1962, **55**, 582–587.

Brackmann, J., & Collier, C. The dependence of probability of response on size of step interval in the method of limits. *J. exp. Psychol.*, 1958, **55**, 423–428.

Bragiel, R. M., & Perkins, C. C., Jr. Conditioned stimulus intensity and response speed. *J. exp. Psychol.*, 1954, **47**, 437–441.

Braly, K. W. The influence of past experience in visual perception. *J. exp. Psychol.*, 1933, **16**, 613–643.

Braun, H. W., Russell, R. W., & Patton, R. A. Duration of decrements in learning and retention following electroshock convulsions in the white rat. *J. comp. physiol. Psychol.*, 1949, **42**, 87–106.

Bridgman, P. W. *The Logic of Modern Physics*. New York: Macmillan, 1928.

Brink, F., Jr. Excitation and conduction in the neuron. In S. S. Stevens (Ed.), *Handbook of Experimental Psychology*. New York: Wiley, 1951.

Broadbent, D. E., Ladefoged, P., & Lawrence, W. Vowel sounds and perceptual constancy. *Nature*, 1956, **178**, 815–816.

Brody, A. L. Statistical learning theory applied to an instrumental avoidance situation. *J. exp. Psychol.*, 1957, **54**, 240–245.

Brogden, W. J. Sensory pre-conditioning with human subjects. *J. exp. Psychol.*, 1947, **37**, 527–539.

Brogden, W. J. Sensory conditioning measured by the facilitation of auditory acuity. *J. exp. Psychol.*, 1950, **40**, 512–519.

Brogden, W. J. Animal studies of learning. In S. S. Stevens (Ed.), *Handbook of Experimental Psychology*. New York: Wiley, 1951a, 508–612.

Brogden, W. J. Some theoretical considerations of learning. *Psychol. Rev.*, 1951b, **58**, 224–229.

Brogden, W. J., & Gregg, L. W. Studies of sensory conditioning measured by the facilitation of auditory acuity. *J. exp. Psychol.*, 1951, **42**, 384–389.

Bronk, D. W. The mechanism of sensory end organs. *Res. Publ. Assoc. nerv. ment. Dis.*, 1935, **15**, 60–82.

Brown, D. R. Stimulus-similarity and the anchoring of subjective scales. *Amer. J. Psychol.*, 1953, **66**, 199–214.

Brown, F. A., Jr. Living clocks. *Science*, 1959, **139**, 1535–1544.

Brown, J. F. Ueber gesehene Geschwindigkeiten. *Psych. Forsch.*, 1928, **10**, 84–101.

Brown, J. F. The visual perception of velocity. *Psych. Forsch.*, 1931, **14**, 199–232.

Bruell, J. H., & Albee, G. W. Effect of asymmetrical retinal stimulation on the perception of the median plane. *Percept. mot. Skills*, 1955a, **5**, 133–139.

Bruell, J. H., & Albee, G. W. Notes toward a motor theory of visual ego-centric localization. *Psychol. Rev.*, 1955*b*, **62**, 391–400.

Bruell, J. H., & Albee, G. W. A new illusion of apparent movement and the concept of retinal local signs. *J. Psychol.*, 1956, **41**, 55–59.

Bruner, J. S., & Goodman, C. C. Value and need as organizing factors in perception. *J. abnorm. soc. Psychol.*, 1947, **42**, 33–44.

Bruner, J. S., Goodnow, J. J., & Austin, G. A. *A Study of Thinking*. New York: Wiley, 1956.

Bruner, J. S., & Postman, L. Symbolic value as an organizing factor in perception. *J. soc. Psychol.*, 1948, **27**, 203–208.

Brunswik, E. Probability as a determiner of rat behavior. *J. exp. Psychol.*, 1939, **25**, 175–197.

Brunswik, E. Organismic achievement and environmental probability. *Psychol. Rev.*, 1943, **50**, 255–272.

Brunswik, E., & Herma, H. Probability learning of perceptual cues in the establishment of a weight illusion. *J. exp. Psychol.*, 1951, **41**, 281–290.

Bühler, C. Maturation and motivation. *Personality*, 1951, **1**, 184–211.

Bühler, K. The skywise and neighborwise navigation of ants and bees. *Acta Psychologica*, 1951–1952, **8**, 225–263.

Bühler, K. The essentials of contact navigation. *Acta Psychologica*, 1954, **10**, 278–316.

Bunch, M. E. The concept of motivation. *J. gen. Psychol.*, 1958, **58**, 189–205.

Burnett, N. C., & Dallenbach, K. M. The experience of heat. *Amer. J. Psychol.*, 1927, **38**, 418–431.

Burnham, R. W. Bezold's color-mixture effect. *Amer. J. Psychol.*, 1953, **66**, 377–385.

Burns, M., & Dallenbach, K. M. The adaptation of cutaneous pain. *Amer. J. Psychol.*, 1933, **45**, 111–117.

Burrow, T. Emotion and the social crisis: a problem in phylobiology. In M. L. Reymert (Ed.), *Feelings and Emotions*. New York: McGraw-Hill, 1950.

Burtt, H. E., & Falkenburg, D. R. The influence of majority and expert opinion on religious attitudes. *J. soc. Psychol.*, 1941, **14**, 269–278.

Buss, A. H. Some determinants of rigidity in discrimination-reversal learning. *J. exp. Psychol.*, 1952, **44**, 222–227.

Buss, A. H. The effect of item style on social desirability and frequency of endorsement. *J. consult. Psychol.*, 1959, **23**, 510–513.

Butler, J. M. The interaction of client and therapist. *J. abnorm. soc. Psychol.*, 1952, **47**, 366–378.

Butler, R. A. Incentive conditions which influence visual exploration. *J. exp. Psychol.*, 1954, **48**, 19–23.

Buytendijk, F. J. J. The phenomenological approach to the problem of feelings and emotions. In M. L. Reymert (Ed.), *Feelings and Emotions*. New York: McGraw-Hill, 1950.

Cahn, E. *The Moral Decision*. Bloomington: Indiana University Press, 1956.

Caldwell, W. E. The mathematical formulation of a unified field theory. *Psychol. Rev.*, 1953, **60**, 64–72.

Cameron, N. The functional psychoses. In J. McV. Hunt (Ed.), *Personality and the Behavior Disorders*. New York: Ronald, 1944.

Campbell, D. T., & Kral, T. P. Transposition away from a rewarded stimulus card to a nonrewarded one as a function of a shift in background. *J. comp. physiol. Psychol.*, 1958, **51**, 592–595.

Campbell, D. T., Hunt, W. A., & Lewis, N. A. The effects of assimilation and contrast in judgments of clinical materials. *Amer. J. Psychol.*, 1957, **70**, 347–360.

Campbell, D. T., Lewis, N. A., & Hunt, W. A. Context effects with judgmental language that is absolute, extensive, and extra-experimentally anchored. *J. exp. Psychol.*, 1958, **55**, 220–228.

Cannon, W. B. *The Wisdom of the Body*. (2nd ed.) New York: Norton, 1939.

Canter, R. R., & Hirsch, J. An experimental comparison of several psychological scales of weight. *Amer. J. Psychol.*, 1955, **68**, 645–649.

Cantril, H. The intensity of an attitude. *J. abnorm. soc. Psychol.*, 1946, **41**, 129–135.

Carmichael, L. Ontogenetic Development. In S. S. Stevens (Ed.), *Handbook of Experimental Psychology*. New York: Wiley, 1951.

Carmichael, L., & Dearborn, W. F. *Reading and Visual Fatigue*. Boston: Houghton Mifflin, 1947.

Carmichael, L., Kennedy, J. L., & Mead, L. C. Some recent approaches to the experimental study of human fatigue. *Proc. nat. Acad. Sci.*, 1949, **35**, 691–696.

Carr, H. Maze studies with the white rat. 1. Normal animals. *J. Animal Behav.*, 1917, **7**, 259–275.

Carr, H. A. *Psychology*. New York: Longmans (David McKay Co.), 1925.

Carr, H. A., & Kingsbury, F. A. The concept of traits. *Psychol. Rev.*, 1938, **45**, 497–524.

Carterette, E. C. Loudness adaptation for bands of noise. *J. acoust. Soc. Amer.*, 1956, **28**, 865–871.

Cartwright, D. Decision-time in relation to the differentiation of the phenomenal field. *Psychol. Rev.*, 1941a, **48**, 425–442.

Cartwright, D. The relation of decision-time to the categories of response. *Amer. J. Psychol.*, 1941b, **54**, 174–196.

Cattell, R. B. Concepts and methods in the measurement of group syntality. *Psychol. Rev.*, 1948, **55**, 48–63.

Cattell, R. B., & Luborsky, L. B. Personality factors in response to humor. *J. abnorm soc. Psychol.*, 1947, **42**, 402–421.

Chapanis, A. The reconstruction of abbreviated printed messages. *J. exp. Psychol.*, 1954, **48**, 496–510.

Chapman, D. W., & Volkmann, J. A social determinant of the level of aspiration. *J. abnorm. soc. Psychol.*, 1939, **34**, 225–238.

Chein, I. The genetic factor in ahistorical psychology. *J. gen. Psychol.*, 1947, **36**, 151–172.

Christensen, P. R., Guilford, J. P., & Wilson, R. C. Relations of creative responses to working time and instructions. *J. exp. Psychol.*, 1957, **53**, 82–88.

Christman, R. J. Shifts in pitch as a function of prolonged stimulation with pure tones. *Amer. J. Psychol.*, 1954, **67**, 484–491.

Clausen, J. An evaluation of experimental methods of time judgment. *J. exp. Psychol.*, 1950, **40**, 756–761.

Clausen, J. Gjesvik, A., & Urdal, A. Repetition effect in pain threshold determination. *J. gen. Psychol.*, 1954, **51**, 185–192.

Clay, H. M. Changes of performance with age on similar tasks of varying complexity. *Brit. J. Psychol.*, 1954, **45**, 7–13.

Cobliner, W. G. Intra-communication and attitude: a methodological note. *J. Psychol.*, 1955, **39**, 253–267.

Cofer, C. N. Verbal behavior in relation to reasoning and values. In H. Guetzkow (Ed.), *Groups, Leadership and Men*. Pittsburgh: Carnegie Press, 1951.

Cofer, C. N., & Shevitz, R. Word-association as a function of word-frequency. *Amer. J. Psychol.*, 1952, **65**, 75–79.

Coffin, T. E. Some conditions of suggestion and suggestibility: a study of certain attitudinal and situational factors influencing the process of suggestion. *Psychol. Monogr.*, 1941, **53** (Whole No. 4).

Cohen, J. *Humanistic Psychology*. London: Allen & Unwin, 1958.

Cohen, J., Hansel, C. E. M., & Sylvester, J. D. A new phenomenon in time judgment. *Nature*, 1953, **172**, 901–903.

Cohen, J., Hansel, C. E. M., & Sylvester, J. D. Interdependence of temporal and auditory judgments. *Nature*, 1954, **174**, 642.

Cohen, J., Hansel, C. E. M., & Sylvester, J. D. Interdependence in judgments of space, time, and movement. *Acta Psychologica*, 1955, **11**, 360–372.

Combs, A. W. A phenomenological approach to adjustment theory. *J. abnorm. soc. Psychol.*, 1949, **44**, 29–35.

Coombs, C. E. Some hypotheses for the analysis of qualitative variables. *Psychol. Rev.*, 1948, **55**, 167–174.

Coser, L. *The Functions of Social Conflict*. New York: Free Press, 1956.

Cowen, E. L., & Beier, E. G. The influence of "threat-expectancy" on perception. *J. Pers.*, 1950, **19**, 85-94.

Crespi, L. P. Quantitative variation in incentive and performance in the white rat. *Amer. J. Psychol.*, 1942, **55**, 467–517.

Crespi, L. P. Amount of reinforcement and level of performance. *Psychol. Rev.*, 1944, **51**, 341–357.

Crutchfield, R. S. Conformity and character. *Amer. Psychol.*, 1955, **10**, 191–198.

Culbert, S. S. Directional after-effects following systematic distortion of the visual field. *J. Psychol.*, 1954, **37**, 81–93.

Culbert, S. S., & Posner, M. I. Human habituation to an acoustical energy distribution spectrum. *J. appl. Psychol.*, 1960, **44**, 263–266.

Culler, A. J. Interference and adaptability. *Arch. Psychol.*, 1912 (Whole No. 24).

Darrow, C. W. The equation of the galvanic skin reflex curve. I. The dynamics of reaction in relation to excitation-background. *J. gen. Psychol.*, 1937, **16**, 285–309.

Darrow, C. W. Cerebral concomitants of autonomic changes: observations on anterior-posterior cerebral dominance. Discussion on "recent advances in autonomic nervous system psychophysiology." Symposium held at the 1952 meetings of the American Psychological Association, Washington, D.C. (J. I. Lacey, Chairman).

Darrow, C. W., & Henry, C. E. Psychophysiology of stress. *Human Factors in Undersea Warfare*. Washington, D.C.: National Research Council, 1949.

Darrow, C. W., Vieth, R. N., & Wilson, J. Electroencephalographic "blocking" and "adaptation." *Science*, 1957, **126**, 74–75.

Dashiell, J. F. Affective value-distances as a determinant of esthetic judgment-times. *Amer. J. Psychol.*, 1937, **50**, 57–67.

Datel, W. E., & Seward, J. P. On the persistence of ear-scratching response in the rat. *J. abnorm. soc. Psychol.*, 1952, **47**, 58–61.

Davidon, R. S. The effects of symbols, shift, and manipulation upon the number of concepts attained. *J. exp. Psychol.*, 1952, **44**, 70–79.

Davis, R. C. Motor effects of strong auditory stimuli. *J. exp. Psychol.*, 1948, **38**, 257–275.

Davis, R. C. Motor responses to auditory stimuli above and below threshold. *J. exp. Psychol.*, 1950, **40**, 107–120.

Davis, R. C. The stimulus trace in effectors and its relation to judgment responses. *J. exp. Psychol.*, 1952, **44**, 377–390.

Davis, R. C. The domain of homeostasis. *Psychol. Rev.*, 1958, **65**, 8–13.

Davis, R. C. & Van Liere, D. W. Adaptation of the muscular tension response to gunfire. *J. exp. Psychol.*, 1949, **39**, 114–117.

Day, R. H. The effect of size of target on accuracy of aim. *Amer. J. Psychol.*, 1954, **67**, 659–667.

Deese, J. Some problems in the theory of vigilance. *Psychol. Rev.*, 1955, **62**, 359–368.

De La Garza, C. O., & Worchel, P. Time and space orientation in schizophrenics. *J. abnorm. soc. Psychol.*, 1956, **52**, 191–194.

Delgado, J. M. R. Positive reinforcement induced by intracerebral stimulation in the monkey. *J. comp. physiol. Psychol.*, 1958, **51**, 6–10.

Delgado, J. M. R., Roberts, W. W., & Miller, N. E. Learning motivated by electrical stimulation of the brain. *Amer. J. Physiol.*, 1954, **179**, 587–593.

Dempsey, E. W. Homeostasis. In S. S. Stevens (Ed.), *Handbook of Experimental Psychology.* New York: Wiley, 1951.

DeSoto, C. Two-category judgments of sequences of stimuli of two values. *J. exp. Psychol.*, 1958, **55**, 34–38.

Dey, M. K., & Ammons, R. B. Stimulation-maturation prediction of distribution of phenomena in compensatory pursuit. *Can. J. Psychol.*, 1956, **10**, 139–146.

Djang, S. The role of past experience in the visual apprehension of masked forms. *J. exp. Psychol.*, 1937, **20**, 29–59.

Dobzhansky, T. The genetic basis of evolution. *Sci. Amer.*, 1950, **182**, 32 ff.

Dole, Gertrude. Endocannibalism among the Amahuaca Indians. *N.Y. Acad. Sci.*, 1962, **24**, 567–573.

Dollard, J., & Miller, N. E. *Personality and Psychotherapy.* New York: McGraw-Hill, 1950.

Dollin, Adelaide, & Sakoda, J. M. The effect of order of presentation on perception of TAT pictures. *J. consult. Psychol.*, 1962, **26**, 340–344.

Doughty, J. M. The effect of psychophysical method and context on pitch and loudness functions. *J. exp. Psychol.*, 1949, **39**, 729–745.

Drever, J. Early learning and the perception of space. *Amer. J. Psychol.*, 1955, **68**, 605–614.

Droba, D. D. A scale of militarism-pacificism. *J. educ. Psychol.*, 1931, **22**, 96–111.

Duffy, Elizabeth. Emotion: an example of the need for reorientation in psychology. *Psychol. Rev.*, 1934, **41**, 184–198.

Duffy, Elizabeth. An explanation of "emotional" phenomena without the use of the concept "emotion." *J. gen. Psychol.*, 1941*a*, **25**, 283–293.

Duffy, Elizabeth. The conceptual categories of psychology: a suggestion for revision. *Psychol. Rev.*, 1941*b*, **48**, 177–203.

Duffy, Elizabeth. Leeper's motivational theory of "emotion." *Psychol. Rev.*, 1948, **55**, 324–328.

Duffy, E., & Lacey, O. L. Adaptation in energy mobilization: changes in general level of palmar skin conductance. *J. exp. Psychol.*, 1946, **36**, 437–452.

Dulsky, S. G. The effect of a change of background on recall and relearning. *J. exp. Psychol.*, 1935, **18**, 725–740.

Duncan, C. P. On the similarity between reactive inhibition and neural satiation. *Amer. J. Psychol.*, 1956, **69**, 227–235.

Duncker, K. Experimental modification of children's food preferences through social suggestion. *J. abnorm. soc. Psychol.*, 1938, **33**, 489–507.

Duncker, K. On problem solving. *Psychol. Monogr.*, 1945, **58** (Whole No. 270).

Dusek, E. R., Teichner, W. H., & Kobrick, J. L. The effects of the angular relationships between the observer and the base-surround on relative depth-discrimination. *Amer. J. Psychol.*, 1955, **68**, 438–443.

Dyson, F. J. Innovation in Physics. *Sci. Amer.*, 1958, **199**, 74–99.

Edelberg, R. The relationship between the galvanic skin response, vasoconstriction, and tactile sensitivity. *J. exp. Psychol.*, 1961, **62**, 187–195.

Edwards, A. L. A critique of "neutral" items in attitude scales constructed by the method of equal appearing intervals. *Psychol. Rev.*, 1946, **53**, 159–169.

Ellson, D. G. Hallucinations produced by sensory conditioning. *J. exp. Psychol.*, 1941*a*, **28**, 1–20.

Ellson, D. G. Experimental extinction of an hallucination produced by sensory conditioning. *J. exp. Psychol.*, 1941*b*, **28**, 350–361.

Engen, T. An evaluation of a method for developing ratio-scales. *Amer. J. Psychol.*, 1956, **69**, 92–95.

Engen, T., & Levy, N. The influence of standards on psychophysical judgments. *Percept. mot. Skills*, 1955, **5**, 193–197.

Engen, T., & Tulünay, Ü. Some sources of error in half-heaviness judgments. *J. exp. Psychol.*, 1957, **54**, 208–212.

Eriksen, C. W., & Hake, H. W. Multidimensional stimulus differences and accuracy of discrimination. *J. exp. Psychol.*, 1955, **50**, 155–160.

Eriksen, C. W., & Hake, H. W. Anchor effects in absolute judgments. *J. exp. Psychol.*, 1957, **53**, 132–138.

Essenberg, J. M. The deterioration of intelligence of albino rats chronically poisoned by nicotine. *J. Psychol.*, 1955, **40**, 209–213.

Estes, W. K. Toward a statistical theory of learning. *Psychol. Rev.*, 1950, **57**, 94–107.

Estes, W. K. Learning. *Annu. Rev. Psychol.*, 1956, **7**, 1–38.

Estes, W. K., & Burke, C. J. A theory of stimulus variability in learning. *Psychol. Rev.*, 1953, **60**, 276–286.

Estes, W. K., & Burke, C. J. Application of a statistical model to simple discrimination learning in human subjects. *J. exp. Psychol.*, 1955, **50**, 81–88.

Estes, W. K., Burke, C. J., Atkinson, R. C., & Frankmann, J. P. Probabilistic discrimination learning. *J. exp. Psychol.*, 1957, **54**, 233–239.

Estes, W. K., & Straughan, J. H. Analysis of a verbal conditioning situation in terms of statistical learning theory. *J. exp. Psychol.*, 1954, **47**, 225–234.

Evans, R. M. *An Introduction to Color.* New York: Wiley, 1948.

Evans, R. M. The expressiveness of color. *Educ. Theatre J.*, 1954, **6**, 327–330.

Ex, J., & De Bruijn, G. L. An experimental study of the influence of mental set on the perception of identity and substitution. *Acta Psychologica*, 1956, **12**, 198–207.

Eysenck, H. J. The general factor in aesthetic judgments. *Brit. J. Psychol.*, 1940, **31**, 94–102.

Eysenck, H. J. The appreciation of humor: an experimental and theoretical study. *Brit. J. Psychol.*, 1942, **32**, 295–309.

Farnsworth, P. R. Shifts in the value of opinion items. *J. Psychol.*, 1943, **16**, 125–128.

Fehrer, E. Shifts in scale values of attitude statements as a function of the composition of the scale. *J. exp. Psychol.*, 1952, **44**, 179–188.

Feigenbaum, E. A., & Simon, H. A. Comment: The distinctiveness of stimuli. *Psychol. Rev.*, 1961, **68**, 285–288.

Ferguson, L. W. An analysis of the generality of suggestibility to group opinion. *Charact. & Pers.*, 1944, **13**, 237–243.

Fernberger, S. W., The use of equality judgments in psychophysical procedures, *Psychol. Rev.*, 1930, **37**, 107–112.

Fernberger, S. W. On absolute and relative judgments in lifted weight experiments. *Amer. J. Psychol.*, 1931, **43**, 560–578.

Festinger, L. The psychological effects of insufficient rewards. *Amer. Psychologist*, 1961, **16**, 1–11.

Fey, W. F. Correlates of certain subjective attitudes toward self and others. *J. clin. Psychol.*, 1957, **13**, 44–49.

Fiske, D. W., & Rice, L. Intra-individual variability. *Psychol. Bull.*, 1955, **52**, 217–250.

Fitts, P. M. Engineering psychology and equipment design. In S. S. Stevens (Ed.), *Handbook of Experimental Psychology.* New York: Wiley, 1951.

Fitts, P. M. The information capacity of the human motor system in controlling the amplitude of movement. *J. exp. Psychol.*, 1954, **47**, 381–391.

Fitts, P. M., & Deininger, R. L. S-R compatibility: correspondence among paired elements within stimulus and response codes. *J. exp. Psychol.*, 1954, **48**, 483–492.

Fitts, P. M., & Seeger, C. M. S-R compatibility: spatial characteristics of stimulus and response codes. *J. exp. Psychol.*, 1953, **46**, 199–210.

Flaherty, B. E., Flinn, D. E., Hauty, G. T. & Steinkamp, G. R. Psychiatry and space flight. School of Aviation Medicine, USAF Aerospace Medical Center (ATC), Brooks AFB, Texas, 1960, 60–80, 1–9.

Fletcher, J. M. Homeostasis as an explanatory principle in psychology. *Psychol. Rev.*, 1942, **49**, 80–87.

Frank, J. D. Recent studies of level of aspiration. *Psychol. Bull.*, 1941, **38**, 218–225.

Franz, S. I. How the brain works. Faculty research lecture. Los Angeles: University of California Press, 1929.

Frazier, C. H. Surgery of peripheral nerves. *Surgery, Gynecology, and Obstetrics,* 1917, **24**, 147–150.

Fredericson, E. Distributed versus massed experience in a traumatic situation. *J. abnorm. soc. Psychol.,* 1950, **45**, 259–266.

Freed, A., Chandler, P. J., Mouton, Jane S., & Blake, R. R. Stimulus and background factors in sign violation. *J. Pers.,* 1955, **23**, 499.

Freedman, J. L., & Mednick, S. A. Ease of attainment of concepts as a function of response dominance variance. *J. exp. Psychol.,* 1958, **55**, 463–466.

Freeman, J. T. Set or perceptual defense? *J. exp. Psychol.,* 1954, **48**, 283–288.

French, R. S. The discrimination of dot patterns as a function of number and average separation of dots. *J. exp. Psychol.,* 1953, **46**, 1–9.

Freud, S. *A General Introduction to Psychoanalysis* (Trans. J. Riviere). New York: Boni and Liveright, 1920.

Freud, S. *New Introductory Lectures on Psychoanalysis.* New York: Norton, 1933.

Freud, S. The antithetical sense of primal words. In E. Jones (Ed.), Collected Papers. London: Hogarth, 1953, Vol. IV, 184–191.

Frick, J. W., Guilford, J. P., Christensen, P. R., & Merrifield, P. R. A factor-analytic study of flexibility in thinking. *Educ. psychol. Measmt,* 1959, **19**, 469–496.

Fröbes, J. *Lehrbuch der experimentellen Psychologie.* St. Louis: Herder, 1923, Vol. I.

Fry, G., & Robertson, V. M. Alleged effects of figure-ground upon hue and brilliance. *Amer. J. Psychol.,* 1935, **47**, 424–435.

Furth, H. G. The effect of the size-weight illusion on adaptation level. *J. exp. Psychol.,* 1960, **60**, 150–154.

Gaier, E. L., & Bass, B. M. Effects of city familiarity on size estimation. *Psychol. Rep.,* 1956, **2**, 35–38.

Galambos, R., & Allen, R. Action of middle ear muscles in normal cats. *Fed. Proc.,* 1958, **17**, 50.

Gamow, G. *One Two Three . . . Infinity.* New York: Mentor Books, 1957.

Gardner, R. W., Holzman, P. S., & Siegal, R. S. Some variables affecting size judgments. *Percept. mot. Skills,* 1956, **6**, 285–290.

Garner, W. R. Informational analysis of absolute judgments of loudness. *J. exp. Psychol.,* 1953, **46**, 373–380.

Garner, W. R. Context effects and the validity of loudness scales. *J. exp. Psychol.*, 1954, **48**, 218–224.

Garvey, W. D. The intelligibility of speeded speech. *J. exp. Psychol.*, 1953, **45**, 102–108.

Gelb, A. Versuche auf dem Gebiet der Zeit- und Raumanschauung. *Ber. über d. VI Kongr. f. exp. Psychol. in Göttingen.* Leipzig: 1914, 36–42.

Gelb, A. Die Farbenkonstanz der Sehdinge. In G. Embden and A. Ellinger (Eds.), *Handb. d. norm. path. Physiol.*, 1929, **12**, 594–678.

Gelb, A., & Goldstein, K. Zur Psychologie des optischen Wahrnehmungs- und Erkennungsvorganges. *Arch.f.d. ges. Neurol. u. Psychiat.*, 1920, **41**, 1–142.

Gengerelli, J. A. Apparent movement in relation to homonymous and heteronymous stimulation of the cerebral hemispheres. *J. exp. Psychol.*, 1948, **38**, 592–599.

George, C. E., & Bonney, W. C. Rorschach's affect-color hypothesis and adaptation-level theory. *Psychol. Rev.*, 1956a, **63**, 294–298.

George, C. E., & Bonney, W. C. Consistency of personality in the framework of adaptation-level theory. *Navy Tech. Rep.*, 1956b, Contract NR 174-054.

Gernandt, B. E., & Thulin, G. A. Reciprocal effects upon spinal motoneurons from stimulation of bulbar reticular formation. *J. Neurophysiol.*, 1955, **18**, 113–129.

Gesell, A. The ontogenesis of infant behavior. In L. Carmichael (Ed.), *Manual of Child Psychology.* New York: Wiley, 1946.

Getman, F. H. *Outlines of Theoretical Chemistry.* New York: Wiley, 1922.

Gibbs, C. B. Transfer of training and skill assumptions in tracking tasks. *Quart. J. exp. Psychol.*, 1951, **3**, 99–110.

Gibbs, C. B. The continuous regulation of skilled response by kinesthetic feedback. *Brit. J. Psychol.*, 1954, **45**, 24–39.

Gibson, Eleanor. Improvement in perceptual judgments as a function of controlled practice or training. *Psychol. Bull.*, 1953, **50**, 401–431.

Gibson, Eleanor, & Bergman, R. The effect of training on absolute estimation of distance over the ground. *J. exp. Psychol.*, 1954, **48**, 473–482.

Gibson, J. J. Adaptation, after-effect and contrast in the perception of curved lines. *J. exp. Psychol.*, 1933, **16**, 1–31.

Gibson, J. J. Adaptation, after-effect and contrast in the perception of tilted lines. I. Quantitative studies. *J. exp. Psychol.*, 1937a, **20**, 453–467.

Gibson, J. J. Adaptation with negative after-effect. *Psychol. Rev.*, 1937b, **44**, 222–244.

Gibson, J. J. A critical review of the concept of set in contemporary experimental psychology. *Psychol. Bull.*, 1941, **38**, 781–817.

Gibson, J. J. Perception of visual surfaces. *Amer. J. Psychol.*, 1950a, **63**, 367–384.

Gibson, J. J. *The Perception of the Visual World.* Boston: Houghton Mifflin, 1950*b.*

Gibson, J. J. What is a form? *Psychol. Rev.,* 1951, **58,** 403–412.

Gibson, J. J., & Cornsweet, J. The perceived slant of visual surface—optical and geographical. *J. exp. Psychol.,* 1952, **44,** 11–15.

Gibson, J. J., Purdy, J. J., & Lawrence, L. A method of controlling stimulation for the study of spatial perception: the optical tunnel. *J. exp. Psychol.,* 1955, **50,** 1–14.

Gibson, J. J., & Robinson, Doris. Orientation in visual perception; the recognition of familiar plane forms in differing orientations. In J. J. Gibson (Ed.), *Stud. Psychol. Smith Coll.; Psychol. Monogr.,* 1935, **46,** 39–47 (Whole No. 210).

Gibson, William. Confessions of a turtle. Address, American Psychological Association annual convention, 1959. Symposium: Fertility and infertility in the artist (George Klein, Chairman).

Gilbert, G. M. Inter-sensory facilitation and inhibition. *J. gen. Psychol.,* 1941, **24,** 381–407.

Gilinsky, A. S. Relative self-estimate and the level of aspiration. *J. exp. Psychol.,* 1949, **39,** 256–259.

Glaze, J. A. The association value of nonsense syllables. *J. genet. Psychol.,* 1928, **35,** 255–269.

Goldberg, S. C. Three situational determinants of conformity to social norms. *J. abnorm. soc. Psychol.,* 1954, **49,** 325–329.

Goldings, H. On the avowal and projection of happiness. *J. Pers.,* 1954, **23,** 30–47.

Goldstein, H., & Spence, K. W. Performance in differential conditioning as a function of variation in magnitude of reward. *J. exp. Psychol.,* 1963, **65,** 86–93.

Goldstein, K., & Scheerer, M. Abstract and concrete behavior; an experimental study with special tests. *Psychol. Monogr.,* 1941, **53** (Whole No. 2).

Goldstein, M., & Rittenhouse, C. H. Knowledge of results in the acquisition and transfer of a gunnery skill. *J. exp. Psychol.,* 1954, **48,** 187–196.

Goldstein, R., & Solomon, R. L. A serial position effect in "incidental learning." *J. gen. Psychol.,* 1955, **53,** 293–298.

Goldstone, S. Psychophysics, reality and hallucinations. In L. J. West (Ed.), *Hallucinations.* New York: Grune & Stratton, 1962.

Goldstone, S., Boardman, W. K., & Lhamon, W. T. Intersensory comparison of temporal judgments. *Amer. J. Psychol.,* 1959, **57,** 243–248.

Goldstone, S., Goldfarb, J., Strong, J., & Russell, J. Replication: the effect of subliminal shock upon the judged intensity of weak shock. *Percept. mot. Skills,* 1962, **14,** 222.

Gonzalez, R. C., Gleitman, H., & Bitterman, M. E. Some observations on the depression effect. *J. comp. physiol. Psychol.*, 1962, **55**, 578–581.

Goodnow, J. J., & Postman, L. Probability learning in a problem-solving situation. *J. exp. Psychol.*, 1955, **49**, 16–22.

Gottschaldt, K. Ueber den Einfluss der Erfahrung auf die Wahrnehmung von Figuren. II. *Psychol. Forsch.*, 1929, **12**, 1–87.

Graham, C. H. Behavior, perception, and the psychophysical methods. *Psychol. Rev.*, 1950, **57**, 108–120.

Graham, C. H., & Kemp, E. H. Brightness discrimination as a function of the duration of the increment in intensity. *J. gen. Physiol.*, 1938, **21**, 635–650.

Graham, L. F., & Helson, H. Effect of background reflectance on bisection of a lightness interval. Unpublished study.

Granit, R. Centrifugal and antidromic effects on ganglion cells of retina. *J. Neurophysiol.*, 1955, **18**, 388–411.

Granit, R., & Kaada, B. R. Influence of stimulation of central nervous structures on muscle spindles in cat. *Acta physiol. Scand.*, 1952, **27**, 130–160.

Grant, D. A., & Schipper, L. M. The acquisition and extinction of conditioned eyelid responses as a function of the percentage of fixed-ratio random reinforcement. *J. exp. Psychol.*, 1952, **43**, 313–320.

Green, E. J. An anchoring effect in the operant responding of rats. *Amer. J. Psychol.*, 1954, **67**, 141–142.

Green, R. F. Transfer of skill on a following tracking task as a function of task difficulty (target size). *J. Psychol.*, 1955, **39**, 355–370.

Gregg, L. W., & Brogden, W. J. The effect of simultaneous visual stimulation on absolute auditory sensitivity. *J. exp. Psychol.*, 1952, **43**, 179–186.

Griffith, R. M. Odds adjustment by American horse-race bettors. *Amer. J. Psychol.*, 1949, **62**, 290–294.

Grinker, R. R., & Spiegel, J. P. *War Neuroses in North Africa.* New York: Josiah Macy, Jr. Foundation, 1943.

Guilford, J. P. A generalized psychophysical law. *Psychol. Rev.*, 1932, **39**, 73–85.

Guilford, J. P. The affective value of color as a function of hue, tint, and chroma. *J. exp. Psychol.*, 1934, **17**, 342–370.

Guilford, J. P. *Psychometric Methods.* (1st ed.) New York: McGraw-Hill, 1936.

Guilford, J. P. *Psychometric Methods.* (2nd ed.) New York: McGraw-Hill, 1954a.

Guilford, J. P. System in the relationship of affective value to frequency and intensity of auditory stimuli. *Amer. J. Psychol.*, 1954b, **67**, 691–695.

Guilford, J. P. Creative abilities in the arts. *Psychol. Rev.*, 1957a, **64**, 110–118.

Guilford, J. P. A revised structure of intellect. *Rep. psychol. Lab.*, No. 19, Los Angeles: University Southern California, 1957*b*.

Guilford, J. P. *Personality*. New York: McGraw-Hill, 1959.

Guilford, J. P., & Cotzin, M. Judgment of difficulty of simple tasks. *Amer. J. Psychol.*, 1941, **54**, 38–52.

Guilford, J. P., & Dingman, H. F. A validation study of ratio-judgment methods. *Amer. J. Psychol.*, 1954, **67**, 395–410.

Guilford, J. P., & Dingman, H. F. A modification of the method of equal-appearing intervals. *Amer. J. Psychol.*, 1955, **68**, 450–454.

Guilford, J. P., and Park, D. G. The effect of interpolated weights upon comparative judgments. *Amer. J. Psychol.*, 1931, **43**, 589–599.

Guilford, J. P., & Smith, Patricia C. A system of color preferences. *Amer. J. Psychol.*, 1959, **72**, 487–502.

Guth, S. K. Brightness relationships for comfortable seeing. *J. opt. Soc. Amer.*, 1951, **41**, 235–244.

Haber, R. N. Discrepancy from adaptation-level as a source of affect. *J. exp. Psychol.*, 1958, **56**, 370–375.

Hagbarth, K. E., & Kerr, D. I. B. Central influence on spinal afferent conduction. *J. Neurophysiol.*, 1954, **17**, 295–307.

Hahn, E. L., & Bartley, S. H. The apparent orientation of a luminous figure in darkness. *Amer. J. Psychol.*, 1954, **67**, 500–508.

Hake, H. W., & Hyman, R. Perception of the statistical structure of a random series of binary symbols. *J. exp. Psychol.*, 1953, **45**, 64–73.

Hall, J. F. *Psychology of Motivation*. Philadelphia: Lippincott, 1961.

Hall, K. R. L. Perceiving and naming a series of figures. *Quart. J. exp. Psychol.*, 1950, **2**, 153–162.

Halsey, R. M., & Chapanis, A. Chromaticity-confusion in a complex viewing situation. *J. opt. Soc. Amer.*, 1954, **44**, 442 ff.

Hanes, R. M. A scale of subjective brightness. *J. exp. Psychol.*, 1949*a*, **39**, 438–452.

Hanes, R. M. The construction of subjective brightness scales from fractionation data: a validation. *J. exp. Psychol.*, 1949*b*, **39**, 719–728.

Harlow, H. F. The formation of learning sets. *Psychol. Rev.*, 1949, **56**, 51–65.

Harlow, H. F. Mice, monkeys, men, and motives. *Psychol. Rev.*, 1953, **60**, 23–32.

Harris, A. J. An experiment on affective contrasts. *Amer. J. Psychol.*, 1929, **41**, 617–624.

Harris, J. D. The effect of interstimulus interval on intensity discrimination for white noise. *Amer. J. Psychol.*, 1949, **62**, 202–214.

Harris, J. D. *Some Relations between Vision and Audition*. Springfield, Ill.: Charles C Thomas, 1950.

Harris, J. D. The decline of pitch discrimination with time. *J. exp. Psychol.*, 1952, **43**, 96–99.

Harris, J. D., & Rawnsley, A. I. The locus of short duration auditory fatigue or "adaptation." *J. exp. Psychol.*, 1953, **46**, 457–461.

Hartman, B. O., & Fitts, P. M. Relation of stimulus and response amplitude to tracking performance. *J. exp. Psychol.*, 1955, **49**, 82–92.

Hartman, E. B. The influence of practice and pitch-distance between tones on the absolute identification of pitch. *Amer. J. Psychol.*, 1954, **67**, 1–14.

Hartmann, G. W. Learning as a function of the spatial interval between discriminanda. *J. genet. Psychol.*, 1936, **49**, 249–253.

Hartmann, L. Neue Verschmelzungsprobleme. *Psych. Forsch.*, 1923, **3**, 319–396.

Hastings, W., Wright, D. G., & Glueck, B. C. *Psychiatric Experiences of the Eighth Air Force.* New York: Josiah Macy, Jr. Foundation, 1944.

Hauty, G. T. Psychological adaptability: standardization of a psychomotor test and consideration of transfer effects. USAF School of Aviation Medicine, Project No. 21-0202-0005, Report No. 2, Randolph Field, Texas, 1953.

Hayakawa, S. I. *Language in Action.* New York: Harcourt, Brace & World, 1941.

Head, H. *Aphasia and Kindred Disorders of Speech.* London: Cambridge Univ. Press, 1926.

Hearnshaw, L. S. Temporal integration and behavior. *Bulletin*, 1956, 1–20.

Hebb, D. O. *The Organization of Behavior.* New York: Wiley, 1949.

Hebb, D. O. Drives and the C.N.S. (conceptual nervous system). *Psychol. Rev.*, 1955, **62**, 243–254.

Hecht, S. Sensory adaptation and the stationary state, *J. gen. Physiol.*, 1923, **5**, 555–579.

Hecht, S. The nature of the photoreceptor process. In C. Murchison (Ed.), *Handbook of General Experimental Psychology.* Worcester, Mass.: Clark University Press, 1934.

Heider, F. Attitudes and cognitive organization. *J. Psychol.*, 1946, **21**, 107–112.

Heim, A. W. Adaptation to level of difficulty in intelligence testing. *Brit. J. Psychol.*, 1955, **46**, 211–224.

Heim, A. W. Psychological adaptation as a response to variations in difficulty and intensity. *J. gen. Psychol.*, 1957, **56**, 193–211.

Heinemann, E. G., & Marill, T. Tilt adaptation and figural after-effects. *J. exp. Psychol.*, 1954, **48**, 468–472.

Heintz, R. K. The effect of remote anchoring points upon the judgments of lifted weights. *J. exp. Psychol.*, 1950, **40**, 584–591.

Helson, H. The Psychology of *Gestalt. Amer. J. Psychol.*, 1925, **36**, 342–370, 494–526; 1926, **37**, 25–62, 189–216.

Helson, H. A child's spontaneous reports of imagery. *Amer. J. Psychol.*, 1933, **45**, 360–361.

Helson, H. Demonstration of pupillary, accommodative, and consensual reflexes through changes in apparent size of a pinhole. *J. gen. Psychol.*, 1935, **13**, 186–188.

Helson, H. Fundamental problems in color vision. I. The principle governing changes in hue, saturation, and lightness of non-selective samples in chromatic illumination. *J. exp. Psychol.*, 1938, **23**, 439–476.

Helson, H. Color tolerances as affected by changes in composition and intensity of illumination and reflectance of background. *Amer. J. Psychol.*, 1939, **52**, 406–412.

Helson, H. Some factors and implications of color constancy. *J. opt. Soc. Amer.*, 1943, **33**, 555–567.

Helson, H. Adaptation-level as frame of reference for prediction of psychophysical data. *Amer. J. Psychol.*, 1947, **60**, 1–29.

Helson, H. Adaptation-level as a basis for a quantitative theory of frames of reference. *Psychol. Rev.*, 1948, **55**, 297–313.

Helson, H. Design of equipment and optimal human operation. *Amer. J. Psychol.*, 1949, **62**, 473–497.

Helson, H. Perception. In H. Helson (Ed.), *Theoretical Foundations of Psychology.* New York: Van Nostrand, 1951.

Helson, H. *Perception and personality—a critique of recent experimental literature.* Report No. 1, Project No. 21-0202-0007, USAF, School of Aviation Medicine, Randolph Field, Texas, 1953.

Helson, H. An experimental approach to personality. *Psychiat. Res. Rep.*, 1955a, **1**, 89–99.

Helson, H. Color and seeing. *Illum. Eng.*, 1955b, **50**, 271–278.

Helson, H. Adaptation-Level Theory. In S. Koch (Ed.), *Psychology: A Study of a Science.* Vol. I. *Sensory, Perceptual, and Physiological Foundations.* New York: McGraw-Hill, 1959.

Helson, H. Studies of anomalous contrast and assimilation. *J. opt. Soc. Amer.*, 1963, **53**, 179–184.

Helson, H., Blake, R. R., & Mouton, J. S. An experimental investigation of the "big lie" in shifting attitudes. *J. soc. Psychol.*, 1958a, **48**, 51–60.

Helson, H., Blake, R. R., & Mouton, J. S. Petition-signing as adjustment to situational and personal factors. *J. soc. Psychol.*, 1958b, **48**, 3–10.

Helson, H., Blake, R. R., Mouton, J. S., & Olmstead, J. A. Attitudes as adjustments to stimulus, background, and residual factors. *J. abnorm. soc. Psychol.*, 1956, **52**, 314–322.

Helson, H., Dworkin, R. S., & Michels, W. C. Quantitative denotations of common terms as a function of background. *Amer. J. Psychol.*, 1956, **69,** 194–208.

Helson, H., & Grove, Josephine. Changes in hue, lightness, and saturation of surface colors in passing from daylight to incandescent-lamp light. *J. opt. Soc. Amer.*, 1947, **37,** 387–395.

Helson, H., & Guilford, J. P. The relation of visual sensitivity to the amount of retinal pigmentation. *J. gen. Psychol.*, 1933, **9,** 58–76.

Helson, H., & Helson, H. B. Some common features of concrete and abstract thinking. *Amer. J. Psychol.*, 1946, **59,** 468–472.

Helson, H., and Himelstein, P. A short method for calculating the adaptation-level for absolute and comparative rating judgments. *Amer. J. Psychol.*, 1955, **68,** 631–637.

Helson, H., & Jeffers, V. B. Fundamental problems in color vision. II. Hue, lightness, and saturation of selective samples in chromatic illumination. *J. exp. Psychol.*, 1940, **26,** 1–27.

Helson, H., & Joy, V. Domains of lightness, assimilation and contrast effects in vision. *Psychol. Beitr.*, 1962, **6,** 405–415.

Helson, H., & Judd, D. B. A study in photopic adaptation. *J. exp. Psychol.*, 1932, **15,** 380–398.

Helson, H., Judd, D. B., & Warren, M. H. Object-color changes from daylight to incandescent filament illumination. *Illum. Eng.*, 1952, **47,** 221–233.

Helson, H., Judd, D. B., & Wilson, M. Color rendition with fluorescent sources of illumination. *Illum. Eng.*, 1956, **51,** 329–346.

Helson, H., & Kaplan, S. Effects of background reflectance on transposition of lightness discrimination. Unpublished study, 1950.

Helson, H., & King, S. M. The *Tau* effect: an example of psychological relativity. *J. exp. Psychol.*, 1931, **14,** 202–217.

Helson, H., & Michels, W. C. The effect of adaptation on achromaticity. *J. opt. Soc. Amer.*, 1948, **38,** 1025–1032.

Helson, H., Michels, W. C., & Sturgeon, A. The use of comparative rating scales for the evaluation of psychophysical data. *Amer. J. Psychol.*, 1954, **67,** 321–326.

Helson, H., & Nash, Myrtle C. Anchor, contrast, and paradoxical distance effects. *J. exp. Psychol.*, 1960, **59,** 113–121.

Helson, H., & Rohles, F. H., Jr. A quantitative study of reversal of classical lightness-contrast. *Amer. J. Psychol.*, 1959, **72,** 530–538.

Helson, H., & Self, H. C. A study of coloured shadows. Maxwell Color Centenary, Imperial Coll., London, 1961, pp. 23–24.

Helson, H., & Steger, J. A. On the inhibitory effects of a second stimulus following the primary stimulus to react. *J. exp. Psychol.*, 1962, **63,** 201–205.

Helson, Ravenna M., & Cover, H. Specificity-generality of classificatory categories as a variable in recall. *Percept. mot. Skills,* 1956, **6,** 233–236.

Henle, M. An experimental investigation of past experience as a determinant of visual form perception. *J. exp. Psychol.,* 1942, **30,** 1–22.

Henneman, R. H. A photometric study of the perception of object color. *Arch. Psychol.,* 1935, No. 179.

Henry, E. M., & Rotter, J. B. Situational influences on Rorschach responses. *J. consult. Psychol.,* 1956, **20,** 457–462.

Henry, L. K. The role of insight in plane geometry. *J. educ. Psychol.,* 1934, **25,** 598–610.

Hermans, T. G. The relationship of convergence and elevation changes to judgments of size. *J. exp. Psychol.,* 1954, **48,** 204–208.

Hernàndez-Peòn, R., Scherrer, H., & Jouvet, M. Modification of electric activity in cochlear nucleus during attention in unanesthetized cats. *Science,* 1956, **123,** 331–332.

Heron, W. The pathology of boredom. *Sci. Amer.,* 1957, **197,** 52–56.

Herrick, C. J. *Neurological Foundations of Animal Behavior.* New York: Holt, Rinehart and Winston, 1924.

Hess, W. Reactions to light in the earthworm, *Lumbricus Terrestris. J. morphol. Physiol.,* 1924, **39,** 515–542.

Hilgard, E. R. *Theories of Learning.* New York: Appleton-Century-Crofts, 1948.

Hilgard, E. R. The role of learning in perception. In R. R. Blake & G. V. Ramsey (Eds.), *Perception: An Approach to Personality.* New York: Ronald, 1951.

Hilgard, E. R. Intervening variables, hypothetical constructs, parameters, and constants. *Amer. J. Psychol.,* 1958, **71,** 238–246.

Hilgard, E. R., & Marquis, D. G. *Conditioning and Learning.* New York: Appleton-Century-Crofts, 1940.

Hinckley, E. D., & Rethlingshafer, D. Value judgments of heights of men by college students. *J. Psychol.,* 1951, **31,** 257–262.

Hirsh, I. J., Bilger, R. C., & Deatherage, B. H. The effect of auditory and visual background on apparent duration. *Amer. J. Psychol.,* 1956, **69,** 561–574

Hofmann, F. B. *Die Lehre vom Raumsinn des Auges.* Berlin: Julius Springer, Erster Teil, 1920; Zweiter Teil, 1925.

Hofstätter, P. R. *Sozialpsychologie.* Berlin: Walter de Gruyter & Co., 1956.

Hogan, F., & Moulton, S. Men who need your friendship. *Coronet,* March, 1949, Pp. 27–31.

Hollingworth, H. L. The central tendency of judgment. *J. philos. psychol. & sci. Meth.,* 1910, **7,** 461–469.

Holtzman, W. H. Progress report on the development of an inkblot test. Personal communication.

Holway, A. H., & Boring, E. G. The moon illusion and the angle of regard. *Amer. J. Psychol.,* 1940a, **53**, 109–116.

Holway, A. H., & Boring, E. G. The apparent size of the moon as a function of the angle of regard: further experiments. *Amer. J. Psychol.,* 1940b, **53**, 537–553.

Holway, A. H., Smith, J. E., & Zigler, M. J. On the discrimination of minimal differences in weight: II. Number of available elements as variant. *J. exp. Psychol.,* 1937a, **20**, 371–380.

Holway, A. H., Smith, J. E., & Zigler, M. J. On the discrimination of minimal differences in weight: III. The role of frequency. *J. exp. Psychol.,* 1937b, **21**, 423–432.

Hovland, C., Harvey, O., & Sherif, M. Assimilation and contrast effects in reactions to communication and attitude change. *J. abnorm. soc. Psychol.,* 1957, **55**, 244–252.

Hovland, C. I., Lumsdaine, A. A., & Sheffield, F. D. *Experiments in Mass Communication.* Princeton University Press, 1949.

Hovland, C. I., & Sherif, M. Judgmental phenomena and scales of attitude measurement; item displacement in Thurstone scales. *J. abnorm. soc. Psychol.,* 1952, **47**, 822–832.

Hovland, C. I., & Weiss, W. Transmission of information concerning concepts through positive and negative instances. *J. exp. Psychol.,* 1953, **45**, 175–182.

Howes, D. H., & Solomon, R. L. A note on McGinnies' "Emotionality and perceptual defense." *Psychol. Rev.,* 1950, **57**, 229–234.

Howland, D., & Noble, M. E. The effect of physical constants of a control on tracking performance. *J. exp. Psychol.,* 1953, **46**, 353–360.

Hugelin, A., Dumont, S., & Paillas, N. Tympanic muscles and control of auditory input during arousal. *Science,* 1960, **131**, 1371–1372.

Hull, C. L. *Principles of Learning.* New York: Appleton-Century-Crofts, 1943a.

Hull, C. L. *Principles of Behavior.* New York: Appleton-Century-Crofts, 1943b.

Hull, C. L. Stimulus intensity dynamism (V) and stimulus generalization. *Psychol. Rev.,* 1949, **56**, 67–76.

Hull, C. L. *Essentials of Behavior.* New Haven: Yale University Press, 1951.

Humphrey, G. Extinction and negative adaptation. *Psychol. Rev.,* 1930a, **37**, 361–363.

Humphrey, G. Learning and the living system. *Psychol. Rev.,* 1930b, **37**, 497–510.

Humphrey, G. A note on the applicability of Le Chatelier's rule to biological systems. *Psychol. Forsch.*, 1930c, **13**, 365–367.

Humphreys, L. G. Acquisition and extinction of verbal expectations in a situation analogous to conditioning. *J. exp. Psychol.*, 1939, **25**, 294–301.

Humphreys, L. G. The organization of human abilities. *Amer. Psychologist*, 1962, **17**, 475–483.

Hunt, J. McV., & Quay, H. C. Early vibratory experience and the question of innate reinforcement value of vibration and other stimuli: a limitation on the discrepancy (burnt soup) principle of motivation. *Psychol. Rev.*, 1961, **68**, 149–156.

Hunt, W. A. Ambiguity of descriptive terms for feeling and emotion. *Amer. J. Psychol.*, 1935, **47**, 165–166.

Hunt, W. A. Anchoring effects in judgment. *Amer. J. Psychol.*, 1941, **54**, 395–403.

Hunt, W. A., and Flannery, J. Variability in the affective judgment. *Amer. J. Psychol.*, 1938, **51**, 507–513.

Hunt, W. A., and Volkmann, J. The anchoring of an affective scale. *Amer. J. Psychol.*, 1937, **49**, 88–92.

Hunter, I. A. M. L. An experimental investigation of the absolute and relative theories of transposition behavior in children. *Brit. J. Psychol.*, 1952, **43**, 112–128.

Hunter, I. A. M. L. The influence of mental set on problem solving. *Brit. J. Psychol.*, 1956, **47**, 63–64.

Hunter, W. S. Some labyrinth habits of the domestic pigeon. *J. Animal Behav.*, 1911, **1**, 278–304.

Hurvich, L. M., & Jameson, D. An opponents-process theory of color vision. *Psychol. Rev.*, 1957, **64**, 384–404.

Husserl, E. Ideen zu einer reinen Phänomenologie und phänomenologischen Philosophie. *Jahrb. f. Philos. u. phänom. Forsch.*, 1913, **1**, 1 ff.

Immergluck, I. The role of set in perceptual judgment. *J. Psychol.*, 1952, **34**, 181–189.

Irwin, F. W. Motivation. In H. Helson (Ed.), *Theoretical Foundations of Psychology*. New York: Van Nostrand, 1951.

Irwin, F. W., & Mintzer, M. G. Effect of differences in instructions and motivation upon measures of the level of aspiration. *Amer. J. Psychol.*, 1942, **55**, 400–406.

Irwin, F. W., & Smith, W. A. S. Further tests of theories of decision in an "expanded judgment" situation. *J. exp. Psychol.*, 1956, **52**, 345–348.

Jacobson, E. Neuromuscular controls in man: methods of self-direction in health and in disease. *Amer. J. Psychol.*, 1955, **68**, 549–561.

Jaffe, R. Kinesthetic after-effects following cerebral lesions. *Amer. J. Psychol.*, 1954, **67**, 668–676.

Jaffe, R. The influences of visual stimulation on kinesthetic figural after-effects. *Amer. J. Psychol.*, 1956, **69**, 70–75.

Jahoda, G. Assessment of abstract behavior in a non-western culture. *J. abnorm. soc. Psychol.*, 1956, **53**, 237–243.

James, H. An application of Helson's theory of adaptation level to the problem of transposition. *Psychol. Rev.*, 1953, **60**, 345–352.

James, W. *The Principles of Psychology.* New York: Holt, Rinehart & Winston, 1890.

Jameson, Dorothea, & Hurvich, L. M. Complexities of perceived brightness. *Science*, 1961, **133**, 174–179.

Jelliffe, S. E. The ecological principle in medicine. *J. abnorm. soc. Psychol.*, 1937, **32**, 100–121.

Jenkin, N. Affective processes in perception. *Psychol. Bull.*, 1957, **54**, 100–127.

Jenkins, W. O., & Postman, L. An experimental analysis of set in rote learning: retroactive inhibition as a function of changing set. *J. exp. Psychol.*, 1949, **39**, 69–72.

Jenkins, W. O., & Rigby, M. K. Partial (periodic) versus continuous reinforcement in resistance to extinction. *J. comp. physiol. Psychol.*, 1950, **43**, 30–40.

Jensen, A. R. Personality. *Annu. Rev. Psychol.*, 1958, **9**, 295–322.

Jensen, E. M., Reese, E. P., & Reese, T. W. The subitizing and counting of visually presented fields of dots. *J. Psychol.*, 1950, **30**, 363–392.

Johansson, G. Configurations in the perception of velocity. *Acta Psychologica*, 1950, **7**, 25–79.

Johnsgard, K. W. The role of contrast in stimulus intensity dynamism (V). *J. exp. Psychol.*, 1957, **53**, 173–179.

Johnson, D. M. Generalization of a scale of values by averaging of practice effects. *J. exp. Psychol.*, 1944, **34**, 425–436.

Johnson, D. M. Learning function for a change in the scale of judgment. *J. exp. Psychol.*, 1949, **39**, 851–860.

Johnson, D. M. *The Psychology of Thought and Judgment.* New York: Harper & Row, 1955.

Johnson, H. M. Some properties of Fechner's "intensity of sensation." *Psychol. Rev.*, 1930, **37**, 113–123.

Jones, F. N. Space-time relationships in somesthetic localization. *Science*, 1956, **124**, 484.

Jones, F. N., & Jones, M. H. A second factor analysis of visibility data. *Amer. J. Psychol.*, 1950, **63**, 206–213.

Jones, H. E. The study of patterns of emotional expression. In M. L. Reymert (Ed.), *Feelings and Emotions.* New York: McGraw-Hill, 1950.

Jones, L. V., Peryam, D. E., & Thurstone, L. L. Development of a scale for measuring soldiers' food preferences. *Food Research,* 1955, **20**, 515–520.

Jones, L. V., & Thurstone, L. L. The psychophysics of semantics: an experimental investigation. *J. appl. Psychol.,* 1955, **39**, 31–36.

Joos, G. *Theoretical Physics* (Trans. I. M. Freeman). New York: G. E. Stechert & Co., 1934.

Joseph, H. W. B. *An Introduction to Logic.* New York: Oxford Univ. Press, 1916.

Jourard, S. M., & Secord, P. F. Body size and body-cathexis. *J. consult. Psychol.,* 1954, **18**, 184.

Jourard, S. M., & Secord, P. F. Body-cathexis and the ideal female figure. *J. abnorm. soc. Psychol.,* 1955, **50**, 243–246.

Judd, D. B. Hue saturation and lightness of surface colors with chromatic illumination. *J. opt. Soc. Amer.,* 1940, **30**, 2–32.

Judd, D. B. Some color demonstrations I have shown. *J. opt. Soc. Amer.,* 1959, **49**, 322–328.

Judd, D. B. Appraisal of Land's work on two primary color projections. *J. opt. Soc. Amer.,* 1960, **50**, 254–268.

Jung, C. G. *Psychological Types.* New York: Harcourt, Brace & World, 1923.

Kahn, L. A. A discussion of some causes of operational fatigue in the Army Air Forces. *Psychol. Bull.,* 1947, **44**, 34–53.

Kanner, L. Behavior disorders in childhood. In J. McV. Hunt (Ed.), *Personality and the Behavior Disorders.* New York: Ronald, 1944.

Kaplan, S., & Helson, H. A study of judgment in pre- and post-lobotomized patients. Unpublished study, 1950.

Kardos, L. Ding und Schatten. *Z. f. Psychol.,* 1934, Ergbd. 23.

Katz, D. Die Erscheinungsweisen der Farben und ihre Beeinflussung durch die individuelle Erfahrung. *Z. f. Psychol.,* 1911, Ergbd. 7.

Katz, D. *The World of Color* (Trans. R. B. MacLeod & C. W. Fox). London: Kegan Paul, 1935.

Katz, D. *Studien zur experimentellen Psychologie.* Zurich: 1953.

Kaufman, E. L., Lord, M. W., Reese, T. W., & Volkmann, J. The discrimination of visual number. *Amer. J. Psychol.,* 1949, **62**, 498–525.

Kelly, J. G., & Helson, H. Judgments of lightness under conditions of bright and dim illumination. Unpublished study, 1955.

Kendler, H. H., Greenberg, A., & Richman, H. The influence of massed and distributed practice on the development of mental set. *J. exp. Psychol.,* 1952, **43**, 21–25.

Kendrew, E. N. A note on resistance of moods. *Brit. J. Psychol.,* 1935, **25**, 165–173.

Kerr, D. I., & Hagbarth, K. E. An investigation of olfactory centrifugal fiber systems. *J. Neurophysiol.,* 1955, **18**, 362–374.

Kimble, G. A. Social influence on Rorschach records. *J. abnorm. soc. Psychol.*, 1945, **40**, 89–93.

Kimble, G. A. Reinforcement theory. *J. counsel. Psychol.*, 1956, **3**, 112–115.

Kinsey, A. C., Pomeroy, W. B., & Martin, E. *Sexual Behavior in the Human Male.* Philadelphia: Saunders, 1948.

Kleint, H. Versuche über die Wahrnehmung. *Z. f. Psychol.*, 1937, **141**, 9–44.

Kleint, H. Versuche über die Wahrnehmung. *Z. f. Psychol.*, 1938, **142**, 259–290.

Klüver, H. Karl S. Lashley. *Res. Publ. nerv. men. Dis.*, 1958, **36**, 14–15.

Knox, G. W. Investigations of flicker and fusion. II. The effect of stimulus patern on the CFF. *J. gen. Psychol.*, 1945, **33**, 131–137.

Koch, S., The current state of motivational psychology. *Psychol. Rev.*, 1951, **58**, 147–154.

Koester, T., & Schoenfeld, W. N. The effect of context upon judgments of pitch differences. *J. exp. Psychol.*, 1946, **36**, 417–430.

Koffka, K. Perception: An introduction to the Gestalt-Theorie. *Psychol. Bull.*, 1922, **19**, 531–585.

Koffka, K. *Principles of Gestalt Psychology.* New York: Harcourt, Brace & World, 1935.

Kohler, I. Ueber Aufbau und Wandlungen der Wahrnehmungswelt. *Oesterr. Akad. d. Wiss. Philos.-Histor. Kl., Sitz. Ber.*, 1951, **227**, 1–118. Not seen; quoted by Werner and Wapner, 1955.

Kohler, I. Die Methode des Brillenversuchs in der Wahrnehmungs-psychologie mit Bemerkungen zur Lehre von der Adaptation. *Z. f. exp. u. angew. Psych.*, 1956, **3**, 381–417.

Köhler, W. *The Mentality of Apes.* New York: Harcourt, Brace & World, 1925.

Köhler, W., & Fishback, J. The destruction of the Müller-Lyer illusion in repeated trials: I. An examination of two theories. *J. exp. Psychol.*, 1950a, **40**, 267–281.

Köhler, W., & Fishback, J. The destruction of the Müller-Lyer illusion in repeated trials; II. Satiation patterns and memory traces. *J. exp. Psychol.*, 1950b, **40**, 398–410.

Köhler, W., & von Restorff, H. Analyse von Vorgängen im Spurenfeld. II. Zur Theorie der Reproduktion. *Psych. Forsch.*, 1935, **21**, 56–112.

Köhler, W., & Wallach, H. Figural after-effects: an investigation of visual processes. *Proc. Amer. Philos. Soc.*, 1944, **88**, 269–357.

Kolers, P. A. Sublimation in problem-solving. *Amer. J. Psychol.*, 1957, **70**, 437–441.

Krech, D., & Crutchfield, R. S. *Theory and Problems of Social Psychology.* New York: McGraw-Hill, 1948.

Kretschmer, E. *Physique and Character*. New York: Harcourt, Brace & World, 1926.

Kretschmer, E. *The Psychology of Men of Genius* (Trans. R. B. Cattell). New York: Harcourt, Brace & World, 1931.

Künnapas, T. M. Influence of frame size on apparent length of a line. *J. exp. Psychol.*, 1955, **50**, 168–170.

Künnapas, T. M. The vertical-horizontal illusion and the visual field. *J. exp. Psychol.*, 1957, **53**, 405–407.

Kuo, Z. Y. A psychology without heredity. *Psychol. Rev.*, 1924, **31**, 427–448.

Kurtz, K. H., & Hovland, C. I. The effect of verbalization during observation of stimulus objects upon accuracy of recogniton and recall. *J. exp. Psychol.*, 1953, **45**, 157–164.

Ladefoged, P., & Broadbent, D. E. Information conveyed by vowels. *J. acoust. Soc. Amer.*, 1957, **29**, 98–104.

Land, E. H. Color vision and the natural image. Part I, *Proc. Nat'l Acad. Sci.*, 1959a, **45**, 115–129; Part II, *idem*, 636–644.

Land, E. H. Experiments in color vision. *Sci. Amer.*, 1959b, **200**(5), 84–99.

Landis, C., & Clausen, J. Changes in sensory and motor performance induced by active psychiatric treatment. *J. Psychol.*, 1955, **40**, 275–305.

Landis, C., Zubin, J., & Mettler, F. A. The functions of the human frontal lobe. *J. Psychol.*, 1950, **30**, 123–138.

Lanier, L. H. The interrelations of speed of reaction measurements. *J. exp. Psychol.*, 1934, **17**, 371–399.

Lashley, K. S. Basic neural mechanisms in behavior. *Psychol. Rev.*, 1930, **37**, 1–24.

Lashley, K. S. Coalescence of neurology and psychology. *Proc. Amer. Philos. Soc.*, 1941, **84**, 461–470.

Lashley, K. S., Chow, K. L., & Semmes, J. An examination of the electrical field theory of cerebral integration. *Psychol. Rev.*, 1951, **58**, 123–146.

Lauenstein, O. Ansatz an einer physiologischen Theorie des Vergleichs und der Zeitfehler. *Psych. Forsch.*, 1933, **17**, 130–177.

Lawrence, D. H. The transfer of a discrimination along a continuum. *J. comp. physiol. Psychol.*, 1952, **45**, 511–516.

Lawson, R. Brightness discrimination performance and secondary reward strength as a function of primary reward amount. *J. comp. physiol. Psychol.*, 1957, **50**, 35–39.

Lazarus, R. S., & McCleary, R. A. Autonomic discrimination without awareness: A study of subception. *Psychol. Rev.*, 1951, **58**, 113–122.

Leeper, R. Cognitive Processes. In S. S. Stevens (Ed.), *Handbook of Experimental Psychology*. New York: Wiley, 1951.

Lefford, A. The influence of emotional subject-matter on logical reasoning. *J. gen. Psychol.,* 1946, **34,** 127–151.

Lefkowitz, M., Blake, R. R., & Mouton, J. S. Status factors in pedestrian violation of traffic signals. *J. abnorm. soc. Psychol.,* 1955, **51,** 704–706.

Leuba, C. Toward some integration of learning theories: the concept of optimal stimulation. *Psychol. Rep.,* 1955, **1,** 27–33.

Leventhal, A. M., Morrell, R. F., Morgan, E. F., Jr., & Perkins, C. C., Jr. The relation between mean reward and mean reinforcement. *J. exp. Psychol.,* 1959, **57,** 284–287.

Levin, M. M. Inconsistent cues in the establishment of perceptual illusions. *Amer. J. Psychol.,* 1952, **65,** 517–532.

Levine, J., & Butler, J. Lecture vs. group decision in changing behavior. *J. appl. Psychol.,* 1952, **36,** 29–33.

Levine, R., Chein, I., & Murphy, G. The relation of the intensity of a need to the amount of perceptual distortion: A preliminary report. *J. Psychol.,* 1942, **13,** 283–293.

Lewin, K. The conflict between Aristotelian and Galileian modes of thought in contemporary psychology. *J. gen. Psychol.,* 1931, **5,** 141–177.

Lewin, K. *Field Theory in Social Science.* New York: Harper & Row, 1951.

Lewin, K., Dembo, T., Festinger, L., & Sears, P. S. Level of aspiration. In J. McV. Hunt (Ed.), *Personality and the Behavior Disorders.* New York: Ronald, 1944.

Lewis, C. D. The making of a poem. *Saturday Evening Post,* 1961, **234,** No. 3, Pp. 18 ff.

Lewis, D. R. Psychological scales of taste. *J. Psychol.,* 1948, **26,** 437–446.

Lewis, H. B. Studies in the principles of judgments and attitudes: IV. The operation of "prestige suggestion." *J. soc. Psychol.,* 1941, **14,** 229–256.

Lichtenberg, P. Time perspective and the initiation of cooperation. *J. soc. Psychol.,* 1956, **43,** 247–260.

Licklider, J. C. R. Basic correlates of the auditory stimulus. In S. S. Stevens (Ed.), *Handbook of Experimental Psychology.* New York: Wiley, 1951.

Liddell, H. S. Animal origins of anxiety. In M. L. Reymert (Ed.), *Feelings and Emotions.* New York: McGraw-Hill, 1950.

Lifson, K. A. Errors in time-study judgments of industrial work pace. *Psychol. Monogr.,* 1953, **67** (Whole No. 355).

Lillie, R. S. *General Biology and Philosophy of Organism.* University of Chicago Press, 1945.

Lindsley, D. B. Psychological phenomena and the electroencephalogram. *Clin. Neurophysiol.,* 1952, **4,** 443–456.

Lindsley, D. B. Physiological Psychology, *Annu. Rev. Psychol.,* 1956, **7,** 323–348.

Lloyd, D. P. C. Electrical properties of nerve and muscle. In J. F. Fulton (Ed.), *Howell's Textbook of Physiology*. Philadelphia: Saunders, 1946a.

Lloyd, D. P. C. Principles of spinal reflex activity. In J. F. Fulton (Ed.), *Howell's Textbook of Physiology*. Philadelphia: Saunders, 1946b.

Loewenstein, W. R. Modulation of cutaneous receptors by sympathetic stimulation. *J. Physiol.*, 1956, **132**, 40–60.

Logan, F. A. *Incentive*. New Haven: Yale University Press, 1960.

Logan, F. A., Beier, E. M., & Ellis, R. A. The effect of varied reinforcement on speed of locomotion. *J. exp. Psychol.*, 1955, **49**, 260–266.

Long, L. A study of the effect of preceding stimuli upon the judgment of auditory intensities. *Arch. Psychol.*, 1937, **30** (Whole No. 209).

Lord, E. Experimentally induced variations in Rorschach performance. *Psychol. Monogr.*, 1950, **64**, 1–34.

Luchins, A. S. Mechanization in problem solving: the effect of *Einstellung*. *Psychol., Monogr.*, 1942, **54** (Whole No. 248).

Luchins, A. S. On agreement with another's judgments. *J. abnorm. soc. Psychol.*, 1944, **39**, 97–111.

Luchins, A. S., & Luchins, E. H. New experimental attempts at preventing mechanization in problem solving. *J. gen. Psychol.*, 1950, **42**, 279–297.

Luchins, A. S., & Luchins, E. H. *Rigidity of Behavior: A Variational Approach to the Effect of Einstellung*. Eugene: University of Oregon Books, 1959.

MacAdam, D. L. Measurement of the influence of local adaptation on color matching. *J. opt. Soc. Amer.*, 1949, **39**, 454–459.

MacAdam, D. L. Loci of constant hue and brightness determined with various surrounding colors. *J. opt. Soc. Amer.*, 1950, **40**, 589–595.

Mace, C. A. The influence of indirect incentives upon the accuracy of skilled movements. *Brit. J. Psychol.*, 1931, **22**, 101–114.

Mace, C. A. Homeostasis, needs, and values. *Brit. J. Psychol.*, 1953, **44**, 200–210.

Macfarlane, J. W., & Tuddenham, R. D. In H. H. Anderson and G. L. Anderson (Eds.), *An Introduction to Projective Techniques*. New York: Prentice-Hall, 1951.

Mach, E. *Analysis of Sensations*. Chicago: Open Court, 1914. (German ed. Jena, 1886.)

MacKay, D. M. On comparing the brain with machines. *Amer. Scientist*, 1954, **42**, 261–268.

MacKay, D. M. Towards an information-flow model of human behavior. *Brit. J. Psychol.*, 1956, **47**, 30–43.

MacKinnon, D. W. The Structure of Personality. In J. McV. Hunt (Ed.), *Personality and the Behavior Disorders*. New York: Ronald, 1944.

Mackworth, N. H. Some recent studies of human stress from a marine and naval viewpoint. *Inst. Marine Eng'ng Trans.*, 1952, **64**, 1–10.

MacLeod, R. B., & Roff, M. F. An experiment in temporal disorientation. *Acta Psychologica*, 1935, **1**, 381–423.

Malmo, R. B. Experimental studies of mental patients under stress. In M. L. Reymert (Ed.), *Feelings and Emotions*. New York: McGraw-Hill, 1950.

Mann, R. D. A review of the relationships between personality and performance in small groups. *Psychol. Bull.*, 1959, **56**, 241–270.

Marimont, Rosalind B. Model for visual response to contrast. *J. opt. Soc. Amer.*, 1962, **52**, 801–806.

Marks, E. S. Skin color judgments of Negro college students. *J. abnorm. soc. Psychol.*, 1943, **38**, 370–376.

Marple, C. H. The comparative susceptibility of three age groups to the suggestion of group vs. expert opinion. *J. soc. Psychol.*, 1933, **4**, 176–186.

Masling, J. The influence of situational and interpersonal variables in projective testing. *Psychol. Bull.*, 1960, **57**, 65–85.

Maslow, A. H., & Mintz, N. L. Effects of esthetic surroundings: I. Initial effects of three esthetic conditions upon perceiving "energy" and "well-being" in faces. *J. Psychol.*, 1956, **41**, 247–254.

Maxwell, R. S. Remembering in social groups. *Brit. J. Psychol.*, 1936, **27**, 30–40.

McClelland, D. C., & Atkinson, J. W. The projective expression of needs. I. The effect of different intensities of the hunger drive on perception. *J. Psychol.*, 1948, **25**, 205–222.

McClelland, D. C., Atkinson, J. W., Clark, R. A., & Lowell, E. L. *The Achievement Motive*. New York: Appleton-Century-Crofts, 1953.

McDougall, W. *An Introduction to Social Psychology*. Boston: Luce, 1908.

McGarvey, H. R. Anchoring effects in the absolute judgment of verbal materials. *Arch. Psychol.*, 1942, **43** (Whole No. 281).

McGinnies, E. Emotionality and perceptual defense. *Psychol. Rev.*, 1949, **56**, 244–251.

McGregor, D. The major determinants of the prediction of social events. *J. abnorm. soc. Psychol.*, 1938, **33**, 179–204.

McNemar, Q. Opinion-attitude methodology. *Psychol. Bull.*, 1946, **43**, 289–374.

McQueen, R. Examination deception as a function of residual, background, and immediate stimulus factors. *J. Pers.*, 1957, **25**, 643–650.

McQueen, R., & Pearson, W. O. Stimulus-word changes in picture-frustration situations. *Percept. mot. Skills*, 1959, **9**, 407–410.

McReynolds, P. Thinking conceptualized in terms of interacting moments. *Psychol. Rev.*, 1953, **60**, 319–330.

Mednick, S. A. A learning theory approach to research in schizophrenia. *Psychol. Bull.*, 1958, **55**, 316–327.

Meehl, P. E. Wanted—a good cookbook. *Amer. Psychologist*, 1956a, **11**, 263–272.

Meehl, P. E. When shall we use our heads instead of the formula? APA Convention, 1956b.

Meier, G. W., Foschee, D. P., Wittrig, J. J., Peeler, D. F., & Huff, F. W. Helson's residual factor versus innate S-R relations. *Psychol. Rep.*, 1960, **6**, 61–62.

Merton, R. K., and Lazarsfeld, P. F. (Eds.) *Continuities in Social Research.* New York: Free Press, 1950.

Meyer, D. R. The effects of differential reward on discrimination reversal learning by monkeys. *J. exp. Psychol.*, 1951, **41**, 268–274.

Michels, W. C. An interpretation of the bril scale of subjective brightness. *J. opt. Soc. Amer.*, 1954, **44**, 70–74.

Michels, W. C., & Doser, B. T. Rating scale method for comparative loudness measurements. *J. acoust. Soc. Amer.*, 1955, **27**, 1173–1180.

Michels, W. C., & Helson, H. A reformulation of the Fechner law in terms of adaptation-level applied to rating-scale data. *Amer. J. Psychol.*, 1949, **62**, 355–368.

Michels, W. C., & Helson, H. Man as a meter. *Physics Today*, 1953, **6**, 4–7.

Michels, W. C., & Helson, H. A quantitative theory of time-order effects. *Amer. J. Psychol.*, 1954a, **67**, 327–334.

Michels, W. C., & Helson, H. A reconciliation of the *veg* scale with Fechner's law. *Amer. J. Psychol.*, 1954b, **67**, 677–683.

Michels, W. C., & Patterson, A. L. *Elements of Modern Physics.* New York: Van Nostrand, 1951.

Michotte, A. E. The emotions regarded as functional connections. In M. L. Reymert (Ed.), *Feelings and Emotions.* New York: McGraw-Hill, 1950.

Miles, W. R. Psychological aspects of ageing. *Problems of Ageing.* (2d ed.) 1942.

Miller, C. A., & Engen, T. Supplementary Report: Context effects on absolute judgments of length. *J. exp. Psychol.*, 1960, **59**, 276–277.

Miller, D. R. Predictions of behavior by means of the Rorschach test. *J. abnorm. soc. Psychol.*, 1953, **48**, 367–375.

Miller, G. A., Bruner, J. S., & Postman, L. Familiarity of letter sequences and tachistoscopic identification. *J. gen. Psychol.*, 1954, **50**, 129–139.

Miller, J. G. Discrimination without awareness. *Amer. J. Psychol.*, 1939, **52**, 562–578.

Miller, N. E. Comments on theoretical models. *J. Pers.*, 1951, **20**, 82–100.

Miller, N. E. Liberalization of basic S-R concepts: Extensions to conflict behavior, motivation and social learning. In S. Koch (Ed.), *Psychology: A Study of a Science,* Study 1, Vol. 2. New York: McGraw-Hill, 1959.

Miller, N. E. Learning and performance motivated by direct stimulation of the brain. In D. E. Sheer (Ed.), *Electrical Stimulation of the Brain.* Austin: Texas University Press, 1962.

Minami, H., & Dallenbach, K. M. The effect of activity upon learning and retention in the cockroach. *Amer. J. Psychol.*, 1946, **59**, 1–58.

Minturn, A. L., & Reese, T. W. The effect of differential reinforcement on the discrimination of visual number. *J. Psychol.*, 1951, **31**, 201–232.

Mintz, A. Non-adaptive group behavior. *J. abnorm. soc. Psychol.*, 1951, **46**, 150–159.

Mintz, N. L. Effects of esthetic surroundings: II. Prolonged and repeated experience in a "beautiful" and an "ugly" room. *J. Psychol.*, 1956, **41**, 459–466.

Moore, H. T. The comparative influence of majority and expert opinion. *Amer. J. Psychol.*, 1921, **32**, 16–20.

Moore, T. V. *Cognitive Psychology.* Philadelphia: Lippincott, 1939.

Morgan, C. T. *Physiological Psychology.* New York: McGraw-Hill, 1943.

Morin, R. E., & Grant, D. A. Learning and performance on a key-pressing task as a function of the degree of spatial stimulus-response correspondences. *J. exp. Psychol.*, 1955, **49**, 39–47.

Morinaga, S., & Noguchi, K. Analysis of factors determining the perceptual judgment of lightness. *J. Coll. Arts and Sci.*, Chiba University (Japan), 1960, **3**, 41–48.

Mosier, C. I. A psychometric study of meaning. *J. soc. Psychol.*, 1941, **13**, 123–140.

Mouton, J. S., Blake, R. R., & Olmstead, J. A. The relationship between frequency of yielding and the disclosure of personal identity. *J. Pers.*, 1956, **24**, 339–347.

Mouton, J. S., & Helson, H. Total impression as a function of the dimensions of esthetic objects. Unpublished study.

Muenzinger, K. F. Reward and Punishment. *Univ. Colo. Stud., Gen. Sec.*, 1946, **27**(4), 1–16.

Mukerji, N. An investigation into the perception of height by rats. *Brit. J. Psychol.*, 1956, **47**, 140–143.

Müller, G. E. *Zur Analyse der Gedächtnistätigkeit und des Vorstellungsverlaufes.* Tl. II. *Z.f. Psychol.*, 1917, Ergbd. 9, 1–682.

Murdock, B. B. The distinctiveness of stimuli. *Psychol. Rev.*, 1960, **67**, 16–31.

Murphy, G. An experimental study of literary versus scientific types. *Amer. J. Psychol.*, 1917, **28**, 238–263.

Murphy, G. *Personality: A Biosocial Approach to Origins and Structure.* New York: Harper & Row, 1947.

Murphy, G. *Human Potentialities.* New York: Basic Books, 1958.

Murphy, Lois. Empathy in children. In L. Carmichael (Ed.), *Manual of Child Psychology.* New York: Wiley, 1946.

Murray, H. A. *Explorations in Personality: A Clinical and Experimental Study of Fifty Men of College Age.* New York: Oxford Univ. Press, 1938.

Murray, H. A. *Thematic Apperception Test.* Cambridge, Mass.: Harvard University Press, 1943.

Murstein, B. I. A conceptual model of projective techniques applied to stimulus variations with thematic techniques. *J. consult. Psychol.,* 1959, **25,** 3–14.

Nachmias, J. The effect of stimulus-heterogeneity on free recall. *Amer. J. Psychol.,* 1958, **71,** 578–582.

Nafe, J. P. An experimental study of the affective qualities. *Amer. J. Psychol.,* 1924, **35,** 507–544.

Nash, M. C. An experimental test of the Michels-Helson theory of judgment. *Amer. J. Psychol.,* 1950*a,* **63,** 214–220.

Nash, M. C. A quantitative study of effects of past experience on adaptation-level. Ph.D. dissertation, Bryn Mawr College, 1950*b.*

Needham, J. G. Prior entry within a single sense department. *J. exp. Psychol.,* 1934*a,* **17,** 400–411.

Needham, J. G. The time-error in comparison-judgments. *Psychol. Bull.,* 1934*b,* **31,** 239.

Needham, J. G. Rate of presentation in the method of single stimuli. *Amer. J. Psychol.,* 1935, **47,** 275–284.

Needham, J. G. Some conditions of prior entry. *J. gen. Psychol.,* 1936, **14,** 226–240.

Nellis, Barbara S. Effects of object- and background-tilt on perception of form. Ph.D. dissertation, University of Texas Library, Austin, 1958.

Newcomb, T. M. An approach to the study of communicative acts. *Psychol. Rev.,* 1953, **60,** 393–404.

Newhall, S. M. The ratio method in the review of the Munsell colors. *Amer. J. Psychol.,* 1939, **52,** 394–405.

Newhall, S. M. Preliminary report of the O.S.A. subcommittee on the spacing of the Munsell colors. *J. opt. Soc. Amer.,* 1940, **30,** 617–645.

Newhall, S. M. The reversal of simultaneous brightness contrast. *J. exp. Psychol.,* 1942, **31,** 393–409.

Newhall, S. M., Nickerson, D., & Judd, D. B. Final report of the O.S.A. subcommittee on the spacing of the Munsell colors. *J. opt. Soc. Amer.,* 1943, **33,** 385–418.

Nissen, H. W. Phylogenetic comparison. In S. S. Stevens (Ed.), *Handbook of Experimental Psychology.* New York: Wiley, 1951.

Noble, C. E., & Broussard, I. G. Effects of complex transformations of feedback upon simple instrumental behavior. *J. exp. Psychol.,* 1955, **50,** 381–386.

Noble, M. E., Fitts, P. M., & Warren, C. E. The frequency response of skilled subjects in a pursuit tracking task. *J. exp. Psychol.,* 1955, **49,** 249–256.

North, A. J., & Jenkins, L. B. Reading speed and comprehension as a function of typography. *J. appl. Psychol.*, 1951, **35**, 225–228.

Nyssen, R., & Bourdon, J. A new contribution to the experimental study of the size-weight illusion. *Acta Psychologica*, 1956, **12**, 157–173.

Ogden, R. M. *The Psychology of Art.* New York: Scribner, 1938.

Olds, J. Self stimulation of the brain. *Science*, 1958, **127**, 315–324.

Oort, J. H. The crab nebula. *Sci. Amer.*, 1957, **196**, 52–60.

Osgood, C. E., & Stagner, R. Analysis of a prestige frame of reference by a gradient technique. *J. appl. Psychol.*, 1941, **25**, 275–290.

OSS Assessment Staff. *Assessment of Men.* New York: Holt, Rinehart and Winston, 1948.

Pan, S. Influence of context upon learning and recall. *J. exp. Psychol.*, 1926, **9**, 468–491.

Parducci, A. Learning variables in the judgment of single stimuli. *J. exp. Psychol.*, 1954, **48**, 24–30.

Parducci, A. Direction of shift in the judgment of single stimuli. *J. exp. Psychol.*, 1956a, **51**, 169–178.

Parducci, A. Figural after-effects with tachistoscopic presentation. *Amer. J. Psychol.*, 1956b, **69**, 635–639.

Parducci, A. Incidental learning of stimulus frequencies in the establishment of judgment scales. *J. exp. Psychol.*, 1956c, **52**, 112–118.

Parducci, A. Restriction of range in the judgment of single stimuli. *Amer. J. Psychol.*, 1957, **70**, 272–275.

Parducci, A. An adaptation-level analysis of ordinal effects in judgment. *J. exp. Psychol.*, 1959, **58**, 239–246.

Parducci, A., Calfee, R. C., Marshall, Louise M., & Davidson, Linda P. Context effects in judgment: adaptation level as a function of the mean, midpoint, and median of the stimuli. *J. exp. Psychol.*, 1960, **60**, 65–77.

Parducci, A., & Marshall, Louise M. Assimilation vs. contrast in the anchoring of perceptual judgments of weight. *J. exp. Psychol.*, 1962, **63**, 426–437.

Paterson, D. G. *Physique and Intellect.* New York: Appleton-Century-Crofts, 1930.

Paterson, D. G., & Ludgate, K. E. Blond and brunette. *J. Pers. Res.*, 1922, **1**, 122–128.

Paterson, D. G., & Tinker, M. A. The part-whole proportion illusion in printing. *J. appl. Psychol.*, 1938, **22**, 421–425.

Pavlov, I. P. *Conditioned Reflexes.* (G. V. Anrep, Trans. and Ed.) London: Oxford Univ. Press, 1927.

Payne, R. B., & Hauty, G. T. The effects of experimentally induced attitudes upon task proficiency. *J. exp. Psychol.*, 1954, **47**, 267–273.

Payne, R. B., & Hauty, G. T. Effect of psychological feedback upon work decrement. *J. exp. Psychol.*, 1955a, **50**, 343–351.

Payne, R. B., & Hauty, G. T. Factors affecting the endurance of psychomotor skill. *J. Aviation Med.*, 1955*b*, **26**, 382–389.

Peak, Helen. Time order error in successive judgments and in reflexes. I. Inhibition of the judgment and the reflex. *J. exp. Psychol.*, 1939, **25**, 535–565.

Peak, Helen. The time order error in successive judgments and in reflexes. II. As a function of the first stimulus of a pair. *J. exp. Psychol.*, 1940*a*, **26**, 103–115.

Peak, Helen. Time order error in successive judgments and in reflexes. III. Time error theories. *J. exp. Psychol.*, 1940*b*, **47**, 1–20.

Peak, Helen. Attitude and motivation. *Nebraska Symposium on Motivation*. Lincoln: University of Nebraska Press, 1955.

Peak, Helen. Psychological structure and psychological activity. *Psychol. Rev.*, 1958, **65**, 325–347.

Pedley, P. E., & Harper, R. S. Pitch and the vertical localization of sound. *Amer. J. Psychol.*, 1959, **72**, 447–449.

Perkins, C. C., Jr. The relation between conditioned stimulus intensity and response strength. *J. exp. Psychol.*, 1953, **46**, 225–231.

Peterson, L. R., & Peterson, M. J. The role of context stimuli in verbal learning. *J. exp. Psychol.*, 1957, **53**, 102–105.

Pfaffmann, C., & Bare, J. K. Gustatory nerve discharges in normal and adrenalectomized rats. *J. comp. physiol. Psychol.*, 1950, **43**, 320–324.

Phares, E. J., & Rotter, J. B. An effect of the situation on psychological testing. *J. consult. Psychol.*, 1956, **20**, 291–293.

Philbrick, E. B., & Postman, L. A further analysis of "learning without awareness." *Amer. J. Psychol.*, 1955, **68**, 417–424.

Philip, B. R. Time errors in the discrimination of color mass by the ranking method. *J. exp. Psychol.*, 1940, **27**, 285–302.

Philip, B. R. The Weber-Fechner law and the discrimination of color mass. *J. exp. Psychol.*, 1941, **29**, 323–333.

Philip, B. R. The frame of reference concept. *Can. J. Psychol.*, 1949, **3**, 73–79.

Philip, B. R. The effect of general and of specific labelling on judgmental scales. *Can. J. Psychol.*, 1951, **5**, 18–28.

Pickford, R. W. Experiments on the relation of dissonance and context—part one. *Quart. J. exp. Psychol.*, 1948, **1**, 57–67.

Pierce, A. H. *Studies in Space Perception.* New York: Longmans (David McKay Co.), 1901.

Piéron, H. Sensory affectivity. In M. L. Reymert (Ed.), *Feelings and Emotions.* New York: McGraw-Hill, 1950.

Piéron, H. Les échelles subjectives. Peuvent-elles fournir la base d'une nouvelle loi psychophysique? *L'Année Psychologique*, 1959, **59**, 1–34.

Plutchick, R. The role of muscular tension in maladjustment. *J. gen. Psychol.*, 1954, **50**, 45–62.

Podell, J. E. A comparison of generalization and adaptation level as theories of connotation. *J. abnorm. soc. Psychol.*, 1961, **62**, 593–597.

Polya, G. *How to Solve It: A New Aspect of Mathematical Method.* Princeton University Press, 1948.

Polyak, S. L. *The Retina.* University of Chicago Press, 1941.

Poppelreuter, W. Zur Psychologie der optischen Wahrnehumung. *Z.f.d. ges. Neurol. u. Psychiat.*, 1923, **83**, 26–152.

Porter, J. P. Further study of the English sparrow and other birds. *Amer. J. Psychol.*, 1906, **17**, 248–271.

Postman, L. Time-error as a function of the method of experimentation. *Amer. J. Psychol.*, 1947, **60**, 101–108.

Postman, L., Adams, P. A., & Phillips, L. W. Studies in incidental learning: II. The effects of association value and of the method of testing. *J. exp. Psychol.*, 1955, **49**, 1–10.

Postman, L., & Adis-Castro, G. Psychophysical methods in the study of word recognition. *Science,* 1957, **125**, 193–194.

Postman, L., & Bruner, J. S. Perception under stress. *Psychol. Rev.*, 1948, **55**, 314–323.

Postman, L., & Bruner, J. S. Multiplicity of set as a determinant of perceptual behavior. *J. exp. Psychol.*, 1949, **39**, 369–377.

Postman, L., & Crutchfield, R. S. The interaction of need, set, and stimulus-structure in a cognitive task. *Amer. J. Psychol.*, 1952, **65**, 196–217.

Postman, L., & Miller, G. A. Anchoring of temporal judgments. *Amer. J. Psychol.*, 1945, **58**, 43–53.

Postman, L., & Schneider, B. H. Personal values, visual recognition, and recall. *Psychol. Rev.*, 1951, **58**, 271–284.

Pratt, C. C. The spatial character of high and low tones. *J. exp. Psychol.*, 1930, **13**, 278–285.

Pratt, C. C. The time-order error in psychophysical judgments. *Amer. J. Psychol.*, 1933a, **45**, 292–297.

Pratt, C. C. Time-errors in the method of single stimuli. *J. exp. Psychol.*, 1933b, **16**, 798–814.

Pratt, C. C. Repetition, motivation, and recall. *Brit. J. Psychol.*, 1935, **26**, 425–429.

Preston, M., & Baratta, P. An experimental study of the auction value of an uncertain outcome. *Amer. J. Psychol.*, 1948, **61**, 183–193.

Preston, M. G., Spiers, A., & Trasoff, J. On certain conditions controlling the realism and irrealism of aspirations. *J. exp. Psychol.*, 1947, **37**, 48–58.

Price-Williams, D. R. The kappa effect. *Nature,* 1954, **173**, 363–365.

Proshansky, H., & Murphy, G. The effects of reward and punishment on perception. *J. Psychol.*, 1942, **13**, 295–305.

Prosser, C. L., & Sherman, F. G. Cellular mechanisms of physiological adaptation. *Science*, 1958, **127**, 196.

Rambo, W. W., & Johnson, E. L. Practice effects and the estimation of adaptation level. *Amer. J. Psychol.*, in press.

Ratliff, F., & Riggs, L. A. Involuntary motions of the eye during monocular fixation. *J. exp. Psychol.*, 1950, **40**, 687–701.

Razran, G. Stimulus generalization of conditioned responses. *Psychol. Bull.*, 1949, **46**, 337–365.

Restle, F. A. A theory of discrimination learning. *Psychol. Rev.*, 1955, **62**, 11–19.

Rethlingshafer, D., & Hinckley, E. D. Influence of characteristics of judges on their psychophysical judgments. *Amer. Psychologist*, 1954, **9**, 454.

Riedel, G. Ueber die Abhängigkeit optischer Kontraste von Gestaltsbedingungen. *Neue Psychol. Stud.*, 1937, **10**, 1–44.

Rigg, M. R. Favorable versus unfavorable propaganda in the enjoyment of music. *J. exp. Psychol.*, 1948, **38**, 78–81.

Riley, D. A. The nature of the effective stimulus in animal discrimination learning: Transposition reconsidered. *Psychol. Rev.*, 1958, **65**, 1–7.

Rimbaud, A. In J-M Carré (Ed.), *The Life of Arthur Rimbaud* (Trans. J. T. Shipley). New York: Macauley, 1931.

Riss, E. Are hallucinations illusions? An experimental study of non-veridical perception. *J. Psychol.*, 1959, **48**, 367–373.

Ritchie, A. D. *Scientific Method*. New York: Harcourt, Brace & World, 1923.

Roelofs, C. O. Optische Lokalisation. *Arch. f. Augenheilk*, 1935, **109**, 395–415.

Rogers, S. The anchoring of absolute judgments. *Arch. Psychol.*, 1941, **37** (Whole No. 261).

Rose, A. Dark adaptation. *J. opt. Soc. Amer.*, 1951, **41**, 210–211.

Rosenbaum, M. The effect of stimulus and background factors on the volunteering response. *J. abnorm. soc. Psychol.*, 1956, **53**, 118–121.

Rosenbaum, M., & Blake, R. R. Volunteering as a function of field structure. *J. abnorm. soc. Psychol.*, 1955, **50**, 193–196.

Rosenblith, W. A., Miller, G. A., Egan, J. P., Hirsh, I. J., & Thomas, G. J. An auditory afterimage? *Science*, 1947, **106**, 333–334.

Rubenfeld, S., Lowenfeld, J., & Guthrie, G. M. Stimulus generalization in subception. *J. gen. Psychol.*, 1956, **54**, 177–182.

Rubin, E. *Visuell wahrgenommene Figuren*. Copenhagen, 1921.

Rubin-Rabson, G. Item order and difficulty in four verbal subtests of the Bellevue-Wechsler Scale. *J. gen. Psychol.*, 1956, **88**, 167–174.

Ruch, T. C. Vision. In J. F. Fulton (Ed.), *Howell's Textbook of Physiology*. (15th ed.) Philadelphia: Saunders, 1946.

Ruch, T. C. Motor Systems. In S. S. Stevens (Ed.), *Handbook of Experimental Psychology*. New York: Wiley, 1951.

Ruesch, J., & Bateson, G. *Communication: The Social Matrix of Psychiatry.* New York: Norton, 1951.

Russell, B. *Introduction to Mathematical Philosophy.* New York: Macmillan, 1920.

Ryan, T. A. Interrelations of the sensory systems in perception. *Psychol. Bull.*, 1940, **37**, 659–698.

Ryan, T. A., & Schwartz, C. B. Speed of perception as a function of mode of perception. *Amer. J. Psychol.*, 1956, **69**, 60–69.

Sacks, E. J. Intelligence scores as a function of experimentally established social relationships between child and examiner. *J. abnorm. soc. Psychol.*, 1952, **47**, 354–358.

Sakoda, J. M. Factor analysis of OSS situational tests. *J. abnorm. soc. Psychol.*, 1952, **47**, 843–852.

Salzinger, K. Techniques for computing shifts in scale of absolute judgment. *Psychol. Bull.*, 1956, **53**, 394–401.

Sanford, R. N. The effects of abstinence from food upon imaginal processes. *J. Psychol.*, 1936, **2**, 129–136.

Sanford, R. N. The effects of abstinence from food upon imaginal processes: A further experiment. *J. Psychol.*, 1937, **3**, 145–159.

Santayana, G. The Unknowable. Herbert Spencer Lecture for 1923, Oxford Univ. Reprinted in C. Fadiman (Ed.), *Reading I've Liked.* New York: Simon and Schuster, 1941.

Sarason, S. B. *The Clinical Interaction.* New York: Harper & Row, 1954.

Schachter, S. Deviation, rejection, and communication. *J. abnorm. soc. Psychol.*, 1951, **46**, 190–207.

Schachter, S., & Hall, R. Group-derived restraints and audience persuasion. *Human Relat.*, 1952, **5**, 397–406.

Schein, E. The effect of group interaction on judgment of physical stimuli. M.A. Thesis, Stanford University Library, California, 1949.

Schilder, P. *Mind: Perception and Thought in Their Constructive Aspects.* New York: Columbia Univ. Press, 1942.

Schneirla, T. C. Levels in the psychological capacities of animals. In R. W. Sellars, V. J. McGill, and M. Farber (Eds.), *Philosophy for the Future.* New York: Macmillan, 1949.

Scholtz, W. Experimentelle Untersuchungen über die phänomenale Grösse von Raumstrecken, die durch Sukzessiv-Darbietung zweier Reize begrenzt werden. *Psych. Forsch.*, 1924, **5**, 219–272.

Schonell, F. J. *The Psychology and Teaching of Reading.* Edinburgh and London: Oliver and Boyd, 1946.

Schouten, J. F., & Ornstein, L. S. Measurements of direct and indirect adaptation by means of a binocular method. *J. opt. Soc. Amer.*, 1939, **29**, 168–182.

Schrier, A. M., & Harlow, H. F. Effect of amount of incentive on discrimination learning by monkeys. *J. comp. physiol. Psychol.*, 1956, **49**, 117–122.

Schroder, H. M., & Rotter, J. B. Rigidity as learned behavior. *J. exp. Psychol.*, 1952, **44**, 141–150.

Scripture, E. W. *History of Psychology in Autobiography*. (C. Murchison, Ed.) Worcester, Mass.: Clark University Press, 1936.

Sears, R. Experimental studies of projection: 1. Attribution of traits. *J. soc. Psychol.*, 1936, **7**, 151–163.

Sechehaye, M. *Reality Lost and Regained: Autobiography of a Schizophrenic Girl* (Trans. G. Rubin-Rabson). New York: Grune & Stratton, 1951.

Secord, P. F., Bevan, W., & Katz, B. The Negro stereotype and perceptual accentuation. *J. abnorm. soc. Psychol.*, 1956, **53**, 78–83.

Secord, P. F., & Jourard, S. M. The appraisal of body-cathexis: Body-cathexis and the self. *J. consult. Psychol.*, 1953, **17**, 343–347.

Segall, M. H. The effect of attitude and experience on judgments of controversial statements. *J. abnorm. soc. Psychol.*, 1959, **58**, 61–68.

Self, H. C. A quantitative study of colored shadows. Ph.D. dissertation, University of Texas Library, Austin, 1959.

Sells, S. B. The atmosphere effect: An experimental study of reasoning. *Arch. Psychol.*, 1936 (Whole No. 200).

Sells, S. B. Problems of criteria and validity in diagnosis and therapy. *J. clin. Psychol.*, 1952, **8**, 23–28.

Selye, H. The general adaptation syndrome and the diseases of adaptation. *J. clin. Endocrinol.*, 1946, **2**, 117–230.

Selye, H. Stress and the general adaptation syndrome. *Brit. Med. J.*, 1950, **1**, 1383 ff.

Shaffer, L. F. *The Psychology of Adjustment*. New York: Houghton Mifflin, 1936.

Shakow, D. Some psychological features of schizophrenia. In M. L. Reymert (Ed.), *Feelings and Emotions*. New York: McGraw-Hill, 1950.

Sheffield, V. F. Extinction as a function of partial reinforcement and distribution of practice. *J. exp. Psychol.*, 1949, **39**, 511–526.

Sheldon, W. H. *The Varieties of Human Physique*. New York: Harper & Row, 1940.

Sheldon, W. H. *The Varieties of Temperament*. New York: Harper & Row, 1942.

Sheppard, D. Subjective assessments of firmness: the use of a rating scale. *Quart. J. exp. Psychol.*, 1953, **5**, 1–9.

Sheppard, D. The adequacy of everyday quantitative expressions as measurements of qualities. *Brit. J. Psychol.*, 1954, **45**, 40–50.

Sherif, M. *The Psychology of Social Norms*. New York: Harper & Row, 1936.

Sherif, M., & Hovland, C. I. Judgmental phenomena and scales of attitude measurement: Placement of items with individual choice of number categories. *J. abnorm. soc. Psychol.,* 1953, **48,** 135–141.

Sherif, M., & Hovland, C. I. *Social Judgment.* New Haven: Yale University Press, 1961.

Sherif, M., & Sherif, C. W. *Groups in Harmony and Tension.* New York: Harper & Row, 1953.

Sherif, M., Taub, D., & Hovland, C. I. Assimilation and contrast effects of anchoring stimuli on judgments. *J. exp. Psychol.,* 1958, **55,** 150–155.

Sherrington, C. *Man on his Nature.* New York: Macmillan, 1941.

Shipley, T. The horopter in eidetic subjects. *Psychol. Bull.,* 1958, **55,** 171–175.

Sholl, D. A. Regularities in growth curves, including rhythms and allometry. *Dynamics of Growth Processes* (a symposium). Princeton University Press, 1954.

Shuey, H. The fundamental principles of typology. *Psychol. Rev.,* 1937, **44,** 170–182.

Shuford, E. H. A comparison of subjective probabilities for elementary and compound events. The Psychometric Laboratory, University of North Carolina, Chapel Hill, 1959, No. 20. Pp. 1–17.

Siipola, Elsa M. A group study of some effects of preparatory set. *Psychol. Monogr.,* 1935, **46**(210), 27–38.

Siipola, Elsa M. The influence of color on reaction to ink blots. *J. Pers.,* 1952, **21,** 22–47.

Singer, W. B., & Young, P. T. Studies in affective reactions: II. Dependence of affective ratings upon the stimulus situation. *J. gen. Psychol.,* 1941, **24,** 303–325.

Skinner, B. F. *The Behavior of Organisms.* New York: Appleton-Century-Crofts, 1938.

Sleight, R. B. The relative discriminability of several geometric forms. *J. exp. Psychol.,* 1952, **43,** 324–328.

Smedslund, J. *Multiple Probability Learning.* Oslo: Akademisk Forlag, 1955.

Smith, A. A. An electromyographic study of tension in interrupted and completed tasks. *J. exp. Psychol.,* 1953, **46,** 32–36.

Smith, C. B. A comparison of the Urban and comparative rating scale methods of determining thresholds. Unpublished study, University of Texas, 1953.

Smith, C. B. Background effects on learning and transposition of lightness discriminations. Ph.D. dissertation, University of Texas Library, Austin, 1956.

Smith, D. E. P., & Raygor, A. L. Verbal satiation and personality. *J. abnorm. soc. Psychol.,* 1956, **52,** 323–326.

Smith, G. Development as a psychological reference system. *Psychol. Rev.*, 1952, **59**, 363–369.

Smith, M., & Wilson, E. A. A model of the auditory threshold and its application to the problem of the multiple observer. *Psychol. Monogr.*, 1953, **67** (Whole No. 359).

Smith, M. E. Linguistic constancy in individuals when long periods of time are covered and different types of material are sampled. *J. gen. Psychol.*, 1955, **53**, 109–143.

Smith, S., & Guthrie, E. R. *General Psychology in Terms of Behavior*. New York: Appleton-Century-Crofts, 1921.

Snoddy, G. S. Learning and stability. *J. appl. Psychol.*, 1926, **10**, 1–36.

Snygg, D., & Combs, A. W. *Individual Behavior*. New York: Harper & Row, 1949.

Solley, C. M., & Long, J. When is "uh-huh" reinforcing? *Percept. mot. Skills*, 1958, **8**, 277.

Solley, C. M., & Murphy, G. *Development of the Perceptual World*. New York: Basic Books, 1960.

Solomon, R. L., & Wynne, L. C. Traumatic avoidance learning: The principles of anxiety conservation and partial irreversibility. *Psychol. Rev.*, 1954, **61**, 353–385.

Spence, K. W. The differential response in animals to stimuli varying within a single dimension. *Psychol. Rev.*, 1937, **44**, 430–444.

Spencer, D. E. Adaptation in color space. *J. opt. Soc. Amer.*, 1943, **33**, 10–17.

Spranger, E. *Types of Men* (Trans. P. J. W. Pigors). New York: Stechert, 1928.

Squires, P. C. Stereopsis produced without horizontally disparate stimulus loci. *J. exp. Psychol.*, 1956*a*, **52**, 199–203.

Stagner, R. Homeostasis as a unifying concept in personality theory. *Psychol. Rev.*, 1951, **58**, 5–17.

Stagner, R. *Psychology of Industrial Conflict*. New York: Wiley, 1956.

Stagner, R. Homeostasis, need reduction, and motivation. *Merrill-Palmer quart. Behav. & Dev.*, 1961, **7**, 49–68.

Stephenson, W. Methodology of trait analysis. *Brit. J. Psychol.*, 1956, **47**, 5–18.

Stern, Catherine. *Children Discover Arithmetic*. New York: Harper & Row, 1949.

Stern, W. *General Psychology from the Personalistic Standpoint*. New York: Macmillan, 1938.

Stevens, J. C., Mack, J. D., & Stevens, S. S. Growth of sensation on seven continua as measured by force of handgrip. *J. exp. Psychol.*, 1960, **59**, 60–67.

Stevens, J. C., & Stevens, S. S. Warmth and cold: Dynamics of sensory intensity. *J. exp. Psychol.*, 1960, **60**, 183–192.

Stevens, S. S. Mathematics, measurement and psychophysics. In S. S. Stevens (Ed.), *Handbook of Experimental Psychology*. New York: Wiley, 1951.

Stevens, S. S. The direct estimation of sensory magnitudes. *Amer. J. Psychol.*, 1956, **69**, 1–25.

Stevens, S. S. On the psychophysical law. *Psychol. Rev.*, 1957, **64**, 153–181.

Stevens, S. S. Adaptation-level vs. the relativity of judgment. *Amer. J. Psychol.*, 1958, **71**, 633–646.

Stevens, S. S. Cross-modality validation of subjective scales for loudness, vibration, and electric shock. *J. exp. Psychol.*, 1959, **57**, 201–209.

Stevens, S. S. To honor Fechner and repeal his law. *Science*, 1961, **133**, 80–86.

Stevens, S. S. The surprising simplicity of sensory metrics. *Amer. Psychologist*, 1962, **17**, 29–39.

Stevens, S. S., & Galanter, E. H. Ratio scales and category scales for a dozen perceptual continua. *J. exp. Psychol.*, 1957, **54**, 377–411.

Stevens, S. S., & Poulton, E. C. The estimation of loudness by unpracticed observers. *J. exp. Psychol.*, 1956, **51**, 71–78.

Stevenson, H. W., & Iscoe, I. Overtraining and transposition in children. *J. exp. Psychol.*, 1954, **47**, 251–255.

Stevenson, H. W., & Iscoe, I. Transposition in the feeble-minded. *J. exp. Psychol.*, 1955, **49**, 11–15.

Stevenson, H. W., & Zigler, E. F. Probability learning in children. *J. exp. Psychol.*, 1958, **56**, 185–192.

Stewart, E. C. The Gelb effect. *J. exp. Psychol.*, 1959, **57**, 235–242.

Stone, C. P. Losses and gains in cognitive functions as related to electroconvulsive shocks. *J. abnorm. soc. Psychol.*, 1947, **42**, 206–214.

Stone, L. J., & Dallenbach, K. M. The adaptation of areal pain. *Amer. J. Psychol.*, 1936, **48**, 117–125.

Stumpf, C. *Tonpsychologie*. Leipzig: Hirzel, Vol. I, 1883; Vol. II, 1890.

Swartz, P. A new method for scaling pain. *J. exp. Psychol.*, 1953, **45**, 288–293.

Swartz, P., Norris, E. B., & Spragg, S. D. S. Performance on a following tracking task (modified SAM two-hand coordination test) as a function of radius of control cranks. *J. Psychol.*, 1954, **37**, 163–171.

Szafran, J., & Welford, A. T. On the relation between transfer and difficulty of initial task. *Quart. J. exp. Psychol.*, 1950, **2**, 88–94.

Taves, E. H. Two mechanisms for the perception of visual numerousness. *Arch. Psychol.*, 1941, **37**, No. 265.

Taylor, J. A. The relationship of anxiety to the conditioned eyelid response. *J. exp. Psychol.*, 1951, **4**, 81–92.

Taylor, J. A. Level of conditioning and intensity of the adaptation stimulus. *J. exp. Psychol.*, 1956, **51**, 127–130.

Taylor, F. V., & Birmingham, H. P. That confounded system performance measure—a demonstration. *Psychol. Rev.*, 1959, **66**, 178–182.

Teichner, W. H. Recent studies of simple reaction time. *Psychol. Bull.*, 1954, **51**, 128–149.

Terman, L. M., & Cox, C. *Genetic studies of Genius*, I. Stanford University Press, 1925.

Teuber, H-L., & Mishkin, M. Judgment of visual and postural vertical after brain injury. *J. Psychol.*, 1954, **38**, 161–175.

Thomas, D. R., & Jones, C. G. Stimulus generalization as a function of the frame of reference. *J. exp. Psychol.*, 1962, **64**, 77–80.

Thorndike, E. L. *Animal Intelligence: Experimental Studies*. New York: Macmillan, 1911.

Thorndike, E. L. New data on the influence of frequency and of mind set. *J. exp. Psychol.*, 1949, **39**, 395–403.

Thornton, G. R. The effect upon judgments of personality traits of varying a single factor in a photograph. *J. soc. Psychol.*, 1943, **18**, 127–148.

Thornton, G. R. The effect of wearing glasses upon judgments of personality traits of persons seen briefly. *J. appl. Psychol.*, 1944, **28**, 203–207.

Thurstone, L. L. (Ed.) Attitudes toward war. Scale No. 2, Forms A and B (1930) and Scale No. 34, Forms A and B (1931). Univ. of Chicago Press, 1930–1931.

Thurstone, L. L. The prediction of choice. *Psychometrika*, 1945, **10**, 237–253.

Tinbergen, N. *The Study of Instinct*. Oxford Univ. Press, 1951.

Tinker, M. A. Perceptual and oculomotor efficiency in reading materials in vertical and horizontal arrangements. *Amer. J. Psychol.*, 1955, **68**, 444–449.

Titchener, E. B. *A Textbook of Psychology*. New York: Macmillan, 1910.

Tolman, E. C. *Drives Toward War*. New York: Appleton-Century-Crofts, 1942.

Troland, L. T. The colors produced by equilibrium photopic adaptation. *J. exp. Psychol.*, 1931, **4**, 344–390.

Troland, L. T. *The Principles of Psychophysiology*. Vol. II, *Sensation*. New York: Van Nostrand, 1930.

Tucker, D., & Beidler, L. M. Autonomic nervous system influence on olfactory receptors. *Amer. J. Psychol.*, 1956, **187**, 637.

Tuckman, J., & Lorge, I. The best years of life: a study in ageing. *J. Psychol.*, 1952, **34**, 137–149.

Turchioe, R. M. The relation of adjacent inhibitory stimuli to the central tendency effect. *J. gen. Psychol.*, 1948, **39**, 3–14.

Underwood, B. J. An orientation for research on thinking. *Psychol. Rev.*, 1952, **59**, 209–220.

Underwood, B. J., & Richardson, J. Some verbal materials for the study of concept formation. *Psychol. Bull.*, 1956a, **53**, 84–95.

Underwood, B. J., & Richardson, J. Verbal concept learning as a function of instructions and dominance level. *J. exp. Psychol.*, 1956b, **51**, 229–238.

Van Buskirk, W. L. An experimental study of vividness in learning and retention. *J. exp. Psychol.*, 1932, **15**, 563–573.

Volkmann, J., Hunt, W. A., & McGourty, M. Variability of judgment as a function of stimulus-density. *Amer. J. Psychol.*, 1940, **53**, 277–284.

Wallen, R. The nature of color shock. *J. abnorm. soc. Psychol.*, 1948, **43**, 346–356.

Walls, G. L. "Land! Land!" *Psychol. Bull.*, 1960, **57**, 29–48.

Wapner, S., Werner, H., & Chandler, K. A. Experiments on sensory-tonic field theory of perception: I. Effect of extraneous stimulation on the visual perception of verticality. *J. exp. Psychol.*, 1951, **42**, 341–345.

Wapner, S., Werner, H., & Morant, R. B. Experiments on sensory-tonic field theory of perception: III. Effect of body rotation on the visual perception of verticality. *J. exp. Psychol.*, 1951, **42**, 351–357.

Warren, R. M., & Warren, R. P. Effect of the relative volume of standard and comparison object on half-heaviness judgments. *Amer. J. Psychol.*, 1956, **69**, 640–643.

Warren, R. P., & Pfaffmann, C. Early experience and taste aversion. *J. comp. physiol. Psychol.*, 1958, **52**, 263–266.

Watson, J. B. Kinesthetic and organic sensations; their role in the reactions of the white rat to the maze. *Psychol. Monogr.*, 1907, **8** (Whole No. 33).

Watson, J. B. Experimental studies on the growth of the emotions. In C. Murchison (Ed.), *Psychologies of 1925*. Worcester, Mass.: Clark University Press, 1926.

Watson, W. S., & Hartmann, G. W. The rigidity of a basic attitudinal frame. *J. abnorm. soc. Psychol.*, 1939, **34**, 314–335.

Weber, E. H. A new-old illusion. *Ber. über Verhandlungen d. königl. sächsischen Ges. d. Wiss. Leipzig, Math.-Phys. Klasse*, 1851, 99–100.

Wegner, N., & Zeaman, D. Team and individual performances on a motor learning task. *J. gen. Psychol.*, 1956, **55**, 127–142.

Weinstein, A. D., Goldstone, S., & Boardman, W. K. The effect of recent and remote frames of reference on temporal judgments of schizophrenic patients. *J. abnorm. soc. Psychol.*, 1958, **57**, 241–244.

Weiss, B. The role of proprioceptive feedback in positioning responses. *J. exp. Psychol.*, 1954, **47**, 215–224.

Weiss, W., & Margolius, G. The effect of context stimuli on learning and retention. *J. exp. Psychol.*, 1954, **48**, 318–322.

Welch, L., & Kubis, J. The effect of anxiety on the conditioning rate and stability of the PGR. *J. Psychol.,* 1947, **23**, 83–91.

Wenger, M. A. Emotion as visceral action. In M. L. Reymert (Ed.), *Feelings and Emotions.* New York: McGraw-Hill, 1950.

Werner, H. Change of meaning: a study of semantic processes through the experimental method. *J. gen. Psychol.,* 1954, **50**, 181–208.

Werner, H., & Wapner, S. Sensory-tonic theory of perception. *J. Pers.,* 1949, **18**, 88–107.

Werner, H., & Wapner, S. The Innsbrück studies on distorted visual fields in relation to an organismic theory of perception. *Psychol. Rev.,* 1955, **62**, 130–138.

Werner, H., Wapner, S., & Chandler, K. A. Experiments on sensory-tonic field theory of perception: II. Effect of supported and unsupported tilt of body on the visual perception of verticality. *J. exp. Psychol.,* 1951, **42**, 346–350.

Wertheimer, M. Experimentelle Studien über das Sehen von Bewegung. *Z. f. Psychol.,* 1912, **61**, 161–265.

Wertheimer, M. *Productive Thinking.* New York: Harper & Row, 1945.

Wever, E. G., & Zener, K. E. The method of absolute judgment in psychophysics. *Psychol. Rev.,* 1928, **35**, 466–493.

Wherry, R. J. Control of bias in ratings. VII. A theory of rating. Final Report, Sub-project 9, Dept. of the Army, PRB Report 922, Project No. 29545100, Research Contract DA-49–0830SA69, 1952.

White, D. C. Maximizing Color Differences. Ph.D. dissertation, Stanford University, 1949.

White, W. A. *Mechanisms of Character Formation.* New York: Macmillan, 1916.

Whyte, W. H., Jr. *The Organization Man.* New York: Doubleday, 1957.

Wickes, T. A., Jr. Examiner influence in a testing situation. *J. con. Psychol.,* 1956, **20**, 23–26.

Wiener, N. *Cybernetics or Control and Communication in the Animal and Machine.* New York: Wiley, 1948.

Wilde, Oscar. *The Picture of Dorian Gray.* New York: Brentano, 1920.

Wilder, J. The law of initial value in neurology and psychiatry. *J. nerv. ment. Dis.,* 1957, **125**, 73–86.

Williams, G. D. The effect of order of appearance on the appreciation of musical selections. *J. gen. Psychol.,* 1942, **27**, 295–310.

Williams, G. D. The effect of program notes on the enjoyment of musical selections. *J. gen. Psychol.,* 1943, **29**, 261–279.

Williams, R. J. *Biochemical Individuality.* New York: Wiley, 1957.

Wilson, R. C., Guilford, J. P., & Christensen, P. R. The measurement of individual differences in originality. *Psychol. Bull.,* 1953, **50**, 362–370.

Witkin, H. A. Sex differences in perception. *Trans. N.Y. Acad. Sci.,* Series II, 1949, **12**, 22–26.

Witkin, H. A., & Asch, S. E. Studies in space orientation. IV. Further experiments on perception of the upright with displaced visual fields. *J. exp. Psychol.,* 1948, **38**, 762–782.

Witkin, H. A., Lewis, H. B., Hertzman, M., Machover, K., Meissner, P. B., & Wapner, S. *Personality through Perception.* New York: Harper & Row, 1954.

Witkin, H. A., Wapner, S., & Leventhal, T. Sound localization with conflicting visual and auditory cues. *J. exp. Psychol.,* 1952, **43**, 58–67.

Wolpe, J. Need-reduction, drive-reduction, and reinforcement: a neurophysiological view. *Psychol. Rev.,* 1950, **57**, 19–26.

Wong, H., & Brown, W. Effects of surroundings upon mental work as measured by Yerkes multiple choice method. *J. comp. Psychol.,* 1923, **3**, 319–331.

Wood, C. C. Report of an address. *Naval Human Engng. Bull.,* Engineering Psychology Branch, Office of Naval Research, Washington, D.C., September, 1957.

Woodrow, H. Weight-discrimination with a varying standard. *Amer. J. Psychol.,* 1933, **45**, 391–416.

Woodrow, H. The effect of practice upon time-order errors in the comparison of temporal intervals. *Psychol. Rev.,* 1935, **42**, 127–152.

Woodrow, H. Absolute scaling applied to the data yielded by the method of constant stimuli. *J. exp. Psychol.,* 1937, **20**, 1–28.

Woodrow, H. Time perception. In S. S. Stevens (Ed.), *Handbook of Experimental Psychology.* New York: Wiley, 1951.

Woodrow, H., & Stott, L. H. The effect of practice upon positive time-order errors. *J. exp. Psychol.,* 1936, **19**, 694–705.

Woodworth, R. S. *Experimental Psychology.* New York: Holt, Rinehart & Winston, 1938.

Woodworth, R. S., & Schlosberg, H. *Experimental Psychology* (rev. ed.). New York: Holt, Rinehart & Winston, 1954.

Woodworth, R. S., & Sells, S. B. An atmosphere effect in formal syllogistic reasoning. *J. exp. Psychol.,* 1935, **18**, 451–460.

Worchel, P., & Narciso, J. C., Jr. Electroshock convulsions and memory: The interval between learning and shock. *J. abnorm. soc. Psychol.,* 1950, **45**, 85–98.

Worell, L. The effect of goal value upon expectancy. *J. abnorm. soc. Psychol.,* 1956, **53**, 48–53.

Yerkes, R. M. Modes of behavioral adaptation in chimpanzee to multiple-choice problems. *Comp. Psychol. Monogr.,* 1934, **10**, 1–108.

Young, H. H., Holtzman, W. H., & Bryant, N. D. Effects of item context and order on personality ratings. *Educ. psychol. Measmt,* 1954, **14,** 499–517.

Young, P. T. Appetite, palatability, and feeding habits: A critical review. *Psychol. Bull.,* 1948, **45,** 289–320.

Young, P. T. The role of hedonic processes in motivation. In M. R. Jones (Ed.), *Nebraska Symposium on Motivation.* Lincoln: University of Nebraska Press, 1955.

Young, P. T. The role of affective processes in learning and motivation. *Psychol. Rev.,* 1959, **66,** 104–125.

Young, P. T., & Asdourian, D. Relative acceptability of sodium chloride and sucrose solutions. *J. comp. physiol. Psychol.,* 1957, **50,** 499–503.

Young, P. T., & Falk, J. L. The acceptability of tap water and distilled water to nonthirsty rats. *J. comp. physiol. Psychol.,* 1956, **49,** 336–338.

Zaidi, S. M. H. Cognitive behavior under stress. *Psychologia,* 1959, **2,** 57–64.

Zeaman, D. Response latency as a function of the amount of reinforcement. *J. exp. Psychol.,* 1949, **39,** 466–483.

Zigler, M. J. Pressure adaptation-time: A function of intensity and extensity. *Amer. J. Psychol.,* 1932, **44,** 709–720.

Zubin, J. A biometric model for psychopathology. *Current Trends in the Description and Analysis of Behavior.* University of Pittsburgh Press, 1958.

Index of Names

Halsey, R. M., 265 f., 680
Hanes, R. N., 680
Hansel, C. E. M., 83, 160 f., 671
Harlow, H. F., 39, 377, 425 f., 442, 680, 701
Harper, R. S., 155 f., 175, 698
Harris, A. J., 155, 332, 347 f., 680
Harris, J. D., 45, 111, 119, 680, 681
Hartman, B. O., 115, 681
Hartman, E. B., 156 f., 681
Hartmann, G. W., 681, 707
Hartmann, L., 258, 681
Harvey, O. J., 648 ff., 653 ff., 685
Hastings, W., 339 f., 549, 681
Hauty, G. T., 117 f., 243, 377 f., 428, 675, 681, 697, 698
Hayakawa, S. I., 454, 681
Head, H., 86, 681
Hearnshaw, L. S., 85, 494 f., 497 f., 681
Hebb, D. O., 87, 434, 495, 681
Hecht, S., 43, 52, 681
Heider, F., 681
Heim, A. W., 55, 395 f., 398, 421, 491 ff., 681
Heinemann, E. G., 303, 681
Heintz, R. K., 681
Heisenberg, W., 478
Helmholtz, H. von, 238
Helson, H., 5, 15, 17, 32, 45, 55, 60, 62, 79, 81, 83, 107 f., 114, 117 ff., 129, 131, 135, 138, 139, 154, 165 ff., 170, 175, 178, 186, 189, 191, 196 f., 203, 209, 212 f., 215 ff., 224, 226, 233, 239, 252 f., 263, 265, 266 ff., 280 f., 283 ff., 296, 310 ff., 323 ff., 363 ff., 396 ff., 411, 413 f., 421, 426, 428, 473, 475 ff., 477, 505, 559, 599, 609 ff., 615 ff., 622 ff., 631 ff., 647, 652, 661 f., 665, 666, 667, 679, 682, 683, 686, 688, 694, 695
Helson, H. B., 473, 639, 683
Helson, R. M., 469, 684
Henle, M., 684
Henneman, R. H., 684
Henry, C. E., 339, 531, 672
Henry, E. M., 537 f., 684
Henry, L. K., 684
Herma, H., 406 f., 669
Hermans, T. G., 76, 300, 684
Hernàndez-Peòn, R., 247, 684
Heron, W., 242, 684
Herrick, C. J., 684
Hertzman, M., 709

Hess, W., 65, 684
Hilgard, E. R., 388, 392, 684
Himelstein, P., 154, 191, 196, 661 f., 683
Hinckley, E. D., 554 f., 684, 700
Hippocrates, 524
Hirsh, I. J., 45, 322, 684, 700
Hirsch, J., 175, 224, 670
Hitler, A., 621, 627
Hofmann, F. B., 76, 684
Hofstätter, P. R., 66, 684
Hogan, F., 36, 684
Hollingworth, H. L., 95, 685
Holtzman, W. H., 496, 536, 562 ff., 685, 709
Holway, A. H., 76, 103, 685
Holzman, P. S., 676
Houdini, H., 513
Hovland, C. I., 225 ff., 471, 577, 588, 602, 648 ff., 653 ff., 685, 690, 702, 703
Howes, D. H., 237, 483, 685
Howland, D., 685
Huff, F. W., 694
Hugelin, A., 247, 685
Hull, C. L., 7, 13, 65, 412, 414, 685
Humphrey, G., 47, 392, 431, 685, 686
Humphreys, L. G., 406 f., 408, 686
Hunt, J. McV., 434 f., 670, 686, 691, 692
Hunt, W. A., 120 f., 332 f., 371, 375, 648, 653, 656 ff., 670, 686, 707
Hunter, I. A. M. L., 469, 686
Hunter, W. S., 400, 410, 686
Hurvich, L. M., 295 ff., 686, 687
Husserl, E., 252 f., 258, 686
Hyman, R., 123, 680

Iago, 628
Immergluck, I., 686
Irwin, F. W., 120, 150 f., 376, 505, 686
Iscoe, I., 429 f., 705

Jackson, D. D., 510 f., 665
Jacobson, E., 686
Jaffe, R., 78 f., 687
Jahoda, G., 514, 687
James, H., 413 f., 687
James, W., 28, 96, 335, 524, 546 f., 687
Jameson, D., 295 ff., 686, 687
Jeffers, V. B., 5, 683
Jelliffe, S. E., 40, 687
Jenkin, N., 505, 687
Jenkins, L. B., 501, 697
Jenkins, W. O., 408, 687

Index of Subjects

Absolute judgment, 132, 215, 229
Absolute method, 130
  and relative method, 133
Absolute terms, 477
Absolute threshold, 139, 197
Abnormal personality, 580 f.
Abnormality, 389
Abstract system, 508
Abstract thinking, 514 ff.
Acceptance, latitudes of, 650 f.
Acclimatization, 116
Achromatic point, 264
  locus of, 166 ff.
Acoustic structure, 164
Acquiescence, 647
  vs. conventionality, 647
Acting, 511
  and thinking, 455 f., 510 f.
Acuity, visual, 56
Adaptation, 184, 571
  affective, 329 f., 383; alpha, 275; audi-
  tory, 372 f.; behavioral, 57 f.; beta,
  275; biological, 58; central, 46; con-
  cept of, 36 ff.; and constancy, 103;
  and contrast, 47; dark, 43; to difficulty level, 491 ff.; and disparity
  from level, 388; and fatigue, 42; and
  habituation, 372 f.; lateral, 88, 275; in
  Land colors, 275 f.; and learning,
  38 f., 51 ff.; luminance, 186; motor,

50 f.; negative, 47; with negative
  aftereffect, 48, 311; and periodicity,
  109; ratio, 168; to reinforcement,
  449; reflectance, 186, 260 f., 277;
  sensory, 41 f.; series, 219 ff., social,
  58 ff.; steady, 42 ff.; transient, 42 ff.
  See also Adaptation Level
Adaptation level, 22, 32, 37, 120, 186 f.,
  320, 381, 564 f., 587
  aesthetic, 368 ff.; decentered, 159; definition of, 128 f.; displacement of, 128;
  as effective threshold, 224; and figural aftereffects, 313 ff.; functions
  embodying, 189 ff., 197 ff., 204; implications of, 62 f.; lag in, 556; locus
  of, 186 ff.; and point of subjective
  equality, 59; as pooled effect, 58; and
  ratings, 560 ff.; sensory and affective
  compared, 343; shifting, 182 f.; social
  influences on, 595 ff.; theory, 48 f.;
  and transfer of training, 410 ff.; as
  weighted mean, 58 f.
Additivity, paradox, 367 ff.
Adjustment, 38
  to art forms, 370; levels, 126, 395 ff.,
  398, 572, 587
Aesthetics, 362 ff.
  adaptation levels in, 368 ff.
Affects, 241, 328 ff.
  as experiential data, 332 ff., 374 ff.;

Fluorescent light, 354 ff.
colors seen in, 269 ff.
Focalization, 548
Food, 432
color of, 354; intake, 343 f.; preferences, 570
Force, 11
Form, appropriate, 384 ff.
constancy, 298 ff.; perception, 297 ff.; qualities, 239
Formants, 74, 163 f.
Formulas, rational vs. empirical, 20
Fovea, space values of, 305 ff.
Foxboro studies, 104, 106, 114 f.
Fractionation, 177 ff.
order and, 157 f.
Frames, cognitive, 511 f.
properties of, 512; of reference, 9, 37, 126, 569, 580, 582; evaluation of, 133; social, 584
Frequency and affect, 549
Friction, 11, 117, 398
Fry-Bartley effect, 74
Functional relations in social psychology, 594 f.
Functions, mathematical, 6, 7, 17 ff.
psychometric, 31
Fusion, sensory, 74 ff.

Galvanic skin reflex, 140 f., 237 f., 247, 472
Gamma movement, 91
Gelb effect, 282 ff., 293 ff.
Generalization, 8 ff.
gradient, 423 ff.; effect of context on, 423 ff.
Generosity, 379, 572
Genius, 110, 506
Genotype, 259
Geometric mean, 136
Geometry, 513
Gestalt, 1, 4, 13 f., 66, 73, 85, 91, 239 f., 252 ff., 368, 394, 414, 459, 494, 518
ambiguity, 239; properties of, 584 f.; qualität (quality), 584
Gift-giving, 642 ff.
Glassy sensation, 251
Goal, attainment of, 395
gradient, 65; remote, 519; types of, 505 f.
Golden mean, 576
Goldstein-Scheerer test, 514

Gradient, negative, 346
positive, 346; from adaptation level, 128, 130
Gravitation, 25 f.
Graz school, 239
Ground instructions, 323 ff.
Group, attitude, 590
characteristics of, 586 f.; as stimulus, 586 .; level, 587 ff.; measurement of, 590; mind, 584 f.; nature of, 584 f.

Habituation, 47, 373 f., 431 ff.
Half-, loudness, 176
weight, 177 f.
Hallucination, 230, 242, 244 f., 531 f.
peripheral origin of, 532
Halo effect, 564, 566, 569
Handwheel controls, 254 f.
Health, 548
norms, 578
Hearing loss, 112
Heat, 74
Hebb-Williams maze, 480
Hedonic, contrast, 348
intensity, 334; threshold, 382; tone, 387
Height, judgments of, 554
of pitches, 155 f.
Helson-Judd effect, 275
Hering theory, 47
Hero, effect of, 570
Heterogeneity, group, 589
Heteromodal, anchor, 321
interactions, 320 ff.; scaling, 331
Heterostasis, 335 ff.
Higher-order stimuli, 239
Homeostasis, 40 f., 48 f., 52, 103, 106, 336, 455, 581
Honesty, 645 ff.
situational determinants of, 645 ff.
Hope, 505
Hostility, 580
Hue, preferences for, 360 f.
Human factors, 6
interest, 373 f.
Humidity, 428 f.
Humor, 374
bipolar factors in, 374
Hunger, 380
Hypophysectomy, 342
Hypothesis, 12
atomic, 27; goal gradient, 25